HANDBOOK
of POLITICAL
CONFLICT

Theory and Research

EDITED BY
Ted Robert Gurr

The Free Press Series on Political Behavior
Stanley Allen Renshon, General Editor

THE FREE PRESS
A Division of Macmillan Publishing Co., Inc.
NEW YORK

Collier Macmillan Publishers
LONDON

THE FREE PRESS
A Division of Macmillan Publishing Co., Inc.
866 Third Avenue, New York, N. Y. 10022

Collier Macmillan Canada, Ltd.

Library of Congress Catalog Card Number: 79–6145

Printed in the United States of America

printing number

1 2 3 4 5 6 7 8 9 10

Library of Congress Cataloging in Publication Data
Main entry under title:
Handbook of political conflict.

(The Free Press series on political behavior)
Includes index.
1. Violence--Addresses, essays, lectures.
2. Social conflict--Addresses, essays, lectures.
I. Gurr, Ted Robert
JC328.6.H36   303.6   79–6145
ISBN 0–02–912760–2

Contents

Acknowledgments

I should like to thank Stanley Allen Renshon, the editor of the series on political behavior of which this *Handbook* is a part, for repeatedly encouraging me to pursue this project. He, along with Harry Eckstein, Dina A. Zinnes, and several other contributors, also offered helpful ideas about the *Handbook*'s structure, contents, and contributors. A number of authors helped make this a collaborative enterprise by exchanging papers and critiques of one another's work.

The contributors also deserve commendation for putting up with a considerable amount of harrying from the editor. They were subjected to a barrage of comments, some of them rather pointed and categorical, about the substance, organization, and style of their outlines, first drafts, and sometimes second drafts as well. I am flattered that they kept trying to meet what must at times have seemed unreasonable and escalating demands. I also am pleased with the solidity of the results.

This volume is dedicated to my wife, Erika, who died unexpectedly just as we began work on the index. She discovered during our twenty years of marriage that scholarship has its price, and learned again during the preparation of the *Handbook* that part of the price is paid by spouses who have the skill and patience to type manuscripts, check bibliographies, and compile indexes. I have finished the work with the poignant wish that I had given more attention to her during the last three years and less to the *Handbook*.

About the Contributors

Bruce Bueno de Mesquita is associate professor of political science at the University of Rochester. His research interests include international conflict, coalition theory, and South Asian politics. Among his recent publications are *Strategy, Risk, and Personality in Coalition Politics* (1975), *India's Political System* (with Richard L. Park, 1979), *The War Trap*, and articles in such journals as the *American Political Science Review*, *International Studies Quarterly, Journal of Conflict Resolution*, and *Comparative Political Studies*. He currently serves on the editorial boards of the *International Studies Quarterly, Comparative Political Studies*, and *Comparative Strategy*. He has been a fellow of the Guggenheim Foundation and of the American Institute of Indian Studies.

James Chowning Davies, professor of political science at the University of Oregon, is the author of *Human Nature in Politics* (1963) and the editor of *When Men Revolt and Why* (1971). He has written a number of shorter essays on such topics as the causes of revolution, the childhood roots of adult political behavior, political development, political fiction, and ideology. He is currently at work on a theory of stages of political development based on psychological and historical grounds.

Harry Eckstein is IBM Professor of International Studies at Princeton University, where he teaches mainly comparative politics. Among his books are *Patterns of Authority* (with Ted Robert Gurr, 1975) and *Division and Cohesion in Democracy* (1966). He edited and contributed to an early postwar book on political violence, *Internal War: Problems and Approaches* (1966). Among the subjects of his books, monographs, and articles are general comparative politics, the scope of political inquiry, case studies, revolutions, party systems, pressure groups, planning, public medical care, governmental performance, British government and politics, and the historic and contemporary state.

Ted Robert Gurr is Payson S. Wild Professor of Political Science at Northwestern University. His research has focused on political conflict, authority, and institutional change. In 1969 he and Hugh Davis Graham prepared the report, *Violence in America: Historical and Comparative Perspectives*, for the National Commission on the Causes and Prevention of Violence. His 1970 book, *Why Men Rebel*, received the American Political Science Association's Woodrow Wilson Prize as the year's best book in political science. He has written a dozen other books and monographs, among them *Politimetrics* (1972), *Patterns of Authority* (with Harry Eckstein, 1975), and *The Politics of Crime and Conflict: A Comparative History of Four Cities* (with Peter N. Grabosky and Richard C. Hula, 1977).

Edward N. Muller is professor of political science at the University of Arizona, where he teaches courses in political behavior and research methodology. He is the author of *Aggressive Political Participation* (1979). His articles have appeared in the *American Political Science Review*, the *American Journal of Political Science*, *Comparative Political Studies*, *American Behavioral Scientist*, *Quality and Quantity*, and *Politische Vierteljahresschrift*. He is presently working on the dynamic analysis of political attitudes and behavior and on a cross-national study of support for democratic liberties.

Terry Nardin is associate professor of political science at the State University of New York at Buffalo, where he teaches international politics and political theory. He is the author of articles on political violence, international law, and other subjects that have appeared in the *Sage Professional Papers in Comparative Politics*, the *Yale Review*, the *American Political Science Review*, the *British Journal of International Studies*, and elsewhere. He is presently working on a book on international legal and moral theory.

Dennis C. Pirages is associate professor of government and politics and director of the Program in Technology, Resources, and Political Economy at the University of Maryland. He is author or editor of six books including, most recently, *Managing Political Conflict* (1976), *The Sustainable Society* (1977), and *Global Ecopolitics* (1978). He is currently engaged in research on the social and political impact of complex technologies in developing countries.

Mostafa Rejai is professor of political science at Miami University (Ohio), where he has been the recipient of an Outstanding Teaching Award. His most recent publications are *Leaders of Revolution* (1979) and *The Comparative Study of Revolutionary Strategy* (1977). He is a fellow of the Inter-University Seminar on Armed Forces and Society and an associate editor of *Journal of Political and Military Sociology*. He is currently completing the second volume of a three-volume work on revolutionary and political elites.

Bruce M. Russett is professor of political science at Yale University, and editor of the *Journal of Conflict Resolution*. He is a past president of the Peace Science Society (International), and has published fourteen books on international relations.

J. David Singer, professor of political science at the University of Michigan, is one of the pioneers in peace research. He is chairman of the research committee on peace and conflict of the International Political Science Association. He has been at Michigan since 1958, and has also been associated with New York University, Vassar College, Harvard University, the U. S. Naval War College, the University of Oslo, and Geneva's Institute for Graduate Studies in International Relations. Among his books are *Deterrence, Arms Control, and Disarmament* (1962), *Human Behavior and International Politics* (1965), *Quantitative International Politics* (1968), *Beyond Conjecture in International Politics* (1972), *The Wages of War* (1972), and *The Correlates of War*, volumes I and II (1979 and 1980).

Arthur A. Stein, assistant professor of political science at the University of California, Los Angeles, received his Ph.D. in political science from Yale University. His publications include: "The Balance of Power in International History" (1973), "Interdependence: Myth or Reality?" (1973), "Conflict and Cohesion" (1976), "The Politics of Linkage" (1980), and *The Nation at War* (Baltimore: Johns Hopkins University Press, 1980).

Michael Stohl is associate professor of political science at Purdue University. He has published a number of articles and a book, *War and Domestic Political Violence: The American Capacity for Repression and Reaction* (1976), on the relationship between foreign and domestic politics. Recently he has edited a volume on terrorism, *The Politics of Terrorism* (1979), and begun work on the social consequences of the new international economic order. His contribution to this book was completed while he was a research associate of the Richardson Institute for Conflict and Peace Research, Lancaster, England, in 1978–1979.

Ekkart Zimmermann is associate professor in sociology at the University of Wuppertal, West Germany. Among other works in German, he has published articles on status inconsistency (*European Journal of Sociology*), on various topics in the field of conflict research (in *Quality and Quantity, European Journal of Political Research, Armed Forces and Society*), and a comprehensive study on *Political Violence, Crises, and Revolutions: Theories and Research* (1980). Over the next years he will be engaged in cross-national research on crises and crisis outcomes.

Dina A. Zinnes was professor of political science and director of the Center for International Policy Studies at Indiana University until 1980, when she accepted an endowed chair at the University of Illinois. She has written extensively on international crises and arms race modeling. Among her books are *Contemporary Research in International Politics: A Perspective and Critical Appraisal* (1976) and *Mathematical Models in International Relations* (1976, as co-editor). She serves on the editorial boards of a number of journals and in 1979–1980 was president of the International Studies Association.

Introduction

Ted Robert Gurr

THIS HANDBOOK SURVEYS A GENERATION of theoretical and empirical research on the origins, processes, and consequences of political conflict. Two parameters of this survey must be specified at the outset. First, the wide scope of conflict phenomena surveyed in the *Handbook* requires definition and justification. Second, I specify the characteristics that distinguish "empirical research" on conflict from other scholarly work on the subject. The distinctions are only approximations, and in general I have encouraged the contributors to take a broad view of their subjects. The discussion of these basic definitional and boundary issues sets the stage for a detailed outline of the topics reviewed in the *Handbook*. The last two elements of the introduction are more tentative and potentially controversial: I suggest the role of values in conflict research, and sketch some of the major prospects for change in the future directions of conflict research.

DEFINING THE SCOPE OF CONFLICT

Conflict phenomena are the overt, coercive interactions of contending collectivities. This working definition is intended to be broad enough to encompass the full range of threatening, forceful, and violent interactions that occur among groups and nations. There are many other definitions of conflict, some broad (see Fink 1968), some more narrow (see Mack and Snyder 1957). Ours directs attention to interactions that have these four

NOTE: I should like to thank James Chowning Davies, Raymond Duvall, Harry Eckstein, Terry Nardin, Mostafa Rejai, and Ekkart Zimmermann for their helpful comments on an earlier draft of this introduction.

1

distinguishing properties, the first three of which are identified by Mack and Snyder:

1. two or more parties are involved
2. they engage in mutually opposing actions
3. they use coercive behaviors, "designed to destroy, injure, thwart, or otherwise control" their opponent(s) (p. 218)
4. these contentious interactions are overt, hence their occurrence can easily be detected and agreed upon by independent observers.

The essential purpose of this definition is to characterize the range of conflict phenomena or behaviors that are juxtaposed in this *Handbook*. It is not designed to resolve more fundamental (and irreconcilable) debates about what distinguishes conflict from competition, or whether states of minds, intentions, and situations should be included in the domain of conflict studies. (See Fink 1968 for a review of these and other definitional problems.) Our definition also says nothing about how to distinguish more homogenous categories of conflict phenomena. For good or bad, most empirical research on conflict evades the need for abstract definitions and distinctions by employing precise operational definitions of specific kinds of conflict concrete enough to make them subject only to a narrow range of technical criticism. An exception is the substantial and wide-ranging literature on how to define revolution (reviewed by Cohan 1975: chapter 2).

Following the general definition, the scope of the *Handbook* is restricted to research that bears on collective action; most of the extensive research on individual acts of aggression is excluded. The survey is further, though imprecisely, restricted to political conflict. I say "imprecisely" because there are no exact boundaries in the social sciences generally or in conflict research specifically between the political and the nonpolitical. Most theories and research under discussion here are political in the sense that they involve the state, either as a party to conflict or as the object of peoples' demands and perceptions. Little attention is given to extensive research on conflict in the anthropological literature (see, for example, Beals and Siegel 1966), administrative sciences (see K. W. Thomas 1976), or industrial relations (see Ross and Hartman 1960, Hibbs 1976). A broader conceptual approach is developed by Harry Eckstein (1973), in which conflict in all social units, from the family to the state, is "political" insofar as it concerns the exercise of authority. Paradoxically, however, this approach implies that conflict among nations is not political because the international system lacks a central structure of authority.

The conflict phenomena under examination in the *Handbook* include political riots, insurrection, revolution, and war among nations. The effective scope of the subject is broader than this because it is widely assumed in conflict research that to understand collective political action it is necessary to study the dispositions and actions of individuals who participate in it, as well as the structures and processes of conflict situations. This reductionism, which is not shared by all conflict researchers, has been taken one step further to the study of "biopolitics," more specifically to the physiology of human aggression. If we accept that the physiological bases of human behavior are relevant to an understanding of political conflict, then we should be ready to consider arguments that larger systems, including the global ecosystem, also affect social conflict. An ecosystem perspective on social conflict is just beginning to emerge out of work by Choucri and North, Boulding, Ophuls, and a few others cited by Dennis C. Pirages in Chapter 11 of this *Handbook*. But this perspective is far newer and less developed than the behavioral and physiological approach represented in the chapters of Part One.

Several other features of our conception of conflict phenomena also should be noted. The coercive behaviors that give conflict its distinctive character include, in addition to the exercise of violence, the threatening but nonviolent confrontations, verbal challenges, and mock attacks that often precede and sometimes preempt the use of violence. Referring back to the third distinguishing feature of conflict phenomena, above, *threats* to destroy, injure, or thwart opponents often have the same effects as the acts themselves, and therefore are properly part of the field of conflict research. Studies of individual participation in protest and rebellion often focus on people's statements about their willingness to participate rather than actual participation. Studies of civil conflict typically include political demonstrations and strikes whether they are violent or not. And research on international conflict includes studies of threats, sanctions, and other shows of belligerency that fall short of open warfare.

The definition used here makes no assumptions about the objectives of conflict behavior. Some scholars, including Mack and Snyder, assume that conflict is instrumental: "Conflict relations always involve attempts to gain control of scarce resources and positions or to influence behavior in certain directions . . . ." (1957: 218–219, original in italics). No doubt this is true of many individuals and groups engaged in conflict, but it is not readily subject to empirical verification. It runs counter to theory and evidence that people fight for expressive reasons as well: conflict can satisfy anger, thirst for excitement, or desire for group solidarity. A strong case can be made for the proposition that instrumental and expressive motivations both are present in virtually all conflict behavior, and that the volatile character of open conflict is partly a result of the unstable mix of these two kinds of motivations among participants and leaders (on the motives of rebels see Gurr 1970b; on the motives of men at war see Keegan 1976). On these grounds it makes little sense to assume a priori that conflict behavior is either one or the other. It is a theoretical and empirical task to determine how instrumental and expressive motives interact in different conflict situations and processes.

THE DISTINCTIVE CHARACTER OF
EMPIRICAL RESEARCH ON CONFLICT

Anatol Rapoport (1960: 12) has observed that conflict "is a theme that has occupied the thinking of man more than any other, save only God and love." He could have said the same about the prevalence of conflict in the written chronicles of human affairs. The literature on war, revolt, and lesser conflicts is large and of ancient origin. In the fifth century B.C., Herodotus, writing about the Persian Wars, and Thucydides, describing the Peloponnesian Wars and concurrent revolts, set a style and standards for all subsequent Western historiography. In the next century Aristotle formulated a general theory of the causes of revolution in his *Politics*, Book V. But the self-conscious application of scientific methods to the study of conflict phenomena is a twentieth-century enterprise. In fact, well over 90 percent of the works cited in the cumulative bibliography of this *Handbook* have been published since the end of World War II.[1]

The distinctive characteristic of research on conflict in twentieth-century social science is the use of systematic methods of observation and comparative, usually quantitative analysis to develop and test generalizations. In effect, empirical research on conflict couples the historian's craft of description to the theorist's search for valid generalizations.[2] Some such generalizations are descriptive ones, indicating how conflict phenomena are distributed among people or across time and space. Others are causal: they stipulate the antecedents or consequences of conflict phenomena. The general method of empirical research on conflict is always comparative: either there are simultaneous observations of a set of people, systems, or events (the cross-sectional approach) or there are multiple observations of one or several individuals, groups, or systems across time (the longitudinal approach). Such observations are frequently but not always reducible to quantitative measures: numbers facilitate precise analysis, but they are not essential to it. Some elegant theories about revolution, for example, have been derived from the systematic but nonquantitative comparison of a handful of cases, for example, by Crane Brinton (1938), Barrington Moore, Jr. (1966), and Skocpol (1979). And in principle a carefully designed "crucial case study" is sufficient to provide a strong test of a lawlike generalization (see Eckstein 1975).

Probably the most visible of the distinguishing traits of contemporary conflict research is the widespread reliance on quantification. The conflict phenomena of interest are measured, and statistical techniques are employed to develop and test generalizations about them. The earliest work employing these techniques was carried out in the decades between

World Wars I and II. Beginning in the 1930s, an English mathematician, Louis Fry Richardson, began compiling information on arms races and wars in a search for mathematical regularities that might make it possible to anticipate and thus avoid wars. And in 1937 the émigré Russian sociologist Pitirim Sorokin published the results of a vast study of the variable incidence of war and internal disturbances in twelve countries and empires over a span of twenty-four centuries, intended to show the effects of changes in idea systems on conflict. At the same time another pioneer, Quincy Wright, was compiling quantitative information for his *A Study of War* (1942).

In the aftermath of World War II there was a strong interdisciplinary movement to bring more of the theories and methods of social research to bear on the problems of international conflict. Though the focus was war and its avoidance, this research drew upon and commingled with research traditions in psychology (the study of aggression and intrapersonal conflict), sociology (intergroup conflict), economics (labor–management conflict), and formal studies (theories of games, bargaining, decision-making). Among the significant contributors to conflict studies in the 1950s and early 1960s were Jessie Bernard, Lewis A. Coser, Ralf Dahrendorf, and Johan Galtung, who introduced sociological perspectives; Kurt Lewin in social psychology; Kenneth Boulding, with a background in economics; and Anatol Rapoport, a game theorist. Those who focused on war per se were mostly political scientists: Quincy Wright continued his work on the subject, joined by a cadre of younger scholars like Klaus Knorr, Robert North, Bruce M. Russett, and J. David Singer. Much of the new theoretical and empirical work appeared in the *Journal of Conflict Resolution*, which began publication in 1957. The Peace Research Society (International) was founded in the early 1960s and published its first volume of proceedings in 1963. The following year the *Journal of Peace Research* was established at the International Peace Research Institute in Oslo.

Political violence within nations was the subject of a scattering of comparative and theoretical studies that appeared during the 1940s and 1950s, but it was the spate of revolutionary wars in the Third World and riotous protest in Western democracies that gave the major impetus to research on the subject in the 1960s. In addition to drawing on the conflict research traditions noted above, the study of violent conflict within nations could make use of a large body of historical research on revolutions. In 1962 James C. Davies published an influential theory of revolution and in 1964 there appeared a major collection of theoretical essays on internal war reflecting the work of a group of scholars at Princeton's Center of International Studies (Eckstein 1964). The first of a new generation of quantitative studies began to appear at the same time. Rudolph J. Rummel reported on the "dimensions of conflict behavior within and between nations" (1963) and Russett used a new collection of aggregate data gathered by the World Data Analysis Program at Yale University to make a cross-national analysis of the relationship between "inequality and instability" (1964). Since then the growth of published research has been exponential, although it showed evidence of leveling off in the late 1970s.

Research on individual participation in protest and rebellion, like empirical research on war and political violence, is a newly emphasized subject with significant scholarly antecedents. Studies of individual revolutionary leaders have long been in vogue among historians and biographers; in the last generation some psychiatrists and political scientists have begun to derive comparative generalizations from this material. The historians also have a valid claim to priority in studies of the common people who participate in conflict. Two especially active fields of historical study are the role of peasants in revolts (see, for example, AlRoy 1966, Paige 1975, and Wolf 1969) and the composition of crowds in classic and modern revolutions (see the works cited by Rejai in Chapter 3 of this *Handbook*). The major recent innovation in research on this topic is the use of systematic sampling and interview techniques to elicit information from actual or potential participants in protest and rebellion. Such work was begun in the mid-1960s by American sociologists and political scientists in the aftermath of the black riots and rebellions. Such research now is cross-national in scope and deals with more fundamental issues than the immediate perceptions and grievances of rioters.

This, then, is the scope of the generation of empirical research on political conflict surveyed in this *Handbook*. It includes theoretical generalizations about the origins, processes, and outcomes of political conflict; and the accumulation of comparative evidence about these issues. Most of this research has been done during the thirty years since 1950, but the basic questions posed are much older and so are some of the pioneering studies. Social scientists did not "discover" conflict in the 1950s. What attracted them was the dawning hope that the theories and methods of empirical social science might make conflict more generally understandable, hence more tractable.

PEACE AND CONFLICT RESEARCH

In this *Handbook* "conflict research" subsumes most of the subject matter of peace research. The nominal distinction between peace and conflict research is that the former emphasizes a positive quest for peace, especially among nations, rather than a concern with the phenomena of conflict per se. If this nominal distinction had substantive import, we would expect peace researchers to work with "theories of peace" in contrast to "theories of conflict." In fact, the substantive differences between the work of those who call themselves peace researchers and the work of other conflict researchers are slight; they differ mainly in their intellectual and political orientations. Since the late 1960s "peace research" has signified a critical orientation toward existing patterns of national and international power; skepticism about the impartiality of neopositivist social science, on grounds that it often serves the status quo; and a commitment in principle to research that leads toward the restructuring of power in favor of disadvantaged societies and classes. The emergence of this critical tendency in conflict research is discussed by Terry Nardin in Chapter 12. Most who now call themselves peace researchers are Europeans. The majority of conflict researchers, especially in North America, retain both their commitment to the norms of scientific objectivity and the division of theory from practice, though personally they often are as critical and as partisan as peace researchers. The distinction between the critical posture of peace researchers and the positivist commitments of other conflict researchers was highlighted in 1972 when the members of the Peace Research Society (International) voted to rename it the Peace Science Society (International).

The substantial majority of scholars whose work is evaluated in this *Handbook* probably do not self-consciously identify themselves as either peace or conflict researchers. These divisions are tangential to our purpose, which is to survey systematic theory and evidence about the conditions, patterns, and consequences of open political conflict. It is the subject matter, and a systematic approach to it, which gives unity to the *Handbook*.

HOW THE HANDBOOK IS ORGANIZED

In the preceding sketch of the development of empirical conflict research I suggested that war was studied in this perspective earlier than was political violence within nations, and that individual participation in conflict is the most recent subject of research. When I outlined and sought contributions for this *Handbook*, however, I did so by beginning at the individual level and moving up through the levels of analysis to the international system. As a result the skeleton of the *Handbook*'s organization consists of three parts that comprise four conceptually distinct but overlapping levels of analysis: the individual level, subject of Part One; the group and national levels, which are combined in Part Two as they are in most empirical research; and the international system, in Part Three. Part Four comprises essays on the implications of conflict research for practice, in both personal and policy senses. Within each of these parts there is no fixed division of labor. At the outset I specified a set of more or less coherent topics, based on my perception of the natural intellectual divisions of conflict research, but in the final analysis the contributors decided on the scope of their essays—though not without editorial guidance. These are the general topics of the *Handbook*, and a sketch of their subjects:

1. *Individual participation in conflict.* Empirical research on this topic, the subject of Part One, is concerned with the identities, traits, and

perceptions of people who participate in conflict. People's potential for aggressive behavior is the subject of a growing body of physiological research, reviewed by James Chowning Davies in Chapter 1. Whether individuals actually participate in protest and rebellion is a function of their motivations and perceptions, variables which depend in turn upon their life histories and present circumstances. Two chapters explore the relevant evidence. In Chapter 2 Edward N. Muller evaluates survey evidence about the importance of relative deprivation, political attitudes, and socioeconomic factors as determinants of participation in aggressive political action in contemporary Western societies. In Chapter 3 Mostafa Rejai summarizes his own and others' studies of the traits, life cycles, and ideological orientations of revolutionary leaders and followers. This micro-level research, as it is sometimes called, entails comparisons among individuals within specific societies; comparisons of activists and leaders across time and societies; and, in a few studies, comparisons of the aggregate properties of individual participants in political conflict in a number of different societies.

2. *Conflict within nations.* There are two distinct foci of research on conflict within nations: the groups that are party to conflict, and the national system as such. Most conflict research by sociologists and social historians has been preoccupied with the organization, growth, actions, and fate of political and socioeconomic groups in conflict. Systematic research on conflict groups usually compares groups either simultaneously or over time within a single society. Cross-cultural research on conflict groups is less common, consisting mainly of comparative studies of revolutionary movements. A distinctive feature of most research on conflict groups is the treatment accorded to political regimes: the state and its supporters are conceptualized as the dominant sociopolitical group, in actual or potential conflict with nonelite groups.

Conflict research by political scientists usually takes the nation–state or society, rather than groups within nations, as the unit of analysis. At this level of analysis the state ordinarily is regarded as the central or defining element of the social and political system. Its role in conflict is usually seen as the target and manager of conflict behavior rather than as a protagonist. Research in this perspective includes many cross-sectional comparative studies of nations and a smaller but increasing number of longitudinal studies that trace conflict in one or several countries over time. The main questions have to do with how the socioeconomic and political characteristics of countries affect the shape and extent of violent conflict. A newer body of research asks whether and how conflict affects society. Another important development in research on national conflict is the recognition that the structure of the international system and specific interdependencies among nations have significant effects on the causes and outcomes of conflict within nations.

The theoretical presuppositions of research on conflict within nations are examined by Harry Eckstein in Chapter 4. He questions the assumption of most group conflict researchers that violent conflict is inherent in political and social arrangements and contrasts it with the prevailing view of political scientists that violent conflict is contingent on the occurrence of abnormal social conditions. Ekkart Zimmermann surveys the ample quantitative research on the correlates of civil conflict in Chapter 5, most of it exemplifying the national rather than the group level of analysis. The theories and evidence surveyed by Eckstein and Zimmermann are concerned mainly with "why people rebel." The obverse question concerns "why states use coercion," a subject that has only recently begun to attract significant attention from conflict researchers. An essay on this topic by Raymond Duvall was completed too late to include here and will appear elsewhere. Another new and largely uncharted field of conflict research is the analysis of the outcomes of conflict, which I review and attempt to synthesize in Chapter 6. Some of this work asks about the fate of groups caught up in conflict, some of it examines the impact of conflict on governmental policies and on the social, economic, and political characteristics of the nation.

3. *International conflict.* War and lesser forms of international conflict are the subject of three distinct clusters of theoretical and comparative research: (a) the linkage between internal and international conflict; (b) the causes and effects of nations' involvement in warfare; and (c) the conditions that determine the levels of conflict in the international system as a whole. Research on these subjects is largely the province of political science and international relations, to which can be added a few distinguished contributions by anthropologists and others. In Chapter 7 Michael Stohl reviews the large corpus of quantitative research on the correlation of internal and external conflict. The theoretical basis of most of this work is poorly developed, he observes, and the weight of evidence is that there are no strong, global relationships of any kind between civil and international conflict—though many specific ones. The quantitative empirical literature on causes of war is surveyed in Chapter 8 by Dina A. Zinnes, who shows that there has been modest progress toward explaining the varying incidence of war among nations and over time in the international system. A general evaluation of the state of theory about international conflict is provided in Chapter 9 by Bruce Bueno de Mesquita, who is sharply critical of the logical foundations and structure of balance-of-power, polarity, arms-race, deterrence, and other theories. Considerably less research has been done on the outcomes and consequences of war than on its causes. The evidence and speculation evaluated by Arthur A. Stein and Bruce M. Russett in Chapter 10 are wide-ranging, but theoretical certainty and cumulative findings are largely lacking.

4. *The practical implications of conflict research.* Part Four of the

Handbook consists of three chapters, in style and subject quite different from most others. In Chapter 11 Dennis C. Pirages asks what has been learned about conflict management and surveys a variety of research identifying the kinds of structures and processes that reduce levels of conflict, whether within organizations or in national political life. He also identifies strategies by which those in power and others can minimize disruptive conflict and pursue peaceful change. I invited Terry Nardin to consider the connections between theory and practice in conflict research from a more abstract viewpoint. His response, in Chapter 12, is an analysis of the character and limitations of research on conflict, which concludes that both conflict researchers and their critics have too often confused the search for understanding with practical concerns: "The vocation of the theorist is not to change the world but to interpret it." In the last chapter J. David Singer comments on the same issue from a different perspective. His view is that conflict research can and should be brought to bear on policy issues in the quest for peace, but in a mode that is professional rather than polemical.

Some aspects of peace and conflict research have received less attention in this review than others. The socioeconomic characteristics of contemporary rioters and demonstrators are the subject of a significant amount of sociological research which is noted only in passing. No evaluation is offered of the empirical work, mainly by sociologists, on the differential incidence of riots in American cities during the 1960s (a recent contribution citing the principal earlier studies is Midlarsky 1978). The vast comparative literature on the incidence and causes of coups d'état is not treated separately; neither is the newer literature on terrorism. Zimmermann has recently completed a broad survey of cross-national research on coups (1980), and a useful bibliographic essay on terrorism research through 1977 is provided by Bell (1978: 280–285). I offer no apologies for these omissions; these are specialized areas of concentration in conflict research that did not warrant separate review chapters, given the constraints placed on the *Handbook*'s length, but ones whose major features I expected to be noted by contributors dealing with more general subjects.

The *Handbook* also lacks a separate essay on methodological issues in conflict research. This cluster of topics includes the scope and quality of conflict data, evaluation of the measurement of theoretical variables, consideration of the relative merits of cross-sectional and longitudinal research designs, and assessment of the statistical models and methods in use. The omission is deliberate: since methodological issues are specific to particular subjects in conflict research, I asked contributors to discuss them wherever appropriate to their topics. The reader interested in a useful methodological critique of research on conflict within nations should read David Snyder's 1978 essay in the *Journal of Conflict Resolution*.

There is only one significant omission that I regret. No essay in this *Handbook* offers a full, careful review of the general, formal approach to conflict theory pioneered by scholars like Boulding (1962), Rapoport (1960), and Schelling (1963). Richardson's mathematical models of arms races (surveyed in Rapoport 1957) are another narrower example. I expected that insofar as contributors found formal models relevant to their subjects, they would consider them. In fact, only arms-race models are considered, and these only from one particular perspective, by Bueno de Mesquita in his review of theories of international conflict. The fact is that general, formal models of conflict processes, though widely cited in the literature, only recently have begun to influence empirically minded researchers, most of whom have preferred soft theory and hard evidence over formal theory. There is evidence now of a quickening of interest in formal approaches to conflict and of the explicit marriage of these approaches to empirical inquiry, represented, for example, in Zinnes's recent work (see Zinnes 1976: section III). A number of different kinds of formal theory are being used in this way, including dynamic systems models (Salert and Sprague 1978) and simulations (Bennett and Alker 1977; Bremer and Mihalka 1977); deterministic action–reaction models (Jackson et al. 1978; Schrodt 1978); mathematical diffusion models (Duncan and Siverson 1975; Midlarsky 1978); rational-choice theories (Altfield and Bueno de Mesquita 1979; Bueno de Mesquita 1980); and catastrophe theory (Holt, Job and Markus 1978). The use of quantitative analysis to test formal theories seems now to be the most promising of all the gleams on the horizon of empirical conflict research.

VALUES AND CONFLICT RESEARCH

There are strong antitheses between empirical conflict research and its subject matter. Conflict by its nature involves opposed values, whereas conflict research aims at objective description and explanation. Acts of conflict are intensely emotional while the abstract theories, quantitative measures, and statistical analyses of conflict studies are remote from the rage, terror, and pain of people caught up in open conflict. It is important to understand that the dispassionate scientific objectivity of much of the research reviewed in this *Handbook* rests on and is intended to serve the values of the researchers.

The first assumption of most conflict researchers is that the procedures of social science make it possible to achieve a general, analytic description and understanding of the properties and processes of conflict. Most researchers do not regard valid understanding as an end in itself but as a means toward the realization of personal values, which are often pacifist, humanitarian, and egalitarian. It is quite common to hear conflict researchers justify their choice of subjects and the use of scientific procedures by reference to the presumed instrumentality of knowledge, if not for them personally then for the students they teach, or the activists who learn of it, or policy makers who, the researchers expect, will act in ways that enhance peace. When I first invited contributions for the *Handbook* several years ago, I suggested to contributors that the following principles represented the views of the majority of scholars doing research on conflict:

1. conflict is inevitable in all social systems; violent conflict is not
2. conflict is potentially creative as well as destructive; conflict research should aim at enhancing the creative and nonviolent consequences of conflict and minimizing its destructive consequences
3. the development and testing of empirical theory about the conditions of conflict and peace are the ultimate intellectual objectives of conflict analysis
4. neopositivist approaches to conflict analysis alone are not likely to save humankind from itself, but it is unlikely that humankind can save itself without them
5. normative concerns in the scientific analysis of conflict should be limited, as far as possible, to the choice of subject and to the application of resultant knowledge; the irreducible normative connotations of conflict theory should be made explicit
6. the net reduction of human misery is the ultimate social objective of conflict analysis.

Two aspects of these principles are particularly problematic. One is whether the concepts and procedures used in conflict research, the interpretations of findings, and therefore the knowledge obtained are a function of the researcher's values. Critical essays have shown how scholars' values can affect every phase of social research, from conceptualization (see Nardin 1973) and measurement to the interpretation of statistical data and analyses (see especially Beardsley 1979). The conventional prescription for dealing with this issue is that scholars should state their value premises explicitly in their research reports so that others can judge and discount the effects accordingly. But if the influences of values are in fact pervasive and ineradicable (which may plague some kinds of conflict research more than others), this is a flabby and inadequate response. A more rigorous and demanding alternative might be to formulate alternative theories about the conflict phenomena at issue designed explicitly to facilitate the attainment of contending values, just as we often formulate competing hypotheses. From each point of view the researcher would devise alternative definitions of key terms, employ different measures and research designs, and offer competing interpretations of results. Philip

Beardsley has suggested how this might be done in his articles (1974; 1979) and in his unpublished manuscripts. It would be difficult to do and hard to get published, but if a few key studies were carried out or replicated in this way—using alternative normative perspectives—we should be better able to say whether some of the essential findings of conflict research are indeed independent of normative context.

The second problematic feature of these principles is their optimistic assumption that knowledge-in-practice will have such hoped-for results as the enhancement of conflict's creative consequences and the reduction of human misery. Some will be skeptical on grounds that the results of social research are either trivial or are ignored in practice. Even if results are significant and potentially fateful for social action, there is much controversy about the most suitable way to apply them and about whether or not the student of conflict should also be an activist or an adviser, and if so to whom (see the contributions to Fink and Boulding 1972).[3]

One manifestation of these tensions is a transatlantic debate between those who argue that peace and conflict research should be designed in such a way that results are of potential advantage to underdogs, and others, whose objective is the more even-handed dispensation of knowledge. A personal example illustrates the problem. A decade ago I proposed a theory about "why men rebel" which, I speculated, was "as likely to be read by rebels as by rulers and suggest[ed] as many courses of effective action for one as the other" (Gurr 1970b: x). In a rejoinder, Tord Høivik of the International Peace Research Institute (Oslo) argued that social theory should serve the oppressed, not the oppressors (personal communication 1973; see also Wolin 1973). I would be pleased if my theory were incapable of being applied by "oppressors," but no conceivable formulation of the theory—or other empirical theories of civil conflict—could guarantee that result. For one, it is impossible to accept Høivik's implicit assumption that rebels always are oppressed and rulers necessarily are oppressors. Second, only clandestine research in the service of one party to conflict can have uniquely one-sided effects. In a world of freely circulating ideas it is inevitable that theories of both revolution and counterinsurgency, for example, will be studied by all parties to conflict, both to design strategy and to anticipate what opponents will do. Confronted by such dilemmas about the uncertain uses of social theory, our only sanctuary seems to be to reaffirm that the scholar's first obligation is to seek valid understanding. We may accept other obligations as well, but in my view this one is most fundamental.

THE FUTURE OF CONFLICT RESEARCH

Since conflict is a relatively new subject for systematic social research it should not be surprising that it suffers from growing pains. A common theme of the contributors to this *Handbook* is dissatisfaction with the present state of theory and empirical findings. The commentaries on theory reflect a level of contentiousness among conflict theorists that resembles their subject matter. Eckstein criticizes theorists of internal conflict for failure to recognize and deal with a fundamental "choice point" in theory; Davies challenges theorists who do not take account of psychological factors in conflict situations. Bueno de Mesquita diagnoses fundamental logical flaws in theories purporting to explain international conflict. Many contributors note the failure of theorists at all levels to specify concepts adequately or to identify the circumstances under which their theories can be expected to be applicable.

The evaluations of empirical research are almost as sharp. Research on the characteristics of revolutionary leaders and followers is mainly descriptive and too often is forced into the procrustean bed of psychoanalytic interpretation (Rejai). Empirical research on who participates in protest and why aspires to test theoretical arguments about the relative importance of deprivation, calculated self-interest, and political beliefs but is flawed because participation usually is measured by reference to intentions rather than action and because at least one of the explanatory variables—relative deprivation—has been mismeasured in most research done to date (Muller). Most empirical studies on the causes of civil conflict explicitly confront theoretical issues, but the quality of aggregate conflict data is suspect and causal variables often are measured imprecisely and at a different level of analysis than that specified in theory (Zimmermann). Empirical research on the outcomes of internal and international conflict thus far is fragmentary and largely divorced from such theoretical speculation as exists on the subject (Gurr, Stein and Russett). A great deal of quantitative research on conflict linkages and on the determinants of war has been carried out in the last twenty years without precise theoretical guidance and without much cumulation of evidence (Stohl, Zinnes).

Critical though the contributors are about much of conflict research, most of them also point to general precepts and exemplary studies that should improve future research on the subject. It is after all the nature of social research to proceed by a noisy and messy process of thesis and rejoinder, experiment and counterexperiment, in which the weakness of each body of work provides the subject matter for the next round of theoretical revision and empirical advancement. If the remedies proposed here for the flaws of conflict research are taken seriously in future, they should lead to these general kinds of improvement:

1. *Theory and empirical research will be more closely articulated.* Theorists will be more universally concerned about formulating generalizations that are susceptible to empirical assessment. More important, because less widely done now, empiricists will give more careful attention to specifying and evaluating theoretical systems of hypotheses,

rather than testing isolated hypotheses or searching for descriptive generalizations. A number of imbalances between theoretical and empirical research also will be remedied: empirical work will flourish in areas such as revolutionary processes and outcomes that are rich in theory but poor in evidence, while theoretical work should move ahead on subjects like revolutionary participation and internal–external linkages where empirical evidence has accumulated in advance of plausible and well-specified theory.

2. *There will be better theoretical integration across levels of analysis.* It is widely though not universally accepted that psychological factors need to be taken into account in macro-theories of conflict. Similarly, conflict researchers are moving toward a better theoretical understanding of how international factors affect conflict within nations, and of how the dynamics of political and economic systems affect conflict between nations. At the outer limits, theory is being or will be developed to specify how conflict and cooperative behavior are influenced by the biological equipment of the human species and by the dynamics of the global biosphere. Many theories now attempt to move across levels of analysis. The expectation is that more will do so across more levels of analysis and in more empirically provocative and convincing ways.

3. *Conflict research will increasingly take the long view as well as the large one.* There are promising instances of longitudinal research on conflict, especially on patterns of war, revolutionary change, and political development and stability. We should expect, and work for, the development of more substantial bodies of theory about the dynamics and the historical tendencies of conflict (for two very different approaches see Davies 1977b,c, and Tilly 1978, chapter 6). Few contemporary scholars have taken up the challenge of Sorokin's work, more than forty years ago, to link and explain millennial changes in social organization, culture, and conflict. The "long view" in macro-research may be measured in centuries; in research on individuals and groups in conflict it is more likely to require the study of life-cycles of personal commitment, group mobilization, and challenge-and-response sequences that span a few years or decades. The temporal span of dynamic studies will depend on the units and questions under examination; the principle is that research on conflict will be extended both backward and forward in time.

4. *The technology of quantitative conflict analysis will continue to improve.* Analytic techniques have come a long way from the graphic depictions and simple correlational analyses of early empirical research on conflict. Testing the complexities of the best current theories requires the full armamentorium of advanced regression techniques, including especially time-series analysis and the estimation of simultaneous-equation models. These and other statistical methodologies have gained acceptance and usage in conflict research at a pace in advance of the development of

suitable data. At every level of analysis, from riot participation to warfare, researchers have devised good and expensive procedures for gathering reliable conflict data. But they are not always able to afford to employ them and rely instead on dubious or approximate data. Data on the myriad theoretically specified causes and correlates of conflict are also problematic: too many theoretically important causal variables have been indexed in indirect and imprecise ways. Nonetheless there are definite upward trends in the quality of data being used in causal analyses at the individual, collective, and systemic levels. I hope and expect that quantitative researchers will continue to use better data and more sophisticated modes of analysis to evaluate more precisely formulated theories. Insofar as they do, our understanding of conflict and conviction about the validity of our findings will be enhanced.

NOTES

1. Mack and Snyder's 1957 review of the literature on social conflict includes 44 primary references, all but two of them published after 1945. A more comprehensive review of conflict theory by Fink (1968) cites 125 works, 20 of them published before 1945; about half of the 20 are general texts or treatises that include some discussion of conflict or competition. The cumulative bibliography of this *Handbook* includes an estimated 673 items dealing with the conflict behavior of individuals, groups, states, or the international system. (I did not count general works and those that deal only peripherally with conflict behavior.) These are their years of publication:

before 1920	8	1955–1959	21
1920–1929	3	1960–1964	61
1930–1939	8	1965–1969	148
1940–1949	14	1970–1974	295
1950–1954	13	1975–	249

    The distribution may be distorted somewhat because minor, early studies tend to get displaced from scholarly memories and bibliographies by better and more recent ones. But the general pattern surely is valid: a veritable explosion of conflict research began in the early 1960s.
2. I am not suggesting that systematic social research in general or on conflict specifically is exclusively a twentieth-century enterprise. Sir Henry Maine, Karl Marx, and Max Weber are among the most eminent of the nineteenth-century scholars who were systematic in their use of evidence and formulation of generalizations about subjects peripheral or central to conflict. Emile Durkheim was one among many French social researchers who made extensive use of quantitative data. What is distinctive, though not absolutely unique, about contemporary conflict research is the choice and use of methods.
3. The issue is neither new nor peculiar to conflict research. Max Weber, for example, wrestled with the problem in his 1918 essays on "Politics as a Vocation" and "Science as a Vocation" (in Gerth and Mills 1946). A contemporary exposition of the Weberian dilemma is Eckstein 1967.

PART ONE

Psychosocial Foundations of Conflict Behavior

CHAPTER 1

Biological Perspectives on Human Conflict

James Chowning Davies

$$B = f(OE)$$

ALL HUMAN BEHAVIOR, including conflict behavior, is a function or product of the interaction of the organism and the environment: $B = f(OE)$. Observable acts may involve conflict between individuals, between individuals and groups, or between groups. So considered, conflict is simply environmental interaction: we see a policeman and a demonstrator fighting; a crowd lynching a deviant; class fighting class; and nation fighting nation. Each party to such conflict is environment to the other. But organic forces within individuals (mainly in their brains) are always interacting with environmental forces (mainly in the society and culture) and may be critical in such violent events. The innate desire to stay alive may be a critical factor in a bread riot. The perhaps innate desire to be treated with equal dignity may be a critical factor in a conflict within or between nations in which ethnic, religious, or socioeconomic groups look upon each other as subordinate or superior.

To seek to understand political conflict in any depth, it is just as necessary to analyze the organism–environment interaction as, in studying basic physical events (like the formation and destruction of such compounds as water or salt), it is necessary to analyze the interaction between the particles that compose atoms (electrons, protons, muons, and so on) on the one hand and the environment of atoms (other atoms, compounds,

NOTE: For indispensable early encouragement more than a decade ago, I am still much indebted to Philip W. Davies and Roger W. Sperry. For help and encouragement en route, I am likewise indebted to José M. R. Delgado, Paul D. MacLean, Denis A. Snook, Vicki Van Nortwick, John C. Wahlke, and Armand L. Zanecchia.

molecules, temperature, pressure, critical mass, and so on) on the other. By far the greatest portion of theory and research in social and political conflict has concentrated on the environmental half of the equation. In this chapter, I will seek to show ways in which biology can help us understand the other half.

The study of conflict calls for examining the organic half of the equation, notably for the following reason. Stable environmental forces tend to normalize human interactions and to make them unchanging. An environment may become unstable for three reasons: because of an external natural change, such as drought or disease; because of internal changes within the developing human organism that destabilize the natural and the social-cultural environment; and because of changes in the environment that produce changes within the developing human organism. A sudden scarcity (or abundance) of food affects the physical and mental health of people. The growth of technology, which can vastly affect the food supply, is one of numerous products of human social integration and intelligence—which phenomena are in part products of the organic development of human beings. And such organic development is in turn dependent on the gradual evolution of society and culture.

The process is an interaction, which is to say that internal demands to alter the environment are themselves partly the result of organic forces. Social theory and research that neglects the organism is not wrong or even necessarily futile: it is merely incomplete and likely to neglect the deepest demands for change, those that arise within the human organism. Environmental frustration of these demands produces internal tension that sometimes explodes into violence. The organic roots of these demands and tension are a necessary part of the analysis of conflict, particularly violent conflict.

Biological considerations in the study of political conflict are rather new. Because of this, I will first clarify the linkage between private and public conflict, in familial and historical contexts; then propose a theoretical framework relating biological to other modes of studying conflict, in which I will try to clarify some definitions and distinctions; and then go into a consideration of research in the brain's two major subsystems (nerves and endocrines). Then I will discuss some of the grossest environmental influences on the brain (physical, emotional, and cognitive deprivation) and take a critical look at sociobiological perspectives. Finally I will present a theory of basic human motivation as it may help understand the organic, species-wide drives that lead people into conflict when the drives are not adequately satisfied.

SOME LINKAGES BETWEEN PRIVATE AND PUBLIC CONFLICT

Conflict is present during periods of political stability, but it is continuously resolved in interactions that are usually neither hostile nor violent.

During such periods, analysis that concentrates on environmental forces is often adequate, for a couple of reasons. First, the natural and social environment is generally supportive of the innate, that is the organic, needs, demands, and expectations of human beings. A supportive environment thus reduces tensions that reflect unfulfilled, frustrated demands and thereby stabilizes, normalizes, conventionalizes human interactions. Second, people evidently enjoy stability, normality, and good will in their sometimes conflictful interactions—unless these interactions become deeply frustrating to people at a particular stage of their individual and collective development, when one-time friends may become enemies.

Tensions that reflect deep and widespread frustration therefore tend to build slowly within a people, a nation, and they lead to political conflict when people blame the government for their frustration—and to violent political conflict when the government's *non*response to popular demands is accompanied by coercion. It is notably during these periods of deep, prolonged, and widespread frustration that we need to look inside the human organism. We can then see what new demands, when sufficiently frustrated, turn usually amiable people into angry, determined, and elementally intelligent beings whose immediate goal is the rearrangement of long-established, long-comfortable values, habits, skills, customs, structures, socioeconomic institutions, and even government. Jefferson said in the American Declaration of Independence in 1776 that "mankind are more disposed to suffer, while evils are sufferable, than to right themselves by abolishing the forms to which they are accustomed." Our concern is with the forces inside people that cause them to stop suffering evils and to alter or abolish the political forms to which they are accustomed.

Intense conflict is associated with instability and violent conflict with extreme instability, a relationship that is sometimes supposed to be profoundly causal. However, it is almost a redundancy to say that instability causes conflict: it is almost like saying a forest burns because it has caught on fire. The more causal question is: what causes conflict to heat up to the point where it ignites into hatred and violence? What, in sum, causes violent civil strife, both within and between nations?

It is scientifically uneconomic to suppose that the basic organic causes of both nonviolent and violent conflict are qualitatively different, just as it is scientifically uneconomic to suppose that there are altogether different sets of causes for conflict between two individuals and between large groups of individuals. The fiery or icy anger that has as its object injury to another individual is not altogether different from the anger whose object is the overthrow of a government. Anger is anger. Its causes vary but seem always to result from frustration. Its objects vary, but even so there is a large amount of overlap between the causes of interindividual and of intergroup conflict. Let me give an example to indicate what I mean by the kinship, though of course not the identity, between the organic roots of interindividual and intergroup conflict.

An infant child is typically contented with the kinds and amounts of nurturance its parents provide—if these are sufficient. But as the child enters adolescence, he or she wants to become less dependent on parents for nurturance, friendship, and recognition. For example, he or she wants to form attachments with young people of the opposite sex, a desire that nurturant, responsible parents are wont to regard with concern. Parents want to see that their children do not get "in trouble" on dates; the children want to do as they themselves see fit. The conflict may be verbalized in a variety of ways, but the least likely way is for the adolescents (and their parents) to acknowledge that the adolescents' sex glands have commenced to alter long-established parent–child interaction patterns. Sometimes, we may suppose, the parents talk to each other in bed about the kind of nighttime activity they fear in their children, and then they themselves proceed to fulfill the same sex needs. The parent–child conflict *may* take violent form, but in no event is it resolved until the child's new and organically based needs are fulfilled by his or her leaving home, marrying, and settling down with a spouse. When the conflict is happily resolved, social habits and customs have successfully interacted with organic demands. But the necessary organic roots of the conflict between parents and children are typically ignored.

For a macrocosmic example, we can take an event that unfolded over centuries, an event that is parochially referred to as the Protestant Reformation of the sixteenth and seventeenth centuries in Germany and Western Europe. The Wars of the Reformation, lasting from about 1525 (the German Peasant War) to 1648 (the Treaties of Westphalia), involved much more than a war between Protestants and Catholics. Estimates of the deaths during the 124-year period range as high as a quarter of the population of Germany. It makes little sense to suppose that such an intense and protracted conflict can be explained by ideological or doctrinal differences. Both Catholics and Protestants justified their part in the conflict by references to the same Bible, which both sides regarded as the Word of God. Nor can the corruption of the Roman church, which so deeply disturbed Luther and his followers, serve as a deep or adequate explanation for such a long and bloody conflict. To these explanations we have to add changes in economic and social institutions. But then, to get to fundamentals, we have to consider what caused these institutional changes.

Standard historical or sociological explanations for the Protestant Reformation concentrate on various aspects of the environment as it developed and stabilized out of the gradual disintegration and decay of the Roman Empire. The feudal and manorial socioeconomic and political system was a response in part to the inability of the Roman Empire to maintain physical security and some social and economic coherence over the broad land-mass of Europe and the Mediterranean basin. The feudal-manorial system endured for well over a thousand years after the Roman Empire decayed. Indeed the system still persists in much of Latin America, to which it was carried inside the heads of the Portuguese and Spanish conquerors, and in other parts of the world in which feudalism was some kind of advance over what it replaced.

The forces that led to the decline of feudalism as a set of institutions, as a system, must have been very powerful. They had to overcome more than a millennium of what stimulus-response psychology would call operant conditioning. They had to overcome the long-accustomed and continuing provision by feudalism of a reasonably secure environment, and a society in which people were secure as group members who knew each other on a face-to-face basis. Many of these forces (such as the growth of commerce, banking, the specialization of economic function, and thus the growth of trade in goods produced on farms and in factories) were environmental. But some of them were internal and must have been very powerful, or they would not have been able to overcome more than a millennium of conditioning. And the conflict of forces became savagely violent.

If, as suggested, there is not adequate reason to assume that the organic and environmental forces that produce tension between growing children and their parents are altogether different from the organic and environmental forces that produce tension in developing societies, then there is a basic question: how can these forces be conceptualized and how can they be studied?

HOW CAN CONFLICT BE STUDIED?

In order to put the biological aspect of the study of conflict into perspective, we may order the entire range of forces that produce conflict in the following categories.

1. *The human organism as an "isolated" system.* Basically this refers to those forces within the individual organism that originate in the genes. However, we need to remember that the genetic structure of organisms is inherited from parent cells and thus also is an organism–environment interaction. This has been studied mainly by the branches of biology known as genetics and, more recently, microbiology and physiology. The last of these concentrates on what is imprecisely called the nervous system.

2. *The human organism in its developmental context.* This refers to the organism as it affects and is affected by the more or less continuous interactions with other human beings. These developmental processes begin before birth, in intrauterine contact between mother and fetus, and continue throughout life. Investigators in this category range from physiologists to motivational psychologists like Freud and Maslow and developmental psychologists like Piaget and Erikson.

3. *Small groups of individuals in face-to-face, direct, unmediated—that*

is, proximal—contacts. This refers to the behavior of individuals as members of proximal groups. Examples: the interactions of parents and children, husbands and wives, sisters and brothers, the members of a class in a schoolroom, the members of a street gang, and the members of a revolutionary group. This category overlaps with both category 2 and category 4. Anthropologists, sociologists, and social psychologists are among the main students of such interactions.

4. *Large groups of individuals in non-face-to-face, mediated—that is, distal—contacts.* This refers to the more loosely tied members of such groups as political parties, socioeconomic classes, castes, and the nonelite adherents of revolutionary movements. In such group interactions, people are not in frequent proximal contact as Democrats or Republicans, businessmen or working men, Untouchables or Brahmans, but nevertheless share many of the expectations, values, and behavior patterns of others in the group. Marx is the classic originator of this mode of analysis, along with many other social scientists in several disciplines.

Most conflict theory and research has concentrated on the last two of the above categories. Marx's theory of class conflict falls in the last of them, as does his research into the immiserization of rural people who were forced by the closing of common lands and other factors to move into cities and to work in factories. Theory and research in such events as the American black rebellion of the 1960s and in national revolutions also falls mostly into the last category. Other conflict research relates the third to the fourth, examining linkages between behavior patterns established, for example, within the family and social (but rarely political) conflict.

This chapter deals mainly with forces of the first two kinds as they pertain to political conflict. It concentrates on biological rather than psychological theory and research, even though many psychologists are now using biological concepts and techniques. The more usual kind of pertinent psychological work is the subject of later chapters in this book.

There is some disagreement and much unclarity among social scientists as to the genetic, organic factors that affect behavior. The nature of mankind has been the subject of philosophical study since at least Aristotle. If human nature is defined as those components of overt behavior that are genetically programmed and therefore universal to the species, physiologists have of course been studying human and animal nature even though they prefer more exact and limited concepts. There is little use in making conclusive jumps from the genes to political conflict and thus to fall into the unavoidable error of saying that behavior *x* is *the* consequence of gene *a*. There is nevertheless much research by physiologists and other biologists that helps explain conflict, and we will here attempt to make tentative inferences from some of it.

What this chapter is about may be best understood by noting what a

Nobel laureate and biologist, Peter Medawar, wrote. A political scientist who is interested in biology and politics, W. J. M. Mackenzie, quoted Medawar thus:

> If we write down a list of empirical sciences in the order:
> 1. Physics
> 2. Chemistry
> 3. Biology
> 4. Ecology/Sociology
> it seems to be arguable that each science is a special case of the one that precedes it. . . . As we go down the list in the hierarchy of empirical sciences, every statement which is true in physics is true also in chemistry and biology and ecology and sociology. Likewise any statement that is true in biology . . . is also true in sociology. [Mackenzie 1978: 92]

Without depreciating the causal significance of a host of extraorganic forces—those that fall mainly within the third and fourth categories above—in this chapter we concentrate on those organic tendencies that bear a relationship to political behavior that is comparable to that between basic physical principles (like conductance or the electrical properties of ions) and biology. These organic tendencies, researched empirically by biologists, pertain to what philosophers have abstractly called human nature.

BRAIN AND OTHER BIOLOGICAL RESEARCH

The kind of biological research that seems to be most promising in the long run for helping explain conflict is brain research. It deals, inter alia, with tracing electrically and chemically the sequence of events within the brain that have violent behavior as their output. The most relevant brain theory and research involves the working of what is called the limbic system or the emotional brain and also involves the functions of some of the hormones. The human limbic system and hormones are strikingly similar to those of the higher and even of the lower vertebrates—similar, that is, to the brains of not only primates and other mammals but also birds and even reptiles. This research falls mainly within the first category above.

Another kind of biological research can also be fruitful for understanding conflict. It necessitates more inference about what is going on physically and chemically within the brain but it involves systematic laboratory study of the effects of external, that is, environmental events in more or less controlled circumstances. Research with laboratory rats, cats, dogs, and monkeys—in which the animals remain intact—is also promising, and it falls within the first two categories.

Animal research in more natural and therefore uncontrolled circumstances can also help understand conflict. However, the very fact that the research is undertaken in normal circumstances makes it hard to separate out three sets of factors:

1. those environmental forces that are powerfully and widely operant, such as profound socioeconomic and political change or natural disaster
2. those environmental forces that reflect the organism's early experience—from conception to maturity—which seem to be innate but are actually environmental, such as malnutrition and emotional deprivation during the first days, months, and years of life
3. truly organic forces, such as the innate needs for nutrition and for attachment to other human beings and for recognition as (semi-) autonomous individuals who want to take part in determining their own destinies.

A common error is to single out one observable behavior of an intact, nonlaboratory animal, to note that it appears under a variety of real-life circumstances, to classify it as conflictful or cooperative, and then to conclude that it is manifestly an innate, genetic tendency. Manifest it is; innate it only may be. Another common error, shared it seems by most biologists and some social scientists, is to reduce the innate drives of Homo sapiens to self- and species-preservation. These drives or motives or goals are characteristics of all life forms. Research based on the assumption that humans have only these innate drives does not help to explain political or other kinds of conflict arising over issues beyond survival.

Particularly in analysis of political strife, it is easy to overlook the historic circumstances in which conflict occurs. In the middle of the seventeenth century, Hobbes (1651) concluded that humans are innately quarrelsome and violent. He wrote during a period of enormous change. A still largely subsistence and feudal economy was being replaced by an exchange and capitalist economy, with its division of labor. An absolute monarchy was being replaced by parliamentary rule. The enclosure of common lands converted areas that the rural poor used for their own providence to lands producing grains and wool for sale by landowners in the urban market. Poor people were forced to migrate to cities, where they had to fight to stay alive. Political elites meanwhile enjoyed a murderous pursuit of power. Evidently assuming that such circumstances were normal, Hobbes regarded them simply as the product of innate human aggression.

In the twentieth century, which has been perhaps as violent as the sixteenth and seventeenth, some writers have come to the Hobbesian conclusion. Again without a sense of historic context or of the profound developmental processes about which Marx had theorized, Einstein and Freud (1932), Lorenz (1963), and Ardrey (1961, 1966) all pessimistically concluded that man is innately aggressive. With Hobbes, they shared a tendency to ignore the deep social, economic, and political forces that have helped to produce the sometimes savage wars and revolutions of our time. Skipping over all these intervening, developmental variables—these changes in environmental forces as they interact with human beings who themselves are developing from less to more mature stages—such writers have blamed everything on the genetic structure of Homo sapiens.

Similarly, but optimistically, Rousseau, Marx, and (as we shall see later in this chapter) Edward O. Wilson have all made the same many-linked, noncontextual inferences. Man is born free, said Rousseau in *The Social Contract* (1762a), and he is everywhere in chains—because of social-systemic constraints as they would now be called. But then in *Emile* (1762b), Rousseau described the three forces—two of them environmental—that could liberate humans: their heredity, their upbringing (socialization as we now call it), and the direct experience of their "surroundings" (Rousseau 1762b: 6). Liberate poor people from bondage to capitalism, with its degrading and stultifying labor, Marx said, and they will live amicably, freely, and with spontaneity. And Wilson has contrived to link the genetically determined desire to survive to a conclusion that people are genetically unselfish. They may be, as I think they are under certain circumstances; and they may be selfish under certain circumstances. But Wilson has not forged many of the links between the genes and altruistic behavior.

Inference is inescapable. In a post-Einsteinian, Heisenbergian world, one can never assume that the occurrence of an event predicts with certainty the repetition of that event. But inference is better understood if one is aware of and specifies the sequence of steps in the process of inferring and if one thereby reduces the uncertainty of one's inferences. John Paul Scott (1975a: 247–255; 1975b) has contributed to an awareness of the problem of making inferences between innate organic forces and manifest behavior. He conceives five levels of systems: 1) genetic systems, 2) physiological systems, 3) systems of organization in individual behavior, 4) social systems, and 5) ecosystems. He stresses that the causes of confict cannot be reduced to any one of these systems; that they are all involved; and that to make inferences from one system to overt behavior is reducing analysis to the old heredity-environment dilemma.

Scott calls his orientation "polysystemic," saying that factors at each level contribute—separately, consecutively, and collectively—to the end product of conflict behavior. While it may be reassuring to suppose that there is indeed one cause or even one system of causes of conflict, reality does not seem to be that simple. If it were, social scientists would by now have produced a rigorous conflict theory that could be confirmed with the relative ease that established Einstein's theory of relativity. And we could have long since settled on just what are the factors that cause conflict, violent conflict, and violent political conflict.

This chapter concentrates on the organism as an "isolated" system and as a system in its natural and social contexts, and it comes to some tentative conclusions about organic influences. The chapter also hypothesizes about the basic needs of the human organism that, when frustrated, increase the likelihood of conflict. But this chapter does not conclude that humans have an innate desire to injure and destroy one another, nor does the statement of hypotheses have any purpose other than the useful one of focusing discussion and encouraging research that can confirm or disconfirm theory.

PHYLOGENY, ONTOGENY, AND EPIGENESIS

In addition to a scheme that establishes levels of analysis, there is another set of basic concepts—phylogeny, ontogeny, and epigenesis—that is crucial to developing durable and fundamental analysis of conflict. All three of these concepts are from biology, rooted perhaps in Charles Darwin's theory on *The Origin of Species* (1859). And Karl Marx, who wanted to dedicate his *Capital* (1867) to Darwin, was perhaps the first social scientist to see an orderly sequence in the genesis of socioeconomic systems, from primitive to feudal to capitalistic. Erik Erikson (1963: 269–274) made ontogeny and epigenesis central concepts in his theory of the development of human beings. A skeletal statement of a theory of stages of human political development is presented at the end of this chapter. The relationship of phylogeny, ontogeny, and epigenesis to theory and research in conflict, which is both consequence and cause of development, is introduced here.

Phylogeny is a broad term used to describe the evolution of life from its most primitive origins in single-celled organisms, billions of years ago, to its most recent and complex manifestation in the form of Homo sapiens. Phylogeny describes the process that Darwin analyzed in his 1859 theory. He noted the interaction between organisms and their environment, in stating his principle of natural selection, arguing that those species survived that adapted most successfully to their particular circumstances.

Ontogeny describes the process by which not a species but a particular individual develops from its primitive origin as a zygote to its maturity as a fully developed adult. The ontogeny of individuals and the phylogeny of species are not identical but comparable. For example, in humans there is a stage when the embryo in the womb has some of the characteristics of a chick developing in its shell (e.g., in the emergence at one end of nervous tissue, which becomes a brain attached to a spine). This similarity between phylogeny of species and physical ontogeny of individuals has theoretical implications for comparable processes in the evolution of socioeconomic and political systems and in the mental development of individuals— unless one believes that the development of individuals is never a cause but is always merely a consequence of the evolution of social systems. A theory of the phylogenetic development of systems as they interact with the ontogenetic development of individuals is indeed a theory. But if the interaction is indeed two-way, it suggests that processes of conflict, as they accompany change and development, involve forces that generate within human beings as part of their genetic inheritance and not only as the consequence of their social conditioning. In short, if the interaction is two-way, biology does indeed relate to the study of conflict.

Epigenesis is the process whereby each successive stage of development of an organism depends on the prior occurrence of the preceding stage. That is, if the normal sequence of development is from stage one to stage two, then stage three cannot successfully occur without the organism achieving stage two; and stage two cannot occur without the achievement of stage one. An embryonic limb in a vertebrate, for example, cannot ordinarily develop without the prior development of the spine. As Erikson applied epigenesis to mental development (Erikson 1963: 269–274), the first stage is "oral–sensory," in which basic trust or mistrust develops; the second is "muscular–anal," in which autonomy and shame and doubt begin to develop; and the third is "locomotor-genital," during which initiative and guilt begin to develop. If there is a failure at an earlier stage, it will inhibit or distort the development of later stages.

An example of the applicability of epigenesis as a concept to the study of conflict *as a concomitant of development* is the case of Haiti. It achieved its independence following a revolt of slaves against their French colonial owners a few years after the beginning of the French revolution. A pattern of violence became established that lost its connection with the period of transition from slavery to freedom and became institutionalized. The result was the perpetuation—for more than a century and a half—of violence that inhibited development beyond slavery: in effect the whole of Haitian society became enslaved to its violent elite (James 1939; Rotberg 1971: 49–64, 223–245, 342–368), even after Haiti liberated itself and emancipated all its slaves.

PHYSIOLOGICAL PERSPECTIVES ON AGGRESSION

As one often ill-defined or undefined aspect of conflict, the term "aggression" merits specification before we proceed any further. In this chapter, the term is used to mean a tendency to engage in hostile and intentionally destructive acts (Davies 1973: 235–237). The purpose of aggressive acts is to injure or kill other live creatures or to damage or destroy inanimate objects. Aggressive acts are here distinguished from the more general set of assertive acts by the intent that is involved: there is destructive intent in aggressive acts but no such intent, per se, in assertive ones. It is sometimes hard to distinguish the two kinds of action, but if the distinction is not made, then all acts that result in harm are deemed aggressive or all acts in-volving positive interaction may be considered aggressive, even if they result in *un*intended harm to the object of the action.

The distinction between aggressive and assertive acts has been glossed over so often that their intent becomes either conceptually irrelevant or befuddled. By intent I mean no more than goal-oriented behavior. A worm that has learned the correct path to food in a Y-maze is here deemed to have intent, as it turns at the junction toward the food. On the other hand, a person who accidentally runs his or her car into a shop window, killing the proprietor and destroying goods displayed in the window, is not here deemed to have engaged in aggressive action, despite the destruction. Political acts also may have consequences beyond the apparent intent. It is relatively easy to infer destructive intent on the part of the crowd that burned the Bastille in Paris on 14 July 1789, but it is quite difficult to infer that the crowd intended (unconsciously or consciously) to start more than a fire—that is, to start a revolution. In sum, intent may be unconscious or conscious (the worm in the maze versus the crowd at the Bastille), and the intended goal (destruction of the Bastille) may not contain the conse-quences of the act (revolution). For such reasons, it is very difficult to make inferences from observed acts to forces generated within the organism, but if we are aware neither of our premises nor of our in-ferences, our conclusions as to the innateness of aggressive (intentionally destructive) acts are specious.

Some writers, for example Scott (1970, 1977), have abandoned the term "aggressive," using in its place the term "agonistic." But such a change in terms, without facing the question of intent, seems to make it impossible to distinguish actions of quite contradictory sorts: it becomes impossible to distinguish the act of love from the act of rape. The terminology followed in this chapter defines the more general category of action as assertive, in-cluding therein action whose intent may be either constructive or destruc-tive or both. What Scott and others call agonistic approximates what is here called assertive.

One class of assertive actions includes those whose intent is positive, con-structive, and binding—friendly actions in which both or all parties sense benefit. Another class of assertive acts includes those whose intent is negative, destructive, and bond-breaking. These are here called aggressive. However, acts intended to harm others who threaten satisfaction of one's basic needs (physical or other kinds) are indeed aggressive but not neces-sarily wrongful—unless one supposes that it is always wrong to resist the efforts of other people who frustrate the satisfaction of one's own needs. Aggression in the form of revolution, and in the name of equality, was justified by Thomas Jefferson in 1776; and his arguments based on the in-nate equality of humans have been used in many other nations since 1776. This chapter tries to narrow the gap between levels of systems and levels of

analysis by taking a look at how the brain works. It recommends that inferences about the innateness of aggressive tendencies be explored in
greater depth than has been thus far achieved by either students of
philosophy or those who have come to their conclusions by studying intact
animals.

THE BRAIN: THE CENTRAL CONTROL SYSTEM

In this chapter we will review some of the most important findings about
the physiology of the brain and, with some caution, explicate the significance of these findings for understanding the roots of aggression. First we
will look at the two parts of the central control system (CCS): the central
nervous system (CNS) and the endocrine system (ES), concentrating on the
parts of the CCS that relate most directly to aggressive behavior. Then we
will look at what may be called biosocial perspectives, in which the work
of ethologists and geneticists helps broaden our understanding of genetic
forces operating in the brain. The findings of these researchers are based
on observation of the behavior of intact animals and the "behavior" of the
genes. And then we will spell out some of the implications for a deeper,
less mood-dominated, more realistic understanding of just what are roots,
what is the soil which nurtures the roots, and what is the ever ambiguous,
ever ambivalent product. It is well to bear in mind that none of the
research into the brain invalidates the evidence of environmental, particularly social, effects. Brain research and ethological research comple-
ment but do not necessarily invalidate theory and research of traditional
social science.

THE NERVES: THE CENTRAL NERVOUS SYSTEM

Human beings have the most highly developed and intricate brain of
any species. Estimates of the number of neurons in the human brain range
up to a hundred billion contained in a brain mass weighing about three
pounds (1.36 kilograms). In addition to the 100,000,000,000 or so neurons
(Hubel 1979:45) there are interconnections between neurons. These dendrites in some parts of the brain establish connections between one neuron
and up to tens of thousands of other neurons (Cragg in Granit 1977: 41). It
is surely an understatement to say that the number of possible connections
between neurons is enormous. And so the potential range of memories and
of combinations of old and new stimuli that can be involved in the making
of decisions is greater than the memory bank and programming parts of
any computer.

The enormous range of processes of observing, evaluating, organizing,
and decision making that the cortex of the brain makes available to every
human is consistent with our self-images as all-knowing and all-powerful
beings. If these self-images were the sole consequences of the extraor-

dinarily developed human cortex, people might indeed have the incessant desire to dominate that Hobbes said is a basic human characteristic. Fortunately there are massive but still largely uncharted nerve tracts linking the rational ("information-processing") and the emotional parts of the brain. This is the organic basis for a manifest behavioral fact: humans are not just intellectually or rationally but also emotionally interactive. They exhibit love and hatred, hope and despair, optimism and pessimism, and a range of combinations of these and other emotions. If there were not this organic substrate—this innate linkage—between the emotional and rational parts of the brain, we would indeed have to explain organized society on altogether environmental terms. The beginnings of orderly cooperation antedate by eons the calculus of cooperation. Without the emotional link, whose environmental strengthening, as we shall see, begins at birth, the formation and maintenance of society is inconceivable. Without the rational link, the scale and degree of integration is inconceivable.

A physiologist, Paul MacLean (1967, 1972), has divided the brain into three basic parts: the reptilian, paleomammalian, and neomammalian. These three parts are functionally and in some degree structurally distinguished in Figure 1–1. The reptilian part is so named by MacLean because in it are contained behavioral functions that humans share with reptiles. That is, reptiles have been found to manifest these and other behaviors: (1) the establishment and marking of territory; (2) defense of territory; (3) fighting; (4) the formation of groups; (5) the establishment of social hierarchy; (6) courtship; (7) mating; (8) the breeding and sometimes the care of offspring. An anthropocentric view would describe these behaviors of reptiles as humanoid. MacLean's nomenclature reminds us better of the continuity between the behavior of human beings and those of some of the lowest vertebrates.

Between the most primitive, reptilian part and the most advanced, neomammalian part of the brain (otherwise called the neocortex, the "new" cortex, where information is processed and decisions are made) lies the part which is most critical for our analysis. This is the limbic system, otherwise and more or less interchangeably designated as the paleocortex, the "old" cortex, or the paleomammalian system. A brilliant nineteenth-century French brain surgeon, Paul Broca, called this in-between part of the brain the limbic system because it constitutes the border zone between the most primitive and most advanced parts: it is the zone which more than any other part of the brain is the seat of the emotions.

Following Broca and Papez (1937), MacLean (1972), Delgado (1969), and many others have done extensive research within the limbic system, some of which is discussed here. To the extent that conflict behavior involves emotion, the limbic system is involved, and it is hard to conceive of emotion-free conflict behavior. However, it must always be borne in mind that there are large bundles of nerves connecting the limbic system with

FIGURE 1–1. The phylogenesis of the mammalian brain as conceptualized by Paul D. MacLean. In its evolution, the human forebrain expands in hierarchic fashion along the lines of three basic patterns that may be characterized as reptilian, paleomammalian, and neomammalian. Reproduced by permission of the author.

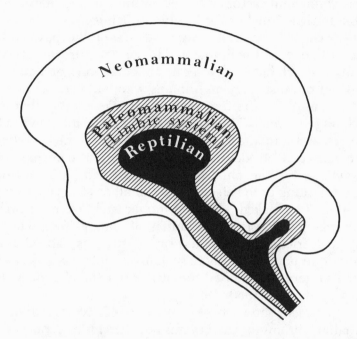

the neocortex and with the most primitive, "reptilian" parts of the brain. One implication of these interties is that, physiologically speaking, there are probably few behaviors that are quite free of either the information-processing and decision-making functions of the neocortex or the most primitive "instincts" of the sort that MacLean listed for reptiles. Another implication is that, to the extent that the primitive and the limbic systems "dominate" overt behavior, people may not be totally aware and in control of their reasons for behaving as they do, notably in times of stress that attend conflict. Some of the research reported below, which shows the behavioral consequences of direct intervention in the limbic system, thus establishes physiologically what Freud established psychologically: namely, that unconscious and often uncontrolled forces within human beings are among the major determinants of behavior. Freud discovered the unconscious origins of adult mental conflict in the (ontogenetic) development of humans as infants and children. What Broca, Papez, MacLean, and many others have done is to establish the similarities of brain structure and function between humans and lower vertebrates. They thereby have indicated that the emotional and some of the cognitive capabilities of humans are phylogenetically rooted in the evolution of all vertebrate and, perhaps ultimately, all sensate species. Crews's research (1979) illustrates the point by showing the interaction among neural structures, sex hormones, and various environmental factors in a species of lizard. These combine to produce certain complicated sex behaviors. We can infer that the neural structure in the lizard's limbic system, its sex hormones, and various environmental factors interact within this reptilian brain in ways comparable to their functioning in human beings.

Some neurological research gives evidence of the powerful, at times overriding, influence of the limbic and lower structures on overt behavior. Some of this research has involved experimental work on animals; some of it has involved brain surgery on humans who had become uncontrollably violent. An example of the first involved chickens in a laboratory. They had been living "normally" in cages and were amicable toward the people doing the research. In the experimental phase of the investigation, the researchers placed electrodes in the chickens' brainstems (part of the "reptilian" brain). After the chickens had recovered their normal routine following implanting of the electrodes, a small electric charge was fed into the electrode. The chickens changed immediately from normal to attack behavior, pecking viciously at the human attendants with whom they had previously been friendly. One could say that it was natural and right for the chickens to respond violently to such involuntary surgery, except that it was not the surgery that caused the attack but the electrical charge (von Holst and von St. Paul 1960, 1962).

A later experiment shows some of the complexity of emotional response in "mammalian" brains (of cats) that is not evident in "reptilian" brains (of chickens). The experiment also shows a change from nonviolent to violent behavior, merely as a function of increased electrical stimulation. The investigators selected nine cats that "did not spontaneously kill rats," and under anesthesia surgically implanted electrodes into the fastigial nucleus, a part of the cerebellum, which is near but not part of the limbic system. The electrodes were attached by wires to a device for putting a precisely measured current into the fastigial nucleus. The investigators measured the heartbeat and blood pressure to get an index of response to the forty-second electrical stimulation. At a current of 40μA they found no response among the gentle cats, other than alertness and sometimes sitting or standing up. An increase in the current by only 10μA to 50μA produced self-grooming. Increasing the current to 60μA elicited eating in five of the nine cats. After increasing the current to 70μA—just 30μA above the level of stimulation that elicited only alertness—seven of the cats savagely attacked a rat placed in the cage, until the current was turned off. When the current was turned on again, they attacked the rat again (Reis et al. 1973).

Other research has been done in vertebrates high on the phylogenetic scale with techniques that make it possible to control the electricity without wires, which restrict the movement of the experimental animals. José Delgado, first at the Yale Medical School and then in his native Spain, has done much research that is relevant to physiological understanding of conflict. Only a small fraction of it can be discussed here. For example, Delgado implanted an electrode in the brain of a "brave bull," the name given to the breed of domestic cattle that is genetically selected for readiness to attack humans in the bull ring. The electrode in the bull's brain was connected to a radio transceiver implanted outside the skull. The electrode was activated by a radio transmitter held in the experimenter's hand. When the brave bull started to charge, the experimenter turned on the signal to the bull's brain. The bull stopped in mid-charge (Delgado 1969: 168, 170–171).

In another experiment Delgado worked with a group of monkeys housed in a single cage. At the outset of the study the usual social power structure existed in which the alpha monkey, the top monkey in the hierarchy, was unchallenged in his possession of food or a place in the cage. He chased the others but was not usually himself chased. The experiment, using the same technique of remote radio control, added another component: the transmitter was attached to a wall inside the cage, so that it could be activated by the monkeys themselves. A current was applied for five seconds, once each minute, during the training period. Later, a female discovered that if she pressed the lever that activated the radio signal to the alpha monkey's brain (the caudate nucleus, a part of the limbic system), he stopped acting in ways that maintained his dominance over her and the other monkeys. After pushing the lever, she could do what no subordinate monkey would dare do to an alpha: she looked him straight in the eye. After the effect of the signal had worn off, the alpha monkey was boss again (Delgado 1969: 164–167). This experiment suggests that subordinate monkeys, without reading the Declaration of Independence, would rather be equal.

Another line of research, which developed independently of the work of Delgado and others, had as its focus what James Olds called "the pleasure centers" of the brains of laboratory rats. These centers are located in various regions of the hypothalamus, a central structure in the limbic system. Olds and his associates mapped the precise areas within the hypothalamus where electrical stimulation had its strongest and weakest effects. When stimulated in some areas, with a current ranging from 5 to $10\mu A$, the rats found the sensation so pleasant that they would keep pressing the bar that activated the electrical impulse until they dropped from exhaustion. In at least one instance, a rat that was stimulated in a very sensitive part pressed the bar almost two times per second, for a total of about 2000 times per hour, for twenty-six hours, and then after sleeping for about six hours resumed pressing the pleasure electrode (Olds 1958: 319).

The mapping of areas of the hypothalamus was so precise that Olds and associates clearly distinguished some of the emotional from the nonemotional areas of the brain. They discovered that an electrode placed in a part of the limbic system produced a maximum positive response of 7000 bar presses per hour. An electrode placed in a part of the cortex produced a rapidly diminishing positive response of 200 per hour. In some areas next to positive areas, the response was immediately negative and was followed by no more than one or two attempts to repeat the stimulus (Olds 1958: 316). Although the pleasure induced apparently was not primarily sexual, rats that were castrated after learning the self-stimulation routine required $55\mu A$ to self-stimulate. When these castrated rats were injected with testosterone, the charge needed for self-stimulation went down to $15\mu A$. That is, there was some positive internal linkage between the sex hormone and the pleasure the rats themselves were able to produce when they activated an electrode that had been implanted in their brains.

The role of the limbic system in emotional behavior has been demonstrated with and without implanted electrodes in human beings. In one case, the stimulus to the hypothalamus was evidently not pleasurable but painful. A hitherto mentally healthy Philadelphia attorney began to assault people to whom he took offense at cocktail parties and to use his car to pursue and punish impolite drivers on the freeway. Brain surgery was finally decided upon; the attorney died in the hospital. Autopsy revealed a massive tumor surrounding the hypothalamus (Alpers 1937). In another case, an adolescent girl had been hospitalized after stabbing someone in the heart with a knife. In the hospital, she attacked a nurse with a pair of scissors. In subsequent surgery, a probe with electrodes discovered the place in the brain (in the amygdala, a part of the limbic system) where stimulation produced a violent response. This place was cauterized and thereby destroyed. The girl had only one mild rage episode during the first year after the operation and none during the second (Mark and Ervin 1970: 97–108).

The success of such intervention is uncertain, but aside from success or failure and the moral implications of undertaking such action (Chorover 1973), it is increasingly clear that what goes on in the brain, particularly in the limbic system, is a direct response to either internal or external stimulation of various parts of the brain. When the stimulation is extremely unpleasant, the likelihood of a violent response increases.

Research of the kind just described indicates several things. There is continuity between both the brains and the behavior of various animals (ranging from chickens to rats and monkeys) and human beings. When stimulated by an electrode under laboratory circumstances, an angry chicken strikes out against whatever is nearest to it. A cat when similarly stimulated first grooms itself, then eats, and—when the current is just a little stronger—kills a convenient rat. A human being with pre-existing violent tendencies, when stimulated by an electrode implanted in the part of the circuitry that is active during violent behavior, will act violently; and when the area stimulated is cauterized and thereby deadened, the tendency to violent behavior is for a time at least stopped. When rats are stimulated in certain areas of the brain, they find the sensation so pleasant that only extreme physical exhaustion stops them. In all these cases, the part of the brain that was stimulated was in or near the limbic system—that is, the emotional brain.

Another significant factor in this research is that the electrode was not in the forebrain, the neocortex, that is, the part of the central control system that processes information received from other parts of the brain, notably the limbic system, and from sources external to the organism. As the main information-processing and decision-making part of the CCS, the neocortex is nevertheless involved in violent and nonviolent behavior. If the limbic system were indeed paradoxically an autonomous part of the brain, we could regard emotional behavior as independent of other kinds of behavior. But, as we have noted, the limbic system is intertied with the neocortex by large bundles of nerves. We could infer from this that the neocortex is a slave of the limbic system, that intelligence is controlled by emotion. It is more accurate to say that there is two-way interaction: that emotions and the limbic system affect thought and the neocortex, and that thought and the neocortex affect emotions and the limbic system. The effects of prefrontal lobotomy are a case in point. This now abandoned surgical procedure involved making gross cuts in but not removing the prefrontal lobes of the cortex, the parts that are most highly developed in humans and thus are most inherently characteristic of human beings. The effects of prefrontal lobotomy included, in some if not most cases, the dulling of emotional life to a state described as vegetablelike.

Related research using dogs and cats has produced results comparable to the effect of prefrontal lobotomy. Walter Cannon, Philip Bard, and others did pioneering work on the interties between the emotional and the control parts of the brain. When a main trunk of nerves was cut quite low in the brain (not higher and therefore not nearer the cortex), laboratory animals became snarling, growling, internally uncontrolled and *un*-dangerous creatures. They reacted angrily, but only in a very general way, to virtually any kind of stimulus. But when the cut was made higher up, the animals became veritable engines of destruction, sizing up in a coordinated way whomever was near and waiting for the first opportunity to strike.

What this research suggests is that the control part of the brain, the cortex, is not only activated by the emotional brain but also acts upon the limbic system as a limiter, a controller of emotional responses. (For an excellent summary of relevant research, see Zanchetti 1967.) Delgado (1969: 148) also has emphasized the interrelationship between the forebrain and the emotional brain, and by implication the role of the cortex, in controlling emotional responses. He points out that damage to parts of the cortex (the sensory and motor parts) does not interfere with emotional responses but that damage to the frontal lobes does—and that stimulation with an electrode inserted into the frontal lobes may elicit a friendly response.

The point of all this is that there is growing physiological evidence that the pathways between the thinking or data-processing and the emotional parts of the brain (roughly, the forebrain or the neocortex and the midbrain or the limbic system) form a two-way street, with thought affecting feeling and feeling affecting thought. This evidence is consistent with the commonly held notion that there is no such thing as affect-free thought or thoughtless emotion. After considering some other aspects of physiological analysis of behavior, I will return to some theoretical implications of the two-way street concept.

THE ENDOCRINES AS THE OTHER HALF OF THE CONTROL SYSTEM

Many of the endocrines—the glands that secrete hormones into the bloodstream and the nervous system—affect the functioning of other endocrines and many are interconnected with nerves. We cannot consider all the endocrine glands, but some are related to conflict behavior closely enough to require that their functions be spelled out.

Two classes of hormones appear to be related most directly to the kinds of behavior that have an aggressive component, that is, contain the intent to do harm. The two classes are the catecholamines and the steroids. These two classes of hormones can no more claim to be totally responsible for aggression than can any other part of the central control system (or of the environment), but they always seem to be involved in the sequence of events inside that occur between frustration and aggression.

The catecholamines.   There are three of these: dopamine, which produces noradrenaline or norepinephrine (NE), which in turn produces adrenaline or epinephrine (E). NE and E are mainly produced and stored in the adrenal medulla (the core of the adrenal glands, which sit atop the kidneys). But they are also produced and stored in the pituitary gland (the hypophysis), which is located underneath the hypothalamus in the brain, and also at certain nerve endings, in both the brain and elsewhere. They are released when the organism—indeed when the person—is under stress or tension as the result of some kind of challenge or threat. When signaled by the hypothalamus, NE and E are released almost instantaneously at the sympathetic nerve endings, thereby activating the organs and tissues linked to the sympathetic nervous system. The adrenal medulla, also neurally linked to the hypothalamus, releases NE and E into the bloodstream, thereby preparing the entire organism—including the brain—to respond to challenge or threat. The secretion at nerve endings is a very fast, emergency process; the secretion into the bloodstream is a follow-up mechanism, sustaining a state of tension for prolonged periods.

The effects of the two hormones overlap. NE constricts blood vessels in both striated (skeletal) and smooth (organ) muscle tissue, accelerates the heartbeat, relaxes the intestines, and releases sugar into the bloodstream. E has less tendency to constrict blood vessels in striated muscle tissue, greater tendency to make the heart beat faster, and greater tendency to release sugar into the bloodstream. Both NE and E generally increase the metabolic rate of the entire body, making it more ready to respond to challenge or threat. In humans, at least, E has a greater tendency to produce anxiety, that is, internal tension producing an internalized response rather than overt action on persons or objects in the environment. Thus in humans, E has the effect of producing more prolonged and deliberated action in response to challenge or threat. There is, in short, a greater tendency for NE to externalize responses and for E to internalize them.

A comparison of the proportions of NE and E typically secreted in various species indicates the following: in man, it is about 25 percent NE and 75 percent E; in lions, somewhat more NE than E; and in whales and chickens, about 80 percent NE and 20 percent E. From this we can infer that there is a hormonal relationship between the greater tendency of lower animals to respond to challenge or threat by immediate fight or flight, whereas in humans there is more tendency to internalize and reflect on the kinds and timing of response that will be most appropriate.

Some experiments with higher vertebrates show the necessary role the catecholamines play in behavior under stress. In one laboratory experiment, rats were put in a state of prolonged stress by being made to fight constantly. The result was greatly increased uptake (storage and use) of NE in the cortex of the rats' brains. The effect lasted from four to six weeks, after which the NE levels in the cortex returned to normal. The experimenters speculated that "when 'normal' or 'abnormal' changes in mood or mental function occur as sequelae to chronic psychosocial stress, one important underlying mechanism may be a sustained alteration of the normal neuronal uptake of norepinephrine in the brain" (Henley et al. 1973: 1052).

In the above experiment, a stressful environment produced increased levels of NE in the brain. Another experiment showed the effects on behavior under stress when NE levels were artificially reduced. The experimenters removed six adult female and two dominant male macaque monkeys from their natural surroundings on a small Caribbean island. In a part of the midbrain of three females and one male they implanted a thin tube, a cannula, and then injected a chemical (6-hydroxydopamine) that destroys NE. The other three females and one male did not get 6-OHDA. After they recovered from the surgery, all eight monkeys were released and observed to see how they reintegrated into the groups from which they had been removed. Within 15 minutes, three of the four nontreated monkeys had made their way back to their groups; the fourth was back within a few hours. All four returned to normal interaction patterns.

The four monkeys treated to reduce NE levels in their brains were another story. Two of them at first did not go back to their own groups; one of these two (a female) was driven into the sea (but not drowned) by males in the strange group. During the first five days after release, the treated monkeys groomed other monkeys and themselves at about half the normal rate, and they made threats and attacks at about a sixth the normal rate. In neither grooming nor fighting behavior had the four treated monkeys returned to normal ten days after release. The one treated male, previously one of the dominant males in his group, became a loner, hanging on to his original group by its edges (Redmond et al. 1973).

The optimum amounts of NE and E are related to normal moods, normal mental vitality. Depression, the condition that evidently attended the monkeys treated with NE-depleting 6-OHDA, is best conceived as being at one end of a continuum, with mania at the other. Reserpine, which, like 6-OHDA, depletes the catecholamines, when given to monkeys produced an isolated huddling, which experimenters called despair. Reserpine given to hypertensive human patients produced depression in some 15–20 percent of the patients. Another drug (alphamethylparatyrosine), which depletes dopamine and NE, produced a decrease in social initiative and interaction in humans.

Whatever the possibilities of hormonal imbalance, it is clear that a deficiency of catecholamines is related to depression and an overabundance is related to manic reactions. If the imbalance is a consequence of a congenital disorder or, in the case of the Caribbean monkeys, of experimental intrusion into a normal brain, one can say that a manic rage is the abnormal product of the natural or induced internal disorder. But if the imbalance is evident after extreme environmental stress, as in the case of the rats whose NE levels were elevated for three to four weeks after they were compelled to fight constantly, then we can suppose that the hormonal imbalance is a product of environment—caused stress. The imbalance, a normal reaction to such stress, increases the likelihood of a violent reaction to much stress, that is, increases the likelihood of a violent reaction to frustration. In that very crucial sense, violent reaction is natural and normal. That is, in a normal organism with a normal CCS, excessive stress will produce an angry, even a violent response. This says little more than what psychologists have said when they argue that frustration produces aggression, but it shows that there is indeed an organic substrate for the behavior: that some palpable, researchable events are taking place that correlate with and underlie the overt behavior of people in conflict situations. In contrast to testosterone, discussed below, one cannot say that NE causes aggressive behavior, only that it helps the body to respond aggressively.

The steroid derivatives. Hormones of the second category relevant to aggression and conflict are the steroids, notably the sex hormones. All the sex steroids are derived from cholesterol that is converted into either the female hormones (the estrogens, notably progesterone and estradiol) or the male hormones (the androgens, notably androstenedione and testosterone). From birth to death, human females and males produce and use both estrogens and androgens. The absolute and relative amounts of these hormones vary as a function of sex and age. Both the catecholamines and the steroids are produced in the adrenal glands, the catecholamines in the adrenal medulla (the inside of the adrenal glands) and the steroids in the adrenal cortex (the outer part of the adrenals). The sex hormones are also, of course, produced in the sex glands.

Physical differences between females and males are commonly and accurately attributed to genetically differentiated sexual development. At puberty, this includes maturation of primary and secondary physical characteristics of manhood and womanhood resulting from changed hormonal secretions. Few people dispute that the physical differences between men and women are in part a consequence of glandular and hormonal differences. What is less commonly accepted is that men and women also differ in behavioral tendencies that, like physical differences, are partly a consequence of innate glandular and hormonal differences. It is not yet possible to sort out from these genetically determined differences the effects of social and cultural environment as it has interacted over eons to reinforce or to change organically established distinctions between female and male. The present impossibility does not rest only on the prescriptive assertion with which this chapter opened: $B = f (OE)$. Rather, both the impossibility and the assertion rest on the fact that interaction between organism and environment began not with the intrauterine conception of human beings but with the origin of life itself on the planet.

The research below indicates that environmental factors operate in sex-related behavior, and it just as emphatically indicates that the organic, genetic distinctions between females and males do have significant effects on the differences in their behavior. Further research will help clarify just which differences are organic and which are environmental.

One line of experiments that link the steroids to aggression and conflict involves interfering with the normal effect of the sex hormones in mice. In one procedure testosterone proprionate or, alternatively, estradiol was injected into three-day-old mice that were intact, that is, not ovariectomized. After this one-time injection, the mice were returned to their mothers and allowed to mature normally. At age eighty to ninety days, individual mice were paired: males with males, females with females, and males with females. Nearly all the paired males, whether or not injected with the androgen, fought. Half the paired males injected with estrogen fought and the other half did not. One of the female pairs that were not injected with either steroid fought. More than a fourth of the female pairs injected with testosterone *or* with estradiol fought.

But perhaps the most striking result occurred when females injected as neonates with testosterone were paired with uninjected males. Half of these masculinized females fought with their male partners. Four of these pairings resulted in the wounding of the males, one of them being killed by his female partner. One of these female–male pairs resulted in the androgenized female being wounded (Bronson and Desjardins 1968). Two things are suggested by this experiment: that both excessive androgen and excessive estrogen in neonate mice affect behavior in the direction of making it more aggressive and that the male hormone is enormously potent in producing aggressive behavior.

Among other experiments relating testosterone levels to aggressive behavior are these. When male rats were castrated at birth as adults they failed to do what is fairly common among mature males: they failed to kill rat pups. And even when the mature castrated males were injected with testosterone, they did not try to kill pups (Rosenberg et al. 1971). In addition to indicating that testosterone is one cause of aggressive behavior in rats, the experiment indicates that the *time* when testosterone has its effects (whether naturally present at birth or injected in adults) is critical. Two other experiments, done with monkeys, pertain to the testosterone–aggression linkage and to the time when testosterone is injected. When pregnant monkeys were given an injection of testosterone during the middle of the gestation period (from the 39th to the 105th day of a 168-day pregnancy), female fetuses were *permanently* affected—by the presence of testosterone in the blood crossing the placenta. During the growth period, from 3½ to 15 months after birth, young female monkeys with their prenatal dose of testosterone were consistently more likely to act like males than were young females that had not been given a prenatal dose of testosterone. The treated ones, more often than untreated females but less often than untreated males, tended to initiate play, to play rough, to chase other monkeys, and to make threatening gestures (Goy 1970: 201–205).

From these experiments with high vertebrates there is good evidence that the male sex hormones tend to produce masculine behavior, defining "masculine" as that which includes taking the initiative in interactions like chase, rough play, and fight. It cannot be argued that the experiments were free of influences external to the organism, but they do point to innate components of overt aggressive acts. It is evident that male sex hormones tend to produce assertive and even aggressive behavior.

To this can be counterproposed the argument that, because of the subtle and unsubtle, unconscious and conscious efforts to socialize even young children into sex-differentiated roles, it is specious to conclude anything about any effect of androgens and estrogens on the behavior of men and women. It is indeed certain that girls and boys are socialized to behave differently, perhaps in all societies (Blum and Fisher 1978), but unless anthropologists unearth evidence that when the species Homo sapiens first emerged there was no sex-linked behavior, or that Neanderthal or other anthropoid species read somewhere about masculinity and adapted their behavior accordingly, it makes more sense to suppose a similarity in the effect of the androgens and estrogens among all such higher vertebrates as mice, monkeys, and humans.

There is some evidence that nonenvironmental factors function even in normal, intact humans to producing hostile predispositions to respond. The Buss–Dunker Hostility Inventory was administered to two groups of men, one aged 17–28 and the other 31–66. Both the capacity to express aggressive attitudes and the actual expression of such attitudes correlated positively with testosterone levels among the younger group. Among the older group, there was no such correlation (Persky, Smith, and Basu 1971).

The difference between the correlation and the noncorrelation may be explained partly by the change in balance between the levels of androgens and estrogens in the blood as a function of age and sex. According to one study, men between the ages 16 and 43 have about 0.6 ug./100ml. of testosterone in their blood. This figure drops by about 20 percent for men between the ages of 46 and 92. Women (age not specified) have about a fourth of this amount (0.14 ug./100ml) and castrates about a sixth (0.10) (Ganong 1969: 354). Correlatively, men have between a fourth and a tenth as much estrogen as women until the age of about 45 to 50. However, after menopause women have between a third and a half of the serum estrogen level that men do between the ages 45 and 65 (Ganong 1969: 363–364). In sum, testosterone levels fall with age among men; estrogen levels fall with age among women but rise with age among men.

There is additional evidence about the relationship between the androgen–estrogen balance and aggression (Sobel 1978). The violent crime rate among women is much smaller than among men, but at least one study says that about six out of ten violent crimes committed by women occur in the week before menstruation, during the very part of the cycle when estrogen levels drop in women (cited in Moyer 1971: 88–89). In another study fifteen women reported that their own aggressiveness was high during the beginning, postovulatory, and end phases of the menstrual cycle (Moos et al. 1969: 39).

If this chapter were to be considered a legal brief, one might conclude that there is abundant evidence that men are more assertive than women and that *the* basic reason is a difference in the levels of the sex hormones. It seems to me that there is an apparent difference in the degree of assertiveness in men and women, indeed such an apparent difference as to make research on the topic a belaboring of the obvious, by examining overt behavior rather than looking for causes. But it also seems to me that there is at least *one* genetic, organic reason for male assertiveness because the physiological evidence is rather strong not simply among humans but also other higher vertebrates. Sex hormone research does not belabor the obvious when it compares quantitatively the amounts of androgens and estrogens in men and women of various ages and when that research correlates these amounts with differences in behavior.

Correlatively, it seems from both laboratory research with higher vertebrates other than humans and psychological research among humans that women are more nurturant than men. That is, women are more likely to be found caring for children and protecting them from attack, not only from their siblings and their fathers but also from any other source of possible injury. The fact that husbands and fathers are also protective of women, wives, and mothers does not establish that they are as nurturant as women (Davies 1977a: 152–154).

If these tentative inferences are reasonable, they help to explain such facts as the greater tendency among men to take active part in politics—though the cultural factor is without any question a very strong one, even in societies that have abandoned formal discriminations against women. These suppositions about hormone-related behavior differences between men and women also help explain such facts as the greater tendency among men to commit violent crimes—and to engage in political conflict, including the violent kind.

One major precaution. What is said above does not say anything per se about whether men are more (or less) inclined than women to engage in harmful action. It says that men are more assertive and violence-prone than women and that physical assertiveness and aggression are associated with testosterone levels. Among both men and women there can be intent to harm, without intent to do so physically. While there is no evidence that women are free of aggressive tendencies, physical aggression is the most obvious kind and appears to be a male tendency. Perhaps the basic propositions calling for research on the sex-hormone factor in aggression are these: humans of both sexes are capable of aggressive, that is, intentionally harmful action; and men are more inclined to engage in *violent* aggressive action, in politics as elsewhere.

ENVIRONMENTAL EFFECTS

In the section above, we have considered research on the most direct relationships between organic determinants and overt behavior. That is, we have considered the overt consequences of activation of segments of the CNS, the neural part of the CCS, and of some parts of the ES, the endocrine part of the CCS. We have noted that the emotional or paleomammalian brain (limbic system) closely interacts with the information storage, retrieval, and processing parts of the brain and that it cannot be unequivocally stated that either the limbic system or the neocortex totally determines behavior. And we have noted that the most relevant hormones—the catecholamines (notably norepinephrine and epinephrine) and the steroids (notably estrogens and androgens) similarly have enormous effect on aggressive behavior—and similarly cannot be said unequivocally to control such behavior or any other. The CCS is the total organic unit, and no single part of either its neural or endocrine subsystems is altogether in control. And the organism vis-à-vis the environment is not altogether in control. The organic roots of human behavior, as seen by physiologists, are numerous indeed.

In this section, we will consider some of the environmental effects that have the most enduring and fateful consequences for all political behavior, including violent political conflict. The first category of such influences pertains to physical nutrition, the second to emotional nutrition, and the third to stimulus or cognitive nutrition.

PHYSICAL HUNGER

The physical devastation of war and revolution has among its most immediate and most enduring effects simple malnutrition. Hungry adults behave differently from well-fed adults. Hungry children not only behave differently from well-fed children but also behave differently from well-fed children when both reach adulthood. Deprivation of bodily needs produces mental damage, either temporarily (in the case of deprived adults) or permanently (in the case of children).

During World War II, experiments in semistarvation at the University of Minnesota studied the effects of deprivation in adequately fed, middle-class war resistors who volunteered to go on a half-normal diet of about 1500 calories per day for a twenty-four-week period. Their behavior was studied carefully, before, during, and after this critical period. One rather typical subject among the thirty-two volunteers, who weighed 142 lbs. (65 kg.) before commencing the 1500-calorie diet, lost 27 lbs. (12 kg.) during the 24 weeks. From high spirits and unimpaired mental energy and acumen up to the fourth week, he became restless, irritable, and unable to concentrate on anything other than food by the twelfth week. When his girlfriend came to visit him during the eighteenth week, he could not establish rapport with her. He had almost stopped writing her by the twenty-fourth week and had lost all interest in his earlier plan to do postwar relief work. His self-confidence was greatly diminished, and even early in the experiment he said: "I think it is a good idea to put strong checks on us." In his hunger-derived and hunger-preoccupied anxiety, he wanted to divest himself of power. Hunger made him feel alone, a little afraid, and very withdrawn (Keys et al. 1950: chapters 37 and 38; Brozek 1953).

Hunger and famine or death from malnutrition has for centuries been the prime fact of life for large portions of the human race. During times of both internal and international political conflict, extreme and chronic hunger has resembled that which the subjects of the Minnesota semistarvation experiments "enjoyed." During other times, such hunger has been similarly debilitating, and perhaps more enduring in its consequences. We are talking about perhaps 60 percent of the world's population: an estimate made in the 1960s indicates that some 300 million of the 500 million children of preschool age were (and probably are) mildly or severely underfed (Behar 1968: 40). Most of those who are severely underfed, particularly in their childhood, are in the developing parts of the world where old social ties have begun to disintegrate and new ties have not yet become firmly established.

Among a cohesive, integrated population in which there is a high degree of involvement and commitment to the community, the disintegrating effects of physical deprivation may be dramatically ameliorated. Within eleven weeks after the German campaign against the Soviet Union began on 22 June 1941, the northern city of Leningrad was put under a siege that lasted over sixteen months, from September 1941 to January 1943, including all of one winter and part of another. Leningrad's population when the siege started was about 2.5 million; at the end of 1943, it was about 600,000—a fourth of what it had been before the blockade began. Part of the reduction involved people who were evacuated, but the best guess that came out of the chaos of such an unforeseeable event is that about one million died of starvation and a third to half of that number died from other causes (Salisbury 1969: 593–594; but see also Pavlov 1965: xiv).

A million deaths in Leningrad means that at least 40 percent of the population ended the journey whose first steps were studied in the Minnesota semistarvation experiments. More exactly it means that more than half the population did not succumb to the final disintegrating social and political consequences of extreme hunger, including cannibalism (Salisbury 1969: 550). With a high degree of coercion but also with a high degree of community commitment, the inhabitants and the city survived one of the most terrible and violent attacks on human survival in the history of the human race.

A similar case, also during World War II, involved the dire threat to survival of Dutchmen as individuals and as a nation during the terrible "hongerwinter" of 1944–1945, when the nation was virtually stripped of food stuffs (Stein et al. 1972). Because of a transport embargo imposed on Western Holland by the German occupying forces, no food got to the large cities of Amsterdam, Rotterdam, and The Hague. The *national* average daily caloric intake was close to that of the Minnesota subjects, and the average daily caloric intake in Western Holland went down as low as 700, or half the national average. Again, as in Leningrad, the Dutch cities maintained their cohesiveness. But again, as in Leningrad, there was outside moral support, on the national and international levels, which very possibly had some real part in preventing the disintegration.

A later study of Dutch army recruits who had been gestated, born, or as infants raised in Western Holland found none of those real and permanent effects of early-childhood starvation. The recruits from Western Holland showed no greater or different mental retardation than recruits from the rest of the nation (Stein et al. 1972). But of course the rest of the nation was on a semistarvation diet and the study made no comparison with recruits in a well-fed nation. There is no statistical evidence of how many Dutch parents sacrificed their own health in order to give their children a good start in life.

From studies of the concentration camps we know well about the socially fragmenting consequences of thrusting people into conditions where their physical survival depends on their seeking only to survive as individuals (E.A. Cohen 1953, Kogon 1950). We also have been reminded that even in such extreme circumstances, there were occasional, short-lived revolts within some of the concentration camps, notably Treblinka (J. F. Steiner 1967).

The most extreme conditions seem to have prevailed in circumstances like in Holland and Leningrad, where there was extreme and more prolonged semistarvation, and where, *un*like Holland and Leningrad, there was internally and externally none of the social support that helped pull Holland and Leningrad through, during a war in which Europe was the main theater and the entire world was the audience.

These extreme conditions prevailed for a time in a small part of Africa in the 1960s, and few people in the world knew or empathized. In an area bordering on Kenya, Uganda, and Sudan, the forced removal from their traditional living area of a small group of people in the hunting and gathering stage of subsistence combined with a years-long desiccating drought to produce catastrophe. These "Mountain People," as Turnbull (1972) called them, experienced the ultimate in social disintegration: young people literally snatched food from the mouths of old people, thereby saving themselves by precipitating death among their elders.

These effects of starvation are dramatic, but probably such depredations of war and famine are of less chronic social and political significance than the effects of malnutrition for the approximately 60 percent of the young people in the world who experienced it in their childhood. Those who experience starvation as adults (as in Leningrad and Holland and the concentration camps) suffer from apathy and, in extreme cases, from social breakdown. But for the most part the damage is transitory: their bodies recover rather well and their societies get knit back together. Leningrad and Holland recovered from their severe deprivation, and the new state of Israel was born out of the death pits in the concentration camps.

The effects of malnutrition on previously well-fed individuals in highly integrated communities are severe, but the long-term effects are worse on individuals when both the technology of nutrition and the degree of communal integration are primitive. The effects of malnutrition on political development and conflict are complex and remain unknown in any detail. We know that political participation rates are lower for people in developed nations who are poor than for those who are not. And we are probably right in inferring that political involvement in developing nations since at least the American and French revolutions, during the period when national polities are forming, is less among poor, ill-fed, and very insecure people than among prosperous, well-fed, more secure people. If so, we can say in grossest terms that there is a strong but not yet ascertained correlation between nutrition levels, when they are consistently low for large portions of national populations, and rates of participation in both nonviolent and violent politics.

We may also guess that those individuals who are most active in a military–political way when their nations are gestating are above the national average in nutrition levels. At least, we do know with some certainty, from the study of guerrilla communists in the 1950s in Malaya (Pye 1956) and from the study of political participation in both developing and developed nations (Almond and Verba 1963, esp. ch. 9; and Inglehart 1977), that those who are more active—whether as dissenters or as conservatives—are from families of relatively higher socioeconomic status and so are presumably better nourished. But the bridges between knowledge of participation in both nonviolent and violent civil conflict on the one hand and nutrition on the other remain to be built.

We can, however, be rather specific about the effects of malnutrition on the development of the brain in other mammals. In one laboratory study, pregnant guinea pigs were put on semistarvation rations (one-third their normal diet), commencing halfway through the gestation of their embyros. More than half the fetuses were either aborted or stillborn. Of those that survived birth, the average body weight was about half normal. The brain weight was about 85 percent of normal (Martin 1973). In another study of normally gestated newborn laboratory rats that were deliberately and drastically underfed for 24 days, body weights were about a third of normal, and brain weights were 78 percent of normal (Cragg 1972: 146).

In still another experiment, normally gestated rats were divided into three categories. In the first, the neonates were underfed for the first 21 days and then fed normally. The number of cells in their brains and other organs was permanently reduced. In the second, the neonates were fed normally for the first 21 days and then underfed for 21 days. They suffered a decrease in number of cells in all organs except brain and lungs. Those fed normally for 64 days from birth and then underfed for 23 days suffered no loss in number of cells in brain or other organs (Winick and Noble, in Winick 1974: 255–256). These findings provide neurological depth to the surface statements about the enduring consequences of malnutrition at the earliest stages of life. However, not all vertebrates develop at the same rates in all parts of their anatomy and there is still very limited knowledge of the effects on human brain development of malnutrition during various pre- and postnatal periods.

In human beings, the brain contains about two-thirds the adult number of cells at birth and nearly the complete number by the age of one year, when the brain reaches about 80 percent of its adult weight. The most rapid growth of brain cells in humans takes place during the second half of the first postnatal year. The overt consequence is suggested by one study reporting that 19 children undernourished for more than four months during their first year were an average of about 30 points lower in their mental development quotients at the age of 4½ years than those who had not experienced such malnourishment (Martin 1973: 767–778). Early semistarvation in humans retards cell division and cell size in the brain. There is little chance of the brain ever growing to normal intelligence levels following semistarvation during the critical first year of life when brain cells are still growing in number (Winick and Rosso 1975).

Another explanation suggests why those who are malnourished in infancy are apt to be dull. Neurons in the CNS have dendrites—offshoots—that link them via synapses with as many as thousands of other neurons. One study reported finding about the same number of neurons among starved as among nonstarved rats, but stated that the number of synapses was down 38 percent (Cragg 1972). The number of synapses of each neuron determines the number of neurons that are interconnected, and thereby limits the number of choices that the brain can make. This is to say that one component of political behavior—deciding what to do—is limited in the case of malnourished people. One possible implication is that on the relatively infrequent occasions when the malnourished majority of the world's population does get involved in the politics of their nations, their decisions are apt to be more categorical, both in kind and in intensity, than are decisions of the well-fed minority.

EMOTIONAL HUNGER

These reports of neurological research can help us understand some consequences of malnutrition for the development of children into adults, and therefore for their political development. The consequences of emotional deprivation intertie with nutrition in ways that are not yet very well known on the physiological level of analysis. We know rather well, from Harlow's study (1958, 1959) of infant monkeys, that emotional deprivation during early childhood is an enduring trauma of the sort that would portend, in the human case, enormous difficulty in the knitting together of a community of any size, from the nuclear family to the nation. There is too high a correlation between an emotionally disturbed childhood and criminal delinquency—the extreme form of social alienation—for us to suppose that the effects of emotional deprivation do not spill over into politics. But systematic quantitative research remains to be done.

Research on the phenomenon of kwashiorkor and its consequences, when judged in the light of some physiological research, raises but does not answer the question of how enduring the emotional trauma, when linked with malnutrition, may indeed be. Kwashiorkor, "the weaning disease," as the West African word may be translated, is a trauma that occurs not only in Africa but also in some parts of Latin America and among some Navajo children in the United States (Chase and Metcalf 1975: 279). In the African research, Geber (1973) reported that infant children in Uganda are given the nearly ideal starting diet of their mothers' milk and in addition a large and also healthy amount of their mothers' attention. Then, at age 12 to 18 months, the small children are abruptly weaned and abruptly separated from their mothers, typically being sent either to another part of the same village or to another village. The diet on which these children are weaned is low in protein and high in carbohydrate. The emotional weaning is a shift from intimacy with the mother to associations that are warm but much less familiar and secure. In the Geber study, 40 percent of the children so weaned died. This is consistent with the death rate of infants whom Spitz (1949, 1965) studied. These infants, in a foundling home, were attended by nurses in a ratio of eight to ten infants per nurse. Though well fed, by the age of two 37 percent of these emotionally fractionated foundlings (34 out of 91) had died.

A seemingly insignificant phenomenon appeared not only among the survivors of the foundling home that Spitz studied but also among the mother-deprived monkeys that Harlow studied. These apparently permanently damaged young children and monkeys varied in mood between total withdrawal and occasional fits of rage. During the latter, they would rage at any person or monkey near them and, in the case of Harlow's monkeys, would internalize their rage by biting themselves so much and so deeply that in some instances bone in their arms or hands was exposed. This alternation between rage and withdrawal possibly compares to mania-depression among adults and certainly compares to a process which Bowlby (1969, 1973) studied. He found this sequence of events when a child was separated from its mother: first there was intense anxiety, even panic, with the child crying frantically for its mother. Then there was a period of rage—anger at being thus abandoned. Then there was a period of withdrawal and despair—the child "completing" its adaptation to abandonment and solitude.

The sequence of mental events in emotionally deprived small children is thus pretty well known. The provocative question is whether oscillation in mood, from depressed withdrawal to manic rage, occurs among adults who have as children experienced more moderate emotional deprivation. Or are mood oscillations in general publics rather uniformly distributed among the population, independently of childhood emotional trauma?

Although to my knowledge not systematically studied, there *are* quite evidently mood oscillations in general publics. The 1960s and early 1970s in the United States was a period of intense political involvement. The general public and special publics were excited by and about a sequence of events that included the black rebellion, the student rebellion, the war in Vietnam, and the profound presidential crisis of Watergate. Dating perhaps from Nixon's resignation in August 1974, there was a swing in mood toward withdrawal. In Russia during most of 1905, following the defeat in the war with Japan, there was intense and widespread political involvement. Sporadic uprisings throughout the empire blended into one another to such a degree as to make it appropriate to say that in 1905 the entire nation was in a mood of intense involvement and turmoil, one which lasted for about five years (Masaryk 1919: vol. 1, 174–197; Davies 1962: 10–13). By 1910 the nation appeared to be exhausted and people turned away from politics, until the August 1914 war moved just thirty months later into the February 1917 revolution.

It would be simplistic to say that the behavior of millions of individual citizens during swings from involvement to withdrawal can be explained as the product of events going on within their brains, but it would be absurd to deny that events are taking place within people's heads or to deny that there is a synchrony of great political significance. The etiology in most cases presumably is public and social in origin: people are reacting similarly to events that affect them all. Nevertheless their moods do swing, just as surely as do the moods of emotionally deprived children, though presumably in much smaller degree.

The kinds and amounts of early childhood deprivation, nutritional as well as emotional, of adults in a nation experiencing severe socioeconomic and political crisis correlate hypothetically with kinds and amounts of involvement in (violent) political conflict. Generally the more deprived are likely to be less involved, in normal and critical times. However, the question remains whether such deprived people, usually mere spectators of political action, for relatively brief periods may become more intensely and violently involved than those who are less deprived.

If physically and emotionally deprived people do become involved episodically, then rank-and-file revolutionaries may stem disproportionately from the ranks of people thus deprived. They would enter the political scene, during times of great crisis, in one gigantic effort and then leave it to those cadres who are better nourished, physically and emotionally. The nonelite form the solid base of the kind of resistance that topples regimes—the crowds of people who storm the Bastille, invest royal palaces in Russia and Iran, or pillage and burn down buildings that symbolize the "unchallengeable" power of the established elite and regime. Perhaps such nonelite revolutionaries tend more often to have experienced nutritional and/or emotional deprivation in their early childhood than those who either do not get so involved or who, as leaders and cadres, are continuously, nonsporadically involved.

Indeed, there are the beginnings of research into relationships between nutritional and emotional deprivation on the one side and social-political involvement on the other. D. C. Schwartz (1973a) studied health data on 2,000 high-school students. He found that the 5 percent in poor health were less involved both in student politics and in national politics, and knew less about political issues than their healthier peers. Knutson (1972: 334–345) found that both physically (including nutritionally) and emotionally deprived individuals were more likely than others to exhibit anxiety, dogmatism, a sense of the world being threatening, a sense that there was little point in their getting involved in politics, and also were unlikely to get involved in politics. And on each of these measures, those who were physically deprived were more anxious, dogmatic, threatened, inefficacious, and uninvolved than were those who were emotionally deprived. The effect of physical deprivation was stronger than the effect of emotional deprivation, and both severely stunted the vitality and sense of being able to do something politically significant.

Another pioneering study, comparing some moderately poor people with very poor people living on a West Indies island, showed similar long-range consequences of physical deprivation. Aronoff (1967) compared cane-cutters with fishermen on this island. The cane-cutters were considerably poorer than the fishermen, with less to eat and less protein in their diets. The cane-cutters were living on a plane not much above survival; the fishermen, while still poor, were physically much better off. The cane-cutters were more likely than the fishermen to have stayed with the mother a long time, to have lost brothers and sisters by death, to be concerned about their health, not to be concerned with social ties, to have a negative image of themselves, and to have a relatively unstable family life (both in family of origin and of procreation). The simple fact of malnutrition appears to have had a wide-ranging series of consequences for the cane-cutters' lives. They were evidently far from having anything to say or do politically. However, if there is a revolt on that island, they may act intensely but briefly.

So far I have dealt with research that describes the effects of early-childhood deprivation on the brain and the body. The deprivation we have looked at is both nutritional and emotional. The long-range damage to the brains of rats and humans is apparently more irreversible when the animals, including humans, were at their youngest, and the effects less irreversible when the damage was done later in development toward maturity. We have noted, for example, that the effect of prenatal semistarvation on rats is worse than starvation at birth and starvation at birth is worse than starvation some weeks later, when it is preceded by normal feeding.

We noticed similar effects when the deprivation is not of food but of affection, and we can add that normally raised children are better able to endure separation from mother at age five than at earlier ages (Bowlby 1973: 33–39).

COGNITIVE NUTRITION

One basic implication of such preliminary findings is that there are critical periods during which the environment must provide what the developing organism needs at that time and that if the environment does not provide it then, the damage may be permanent. This applies not only to emotional attachments in which deprivation may produce death or alteration between moods of rage and withdrawal. It applies also to the ability to distinguish objects so as to respond selectively to them. Eckhard Hess (1973: 192–198) found that the time of exposure to a motherlike stimulus not only determined whether an attachment could be formed but also limited the ability to perceive the stimulus. Some of this loss of ability to attach and to discriminate was related by Hess (1973: 158–159) to the fact that the development of dendrites as offshoots of neurons takes place at a very early age and, if it does not then occur, virtually never takes place.

Learning is a basic mental process that has consequences for all behavior, including conflict behavior of the political kind that this book is about. We have already mentioned that when Cannon and associates (see Zanchetti 1967: 602–614) cut the connections between the forebrain and the midbrain of dogs, the dogs were reduced, in the face of threat, not to amicable creatures, but to animals that could not focus their defensive reaction. To make an appropriate response, the dogs needed the parts of the brain that made it possible to respond effectively to threat. This specificity in turn means that vertebrates at least have to *learn* how to respond. And learning involves the establishment of memory—more exactly, of long-term memory, in the cerebellum, cerebral cortex, and parts of the limbic system.

There is apparently the same complex interaction between different parts of the brain, notably between the forebrain and the limbic system, during the process of memory formation as there is in other mental processes. In real life, people tend to forget totally events that are literally too shocking to recall. In a sense, people do not *want* to recall them. Automobile accidents are completely blocked out of the memory of those who went through them. People who have committed violent crimes often have no recollection of the action involved in killing or raping someone. Veterans of combat similarly block out shocking experiences. These traumatic experiences have been buried in the unconscious by mental processes not yet well understood physiologically.

Freud and his successors made the profound discovery that there is a basic division between the conscious and unconscious mind and that unpleasant memories indeed exist—that is, are not destroyed as is the case in true amnesia but may remain in the unconscious. Here, as in other mental phenomena, there is an interaction between organism and environment, but so far as 1 know, it is not clear why some traumata produce true amnesia in some people and some traumata produce repression and suppression in the unconscious mind. We know that such experiences as anomic violence (in the form of violent crime) and lawful violence (as in combat) are generally traumatic not just to their victims but also to their perpetrators. We know that the blocking out of such events, retrograde amnesia as it is called, can be induced neurally (by very brief but intensive electric shock that produces convulsions) and chemically (by at least one amino acid, proline, and by at least one antibiotic, puromycin). Very little is known about what actually takes place in the process of memory formation, except that it very likely involves permanent physical changes in memory neurons in the brain. These changes are the result of the normal process by which messenger DNA is involved in producing cell tissue, with of course the particular genetic structure of DNA in the memory neurons being necessary to produce the permanently stored memory (Cherkin, Eckhardt, and Gerbrandt 1976; Agranoff 1967). *And this gets to the very heart of the distinction between the organism and the environment, between nature and nurture.* When experience becomes long-term memory, it becomes part of the organism, in the same sense that food may be stored as fatty tissue. Similarly, testosterone may produce an irreversible behavioral effect. Similarly, infantile semistarvation has permanent effects.

This brings us to the question of the innateness of aggression. J. P. Scott (1970, 1971, 1977) has effectively argued, on ethological grounds, against Lorenz's (1963) conclusion, also on ethological grounds, that humans are innately aggressive. Scott emphasizes that aggression is a consequence of organisms' need to eat and reproduce and a consequence of "social dissaggregation," rather than an innate drive itself. However, unless ethological research ascertains the early experience of the animals studied, it cannot tell whether an aggressive response is only a reaction to the current threat or is a response to a prior threatening experience which is triggered by a current stimulus. There can be little doubt that there are at least organic antecedents of aggression (e.g., frustrated basic drives), but that is not the same as saying aggression is an innate tendency. And among adults, aggressive responses also necessarily involve memories—stored information— that have become a permanent part of the brain.

Commonsensically we recognize that focused aggression requires prior experience. For example, it is highly probable that a person who commits a violent crime, who kills in military combat, or who is typically combative or just argumentative is highly specific in his or her selection of targets. By highly specific I do not mean that the aggressively inclined individual necessarily knows the object of attack. The opposite may be the case: that is, knowing the object may inhibit attack. A man may kill or wound or depreciate or ignore a nonthreatening person who reminds him of his hated mother or hated father, or a man may do none of these things to a threatening person who reminds him of his beloved mother or beloved father. But every hostile act, whether committed consciously or unconsciously, against an appropriate or inappropriate object, includes both organic and environmental components. And, I would suggest, in no case is the organism's coherent, unified, focused aggressive response to some aspect of the environment free of stored memories. In stating a "prototheory," I have argued in favor of including innate motivations, neural and hormonal processes, and stored memories in the complex of events in the brain that lead to (violent) political conflict (Davies 1976).

To understand why some stored memories produce positive, amiable responses while others produce negative, hostile responses, we need to know what it is that rewards or punishes the organism. In cases of electroshock, accidents involving serious physical injury, or extreme emotional deprivation, the causes of pathological behavior are rather self-evident, perhaps too self-evident. But our physiological understanding of responses other than those of survival, sex, and elementary social needs is at best rudimentary.

What we do know physiologically about neural, endocrine, and nutritional processes has unfortunately been circumscribed by the preoccupation of the neurosciences with the most elemental needs, those which are sometimes called the urge toward self- and species-preservation or the need to feed and to reproduce (Teitelbaum 1967a, 1967b; Valenstein 1970; Kimble 1973). This leaves out of consideration other needs—higher needs as Maslow called them—which human beings everywhere do indeed seem to have. These higher needs—for nonsexual affection, which has already been studied comparatively by Harlow and others, for dignity and equality, which has not been studied physiologically at all, and for self-actualization—presumably also have organic components, just as the survival and sex needs do.

The organic components of the complex of motivating forces that send people into life-and-death struggles are not adequately explained by analysis that reduces human needs to self- and species-survival. Probably most French soldiers who fought in the Napoleonic wars would have lived better and longer if they had stayed home and organized a revolt against Napoleon. Instead they enthusiastically participated in the French expansion across most of Europe, including a thrust into European Russia. It is a mistake to apply retroactive amnesia to them and to say that, when they were blocked in their effort to capture Moscow and began to retreat westward, they really never intended to head East in the first place. And it would be a like mistake to suppose that Germans who experienced the same initial success and ultimate failure during World War II never really wanted to go West and East, either.

To recapitulate, the ineluctable investigative problem is that these very complex contrivances called human beings are not reducible to either organic or environmental determinants. And they cannot be reduced to the same total set of motivations to survive and procreate that prevail among bugs, worms, fish, and higher vertebrates. And what is more, they cannot be reduced to being passive objects whose predetermined behavior is totally the product of their genes and their environment. That often appears to be the basic assumption of scientific investigation: that all is determined without any possibility of humans making any significant choices, whether consciously or unconsciously. The human brain is too complicated a control system to support such a deterministic assumption. A solid reason against such a conclusion lies not so much in our ignorance of ultimate organic forces in the genes as in the presence of about a hundred billion neurons, loaded with dendrites, in the human brain. Human beings respond selectively to the interaction of their past experiences and their continuing needs to do more than just eat, drink, copulate, and sleep. People make choices and decisions in pursuit of satisfying their needs, and sometimes make them consciously and in the light of their experiences. Whether or not the decisions are wise is not an appropriate subject for consideration here.

BIOSOCIAL PERSPECTIVES

The theory and research considered to this point has been primarily physiological, focusing on brain research and appraising the possible consequences of physical, emotional, and cognitive deprivation for political cooperation and conflict. Now we look at another main stream of socially and politically relevant biological investigation, biosocial research.

There are two major branches in this stream: the new orientation known as sociobiology and the older one (which I have occasionally mentioned), known as ethology. Sociobiology has to do with the implications for social behavior of the findings of those geneticists who have studied organic determinants of the behavior of insects and lower vertebrates. Ethology has to do with the implications for humans of the work of those who have studied organic determinants of the behavior of higher vertebrates in natural environments.

In sociobiology, the chain of inference is very long indeed. Edward O. Wilson and those who have been incited or provoked by his bold major work, *Sociobiology* (1975), have found among many species, of which ants and other "colonial invertebrates" are the most common examples, what they describe as genetically determined altruism. Altruism is defined by Wilson as "self-destructive behavior performed for the benefit of others."

Ants do indeed form a highly integrated society in which the collective welfare of the colony is put above individual welfare. Wilson argues that there seems to be a continuation of altruism among more complex forms of life at the same time that there is generally an increase of selfishness. The roots of conflict, Wilson appears to argue, lie not in selfishness but in group altruism. Individuals tend to cluster with closely related—by extension, ethnically related—kin. These clusters compete destructively with similar groups. And this threatens the survival of any larger aggregate of human beings. Arthur Koestler, not a biologist but a kind of philosopher, made the same point a decade earlier in *The Ghost in the Machine* (1967: 233–253).

On the other hand, Wilson argues, the larger cerebral cortex and therefore greater intelligence of human beings increases the possibility of cooperation. Just how it is that increased intelligence itself, apart from any change in group identity and clustering based on supranational identifications, can accomplish this feat is not adequately explained. Wilson does not consider the need for continued interaction between such innate forces as affection and intelligence—that is to say in physiological terms, interaction between the limbic system and the cortex. The chain of inference is very long indeed in sociobiology, and the weakest link is the rather uninformed view that such geneticists share of systematic psychology and neurophysiology.

Donald T. Campbell (1975), a psychologist working near the visible end of the chain that starts in the genes, has not only examined theoretically some of the intervening links but has also spelled out some of the implications of sociobiology for human evolution. He proposes "sociocultural evolution" as a model and regards the development of civilization as a cumulative process that is separate from natural ("biological") evolution but is dependent on such genetic determinants as "the innate capacity for language, memory, and perhaps group-affiliative tendencies" (1975: 1105). Sociobiology can become a fashionable and transitory pseudoscientific cult, with some people raging favorably or unfavorably about it, as some people did about cybernetics and ethology. Both Wilson and Campbell must share the credit for trying to keep the subject as a basis for dialogue rather than for salvation.

Some ethologists have investigated attachment behavior and conflict behavior, using psychological techniques and concepts with skill and elegance (Eckhard Hess, e.g., cites more than 250 research sources in his chapter in *Imprinting* [1973: 173–187] on "Early Social Experience and Laboratory Imprinting in Birds"). But most ethologists have, with possibly unconscious care, selected for study those manifest behaviors that pessimistically support the inference that the genes themselves of human beings contain aggressive components. Konrad Lorenz is the most egregious among these pessimists. However, at least one ethologist, Eibl-Eibesfeldt, writing within Lorenz's (1979) premise of innate aggression, is optimistic. The research evidence is inadequate to support either pessimism or optimism, or an innateness premise. More judiciously than either the pessimists or optimists, J. P. Scott takes, as we have noted, an agnostic view.

The Wilsonian sociobiologists do not regard aggression as an innate tendency; the Lorenzian ethologists do. It may appear to be trivializing two such major scientific endeavors to note the differing views that leaders in both schools have as to just what is innate. But it is not trivial to observe the ease with which their followers accept as scientific some basic inferences which are stated without systematic, scientific evidence of a host of environmental and at least a few hereditary forces that intervene between genes and behavior.

As it is, there was a great surge of interest in the pessimistic findings of Lorenz and Ardrey at a time in world history, at the end of World War II, when people were appalled by "man's inhumanity to man." More recently, there has been a great surge of interest in the optimistic findings of E. O. Wilson, at a time when people may wish to be reminded of the innateness of altruism and cooperation. The laboratory research that Lorenz and Wilson have done is better than the inferences which they and their followers draw from it. It is likely that there are innate ingredients in what becomes manifest as cooperative or conflictful behavior. This is not to say that cooperation and aggression are innate but that there are innate components which, through a many-linked chain, help produce cooperation and conflict. Cooperation may be partly the consequence of social needs. Conflict may be partly the consequence of the frustration of needs ranging from physical to social, dignity, and even self-actualization needs. But neither sociobiologists nor ethologists have done much to trace the linkages. They have made assertions about what the first links in the chain are and have left the real issue where it has been for a couple of dozen centuries: very much in doubt.

The study of conflict thus faces a continuing dilemma: those who have studied and/or postulated genetic components of behavior have made leaps of inference that are like those which have been made by philosophers for more than two millennia as they have speculated about human nature. The dilemma is reducible, but the evidence adduced by sociobiologists and ethologists alike is still about as inconclusive as the argument between optimistic and pessimistic philosophers about human nature.

Implicit in this chapter has been the premise that physiological research is one of the most promising scientific leads to closer understanding of the organic determinants of behavior. The leading sociobiologist, Wilson, seems to agree with this when he writes, near the end of his massive study, about the inherent conceptual and research problems of the social sciences, which "are more difficult than physics or chemistry by at least two orders of magnitude" (Wilson 1975: 575) and when he says that "the transition from purely phenomenological to fundamental theory in sociology *must await a full, neuronal explanation of the human brain"* (emphasis added).

HUMAN MOTIVATION: A MORE COMPLEX AND HUMAN VIEW

In order to understand fundamentally the causes of conflict that are innate, we would have to understand both genetically and physiologically the energizers to action that are genetically part of the human organism. It is so enormously difficult to do this that we need not wonder why it has not yet been adequately done. It is so enormously important that we need not wonder why people keep making assertions of the sort made by biologists and ethologists who are concerned about society, like Wilson and Lorenz. The case remains moot, but the fact that virtually all the research of behavioral biologists has focused exclusively on motives of self- and species-preservation indicates that the search for basic energizers needs to be broadened. The very act of doing research, or writing, and of arguing as scientists do is at times such a passionate event that it is hard to explain scientific endeavor entirely as the product of a social-cultural environment propitious for investigation and argument. That is, biologists, social scientists, and philosophers who believe humans are concerned only with self- and species-survival fail to consider the organic roots of their own impassioned motivations. They do not investigate merely to earn enough money to eat.

Fortunately we are not left quite so barren of concepts of human motivation as biologists and Social Darwinist writers would leave us. Neither are we left with aphorisms, however valid, like: man does not live by bread alone. Nor are we left with just a philosophical tradition.

In a philosophical tradition we can include Aristotle's comment that out of the family, whose procreation and protection involves concerns with survival, arises social involvement and the pleasure that people take—partly for its own sake—in one another's company. He described the denial of equality as a basic reason for revolution (Aristotle, *Politics*, [ca. 322 B.C.] 1971: 86–87). As we have noted, Jefferson justified revolution on the denial of equality, and his justification has been reinvoked repeatedly in twentieth-century revolutions in developing nations. And Marx's anger against capitalism arose not just over the way it denies poor people life and community but also over the way it degrades them—that is, treats them not equally as human beings but unequally, as animals whose sole concern is survival.

More recently, some social theorists have begun to conceive of basic motivations of human beings in a meta-survival way. William Graham Sumner (1927: 21–28) said that social customs are rooted in four powerful forces that drive all humans and drive them to associate: hunger, love, vanity, and fear. The pioneering sociologist W. I. Thomas ([1927] 1966:

32), who was influenced by Spencer, noted that the individual is affected by his environment but modifies it "by defining situations and solving them according to his wishes and tendencies." And he listed these wishes as the desires for "new experience," "security," "response," and "recognition" ([1923]1966: 119). Pitirim Sorokin, one of the earliest sociologists to study revolution (1925: 33) mentioned what he called the "fundamental inherited impulses": "individual self-preservation, alimentary, sexual, group-defense, and self-expression." And he added that "the fundamental causes of revolutions were circumstances that caused the strongest cramp of one or several of the inherited impulses in very many individuals" (1925: 34).

Writing more than a decade after Sorokin and indeed without reference to the work of either Thomas or Sorokin, the psychologist Abraham Maslow (1943) produced a list of basic human needs that resembles earlier lists. Maslow called these needs "instinctoid." The preferred designation for basic needs here is that they are fundamentally innate, that is, are rooted genetically in the organism and form the internal components, forces, and predispositions of overt acts. I am postulating that all overt behavior, including the political kind, has as a "biological" component one or usually a combination of these basic needs and that all overt acts are oriented toward their satisfaction.

The similarity between lists of basic needs before Maslow, like those generated by W. I. Thomas and Sorokin, and ones prepared by psychologists like William James (1890), William McDougall (1908), and Henry Murray (1938), is part of intellectual history that need not concern us here. And there can be no true or finally validated list. Maslow's major contribution was not primarily a list: it was the idea of hierarchy, with certain needs prepotent over others.

Modifying Maslow's original list a little, I think the following arrangement diminishes some ambiguities in his hierarchy by distinguishing substantive basic needs—those that are ends—from instrumental basic needs—those that are means to those ends.

The substantive needs are generally ordered in the following priority:

1. the physical needs for food, clothing, shelter, health, and physical safety

2. the social-affectional needs for love: for getting, being, and staying together (and including therein the need for perpetuating the species)

3. the self-esteem or dignity needs: for achieving a sense of one's distinct and worthy separate existence

4. the self-actualization needs: for finding and pursuing those activities that are most uniquely suited to one's interest and one's innate potential.

The instrumental needs, also innate in their origins, are

1. security
2. knowledge
3. power

I can see no reason or evidence for supposing that the satisfaction of one of these instrumental needs is sought before or in preference to another and no reason to suppose that they have any priority with respect to each other. That is, people appear innately to desire to be secure in the provision for their physical, love, dignity, and self-actualization needs. They desire also to *know* where and how they are going to get food, etcetera. And they desire to have maximum *control* over their ability to provide for their own needs. But it is not evident that they seek security before knowledge and knowledge before power. Indeed, these three concepts are so close as to be hard to distinguish. The aphorism that knowledge is power expresses this closeness (Davies 1970: 617; 1977b, 1977c).

The question of whether *substantive* needs can be ranked by priority is, however, central and crucial. In common sense, most people agree that the physical needs are prepotent over the others, all of which are mental. But the idea of priority or hierarchy is new enough to have attracted thus far only a small but growing body of research. None of it to my knowledge has been done by physiologists, who remain unnecessarily preoccupied with research pertaining to the motivations of self- and species-preservation. It seems to me more than common sense that there is a hierarchy in mental needs: people do seem to accept degradation rather than be forced into isolation (married people occasionally depreciate one another but remain married because humiliation is more tolerable than isolation). And people do seem to prefer being recognized as worthy individuals before they put the particular, unique stamp on their identity that their chosen occupations, hobbies, and diversions give them—as they strive for fulfillment of their unique, individual selves.

The satisfaction of organically based needs requires a supportive natural and social environment. In Figure 1–2, the priority of substantive needs is presented in relation to the environments in which these needs have to be fulfilled. The figure shows schematically the temporal symmetry, the synchrony, that seems to prevail between aggregates of people and their environmental support systems at successive stages of the development of both. When most people in a society are in the primitive hunting-and-gathering or farming or fishing stage, they spend most of their time doing such things because that is just about all the environment provides. When the environment becomes more complex and "beneficent," people then begin to form increasingly stable, enduring, and cohesive groups and to identify themselves as part of these groups, from extended families to local

FIGURE 1-2. The development of basic needs and of
environmental support systems.

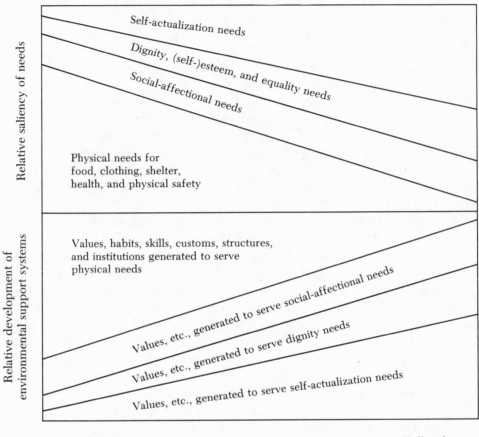

Earliest, least human
development

Fullest human
development

communities (Aronoff 1967), regions, and nations. When these groups
have begun to coalesce, they and the individuals who compose them begin
to demand dignification—esteem in the eyes of others—which gives them,
collectively and individually, self-esteem.

The hypothesis relating stages of development of individuals to stages of
development of societies and polities is itself a derivation of the innate,
"biological" characteristics of Homo sapiens. Without the extraordinary
development of the human brain, it would not be possible for people to
store and learn very intricate and complex patterns of behavior that are
not innate but may appropriately be called second nature. Human behavior, including political behavior, is thus a continuing interaction
between the naturally developing human organism and the developing
environment, as humans by the nature of their brains learn to exploit the
environment, build culture into it in successive stages—all in order to
make it serve and suit the innate needs of human beings.

Stages of political development correspond most obviously to individual development in societies where large numbers of individuals are at approximately the same stage of growth. Stages of political and individual development correspond, but less obviously, in large and complex societies in which there are substantial minorities that are at different stages of development. Perhaps the commonest case is one in which an advanced polity receives immigrants or guest workers from a much less advanced polity, in which the great majority of those who emigrate are moving from extreme poverty and little social integration beyond the local community whence they came. In an advanced society and polity, large aggregates of relative newcomers, because of their preoccupation with the physical and more elemental social needs, will be little involved in the kinds of political activity that presuppose the establishment of integration into regional and national society. These newcomers, living in the same society with people who are already integrated and politically involved, make it more difficult to analyze the kinds and amounts of political behavior among various groups within the society and therefore to generalize as to the overall characteristics of such a complex polity.

To outline the relationship between the organic development of individuals and the development of polities—the relationship between biology and politics—it is appropriate to indicate stages of social development that correspond to stages of individual development on the one hand and of political development on the other. The stages are:

1. Societies in which most people are preoccupied almost entirely with establishing and maintaining their subsistence in relatively intimate and rudimentary groups. Examples: people living in tribal communities in North, Central, and South America and in Africa and Asia; and people living in feudal–manorial villages in premodern Europe, Latin America, and Asia.

2. Societies that have just entered the era of modernization, integration, and industrialization. In these, there are heavy migration rates from rural areas to the slums of rapidly growing cities, and for the overwhelming majority of the population life still revolves around the continued struggle for mere existence. But the setting is new because the struggle to survive depends not on hunting and gathering or on subsistence agriculture but on payment for labor which thereby is exchanged for food and shelter produced by others.

3. Societies in which there is a gradual ordering and routinization of economic, social, and political interactions, involving an intricate division of labor on a heavily industrial base.

4. Societies in which economic, social, and political integration has reached the point where material abundance has become available to the great majority of hitherto poor people.

5. Societies which have achieved material abundance and therefore can begin to move from a materialist to a postmaterialist basis for fulfillment of individual citizens' needs.

The stages of political development that correspond to these stages of individual and social development are:

1. *Primitive anarchy*, in which traditional rules and rulers adequately take care of the relatively infrequent and mild conflicts of a simple face-to-face, subsistence society. In this condition there is a long-established and stable relationship between the rudimentary demands of human beings for self- and species-survival and the political system's ability to adjudicate conflict over these demands.

2. *Anomic anarchy*, in which traditional rules and rulers are cast aside, in what becomes pretty much a war of each against all, in the chaos of life in the slums, whose inhabitants have inadequate occupational and social skills to deal securely with subsistence under the new and challenging circumstances of modernization.

3. *Oligarchy*, in which the prolonged struggle of each against all becomes so intolerable to those engaged in it that they abandon their solitary, anomic anarchy and accept the usually harsh and self-serving, institutionally unresponsible domination of a ruling elite. This elite is tolerated, accepted, even welcomed because it is highly skilled in techniques of production, social organization, and armed force used to compel obedience, and because these skills produce order and material purpose.

4. *Democracy*, in which social integration, induced both voluntarily by those who have learned to live together and involuntarily by elite coercion, proceeds to the point where the general public of once unintegrated people forms solidary groups which oppose coercion by government and gradually make it responsible to the general public.

5. *Civilized anarchy*, in which (a) those rules that are necessary for people to live together in a complex society have been so well integrated within the brains of so many individuals, and (b) the government and governors have become so civilized (nonarbitary, nondiscriminatory, unselfish, limited, and routinized), that there is a vastly diminished need for the previously high levels of coercion (Davies 1977a, 1977b).

The sequential relationship between stages is presented graphically in Figure 1–3. Three things in this figure merit particular attention. The first is that each successive stage depends for its emergence on the successful occurrence of each prior stage. This is—both psychologically and biologically—a matter of epigenesis, which is discussed earlier in the chapter. The theory of development and thus the figure do not suppose

FIGURE 1–3. The sequence of stages of political development.

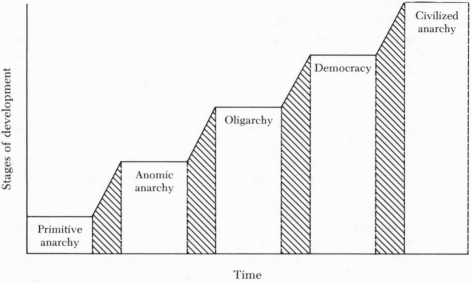

Key: Transition period of relatively high levels of (violent) conflict

that it is possible to skip a stage. The most appropriate analogy is the inability of a ship to pass through a system of locks without going through each lock. The second thing is that there is no instantaneous passage from one stage to the next: the transition takes time. And the third is that the amount of conflict and violence is greatest during the transition periods. Any kind of transition (like adolescence in individuals and industrialization for individuals-in-society) is mentally stressful and presumably involves continuous or repeated rise in catecholamine levels in the brain. When millions of individuals are undergoing transition simultaneously, there is a lot of tension and a lot of raised catecholamine levels.

THE BIOLOGY OF CONFLICT: RETROSPECT AND PROSPECTS

The real and the potential values of biological research to the study of political conflict are still far apart. On the one hand are the efforts of biologists, notably sociobiologists and some ethologists, to make grand inferential leaps from their study of less advanced forms of life to its most advanced form. On the other hand are the efforts of philosophers, social theorists, and motivational psychologists to hypothesize broadly about that which biologists, notably physiologists, are studying in the laboratory: the central control system, that is, the brain.

There are several problems. One is that natural scientists have a disinclination to suppose that when they make grand inferences, they are thinking and writing differently from the philosophers whom they tend to depreciate. Another is that philosophers, social theorists, and social researchers are woefully ignorant of both the substance and the technology of the more advanced natural sciences. Social scientists and sociobiologists are woefully ignorant of both the substance and technology of the neurosciences, of brain physiology. And physiologists continue to take as their motivational model of man a creature concerned with only self- and species-survival.

In spite of such problems, there are some notable beginnings among some social scientists. They have used physiological and ethological or statistical measures to study political phenomena, with a clear determination to focus on the human organism as part of the causal picture of political behavior.

Among the physiologically oriented efforts, let me mention some in which the techniques have involved neither brain probes nor blood samples. They have not gone into the brain but have tested skin conductivity and heart rate, as indicators of responses in the brain to various stimuli. Lodge, Tursky, and associates have indexed changes in skin conductivity and heart rate as these respond to verbal and pictorial stimuli pertaining to ethnic tension (Tursky et al. 1976a: 88–91; 1976b). Change in heart rate has been used to measure what may be a directional change in attitudes toward violence. That is, heart rate may accelerate if the individual likes violence and decelerate if he or she dislikes it (Watts and Sumi 1979: 544–551). Another technique records stress as it can be measured in an individual's voice by an oscillograph called a "Psychological Stress Evaluator," which can detect voice characteristics that are said not to be discriminable by the human ear (Wiegele 1973: 329; Hirsch and Wiegele 1979). Wiegele and his associates have begun to use voice stress analysis to study degrees of tension in speeches by political leaders in the international arena (Wiegele 1978).

Among the ethologically oriented efforts, social scientists have mostly either accepted or rejected the findings of such ethologists as Lorenz and Eibl-Eibesfeldt but have done little research examining the behavior of intact human beings in real-life political contexts. During the 1960s the idea was fashionable that people, like lemmings, tend to reduce intolerable crowding by indulging in suicide and other violence. To assess this idea, a study was conducted relating population density to war-proneness in Europe for a 150-year period following the Council of Vienna, which put an end to the enormous revolutionary and international violence that began in France in 1789. The study reported that in Europe for that period "there does not seem to be much support for the crowding and combat hypotheses at the international level" (Bremer et al. 1973). With a different focus, on the possible relationships between crowding and intranational violence, two investigators, using aggregate data from sixty-five nations, found very low correlations between crowding and civil strife, except on a measure relating people per room to political unrest. They noted that "individual behavior and conditions that motivated this behavior are masked in this kind of analysis" (Welch and Booth 1977: 155–157).

Several things appear to characterize biopolitical research efforts such as these pioneering efforts. The investigators are boldly determined to seek those roots of conflict that rest in the human organism. They have used refined techniques and equipment to test somatic correlates (like heart rate, skin conductivity, and voice) of mental states that are essentially beyond the control of the subjects of their research. Or they gather hard aggregate data that allow for inferences about the states of mind of national populations. All these techniques are appropriate and promising. However, all these research efforts evince the long-established American bias against any theory that is more than one small step removed from the factor-analyzed data under investigation. Researchers do not evidently feel very comfortable with general theories and, aside from their methodologies, do not usually show any inclination to use any of the enormous body of research that has emerged from biology since Darwin and from psychology since William James.

The problem of relating theory to research in a manner that is reciprocally nurturant is not unique to American social scientists. A conference of American and Russian neuroscientists on "Neurophysiological Mechanisms of Goal-Directed Behavior and Learning" was held at the University of California at Irvine in April 1978. The conference evidently challenged the participants not only with relevant work of their counterparts in both countries but also with the more basic question of how to do scientific investigation. As one of the American participants put it: "The big difference seems to be that the Americans have small theories and lots of data, and the Russians have large theories and much less data" (Holden 1978: 633). At least in American social science, the dialogue between theory and research remains for the most part a soliloquy of computerized laboratory and aggregate data. In the Soviet Union it may be mostly a soliloquy of theorizing. In their enduring work, Darwin, Marx, Freud, and Pavlov found it necessary to connect theory and research.

The reasons for neglecting either aspect of scientific endeavor are rarely articulated. What was called political behavior research in the 1950s and 1960s was undertaken by sociologists and political scientists who for the most part gave little evidence of training in psychology, the science of behavior (Davies 1973: 18–27). The biopolitical enterprise can proceed far more efficiently if political researchers and theorists alike learn relevant basic theory and research in psychology and neurophysiology. The task is no facile one, and the use of sensitive and precise electronic equipment is a necessary but woefully insufficient condition for the advancement of biopolitical knowledge.

All this leaves us with a fundamentally tantalizing situation and a set of promising intellectual interactions that have not yet begun in earnest. Motivational psychologists have not explored the neural and hormonal substrates of basic drives beyond survival. Ethologists and psychologists have found just enough evidence of group- and status-oriented behavior in vertebrates (e.g., the dominance hierarchies among primates, dogs, and chickens) to suggest that not only humans but other species have needs beyond survival. Physiologists have found abundant evidence of structural and functional kinship between the limbic system, that is, the emotional brain, in humans and in lower vertebrates (as MacLean noted in labeling parts of the brain the "reptilian brain"). All this suggests that much of human emotional life is organically rooted and phylogenetically based on perhaps billions of years of vertebrate evolution. And psychologists not of the stimulus–response persuasion seem to have abandoned their own knee-jerk reaction of refusing to consider that there are indeed organic components of behavior.

The optimistic side of the interaction between biological and social sciences is that people in both fields, and within various areas in both fields, are no longer just discretely tending their separate gardens. Biologists may be getting a bit self-conscious about their tendency to suppose that they are no more entitled to philosophize than philosophers and are no better at it. Social scientists are indeed becoming more aware of the softness of their disciplines. At least some of them, like Wahlke (1979), have become discontent with the reduction of human behavior to statistical and other mathematical manipulations which are as etiological as recapitulations and predictions of the stock market or of the causes of inflation.

The problems are indeed numerous. There is a need to be able to communicate in common languages. This is not always easy, because social scientists must learn the names of the parts of the vertebrate anatomy that biologists are talking about and become aware of the limited set of motivations that biologists attribute to the vertebrates they study. And there is a need to establish a consensus on the meaning of such basic terms in the study of conflict as "aggressive" or "agonistic."

There is a need also to escape the confining notion that people in one's own field of scientific endeavor are the only ones who really understand anything or say anything that bears on one's own work. And above all, perhaps, there is a need for all investigators to appreciate that all disciplines concerned with analysis of conflict are fundamentally trying to explain the complex behavior of the same species, Homo sapiens, as it has developed socially and politically, from the most primitive and least cultivated conditions to the most advanced and most civilized.

CHAPTER 2

The Psychology of
Political Protest
and Violence

Edward N. Muller

AGGRESSIVE DOMESTIC POLITICAL CONFLICT is a process manifested in outbreaks of protest and violence that may or may not evolve into rebellion (a form of violent power struggle threatening the overthrow of the regime), which in turn may or may not end in revolution (successful rebellion). The variables that determine whether protest and violence lead to rebellion, and whether rebellion is successful, are the characteristics of the *groups* involved in the power struggle: the agents of the regime and the contending dissident organizations. Psychological attributes of *individuals*, such as frustration and alienation, have minimal direct import for explaining the occurrence of rebellion and revolution per se. But if attempts to "psychologize" the explanation of rebellion and revolution are unduly simpleminded, it is equally simple-minded to dismiss psychological variables as being largely irrelevant to the study of aggressive domestic political conflict. Theoretically, at least, there is sound reason to expect that some psychological variables are significant for an understanding of the conditions that make people ready for participation in acts of political protest and violence, that is, political behavior that has revolutionary potential.

This chapter will review research on political protest and violence that has been carried out at the micro level of analysis. Some general methodological issues are raised in the paragraphs immediately below. The first section thereafter considers the evidence bearing upon that most popular of psychological explanations, the thesis that participation in acts of civil disobedience and political violence is primarily a response to frustration. In the second section the focus shifts from studies emphasizing anger born of frustration to research that has investigated psychological variables that provide motivations for political aggression on utilitarian and normative grounds.

Because of the serious ethical problems involved, true experimental designs entailing the manipulation of independent variables and the observation of the dependent variable under controlled conditions have not been used in the study of political protest and violence. All the evidence to be reviewed is correlational (mostly cross-sectional), gathered from responses to questionnaires and personal interviews. Thus, in general, the results of extant micro-level research on determinants of political protest and violence cannot be regarded as decisive from the standpoint of strict canons of scientific inquiry. However, given the nature of the topic, nonexperimental correlational research designs are about the best that can be expected.

A more subtle methodological problem that afflicts some of the micro-level research on political protest and violence is the failure to give serious attention to the quality of the measurement of independent and dependent variables. For example, many tests of the hypothesis that political protest and violence are a response to frustration have been plagued by the use of indicators that correspond poorly to that concept in any theoretically meaningful sense. At the heart of the frustration concept is the idea of unrealized expectations. To infer that objectively disadvantaged persons in society are frustrated is to confuse frustration with a quite different variable, sheer deprivation; to infer that people alienated from their work, from other people, or from societal institutions also are frustrated is to confuse frustration with yet another variable, dissatisfaction. Even when indicators of frustration do measure the degree to which expectations are unrealized, the nature of the expectations often is not considered. Failure to realize expectations in the sense of wishful aspirations is different from failure to realize expectations in the sense of what one believes one is entitled to—that is, one's just deserts. Unrealized just deserts are likely to produce far more intensely felt frustration than unrealized aspirations. Confusing these qualitatively different kinds of frustration, or simply ignoring the distinction, leads to imprecise hypothesis-testing. Thus, when reviewing empirical studies of the association between psychological characteristics of individuals and their participation in political protest and violence, one must be sensitive to the issue of measurement quality and avoid taking all findings at face value.

Of particular importance when evaluating the significance of research findings is the question of how the dependent variable is measured. Many studies have used measures of behavioral potential instead of overt behavior, and some have focused only on attitudes of "militancy" or general approval/disapproval of political protest and violence. Obviously, there is only a thin connection between attitudinal militancy and approval/disapproval measures and participation in aggressive political behavior. Greatest weight should be given to those investigations that use direct measures of actual participation in protest and violence.

DEPRIVATION AND FRUSTRATION

The concept of frustration has been the psychological variable most commonly evoked to account for individual participation in political protest and violence. Following the hypothesis set forth by Dollard et al (1939) that aggression always results from frustration, Davies (1962, 1969), Feierabend and Feierabend (1966) and Feierabend, Feierabend, and Nesvold (1969), and Gurr (1968a, 1970b) have advanced applications of the general frustration–aggression argument to specifically political aggression.

In Davies's view, political violence results from an intolerable gap between what people want (expectations) and what they get (gratifications). Discrepancy between expectations and gratifications is a frustrating experience that, if sufficiently intense and focused on the government, results in either rebellion or revolution. This expectation–gratification discrepancy occurs when expectations and gratifications rise in tandem over a prolonged period, followed by a precipitous drop in gratifications, while expectations continue to increase (the "J-curve" hypothesis of revolution).

Like Davies, the Feierabends see political violence and instability as the result of frustration engendered by discrepancy between expectations and gratifications, but they also postulate that uncertainties in expectations and conflicts between expectations serve as additional sources of frustration. The Feierabends and Nesvold propose that large expectation–gratification discrepancies result from several patterns of change in expectations and gratifications in addition to the J-curve type, including any rapid change in gratifications as well as any pattern of substantial fluctuation.

Equating frustration with discrepancy between expectations and achievements is useful because it ties the concept of frustration specifically to the experience of nonreward (anticipation of a reward that does not materialize or is not satisfactorily consummated), a condition that experimental research has shown leads to attack responses among animals (Amsel 1962; Azrin, Hutchinson, and Hake 1966). But it is desirable to go beyond the stipulation that frustration be equated with unfulfilled expectations, since the concept of expectation is itself ambiguous and open to a variety of specific interpretations. For example, expectations can be pegged to the level of some attractive goal achieved by a reference group, where "reference group" is defined as those others with whom a person identifies and compares himself. A broader standard of comparison is the level of some attractive goal to which a person feels rightfully entitled. In this interpretation of the concept, expectations would be pegged to a person's sense of his or her "just deserts." Gurr uses the just deserts comparison standard in his definition of relative deprivation, arguing that it is preferable to reference group achievement because the latter is more restrictive than the former:

> [Relative deprivation] is widely used in sociological research, where it is usually assumed for operational purposes that value standards are set by reference to some group or status with which an individual does or is thought to identify. It is more generally recognized, however, that value standards can have other sources. An individual's point of reference may be his own past condition, an abstract ideal, or the standards articulated by a leader as well as a "reference group." The definition used here makes no assumptions about the sources of value expectations . . . .[Gurr 1970b: 24–25]

Relative deprivation as conceptualized by Gurr arises when an individual does not attain what he thinks is justifiably due to him; the achievements of a reference group are only one among many possible sources of expectations about a person's just deserts.

Relative deprivation, according to Gurr, is the mechanism that produces frustration of sufficient intensity to motivate people to engage in political protest and violence. He has argued the point quite forcefully:

> The basic relationship is as fundamental to understanding civil strife as the law of gravity is to atmospheric physics: relative deprivation . . . is a necessary precondition for civil strife of any kind. The greater the deprivation an individual perceives relative to his expectations, the greater his discontent; the more widespread and intense is discontent among members of a society, the more likely and severe is civil strife. [Gurr 1970a: 596]

Gurr does qualify the proposition relating relative deprivation to political protest and violence by introducing two additional causal variables: belief in the utilitarian justifiability of protest and violence, and belief in their normative justifiability. These variables are postulated to have an interaction effect such that the strength of the relationship between relative deprivation and participation in protest and violence is weakened when the justification variables take on low values, and strengthened when the justification variables take on high values. Nevertheless, the very strong claim about relative deprivation being *the* root cause of protest and violence has provoked dispute.[1]

OBJECTIVE DEPRIVATION AND FRUSTRATION

McPhail (1971) carried out a secondary analysis of data from ten reports of research on individual participation in five riots: Los Angeles (Watts), 1965; Omaha, 1966; Detroit, 1967; Milwaukee, 1967; and Newark, 1967. A measure of the strength of the association (Cramer's V) was computed for 173 contingency tables showing the relationship between riot participation and variables that McPhail interpreted as indicators of deprivation per se, frustration per se, and combinations of deprivation and frustration. Because only 8 percent of these 173 tests of the deprivation–frustration–aggression explanation revealed even a moderate magnitude of association (.3 or greater), McPhail concluded that "there is considerable reason for rejecting the sociological and popular cliché that absolute or relative deprivation and the ensuing frustration or discontent or despair is the root cause of rebellion" (1971: 1064). McPhail went on to argue that in general social and psychological attributes of individuals were irrelevant to explanation of participation in civil disorders, which in his view was to be accounted for by situational variables such as proximity, the availability of individuals for collective action of any kind, and an "assembling process."

Before we accept McPhail's results as decisive counterevidence, it is important to consider the fact that 50 of the tests entailed measures of objective ("absolute") deprivation. Although Davies, the Feierabends, and Gurr did set a misleading precedent by arguing in their empirical research that frustration and relative deprivation could be reliably inferred from indicators of objective deprivation, this obviously is not the thrust of their theorizing. Discrepancy between expectations and gratifications is a perceptual variable and any proper test of the frustration hypothesis must assess this perception directly. Moreover, of the remaining 123 tests reported by McPhail, those classified under the frustration category (84) apparently did not use any indicators of frustration arising from expectation–gratification discrepancy, while only five of the 39 tests classified under the deprivation and frustration category used indicators of discrepancy between expectations and actual achievement. Of these five, three showed nonsignificant association, one fell in the .10–.19 range, and one was greater than .40—hardly evidence in favor of the frustration explanation, but evidence that constitutes a far less overwhelming refutation. Also, it is worthy of note, in none of these five tests was the concept of expectations defined in the sense of just deserts.

DISCREPANCIES BETWEEN ASPIRATIONS AND ACHIEVEMENTS

A number of studies have employed a ten-step ladder scale developed by Cantril (1965) to measure discrepancy between expectations-as-aspirations and actual achievement. The top rung of the ladder is defined as representing the respondent's conception of the best possible life for him, with the bottom rung representing his worst possible life. The respondent is then asked to place himself on the ladder with respect to his present standing, where he stood five years ago, and where he expects to stand five years hence.

Bowen et al. (1968) used the ladder scale in a study of residents from Cleveland's officially designated poverty areas (N = 500), conducted nine months after the Hough riot in that city. They found no significant relationship between present or future standing on the ladder and a measure of "protest orientation" (the degree to which nonviolent protest is regarded favorably). Also, Crawford and Naditch (1970) used the ladder scale in a study of 18- to 45-year-old black male residents of the Detroit riot area (N = 107), conducted several weeks after the July 1967 riot. They found relationships in the expected direction between present standing on the ladder and a variety of indicators of attitudinal militancy. However, they neither conducted tests of statistical significance nor computed measures of strength of association.

Abeles (1976) has reported results from the administration of the ladder scale to a sample of black adults in the Cleveland "poverty zone" (N = 400), conducted in 1969, and to a sample of adults (N = 530) from predominantly black districts in and adjacent to Miami, conducted in 1968. Measures of past gains (present standing on the ladder minus past standing) and anticipated future gains (future standing on the ladder minus present) were constructed, but only the past-gains measure was related significantly to a measure of attitudinal militancy in the Cleveland data: those in the lower third of the past-gains measure were more likely to be militant than those in the upper third by a difference of 15 percentage points. In the Miami data, significant relationships were found between militancy and measures of both past and anticipated future gains, but the form of the relationship was curiously curvilinear, with the highest militancy scores registered by those in the middle of each "gains" measure. Abeles also analyzed a number of variants of the ladder scale, in which different reference groups were substituted for the "best possible" definition of the top rung. Most of these reference-group versions of the ladder scale were unrelated to militancy and the few significant relationships that did appear were of weak magnitude.

A modification of the ladder scale was included in a study that I conducted in Waterloo, Iowa (Muller 1972), a town that experienced serious civil strife in 1967 and 1968. A disproportionately stratified (by race) probability sample of 503 adults (18 years and older) was interviewed in 1970. Respondents were asked to place themselves on the ladder scale with regard to four welfare values: work situation, total family income, housing accommodations, and chances of being able to get their children a good education. A composite measure of expectation–gratification discrepancy was constructed by summing present standing on the work, income, and housing measures. This variable was regarded as superior to the general ladder scale because it is more sensitive to the number of values in regard to which a respondent might feel relatively deprived. Nevertheless, it showed a statistically significant but trivial correlation ($r = -.234$) with a 0–10 index of potential for political violence. Also, the relationship was found to disappear when the respondent's degree of trust in political authority and belief in the efficacy of past violence were controlled for.

An analysis of measures of change in expectation–gratification discrepancy (Grofman and Muller 1973), using the Waterloo data, did not reveal support for the Davies J-curve hypothesis. (However, time-series survey data would be necessary to carry out a decisive test.) Also, an analysis of data from the Survey Research Center's national election studies during the period 1956–1968 apparently does not support a J-curve explanation of urban riots (Miller et al. 1977; see also the rejoinder by Davies 1978). In the Waterloo data we did find one rather consistent pattern: *any perceived change* in expectation–gratification discrepancy, whether for better or for worse, was associated with an increase in potential for political violence. We called this the V-curve hypothesis, since the pattern of the relationship conformed to a V, with respondents who registered no change scoring lowest on the scale of potential for political violence (the point of the V) and respondents who registered both negative change (increasing discrepancy) and positive change (decreasing discrepancy) scoring progressively higher on potential for political violence as a function of increasing change. However, the fit of this absolute-magnitude-of-change function to the data was not impressive, achieving an r^2 of .10 in only one of three instances (anticipated future change). Nevertheless, it was consistent with a finding reported earlier by Bowen et al. (1968). These findings thus provide some support for the argument of the Feierabends and Nesvold that both deterioration and improvement patterns can produce frustration that leads to political protest and violence.

Blumenthal et al. (1975) administered the ladder scale in 1972 to a sample (age 16 and up) of 283 respondents drawn from residents of Detroit and four southern sampling units: Montgomery, Alabama; East Carroll, Louisiana; Harris, Texas; and Atlanta, Georgia. Their dependent variable was a protest behaviors index: an additive measure of willingness to engage in a protest meeting with a permit, a sit-in, and blocking traffic. They found little or no relationship between the protest behaviors index and present standing, past standing, and future standing on the ladder, and present minus past and future minus present (the possibility of a V curve apparently was not examined in regard to the two change measures).

DISCREPANCIES BETWEEN JUST DESERTS AND ACHIEVEMENT

All the above studies utilized the ladder scale, an instrument that directly indexes perceived discrepancy between expectations and achievement and is sensitive to the intensity of discrepancy. Their results are consistent with the conclusion that McPhail reached from the analysis of far cruder measures: the frustration explanation of political protest and violence simply does not hold up at the micro-level of analysis. But despite these many negative findings, the nagging question still remained: what if frustration were measured in the just-deserts sense of discrepancy between entitlement and achievement? Would this distinction in the definition of value expectations make any difference?

To answer this question unambiguously, research was needed that explicitly compared the ladder-scale method of measuring frustration with a measure of discrepancy between a person's actual achievement and his sense of what was rightfully due to him. Gurr (1970a: 596) had argued that "people become most intensely discontented when they cannot get what they think they deserve, not just what they want in an ideal sense . . . ." The ladder scale, with its definition of the topmost rung as a "best possible" state, seems likely to capture discrepancy between expectations in the sense of an ideal or wishful comparison standard, not a just-deserts standard of comparison. If so, one reason for the failure of measures derived from the ladder scale to display strong and significant associations with political protest and violence variables would be that many people who register high ladder-scale discrepancy are not intensely frustrated. Another reason for the poor performance of the ladder scale might have to do with the nature of the instrument per se. Blumenthal et al. (1975: 105) point out that the "ladder has been severely criticized on the grounds that its questions are too abstract for respondents to comprehend" (1975: 105); they note that in a study of survey questions by Cannell and Robison (1971) the "ladder was found to be more complicated and less likely to be understood by the respondent than any of the other measures investigated." Thus, in designing research to compare the ladder scale with a just-deserts measure, it would seem desirable to use a completely different format for the just-deserts measure.

Another potentially important condition that had not been taken into account in these studies is specification of the source of unfulfilled legitimate expectations. Who or what is held responsible for frustration or relative deprivation? A person could feel that he is receiving substantially less than his just deserts, yet blame it on fate or on himself. In general it seems plausible to assume that if frustration is attributed to any sources other than social structural arrangements—especially, of course, the political system—the effect will be to *decrease* the likelihood of a person engaging in political protest and violence as a response to frustration.

A set of questions designed to measure just-deserts frustration was developed for a study of aggressive political participation that I conducted in the Federal Republic of Germany. Probability and quota samples were drawn of residents from twelve sites (four rural, two urban, six university communities) where opposition to the regime (voting support for extreme left and right political parties in the rural and urban communities, civil disobedience and political violence in the universities) had been manifested at greater-than-average levels during the preceding five years. In the fall of 1974 a first round of interviews was administered to 2,662 respondents by *Infratest*, Munich. The following discussion draws upon findings that have emerged from analysis of these data (Muller 1975, 1979).

Frustration in the sense of discrepancy between a person's just deserts and his achievement was measured by a set of fifteen items. The first item in the series was prefaced by the statement: "Everyone has an opinion about what is properly due to him in life." Then the respondent was asked: "Are your housing conditions as good as those which are properly due to you?" If the response was YES, the interviewer went on to the next value, health and medical care. If the response was NO, the interviewer asked: "Are your housing conditions very much worse, much worse, or only somewhat worse than those which are properly due to you?" This was followed by the question: "And in your opinion, to what extent is the state responsible for your housing conditions?" The respondent answered this question from a list of four options: COMPLETELY, A LOT, SOMEWHAT, NOT AT ALL. This format was repeated in regard to the amount of satisfaction produced by one's daily work, and, finally, in regard to everything important in the life of the respondent. The sequence can be summarized as:

1. Does a person feel that he or she is getting his or her just deserts in regard to important goods and conditions of life?

IF NO:

2. How large is the gap between what a person feels to be his or her just deserts and what he or she is actually getting?

3. How much responsibility does the state have for this condition?

The goods and conditions of life referred to here are the basic material-welfare values of housing, income, and medical care, and the nature of one's work, but the final set of items enables the respondent to report just-deserts discrepancy and structural blame in regard to other goods and conditions of life that are important.

The amount of frustration that a person feels in regard to each stimulus is weighted according to how much responsibility is assigned to the state for this condition. In the sequence shown above, a person giving a YES response at position 1 receives a score of zero, since no just-deserts frustration is experienced. Also, a person who gives a NOT AT ALL response at position 3 receives a score of zero, since the political system is not held responsible for the frustration that is felt and, therefore, this person would have no incentive to take part in aggressive *political* action. Given the existence of frustration in the sense of just-deserts discrepancy, and given the perception that the state has responsibility, the amount of just-deserts frustration a person feels is given twice as much weight under the condition of high structural blame (a COMPLETELY or an A LOT response at position 3) as under the condition of medium structural blame (a SOMEWHAT response at position 3). Each variable scored by this method is an indicator of what is termed "structural just-deserts frustration." The five indicators of structural just-deserts frustration, each ranging from 0–6, were summed to form an overall index of structural just-deserts frustration that could range from 0–30.

Two versions of the ladder scale also were administered. In the first version, the top and bottom of the ladder were defined as the best and worst situation that the respondent could imagine. Somewhat later in the interview schedule the ladder scale was readministered. Respondents were told: "This time imagine that all those people whom you know well are distributed on the ladder. Those who are best off stand at rung 10; those who worst off stand at rung 0. In your opinion, where do you stand?" Here the respondent is comparing his own achievement not with the best to which he aspires but with the best already attained by his friends and neighbors—people like himself with whom he presumably identifies. This permits a test of the contemporary-reference-group hypothesis (see Berkowitz 1972) that it is invidious comparison with one's own kind that is most likely to produce a sense of dissatisfaction or frustration.

The first step in the analysis was to compare relationships between the various ways of indexing frustration. Table 2–1 gives the relevant correlations. The measures of just-deserts frustration (JDF, JDF_s) should correlate negatively with the frustration measures based on the ladder scale (RGG, AG_p), that is, the more the gratification in comparison either with a reference group or with the best that one can imagine, the less the just deserts frustration. If frustration gauged in respect to just deserts is about the same as frustration gauged in respect to achievement of a reference group or to aspirations, then the correlations between these variables should be of a strong magnitude. In fact, however, they are of only moderate magnitude. Also, when the measures of just-deserts frustration are regressed on reference group and aspirational frustration, a strikingly low level of just-deserts frustration is estimated for people who score well into the frustration range on reference group gratification and present aspirational gratification scales (Muller 1979). These results have two important implications. First, just-deserts frustration is clearly different from the reference group and aspirational varieties; in particular, the Cantril ladder scale measure should not, as it has been in the past, be interpreted as a measure of relative deprivation in the sense that Gurr defines the term. Second, people appear to have a tendency to set their just deserts below the achievement attained by the best-off members of their reference group, and below their aspirations (best possible situation); as a consequence, even those who perceive a great discrepancy between their own achievement and that of their reference group, or between their own achievement and that which they would attain if their highest aspirations were realized, do not feel that there is any great discrepancy between what they now have and what they are rightfully entitled to.

TABLE 2–1. Correlations (r) between Just-Deserts Frustration and Other Frustration Measures: West Germany

		Just-Deserts Frustration (JDF)	Structural Just-Deserts Frustration (JDF$_s$)
1.	*Other Measures of Frustration*		
	Reference Group Gratification (Self-placement on the ladder scale in comparison to the best-off and worst-off members of a person's reference group) $\quad$ RGG	− .340	− .318
	Present Aspirational Gratification (Self-placement on the ladder scale in comparison to the best and worst situation imaginable) $\quad AG_p$	− .391	− .363
2.	*Measures of Change in Frustration*		
	Experienced Change (Present minus past aspirational gratification) $\quad AG_p - AG_e$	− .121	− .108
	Absolute Experienced Change $\quad |AG_p - AG_e|$	.155	.139
	Anticipated Change (Future minus present aspirational gratification) $\quad AG_f - AG_p$	.081	.063
	Absolute Anticipated Change $\quad |AG_f - AG_p|$	.211	.190

When looking at change in aspirational gratification (the bottom four rows of Table 2–1), it is worthy of note that, although all the correlations between change variables and just-deserts frustration are of trivial size, those involving the absolute magnitude measures ($|AG_p - AG_e|$, $|AG_f - AG_p|$) are higher than those for the directional change measures ($AG_p - AG_e, AG_f - AG_p$). This suggests that any change, whether deterioration or improvement, is associated with a higher level of just-deserts frustration and that no change is most associated with low just-deserts frustration.

Participation in acts of political protest and violence is a sensitive topic and measurement of it in survey research poses an obvious challenge. Apart from those studies focusing specifically on riot participation, previous research has relied upon a variety of more or less indirect indicators. In the West German study, questions about actual participation in protest and violence were asked and a dependent variable was constructed using behaviors that (1) are antiregime in the sense of being illegal; (2) constitute an attempt to influence the government by inconveniencing it or by disrupting its normal functioning, i.e., behaviors that have political significance; and (3) involve group activity on the part of nonelites. Thus the measure of participation in political protest and violence focuses on civil disobedience and violence, excluding varieties of peaceful and legal protest that may be unconventional but are nevertheless permitted in most industrialized democracies. Also excluded are ordinary labor strikes without political objectives and individualistic actions such as refusal of military service.

A number of steps were taken to reassure respondents that the research was being carried out for purely scientific purposes. The interviews yielded a sufficient number of positive responses to questions about actual participation to warrant the construction of a multi-item index. Five aggressive actions were incorporated into the index: (1) refusal to pay rents or taxes (164 positive responses); (2) participation in wildcat strikes (153 positive responses); (3) seizure of factories, offices, and other buildings (92 positive responses); (4) participation in battles with police or other demonstrators (87 positive responses); and (5) involvement with a group that wants to dislodge the government by violent means (34 positive responses).

Questions also were asked about intention to participate and about the degree to which each action was disapproved in the society at large. These two variables were then used as weighting factors in defining an aggressive political participation measure.

Detailed analysis of the relationships between component items and the composite variable showed that the composite response continuum could be interpreted in a plausible and substantively meaningful way. The continuum can be demarcated roughly into four zones of increasingly aggressive response ranging, low to high, from (1) inactivity and generally negative intention toward participation in aggressive action; to (2) predominant inactivity but positive intention toward performance of civil disobedience; (3) participation limited predominantly to civil disobedience but coupled with positive intention toward political violence; and (4) participation in acts of political violence as well as civil disobedience. Since a sizable majority of respondents scored in the lowest zone of aggressive political participation, the variable was subjected to a logarithmic (*base e*) transformation so as to reduce the skewness of the distribution.

Table 2–2 gives the correlations between the various indicators of frustration and the measure of participation in aggressive political protest and violence. All of the variables based on the ladder scale are weakly correlated with aggressive political participation (*APP*). However, the just-deserts measures show correlations with *APP* of considerably greater, though only moderate, magnitude in an absolute sense. When APP scores are plotted against JDF_s scores (Muller 1979), a clear-cut linear trend is ap-

TABLE 2–2. Correlations (r) between Measures of Frustration and Aggressive Political Participation (APP): West Germany

Measures of Frustration	Correlation with APP	N
RGG	$-.031$	1980
AG_p	$-.149$	2095
$AG_p - AG_e$	$.045$	2074
$\lvert AG_p - AG_e \rvert$	$.152$	2074
$AG_f - AG_p$	$.130$	1753
$\lvert AG_f - AG_p \rvert$	$.164$	1753
JDF	$.401$	2035
JDF_s	$.424$	2179

parent. These results suggest that the weak-to-nonexistent relationships between frustration and political protest and violence, found in previous research, may be largely an artifact of deficient measurement.

To investigate the generality of the findings from the West German study, the ladder-scale measure of aspirational gratification and a variety of just-deserts measures were included in a survey of 1,018 adults in New York City carried out during the spring and summer of 1978. The research design was equivalent to that used in West Germany. Response Analysis Corporation of Princeton, New Jersey, conducted personal interviews with a probability sample of 778 residents of the five boroughs of New York City. In addition, a random sample of 240 upper-division undergraduates, graduate students, and faculty of liberal arts at New York University and Columbia University completed a self-administered version of the instrument.

A quantitative measure of participation in aggressive political behavior was constructed for the New York City study according to the procedures developed in the West German project. As Table 2–3 shows, the measures of frustration in regard to aspirations do not correlate at a statistically significant level with the APP variable in the New York City sample. These results replicate those from the West German study, as well as the other research cited previously. The relationship between frustration in the aspirational sense and individual propensities for political protest and violence is, at best, quite weak.

In the New York City study, just-deserts frustration was measured in two ways. One set of questions, referring to housing conditions, health and medical care, and one's life in general, was equivalent to those used in the West German interview schedule. The job-related questions, income and satisfaction with one's daily work, were changed slightly. In this case, the

TABLE 2–3. Correlations (r) between Measures of Frustration and Aggressive Political Participation (APP): New York City

Measures of Frustration	Correlation with APP	N
1. *Aspirational*		
Present Standing on Ladder	− .065*	598†
Past Standing on Ladder	− .002*	593†
Future Standing on Ladder	− .049*	515†
2. *Just Deserts*		
Housing	.142	970
Health Care	.122	956
Life in General	.151	913
3. *Just Deserts, in comparison to one's level of formal education*		
Income	.271	654‡
Satisfaction with Work	.306	489‡
Occupational Prestige	.289	490‡

* Not significant at .05 level.
† Question administered only to a random half of the general public sample.
‡ Question administered only to employed persons.

just-deserts standard of comparison was defined specifically as level of education. Thus, instead of asking respondents whether they felt they were receiving as much income as they deserved in general, respondents were asked: "Considering your level of education, is your income as good as what you deserve?" And then, if the respondent replied in the negative: "How much worse is your income compared to what you deserve considering your level of education? Is it somewhat worse, much worse, or very much worse?" This format was repeated for the stimuli "amount of say you have about what happens to you in your job" and "occupational prestige." This change was adopted as an experiment to see if the specificity of a just-deserts comparison standard was important. Level of education was selected because in the United States and other industrialized democracies this may well be the most common, specific standard of comparison that people would use when thinking about whether they are receiving their just deserts in regard to job-related concerns such as income and prestige, and perhaps in regard to other valued goods and conditions of life as well.

As Table 2–3 shows, pegging the just-deserts comparison standard to level of education makes an important difference in the degree to which just-deserts frustration correlates with participation in aggressive political behavior. The three employment items, with education as the standard of comparison, correlate highly among themselves (r ranges from .624 to .726) and when combined to form a summated scale, correlate at $r = .331$ with the *APP* variable. Thus the New York City data also provide evidence in favor of the assertion that only just-deserts frustration will bear a nontrivial relationship to individual participation in political protest and violence, although the strength of this evidence obviously is somewhat diluted by the fact that the just-deserts items that are equivalent in the West German and American samples show a quite different magnitude of association.[2]

Other evidence bearing on the relationship between just-deserts frustration and aggressive political action is provided by data from surveys of probability samples of the adult population in Austria, Great Britain, the Netherlands, the United States, and West Germany conducted in 1974 (Barnes et al. 1979). Four versions of the ladder scale were administered to respondents in each country. Two versions entailed placing oneself on the ladder in regard to "all the things that make up your material standard of living" and in regard to "your life as a whole," with the top and bottom rungs assigned the usual aspirational standard of comparison (best and worst possible situation that one can imagine). The other two versions asked respondents to designate the rung on the ladder that corresponded to the material standards and general life situation to which they felt rightfully entitled. The first two questions yielded discrepancy scores that represent aspirational deprivation; the second two questions provide measures of just-deserts deprivation, calculated as the difference between actual standing on the ladder and the entitlement rung. These ladder-scale variables were correlated with a six-category protest potential index (Marsh 1974), ranging from unwillingness to engage in any kind of protest at the low end, through willingness to engage in legally permitted activities in the middle, to willingness to engage in civil disobedience at the high end. The association was uniformly weak across all nations: the correlations between protest potential and absolute ladder-scale scores ranged between .03 (Austria) and $-.12$ (Netherlands); the ladder-scale measures of just-deserts frustration (absolute standing relative to entitlement) correlated with protest potential in a range of $-.13$ (Germany and Austria) to $-.12$ (United States).

A more complex analysis of the British data was undertaken by Marsh (1977), who investigated the relationship between protest potential and the ladder-scale measure of material deprivation in comparison to entitlement, taking into account people's belief in the responsibility of government for equality of wealth and their evaluation of the actual performance of government in evening out differences in wealth between people. It was hypothesized that high protest potential would be most pronounced among individuals who (1) feel that the issue of inequality of wealth is personally important; (2) hold government responsible for improving equality; (3) experience less material satisfaction than they feel entitled to; and (4) are dissatisfied with governmental performance in this area of public policy. Unfortunately, a statistical test of the hypothesis was not performed, although percentage comparisons indicated that respondents who met the above conditions were, indeed, most likely to manifest high protest potential.

Obviously, the results with the ladder-scale measure of just-deserts frustration are discouraging for the thesis that it is only this particular kind of frustration that provides an incentive for participation in political protest and violence. On the other hand, the low correlations could reflect a goodly amount of random measurement error due to the use of the ladder-scale format.

When all the evidence is considered, it seems clear that strong claims about frustration or relative deprivation being the "root" psychological cause of protest and violence must be rejected. The best that can be said for the frustration–aggression hypothesis as applied to aggressive political action is that one kind of frustration—that arising from perceived discrepancy between one's just deserts and one's actual attainment—may bear a modest relationship to individual propensity for participating in political protest and violence.

UTILITARIAN AND NORMATIVE JUSTIFICATION

Gurr (1970b) classifies psychological causes of political protest and violence other than relative deprivation under two very general categories: normative justifications and utilitarian justifications. Attitudes and beliefs that justify aggressive political action because it is intrinsically right or proper provide motivational incentive for such behavior on normative grounds; attitudes and beliefs that justify aggressive action because it is expected to help people achieve their political goals provide utilitarian motivational incentive.

GENERAL THEORIES

Gurr's theory, derived from the frustration–aggression hypothesis, postulates relative deprivation (just-deserts frustration) as a necessary condition of political protest and violence. Just as the frustration–aggression hypothesis (Dollard et al. 1939, N. E. Miller 1941) says that aggression always presupposes the existence of frustration, so does Gurr propose that specifically political aggression will not occur if just-deserts frustration is absent. However, normative and utilitarian justification do play an important role in the determination of individual propensities for political aggression, for the justification variables are expected to amplify or inhibit the effect of just-deserts frustration.

A different theory, proposed by Korpi (1974) following the general theory of motivation formulated by Atkinson (1964), casts relative deprivation in a less important role. In Korpi's view, the direct cause of political protest and violence is utilitarian justification: people engage in such behavior because it has utility for them and because they believe it can be successful. Relative deprivation is related to aggressive action only indirectly, as one of the causes of utility, that is, the greater the relative deprivation, the greater the utility.

In Muller (1978, 1979) I propose a theory based on the work of Fishbein (1967). Three kinds of variables are postulated by Fishbein as the basic determinants of behavior: (1) attitude about an action, defined as the sum of an individual's expectations about the consequences of performing an action multiplied by their subjective value to him; (2) normative beliefs about an action, defined as the individual's own belief in the intrinsic justifiability of the behavior as well as his perception of significant others' (parents, peers) expectations about it; (3) motivation to comply with the norms, reflecting such factors as an individual's personality and his perception of the reasonableness of the expectations of others.

MEASUREMENT OF UTILITARIAN AND NORMATIVE JUSTIFICATION

Fishbein's theory is quite abstract, leaving open the possibility, when applying that theory to aggressive political participation, of operationally defining the general determinants of behavior in a variety of ways. His expectancy-value concept (attitude about the action) is based on the premise that motivational incentive for performing a behavior is provided by expectation that the action will have rewarding consequences, weighted (specifically, multiplied) by the value of performing that action as compared to alternative actions. Belief about the consequences of an action does not have to derive from personal experience; indeed, Bandura's (1973) social learning theory of aggression postulates that vicarious reinforcement for aggression, deriving from observation of the degree to which such action has had rewarding consequences for other groups in the past, is likely to override directly experienced reinforcement, especially in the case of aggressive political action: "Observational incentives play an especially important role in social activism, for here the chances of quick success are poor, but protest behavior is partly sustained by the long-range attainments of groups that have persevered in their efforts" (1973: 206). In my own work (Muller 1972, 1978, 1979) I have operationalized the expectancy-of-success concept by a variable called belief in the efficacy of collective political aggression, defined as the sum of an individual's evaluations of the degree to which a variety of aggressive political actions have been beneficial to the dissident groups involved.

To operationalize the concept of the value of an aggressive action, it seems plausible to assume that the value of behavior that deviates from legally permitted participation will be high when people believe that their ability to influence the government through regular channels is insufficient, and low if the individual believes that involvement in politics is unnecessary or undesirable. For individuals who see themselves as having sufficient capability to influence the government, the value of legally deviant behavior will fall somewhere between these extremes of the continuum, depending upon how the consequences of that kind of action are evaluated. Following this logic, I have proposed (Muller 1978, 1979) that belief in the efficacy of political aggression be weighted by an index of political influence capability such that (1) if political influence capability is thought to be unnecessary, efficacy scores are multiplied by zero, because aggressive action—or any kind of political action—has no value to the individual; (2) efficacy of political aggression scores are given greater weight among people who think their political influence capability is insufficient as compared to people who think their influence capability is sufficient.

This weighting of belief in the efficacy of political aggression by the subjective value of such action is called "utilitarian justification for aggression" in the West German study (Muller 1978, 1979). When aggressive political participation scores were regressed on utilitarian justification for aggression scores, a moderately good fit to a linear function was obtained, as indicated by an r^2 of .234 ($r = .48$). Other research has reported findings congruent with that from the West German study. In the Waterloo, Iowa study (Muller 1972), a measure of belief in the effectiveness of protest and violence was found to explain 21 percent of the variance ($r = .46$) on the potential for political violence scale. Marsh's (1977) British study showed that a measure of belief in the effectiveness of political protest accounted for 27 percent of the variance ($r = .52$) on his protest potential scale. The observation of a moderately strong linear relationship between degree of utilitarian justification for political aggression and aggressive political participation/potential in different political cultures is strong testimony to the importance of this psychological variable in the explanation of why people participate in acts of political protest and violence.

In addition to the expectancy-value concept, Fishbein's theory identifies normative beliefs about the justifiability of an action as a second general determinant of behavior. With regard to political protest and violence, support for the structure of political authority or political system surely must rank among the most important sources of belief in the normative justifiability of aggressive political action. To be sure, not everyone who becomes alienated from the political system will feel that taking aggressive action is proper, but they certainly should be more likely to view it as normatively justifiable than those who support the system.

An eight-item summated scale of political support-to-alienation was administered to respondents in the West German study (Muller 1978, 1979).

This measure showed good reliability (alpha = .822). When the *APP* variable was regressed on political support–alienation, an r^2 of .251 (r = .50) obtained. The slope, however, did not provide a very good summary of the relationship because people scoring in the intermediate range of the support–alienation variable tended to register quite low aggressive participation scores, instead of the intermediate aggressive participation scores predicted by the linear slope. Intermediate to high aggressive participation scores were registered only by persons scoring at very alienated levels of the support–alienation variable. Squaring political support–alienation so as to give greater weight to scores at the alienation end of the continuum produced a more even distribution of deviations about the slope and resulted in an increase in explained variance to 28 percent. This change is not dramatic but does provide some evidence for the possibility that system support in Western societies may have to decline to quite low levels before it will provide any motivation incentive for participation in acts of political protest and violence.

The New York City survey contained a similar measure of support-to-alienation of the political system (Jukam and Muller 1979). This English-language measure showed very good reliability (alpha = .89). In the New York City sample, the political support–alienation variable accounted for 18 percent of the variance (r = .42) in aggressive political participation. However, squaring political support–alienation did not produce any improvement in predictive accuracy. Thus the evidence from comparative hypothesis-testing in different societies indicates that participation in political protest and violence is likely to increase as system support declines, but the strength and form of the relationship may be variable.

The presence of a relationship between attitude about the political system and participation in aggressive political action is hardly surprising. J. D. Wright (1976), however, has argued quite strongly that the evidence for such a relationship is ambiguous. His claim is based mainly on the fact that, in the 1968, 1970, and 1972 University of Michigan Survey Research Center election studies, both he and Citrin (1974) found little or no relationship between the Survey Research Center's trust in government (also called political cynicism) variable (Robinson, Rusk, and Head 1972) and approval/disapproval of civil disobedience and disruptive sit-ins and demonstrations. Also, survey study of American men by Blumenthal et al. (1975) found only a slight relationship between trust in government and the protest behaviors index (gamma = .20) across the entire sample (among black respondents only the gamma correlation was .30). On the other side of the ledger are the results of three local surveys. A study in 1967 of 855 residents of Detroit, Michigan (Aberbach and Walker 1970) found a gamma correlation of .42 between trust in government and response among black respondents to the question of whether or not they could imagine a situation in which they would riot. A 1968 study of 296 students at the University of Iowa (Muller 1970) found a correlation (r) of .412 between trust in government and a measure of the degree to which respondents would avoid participating in acts of disruptive protest and violence. And the Waterloo, Iowa, study (Muller 1972) found that the potential for political violence variable correlated at $r = -.464$ with a trust political authorities variable that included the Survey Research Center's trust in government items along with items measuring affect for the courts and police (this correlation was reduced, though not substantially, when race of respondent was controlled for). To complicate the matter further, when viewed from the cross-national perspective afforded by the Barnes et al.(1979) five-nation study, the relationship between a shortened trust in government variable and the protest potential scale turns out to be exceedingly weak in every country, ranging from a low of $r = .02$ in West Germany to a high of $r = .12$ in the United States.

One plausible explanation for these inconsistent results is simply that the trust in government variable is a poor indicator of affect for the political system, at least in Western societies. As Citrin (1974) has argued, trust in government may be mainly a register of generalized approval/disapproval of incumbent political leaders. If this is true, low political trust would be a weak source of normative justification for participation in acts of political protest and violence because in the democratic regimes where trust in government has been studied, citizens have at their disposal a variety of legal means for changing incumbents of whom they disapprove. Consequently, trust in government per se should be expected to show rather low correlation with measures of attitude about, or participation in, political protest and violence. On the other hand, if many respondents low in political trust also are negative in their system affect, while respondents high in political trust also are high in their system affect, trust in government, because of its association with system attitude, might show a stronger, albeit spurious, correlation with protest and violence. Indeed, results of testing this explanation confirm it in both the West German and New York City studies (Muller and Jukam 1977, Jukam and Muller 1979). For the West German sample, a gamma correlation of .38 between political trust and an index of participation in aggressive political behavior was reduced to $-.06$ when political support–alienation, the measure of system attitude, was controlled for, and a gamma correlation of .66 between political support–alienation and the aggressive behavior index was reduced to only .61 when political trust was controlled for. In the New York City data, a correlation (r) of .19 between trust in government and aggressive political participation was reduced to $-.01$ when political support–alienation was controlled for; the .42 correlation between political support–alienation and aggressive political participation remained at the same value when trust in government was controlled for.

Another source of normative justification for political protest and violence is a person's ideological beliefs. As Gurr has put it: "Men's ideational systems, including their political ideologies, usually incorporate norms about the desirability of violence. They may prohibit the use of violence as an instrument of political competition, or prescribe violence as an historically justified response to political oppression" (1970b: 194). This argument can be extended to aggressive participation in general.

Incentive to participate in political protest and violence on normative grounds should be quite strong when alienation from the political system is reinforced by belief that political aggression is justifiable for ideological reasons. But if a person is not alienated from the political system, it seems likely that normative incentive for political aggression would be relatively weak, even if the person's ideological beliefs condone such action. Also, normative incentive for political aggression on the basis of system alienation might be weakened if a person's ideological beliefs do not condone such action. Finally, of course, when alienation is low and ideological beliefs do not condone aggressive political action, normative incentive should be weak indeed. This line of reasoning implies that the concept of normative justification for political aggression should be defined operationally as the product of degree of alienation from the political system multiplied by the degree of commitment to an ideological position that condones political aggression.

During the 1970s in West Germany and the United States, political protest and violence has been more acceptable to the left than to the right. Broadly speaking, a leftist ideological position has embraced a "social change" orientation that often condones collective political aggression when it is necessary in the interest of social reform; on the other hand, the right has tended to be more concerned with "social control" and to feel that rules should be obeyed instead of challenged. Also, specific leftist ideologies that provide a coherent rationale for collective political aggression—Marxism-Leninism, Maoism, the "New Left" strains of thought that arose in the 1960s—are probably more widely respected on the left than are analogous ideologies on the right.

In the West German and New York City studies (Muller 1978, 1979; Jukam and Muller 1979), respondents' ideological position was measured by the Left-Right scale, a rectangle containing ten boxes labeled LEFT and RIGHT at the two extreme positions. Respondents were asked to check the box that best corresponds to their own position on the left-right ideological continuum. Scores on the political support-to-alienation variable were multiplied by degree of leftist ideological commitment to create an indicator of degree of belief in the normative justifiability of politically aggressive action, called normative justification for aggression. For the West German sample, *APP* scores vary as a linear function of normative justification for aggression and the fit to the slope is quite good (r^2 = .395). Aggressive political participation is almost never high when normative justification for aggression is low; also, hardly any low aggressive political participation occurs when normative justification for aggression is high. The New York City data replicate the West German findings although the fit to a linear function is not quite as strong (r^2 = .275). Examination of the scatterplot for aggressive political participation and normative justification for aggression among New Yorkers reveals the presence of a cluster of six respondents who scored very high on the participation variable and very low on the normative justification variable. These "outliers" depress r^2; why they occurred is a question now being investigated.

In addition to personal normative beliefs, Fishbein's general behavior theory includes the concept of social normative beliefs, defined as "the individual's belief about what 'society' (i.e., most other people, his 'significant others,' etc.) 'says' he should do (i.e., a social or group norm)" (Fishbein 1967: 489). However, there is a disadvantage in adopting this definition, since it focuses on the individual's *subjective perception* of social norms, a perception that may be strongly influenced by the individual's own personal normative beliefs; and if this were the case, then it would be very difficult to disentangle any separate effects that these variables might have on behavior. A definition that avoids this problem equates social normative beliefs with the mean level of belief in the normative justifiability of a given action held by a person's "significant others" or by most other people in his community. Normally, it would be prohibitively expensive to interview the "significant others" identified by each respondent in a survey. An alternative, albeit less satisfactory, strategy is to focus on community-wide norms. In the West Germany study, for example (Muller 1978, 1979), the universities register much higher on the normative justification for aggression variable than do the urban and rural communities. Therefore, a respondent from a university was said to be exposed to a *facilitative* condition of social normative belief in the justifiability of aggression; by comparison, a respondent from an urban or rural community was said to be exposed to an inhibitory condition of social normative belief. Specifically, the social normative beliefs concept was operationalized by a dummy variable, scored "1" if the respondent was from a university community, "0" if the respondent was from an urban or rural community.

The final variable in Fishbein's general behavior theory is a weighting factor, motivation to comply with social normative beliefs. This concept is difficult to define operationally and appears to be of somewhat dubious explanatory value. For example, in one study (Ajzen and Fishbein 1969) the weighting of social normative beliefs by motivation to comply actually reduced the correlations with behavior.

MULTIVARIATE RELATIONSHIPS

Operational models for the general theories of aggressive political participation proposed by Gurr, Korpi, and myself were specified and tested across the West German sample (Muller 1979). Korpi's utilitarian justification theory was specified as

$$APP_{ln} = a + b_0(UJA) + \epsilon, \tag{1}$$

where APP_{ln} is the logged aggressive political participation variable and UJA is the utilitarian justification for aggression variable. The parameters for this model, estimated by ordinary least squares regression, were found to be

$$APP_{ln} = 1.740 + .134\,(UJA), \tag{1a}$$

where $r^2 = .234$ and N = 1915. Clearly, much of the variance on APP_{ln} is left unexplained.

The theory that I derived from Fishbein's work, called the expectancy–value–norms theory, was specified as

$$APP_{ln} = a + b_0\,(UJA) + b_1\,(NJA) + b_2\,(UNV) + b_3\,(A) \tag{2}$$
$$+ c_0\,(UNV^*UJA) + c_1\,(UNV^*NJA) + \epsilon,$$

where NJA is the normative justification for aggression variable; UNV is the indicator of social norms, with the university milieu defined as the facilitative condition and the urban and rural milieus defined as the inhibitory condition; UNV^*UJA and UNV^*NJA are interaction terms representing the possibility that the effect of the justification variables may be enhanced or depressed, depending upon whether social norms are facilitative; and A is a variable called availability (defined as a weighted sum of age, marital status, and employment status, with the highest scores assigned to conditions on these variables that give the respondent the greatest amount of unscheduled time). Variable A is not part of expectancy–value–norms theory but should be included for two reasons. First, "background" characteristics that make people available for participation in collective action generally should be taken into account when the focus is on aggressive collective action. Second, A should be included to provide an indicator of social norms that is not confounded with availability. The problem arises because all of the background characteristics that promote greater availability for collective action of any kind are more likely to be found among individuals at universities than among those in urban and rural communities. In the initial test of the expectancy–value–norms model, the parameter for the UNV^*UJA term was found to be not reliably different from zero, so this term was dropped and the model was reestimated as

$$APP_{ln} = 1.390 + .044 \, (UJA) + .003 \, (NJA) + .236 \, (UNV) + .046 \, (A) \quad \text{(2a)}$$
$$+ .004 \, (UNV^*NJA),$$

where $R^2 = .569$ and N $= 1838$.

Equation 2a shows that the utilitarian justification model expressed by equation 1a is radically underspecified. The variables representing justification for political aggression on normative grounds are estimated to make a very important contribution to prediction of aggressive political participation, independent of the utilitarian justification variable.[3] Moreover, the estimated effect of utilitarian justification for aggression from equation 1a appears from the vantage point of equation 2a to be considerably inflated (the UJA parameter of .134 in equation 1a is reduced to .044 in equation 2a). These results are compelling evidence for the need to include normative justifications in any theory of participation in political protest and violence.

The relative deprivation theory proposed by Gurr asserts that the just-deserts frustration (JDF) variable (the operationalization of the relative deprivation concept) will (1) have a direct effect on aggressive political participation, independent of the justification variables; and (2) will interact multiplicatively with the justification variables. When only utilitarian justification for aggression (UJA) and normative justification for aggression (NJA) are considered, the West German data show that multiplicative interaction terms with just-deserts frustration (UJA^*JDF_s; NJA^*-JDF_s) are not statistically significant in a prediction equation for aggressive political participation, but the parameter estimate for the JDF_s term does reach statistical significance. Inserting the just-deserts frustration variable into the prediction equation for aggressive political participation that already contains the variables from the expectancy–value–norms model (equation 2a) yields the following results:

$$APP_{ln} = 1.389 + .042 \, (UJA) + .0022 \, (NJA) + .010 \, (JDF_s) \quad \text{(3)}$$
$$+ .241 \, (UNV) = .044 \, (A) + .0034 \, (UNV^*NJA),$$

where $R^2 = .572$ and N $= 1838$. Although the JDF_s parameter estimate is statistically significant (in this case, greater than two and one-half times its standard error of .003), it contributes no increase in accuracy of prediction, as R^2 is unchanged at two decimal places.[4] Also, the parameter estimates for the expectancy–value–norms variables remain virtually unchanged with JDF_s in the prediction equation. Thus, the JDF_s term is a superfluous variable and can be deleted from the prediction equation for aggressive political participation. Additional evidence of the super-fluousness of JDF_s can be seen from the standardized regression equation:

$$APP_{ln} = .157\ (UJA) + .150\ (NJA) + .067\ (JDF_s) + .175\ (UNV) \qquad (3a)$$
$$+ .152\ (A) + .252\ (UNV^*NJA),$$

where the standardized coefficient for JDF_s is less than .1, which is a substantively trivial magnitude. Thus these results indicate that just-deserts frustration is most likely only an indirect cause of participation in political protest and violence in West Germany—hardly a necessary condition.

VALIDITY OF THE EXPECTANCY–VALUE–NORMS MODEL

The variables in the expectancy–value–norms model account for nearly three-fifths of the variance in aggressive political participation. For micro-level survey data this is a quite impressive level of predictive accuracy. Predictive accuracy, however, is the least important criterion for assessing the quality of a theory. High predictive accuracy obviously is a desirable feature of any operationalized model for a theory. But predictive accuracy is in part a function of how much variation happens to exist in the independent variables; and the degree of variation in the independent variables is extraneous to the quality of a theory. More important than predictive accuracy is the completeness of the model (have other important causal variables been omitted?), the robustness of its parameter estimates (when omitted variables are entered into the prediction equation, are the parameter estimates for the included variables stable?), and the generality of its parameter estimates (do they reflect laws that hold independent of time and place?).

To assess the completeness and robustness of the expectancy–value–norms model a number of omitted variables were considered. Kaase (1976) has argued that dissatisfaction with the public policy outputs of a given administration is likely to have an effect on participation in political protest and violence if: (1) the policy has broad relevance; (2) the government is assigned responsibility for dealing with it; and (3) it has personal importance for the individual. A policy dissatisfaction index which took these conditions into account was constructed in the Barnes et al. (1979) five-nation study. This variable showed generally weak correlations with the protest potential scale, ranging from a low of $r = .13$ in West Germany and Austria to a high of .27 in the United States.

The West German study contained a similar measure of policy dissatisfaction. In this instance, however, factor analysis of the set of specific policy items revealed the presence of two different dimensions of policy dissatisfaction: a materialist dimension, defined by policies such as providing for economic stability and providing for peace and order in society; and a postmaterialist dimension, defined by policies such as guaranteeing justice for all and ensuring that major institutions are run in accord with democratic principles (on the materialist–postmaterialist distinction see Inglehart 1977). The materialist policy dissatisfaction variable showed virtually no relation with aggressive political participation ($r = .14$), whereas a correlation of moderate strength ($r = .39$) obtained between the participation variable and postmaterialist policy dissatisfaction. When the postmaterialist policy dissatisfaction variable is added to the expectancy–value–norms prediction equation for aggressive participation, it turns out to be a superfluous variable, i.e., the parameter estimate for postmaterialist policy dissatisfaction is significant, but R^2 is not increased and the parameter estimates for the expectancy–value–norms variables remain virtually the same.

Alienation in the sense of powerlessness (low expectancy of control over events) is another variable that has been proposed as an important antecedent of political protest and violence. Ransford (1968), Crawford and Naditch (1970), Seeman (1972), and Crosby (1976, 1979) have argued that the combination of relative deprivation and powerlessness is a psychological condition conducive to individual participation in aggressive political action. Support for this proposition was reported by Ransford (1968) on the basis of data from a sample of Los Angeles blacks (N = 312), where the dependent variable was a measure of willingness to use violence to gain black rights. Others (Caplan and Paige 1968, Caplan 1970, Forward and Williams 1970) have argued just the reverse, namely, that it is a sense of mastery that, combined with the feeling of deprivation, will provoke individuals to take aggressive action. No decisive evidence in favor of either hypothesis has yet been reported. In the West German study, items from the internal–external control of reinforcement scale (Rotter 1966), the usual measure of mastery–powerlessness, were only weakly interrelated. Therefore, a satisfactory measure of mastery–powerlessness could not be constructed.

A variation on the deprivation and mastery theme is the hypothesis that the combination of political distrust and political efficacy will spur individuals to engage in aggressive political action (Gamson 1968, Finifter 1970). Paige (1971) investigated this hypothesis as an explanation of riot participation among black males in Newark; but his measuring instruments, especially the indicator of efficacy, were suspect. The Barnes et al. (1979) cross-national study found that, in all five nations, mean protest potential was highest when a sense of political efficacy was combined with policy dissatisfaction, but no measure of strength of relationship was reported, and no specific test for an interaction effect was conducted. Thus, the importance of a distrust/dissatisfaction–efficacy interaction remains an open question. It was not tested in the West German project because the survey instrument did not include the political efficacy measure.

Turning from psychological antecedents to social background variables, Citrin (1975) and Shanks (1975) have reported that in a San Francisco Bay area survey (N = 963) a measure of personal and political resources, built by combining information about a person's level of education, verbal ability, political interest, and organizational involvement, interacted with an indicator of political alienation in the determination of protest participation: high levels of protest participation result from the combination of high political alienation and high personal and political resources. In the West German study, the interaction between personal and political resources and political support–alienation was found to have a minor effect on aggressive political participation, but when all the variables in the expectancy–value–norms model were considered, the measure of personal and political resources showed neither an additive direct effect nor an interaction effect.

Although direct consideration of these alternative variables did not disclose any deficiencies in the expectancy–value–norms model, analysis of the residuals suggested the presence of an unmeasured, omitted variable that leads some individuals to register medium-to-high aggressive political participation despite low scores on the expectancy–value–norms variables. Perhaps this variable operates at the group rather than individual level, and such persons are responding to group directives instead of to personal motivational incentive.

Of critical importance in evaluating the expectancy–value–norms model is the question of its reproducibility. Do the estimated parameters reflect general laws or do they pertain only to the case of the 1974 sample? The reproducibility of a model is determined by cross-validating it—testing it again for either a different sample from the same population or the same sample at a later point in time.

The West German project contained a cross-validation phase in which 49 percent (N = 1310) of the original respondents were reinterviewed during the fall of 1976, producing three samples for the purpose of cross-validation: the 1974 full sample, the 1974 panel sample, and the 1976 panel sample.

A major difference between the 1974 full sample and the two panel samples is the proportion of persons residing in university and nonuniversity communities. In the 1974 full sample, 42 percent came from university communities. The panel samples contain only 24 percent from university communities. The panel samples also differ considerably from the 1974 full sample in the means and standard deviations of the expectancy–value–norms predictor variables: the panel samples show substantially reduced variation, as indexed by the standard deviation, and lower means. From the standpoint of cross-validating the expectancy–value–norms model estimated for the 1974 full sample, these differences are not at all unwelcome. Because the distributional characteristics of the variables do differ markedly, the panel samples can provide a more stringent test of the cross-validity of the expectancy–value–norms model than would be the case if the samples showed close similarity.

Three considerations are important in the determination of cross-validity for the West German data: (1) the parameters of the expectancy–value–norms model should not fluctuate markedly from sample to sample; (2) when the parameters from the 1974 full sample are used to predict aggressive political participation in the two panel samples, predictive accuracy (as indexed by R^2) should not fluctuate markedly; (3) when the parameters estimated from the 1974 panel sample are inserted into the prediction equation for the 1976 panel sample, and the 1976 panel sample parameters are inserted into the prediction equation for the 1974 panel sample, predictive accuracy also should not fluctuate markedly.

The results of the cross-validation exercise were as follows:

1. The regression weights for the expectancy–value–norms model turned out to be remarkably consistent across samples. Predictive accuracy was reduced for the panel samples (R^2 = .43 for the 1974 panel sample; R^2 = .396 for the 1976 panel sample) as compared with the 1974 full sample (R^2 = .569). This is because the standard deviations of the variables in the panel study are all considerably smaller than the standard deviations of the variables in the 1974 full sample: ceteris paribus, the less the variability in a set of variables, the smaller the multiple correlation coefficient.

2. When the weights from the 1974 full sample were inserted into the prediction equation for aggressive political participation in the 1974 panel sample, the R^2 value was .411. When these weights were inserted into the prediction equation for aggressive political participation in the 1976 panel sample, the R^2 value was .412. This finding is further testimony to the generality of the full sample weights. Also, when the weights from the 1976 panel sample were inserted into the prediction equation for aggressive political participation in the 1974 panel sample, the R^2 was .441, as compared with an R^2 value of .389 obtained when the weights from the 1974 panel sample were used to predict aggressive political participation in the 1976 panel sample. These R^2 values are sufficiently similar to indicate that the weights estimated from the panel samples are essentially interchangeable.

The next step in validating the expectancy–value–norms model entails tests of the model for a different sample from a different population. This phase is presently being carried out with the New York City data.

CONCLUSION

The findings from micro-level research on psychological antecedents of political protest and violence indicate that the frustration–aggression hypothesis has only weak explanatory power when applied to politically aggressive behavior. Most kinds of frustration, not to mention sheer deprivation, are at best weakly associated with individual differences in potential or actual participation in aggressive action. The exception is frustration arising from the belief that one's just deserts are unfulfilled. This feeling of just-deserts frustration, called relative deprivation by Gurr, probably bears an indirect relationship to individual propensities for political protest and violence, but the evidence is by no means decisive even on this point. However, it should be noted that the micro-level evidence bearing on the relationship between subjective deprivation and aggressive political participation has been collected in western societies where the variability of subjective deprivation is presumably lower than in nonwestern locales. Since, ceteris paribus, the less the variability in a set of variables, the smaller are the correlations, it is possible that in nonwestern societies subjective deprivation could play a more important role in the explanation of aggressive participation than has been found to be the case in the studies reviewed here.

Some psychological variables do appear to have rather strong explanatory power. There is nothing esoteric about these variables, and they are less glamorous conceptually than the various frustration and relative deprivation constructs that have been developed, but in western societies they consistently show moderate to strong association with measures of aggression potential/participation. Belief in the justifiability of aggressive action on utilitarian grounds, arising out of expectancy that aggressive action will be beneficial (weighted by its value), and belief in the normative justifiability of aggressive action, arising out of broad-based alienation from the political system and ideological approval of political aggression, are the psychological variables that predispose individuals in general to participate in protest and violence. More simply and tritely put, people rebel when they believe it is right to rebel and that rebellion will pay off. Of course, there is more to the explanation of protest and violence than this simple formula. Prevailing social norms make it more or less likely that individuals who feel political aggression is justifiable on normative and utilitarian grounds will act on their beliefs. If most others in a given social group or community feel that political aggression is unjustified, deviant individuals will be unlikely to go against the grain of prevailing sentiment. Also, the pure availability of time for protest and violence afforded by unemployment, by being a student, or by being unmarried, plays a role in determining propensity for protest. But the basic motivational dynamics appear to be quite logical and obvious.

There are two interesting questions for future research in this area. The first is about the role of organizations. Presumably, the psychological variables of utilitarian and normative beliefs in the justifiability of political aggression create predispositions for participation in political protest and violence. Organizations then activate these predispositions. But what if the predispositions are not there? To what extent can organizational directives mobilize people for protest and violence *independently* of the psychological variables that afford explicit motivational incentive? This will be quite a tricky question to investigate because it involves research designs that bridge the micro- and macro-levels of analysis.

The second question for future research is that of the causes of people's beliefs in the utilitarian and normative justifiability of political aggression. The major determinant of belief in the justifiability of political aggression on utilitarian grounds probably is a macro-level variable, the degree to which government effectively represses dissidents. On the other hand, belief in the normative justifiability of political aggression, especially the system-alienation component, probably requires a far more complicated explanation. Variables such as just-deserts frustration and policy dissatisfaction are obvious candidates for antecedents of system alienation, but the flow of causal influence may be complex. It is quite plausible that system alienation could, through selective perception, predispose individuals to feel that they are not receiving their just deserts and to view the policy performance of incumbent administrations in a negative light. Longitudinal studies certainly, and quasi-experimental research designs probably, will be necessary to answer the question of what causes the causes of aggressive political participation.

NOTES

1. Gurr has subsequently modified this position, giving relative deprivation (called "potential for action") equal status with cultural dispositions and rationalistic calculations in the determination of political protest and violence (see Gurr and Duvall 1976).
2. These just-deserts items have not been weighted by system responsibility. The New York City study contains a more elaborate and complex measure of attribution of responsibility for just-deserts frustration than was used in the West German project. Investigation of the "responsibility" items is not yet complete, but preliminary findings do not show any improvement in correlation with aggressive political participation when the just-deserts variables are weighted by system responsibility.
3. A direct comparison of the relative importance of the two psychological variables can be made by eliminating the other variables from the equation and estimating standardized weights (betas) for the utilitarian justification and normative justification variables. The result is

$$APP_{ln} = .257 \ (UJA) + .516 \ (NJA),$$

where $R^2 = .448$ and N = 1,838. The importance of normative belief in the justifiability of political aggression is further underscored in this comparison, since the independent influence of normative incentive is estimated to be twice as large as the independent influence of utilitarian incentive.

4. Focusing on the set of psychological variables alone, a direct comparison of the relative importance of the frustration variable versus the utilitarian and normative justification variables can be made by estimating standardized weights (betas) in the following equations:

$$APP_{ln} = .381 \ (UJA) + .293 \ (JDF_s) + .013 \ (UJA^*JDFs),$$

where $R^2 = .313$ and $N = 1,899$; and

$$APP_{ln} = .598 \ (NJA) + .187 \ (JDF_s) - .088 \ (NJA^*JDF_s),$$

where $R^2 = .410$ and $N = 1,821$. In both equations the interaction term is included so as to reflect the amplification effect predicted by Gurr's theory. In both instances the amplification effect is trivial. In both instances the independent effect of the frustration variable also is less than that of the justification variables; and this disparity is especially marked when the comparison is between the frustration variable and the normative justification variable.

CHAPTER 3

Theory and Research in the Study of Revolutionary Personnel

Mostafa Rejai

ALTHOUGH REVOLUTIONS HAVE BEEN AMONG the most conspicuous facts of life in the twentieth century, the study of revolutionary personnel—leaders, cadres, rank and file—has been among the most neglected aspects of conflict behavior. While a series of recent works has begun to shed partial light on revolutionary elites, our knowledge of rank and file has not progressed much beyond the stage of intuition and speculation, and information about cadres is virtually nonexistent.

This chapter has three interrelated objectives. First, it presents and evaluates the principal theoretical approaches to the study of revolutionary leadership. Second, it reviews, synthesizes, and critiques current research findings concerning leaders, cadres, and rank and file in revolutions. Finally, it calls attention to the principal lacunae in this area of conflict behavior and to the concomitant need for systematic theoretical/empirical research.

A series of clarifications is in order. First, we are concerned with persons caught up in revolutionary *movements* and the struggle for power, not with those who may appear upon the scene after the power seizure. Thus, for instance, we are interested in Lenin and Stalin but not in Khrushchev and Brezhnev.

Second, for analytic convenience we divide revolutionary personnel into leaders, cadres, and rank and file. Leaders, needless to say, play the

NOTE: I am indebted to Ted Robert Gurr for a searching critique of an earlier draft.

pivotal roles in revolutionary movements. Their special skills lie in ideological mobilization and in organization building of a political, military, or paramilitary nature. Cadres, necessarily a larger group, are intermediate leaders charged with specific aspects of organization, coordination, and discipline. Most important, cadres function as the link between leaders and rank and file, translating and transmitting party policy, and building moral among large numbers of people involved in the drama of revolution. The extent to which these three distinct groups are similar or dissimilar (in terms of social background, for example) is a question to which we shall return later.

Finally, we are interested only in *revolutionary* personnel. As such, we exclude from consideration persons involved in counterrevolutionary (Tilly 1965) or reactionary (Abel 1966, Merkl 1975) movements. Nor are we in a position to consider the general literature of protest, rebellion, and revolt. Indeed, even our treatment of revolutionary personnel will be necessarily selective, drawing only on the more prominent sources.

THEORY

Three theoretical approaches to the study of revolutionary elites may be identified: the psychoanalytic, the psychohistorical, the sociological. The psychoanalytic approach focuses on the inner dynamics of human personality, and it seeks to locate the impulse to revolution in the early psychological experiences of individuals. The psychohistorical approach seeks to move beyond the purely psychoanalytic theories by placing personality dynamics in the context of society and history; it attempts to combine psychological motivation with actual life experiences of an individual through time. The sociological approach—which is most prominently associated with the concept of charisma—stresses certain exceptional or supernatural qualities of individual leaders that sharply distinguish them from the masses while at the same time eliciting the latter's commitment and devotion. Each will be considered in turn.

THE PSYCHOANALYTIC APPROACH

The leader as ego ideal. Pioneered by Sigmund Freud, the psychoanalytic approach constitutes the foundation of some influential contemporary studies of leadership. Though not concerned with revolutionary leaders as such, Freud's *Group Psychology and the Analysis of the Ego* presents a theory of leadership in general. More explicit applications of the Freudian theory to political and revolutionary personalities have been undertaken by Harold D. Lasswell and E. Victor Wolfenstein, among others.

Since group behavior is characterized by irrationality and emotionality, according to Freud, leadership is the key to understanding collective phenomena. He writes that "a group is . . . as intolerant as it is obedient to authority. It respects force and can only be slightly influenced by kindness, which it regards merely as a form of weakness. What it demands of its heroes is strength, or even violence. It wants to be ruled and oppressed and to fear its masters" (Freud 1960: 14).

The mutual ties binding together the members of a group are based upon their common libidinal/emotional (but desexualized) ties to the leader. This, Freud believes, is "the essence of the group mind," determining its cohesiveness and unity. The followers' common identification with the leader shapes their mode of identification toward each other as well.

The followers' emotional ties to the leader stem from persistent tension within their personalities. Specifically, within their psychic apparatus, the ego (rationality principle) is too weak to resolve the eternal conflict between the id (instinctual forces) and the superego (social/moral imperatives). Since the followers are unable to measure up to their own "ego ideal"—as represented by the superego—they come to substitute the leader for the ego ideal.

The psychology of the leader, on the other hand, stands in sharp contrast to that of the members of the group. Most significantly, the leader has no emotional ties to anyone: "he may be of a masterful nature, absolutely narcissistic, self-confident and independent" (Freud 1960: 71).

Freud's theory of leadership is based upon the controversial theory of the "primal horde," according to which, at the beginning of human society, a primal horde of rebellious sons killed their tyrannical father and founded a fraternal society. The need for leadership soon reasserted itself, however, finding expression in totemism and religion, the totem and the deity being the reincarnation of the murdered father. Freud writes: "The leader of the group is still the dreaded primal father. . . . The primal father is the group ideal, which governs the ego in place of the ego ideal" (Freud 1960: 76).

The displacement hypothesis.   Acknowledging the "spectacular and influential nature of Freud's work" (Lasswell 1960:17), Harold D. Lasswell focuses directly upon the psychological dynamics of the political man. Specifically, he views the political personality as the power-centered personality: the political man compensates for his feelings of inadequacy and low self-esteem by a relentless pursuit of power. He values power above all else, for only through the pursuit and exercise of power can he maintain his personal "integrity." Moreover, this private need/motive is displaced upon public objects and rationalized in terms of the public interest (Lasswell 1962: 38; Lasswell 1960: passim).

Lasswell's ground-breaking work on a wide range of clinical case studies led him to postulate several political personality types, most notably the agitator, the administrator, and the theorist. (Although Lasswell uses the term "theorist" in his early work, the context makes clear that what he has in mind is the "ideologue.")

The agitator is committed to principle, highly narcissistic (see Freud), and dependent upon the emotional acclamation of the people. The administrator displaces his private motives upon impersonal and concrete objects; his primary value lies in "the coordination of effort in continuing activity." The ideologue is riddled by doubt, preoccupied with trivialities, and dogmatic: "Deep doubts about the self are displaced onto doubts about the world outside, and these doubts are sought to be allayed by ostentatious preoccupation with truth" (Lasswell, 1960: 175, 263–264).

Lasswell sees persons involved in social movements—revolutions included—in the same light: they displace private motives upon public objects. Anticipating the work of Wolfenstein, he writes: "The affects which are organized in the family are redistributed upon various social objects, such as the state. Political crises are complicated by the concurrent reactivation of specific primitive impulses" (Lasswell 1960: 264).

Oedipal conflict writ large. E. Victor Wolfenstein's study of the "revolutionary personality" is in essence a specific application and amplification of Lasswell's displacement hypothesis, focusing upon the Oedipus complex. Whereas in Freud the rebellious sons channeled their aggression directly against the father, in Wolfenstein they externalize their hostilities to larger arenas.

Wolfenstein employs Erik H. Erikson's model of the eight stages of personality development—oral, anal, genital, latency, adolescence, young manhood, adulthood, maturity—in an effort to locate the motivational dynamics that impel men toward revolutionary action. Wolfenstein searches for similarities and differences in the early life experiences of Lenin, Trotsky, and Gandhi in an attempt to account for their emergence as revolutionary personalities in later years.

According to Erikson, each stage of personality development is marked by a distinctive crisis, the successful resolution of which is a prerequisite for a "mature" transition to the succeeding stage. Focusing upon the genital stage, Wolfenstein identifies the inability to manage its unique crisis—the Oedipus complex—as the root motivation of the revolutionary. This uniformity, he finds, contrasts sharply with the dissimilarities in the life experiences of Lenin, Trotsky, and Gandhi in the other stages of personality development.

Wolfenstein concludes that the revolutionary personality represents the externalization of the rebellion against a parent associated with the Oedipus complex and its projection at the societal level. Thus:

> The basic attribute of this personality is that it is based on opposition to governmental authority; this is the result of the individual's continuing need to express his aggressive impulses vis-à-vis his father and the repressive action of governmental officials. The latter permits the individual to externalize his feelings of hatred. . . . Now the situation is much less ambivalent; governmental authority is clearly malevolent . . . and hence can be fought with a clear conscience. And because . . . the aggressive governmental action came as a conse-

quence of individual actions which were representative [of the way in which government treats the "people"], rather than personal, the individual finds a cause to defend. . . . [At first] the cause is crudely conceived and unelaborated; with time an ideological superstructure is based upon it so that the individual can fulfill his need for self-justification.

In this manner the revolutionist dichotomizes his world, and with it the emotional complex of his ambivalent feelings toward his father. As a consequence his feelings of guilt are substantially reduced, so that in all three cases we saw the men turning from introspection and inaction to vigorous pursuance of their revolutionary vocations. [Wolfenstein 1967: 308–309]

Governmental authority, then, is the functional equivalent of a surrogate father. Each of the three revolutionaries, Wolfenstein notes, fashioned an ideological framework that, among other things, juxtaposed the functional equivalent of a benevolent father (communist society, national independence) to that of a malevolent one (tsarism, British imperialism). The resolution of guilt and ambivalence permits all hate to be directed toward the government, all love toward the "people."

Critique.   Intriguing though they are, the psychoanalytic theories of political and revolutionary personalities are beset with a series of insurmountable difficulties. First, these studies are highly speculative, intuitive, and not always amenable to scientific criteria (for example, replication and verification). This is as true of Freud's "primal horde" and "primal father," as it is of Lasswell's power-seeking and displacement hypothesis and of Wolfenstein's propositions concerning the Oedipus complex and the surrogate father.

Second, these studies provide at best parochial explanations of revolutionary leadership, since they are limited to very few individuals and since they leave out consideration of historical and socioeconomic variables. Third, at times the proposed explanations are so thin as to push the limits of logic and credibility. At no time, for example, does Wolfenstein give a convincing explanation of why it is that some individuals with serious oedipal problems become revolutionaries while others end up on the analyst's couch as they struggle to maintain a routine life style. He does identify Trotsky's first imprisonment and the execution of Lenin's older brother as catalysts that set these men on a revolutionary course. Such unidimensional arguments are hardly adequate, however, since a multiplicity of forces and circumstances must be taken into account.

Finally, the sheer wealth and variety of psychological data necessary for conducting these studies are staggering and more than likely unavailable in most instances.

THE PSYCHOHISTORICAL APPROACH

While the psychoanalytic perspective deals predominantly with the inner dynamics of human personality, the psychohistorical approach attempts to move beyond psychoanalysis by placing personality dynamics in the context of society and history. As pioneered by Erik H. Erikson and practiced by many others, the psychohistorical approach represents, by definition, a fusion of psychology and history. In particular, in Erikson's interpretation, it seeks to juxtapose and interrelate the personality conflicts of a "great man" with the historical problems of a particular era.

Personal crisis and historical drama.   According to Erikson, as we have noted, the human life cycle consists of eight distinct and successive stages of development, each of which evolves in a sociohistorical setting and each of which contributes toward the progressive differentiation—and wholeness—of the human personality as it unfolds through time. Each stage is marked by a distinct "crisis" or "turning point," the successful addressing of which contributes toward the development of a fully psychosocial personality.

Whereas Wolfenstein's approach to Lenin, Trotsky, and Gandhi centered on the genital stage and the oedipal conflict, Erikson's groundbreaking studies of Martin Luther and Mahatma Gandhi focus on the turning points of adolescence (Luther) and adulthood (Gandhi). In Luther's case, the central concern is "identity crisis," the successful resolution of which results in personal wholeness, integrity, and continuity. In Gandhi's case, the focus is "generativity crisis," that is, whether or not one develops the capacity to establish and guide the next generation—either in terms of actual fatherhood or symbolically in terms of accomplishments or "works." In each case, Erikson uses a pivotal "Event" around which to organize his study.

Erikson's work on Luther opens with the account of the Event: a fit Luther is supposed to have had in the choir of his monastery, most likely in his early twenties. Falling to the ground, according to two or three eyewitnesses, Luther raved: "It isn't me!" (German version) or "I am *not!*" (Latin version). Erikson treats this incident as the exemplar of Luther's identity crisis; and he searches for its dynamics in Luther's home life and childhood.

Luther's parents were strict disciplinarians, as were the teachers under whom he studied. Young Martin himself was brooding and aloof, lacked feelings, was rebellious and given to violent moods, and demonstrated a bad temper and an intense capacity to hate. At the University of Erfurt he studied under radical theologians who questioned the strict teachings of the Catholic Church. Having obtained a master's degree, he underwent an abrupt "conversion": in an act of outright defiance of his father, Luther terminated his academic studies and determined to become a monk. Having joined a harsh and austere monastery, he was ordained a priest in 1507, at the age of twenty-three.

Luther's training for priesthood—itself a form of ideological indoctrination—provided him with an opportunity to formulate his distinctive theology as a legitimate weapon with which to attack the Catholic Church. In 1517 Luther nailed his ninety-five theses on the church door in Wittenberg.

In reformulating Christianity, emphasizing the priesthood of all believers, and attacking Church hierarchy, according to Erikson, Luther spoke for countless thousands who had shared the same sentiments but had not dared challenge the established order. As such, Luther was among the few great men "called upon . . . to lift his individual patienthood to the level of a universal one and to try to solve for all what he could not solve for himself alone" (Erikson 1962: 67).

The Event around which Erikson constructs his study of Gandhi is the Ahmedabad textile strike of 1918. Although other authorities—Gandhi himself included—have not assigned such signal importance to the strike, Erikson sees it not only as the cornerstone of labor unionism in India, but also as critical in Gandhi's life and in the fate of nonviolence as a transformative technique (Erikson 1969: passim). The strike, Erikson notes, occasioned the first time Gandhi—then forty-eight years old—fasted for a political issue. A year later, he led the mass movement of national civil disobedience, thereby establishing a spiritual belief in nonviolence as a ritual.

In expounding and practicing nonviolence, according to Erikson, Gandhi was responding to a crisis of generativity characteristic of his adulthood. In fashioning a following, a vast retinue, an extended family, and a nonviolent technique, Gandhi was involved in a process of nation-building as well as of self-creation. In transforming the negative Indian identity of inferiority vis-à-vis the British, he at the same time transformed his own negative self-image based upon persistent feelings of depression, personal despair, and humiliation, and an intense feeling of guilt toward the father (note the famous episode of Gandhi having sexual intercourse as his father lay on his deathbed). In any event, we witness once again the coalescence of historical imperative and personal drama. And we see once again a great man stepping out of conventional boundaries to adapt the historical setting to his personal needs.

Asceticism and displaced libido. A specific psychohistorical study of revolutionary leaders has been undertaken by Bruce Mazlish. Mazlish's starting point is that "there is a cluster of traits" that epitomizes the "revolutionary ascetic" as an ideal type. In delineating this concept, he relies upon the work of Sigmund Freud and Max Weber.

Asceticism, Mazlish argues, has two components: (1) narcissism, and (2) self-denial, self-control, self-sacrifice. Mazlish's discussion of the first component draws directly on Freud's *Group Psychology and the Analysis of the Ego*. Thus, as Freud had indicated, the leader has few libidinal ties to others; he is incapable of feelings and emotions; he is "masterful" and "absolutely narcissistic." However, for Freud's idea of "few libidinal ties,"

Mazlish substitutes the notion of "displaced libido," meaning that the individual has displaced his libidinal ties onto an abstraction. Thus "it is the Revolution, the People, Humanity, or Virtue which the leader glorifies and extols" (Mazlish 1976: 23).

In treating the second component of asceticism, Mazlish draws upon Max Weber. In his *Protestant Ethic and the Spirit of Capitalism,* Weber showed how asceticism as an initially religious concept was transformed into a worldly one and placed at the service of capitalism. Asceticism, Mazlish maintains, was "later put under the banner of revolutionary activity" (Mazlish 1976: 5).

When combined, according to Mazlish, asceticism and displaced libido are highly functional to the vocation of the revolutionary: "We are postulating, in fact, that there is an enormously explosive power in 'revolutionary asceticism,' that the traits of displaced libido and asceticism are highly functional in the real world of revolution" (Mazlish 1976: 34).

The followers of the revolutionary ascetic are bound together by their common identification with the leader and by the hypnotic hold the leader commands over them. The leader's ascetic qualities make him appear "superhuman" and "godlike." He offers not only victory but salvation as well. As such, the masses follow him "blindly" and "slavishly" in search of the millennium.

Having applied the concept of the revolutionary ascetic to Cromwell, Robespierre, Lenin, and Mao, Mazlish concludes that the four are very much alike in the pattern of behavior they exhibited, differing only in the sociohistorical context in which they found themselves.

Critique.   By introducing sociohistorical variables into the discussion of great leaders, the psychohistorical approach overcomes some of the problems of the purely psychoanalytic theory. At the same time it creates fresh problems of its own.

To begin with, much of the intuitive and nonscientific aspects of the psychoanalytic theory remain, as there remain enormous problems of operationalizing many of the psychological categories and of locating the requisite psychohistorical data. Similarly, the problem of the range of explanation remains unresolved as these works, too, are limited to very few individuals.

As far as Erikson is concerned, his studies of Luther and Gandhi are characterized by such "neatness" as to raise questions about their scientific rigor. In each case, as we have seen, he uses an Event that is at best suspect as the turning point that he presents it to be, but that nonetheless provides a seemingly compelling logic around which a tight interpretation is constructed. Thus in each case we end up with the fortuitous coalescence of personal trauma and historical crisis. In this context one appreciates Paul Roazen's reference to the "novelistic" quality of Erikson's work (Roazen 1976: 129).

Mazlish's study of the revolutionary ascetic, though informed by a more elaborate theoretical apparatus, is hardly as sophisticated as he claims. He readily charges the oedipal interpretation of the revolutionary personality with "grossness," "utter simplicity," and "oedipal–schmedipal" (Mazlish 1976: 3, 215), confidently unaware that his own work fares little better.

The point is rather simple. To state that the life of a revolutionary leader is characterized by self-discipline, self-denial, and self-control is to say very little, for these qualities are virtually definitional components of such a personality. A stoic, austere, puritanical life style is widely adopted by revolutionary leaders and widely commented upon by any number of writers. It thus appears, as someone suggested in an entirely different context, that Mazlish has fashioned a sophisticated machine to force an open door.

THE SOCIOLOGICAL APPROACH

The most prominent sociological theory of revolutionary leadership revolves around the concept of charisma. Although "charisma" has become a widely abused term in the English language, finding expression in a variety of forms, our treatment will be limited to the professional literature.

Weber's formulation. The word "charisma" was originally coined by the church historian Rudolf Sohm, who associated it with divinely inspired leaders and used it in an exclusively religious context. According to Sohm, "the charisma is from God . . . and the service to which the charisma calls is a service imposed by God, and an office in the service of the church, and not of any local community" (quoted in Schweitzer 1974: 151–152).

Max Weber—with whom the concept of charisma is most prominently associated—accepted the original religious meaning while adding a secular dimension. Acknowledging that charisma is "often . . . most clearly developed in the field of religion," he proceeded to suggest that "in principle, however, the same state of affairs recurs universally" (Weber 1958: 246). Specifically, according to Weber, charisma refers to a "certain quality of an individual personality by virtue of which he is set apart from ordinary men and treated as endowed with supernatural, superhuman, or at least specifically exceptional powers or qualities. These are . . . regarded as of divine origin or as exemplary, and on the basis of them the individual concerned is treated as a leader" (Weber 1964: 358–359).

Charisma, it follows, is a leader–follower relationship: without the voluntary recognition of disciples and followers, there would be no charisma. "Psychologically," writes Weber, "this 'recognition' is a matter of complete personal devotion to the possessor of the [charismatic] quality, arising out of enthusiasm, or of despair and hope" (Weber 1964: 359).

The basis for the followers' recognition of charismatic authority is superhuman feats—"works," "signs," "proofs," "miracles"—that charisma must regularly exhibit. Otherwise devotion and trust rapidly erode. Weber writes:

> The charismatic leader gains and maintains authority solely by proving his strength in life. If he wants to be a prophet, he must perform miracles; if he wants to be a warlord, he must perform heroic deeds. Above all, however, his divine mission must "prove" itself in that those who faithfully surrender to him must fare well. If they do not fare well, he is obviously not the master sent by the gods. [Weber 1958: 249]

In contrast to traditional and legal–rational authority, charismatic authority rests on an emotional, communal relationship. The organizational component of charisma consists of a voluntary group of disciples and of a followership. Beyond this, there is no formal officialdom, no appointment, no dismissal, no promotion, no career, no salary. There is only a "calling" and a "mission," and "it is the *duty* of those to whom he addresses his mission to recognize him as their charismatically qualified leader" (Weber 1958: 246–247 [emphasis in original]; cf. Weber 1964: 360–361).

Lying outside the established structures of social, political, and economic rationality, charisma involves fundamental innovation and change. Weber states that "within the sphere of its claims, charismatic authority repudiates the past, and is in this sense a specifically revolutionary force." Not bound by the existing order, the charismatic leader "transvalues everything." As such, charismatic authority is most likely to emerge "in times of psychic, physical, economic, ethical, religious, political distress" (Weber 1964: 361–363).

Since charismatic leadership is strictly personal in nature, and since its continued validity rests on "recognition" and "proof," it follows that charisma is a transitory phenomenon. "Indeed," writes Weber, "in its pure form charismatic authority may be said to exist only in the process of originating. It cannot remain stable, but becomes either traditionalized or rationalized, or a combination of both" (Weber 1964: 363–364). The natural fate of charisma, in other words, is its direct antithesis: routinization. As such, the three ideal types of authority—charismatic, traditional, and legal–rational—may coexist in reality.

Charisma and political revolution.   Weber's concept of charisma has set off a controversy of major proportions in social science literature. Scholars have variously accepted Weber's formulation, rejected it, revised it, and applied it in various contexts. Some have discussed charisma in the context of political development, which may involve revolutionary upheavals. Of particular interest in this regard is the work of Ann Ruth Willner.

Accepting Weber's delineation of charisma, Willner stresses the conditions of crisis under which charismatic leaders emerge in colonial or developing societies. Thus "situations of economic deprivation, social stress, political crisis, and psychic stress can crystallize into a collective call by the people for a leader to come to their rescue" (Willner 1968:12). These leaders, she finds, come from diverse social backgrounds. They possess high levels of energy and vitality, high intelligence and motivation, a capacity for originality and innovation, composure under stress, and an ability to evoke cultural myths, symbols, and values. Crisis, in short, leads to the emergence of charisma; charisma, in turn, produces stability and order.

A relatively extensive analysis of revolutionary charisma has been undertaken by Robert C. Tucker. The concept of charisma, he maintains, "is virtually indispensable, particularly for students of revolutionary movements of various kinds." Specifically, Tucker sets out "to develop the theory of charisma into a more workable tool of understanding and research" (Tucker 1968: 732, 735). His principal contribution in this regard is to equate charismatic leadership with charismatic movement:

> Charismatic leadership . . . typically appears in the setting of a social *movement* of some kind or creates such a movement. The charismatic leader is not simply any leader who is idolized and freely followed for his extraordinary leadership qualities, but one who demonstrates such qualities in the process of summoning people to join in a movement for change and in leading such a movement. . . . To speak of charismatic leaders, then, is to speak of charismatic movements; the two phenomena are inseparable. [Tucker 1968: 737–738 (emphasis in original)]

Allowing that a charismatic leader may appear at the outset of a movement or sometime thereafter, Tucker claims that his focus on movement has important implications by placing the emphasis on the leader's early career: "For the student of charisma . . . the pre-power stage of a leader's career is of critical significance" (Tucker 1968: 740). And this career should be explored through interviews with the leader's associates or by means of studying memoirs, autobiographies, and biographies.

Emphasizing that charismatic leaders appear in periods of stress, Tucker writes that "the charismatic leader is one in whom, by virtue of unusual personal qualities, the promise of hope of salvation—deliverance from distress—appears to be embodied. . . . He is in essence a savoir, or one who is so perceived by his followers. *Charismatic leadership is specifically salvationist or messianic in nature*" (Tucker 1968: 742–743; emphasis in original).

Although Tucker claims a great deal for the uniqueness of his treatment of charismatic leadership, it is evident that it is not all that much different from Willner's formulation. Moreover, as we shall presently see, charisma is at best of limited utility in the analysis of revolutionary leaders.

A systematic attempt to revise Weber's concept of charisma has been undertaken by James V. Downton (1973), who approaches charisma as a "psychological exchange" in which both the leader and the follower come to fulfill certain personality needs. Relying on Freud and Erikson, he identifies the sources of the follower's commitment as tensions within his personality. These tensions result from the inability of the ego to mediate effectively the conflict between the id and the superego. On the part of the follower, in other words, ego weakness is the basic stimulus for psychological exchange.

More specifically, Downton identifies two sources of charismatic appeal for the follower: (1) intrapsychic distance: given the disparity between the follower's ego and the goals established by the superego, he substitutes the leader as his ego ideal; (2) identity crisis: an underdeveloped ego ideal leaves the ego with an inadequate identity with which to confront the external world. In either case, identification with the leader counteracts feelings of anxiety, tension, guilt, and insecurity. A charismatic relationship helps develop the follower's personality: it enhances his sense of identity, autonomy, and self-esteem.

The primary personality need of the leader is deference: "the leader comes to see himself as charismatic and lives from day to day on the deferential treatment he sees as rightfully his" (Downton 1973: 230). In return for deference, the charismatic leader performs three roles: (1) he is a "comforter" by offering security; (2) he provides an "ideal" by offering a role model; (3) he is a "spokesman" for a transcedent authority (Downton 1973: 78).

As such, Downton maintains, there are two types of charismatic leadership: revolutionary and institutionalized. Charisma is not only an agent of change, it is also a conservative force. Thus Downton thinks "Weber was wrong in assuming that charismatic authority was synonymous with personal rulership" (Downton 1973: 283).

Critique.   The concept of charisma has come under a barrage of criticisms from all directions. Many scholars have pointed to the ambiguous and elusive nature of Weber's formulations, particularly as it regards the qualities of charisma. Some have objected to the stretching or overextension of the concept to incorporate both the secular and the religious realms, or to associate charisma with persons as well as with sociopolitical institutions. Others have distinguished between "natural" or "pure" charisma on the one hand, and "manufactured" or "fabricated" or "packaged" or "pseudo" charisma on the other—the latter being promoted by the mass media of modern society.

Some scholars have called into question the social scientific utility of the term altogether. For example, K. J. Ratnam argues that the looseness with which "charisma" is used has encouraged "wrong explanations." It has provided some scholars with "the easy way out" by enabling them simply to attribute success to "charisma" without considering that their "explanations follow no recognized criteria" (Ratnam 1964: 341).

The application of the concept of charisma to the analysis of revolutionary leadership is even more problematical. Although the concept is of some intuitive value, its empirical utility is seriously limited. In his massive

Handbook of Leadership, Ralph M. Stogdill omits the coverage of charisma altogether. His rationale is as follows: "This important variant of the leadership role has not been a willing or frequent subject of research that involves measurement and experimentation. Numerous biographical studies of charismatic leaders are available, but they provide comparatively little information that adds to an understanding of leadership" (Stogdill 1974: viii).

A viable theory of charismatic leadership would have to specify criteria for identifying the evidence of charisma, the message that charisma entails, the emotions and commitments that it must inspire or elicit. Moreover, insofar as charisma is a relationship depending entirely upon the "recognition" of the followers, one must be in a position to study followers' responses. Whereas such investigations may be possible in connection with contemporary revolutions where followers are accessible, one must of necessity exclude such countries as China, Hungary, Cuba, and Vietnam, where access to followers is all but impossible. Necessarily, one must also exclude revolutionary movements of the past. In this context, memoirs, autobiographies, and biographies may provide hints and clues, but they are insufficient for purposes of social science research.

Finally, although charismatic figures have appeared in most—perhaps all—revolutions, it is quite clear that not all revolutionary leaders are charismatic, nor are all charismatic leaders revolutionary. Considering the revolutionary movements of the twentieth century, for example, we can identify a handful who may have possessed charismatic qualities—for example, Lenin, Mao, Ho, Castro, Guevara—but by far the majority cannot be called charismatic by any stretch of the imagination.

RESEARCH

LEADERS

If theories of revolutionary leadership leave a great deal to be desired in terms of scientific rigor and explanatory power, the current state of actual research on revolutionary elites is in even worse straits. A great deal has been written about individual leaders of revolutions, the most notable recent examples being Mao, Ho, Castro, and Guevara. A few studies have attempted limited comparisons of a small number of leaders—for example, Wolfenstein's study of Lenin, Trotsky, and Gandhi, and Mazlish's work on Cromwell, Robespierre, Lenin, and Mao. Finally, there have been some studies of the collective leadership of individual revolutions, such as those of Russia, China, and Algeria.

Beyond this, we know surprisingly little about revolutionary elites as a distinct group. With one recent exception (see below), there have been no *quantitative comparative* studies of a significantly large number of revolutionary leaders from a significantly large number of revolutionary upheavals. No scholar has studied revolutionary elites in the manner in which social scientists have studied parliamentary elites, bureaucratic/ managerial/corporate elites, intellectual elites, and the like (see Putnam 1976 and the extensive bibliography cited therein).

Moreover, with rare exceptions (Wolfenstein and Mazlish), studies of revolutionary leaders have uniformly focused on demographic characteristics (age, birthplace, social background, education, occupation, and so on), leaving out consideration of the situational, social, and psychological dynamics under which the leaders emerge. The processes of radicalization of revolutionary leaders constitute a topic that manifestly requires careful and separate treatment. Again, a recent contribution has attempted to fill this void, and its findings will be briefly discussed below.

CHARACTERISTICS OF REVOLUTIONARY ELITES

Current state of research. What we have known about leaders of revolution up to now can be summed up in a few short paragraphs.

Age. Revolutionary leaders are neither very young nor very old, most of them being in their thirties or forties at the time of their revolutions. Crane Brinton, for example, finds that the leaders of the English, French, American, and Russian revolutions were in their thirties and forties (Brinton 1956: 110). George K. Schueller fixes the average age of the Bolshevik Politburo members in 1917 at thirty-nine (Schueller 1965: 111). Robert C. North and Ithiel de Sola Pool put the mean age of the members of the Chinese Politburo in the 1920s as ranging between thirty-three and thirty-seven (North and Pool 1965: 383). Ming T. Lee reports that of the fifty-two founders of the Chinese Communist Party (CCP) in 1921, 94 percent were forty years of age or under and 73 percent thirty years or under (Lee 1968: 115). Robert A. Scalapino establishes the average age of Asian Communist leaders in 1965 as between forty and fifty-five (Scalapino 1965: 15). William B. Quandt reports that the Algerian leaders were in their late thirties and early forties at the time of their revolution (Quandt 1969: 68).

Social and occupational background. Revolutionary leaders are broadly middle class in origin. The English, American, and French revolutions, for example, were thoroughly bourgeois affairs, led by prominent members of the middle and, in some cases, upper class. Brinton reports that among the fifty-six signers of the Declaration of Independence were five physicians, twenty-two lawyers, three ministers, and eleven merchants—and that nearly all were affluent (Brinton 1956: 107).

The middle-class character of revolutionary elites is equally true of communist leaders. Schueller has documented the middle-class origins of a substantial number of the Bolshevik Politburo members (Schueller 1965: 103–104, 119–121). Lee has found that of the fifty-two founders of the CCP, over 90 percent had middle-class backgrounds and were engaged in middle-class occupations (Lee 1968: 117–118, 120). Scalapino reports that

Asian revolutionaries come predominantly from the bourgeoisie (particularly the lower bourgeoisie), and that a majority is active in middle-class occupations (Scalapino 1965: 14). John H. Kautsky discovers that of a sample of thirty-two revolutionary leaders of the Third World, fully thirty (93 percent) occupied middle- and upper-middle-class positions in law, medicine, journalism, education, or government bureaucracy (Kautsky 1969: 446). Quandt finds that the Algerian revolutionaries were exceptional: they came from middle and lower economic strata and held correspondingly low occupations (Quandt 1969: 69, 77–79).

Place of origin.   Revolutionary elites usually come from urban settings, as their middle-class backgrounds would virtually require. Prominent but rare exceptions include Mao Tse-tung and Ho Chi Minh.

Education.   Revolutionary leaders are much better educated than the average populations of their countries. Brinton, for example, has found that of the fifty-six signers of the Declaration of Independence, thirty-three held college degrees, and only four or five had little or no formal education (Brinton 1956: 107). Scalapino reports that most Asian communist leaders have had some higher education and that many can be described as "intellectuals" (Scalapino 1965: 14). Kautsky finds that in his sample of thirty-two revolutionary leaders, twenty-five (78 percent) had received university or advanced professional training, and eighteen (56 percent) had lived or traveled extensively abroad (Kautsky 1969: 445). Lee finds that of the fifty-two founders of the CCP, 42 percent were college graduates, while 82 percent had had at least some college education, and 96 percent had either resided abroad or experienced the "new style" of education (Lee 1968: 115, 119). By contrast, Quandt reports that the educational level of the Algerian leaders was relatively low, most having had only secondary schooling, some only primary education, and only a few college training (Quandt 1969: 69).

A recent contribution.   A large-scale study of revolutionary elites recently has been undertaken by Mostafa Rejai and Kay Phillips (Rejai and Phillips 1979: chapter 5). Space limitations permit presentation of only a fraction of our most general findings. Some of these findings are consistent with the ones presented above, others are not.

The study is based on extensive research and data collection for sixty-four leaders of twelve revolutions that took place in England (1640s), America (1776), France (1789), Mexico (1910), Russia (1917), China (1949), Bolivia (1952), North Vietnam (1954), Hungary (1956), Cuba (1959), Algeria (1962), and France (1968). (Although the inclusion of the last-named revolution may raise an initial question in the reader's mind, the French upheaval of 1968 fully meets the criteria of political revolution. See Rejai 1977: chapters 1, 6).

For each leader we sought data on demographic, situational, and ideological variables. We were interested, among other things, in age, birthplace, family life, socioeconomic status, education, occupation, revolutionary agitation, arrest record, foreign travel, and ideological orientation. (Copies of the twelve-page code sheet will be found in Rejai and Phillips 1979.)

One finding requires only a bare mention: there is not a single female among our revolutionary leaders. While women have played a secondary role in some contemporary revolutionary movements, none has been among the top leadership in any of the twelve cases we studied.

As a group the revolutionaries we studied are slightly younger than anticipated. Rather than being in their thirties and forties, 50 percent of the leaders were under thirty-five years of age at the time of their revolutions, with almost 80 percent being below forty-five. Exposure to revolutionary ideology occurs, however, at much younger ages. Just over 67 percent of the leaders were exposed to revolutionary ideology before the age of twenty, while almost 80 percent had this experience before age twenty-five.

The age of first revolutionary *activity* is also quite young. While 36 percent of the leaders had actually engaged in revolutionary agitation before the age of twenty, almost 84 percent were involved by thirty-five.

Rather than being urban-born (39 percent), most revolutionary leaders came from rural areas (61 percent). This location of birth is likely a consequence of the low level of urbanization in most countries that have experienced revolutions. More important, revolutionary leaders born in rural areas tend to have had early and sustained exposure to urban environments. Specifically, almost 90 percent of these leaders spent four or more years in urban centers, while the remainder spent at least one year in an urban milieu. This exposure to an urban way of life and an urban setting tends to occur early in the lives of the revolutionaries. Over 82 percent of the rural-born leaders were exposed to urban life before the age of twenty. In short, then, although not primarily urban-born, the revolutionary elites we studied did experience urban cultures at early ages and for long periods of time.

As for socioeconomic status, only a small number of revolutionary leaders (19 percent) came from the upper class, while the majority (over 52 percent) were middle class. A surprising 29 percent were drawn from the lower classes, most likely due to the fact that most twentieth-century revolutions have taken place in underdeveloped countries.

Nearly 83 percent of the revolutionary leaders in our study came from large families with three to fifteen siblings. As such, probability considerations would lead one to expect most of them to be middle children. Surprisingly, however, with 33 percent being middle children, fully 31 percent of the leaders were oldest children, 8 percent oldest sons, and 18 percent youngest children. One leader had only one sibling and three had none.

Revolutionary elites tend to be a rather mainstream group with respect to some important social characteristics. For instance, 63 percent of our leaders came from the majority group in their country, only 6 percent came from a small ethnic minority, and 31 percent belonged to a large ethnic minority.

Although the specific religious affiliations of the leaders were quite diverse, some 80 percent belonged to the main religious grouping in their countries. No revolutionary for whom information is available was without formal religious affiliation.

The religious background of revolutionary elites stands in sharp contrast to their religious *orientation* at the time of the revolution. Specifically, almost half (48 percent) had turned atheist, with only 25 percent retaining their Christian religious commitments. No Jewish or Buddhist leader for whom data are available retained his religious origins, while all the Muslims remained steadfast in their religious beliefs.

Revolutionary leaders as a group are well-educated. Less than 20 percent had only primary or secondary education. The education of 18 percent stopped with college, while 41 percent proceeded to postgraduate or professional training. Twenty-one percent were educated in religious, military, or trade institutions.

A relatively high proportion of our revolutionaries (32 percent) was trained in such professions as law, medicine, and education. Almost 12 percent chose the military field, while only 10 percent were in the social sciences, the humanities, and the arts.

The primary occupations of revolutionary leaders were quite diverse. Nearly 29 percent were in such professions as law, medicine, and education. Almost 24 percent (fifteen) can be considered "professional revolutionaries." A relatively large category of twenty-six men (41 percent) were involved in a combination of occupations, including politics and government service. Of these, eleven combined their occupation with that of the professional revolutionary—this in addition to the fifteen cases just mentioned.

A relatively large proportion of revolutionary leaders (41 percent) also had involvement in legal political organizations and activities. By contrast, an overwhelming majority (98 percent) held membership in revolutionary organizations, with almost 94 percent being "intensely" involved in these groups.

Probably related to membership in revolutionary organization is the arrest record of revolutionary elites. Whereas nearly 38 percent of the leaders had no arrest record, 62 percent were arrested at least once, with 18 percent having been arrested four or more times. Needless to say, these arrests were for political agitation rather than for ordinary crimes.

Moreover, imprisonment for illegal activities took a large portion of some leaders' lives. Over 60 percent of all revolutionaries spent at least some time in prison, with 44 percent spending two or more years. Some revolutionaries spent inordinately long periods of time in prison or exile, with Lenin holding the record of twenty-one years.

The revolutionary elites in our sample had extensive exposure to foreign cultures and ideas. Only 23 percent of the leaders had not traveled outside their country of birth, while 25 percent traveled in Europe and another 38 percent traveled to a combination of foreign locales, including the United States, Latin America, Africa, and Asia. In all, 77 percent of the leaders traveled abroad. Moreover, the amount of time spent in foreign lands was rather lengthy: almost 42 percent spent four or more years in foreign settings, with 60 percent spending at least one year abroad.

The diversity of foreign exposure likely accounts in part for the eclectic nature and origin of the ideologies to which the revolutionary elites subscribed. Exposed to a variety of beliefs and values, they were in a position to adapt foreign ideologies to the conditions of their own countries. Over 15 percent of the revolutionaries subscribed to a democratic doctrine, while over 50 percent held some form of Marxist ideology and another 17 percent chose other leftist ideologies such as anarchism, utopian-socialism, and Jacobinism. Not unexpectedly, over 48 percent of the leaders subscribed to a nationalist ideology of some type. The largest number of twentieth-century elites fused variants of Marxism (including Marxism-Leninism or Communism) with forms of nationalism. When combined, these two doctrines have proven the most explosive revolutionary ideology of our time.

EMERGENCE OF REVOLUTIONARY ELITES

Patterns of radicalization. Rejai and Phillips have examined the patterns of radicalization of revolutionary elites and the psychological dynamics that may impel them toward revolution (Rejai and Phillips 1979: chapters 9, 10). This part of the study was limited to thirty-two revolutionaries for whom adequate autobiographical and biographical data were available. Again, space limitations permit presentation of only the gist of our findings.

We analyzed the patterns of radicalization in terms of four components: formative years, school socialization, exposure to foreign cultures, and purely situational dynamics. We found, in contrast to virtually all socialization studies, that formative years are of little explanatory value in the radicalization of revolutionary elites. Nearly half of our leaders experienced tranquil beginnings, the other half stormy childhoods. Similarly, parental conflicts, early rebelliousness, loss of one or both parents, history of family radicalism—all these were associated with revolutionaries who came from tranquil as well as stormy homes.

We found school socialization an equally limited predictor of radicalization. Specifically, we discovered that a small number of revolutionaries was radicalized in school, that those who were so radicalized came from undeveloped or semideveloped lands, and that they held ideologies of nationalism, communism, or a combination of the two. We further found that school was more likely to be a radicalizing agent if one had had a turbulent childhood.

Exposure to foreign cultures, on the other hand, was an important source of radicalization, particularly in the twentieth century. Foreign travel exposes one to a variety of cultures and ideologies, permits one to witness various forms of oppression and exploitation, allows one to heighten one's political consciousness, and makes possible development of standards by which to judge the conditions of one's own country. We also found that travel was more likely to be an agent of radicalization if one had experienced a stormy childhood or school radicalization.

Situational dynamics—responding to circumstances of national crises or emergencies—were also important sources of radicalization for some revolutionaries. Intense, irreversible escalation of systemic conflicts involving major social groups have catapulted into prominence, at times willy-nilly, persons who possessed and exhibited the necessary competencies and skills. There was little by way of prior organization or planning. "Situational revolutionaries" typically are members of the establishment and frequently are involved in the political processes of their societies. Another type of situation setting the stage for the emergence of some revolutionaries lay in the turbulent political histories of their countries, or in the traditionally violent locales in which they lived.

We concluded by venturing the proposition that there is no single pattern in the radicalization of revolutionary elites, and that each revolutionary will encounter a different constellation of experiences. Accordingly, each of the four variables—family, school, travel, situation—may play a role in the emergence of *some* revolutionary leaders. Since each revolutionary will experience life in a more or less unique manner, the particular "mix" among the patterns of radicalization accordingly will vary from case to case. It seems clear, however, that travel and situation command more predictive value than formative years or school socialization.

Psychological dynamics.   The personality development of revolutionary elites, Rejai and Phillips found, is marked by the gradual evolution of a set of psychological dynamics they may share in varying combinations and degrees. Among these dynamics are: (1) vanity, egotism, narcissism; (2) asceticism, puritanism, virtue; (3) relative deprivation and status inconsistency; (4) marginality, inferiority complex, the compulsion to excel; (5) oedipal conflict writ large; (6) estheticism and the romantic streak.

Two characteristics are so universally descriptive of revolutionaries—and so widely discussed in the literature—that they hardly require discussion or elaboration. All our revolutionary leaders were driven by a sense of justice/injustice and a corresponding attempt to right the wrongs. This sense of justice/injustice may be personally rooted, or it may be perceived in societal conditions, or it may be personally based and projected onto the larger society. Similarly, virtually all our revolutionaries were motivated by varieties of nationalism and patriotism. They might seek to maintain the independence and integrity of their nations. They might set out to free their nations from the oppression and exploitation of other nations. They might wish to improve the status, prosperity, power, and prestige of their countries.

Vanity, egotism, narcissism, and a quest for glory and fame typified twenty-three of our thirty-two leaders (72 percent). At times, vanity alternated with humility and self-doubt. At times, it produced a compulsion to excel. At times, it became pathological, generating a persecution complex and a corresponding drive to purge the world of perceived enemies. While self-confident and self-assured, some leaders were noted for their lack of vanity and egotism. Among them were Fidel Castro, Chu Teh, Ernesto Guevara, V. I. Lenin, and Mao Tse-tung (before the 1960s).

Asceticism, puritanism, and a demand for virtue distinguish, again, twenty-three of our thirty-two leaders (including seventeen of the twenty-three characterized by vanity). Self-discipline, self-reliance, self-denial of luxury and comfort, a relentless emphasis on hard work, a commitment to a rugged spartan life—these sum up the concepts of asceticism and puritanism. The objectives in cultivating these qualities are to drive out societal evil, corruption, and sin, and to bring forth the reign of virtue. The reign of virtue, in turn, may be impossible to bring about without coercion, force, and terror.

Relative deprivation and status inconsistency describe twelve of our revolutionaries. Relative deprivation, it will be recalled, refers to a *perceived* discrepancy between aspiration and achievement. As such, it may be based on considerations of a purely personal nature, or it may define a gap between one's actual socioeconomic status and the status to which one aspires, or it may refer to a discrepancy between one's socioeconomic status and political power. This last variety—status inconsistency—is descriptive of a distinct genre of revolutionaries who began as reformers, were consistently disillusioned, came to reject the system as unresponsive and repressive, and turned to revolutionary politics.

Marginality, inferiority complex, and a compulsion to excel define a surprising nineteen of our thirty-two leaders. These men possessed traits or characteristics—physical, social, psychological—that represent deviations from societal norms, expectations, and practices. Traumatic personal experiences, feelings of anxiety and despair, instances of personal humiliation and failure, physical disfigurement, being sickly and frail, being illegitimate-born or a member of a ridiculed minority group—all these may have had the effect of producing an intense need for compensatory mechanisms and an intense desire to excel. Accordingly, involvement in radical activity became a search for integration, support, comfort, acceptance, and belonging that revolutionary movements afford.

Oedipal conflict writ large seems to pertain to only three revolutionary leaders for whom we have adequate data (Lenin, Trotsky, and Mao). Conflict with the father—and the concomitant attachment to the mother—produces feelings of ambivalence, anxiety, and guilt. The politicization of the conflict—the substitution of governmental authority for the father—assuages these feelings and makes the world more manageable. This politicization is usually triggered by a traumatic experience, such as brutal treatment at the hands of the established regime.

Estheticism and romanticism describe fifteen of our thirty-two revolutionaries. Whether expressed in the form of a deep attachment to philosophy, literature, or poetry, or demonstrated in an intense love of nature, or depicted in a passion for music, or revealed in a Don Quixote complex, estheticism and romanticism indicate that our presumably tough and ruthless revolutionaries were gentle and human in many ways as well.

Ranking our psychological dynamics in the order of their frequency of appearance, it is apparent that vanity and asceticism are on the top, followed in this order by marginality, estheticism, relative deprivation, and Oedipus complex. Vanity, asceticism, and marginality have greater explanatory power than estheticism and relative deprivation. Oedipus complex has the least explanatory potential. While the particular "mix" of psychological dynamics varied from revolutionary to revolutionary, vanity, asceticism, estheticism, and marginality occurred with greater frequency than any other traits. As we concluded in connection with our discussion of patterns of radicalization, however, there was no single "mix" in the emergence of revolutionary elites.

CADRES

While studies of revolutionary elites have not progressed as far as one might wish, with rare exceptions the treatment of revolutionary cadres and of rank and file is so undeveloped as to generate acute scholarly dismay. The importance of cadres, for example, is universally recognized—particularly in their roles as transmitters of party policy and agents of mass mobilization, and generally as links between leadership and rank and file. Yet, to our knowledge explicit studies of revolutionary cadres are virtually nonexistent. We have been able to identify three highly diverse investigations of *possible* cadres.

Crane Brinton has offered a study of the most radical group in the French Revolution: members of the Jacobin clubs. We can only speculate that by virtue of club membership—as well as of some of the characteristics discussed below—most Jacobins can be considered cadres.

Brinton's primary data sources are documents of various Jacobin clubs throughout France and French tax rolls for the period 1789–1795. His secondary data come from the writings of French historians on the Jacobins. Brinton identifies three groups of Jacobin clubs. Group I, consisting of twelve clubs and 5,405 members, operated between 1789–1795. Group II, comprising twelve clubs and 4,037 members, was in existence between 1789–1792. Group III, consisting of 42 clubs and 8,062 members, operated between 1793–1795 (Brinton 1930: chapters 2, 3,).

For the ten Jacobin clubs Brinton considered, mean age for members ranged from 38.3 to 45.5 years, with an overall mean of 41.8 years for all ten clubs (Brinton 1930: 56).

In terms of socioeconomic status, Brinton finds that Group I was 62 percent middle class, 28 percent working class, and 10 percent peasantry. Group II was 66 percent middle class, 26 percent working class, and 8 percent peasantry. Group III was 57 percent middle class, 32 percent working class, and 11 percent peasantry (Brinton 1930: 50–51).

The occupations of the Jacobins turn out to be consistent with their socioeconomic status. Specifically, Brinton finds that Jacobins to have held typically middle-class occupations: lawyers, priests, teachers, artists, businessmen, civil servants. His investigation of the tax rolls of the period also confirms the socioeconomic status and occupations of the Jacobins. Brinton finds the Jacobins to have been relatively well off, since as a group they paid higher taxes than the average population (Brinton 1930: 50–55).

Brinton's overall conclusion is that "the Jacobin was neither noble nor beggar . . . but almost anything in between. . . . [T]hey represent a complete cross-section of their community" (Brinton 1930: 70).

Another possible—and exceedingly limited—study of cadres is found in Harlan H. Strauss's investigation of seventy-three revolutionaries who "in any way" (Strauss 1973: 298) participated in the abortive Russian revolution of February 1905. Relying on data from both Russian and Western sources, and employing Q-factor analysis, Strauss identifies six types of revolutionaries: rebel, striker, propagandist, party organizer, upper-level politician, intelligentsia.

The party organizers (N = 14) are of particular interest to us, since in all likelihood they constitute a body of cadres. Strauss's description of this group is instructive: "They were primarily engaged in lower-echelon politics—i.e., the organization of the revolution and revolutionary politics at the local level" (Strauss 1973: 302). By contrast, upper-level politicians (N = 12) cannot be regarded as cadres, since "they participated in revolutionary politics and organizations at national and central committee levels. . . . They were the 'moderates.' . . . [T]hey isolated themselves from the masses" (Strauss 1973: 302).

Reanalyzing the data Strauss presents for the fourteen party organizers (Strauss 1973: 303ff.), we can identify some of their major characteristics. Although the sample is embarrassingly small—and rather idiosyncratic—we present the data in the belief that some information is better than none at all. Of the fourteen cadres, eight were born in urban centers and six came from rural areas. They all became involved in revolution between the ages of sixteen and twenty-seven, eleven having done so by age twenty. As far as their socioeconomic status is concerned, five came from the upper class, five from the middle class, and four from the lower class. As might be expected, they were rather well-educated. Nine had university education, two went to secondary school, and three had only elementary schooling. The initial impetus for revolution came predominantly from the student movement (eight cadres), with three having been radicalized in actual party work and another three in workers' groups.

An impressive study of urban terrorists has been undertaken by Charles A. Russell and Bowman H. Miller. These terrorists are specifically identified as cadres, with a sprinkling of persons in leadership positions. (Although not all terrorists are likely to be committed revolutionaries, we have no way of sorting them out.) Using newspapers, government documents, and other publications, Russell and Miller compiled extensive data for 350 individuals belonging to eighteen terrorist groups in eleven countries (Argentina, Brazil, Germany, Iran, Ireland, Italy, Japan, Palestine, Spain, Turkey, and Uruguay) for the period 1966–1976.

The mean age for the terrorists was twenty-two to twenty-four years. They were predominantly single males, with a few women in "a supportive capacity" (Russell and Miller 1977: 22). They were either born in urban areas or had been long-time urban residents.

As for socioeconomic status, "well over two-thirds" of the terrorists came from middle and upper social strata (Russell and Miller 1977: 25). Their parents characteristically were physicians, lawyers, engineers, government employees, diplomats, clergymen, or military officers. Accordingly, "the vast majority . . . are quite well educated," with two-thirds having had at least some university education (Russell and Miller 1977: 27). These same universities acted, not only as centers of ideological indoctrination, but as recruiting grounds as well. The basic ideologies of the terrorists are anarchism, nationalism, and Marxism-Leninism. However, "it is the combination of these three in specific contexts that produces the variant left-extremist philosophies espoused by most terrorists today" (Russell and Miller 1977: 30). Moreover, these ideologies are fed by personal frustration and relative deprivation.

Russell and Miller close by identifying three trends in terrorist activity: (1) a general lowering of age, (2) an increasing involvement of women, and (3) an increasing involvement of persons from lower socioeconomic and occupational strata, such as electricians, mechanics, and printers.

This is all we know about three groups of possible cadres: thousands of Jacobins from the 1790s, fourteen Russian revolutionaries from 1905, and 350 urban terrorists currently or recently active around the globe. Disparate as they are, it is surprising to find that the three groups have a number of things in common. They came from both urban and rural areas. Their socioeconomic status was heavily middle and upper class, with 25–30 percent coming from the lower class. Accordingly, their level of education was high and they were involved in correspondingly high-status occupations. The communists and the terrorists became involved in revolutionary politics early in life and in the context of student movements. All three groups subscribed to variants of extremist ideologies.

Many of these characteristics, in turn, are strikingly similar to those of revolutionary leaders. To this topic we will return later in this chapter.

RANK AND FILE

To the extent to which they exist, most studies of revolutionary rank and file are marked by a distinctly negative bias. This bias traces back to Edmund Burke, whose blanket denunciation of the French Revolution and those involved in it is too well known to require elaboration (Burke 1955). Briefly, venerating tradition and seeing man as evil and incapable of reason, Burke viewed the French Revolution as the outcome of wicked doctrines expounded by depraved and immoral men with a lust for power.

In his classic study of *The Crowd* (1908)—itself a pejorative label—Gustave Le Bon reached a similar conclusion while traversing a different theoretical route. According to his "law of mental unity of crowds," a group of individuals takes on characteristics quite different from those of the individuals composing the group. Specifically, the crowd develops a "collective mind" in which the unconscious reigns supreme, irrationality and emotionality are heightened, the instincts take over, destructiveness becomes the norm, and individuals act as automatons.

Moreover, crowd behavior is marked by contagion, a phenomenon that "must be classed among those phenomena of a hypnotic order. . . . In a crowd every sentiment and act is contagious, and contagious to such a degree that an individual readily sacrifices his personal interest to the collective interest" (Le Bon 1908: 33–34). Some other characteristics of the crowd are impulsiveness, irritability, and intolerance.

Finally, the crowd has an "instinctive need" for leadership. "A crowd is a servile flock that is incapable of ever doing without a master" (Le Bon 1908: 134). The leaders "are especially recruited from the ranks of those morbidly nervous, excitable, half-deranged persons who are bordering on madness" (1908: 134). Ruling in a tyrannical and despotic manner, the leaders spread contagion and heighten crowd cohesiveness. Accordingly, Le Bon concludes, crowds consist of "barbarians" and "savages" (1908: 19, 36, 40, 237). Crowds are destructive of civilization and the values cherished by rational people.

In his *Psychology of Revolution* (1913), Le Bon reiterates these themes and applies them to the French Revolution. Specifically, he distinguishes two categories of people involved in revolutionary movements. The first group is more or less normal. "The second category, which plays a capital part in all national disturbances, consists of a subversive social residue dominated by a criminal mentality. Degenerates of alcoholism and poverty, thieves, beggars, destitute 'casuals,' indifferent workers without employment—these constitute the dangerous bulk of the armies of insurrection" (Le Bon 1913: 70). Revolutionary crowds attract the "vagabonds, beggars, fugitives from justice, thieves, assassins, and starving creatures" (1913: 99). Mass behavior, Le Bon concludes, represents a "triumph of atavistic instincts." Crowds exhibit "ancestral savagery." They are nothing but "destructive hordes" and "bloodthirsty fanatics" (1913: 66, 72, 73, 76, 103).

Relying on Le Bon, Sigmund Freud developed an analogous theory of group behavior. Freud's theory is more complex, however. And he differs sharply from Le Bon in viewing the leader as "ego ideal."

Among other writers expressing negative views toward mass movements, we may note Kurt Riezler and Eric Hoffer. Riezler considers "the outcasts" and "the fools" as two of the three essential ingredients of revolutionary movements, the third being "the experts." The outcasts are uprooted socially and economically, and hence are resentful of the existing order. The fools have little intellectual independence and are an easy prey for the manipulating leaders (Riezler 1943).

Hoffer flatly asserts that mass movements attract the following groups of people: "(a) the poor, (b) misfits, (c) outcasts, (d) minorities, (e) adolescent youth, (f) the ambitious . . ., (g) those in the grip of some vice or obsession, (h) the impotent (in body or mind), (i) the inordinately selfish, (j) the bored, (k) the sinners" (Hoffer 1958: 30).

More objective—and empirical—studies of revolutionary rank and file have been undertaken by Paul Berman, Dirk Hoerder, Lucian W. Pye, and George Rudé, among others. These works conveniently fall into two groups: Rudé and Hoerder focus on "classic" revolutions (the French and the American); Pye and Berman are interested in communist revolutionary movements (those in Malaya and Vietnam).

Eschewing biased treatments of the crowd, Rudé's *The Crowd in the French Revolution* sets out "to approach the subject in a more detached, or scientific, spirit" (1959: 5). His principal data sources are police records of the Archives Nationales and of the Paris Préfecture de Police for the period 1787–1795.

Rudé finds that, in addition to the *sans-culottes*, the following people were heavily involved in the Revolution: such middle-class groups as owners, *rentiers*, merchants, civil servants, shopkeepers, and "professional men"; such lower-class groups as wage earners, journeymen, metalworkers, dressmakers, cabinetmakers, shoemakers, builders, engravers, cooks, waiters, tailors, hairdressers, porters, and domestic servants (Rudé

1959: 184–185). Accordingly, Rudé notes, the charge that criminals and outcasts were the main force of the revolution cannot be sustained.

Rudé further explores the motivation of revolutionary crowds, emphasizing the interplay and interrelatedness of political and economic forces. On the political side, he identifies the attraction of such new ideas as the "rights of man" and "liberty, equality, fraternity." He writes: "There is therefore little doubt that these revolutionary crowds enthusiastically supported and assimilated . . . the objects, ideas, and slogans of the liberal, democratic, and republican *bourgeoisie* . . . because they appeared to correspond to their own interests in the fight to destroy the old regime and to safeguard the Republic" (Rudé 1959: 119).

On the economic side, Rudé stresses the people's demand for the daily necessities of life. Thus "the inescapable conclusion remains that the primary and most constant motive impelling revolutionary crowds during this period was the concern for the provision of cheap and plentiful food. This, more than any other factor, was the raw material out of which the popular Revolution was forged" (Rudé 1959: 208).

Rudé concludes that "revolutionary crowds, far from being social abstractions, were composed of ordinary men and women with varying needs, who responded to a variety of impulses, in which economic crisis, political upheaval, and the urge to satisfy immediate and particular grievances all played their part" (Rudé 1959: 232–233).

Although Rudé's work is ground-breaking in many respects, his data sources—police records—necessarily yield a biased sample of the French population of the time. Although he is aware of this difficulty, his justification is rather jarring: "While, of course, they [the data] relate only to a small minority of the participants—those arrested, killed, or wounded, or against whom information is laid with the police—the samples thus provided are often sufficiently large to allow one to draw general conclusions from them" (Rudé 1959: 7).

In a later work—*The Crowd in History* (1964)—Rudé seeks to apply the themes developed in *The Crowd in the French Revolution* to a series of "popular disturbances" in France and England and, by implication, to crowd behavior in general. His conclusions are similar to those in the earlier study but, again, the generalizations are subject to question.

Dirk Hoerder has recently attempted to apply Rudé's methodological and theoretical insights to "crowd action" in the State of Massachusetts in the period 1765–1780. He assumes with Rudé "that crowd behavior is rational and goal-directed, that it is guided by a set of traditional norms about social relations and positions of groups within the social structure—that rioters are self-conscious and act according to concepts coming down by oral tradition rather than straight from the magistrates' law books" (Hoerder 1977: 3–4).

Hoerder's data sources consist of "tax lists, court records, official documents, and any other contemporary source available, such as newspapers, private papers, letters, and diaries" (Hoerder 1977: 14). Cognizant of possible biases in the data, Hoerder examines cases of crowd action associated with the Stamp Act, the Townshend Acts, the Boston Massacre, the Tea Party, trade and importation laws, price controls and monopolies, scarcity of provisions, and other generally "intolerable acts."

His conclusions are consistent with those of Rudé. Hoerder finds that a virtually endless list of popular grievances generated a series of crowd actions that began in the urban centers and spread to rural areas. Liberty, property, and natural rights, he argues, were the issues for which most everyone stood up. The "unifying factor," however, was taxation: "since no colonials were left untouched by the tax, resistance was general" (Hoerder 1977: 369). Crowd action involved merchants, artisans, laborers, farmers, landlords. As crowd action increased, so did the level of consciousness among the participants concerning their social and political power.

Hoerder goes beyond Rudé in maintaining that motivation for crowd action was essentially defensive and conservative.

Throughout the colonial period, crowd action was . . . a legitimate and in some instances even a semilegal means of achieving redress of specific grievances. But it always remained an extraordinary means to be used only after all possible legal and regular institutional channels had been exhausted. Individuals, including rioters, were bound by social compact and tradition to observe the written and unwritten laws and codes of their society, which, however, in the course of time could become corrupt. A return to first principles would save society from further corruption. Riots were intended to enforce such principles on those who broke them. They were not means to achieve social change; they could only reinforce patterns of the past. To strive for "innovation" was a social offense. Thus, crowd action, the most intense form of social action, was basically conservative, used to maintain the status quo in a static society. [Hoerder 1977: 368]

While provocative, and while containing a grain of truth, Hoerder's conclusion misses the very meaning of riot and revolution, which by definition seek to undermine or destroy the status quo rather than sustain it.

As noted earlier, Lucian Pye and Paul Berman focus on rank and file in two Asian communist revolutions. Specifically, Pye sets out to identify the types of persons who became attracted to the Malayan Communist Party (MCP), the problems of adaptation to party life, and the processes of disaffection. Accordingly, he presents data on both demographic and motivational variables. The data are drawn from a series of interviews he conducted with sixty Malay Chinese who in the early 1950s left the MCP and voluntarily surrendered to the British authorities—hence the designation

Surrendered Enemy Personnel (SEP). (In 1951, the population of Malaya consisted of about 2,600,000 Malays, 2,000,000 Chinese, and 800,000 Indians.)

Of the sixty SEP, twenty-three held responsible posts in the MCP and thirty-seven were classed among the rank and file. While at least some members of the first group were probably cadres, Pye's data are not presented in such a fashion as to enable us to separate the two groups. He also notes the presence of six women in his sample but, again, does not specify the group to which they belonged.

The demographic data may be quickly summarized. Of the sixty SEP, thirty-six had been born in Malaya, twenty-one in China, and one each in Borneo, Hong Kong, and Sumatra. "The SEP," according to Pye, "had considerably more education than is common among Malayan Chinese in general" (Pye 1956: 149). This finding, however, is not consistent with the SEP's social background, which is identified as primarily lower class (1956: 128). Nor does it coincide with their occupations at the time they joined the MCP, which included students, skilled or semiskilled workers, teachers, barbers, shop clerks, bookkeepers, and the like (1956: 210–211).

As a group, the SEP were intensely dissatisfied with the traditional lives of their parents. Rejecting the old world, they plunged into an intensely competitive situation in search of social advancement and personal security. Survival in the new world rested on adroit manipulation and exploitation of all persons and situations: "they sought to be skillful in adjusting to and handling any situation which arose" (Pye 1956: 134). This extreme opportunism, Pye believes, both drove them to the MCP and was responsible for their defection.

Having become frustrated in their attempts to improve either their social status or their personal security, the SEP turned to radical politics, communist front organizations, and eventually the ubiquitous MCP itself. Dominated by Chinese, the MCP appealed to Chinese pride and identity, and presented itself as an elite organization in which membership was an index of high status.

Once in party ranks, discipline was facilitated by the fact that the SEP attached great importance to form and ritual. Moreover, they were well versed in the Leninist theory of the party and prepared to accept rigid hierarchy and centralized authority. Beyond this, party policy provided for inducement for conformity and severe punishment for deviation. Finally, the SEP's extreme opportunism dictated a behavior pattern consistent with the needs of the situation.

The same opportunism characterized the process of disaffection. The SEP had joined the party, not because of emotional attachment, but for the purely instrumental reasons of social advancement and personal security. Social advancement did not come, however, for hard work did not produce the rapid promotions they expected. Personal security was also in question as dangers of party life became increasingly apparent and as the SEP began to consider the party a lost cause and a corrupt institution. They blamed the party for ruining their lives by preempting the best years of their youth.

While cognizant of the limitations of his sample, Pye provides an interpretation of revolutionary motivation and attitude that is plausible for a particular situation. Whether one can generalize beyond the sixty Chinese Malay communists, as Pye attempts to do, is subject to doubt.

Another important study of revolutionary motivation has been undertaken by Paul Berman (1974). His focus is the People's Liberation Armed Forces (PLAF) of the National Liberation Front of South Vietnam. His data base consists of two series of 1,100 interviews with PLAF prisoners and defectors conducted mostly by the RAND Corporation in 1963–1967.

Berman's approach rests on a dual concern for the individual and the organization. Thus on the one hand he focuses on the cultural, ideological, and motivational dynamics that impel people to join revolutionary organizations, the way they perceive and respond to authority, the extent to which they internalize new norms and values, and the way institutional bonds develop. On the other hand he stresses the manner in which a revolutionary organization establishes its authority and legitimacy, socializes and integrates members, and coordinates their activities.

Berman's principal findings include: (1) PLAF organizational norms were largely consonant with those prevalent in the larger Vietnamese culture; (2) combining coercion and persuasion, PLAF mobilization activities centered on convincing potential members that the basic needs of the Vietnamese "modal personality" would be met; (3) under revolutionary conditions, certain aspects of the Vietnamese model personality were transformed (for example, mastery over fate replaced acceptance of nature, self-sacrifice replaced self-interest), while others remained intact (for example, reverence for communal life and "proper" behavior) because they had counterparts in the traditional culture; (4) while members adapted to PLAF life according to their own motivation and experience, the two dominant modes of adjustment were those of the "committed" and the "conformer"; and (5) whereas the "committed" maintained institutional bonds under the worst of conditions, the "conformers" defected in the face of combat stress.

Berman receives high marks for focusing on a significant and relatively neglected aspect of political revolution and for integrating a wealth of interdisciplinary material concerning organization, motivation, ideology, culture, personality, and related topics. However, the key concept of modal personality is still a suspect notion at best. More important perhaps, although Berman is quite aware of the problem, his data base of interviews with prisoners and defectors necessarily provides a biased sample of revolutionary rank and file in general (the "committed" are completely left out, for example). Hence the data base is inadequate for generalizing about PLAF or about revolutionary organization and motivation as such.

Thanks to the studies of the kind conducted by Berman, Hoerder, Pye, and Rudé, we know more about revolutionary rank and file than we do about cadres. We know, for instance, that revolutionary rank and file is likely to draw upon virtually all segments of the population, except perhaps the upper class. We know that rank and file behavior, far from being random, pathological, or irrational, is goal directed: it is motivated by social, political, and personal norms. We know that, given sufficient intensity, popular grievances may propel ordinary citizens into revolutionary action. We have confirmation that relative deprivation and status inconsistency may operate as acute sources of revolutionary discontent.

To what extent are revolutionary rank and file similar in characteristics and motivations to cadres and leaders? How—and in what manner—do people involved in revolutionary upheavals differ from those involved in other kinds of protest and revolt? To these and related questions we now turn.

LACUNAE

We have examined the state of theory and research in the study of revolutionary personnel, noting at every turn large gaps in knowledge in this area of conflict behavior. Whereas our knowledge of revolutionary elites has been advanced somewhat, we know relatively little about revolutionary rank and file and virtually nothing about revolutionary cadres. A main consideration in this regard is that problems of data collection are so acute as to dishearten even the most enthusiastic researcher. This is particularly the case with cadres and rank and file. How does one identify the cadres? How does one identify that segment of a population that was involved in revolution? How does one gain access to either group? How does one persuade them to respond by giving information about themselves?

These difficulties notwithstanding, improved knowledge of revolutionary personnel requires systematic theoretical and empirical work in several specific areas. Since my current research explores these areas, I share them with the reader in the interest of scholarly communication.

First, insofar as elites play pivotal roles in all revolutions, we are in special need of a theory of revolutionary leadership. Although there are several theoretical approaches to the study of revolutionary elites in the literature, no theory comprehensively and convincingly addresses this area of conflict behavior. Such a theory would need to account for both sociological and psychological variables in the emergence of revolutionary elites: the social and political background from which they come and the motivational dynamics that impel them. It would also pay close attention to certain leadership skills indispensable in the processes of revolution, particularly the capacities for ideological mobilization and organization building. Since universalistic explanations are unlikely, such a theory would best focus on a series of middle-range propositions concerning particular kinds of revolutionary situations, social background characteristics, psychological dynamics, and ideological and organizational skills.

Second, we need to know whether—and to what extent—leaders, cadres, and rank and file differ among themselves, in terms both of demographic characteristics and of the processes by which they are radicalized. As for the former, we have seen that leaders and cadres are similar in a number of respects: they are predominantly middle-aged and middle class, urban-born or urban dwellers, of relatively high education and prestigious occupations, and hold nationalist, communist, or nationalist/communist ideologies. Admittedly the data are better for leaders than for cadres. Nonetheless, given the foregoing similarities, we venture the proposition that the primary differences between leaders and cadres lie in (1) their range of vision, how comprehensively they grasp the social situation, and (2) the degree to which they possess personal skills for organization building and ideological mobilization. As for the rank and file, all we know is that they are drawn from all strata of the population, with the exception of the upper class.

As far as the processes and psychodynamics of radicalization are concerned, we have uncovered much about leaders but very little, in specific terms, about cadres and rank and file. Again, given the demographic similarities between leaders and cadres, we postulate that they share much in the processes and psychodynamics of radicalization. On the other hand, the motivations of rank and file seem to lie in concrete economic and political issues: collective grievances, daily frustrations, food shortages, desire for personal security and social advancement, and the like. Further research on rank and file motivation could be sharpened by taking account of different theoretical approaches for explaining individual participation in conflict behavior in general. Some theories emphasize the importance of relative deprivation (Gurr 1970b) and alienation (D. C. Schwartz 1973b), others maintain that rationalistic calculation of relative advantage is the key factor (Leites and Wolf 1970, Salert 1976), and still others stress the significance of situational factors, such as the characteristics of contending groups (Gamson 1975, Tilly 1978). These theoretical insights should provide a rich source of competing middle-range propositions about the motivational dynamics that draw people into revolutionary upheavals.

A third fruitful area for investigation is whether—and to what extent—leaders, cadres, and rank and file in currently active revolutionary movements differ from their counterparts in the revolutions of the past. Once again, since data problems are likely to be acute, we have to content ourselves with journalistic accounts, government documents, scholarly monographs, and occasional interviews with selected revolutionary personnel. In this context, although in the foregoing pages we have felt obliged to question the data sources and possible biases of a number of studies—and hence their generalizability—we realize that these are the best and perhaps the only data we can hope to come by.

A fourth line of possible inquiry lies in whether—and to what extent—revolutionary leaders, cadres, and rank and file differ from *political* leaders, cadres, and rank and file in general. This is a vast field of study in itself, riddled with problems of data availability, comparability, validity, and reliability. Even limiting such an inquiry to leaders alone engenders enormous problems. Which political leaders does one select—members of parliaments, cabinets, or what? From what time period(s)? From which countries—those that have experienced revolutions, or from any country at all? If the former, does one look for the contemporaries of revolutionary elites in establishment positions, or will any political elite from any time period serve the purpose? These, needless to say, are problems to which one may never find wholly satisfactory answers. Thus some writers may find it convenient simply to speculate that there is no appreciable difference between political and revolutionary elites (for example, Daly 1972: 17).

Finally, underlying the specific areas of possible investigation outlined above are questions about the kinds of theoretical and empirical posture one might adopt. Does one focus in great detail on a few famous revolutionary leaders (cf. Mazlish 1976, Wolfenstein 1967) or does one study hundreds of revolutionaries (cf. Russell and Miller 1977)? And what are the tradeoffs associated with each approach? The smaller the numbers studied, the more manageable the problems of availability, validity, and reliability of information, but the more risky the attempts at generalization and theoretical advance. The larger the numbers studied, the more difficult the data problems but, once these problems have been surmounted, the greater the possibility of theoretical understanding. Again, there is no single answer to the questions posed here. The particular route each scholar takes will depend on his/her specific theoretical and empirical interests, as well as on energy, perseverance, and ambition.

PART TWO

Theory and Research
on Civil Conflict

CHAPTER 4

Theoretical Approaches to Explaining Collective Political Violence

Harry Eckstein

BETWEEN PROBLEMS AND SOLUTIONS in "positive" (if readers prefer, "scientific") inquiry there lies a crucial step. If this step is ignored, as is usual, cumulative theory-building will almost certainly not occur. Instead, one ends up with an accumulation of alternative, untested, generally ambiguous hypotheses.[1] The step I have in mind involves the most fateful aspect of what, in an earlier essay on political violence, I called "problemation" (Eckstein 1963: 23ff.): *the discovery of the most fundamental problem requiring solution if a progressive development of theory about a subject is to occur.* In this essay I will try to show what that basic problem is in studying collective political violence.[2]

Large numbers of social scientists have studied political violence since the early 1960s, when the subject, after one of those long hiatuses that characterize its study, was back in vogue. Production of work has been anything but scant: Zimmerman's magisterial review of the literature (1980) lists about 2,400 items, most of them published since 1960 (though he includes some stones perhaps better left unturned). It might seem odd, then, that an essay should now be devoted to a discussion—not even, as readers will find at the end, a solution—of a "basic," a "primary" problem. But this is not at all odd. The discovery of primary problems usually culminates much work in positive study: it is a critical and difficult achievement. Before core problems can be defined with precision, there usually is much prior observation, speculation, debate, and, especially, diffuse dissatisfaction, a sense of growing mystery rather than of illumination. One gradually comes to see, through long groping, the basic puzzle that a subject presents: where to begin if a genuine unfolding of theory is to occur. Two decades seem a long time to get to that point, but it usually takes much longer (though afterwards progress is swift).

The most basic problem in studying any subject is to choose a fruitful theoretical approach. Usually that choice lies among many candidates, in which case a still more basic problem is to narrow the choice down to viable options. This chapter deals with basic alternative approaches to theories about collective political violence. What then, first of all, is a theoretical approach?

In essence, an approach is, of course, a route or tactic one chooses to follow toward a new or difficult objective. All routes depend primarily on starting points. The starting point in theorizing is always axiomatic in nature, explicitly or implicitly: it involves assumptions deemed fruitful. Any such assumption is an initial commitment that is considered vital if one's goals in inquiry are to be achieved effectively. It is fairly common to call this a "perspective" of inquiry.[3] A perspective is the core of a theoretical approach, which, when fully elaborated, also includes key descriptive concepts, key secondary problems, and the specification of appropriate methods—all matters that depend on the choice of a fundamental perspective and that are more subject to change through feedback from research. A perspective usually takes the form of specifying the basic nature of a subject matter. For instance, physical events are "shaped matter in motion," or markets are "patterns of interaction among rational value-maximizers." Alternatively, a perspective may spotlight a key variable: one facet of a complex subject that is most important to grasp. Since all that constitutes a theoretical approach follows from its axiomatic basis, this essay asks: what are the crucial alternatives among basic perspectives that may be used to elaborate theories about collective political violence, and how can we choose among them?

The discussion cannot be brief, for the subject is enormously consequential, but space dictates that I omit much that ideally should be included. I ignore essentially descriptive case studies, still the main genre in the field, for my interest is in theory. Since my concern is with macro-theory, approaches to the explanation of individual aggression (such as Fromm 1973, Lorenz 1966, Montagu 1973, and Moyer 1969) also are not considered here; because of the linkages between micro- and macro-theory, this is more regrettable.[4] The chapter is concerned with process (especially one aspect of it), and so omits ideologies and personality traits of revolutionary leaders (e.g., Wolfenstein 1967). To make its coverage of the literature manageable I deal with contemporary studies, and only a sample of these.

More seriously, I skirt issues of definition (or, better, delimitation), thus ignoring my own early advice to students of the subject (H. Eckstein 1964: 8–16). But issues of definition and operationalization have always been too intricate for brevity. Early on, the problem was a lack of considered definitions. Now we suffer from overabundance and too much diversity. In any case, the fate of competing definitions will turn in the end on the promise of opposing theoretical approaches to a tentatively conceptualized subject, rather than on abstract discussion: the issue of the "essential nature" of a subject must ultimately determine its conceptualization.

For my purpose here, I will assume that there will be no fundamental quarrels with the following definitional notions:

1. collective political violence involves destructive attacks by groups within a political community against its regime, authorities, or policies (derived from Gurr 1970b: 3–4)
2. revolutions are the extreme cases of collective political violence, in regard to (a) their magnitude (scope, intensity), (b) targets (the political community or "regime"), (c) goals (degree and rapidity of change desired), and (d) the extent to which there is conflict between elites and counterelites.[5]

Most important, I will emphasize one theoretical problem, that of "etiology": why does collective political violence, in general or in particular forms, occur, and why does it occur at different levels of magnitude and intensity? That problem has certainly held center-stage since about 1960, while the study of other phenomena (the "process" of revolution, issues of prudent action by authorities or rebels, determinants of outcomes, problems of postrevolutionary rule) have waxed and waned. Not least, the issue of etiology is the problem on which theoretical approaches now differ most, especially if we include in it the problem of why political violence takes different forms. And we may surmise that the solution of this problem will have important repercussions for all others.[6]

"CONTINGENCY" VERSUS "INHERENCY"

In a very early essay on the etiology of collective political violence—the label then used was "internal war," following French usage in the eighteenth and nineteenth centuries and the language of the Federalist Papers (H. Eckstein 1965: 133)—I discussed a number of options in explaining its causes. Some of the choices to be made were between:

1. "preconditions" or "precipitants"—more remote or more proximate causes
2. "incumbents" or "insurgents"
3. "structural" or "behavioral" (cultural, attitudinal, psychological) factors
4. "specific occurrences" (say, economic depressions) or "general processes" (long-run patterns that may occur in numerous theoretically equivalent forms)

5. "obstacles" to collective political violence or "positive" factors that make for internal-war potential.

The result was a highly tentative eclectic model (not empirically grounded like that in Hibbs 1973) in which internal wars are explained by complex balances of very different and logically heterogeneous factors.

The theme of such complex balances constantly recurs in the literature. Gurr's "simplified" model of the determinants of political violence lists seven factors that may act to enlarge or lessen its magnitude (Gurr 1970b: 320). Another version of his model lists three proximate determinants, but also nineteen factors that determine the values of the more general determinants (Gurr 1970b: 332). In Hibbs's causal universe, positive and negative factors run amok. About thirty factors are directly or indirectly linked to coups, collective protests, and internal wars (Hibbs 1973: 181). The occurrence of these events involves the interplay of all the factors, facilitative and obstructive.

Undoubtedly, all concrete events, physical and social, result from the confluence of just such numerous positive and inhibiting factors. The business of positive theory is not to reproduce this complexity of the concrete, because that route takes one back to what makes experience mystifying in the first place. The task of positive theory is to cut through puzzling complexity to illuminating essentials: to find parsimony within intricacy.[7] How can we do this after so much preliminary study on collective political violence?

The way to start, surely, is to find the most basic branch point for choice in theorizing. My thesis here can be put in a sentence: in studying collective political violence, the first and most fateful choice lies between regarding it as "contingent" or "inherent" in political life.

NATURE OF CONTINGENCY AND INHERENCY

At the outset, I propose a broad thesis about basic branch points in building positive theories, regardless of subject. It seems historically true that primary branch points in theoretical inquiry are all alike: all involve a choice between contingency and inherency. Why so I will try to show momentarily. First, we must understand in a general way the nature of the two notions.

Something is *contingent* if its occurrence depends on the presence of unusual (we might say aberrant) conditions that occur accidentally—conditions that involve a large component of chance. An auto accident clearly is contingent in this sense. Drivers may or may not make mistakes, cars may fatefully malfunction. It is with reason then that we call such occurrences "accidents." Note immediately that contingency does not entail indeterminacy. We can specify that if a particular driver does something, an accident will probably occur. We can also determine general conditions that increase or decrease the probability of accidents. Contingencies thus are not random, and "may–may not" events can sometimes be controlled. Such events, though, do raise questions of explanation and theory in a special form: one wants to know what caused an accident where "normally" none was expected to occur. We are not mystified when a driver gets from here to there without malchance. We want to explain when the opposite occurs. Contingency implies "non-routine," something out of the ordinary, something not understood without special explanation.

Per contra, something is *inherent* either if it always will happen (e.g., entropy) or if the potentiality for it always exists and actuality can only be obstructed. Just when the inevitable occurs or hindrances are removed is decided by contingencies: chance occurrences that hinder or facilitate. As contingency does not entail randomness or inability to control, so inherency does not imply fully predictable determinacy. The decay of an automobile surely is inherent, even without any accidents. When or how it will fall apart, though, is not fully predictable. But basic questions of explanation differ in cases of inherency: we usually want to know why the inherent did not occur sooner, what obstructed or delayed decay and "termination." In contingencies, then, the puzzle is "why"; in inherency it is "why not?"

There is a certain sense in which one could say that contingencies are inherent in entities or events and thus score a debating point. No car, no accident. If you drive, it is always possible that something untoward will happen. An accident could be considered one of a driver's inherent "repertoire" of possibilities. (My terminology comes from a theory of collective violence.) But that would be as fatuous and misleading as saying that walking into the path of a meteorite is included in my inherent repertoire of living. One could say just as fatuously that the final decay of cars generally is contingent, for something circumstantial usually does end them. Everything ends in a circumstance, but obviously it would be disastrous to throw out the second law of thermodynamics on that basis. The reinterpretation of contingency into inherency is verbal flimflam; they are antithetical.

Nevertheless, the silly statements are of some help here. In the concrete world, contingency and inherency are almost always intertwined and hard to disentangle. What seems manifestly contingent to one observer may seem just as obviously inherent to another. This has been the case with studies of collective political violence. Occurrences, at bottom, must always be regarded as the one or the other. Consequently the issue of contingency versus inherency always arises. Both always occur in a mix hard to disentangle, but they cannot, logically, both be equally basic. Any theory that supposes the contrary, or avoids the issue, must end by making experience illogical, hence unintelligible.

Note three matters before the argument is taken farther. First, the distinction between contingency and inherency is often stated in different terminologies. The most common alternative language involves abnormality, irregularity, or aberration versus normality or regularity. In social science, the same distinction has been made as an antimony between "causal" and "purposive" behavior (Coleman 1973: 1–5, Tilly 1978: 6); Hempel's term for the latter is "dispositional" (Hempel 1965: 457ff.) The distinction is between actions caused extrinsically (by contextual factors, and thus contingent) and actions chosen "intrinsically" (upon will, tactics, calculation, or other disposition in actors) from a repertoire of alternatives.[8] Related to the notions of aberration and normality is the concept of "continuity." Thus we have been told that war may be treated as the extreme end of a single political dimension: routine politics continued by other means. War, of course, may also be regarded as lying in a realm separate from regular politics. As stated, these various differences are nominal. Those I employ here are rooted in long philosophic usage.

Second, precisely because contingent and inherent conditions are in most cases mixed in concrete occurrences, the issue usually is not whether something *is* the one or the other, but whether a subject is *better regarded* as basically inherent or contingent. The issue is not, literally, truth but explanatory "fruitfulness": the ability to explain cogently numerous matters through logically related propositions; to allow the subsumption of narrower theories under broader ones; perhaps, above all, to allow the deduction of good, previously unformulated theories. There have, to be sure, been decisive tests of the contingent or inherent nature of certain experiences. Usually, however, they occur long after the experience. (Between Copernicus's brainstorm and Galileo's tests, about sixty years elapsed; between Galileo and Newton, about a century.) In the meantime, one can only choose more or less sensibly—and try to devise projects that allow wiser theoretical choices at the crux.

Third, all kinds of occurrences (of collective violence or anything else) assumed to belong to a general "class" need not be contingent or inherent (see my remarks on this in the conclusion of this chapter). But if answers as to contingency or inherency differ by type of event, it is just about certain that the events do not belong to a single genus. Initially, though, let us assume that occurrences of collective political violence do constitute a broad type, in order not to sacrifice parsimony before we must.

EXAMPLES AND CONSEQUENTIALITY OF THE CONTINGENCY–INHERENCY DISTINCTION

The nature of our primary branch point can be illustrated by analogies to several very disparate fields.

Physical science furnishes the best known example. At the divide between ancient and modern physics are divergent ways of regarding a critical property of objects: their motion. Nothing physical can be explained without a theory of motion, and thus also of rest. Motion can be regarded in Aristotle's manner: as the result of force exerted by (contingent) external movers, so that objects are "normally" at rest, or tend toward it. The alternative—inobvious, but correct—is that motion inheres in objects, so that rest is a condition resulting from a confluence of contingencies. External movers do affect motion, but they affect only its "accidents" (velocities, paths, rest), not motion in itself. It should be evident—as it was to the Inquisition—that the distinction is fateful in the extreme for physical theory, cosmology, and theology, even though particular motions are usually explained fully only by a combination of intrinsic and extrinsic factors. One thing that makes the distinction fateful, as suggested earlier, is that it poses different primary problems. For Aristotelians, the crucial problem involves the occurrence of motion: hence their labored teleological, to us absurd (but long believed) account of gravity. For Galileo the equivalent puzzle is rest, as itself a kind of motion. It would be nicely convenient to put Aristotelian and Galilean notions together in a single formulation. But since objects cannot be both "inertly" moving and unmoving, the result would be messy and illogical, in contrast to the power and elegance of modern physics.

In the life sciences, there exists an analogous core problem. Death (termination, entropy) is inexorable. But how should one regard illness and other disturbances of "normal" functioning? One possibility is the familiar "bacterial" explanation, and its extensions: diseases result from the invasion of organisms by virulent micro-organisms, and disabilities result from diseases, or from accidents, or from the consequences of other external matters (like dominant parents or competitive siblings). Diseases and disabilities are thus contingent—pathological. The alternative is to regard them as particular routine states of the living system: stress on systems is always present; the system defends and usually maintains itself through homeostatic devices, sometimes to avoid disturbance altogether, sometimes to recuperate; thus both illness and health essentially are intrinsic matters of the state of biological systems in interaction with their contexts. As one ages, of course, one becomes more vulnerable to stress, and homeostasis is more difficult to achieve. That does not resolve the fundamental problem: which version of disease and disability, the contingent or the inherent, is the better for all or some pathologies as the base of theory? There is no single, agreed upon view on this issue.[9]

The current debate in structural linguistics between adherents of "deep-structure" theory and "empiricism" furnishes another example. Its consequentiality lies, of course, in that it raises the fundamental issue of the very nature of speech.[10] In politics, as I have argued elsewhere (H. Eckstein 1979), the analogous general branch point is between "culturalist" theories that explain political actions basically by (contingent) learned "orientations," and "rational-choice" theories which postulate an inherent tendency to maximize influence. In studies of social stability and integration, which is close to our subject here, there is a basic confrontation between considering the "normal" state of society to be harmonious or conflictual—for instance, between functionalists and systems theorists, on the one hand, and class theorists, on the other.

TWO ANTITHETICAL EXPLANATION–SKETCHES FOR COLLECTIVE POLITICAL VIOLENCE

How would a contingency theory about collective political violence compare with an inherency theory? At this point, we need broad "explanation-sketches" to illustrate the opposing approaches; in the next section I will summarize actual theories that fit the sketches.

Explanation-sketches (the term is from Hempel 1965: 238) consist of an initial spelling out of laws and initial conditions—scientific *explanantia*—to be filled out and made into a full-fledged theory through research "for which this sketch suggests the direction." Explanation-sketches are more than the initial commitments of theoretical approaches, but much less than final statements of theories.

Contingency theory should conform to the following sketch:

1. The fundamental disposition of individuals (or groups) in politics is toward "peace": the resolution or avoidance of violent conflicts. There would be no governments otherwise (see "contract" theorists). Satisfaction of political values is normally sought through pacific competition (electoral, through interest groups, by petitions, etcetera). Violent conflict is not in the normal "repertoire" of political competition.

2. The disposition toward pacific politics may be blocked and diverted under specifiable and "special" (aberrant) conditions. Given the disposition toward peace, the conditions should not readily occur, least of all in extreme forms of conflict. Collective violence thus involves the blockage of inherent tendencies by peculiar causes.

3. The critical problem in studying collective political violence thus is why it occurs as often as it does.

4. As to "peculiar causes," the pacific disposition may be blocked when some other, discomfiting human disposition (which governments exist to suppress) is activated. This may be a disposition toward aggression or it may be a disposition toward comparing one's condition in life with that of others.

5. It follows that choices of collective political violence are highly "affective" rather than coolly calculated.

6. The tendency to act violently in politics may be increased by cultural patterns—learned modes of action (these are always variable and "contingent," of course). Violent action may be a learned response; and to the extent that this is so, pacific dispositions are more readily diverted.

7. Given the affectivity of collective political violence, two factors should play a rather minor role in its explanation (though they may play some role as "mediating" variables that reduce or increase probability). These are coercive balances between incumbents and their opponents and other factors that facilitate the successful use of violence.

Readers can construct an explanation-sketch for inherency theory by inverting the contingency-sketch, but it will save effort if an equivalent framework is constructed explicitly here:

1. The fundamental disposition of individuals (groups) in politics is to maximize influence, or power, over decisions. This disposition may flow through numerous channels, of which collective violent action is one: extreme but "normal."

2. Since there are alternative channels for seeking power, the choice of violence must be activated, but activation readily occurs—though, of course, not as readily at the extreme of revolution. Collective political violence is a normal response to commonplace conditions.

3. The critical problem for inherency theory, given the normality of violence, is why collective political violence does not occur more often than it does.

4. The activation of the choice of violent channels is a matter of tactical considerations (not arousal of virulent affect).

5. Tactical choice involves cost-benefit calculation. Thus, the violent mode of political competition is chosen if lower-cost channels of influence-seeking are blocked, provided that violent means have a prospect of success that warrants their use. For extreme cases (revolutions) the ideal combination is blocked alternative channels, including those of lower-level violence; high valuation of goals; and perception of low capacity by opponents to inflict high costs.

6. Cultural patterns should play only a minor role; and to the extent that learning plays a role, it should inhibit violence at least as much as promote it, by teaching people that it is a high-cost resource.

7. More objective factors, like coercive balances or facilitating factors, should play a major and primary role in explaining collective political violence.

It should be evident that the two sketches intersect at some points, so that the allure of unparsimonious combination is, as always, considerable. But it should also be evident that what is primary, important, necessary in one case is secondary, minor, chancy in the other. Most important, the sketches lead in quite different directions in research (in logic and, as we will see, in practice): most patently, toward conditions that arouse exceptional types and degrees of affect (especially anger) versus conditions that influence calculations of cost-benefit ratios in choosing modes of political goal-seeking (especially intrinsically high-cost channels). Most fundamental, as in all political theorizing since ancient times, are two antithetical conceptions of political man: as a creature in search of either peace or power.

MAJOR ILLUSTRATIONS FROM STUDIES OF COLLECTIVE POLITICAL VIOLENCE

We proceed to theorists that illustrate the opposed approaches. The theories will not add much to the explanation-sketches. We do not yet have "finished" theories of collective political violence but we do have "evolving" theories—unfortunately, they are becoming more and more complex and logically messy.

CONTINGENCY: THE RELATIVE DEPRIVATION (RD) FAMILY OF THEORIES

Contingency theories of collective violence pivot on the notion of systemic breakdown where homeostatic devices normally provide negative entropy. It has been pointed out, correctly, that this implies sharp discontinuities between routine and nonroutine political activity, that the cause of violent action must be discontinuous (rapid, extensive) change in the context of politics, and that collective and individual behavioral pathologies should significantly covary, the former being a "version" of the latter (Tilly 1978: 23–24). Almost all such theories are subsumable under the notion of relative-deprivation theory, of which Gurr has been the leading exponent.[11]

"Why men rebel." Gurr's RD model can be summarized thus: (1) collective political violence is a form of aggression; (2) aggression results from anger, which is produced by frustration; (3) the fundamental cause of feeling frustration is an imbalance between what one gets and what one considers one's due: in Gurr's language, "discrepancy between men's value expectations and their value capabilities" (Gurr 1970b: 24, also Gurr 1968a: 1104). Obviously, the propensity to feel frustrated and its consequences are in a special sense "inherent." However, it is a dormant disposition until aroused by special extrinsic forces strong enough to overcome the tendency toward pacific acquiescence. The greater the scope and intensity of RD, of course, the more likely is violent behavior per se as well as at high "magnitudes" (see diagram in Gurr 1970b: 320).

The above is only a first step. Aggression is not yet rebellion. It must be politicized if it is to appear as collective political violence, and latency must become actuality. Here, mediating (secondary) variables that do not themselves involve the frustration–anger–aggression nexus come into play. They include: (1) "normative justifications" for political violence or the lack of them, from Sorelian glorifications of violence (Gurr 1970b: 193) to Gandhi's doctrine of nonviolence at the other extreme. Such justifications are themselves, of course, contingent, and unlikely to have consequences without prior frustration (Gurr 1970b: 197–210)[12]; (2) "utilitarian justifications," which are chiefly tactical considerations: estimations of the rational sense in collective violence. These involve calculations of numerous balances concerning the organizations of regimes and dissidents, their respective resources (actual and potential), and the availability of alternative channels of action; (3) a third mediating variable decides whether politicized aggression surfaces as fully actualized collective violence, and involves something obviously tactical (Gurr 1970b: 232ff.): the balance of coercion between regimes and dissidents. The relation of that balance to magnitude of violent political conflict is curvilinear: strife will be greatest if there is an even balance of coercion. At the extremes, where coercion is highly unequal, regimes collapse virtually without being pushed or dissidents lie low out of fear or are quickly put down; (4) Gurr also has at times invoked still other factors, especially environmental conditions that facilitate strife (Gurr 1968a: 1106): transportation networks, geographic traits, demographic characteristics—and, not least, the external support given dissidents.

In a contingency theory, such factors should themselves depend on rather fortuitous circumstances—as they do in Gurr. More important is an implication that must be read into relegating the factors to inferior status of mere mediating variables. Causal-path analysis aside, the implication is that the role of tactical variables diminishes as the more fundamental factor of frustration grows: desperate, impassioned people will not act coolly or be much governed by tactical calculations, even about coercive balances.[13] This is the only logical way to combine rationalistic with essentially arational motivation. Arationality also implies that a major role be assigned to cultural-variable learning. This too occurs in Gurr's theory, the cultural variable being the extent to which a culture of violence, rooted in the past, exists (Gurr 1968a: 231).[14]

Similar theories. Gurr's theory belongs to a large family. Tilly traces its ancestry to Emile Durkheim—though Tilly's treatment of Durkheim (whose puzzle, after all, was solidarity in a differentiated society, not conflict) is debatable (Tilly 1978: 16–18). More obvious precursors among the great sociologists are Gaetano Mosca and Vilfredo Pareto. Pareto traces the decline of elites to the contingency of insufficient cooptation of dangerous, competent members of the nonelite, those in whom the deep-structural residues of combination (organizational skill) and force (ability and will to use coercion) coalesce. The exclusion of such men produces in them a kind of political RD.[15] Mosca propounded Pareto's theory of elite-circulation earlier, though less elaborately. He also argued that the resort to violence is often a reaction to the estrangement of elites from masses: an elite's adoption of foreign ways—a kind of cultural deprivation.[16] Whether or not such estrangement occurs is, of course, no more intrinsic to elitism than is the exclusion of a dangerous counterelite. In Pareto, especially, the most obviously symptomatic indication of contingency, blockage of a normal process, is central.

Among contemporary writers, the most influential member of the family, next to Gurr, probably is Huntington (1968). As in Pareto, the sense of deprivation in Huntington's theory is political, though less a matter of blocked channels than of their paucity or their insufficient capacity to handle "loads." In skeletal form: Huntington argues that revolutions and lesser forms of collective political violence are artifacts of rapid socioeconomic modernization. Such modernization "mobilizes" people and induces them to enter the arena of political conflict. No harm will be done if political channels can handle their demands and activities in pressing them. But if political development lags, blockage occurs and aggressive modes of action are generated. Note the incidence of extreme political violence in conditions of socioeconomic development, especially in centralized monarchies, narrow-based military dictatorships, and in new nations (Huntington 1968: 275).[17]

The notions of overload and adaptation to stress belong to the world of systems theories. Since such theories are essentially concerned with negentropy as a normal state (see J. G. Miller 1965 for a splendid summary), any theory of collective political violence derived from the systems perspective belongs to the universe of contingency (though entropy is inevitable in the very, very long run). C. Johnson (1966) has been perhaps the leading systems theorist of revolution, at any rate if we do not look far beneath his language. The causal chain in Johnson is quite similar to Huntington's, ignoring nominal differences: rapid change leads (sometimes) to system disequilibrium (the overload of mechanisms of homeostasis), which produces individual pathologies as well as collective movements. The sense of deprivation (Johnson actually avoids psychological concepts, and speaks of dysfunction) arises, of course, at the point of overload, or blockage. Similarly, Wolf's account of peasant rebellions (1969), though making more of tactical considerations than Huntington or Johnson, rests on aberration: peasants—not capitalistic "cultivators"—resist the encroachment of market economies; but when traditional peasant life cannot be maintained and alternative arrangements are too ill-developed or restrictive, tensions arise and peasants rebel (Wolf 1969: xiv–xv). Here, aggression is unleashed by a combination of cultural and economic frustrations.[18]

We can perhaps best divide the members of the family of contingency theories according to whether their normal model is essentially macro-cosmic or micro-cosmic. In the first case, notions of systems and of their aberrations under conditions of extrinsically imposed strain are used to identify pathologies. In the latter case, apart from cultural learning,[19] the micro-condition is more manifestly and explicitly a sense of deprivation, relative to others or to more abstract conceptions of what is justly due.

Thus Gurr's theory is micro-cosmic (individual), and Huntington's and Johnson's, macro-cosmic (societal) in emphasis; but they converge at the explanandum, *collective* political violence.

INHERENCY: THE COLLECTIVE ACTION (CA) FAMILY OF THEORIES

Inherency theories of collective political violence at present are less common than contingency theories. They seem more numerous than they actually are because of a proliferation of labels for the same thing: resource-mobilization theory, political-process theory, theories of group dynamics, mobilization theory, strategic interaction models, and political contention theory. "Collective action theory" is used here because the postulate of the approach is that violent collective action is not aberrant but simply one of many alternative channels of group activity; like any other it is chosen by tactical calculation. Thus it belongs on a continuum or is part of a repertoire: different, sometimes extreme, but not off the normal scale.

"From mobilization to revolution." CA theory is chiefly the work of Charles Tilly and his associates; its *summa* is Tilly's recently published *From Mobilization to Revolution* (1978). An earlier and more succinct overview appeared in 1975. Again, what I present here is a skeleton of a theory that, like Gurr's, has grown in complexity to accommodate data and objections, to the detriment of logical elegance.

Tilly begins with a simple conception of the polity. Polities have members, who have formal access to the political decision-making process, and challengers, who do not (Tilly 1978: 53).[20] All are contenders for power—with members, of course, enjoying privileges. Members use their resources in a game of continuous jockeying to enhance their power; challengers try, as a condition to all else, to get into the game. To be allowed to play, there are entrance fees. The higher the fees, the greater the pressure needed to become members; and at some point of cost-efficiency, violent action among contenders occurs, with revolution as the most extreme, but normal, form of such action.[21]

This is the barest précis. Some key points need to be added. Before any collective action (say, a strike, election, demonstration, charivari, riot) can occur, there must be a confluence of shared interests (Tilly 1978: 59–62)—though Tilly deliberately skirts the issue of how collective interests come to be perceived and pursued (1978: 62), perhaps wisely, given his purpose. The interests must possess organization: a combination of shared categoric traits and a pattern of frequent interaction, or network (1978: 62–69). Beyond this, organized interests must be mobilized; by this Tilly means the possession and use of resources that may help achieve goals (1978: 69–84).[22] Even at this point, collective action will not occur unless there is sufficient opportunity for it (1978: chapter 4). This is essentially a matter of power to repress (especially of credible threats) or, more generally, to make collective action costly. The obverse of repression is, of course, facilitation, not in the sense that Gurr usually employs the term, but with emphasis on political toleration of, or help to, the activities of groups in conflict.

There remains the question of what (if not contingent matters like anger or strain) activates violent collective action, particularly in the more extreme form of revolution rather than lower-cost actions. The answer is a process (1978: 201ff.): (1) contenders (insiders or outsiders), organized around some specially motivated core group, make claims incompatible with a polity's survival in its existing form[23]; (2) the claims gain increasing acceptance, usually under conditions of alienation resulting from governmental malfunctioning: failures to meet obligations (provide benefits) or unexpected demands for resources (usually taxes); note here the intrusion of a glaring contingency—but only (as in Galilean motion) as an accelerator or as something that channels activity into a special path; (3) threatened authorities either cannot, or will not, or will not efficiently, block the potential for extreme action by suppression; hence (4) a condition of multiple sovereignty comes to exist. That condition never occurs after a short-run breakdown; it is always the result of a long-run chain of events. Multiple sovereignty involves mutially exclusive claims to legitimate governmental control, accepted by many (on both sides); often it is manifest in the establishment of parallel governments; and a struggle for partners in coalition occurs. Upon the reintegration of sovereignty, the process ends.

Apart from challengers' egregious "claims to resources," mysterious in origin, it seems plain that the crucial force that channels collective actions to violent political actions, once the (obvious) conditions of any such actions exist, is governmental inefficiency, timidity, and weakness. Revolutions thus occur when obstacles to strong pressures are unblocked; they are not, as typical contingency theorists believe, the very result of blockage. Hence the assertion in our explanation-sketches: for inherency theory, the pivotal problem is what *prevents* extreme conflict from taking place; in contingency theory, the issue is what *causes* it at all.

Relatives of CA theory.   Tilly himself locates the ancestry of his theory in John Stuart Mill (Tilly 1978: 24–25)—with a mandatory nod also to Marx and Marxists (1978: 42–46), for whom inherency takes more the form of ineluctable historical process. Mill and the Utilitarians are aboriginal CA theorists in that they regard all action as based on the rational pursuit of self-interest (pleasure), in contrast to Durkheim's notion of aberrant phases in the unfolding of the division of labor, or Weber's notion of chiliastic traumas in the unfolding of a disenchanted world.[24]

Among contemporary writers, we find versions of CA theory in numerous strategic interaction models of behavior (for references, see Tilly 1978: 29–35). Such models treat forceful courses of action, such as strikes, not as releases for potent emotions but as moves in games—they involve bargains, coalitions, lying low or pouncing, to maximize one's take. Hirschman's elegant *Exit, Voice, and Loyalty* (1970) resembles Tilly's in that Hirschman accounts for "secession" from a social entity, protests (opposition) of various kinds within such entities, and acquiescence as a "repertoire" of responses to discontent; choice among them is considered a matter essentially of cost calculation. In an unfortunately discursive but fascinating work on violence by American blacks during the sixties, Nieburg (1969) argues at least implicitly in a similar vein. People prefer low-risk methods of resolving conflicts; the discovery of a method that offers a decent chance of success at low risk is a matter of trial and error (strategic interactions, in less plain words). In that process, violence may be used, usually under conditions of rapid social change, new group formations, and high levels of social uncertainty. In-groups and out-groups maneuver toward some new political balance, until a proper new low-risk mode of resolving conflicts is found; if not found, a life-and-death struggle for domination occurs. Violence here is, as in all CA theories, a "move" likely to be made if expected costs do not exceed expected benefits—more accurately, violence is used if it is the best available course of action. For manifest reasons, it often is for systematically disadvantaged groups. Nieburg's work represents a special form of rational choice: the choice of actions occurs not so much by hard calculation as by experience—trial-and-error among a set of (abstractly) equivalent actions.

EVALUATION

We can now come to the crux. How can one make a reasoned choice at the branch point?

Unfortunately, there is no simple, workable way. One might simply reflect on the actual incidence of collective political violence. But that leads nowhere. One reason is logical. One might, superficially, expect something "inherent" to occur more often than something "contingent," but after a bit more thought it is clear that this is not necessarily so: contingencies can frequently occur (like physical "rest") and inherent tendencies may not generally be unblocked. (That is why people so often leap, like Aristotle, into obvious, but mistaken, positions. Concrete nature is masterful at deceit.) In actuality, violent actions occur very often; but they do not occur as often as alternatives. Sorokin (1937: 409–475) found, over two millennia, about one year of violent disturbance out of every four. From this it may follow that it does not take much to make violence occur contingently or that it does not take much to block the tendency toward it or make other actions more attractive.[25]

It also goes without saying that studies by the theorists themselves fit whatever tack they choose—though sometimes in an eyebrow-raising way.

Gurr, for instance, consistently does get good statistical results. But so does Tilly, when he confronts his models with data (which he does less well than Gurr). This is hardly surprising, since their models must come together at some point of explanation of concrete events, which, as stated, do nearly always have both contingent and inherent causes. At the same time, difficulties of research findings, even if manifest, are often glossed over or interpreted in a dubious way. To my knowledge, Tilly and collaborators have never succeeded in solving a crucial problem early recognized: finding "reliable procedures" for enumerating contenders, measuring mobilization, and specifying the relationship of groups to existing structures of power. Operationally, the theory is in limbo at all crucial points. Gurr, on the other hand, has been much criticized for his choice of "indicators" of RD. Deprivation is a "state of mind" that Cantril (1958) studies psychologically, but that is inferred in Gurr from objective (economic and political) indices. That begs many questions. One also wonders about: (1) the fact that Gurr and Duvall (1973) account for 75 percent of the variance in "civil conflict" across eighty-six countries in the early 1960s with five "causes" and eleven variables, in a simultaneous equation model—which could be worse, but hardly is conclusive; (2) the fact that mediating (secondary) variables in work by Gurr always account for a good deal of the variance in magnitude of civil strife, with social-structural facilitation always a significant variable—a result that CA theorists surely can turn to their own account.

At the very outset, then, we confront ambiguity. We should try to reduce it by inspecting available data bearing logically on one theory or the other. I will do so by discussing a number of selected issues, potentially helpful in choosing at the branch point.[26]

ALTERNATIVE CHANNELS

If CA theory is the fruitful tack, a clear relationship should show up between the incidence of collective political violence and the availability of alternative channels for making and realizing "claims." We may thus posit that democracies ("open" polities) will rank low on the dependent variable. By extension, political violence should at least decline discernibly in cases of regular electoral competition. But since the less advantaged do not have equal access even in open polities one should find them playing a specially important role in political violence—following the cliché that violence is the resort of the weak: everyone's equal capacity, in Hobbes's state of nature.

The matter of alternative channels would seem immediately vital for anyone who considers all collective actions a set, or repertoire, of equivalent events. However, astonishingly little has been done with the subject by Tilly: some secondary analyses of lower-class actions such as strikes (see especially Tilly 1978: 15ff.) and food riots (1978: 185–187), and a study of the connection between elections, organized associations, and the occurrence of "demonstrations" (1978: 167–171). We do have more direct evidence—though the subject cries for far more investigation by all inquirers into our subject.

In general, the data run counter to CA theory. Hibbs (1973: 118–121) found virtually no statistical relationship between democratic polities and magnitude of political violence, either of the milder protest variety or with more virulent internal wars. To avoid the possibility that findings were distorted by including "ill-developed" democracies, a relationship was sought between levels of political violence and democratic development, in the well-known manner of McCrone and Cnudde (1967) and Neubauer (1967). Again, no significant relationship emerged with protest, and a weak negative association with internal war was convincingly explained away as spurious. Worse, a positive association turns up between elections and political violence (Hibbs 1973: Table 7.1; also, of all people, Snyder and Tilly 1972), suggesting, perhaps, that electoral processes activate emotions appropriate also to other outlets. Hibbs also finds that effective exclusion from valued political positions due to ethnic, religious, or linguistic traits usually leads only to mild forms of protest—a finding that also turns up in Gurr (1966: 71).

In the most recent, and most persuasive, study of the subject by Gurr (Graham and Gurr, 1979), the results are more complex, but still of scant comfort to CA theorists. One critical finding is that democracies typically had more extensive "civil conflict" (a broad notion that ranges from demonstrations to guerrilla wars) than autocracies. (For simplicity's sake I ignore a third type that Gurr calls "elitist.") On the other hand, democratic civil conflicts were much less deadly. The first finding clearly impugns CA theory. However, the second provides CA theorists with a measure of comfort, since it must be due to a toleration in democracies of protests that, in repressive regimes, never surface, or else are forced to take virulent forms. RD theorists can rejoin that grievances in democracies are generally less serious (most obviously, because of lesser political deprivation per se). They can also sensibly hold that the greater deadliness of civil conflicts in autocracies may be a result of the actions of regimes, not of dissidents; this depends, obviously, on who is killed, and under what circumstances.

Two other relevant points: the old saw that violence is the political means of the impoverished—the basis of the McCone Report about the Los Angeles riots in the mid-1960s—simply does not stand up to close examination (e.g., Fogelson 1971: 30; Caplan and Paige 1968: 19–20). There is also the much documented fact that revolutionary leaders do not much differ socioeconomically from other salient political figures, and that they differ more in regard to social marginality than in regard to resources at their disposal.

It seems evident—logically and empirically—that CA theorists must deflate many quantitative findings about the effects of alternative channels by stressing facilitation. Open polities do not block propensities to act of many, or any, kinds as much as closed polities. So they produce more collective political actions of all sorts. And the more advantaged and powerful have more means for deadly violence, no less than other actions: particularly military elites, who are more likely to act politically in closed polities. Our first test thus is one-sided in statistical results, but not hard to argue away.

FACILITATION

It seems necessary then to look hard at the CA theorist's chief route of escape: facilitation—that is, how difficult or how easy pertinent circumstances make it to use collective violence in politics. Here, contingency theorists sometimes seem to turn the tables on themselves. Consider Gurr. In his early (now much modified) report (1968a: 1121), certain highly contextual factors presumed related to the possibility of violence (e.g., transportation networks, density of population, other geographic characteristics, and "external support of insurgents") account for more variance in magnitude of civil strife than anything else (twice as much as persistent deprivation!). Similarly, such facilitating factors as the distribution of value-stocks, complexity and cohesion of organization, number and scope of values (resources), are likely to decrease strife if regimes are better equipped and to increase it to the extent that dissidents possess them. In later work, facilitative matters still seem to have crucial effects on whether dissidence is peaceful or violent.

A picture begins to emerge. Having less costly channels available does seem to affect the choice of violent means: so, score a point for inherency. But the cost of violence does not much reduce deadly conflict in democracies, and still less in autocracies, where presumably it is likely to cost more: so, score a point for the other side. All would seem to depend then on what to regard as fundamental. I know no way to decide that issue yet, since CA theory incorporates facilitation (viz., opportunity), as does RD theory. The most we can say is that violence is more likely if easier to engage in and perceived to be more likely to succeed. Tactics play a role—but perhaps only for people afflicted by high RD. It seems necessary, then, to look at other issues that might break what, so far, appears to be a tie.

THE BALANCE OF COERCION

The most manifest "facility" for collective political violence is the ability and willingness of regimes to repress, relative to that of dissidents to be destructive. We should, of course, expect the balance of coercion to make a difference both in a contingency-sketch of political violence and in its opposite. For contingency theory, though, the tactical consideration involved is of lesser import: as stated earlier, very angry men are not likely to act coolly, even in the face of what Tilly calls "threat." For CA theories, *per contra*, little would seem more important. What does the evidence suggest?

To begin with, we are handicapped by a flaw in method: the almost universal tendency to use the coercive capacities of regimes as measures of the coercive balance between authorities and dissidents. One exception is an article by Gurr (1970a). Gurr uses measures of loyalty and dissidence by military forces, and weighs familiar measures of the coercive potential of regimes against foreign support of dissidents and aspects of dissident groups, such as their size and organization, that may be assumed to have a bearing on coercive capacity (Gurr 1970a: 138). The results Gurr obtains actually seem to offer some support to CA theorists, but not much. The coercive capacity of dissidents does "enhance the prospects for rebellion," the most extreme category of dissidence, whereas that of authorities reduces it. This is what CA theorists would expect. However, (1) regime coercion has "very little effect" on other forms of protest; (2) a different balance, concerning "institutional support" (support by "dense" and pervasive networks of organizations) consistently explains more; (3) throughout, the combined factor of institutional/coercive balance fares only a little better or worse in regard to different kinds of collective violence than a quite different explanatory variable, "justification," which includes both tactically relevant factors (e.g., success of past strife) and nontactical ones (legitimacy), but with the latter yielding better results than the former; (4) dissident coerciveness enhances the likelihood of rebellion much more than regime coercion inhibits it; (5) the latter has virtually no effect on lesser forms of strife.

What follows? Perhaps nothing, for operational reasons: leaving aside questions of data sources and scaling, Gurr's evidence comes from twenty-one Western countries over a mere five-year span (1961–1965). However, the clear and strong result that CA theory would seem to call for manifestly fails to turn up. Also, CA theorists must make much of the capacity to inflict high costs (as pointed out in the explanation-sketch for inherency theory above); one therefore should not find that regime coercion is, as it seems to be, the least weighty explanatory factor in all types of strife. After an initial leaning toward CA theory, one thus is led to a contrary conclusion—though that, again, is offset by Gurr's conclusion that "variations in deprivation are not an important direct determinant of total strife, turmoil, or violent strife" (1970a: 142). Deprivation exists in the remote background, waiting to be "converted."

CA theory would be best supported by finding a strongly curvilinear relation between conflict and coercion. If one or another side greatly outweighs the other's capacity for coercion, rebellions should not start or regimes ought quickly to collapse, at low cost. The most intense conflicts ought to occur where coercive capacities are closely matched. Granted difficulties in the available data, the most recent study (by Gurr et al., forthcoming) shows only slight curvilinearity. In addition, some other results that are very odd from the standpoint of CA theory turn up: in general, a positive relationship seems to exist between governmental coercion and conflict. This includes the finding that the cumulative application of sanctions increases conflict, even at the extreme of sanctions, and that the use of sanctions has no discernible time-lagged effect on conflict. These findings are contrary to Gurr's earlier position (1970b: 251) or that of the Feierabends (1971: 429). However, they are strongly supported by Hibbs (1973: 86–87). And they are more consistent with contingency theory than the earlier position.

The unsatisfactory state of the available evidence does provide an escape hatch to CA theorists, at least for now. The tendency, though, has been for coercive balance to be of less importance as studies have improved. Most damaging, perhaps, has been the tendency of CA theorists themselves to argue away inconvenient findings by making fuzzy what should be especially clear in their theories. The problem is illustrated by Tilly's *magnum opus* (1978: 106–115), in which repression is treated with unusual convolution—and by aphorism: for instance, "governments which repress also facilitate." Ultimately, Tilly resorts to a promising line of argument, one that involves historical patterns of repression. The special variable involves abrupt changes in such patterns. Unfortunately, the hypothetical relationship is either to "encourage" or "discourage" types of collective action (again, excepting only the obvious exception: very high levels of successful repression). That is simply not permissible—not, anyway, without a lot of added theory.

On the whole, contingency theory emerges healthier than inherency theory from our third test. But we cannot escape the problem of adequate data. For this reason, CA theorists need not throw in their towel yet. We need far more and better light on the issue. We want it especially from CA theorists themselves, the matter being critical for theories in which "causation" and "channeling" (or blockage) are the same thing. This is useful to know, but leaves our issue still undecided.

WHEN MEN REBEL

I referred above to Tilly's use of the historical pattern of repression as an explanatory factor. His doing so may be subsumed under a more general, widely followed line of assessment: to find out *why* men rebel we may be helped by studying *when* they do so. As we shall see, this involves a set of diverse tests that could also be invoked separately. Each, though, fits a general deduction from our two explanation-sketches:

1. for contingency theory: Collective political violence, or such violence in its more extreme forms, should occur when, as the result of some

temporal pattern, the specified contingency, such as RD, is or may be expected to be particularly great

2. for inherence theory: Collective political violence, or its more extreme forms, should occur when, as a result of a temporal pattern, (a) the costs of violent collective action are expected to be especially low, or (b) nonviolent actions in pursuit of highly valued goals have been shown to be unproductive.

There is much historical precedent for seeking explanations of political violence in the nature of historical moments of such violence. The classic source is Tocqueville. His basic argument in *The Ancient Regime* (1856) is familiar:

> Revolution does not always come when things are going from bad to worse. It occurs most often when a nation that has accepted, and indeed has given no sign of even having noticed the most crushing laws, rejects them at the very moment when their load is being lightened. . . . Usually the most dangerous time for a bad government is when it attempts to reform itself.

This argument is the theme for numerous variations. We will consider the most important:

Rapid change.   There is a large family of theory that attributes extreme and destructive political behavior to an obviously "contingent" condition: unusually rapid, hence unusually unsettling, socioeconomic conditions. Frustrations are likely to arise under such conditions because of disorientation (anomie) per se, and because of the familiar occurrence of an excessive rise in expectations. At a minimum, the conditions of any contingency theory are more likely to be satisfied when change is rapid (and abrupt) than under more settled circumstances.

Olson's influential article on the consequences of rapid economic growth (1963) is prototypical of this view. A political, and otherwise modified, version of Olson's argument is Huntington's mobilization–institutionalization hypothesis.[27] Both arguments are backed by persuasive reasoning, as well as the usual selectively chosen, *post hoc* illustrations. However, the evidence once again is surprisingly inconclusive; in general, only illustrations are used, and illustrations can be found of almost anything that is not wholly absurd.

Tilly and Johnson both have pointed out that contingency theorists should expect a high correlation, in cases of rapid change, between individual pathology (crime) and the collective variety (political violence). One can see why this should be so, the causes of individual and collective aberration (such as frustration) being presumably the same. But again, though the point seems crucial, evidence is strangely meager, and, for us, confusing. Gurr's work of 1970b cites a study that reports a decline in aggressive crimes (by blacks and against blacks) during periods of civil rights demonstrations (Gurr 1970b: 310, note 92). That fact, though, can be interpreted almost any way one chooses—though, superficially, it runs against the expectations of contingency theory. By way of compensation, Tilly and Lodhi find a correlation of the two (1973: 296), but they emphasize that it is low. Perhaps, though, this is the correct expectation—anyway for them—since CA theorists regard different responses to similar conditions as alternatives in a repertoire of actions. If so, individual and group violence should be associated, but not very closely, for some people will choose the one response and others its alternative. Obviously, we need here both better data and better reasoning.

In any case, an impressive number of studies suggests that there is no simple, direct relationship between rates of socioeconomic change and political violence. The relationship, again, seems unusually ambiguous. Tanter and Midlarsky (1967) found a negative relationship between economic growth and, as they use the term, "revolutions" in Latin America, but a positive relationship in the Middle East and Asia. Bwy (1968b) confirms the Latin-American result, but argues that a different relationship among the variables holds for less developed countries. Flanigan and Fogelman (1970) find a negative relationship; Alker and Russett (1964) find the same. On the other hand, the Feierabends and Nesvold (1969) report a high association between rate of modernization and "instability." Hibbs (1973) finds different relations between rapid change and different types of political violence. And so it goes, in a very extensive set of works.

With enough ingenuity, one could probably trace this extreme confusion to different uses of concepts and measures. But if the relationship between the variables were very strong, mere differences in preferred measures ought not to produce such wildly divergent findings.

Adaptation to change. The virulent potential effects of most stresses may, of course, be offset by the proper adaptation of "systems." If socioeconomic change is similar, differences in "adaptation" to it should be matched by differences in its consequences, including collective political violence. An example is the apparent relation (to be sure, small) between historical bourgeois radicalism and the relative lack of opportunities to become ennobled (see Shapiro and Dawson 1972: 180)—a nice example of Pareto's hypothesis.

More to the point here is Barrington Moore's thesis that political outcomes (in Moore's case, the nature of regimes, but, by implication, also political processes more generally) depend chiefly on the adaptation of the traditional landed upper classes to "bourgeoisification"—economic modernization, as most of us think of it (Moore 1966: 429ff.). That famous thesis fits, *post hoc*, eight widely assorted cases. But it has run into trouble when extended to other cases (or when examined more closely): by Tilton (Sweden) and Rokkan (the smaller countries in general); note also the crushing critique by Skocpol (1973). Moore's thesis can also be logically subsumed under either contingency theory, if change is emphasized, or inherency theory, if his argument is interpreted as hinging on choices of coalitions. Note, too, that despite the long vogue of "systems" theories in political science, operationally rigorous work on stress due to change, and adaptations to such stress, is just about nonexistent.

Structural imbalance. As implied earlier, Huntington's thesis rests on the notion of a "balance" of structures rather than on rapid mobilizing as such. This, in a sense, combines the variables of change and adaptation to change. Huntington's theory, of course, places the most inflammatory point in polities where the divergence between mobilization and institutionalization is greatest. As the space between the two narrows, collective political violence should decline. Like Moore, Huntington illustrates his argument. The evidence of other studies, however, runs strongly against him.

Schneider and Schneider (1971) accept Huntington's basic argument on the basis of a cross-national study, but their evidence leads them to reject the corollary that "mobilization" should be slow if it is to be balanced by "institutional" adaptations; this is damaging evidence, for one can easily show that the corollary is inherent in the postulate. Sanders (1973) concocts a resounding empirical refutation and also presents a strong critique of Huntington's conceptualization (which, of course, weakens the empirical refutation). Other important empirical rebuttals may be found in Yough and Sigelman (1976) and Duvall and Welfling (1973). Huntington himself distinguishes among "western" and "eastern" types of polities, to which his thesis (presumably) applies differently, and adds some very ill-fitting variables that confuse the nontactical character of his theory: the failure of elite-circulation and the effects of foreign wars and interventions (Huntington 1968: 273, 308).

Unfortunately, again, there seem to be no other theories of structural "imbalance" that have sufficient empirical support to allow a more definite verdict about this mode of theorizing; nor are other possibilities worked out as fully as is Huntington's theory (really, itself an "explanation-sketch").

The J-curve. One major hope remains: that we can infer the conditions of collective political violence from some less simply wrought theory of change—some theory that finds the point of explosion at a particular point, or range, on a curve of change. The leading exposition of such a view is Davies's J-curve theory (1962).

The theory is that revolution is likely when periods of prolonged improvement, the historical pattern most likely to raise expectations, are interrupted by abrupt reversals; then frustrations due to unrequited expectations become intolerable. The J-curve theory, needless to say, involves contingency in its most pristine form, especially considering that it has never been diluted with logically confusing factors suggesting tactical choice—all honor to Davies for theoretical courage. What is the state of the evidence regarding the theory?

The supporting evidence should be very strong, for all contingency theory implies that the condition described by Davies frustrates and angers very deeply. In Davies's original formulation four cases were invoked—once again, as illustrations. Later, four other cases were added (see Davies in Graham and Gurr 1969). In an impressive independent check, Grofman and Muller (1973) provide a clear measure of support, using data on individuals. But they also find strong evidence for a "relative gratification" theory of conflict behavior (drop–rise, or V-curve, theory). Still, their study manifestly remains within the realm of contingency theory, and rests on reasoning analogous to, though not wholly the same as, that of Gurr and Davies.

The chief problem with J-curve theory is the abundance of countercases. Consider, for example, the many countries in which the Great Depression of the 1930s did not increase political violence. Surely, the effects of sudden depression, following the orgiastic recovery of the 1920s were crucial—and no more in Germany than in all the countercases. Moreover, Tilly (1978: 207) provides, of all things, a tactical interpretation of the meaning of the J-curve patterns of change. Unfortunately, it seems labored: members should "break commitments where least dangerous." This begs crucial questions: What commitments, and to whom? Moreover, the interpretation accepts the importance of contingent frustration and simply counsels increased coercion in the right place.

Group dynamics.   The question of when men rebel obviously has led, again, to puzzlement, if viewed from the standpoint of contingency theory. Does inherency theory, then, fare better with the question of timing? For RD theorists and their kin, the flashpoint of collective political violence should occur at a point of social process when rage or despair are most acute—when expectations and capabilities are most distant. For CA theorists, in contrast, violent action, being relatively high in cost in most circumstances, should generally be chosen after lower-cost channels are perceived as ineffectual, provided only that the balance of coercion does not manifestly rule out successful violence.

A tactical scenario that makes the resort to violence especially likely can readily be constructed. A group of contenders makes political claims cheaply: say, by petition. No response is made by authorities. Pressure is stepped up, perhaps through a stoppage of work; but still no response. A more dangerous organized demonstration is used next. The authorities remain intransigent and call out some squads of police to indicate determination. A more intense demonstration occurs; perhaps now some undisciplined elements or provocateurs throws rocks or do some looting. The authorities call on police and militia; heads are broken. At this point it will be clear that only violent collective action has any prospect of success at all. And, given some chance of success and intensity of claims, the high-cost method will be used. The moral is that negative sanctions precede collective political violence. On this point, CA theorists have differed from RD theorists almost from the beginning, for manifest reasons (see especially Tilly 1971).[28]

Tilly's argument along the lines just sketched is predated by the report of the National Advisory Commission on Civil Disorders (1968). The report held that intervention by the police "almost invariably" preceded larger-scale violence—though, of course, the police might simply be acting in learned anticipation of what might occur anyway. A more convincing finding occurs in Hibbs (1973: 181): milder forms of aggression do generally escalate if regimes use coercion; in fact, that is the strongest of all factors leading to "internal war" in Hibbs's eclectic model. Hibbs, though, can hardly be conclusive on the point at issue here. For one thing, it is not peaceful action that is converted by force; but aggressive action into more aggressive action: the optional channels *start* with violent behavior. In addition, Hibbs's data are cross-sectional; they do not follow the same conflicts over time. And, again, there is empirical support also for the other side. Tilly and partners themselves have presented contrary evidence (Tilly 1975a: 78, 285): repression, they argue, works—though, needless to say, they use the point to support the tactical-choice argument. This is a fine example of how one may read the same evidence in contrary ways if one starts from antithetical bases—hence the bases of theory matter a great deal. Repression is used and violent action stops; a routine channel is blocked or aberrant anger is suppressed. The evidence fits both conclusions equally—and we remain ambiguously suspended between antitheses.

War. A different argument for inherency involves the removal or weakening of coercive blockages, rather than gradual escalation as a forceful response to repression. A tendency may be present and emerge when resistance to it weakens, or actions may occur to overcome resistance when otherwise behavior would be more moderate.

When is coercion, as an obstacle to turbulent political action, likely to be unusually low? The most obvious answer is that the coercive potential of regimes will be exceptionally low when military forces have disintegrated, leaving the field free to less potent groups. This condition is likely after defeat in war, at least if occupation forces do not step in to help incumbent authorities (see, among others, Huntington 1968: 304–308, Arendt 1963, Seton-Watson 1951, and Hagopian 1974).

Examples of revolutions after lost wars abound: France in 1871; Russia in 1905 and 1917; Turkey in 1918; China after World War II. Unfortunately, countercases can be invoked just as readily: Japan or Italy after the last great war, for instance. Perhaps these cases only show that losing a war is not a sufficient condition for revolution; but then, neither is it a necessary condition, or even a "normal" occurrence (e.g., France, 1789;

Mexico, 1910; Cuba, 1959, etcetera). Anyway, the argument surely is more pertinent to the outcome of revolutionary conflicts than to their inception. This is Hammond's point about communist take-overs (1975: 640–641) and, more broadly, that of D. E. H. Russell's study of twenty-eight "mass rebellions" since 1906 (1974). Consider also Trotsky's familiar argument that the armed forces usually reflect popular conditions. If so, they would always facilitate violent action, if there is sufficient popular disposition to use it.

LEARNING: THE "CULTURE OF VIOLENCE"

Contingency theories belong, in social analysis, to the same family as culturalist theories—theories based on learned orientations to action. Inherency theories are related to rationalist theories—based on the notion that actions are chosen by calculations of cost-efficiency.

There is much writing about the role of learning and culture in relation to political violence. Bandura (1973) is the leading exponent of the view that using violence individually is learned, and he makes a good case. On the macro-level, though, we should expect ambiguous findings about the relation of present to past violence. The use of violent action might, logically, become a learned response, but it might also teach people that its costs tend to be disproportionately large, even if successful. The problem here (as with violence by authorities: repression) is that any curve, or none, can support the cultural interpretation. Much, in other words, is made in the literature of "cultures" of violence, but nothing definitive for the debate between contingency and inherency theories is likely to emerge from studies linking past to present violence.

This point fits findings. At best, a moderate relationship tends to turn up, as in Gurr's work (1968a: 1121). Still, Gurr later (1970b: 170, 176–177) strongly argues the "culture-of-violence" hypothesis on "varied evidence and arguments"—which, as I read them, support equally well utilitarian explanations of violence. Another recurrent theme in studies of the culture of violence, as we should expect, is that "it depends." For instance, statistical relations seem to vary, for some reason, with geographic areas. In Africa, past rebellions are associated with reduced "turmoil" (Welfling 1975: 887); but Latin America is different, and Western Europe different again. Welfling (with Duvall) squares the circle on the basis of type of collective violence: turmoil, it is argued, feeds on itself whereas "elitist" kinds of violence reduce the likelihood of later violence. But they do not do so through learning; rather, the cause seems to be the tactical factor of suppression (Duvall and Welfling 1973: 692). Hibbs also reports quite contrary findings for "protest" and "internal war" (1973: 159 and 163); in his study, conflict akin to the "elitist" type in Welfling seems to be increased by the existence of a "culture" of violence.

As I argued, this contrariness can be accommodated to the premises of contingency theory. But to accommodate the evidence, we will have to specify when violence teaches violence or the imperative of peace. This will be difficult, at best. At present, the evidence may be regarded as typical of the too often ambiguous findings in the literature.

CONCLUSION

We began with an explication of a recurrent antithesis at the basic branch points of theorizing about any subject. We went on to a version of that branch point especially tailored to explaining collective political violence. We found that theories in the field do divide along the lines indicated And we reviewed many empirical studies that bear on expectations deduced from the postulates of the antithetical approaches. No clear result emerged. Granted, conditions such as inequalities, unsatisfied demands, discrimination, and societal cleavages are related consistently to degrees of conflict. What remains mysterious, in the end, is the basic nature of the link between causes and effects—not least, therefore, understanding why similar conditions so often have dissimilar results.

The findings do not point strongly toward the superior fertility of a particular species of theorizing. "Fertility" in this connection is, first, the capacity of an approach to provide consistently superior explanations of many aspects of an independent variable—explanations that are themselves logically consistent, or entailed by a higher-order theory. Second, fertility is the ability of such higher-order theory deductively to yield new, and good, lower-order theoretical relations. On the whole, contingency theory probably has fared better than inherency theory. That may only be a by-product of its more frequent use or it may result from a lesser empirical bent among inherency theorists. More important, we consistently found ambiguities in data bearing on the contingency perspective, no less than its antithesis—problems of interpreting correctly their implications; and often findings that were offset or made doubtful by other findings. Also, relationships that should have been clear and strong frequently were opaque and weak.

Something, then, must be amiss—at least if the premise of this essay concerning basic theoretical choice in studying collective violence is correct. I will conclude with some speculations on what the problem might be.

Surely, the difficulty is not any lack of studies or data. We are inundated with both, and the data cover a vast range of variables, history, geography, and types of polities.

Somewhat more likely (though I doubt it) is that we arrived at a confusing result because the empirical studies cited were an inadequate sample. They certainly do not exhaust the literature and are a mix of methodologically good, bad, and indifferent studies. This implies a challenge to specialists in the field: before embarking on new empirical studies, identify the high-quality works in both approaches and analyze their procedures and results from the perspective sketched here.

Another strong possibility is that confusion has emerged because of a taxonomic error. We have treated cases of collective political violence as a single class—as Tilly treats a still much larger universe: all collective actions. Even if this is typologically plausible, doing so may be theoretically confusing: as suggested early in this essay, certain kinds of political violence might better be treated as "contingent," others as "inherent." We did frequently find such results in the literature, especially between lesser and greater types of strife. For reasons of parsimony, we ought perhaps to resist using this possibility, but evidence might compel resorting to it. In any case, here is another challenge for analysis.

A third likely difficulty—one common in the social sciences, and one that may well condemn to futility exercises like those just suggested—is method: an overdose of induction. One doubts that underlying determinants can ever be mechanically teased out of the complexity of highly disparate events, no matter how sophisticated the quantitative methods used. A related problem is deliberate eclecticism. Choosing eclecticism at the outset virtually guarantees confusion in the end, and thus seems self-defeating—even perverse.

Although we have not found a hero, we have surely found a villain: prehedged models, or models ground out mechanically from motley data. The resulting "modeled" world appears about as complex (and thus mystifying) as the concrete world it models. In Hibbs (1973: 181), we find no illuminating simplification: we find only a complex world of variables, vertiginous with arrows and proportions. The artfulness of nature wins out over that of theory because, *contra* Bacon, nature is not "put to the test." One should not be too censorious about this, since Hibbs's deliberate aim is eclecticism. Gurr's "model,"—more surprisingly, because based on an elegantly parsimonious theory—is not much less complex. Is not the reason fear of potential disconfirmation, even at the cost of mixing up a highly plausible line of analysis with its antithesis?

The result always is a realized intention: a model that "fits" the data. But if such a model is irrefutable in principle, it will fit only without really illuminating experience. That, I suggest, is inadvertently the case in Gurr's work, however tenacious and ingenious the work has been. Try to refute the following, which is essential RD theory, à la Gurr:

1. no political violence can occur without politicized discontent (satisfied people do not rebel)
2. no discontent will exist unless somebody feels deprived
3. politicization involves both normative and utilitarian (tactical) considerations

4. even so, little or nothing will happen when facilitative and coercive resources available to dissidents and authorities are distributed one-sidedly.

Admittedly, this is a great simplification. But it surely shows, by omitting inessentials, how RD theory has been insulated against tactical accounts of collective political violence by incorporating them.

Tilly, too, has increasingly complicated his theoretical model, as well as swallowed up inconvenient data by reinterpretations. A still greater difficulty that emerges in his work, and also disarms invalidation, is a kind of clever triviality (in the philosophic sense). Something *seems* to be said to explain a mystifying set of events. But except for labels (members, challengers, etcetera) we know it already, and so remain mystified. No substantial violent action will occur unless:

1. some group wants something it does not have

2. a fair number of people agree that their claim is justified

3. the group is not successfully suppressed to begin with

4. the group controls some suitable resources (and wants to control more).

And who does not know that extreme rebels lay claim to nothing less than sovereign authority, against the claims of incumbent authorities? I do not mean to be sardonic. The point of the argument is that the "interesting" issues (those that really need explaining) always are a step removed from those Tilly faces: why do "outgroups" actually (not latently) come to want "in," where before they acquiesced? Under what conditions do people come to perceive the illegitimacy of a pattern of governmental authority, rather than continue to acquiesce?

A conclusion seems to emerge. The literature, even if differently surveyed, will probably be inconclusive for us, because a well-defined choice among theoretical approaches has not been faced at all by the many scholars of collective political violence. Perhaps this is due to failure to recognize that such a choice exists. If so, this essay, though it has no "result," should help. More immediate reasons are the understandable desire to be "right," which, in a messy world, is easier to achieve with messy theory than with parsimonious theory. If not tautological, our explanations of collective political violence thus far have been too close to descriptions: too close, that is, to being depictions of the concrete, in the jargon of either contingency or inherency theory. On that basis, explanation hardly can fail; but it also cannot succeed in getting to, or even near, essentials. The remedy is to regard theory as what it is: a tool of explanation, not something that models all facets of the concrete. We want deliberate one-sidedness that may fall in clean, competitive tests, not deliberate, or face-saving, eclecticism. If the choice of a theoretical approach is a choice among conceptions of the essential nature of a set of phenomena, studies that circumnavigate that issue can only defeat us— unless I totally misunderstand the powers of multivariate methods.

We *can* choose between the two most basic models of political man: peace-seeking man versus power-seeking man.[29] But in my view we cannot do it effectively by incorporating both in our initial models. If we do that, results pointing to both assuredly will turn up, both being at work—as they are also in physical motion, language, or the malfunctioning of organisms. Nor can we do it by largely arbitrary commitments. Political "theorists" have always dealt with basic branch points in one way or the other. Thus they have come to no resolution at the foundations of theory; rather, they simply have divided "members" and "challengers" into disciplinary factions, always for suspect reasons—the worst of which is not facing up thoughtfully, with open minds, to the problem of primary theoretical choice.

One way to do so would be to work along a given line to see how far it leads. All considered, I would at present choose contingency theory in the RD version—but in a much more simplified form than Gurr and his associates have used, recognizing that the goal is to construct good "theory," which is an abstract tool of understanding, not to reconstruct concrete reality in all its nuances and complexities. Once the essentials are known, the nagging complexities will (on past scientific evidence) fall into place more persuasively.

NOTES

1. Readers will find many illustrations of ambiguity in the section on evaluation, below.
2. My formulation of the problem was worked out some years ago. Recently another social scientist, Tilly (1978: 6) has stated a similar view, but in a more offhand fashion.
3. "Initial" does not literally mean at the beginning of study. As stated, one usually learns how best to begin by doing and learning. Also, only finished results can tell one definitively whether an initial choice was wise or not. "Perspectives" thus are both first and last things and usually change through work—though most people cling to initial theoretical choices as one clings to religious or political dogmas.
4. However, the essays in the first part of this *Handbook* deal with the subject.
5. No doubt this leaves loose ends: e.g., should political "violence" really be distinguished from nonviolent actions? What about violent coercion by authorities? How does one measure "extreme" collective political violence? Let us leave the ends loose. If they affect our discussion, they will be confronted when required.
6. I also do not want to get involved in methodological disputes, though many confuse methods with approaches to theory. The assumption that underlies

this view is that good positive theory may be *discovered* by induction. I am on record about this view, which I consider deeply mistaken (H. Eckstein 1975). Thus I ignore work that involves technical manipulation of data (e.g., Rummel 1963) and the "approach"—but not results—of what Hibbs (1973) calls "eclectic model specification." My essay is written precisely to cut through "eclecticism," while Hibbs makes intrinsic avoidance of theoretical commitment a virtue.

7. It can be shown that high parsimony is an absolute requisite of scientific explanation. But this is a side-issue here. For discussion of the point see H. Eckstein 1975.

8. These labels strike me as unfortunate. Surely no one means to say that actions aiming at purposes are uncaused—especially if they are rationally tactical—or that exogenous factors do not affect purposes (goals).

9. At issue, of course, is general theory, not accounts of particular cases. No one could explain a cut finger or a cold through "normal" entropy. It is distinctly likely, though, that many diseases resist understanding because we proceed from basic premises bound to be fruitless—usually those of exogenous, contingent causation.

10. The fatefulness of the question is reflected, as earlier in physics, by extreme acrimony and the extension of the argument into the realm of political morality.

11. Gurr's macro-theory was influenced mainly by the psychological theories of Berkowitz (see esp. 1962, 1969).

12. For a brief enumeration of "contingencies" that politicize what otherwise may not enter the political domain, see Gurr 1970b: 230.

13. There is internal evidence in Gurr's work that the "tactical" variables were in fact rather late concessions to the counterarguments of rational-choice theorists (see, for instance, Gurr 1970b: 210, n. 54).

14. This summary omits most of the nuances of a still evolving set of empirical and theoretical works. But I suspect that a fuller summary would serve my purpose of displaying contingency theory less well; for Gurr has not resisted the temptation to increase explanatory power (and disarm objections) by incorporating others' models, even if antithetical. I will try to show in the Conclusion, below, that the reasons for doing so are not overwhelming—logic aside.

15. Pareto could readily incorporate Tocqueville's account of how expectations rise and boil over into his theory of the circulation of elites. And Tilly would have been well-advised to trace Gurr's origins to Tocqueville.

16. I elaborate this point in H. Eckstein 1965: 146–147.

17. Huntington sometimes writes as if blockage were "normal" if modernization is rapid. However, modernization itself may be gradual and can be coped with politically. His theoretical account thus remains fundamentally contingent.

18. Other important members of the family, omitted here only because of space, are Galtung 1964 (rank-disequilibrium theory), and D. C. Schwartz 1972 (cognitive-inconsistency theory applied to revolution).

19. For learning theory of aggression, see especially Bandura (1973).

20. It is not quite clear to me whether the "masses" are a separate category, or challengers, nor does it much matter.

21. Political violence, in Tilly, may take three forms (1975: 506–507): competitive (two groups attack each others' resources), reactive (a group responds to attack), or proactive (a group attacks to obtain resources). Each of these types comes in modern (associational) and nonmodern (communal) versions; therefore, types of political violence can be distinguished historically and associated with social development—but not at all in the manner of Huntington or Johnson.

22. Tilly uses the terms "organization" and "mobilization" largely in his own way, only loosely related to more familiar ways. Readers should not assume that Tilly can be fully understood without going into terminological (and other nuances) at the source.

23. We would, of course, like to know what makes claims indigestible, but are told almost nothing about this—no doubt because the emphasis remains on process, not content.

24. One could trace the approach's ancestry farther back, to "contract theory," as does Rogowski (1974: 51ff.). Rogowski's work, incidentally, plausibly explains the basic "increased claims" within the framework of a rationalistic, or "tactical," model, and thus complements Tilly.

25. We may ignore here methodological problems of such assessments. They are familiar, and different methods probably would not make much difference to the general picture.

26. In drafting the essay, I worked out sixteen such issues. They are not equally illuminating, and, in any event, too many for the space I have been allotted. So only five are used—but one involves five separate, though related, issues.

27. The added modification lies in the possibility (but improbability) that "institutional" capacity might handle rapidly increased mobilization.

28. The use of negative sanctions should not invariably lead to escalation by dissidents: the sanctions may succeed.

29. Here, let me make a very brief proposal. To choose among theoretical approaches we need deliberately simple, antithetical models, and to test them in fair competition, in well-selected cases, and in ways precluding ambivalent results. How this might be done I have described in a separate essay (H. Eckstein 1979), which is also the design of a (potential) project. It happens that the issue of that essay is support for regimes—"legitimacy." But that is simply the obverse of dissidence. It also happens that the essay constructs a clean (and, I think, compelling) contingency model and, as its antithesis, a clean (also compelling) inherency model; it also tries to show how to go about resolving the theoretical antithesis by "strong" tests. If the work is done (which is at present contingent) the choice at the branch point discussed here will follow from it—for Tilly is right: a theory of violent politics must also, *mutatis mutandis*, be a theory of peaceful politics. (The proposal may smack of self-advertisement but should need no apology, for the essay cited resulted from reflections on my own failures.)

CHAPTER 5

Macro-Comparative Research on Political Protest

Ekkart Zimmermann

POLITICAL PROTEST IS DEFINED HERE as consisting of relatively shortlived, mostly (but not exclusively) violent activities by or on behalf of a group of people "against a regime, government, or one or more of its leaders; or against its ideology, policy, intended policy, or lack of policy; or against its previous action or intended action" (Taylor and Hudson 1972: 66). Protest becomes political: (1) through the targets chosen for demonstration, e.g., national or local policies, national or local officials, public buildings; and/or (2) through the reaction of the targets or of persons responsible for their protection; and/or (3) through the reaction of the public at large. The higher the number of protesters and the more radical their demands, the more likely protest is to trigger political reactions by state authorities and demands for political action by the public at large, expressed through political parties and mass media.

A very small number of people pursuing extremely radical goals may also be treated as political demonstrators, as in the case of some contemporary political terrorists in many western countries. These terrorists often make skillful use of the mass media to advertise their acts as "political" in nature. Small in number, they pretend to speak for larger "oppressed" segments of the population. A large gathering of people, on the other hand, demanding change from a private factor, e.g., a corporation, may be considered a nonpolitical phenomenon. Obviously, it is a delicate question

NOTE: I am grateful to Ted Robert Gurr for his detailed critiques of earlier versions of this chapter.

167

where to draw a boundary between nonpolitical and political protest. *Ceteris paribus*, the greater the involvement of the state, its institutions, and its actors in a society, the greater the tendency for protests in that society to become political. The use of violence on behalf of protesters also increases the probability that their action will be judged as political protest, simply because legal norms of behavior and the state monopoly of violence (Weber 1964b: 1043) are violated.

Conversely, state authorities often step in early to prevent or dispel peaceful protests. Sometimes they do this by making erratic use of their own coercive powers, thus increasing anger among protesters and eventually turning a peaceful demonstration through their own nonneutral intervention into a violent political conflict. Two general possibilities have to be distinguished here: (1) the objects originally attacked are nonpolitical ones as defined above, or (2) they are of a political nature, but the protest is (intended to be) carried out in a peaceful manner.

Many protests (e.g., demonstrations, political strikes) are nonviolent unless authorities intervene in a coercive way that elicits resistance. In other instances, violence is purposively initiated on behalf of the protesters. Thus violence may be used by neither, one, or both parties to protest: it may be used in a proactive or reactive way (see D. Snyder 1976 for this distinction with respect to governmental coercion only). Various sequences of action and reaction are possible. At present, our empirical knowledge as to the types and frequencies of escalating and de-escalating *processes* in political protest is rather limited because of the strategies of data aggregation that have prevailed in cross-national studies (see below). Data collectors such as Gurr (see Gurr et al. 1978), Feierabend and Feierabend (1966), and Taylor and Hudson (1972) have included episodes of violent and nonviolent protest in their data, even though theoretically Gurr as well as Feierabend and Feierabend seem to be more interested in the patterns and causes of violent political protest. In this chapter I also focus on violent political protests, but include instances of nonviolent protests, too. Insofar as violence is a more radical means of exerting political influence, it might be that we are concerned with the more intense forms of political protests.

Protest as used here comprises such events or chains of events as political demonstrations, antigovernment riots, political strikes (often called general strikes), and political clashes. Of course, these terms originated as journalistic labels, but they have been given more precise scholarly definitions (Rummel 1963, Gurr et al. 1978, and others). Some more general terms for protest used in journalistic accounts are "disturbances," "disorders," and "mob action." Academic usage favors more precisely defined general concepts such as "hostile outbursts" (Smelser 1963), "collective action" (Tilly 1978), and "turmoil" (Gurr 1970b). The last concept is used more or less interchangeably with "protest" in cross-national research. Turmoil is generally defined as "relatively spontaneous, partially organized or unorganized strife with substantial popular participation and limited objectives" (Graham and Gurr 1969: 799). The emphasis here, however, is on *political* protest, that is, that turmoil which either is focused explicitly on the political system or becomes political through the reaction of the authorities and the public at large.

Protests are characterized foremost by their relatively low degree of organization, if compared to more intense forms of political dissent such as internal wars, guerrilla warfare, or armed attacks. Even coups as one form of conspiracy, just like other clandestine activities, have to be planned and carried out carefully if they are to be successful. However, protests are not always totally disorganized, contrary to what is suggested in the following definition of riots: "events involving relatively spontaneous, shortlived but violent activity, in which the generalized aims of the insurgents or the objects of their aggression are not coherently specified" (Morrison and Stevenson 1971: 350). Protests totally lacking in organization and pursuing aims "not coherently specified" represent only one extreme. Since protest activities entail costs on the part of participants, cost-benefit calculations usually play a role, and this, at least for the core group of protesters, means organization, even if in rudimentary form. As any experienced union member will confirm, protests in contemporary societies are more likely to be successful when they are well-controlled, when realistic (modest) goals are pursued, and when little use is made of violence. This does not mean, however, that violent protests are of themselves less successful than nonviolent protests (see Gamson 1975).

Protest events in themselves seldom last more than a day. This does not preclude the possibility of protest campaigns, a series of relatively short demonstrations over a single issue. Thus, if one compares political protest to rebellion, it may be characterized by its short duration, low degree of organization, and limited goals. "*Protest* arises from conflict over limited issues, such as opposition to particular policies or personnel of a government, or antagonisms between groups competing for political influence. *Rebellion* centers on more fundamental issues, especially struggles over who shall govern and by what means" (Gurr 1979: 50). Whereas the labels applied vary between protest or turmoil on the one side, and rebellion and internal war (Hibbs 1973) on the other, the types of conflict subsumed under the first category consistently tap less far-reaching political issues in a polity than those in the second category. In the latter instance more fundamental issues are at stake, issues that quite likely meet strong resistance and therefore require dissidents to build up organizational resources if their goals are to be achieved.

Much of political scientists' empirical research on protest has focused on the cross-national patterns of political protest, on their distribution across time and place. Factor-analysts such as Rummel (1963), Tanter (1966), and Banks (1972) have dealt with the question whether conflict events cluster in certain patterns. Some of Gurr's work (e.g., Gurr 1969; 1979) deals with patterns of political conflict in various categories of nation–states. Other studies (Gurr 1968a; 1968b; 1972a; Gurr and Duvall 1973; and Gurr and Lichbach 1979; Hibbs 1973) analyze the conditions that influence the magnitudes of protest at the national level. Others have traced historical changes in the forms of political protest, notably the sociologist and social historian Charles Tilly (e.g., Tilly, Tilly, and Tilly 1975). He and other researchers have also looked at the kinds of people and groups participating in political protests. Studies of preindustrial crowds, of American blacks, and of students provide the most notable examples of contemporary scholarly work on this topic. Another emerging area of concern is the history of groups involved in conflict. Instead of asking "Why and how men rebel," as is done in the above studies, the question is "What happens when men rebel?" What are the outcomes of violent conflict? Does it pay for protesting groups to use violence in political confrontations? Few studies have been accomplished in this field of research (see Gamson 1975 and Zelditch 1978 for a critique, and chapter 6 in this *Handbook* for a review).

Subsequent sections of this chapter report empirical evidence and theorizing bearing mainly on cross-national patterns and group participation. Many of the differences among theoretical approaches, findings, and points of criticisms found in the literature are due to these different foci of research. These, in turn, require somewhat different strategies of data collection and analysis (e.g., time series data within a few countries, as in case of Tilly's studies, versus cross-national aggregated data-sets in case of Gurr's "world patterns" approach). Thus criticism raised against either approach should be seen in proper perspective. The approaches are complementary rather than mutually contradictory. Theoretically, for example, Tilly's attacks (1971; 1975a) on Gurr's relative deprivation approach (Gurr 1970b) seem to be overdrawn, since Gurr (1970b: chapters 8 and 9) deals with many of the variables supposedly neglected. Moreover, Tilly's solidarity-resource mobilization approach, with its emphasis on group dynamics, can be combined with Gurr's emphasis on discontent and beliefs, as antecedent conditions in an account of violent political conflict more powerful than either approach offers separately.

The focus of this survey is national patterns of political protest. We are concerned with: (1) variations in the forms and magnitudes of political protest among countries and across time; and (2) with theoretical explanations for these variations. The unit of analysis ordinarily is the nation–state. These analyses use measures of conflict aggregated at the national level, usually covering several years of observation.

PATTERNS OF PROTEST: SOME DESCRIPTIVE EVIDENCE

One of the first questions addressed by cross-national studies was whether there are common dimensions to conflict behavior, whether some kinds of events tend to occur together, but independently of other kinds of events. A number of factor-analytic studies have addressed this question, using such measures as countries' numbers of assassinations, general strikes, guerrilla wars, major government crises, purges, riots, "revolutions," demonstrations, mutinies, coups, acts of terrorism and sabotage, conflict deaths, and so forth (Rummel 1963, 1966; Tanter 1965, 1966; Feierabend, Feierabend, and Litell 1966; Bwy 1968b; Hibbs 1973; Hazlewood 1973a; Gurr and Bishop 1976; Jackman and Boyd 1979). The results tend to support Rummel's finding, reported in 1963,

> in the sense that three-factor solutions delineating "turmoil," "revolutionary" and "subversive" dimensions are possible at varying points of time after World War I, but the precise structure of the latter two dimensions tends to vary through time, while Tanter's two-fold distinction between "turmoil" and "internal warfare" dimensions remains relatively invariate throughout the contemporary era. [Banks 1972: 50]

There is, of course, some variation in the findings (see Zimmermann 1976 for a review), especially in the African context (Collins 1973; Morrison and Stevenson 1971). But most differences deal with whether internal conflict can be reduced to two rather than three dimensions. The events we call protests almost invariably load highly on a single factor, independently of measures of coups, conflict deaths, armed attacks, and so forth. The latter events sometimes load highly on a single "internal war" factor, while other studies find them distributed among several different factors. Thus, independently of periods of observations, of conflict indicators, and of methods of factor extraction used, the measures that represent the less organized, more limited forms of (violent) political conflict cluster together even more closely than do the indicators of more intense forms. Researchers thus seem justified on empirical grounds to analyze political protest as a distinct type of violent political conflict.[1]

Political protest, characterized as a set of covarying conflict events, has served as explanandum in more than a dozen cross-national studies. Before these analyses are taken up, however, more descriptive information on the patterns and magnitudes of protest is needed. Gurr has made one of the most recent and comprehensive collections of data on manifest political conflict. It includes eighty-seven nations and dependencies between 1961–1970.[2] Manifest political conflict is defined as "collective confrontations and attacks between at least 100 actors contending over political structures, incumbents, or policies" (Gurr et al. forthcoming, Gurr et al. 1978). Two conflict dimensions are distinguished: *protest* and *rebellion* (see Gurr's definitions, above). The protest and rebellion variables are not constructed on the basis of a factor analysis, but rather on theoretical grounds that are consistent with empirical evidence. Hibbs (1973) treats military coups as a separate (dependent) variable in his analysis of mass political violence since it involves elite actions. According to Gurr's findings (1974: 64–66), however, participation of renegade members of the political elites is prevalent in most forms of rebellion, not just in cases of military coups.

Gurr strongly advocates the use of measures of conflict that go beyond event counts (as reported by Rummel 1963; Taylor and Hudson 1972, and others) to take into account the properties of events. From measures of the properties of events it often is possible to derive aggregated measures of the properties of conflict for a country as a whole. Gurr uses data on man-days of participation and deaths in conflict events in this way:

> The *extent* of MCP [manifest political conflict] is measured by summing the man-days of participation in all reported conflict events for a country. Each event's man-days are estimated by multiplying the reported number of nongovernmental participants by the event's duration in days. . . . The *intensity* of MPC is measured by summing the deaths reported in all conflict events for a country. . . . Both man-days and deaths are weighted by the country's population: man-days per 100,000 population, deaths per 10 million. . . . The man-days and deaths measures are combined, with each given equal weight, into a total MPC score. [Gurr and Duvall 1973: 142–143]

In some of Gurr's analyses these properties are estimated separately for protest and for rebellion events. Event counts, in contrast to the measurement of properties, may be unreliable due to underreporting in sources and the fact that "events" frequently are waves of associated events. Gurr characterizes his approach as "molecular, based on the conflict behavior of groups, while that of event-counters is atomistic and based on one-day-at-a-time tabulation of specific actions" (Gurr et al. forthcoming). On the other hand, there is an inflationary bias if one uses man-days instead of mere event counts as the basic operational unit, as "only some people participate in an act of protest or rebellion from beginning to end" (Gurr et al. forthcoming). In general, aggregate measures of the extent and intensity of political conflict "should be accurate enough to map the general contours of conflict in a country, and to distinguish among the general properties of conflict from one country to another" (Gurr et al. 1978: 4). Errors due to nonreporting or underreporting in the sources should tend to offset one another through the aggregation process.

Gurr's analysis of 1,525 episodes of protest in the 1960s shows that their component events seldom lasted more than a day and rarely resulted in fatalities. (Note that "episodes" include waves of linked events in which the same group and issue were involved.) Peaceful demonstrations and riots were about equally common; an estimated 3,400 people died in the 627 episodes of rioting. Political strikes numbered 107 and usually mobilized more dissidents than any other form of protest or rebellion, but they seldom were violent. (These and the following generalizations are from Gurr 1979 and Gurr et al. forthcoming, Part II.)

The most instructive results come from comparison of the properties of these protest episodes in different groups of countries. The type of political system sharply affects protest, for example. Gurr distinguishes elitist countries (31 unstable, Third-World regimes) from democracies (N = 37, in all world regions) and autocracies (N = 19, including communist countries), based on an earlier study by Banks and Gregg (1965). Conflict in the typical elitist country in the 1960s was 25 times more extensive (in terms of man-days of participation, weighted by population) than in the typical democracy, and 40 times as intense (in terms of proportional deaths) as in the typical autocracy (Gurr 1979: table 2.5; these and subsequent comparisons are based on the median values within each group of countries). The democracies were distinctive in having more extensive but less deadly protest than the autocracies. Comparisons based on levels of economic development showed that rebellion was far less extensive and less intensive in the most developed countries than in others, whereas differences in protest were much less: the most developed countries (and the democracies) had proportionally almost as many man-days of protest per 100,000 population as the least developed countries.

Other comparisons focus on the kinds of classes and groups involved in protest and the apparent motives of protestors. With respect to class participation,[3] Gurr reports that middle-class groups, including students, reportedly took part in 77 percent of all episodes of protest (59 percent if students are not counted as middle-class), compared with working-class participation in 60 percent of them. Dissident members of the governing classes played a role in only 6 percent of all protest (usually as participants in general strikes) but reportedly were involved in 49 percent of all rebellions. These are among the general conclusions Gurr draws from these and other data on class participation in conflict:

> Protest in the contemporary world is not solely or primarily a lower-class phenomenon. Public protest cuts across class lines to mobilize discontented people whatever their social status. [Gurr 1979: 64]

> Since it is the presence of . . . renegade members of the political elite, officialdom, and security forces that makes the difference between protest and rebellion, they might be more truly said to be the "dangerous classes" of the 1960's. The lower and middle classes acting alone seem much more disposed to protest over limited issues. [Gurr et al. forthcoming]

Other comparisons were made of the proportions of man-days of protest that were mobilized by different kinds of groups. In the most developed countries, for example, associational groups (economic and open political organizations)

> mobilized just over 50 percent of all political dissidence compared with only 30 percent in the least-developed countries. Dissidence in the least-developed countries was relatively more likely to originate with communal and clandestine groups, and more likely than in any other group of countries to show up within the government itself. The one anomalous result is that communal and territorial groups were a significant source of dissidence in the wealthiest countries. This reflects the activities of communal and regional dissidents throughout Western Europe and North America in the 1960s, including minority groups in the United States, the Quebecois in Canada, Catholics in Northern Ireland, Scottish and Welsh nationalists in Britain, the German-speaking people of Northern Italy, Bretons in France, and even advocates of autonomy for Switzerland's Jura region. [Gurr 1979: 68]

With respect to motives of political protesters, the following quotation sums up some of the main findings:

> In democratic countries, dissidents very rarely had revolutionary objectives; reformist demands were ten times more common. Autocratic governments faced proportionally three times as much revolutionary opposition, but were less likely to hear reformist demands than the democratic governments. Even so, the rulers of authoritarian countries confronted far less revolutionary opposition than the rulers of the elitist countries, where revolutionary objectives accounted for almost as much dissident activity (32 percent) as reformist ones (38 percent). . . . The less developed a country, the more likely was conflict waged over the revolutionary issues of who should rule and how, and the less likely it was to be limited to questions of policies and personnel. [Gurr 1979: 69]

Concerning the fatalities incurred in civil conflict, there is one outstanding result, namely that dissidents suffered on the average about 70 percent of all reported deaths in domestic political conflict (based on data from fifty countries during 1966–1970). Somewhat lower figures were characteristic of democratic (59 percent) and highly developed countries (61 percent). This tilt against dissidents is confirmed in Tilly's longitudinal analyses of conflicts in four countries during the nineteenth and twentieth centuries. When deaths occurred during acts of political violence, they were mostly due to activities of state agents:

> Because a number of events we have studied in Germany, Italy, and France would not have been violent if troops and police had not attacked, it is likely that some of the apparent differences between Great Britain and other countries results from greater British constraints on military and police violence. [Tilly, Tilly, and Tilly 1975: 280]

"World around, rebellion in the 1960s was more than one hundred times deadlier than protest, though in the most-developed and European nations protest was deadlier than rebellion simply because there was proportionally so much more of it" (Gurr et al. forthcoming). Finally,

> conflict was distinctly more brutal and one-sided in autocratic regimes, where dissidents made up 85 percent of the fatalities, than in the democratic regimes. There was a similar disparity between the highly-developed countries and the moderately developed ones. Since the armies and police forces of all these groups of countries are relatively large and well-equipped, the differences are almost surely attributable to policies of restraint on the part of the authorities of the developed democracies—restraint that has its counterpart in the preference of dissidents in these countries for protest over rebellion. [Gurr et al. forthcoming]

As we turn to theoretical explanations of political protest, many results bearing on these observations will be referred to. It should be pointed out that only some of the descriptive materials cited above have been used so far in causal analyses (see Gurr and Duvall 1973, Gurr and Lichbach forthcoming, Gurr et al. forthcoming). In the meantime the data are available through the Inter-University Consortium for Political and Social Research (see Gurr et al. 1978), so that researchers may carry out their own analyses of the patterns and determinants of various forms of violent political conflict.

EXPLAINING PROTEST ON A MACRO-POLITICAL CROSS-NATIONAL BASIS

In subsequent paragraphs a number of explanatory variables will be traced briefly through the literature (see Zimmermann 1980 for a more extensive discussion dealing also with explanations of rebellion/internal war). Since some of these variables are also incorporated into more complex theoretical approaches to the explanation of protest, at times some critical remarks concerning these "paradigmatic" works will be inserted into the discussion. In general, however, analytical and empirical criteria serve as a guideline in our discussion not as *in toto* evaluations of specific approaches. Also it should be noted that summary measures of all violent political conflict are used in some of the studies cited, rendering impossible direct comparisons with studies that focus on protest alone. Moreover, protest and rebellion (the latter being the more intense form of manifest political conflict) sometimes are joint explananda in cross-national analyses of political conflict. Consequently, the discussion will also occasionally bear on the phenomenon of rebellion and explanations thereof.

SOCIOECONOMIC DEVELOPMENT

If dissident political action is to be explained at the level of the polity, socioeconomic development ranks as a key theoretical variable. There are, however, a number of results that partly contradict each other and render simple predictions derived from modernization theories incorrect or insufficient. Most researchers treat socioeconomic development (and change) as a whole and do not separate its social and economic aspects, as they often are interrelated and therefore difficult to disentangle. For theoretical reasons (Huntington 1968), however, one should distinguish the two aspects, as one does in separating socioeconomic development (or change) from political development (or change; discussed below). There are at least three competing general hypotheses about the impact of socioeconomic development on political protest.

1. The most widespread hypothesis states that there is a negative linear relationship between economic development and political violence. One easily could cite a long list of authors—Aristotle being one of the first—who relate socioeconomic development to political stability (Lipset 1959, Cutright 1963, McCrone and Cnudde 1967, Neubauer 1967, Pride 1970, Flanigan and Fogelman 1971, Cnudde 1972). There is also considerable empirical evidence across various samples, periods, and indicators that "modern" nations tend to have less political violence than underdeveloped countries. Various findings corroborate the hypothesis of a negative relationship between socioeconomic development and political violence:

Source	Number of Nations	Period
Banks 1972: 48–49	51	1922–1963
Tanter 1965: 175	70	1955–1960
Terrell 1971: 337	68	
Parvin 1973	26	
Feierabend, Feierabend, and Nesvold 1969: 684–685	68	1948–1965
Von der Mehden 1973	40	1960–1965
Alker and Russett 1964: 272, 288, 307	74	

Studying political and economic development in sixty-five nations from 1800 to 1960, Flanigan and Fogelman (1970) group their countries into four types according to the level of development and the periodization of the developmental process and report the following result:

Countries which began their development relatively early and have reached high levels of development by the mid-twentieth century are less likely to experience domestic violence than those which have been developing only in the current century; and both groups of countries experience less violence than countries which began to develop only recently. [Flanigan and Fogelman 1970: 14]

2. One alternative hypothesis predicts a curvilinear relationship between socioeconomic development and political violence, with political violence reaching its maximum during mid-levels of economic development. "It is at this middle stage that awareness of modernity and exposure to modern patterns should be complete, that is, at a theoretical ceiling, whereas achievement levels would still be lagging far behind" (Feierabend and Feierabend 1966: 257). Using a sample of 130 countries, Adams (1970) reports a curvilinear relationship (see also Alker and Russett 1964: 307) between GNP per capita in the early 1960s and the extent of political violence during 1946–1965. On a close examination of the seventy-one least developed countries, a negative linear relationship is found when the Asian and Arabian countries ("poor but relatively deprived") are analyzed together with the developed countries, and a positive relationship in mostly African countries ("poor and unaware," as quoted from Gurr 1972b: 37–38). As the "traditional" end of the modernity continuum is often insufficiently defined in these studies, some of these results may be artifacts. Testing for various possible relationships between socioeconomic development and political violence in his study of 108 nations during 1948–1967, Hibbs (1973: 28) found some evidence for a weak curvilinear relationship (see also Gurr and Ruttenberg 1967: 66–68; N = 119 nations, period: 1961–1963). In a multivariate analysis, however, socioeconomic development (GNP per capita) loses its explanatory power, as it contributes only indirectly to a reduction of the amount of political violence (see Figure 5-2 below). In other respects, it increases the amount of political violence: Communist Party membership is larger in more developed nations, and it in turn correlates directly with the amount of collective protest.

3. Political protest, as distinct from rebellion, does *not* tend to level off as a polity becomes economically more developed. Since the economically most developed countries are democracies and since political protest is tolerated in democracies, economic development might have a positive net impact on the man-days of political protest in spite of the inhibiting conditions of economic development.[4]

If there is one basic finding, it is that economically developed countries in general experience less intense forms of political violence:

> GNP per capita in the early 1960's correlates − .55 with conflict deaths per 10 million in 1961–1965, showing that the wealthier a nation, the less intense conflict is likely to be. Per capita GNP has a weaker − .42 correlation with man-days of conflict, which is consistent with our observation that wealth helps transform civil conflict—by making it less deadly—but is not so likely to reduce its extent. [Gurr 1979: 62]

The relationship between being a poorer nation and having more intense political violence does not, of course, imply that it is the poorest groups (with Marx, the *Lumpenproletariat*) in these countries that resort to political violence. Within poorer nations acts of political violence may very well occur in the more "prosperous" regions (for some evidence, see Huntington 1968: 44 ff.). One must avoid the danger of group fallacy (on the national, regional, or other levels) so easily subscribed to in interpretations of cross-national research.

SOCIOECONOMIC CHANGE

Causal analysis implies more than merely static analysis; it calls for analysis of change in variables, too. Relating the level of socioeconomic development to political protest without taking rates of socioeconomic change into consideration is as likely to lead to erroneous conclusions as dealing with measures of change without taking into consideration the socioeconomic level at which these changes take place. Conflict researchers have not always followed these rules so that some results reported in the literature remain ambiguous at least.

The theoretical argument here has been forcefully put by Huntington:

> In fact, *modernity breeds stability*, but *modernization breeds instability*. It is not the absence of modernity but the efforts to achieve it which produce political disorder. If poor countries appear to be unstable, it is not because they are poor, but because they are trying to become rich. [Huntington 1968: 41; italics added; cf. also Alker and Russett 1964: 307]

Huntington claims that the relationship between poverty and instability (on the national level) is one that leads to spurious inferences (Huntington 1968: 39–59). The level of socioeconomic development as well as the degree of political institutionalization have to be controlled if valid conclusions about the impact of socioeconomic change are to be drawn.

In the literature either summary measures of socioeconomic change or very specific features of socioeconomic change have been related to the respective dependent variables.

1. Olson (1963) proposes the hypothesis that rapid economic change leads to "social dislocation," which in turn is said to create alienation and a susceptibility to political radicalism among large portions of the population (see Kornhauser 1959; for a critique, see Gusfield 1962 and Pinard 1968). Yet, a number of—not necessarily representative—studies bearing on the effects of migration and urbanization (and thus indirectly on alienation theory) lead Nelson to this contrary conclusion:

> The assumptions that migrants are uprooted and isolated in the city are grossly overdrawn. The assumption that most are disappointed and frustrated by economic conditions is simply wrong. Some migrants undoubtedly are disillusioned, but lack of widespread contacts plus political inexperience and traditional patterns of deference makes it most unlikely that newcomers' frustrations will be translated into destabilizing political action. [Nelson 1970: 399; see also Nelson 1976 for a multifold picture drawing on examples from many developed countries; Cornelius 1969, 1974; finally see Weiner 1967, Oberschall 1969]

In the context of rapid urbanization two causal processes are said to be at work (see also Tilly 1973a: 103), each of which may increase the likelihood of conflict: (1) the new environment can mean austerity for the newly arrived, calling for increased discipline, which may breed discontent; (2) through contacts with the mass media and more modern social groups, the new environment creates higher levels of aspiration than can be realized. At least the first hypothesis cannot be supported with the data currently available. The "revolver approach" (White 1973: 49, following Pye) rather has to be replaced by the notion of the "supportive migrant" who is more interested in finding out about his new environment and adjusting to it than he is willing or able to command the resources necessary to carry out political protest. Also, for the first-generation migrant *actual* personal living standards in the city may be higher than in the countryside.

2. If political violence is to occur in mobilized segments of the population, it may be expected from the second (or later) generation(s) of migrants (see the analysis in Huntington 1968: 278–283) who have been "mobilized" but remain—in the terminology of Deutsch (1966)—"differentiated." There is more evidence for the latter argument (but see also Nelson 1969: 35–44 and Cornelius 1971: 107–108 for some counterevidence) than for the more popular and stereotypic urbanization → alienation → radicalization hypothesis. But even the second-generation hypothesis might prove to be a gross simplification of reality. "In those countries where urban participation rates are higher, the apparent direct relationship is spurious, a result of differences in education and occupation. When these factors are held constant, locality, size and length of urban residence appear to have no significant independent effect on political participation" (Huntington and Nelson 1976: 47, drawing on results of a six-nation study by Inkeles).

Any kind of monocausal approach leads to questionable interpretations of socioeconomic and political modernization processes. A number of empirical results refute the idea that rapid socioeconomic change leads directly to political violence or political instability. For more prosperous Latin American countries Bwy (1968b; for critiques see Snow 1968 and West 1973: 73 ff.) reports a negative relationship between the rate of economic growth and his two dependent variables, organized and anomic violence. In countries on a lower level of economic development, however, this relationship is reversed. Flanigan and Fogelman (1970) find a negative relationship between rate of economic development ("rates of change in agricultural employment in the twentieth century") and political violence as do Alker and Russett (1964: 321, N = 33 countries). Feierabend, Feierabend and Nesvold (1969), however, report a linear relation (r = .67) between their rate of modernization measure and political instability, with the notable exception of national income. Hibbs (1973) found a weak negative relationship between rate of economic change (change in energy consumption per capita, 1955–1965) and political violence, but only in the case of collective protest (this relationship also holds in Hibbs's multivariate analysis).

When using rate of change of urbanization ("% change in population in cities of 20,000 or more residents per 1,000 population 1955–1960") as the independent variable, contrary to much speculation no "significant" relationships emerge in Hibbs's study (1973; N = 58 countries). Gurr et al. (forthcoming; N = 84 countries) report a weak negative relationship between new city dwellers (1950–1960) and political violence (1961–1965) in all its forms, except for the Euromodern countries. Nevertheless, there may be some truth in the proposed relationship between (rapid) urbanization and political violence: in some cities, especially those with relatively fewer resources, there may be a positive effect on political violence, whereas in more affluent cities there may be no relationship or even a negative one, due to the integrative power of these cities.

Altogether, there is no consistent positive or negative relationship between rapid urbanization and political violence at either the national or the group level. Tilly, who studied the relationship between urbanization processes and political violence in nineteenth-century France also provides evidence against the urbanization → alienation → radicalization hypothesis. "There is, if anything, a negative correlation over time and space between the pace of urban growth and the intensity of collective violence" (Tilly 1969: 33; see also Tilly, Tilly, and Tilly 1975). Ambiguous or at least inconsistent results must also be reported as we turn to the evaluation of other specific hypotheses bearing on the theoretical relationship between socioeconomic change and political protest.

3. Gurr et al. (forthcoming) found significant positive relationships between the growth of the total population (and the growth rate of the urban population; both for 1950–1960) and his dependent variables, man-days of participation and magnitude of protest (1961–1965; N = 84). When geocultural area is controlled, however, somewhat inconsistent patterns emerge. In Hibbs's study (1973), population growth (average annual percentage change in population, 1955–1965) also proves to be a positive and significant determinant of both collective protest and internal war. In Hibbs's final model specifications, however, population growth loses its explanatory power. Welch and Booth studied the relationship of spatial density to two forms of political violence (using Gurr's data for 1961–1963, N = 65 countries; see Gurr with Ruttenberg 1967) and report that "this variable is strongly related to both incidence and intensity of political violence" (Welch and Booth 1974: 155). Data at the individual level will, of course, have to be collected, especially as to how (objective) spatial density is socially reacted to, before any definite judgment about the impact of this variable can be made.

4. Another hypothesis about the effects of rapid socioeconomic change links increases in mass media exposure and education with instability.

Some authors, however, find a negative relationship between educational opportunities and political violence (see Gurr 1968a: 1110, and Gurr with Ruttenberg 1967: 76, whose empirical findings contradict their original assumption, 1967: 58). Interestingly, the same indicators are used by different researchers to index contrary theoretical notions.

We shall deal with the (alleged) effects of increased exposure to mass media first. It has often been stated that modernization starts with new communication processes. As Huntington puts it: "Urbanization, increases in literacy, education, and media exposure all give rise to enhanced aspirations and expectations which, if unsatisfied, galvanize individuals and groups into politics" (Huntington 1968: 47). The empirical evidence as to the effects of mass media exposure, however, is inconclusive. Parvin (1973) reports a positive relationship between the number of radios per capita and political violence (N = 26 countries). Taylor (1969; N = 117 countries), on the other hand, found no relationships (with European countries being the exception) between level and rate of communications development (newspaper circulation and radios per 1,000 population, 1960; rates of change 1960–1965, respectively) and the dependent variables turmoil, internal war (data from Taylor and Hudson 1972, 1958–1965), and political instability (defined in terms of changes in government). When the European countries are analyzed separately, the *level* of communication development is negatively related to conflict ($\gamma = -.40$) while the *rate of change* is positively related ($\gamma = .35$). Gurr et al. (forthcoming) report negative or negligible relationships between expansion of the mass media (increases in radio audience and in daily newspaper circulation, both for 1953–1963 and weighted for population) and measures of political violence in 1961–1965.

There is, of course, an important alternative to the hypothesis that increased media coverage leads to rising expectations. The rival hypothesis predicts that retreat rather than protest is the more likely reaction to the new stimulus of mass media. "Through the media the masses can retreat into fantasy or a more successful vicarious existence. Rather than being stimulated and then frustrated by the media, the masses are seen to be lethargized and then diverted from more constructive activities" (Frey 1973: 387). As of now, cross-national evidence bearing on this rival hypothesis does not seem to be available.

5. The underlying hypothesis as to the effects of increases in education can be stated as follows:

> The expansion in the educational system and the comparatively limited growth in the economy and in the occupational structure [lead to] a vast and nearly uncontrollable increase in the number of unemployed and underemployed school leavers, whose political orientation toward the polity is marked by disaffection and alienation and whose behavioral disposition is basically anomic. [Coleman 1965: 29]

In the study of Gurr et al. (forthcoming) there is evidence of a significant global relationship between the expansion in primary school enrollment ratios from the 1930s to 1960, and expansion in the proportion of males between five and nineteen in primary and secondary schools, 1950–1960, and the magnitude of rebellion in the 1960s. The relationships with man-days of participation and magnitude of protest are weaker. For Latin American as well as African countries Morrison and Stevenson (1974) also report several positive relationships between educational facilities and various indicators of political violence. Other evidence, however, drawing on a more complex theoretical explanation (Sofranko and Bealer 1972) is negative. Further cross-national studies on the relationship between increases in education and political protest should take into consideration the context in which educational changes are taking place. Increases in education that occur in an expanding economy offering opportunities of social and geographical mobility have to be distinguished from those changes taking place in "narrowing" markets, especially for academic title-holders.

6. So far we have implicitly assumed positive socioeconomic change, at least at the polity level (not necessarily at the group level). Hypotheses on the impact of socioeconomic change, however, may also refer to declines in the rates of economic growth or, more important, to absolute declines. Marxist crisis theory has provided the most often quoted explanation in this context. Yet, a positive relationship between socioeconomic decline and political protest may hold for reasons other than stated in Marxist theorizing about the decay of late capitalism (e.g., social-psychological mechanisms of relative deprivation; see Grofman and Muller 1973). Cross-national evidence (Gurr and Duvall 1973) seems to show that there is a positive relationship between measures of short-term economic decline and political violence. Hibbs (1973), however, found no indication for this contention. In the case of strikes he also reports results inconsistent with the hypothesis under review: as the labor market tightens and the percentage of the civilian unemployed increases, there is a deterent effect on the volume of strikes (Hibbs 1976, 1978: 157; Tilly 1978: 166). On the other hand, industrial conflict "responds to movements in real wages" (Hibbs 1976: 1057; N = 10 advanced industrial societies between 1950 and 1969) which is, however, not identical in explanatory terms with economic decline. Hibbs favors an explanation by mechanisms of " 'memory' persisting several periods back through time, in the sense that a change in real wages affects strike activity over a number of subsequent years" (Hibbs 1976: 1057). Furthermore, only effects on *political* strikes would be of relevance to political protest, and they are not separately analyzed in cross-national aggregate analyses of strikes.

In general it seems that rapid socioeconomic change cannot be considered to be an important direct determinant of political violence. Neither the rate of economic growth nor that of economic decline are consistent predictors of the dependent variables. This summary is contrary to much that has been written about the impact of these variables. Perhaps some of the puzzles created by these inconsistent results will be solved if socioeconomic level is controlled for when relating socioeconomic change to political violence or political protest. The hypothesis is that there are negative relationships between socioeconomic changes and political violence in more developed countries and positive relationships in less developed countries.

The diverse impacts of socioeconomic change also need to be differentiated. Rarely is any one kind of change uniform in its effects. Socioeconomic change may be seen as beneficial by some societal groups while other groups who also stand to benefit from it may nonetheless see it as detrimental to them. And it may unambiguously weaken the position of some groups, which thus react to change in a hostile way. Due to the aggregation process used in the cross-national macro-political studies on political protest, these differential effects are lost. Moreover the differential effects probably vary according to countries' level of modernization. Socioeconomic change seems to be more often opposed in countries in the midst of the modernization process than in the most developed societies. Moreover, the latter tend to be better able to compensate groups that suffer negative effects of socioeconomic change.

It also is important to examine the differential impact of socioeconomic change on distinctive ethno-cultural or ethno-religious groups. Such groups often are the object of political and economic discrimination. If negatively affected by change, they may protest or rebel with an intensity that is due only partly to change itself.

If Huntington's thesis quoted at the beginning of this section is to be rigorously tested, longitudinal analyses instead of comparisons of different cross-sections also are needed. It must be determined whether political violence or political protest fades away as specific societies become modern, instead of comparing the political protest scores of more developed polities with those of less developed ones.

In sum, under *some conditions* socioeconomic change might lead to an increase in political protest, for instance, if it leads to the dislocation of social groups that are strong enough in their cultural and/or religious and/or ethnic identity to sustain prolonged resistance. Thus one should look for data on the history of specific protesting groups. Researchers should concentrate on the intervening conditions (some of which will be considered below) between these independent variables and phenomena of political violence. In other circumstances socioeconomic change has beneficial effects that outweigh its destabilizing effects. Cross-national analyses that blur these and other distinctions and substitute cross-sectional data analysis for longitudinal study simply are beside the point.

POLITICAL DEVELOPMENT

The "fads and foibles," to use Sorokin's words, in research on political development have much in common with those in modernization research in general. Thus the criticisms made of modernization research also bear on studies of political development (see Zimmermann 1980 for references). Of importance in the present context is the distinction between democratic political order and nondemocratic political order, and the impact of these forms of political authority on political protest or rebellion, respectively.

1. Democratic political conditions do not guarantee the absence of political protest (see the findings in Gurr 1979 and the discussion *supra*) partly because dissidents can use civil liberties (which are absent in totalitarian and most autocratic systems) to build up their organizations and to carry out their activities. These protest-enhancing conditions notwithstanding, there are eight democracies (in declining order: Netherlands, Costa Rica, New Zealand, Denmark, Switzerland, Taiwan, Finland, and Malagasy) and four totalitarian systems (Bulgaria, Hungary, East Germany, and Rumania) among the twelve countries with the least extent of political protest (man-days of participation) during the 1960s (Gurr et al. forthcoming).

2. Democracies may not discourage political protest, but they are successful in eliminating or strongly reducing the probability of rebellion. Hibbs (1973; N = 67 countries), for one, has shown this employing Cutright's (1963) index of political development, although the relationship disappears if economic development is controlled for. Yet, using elite electoral accountability and electoral turnout as indicators of democracy as well as an interaction term of both, Hibbs (1973: 118) finds no support for Lipset's hypothesis linking democracy with stability. Studying the period from 1800 to 1960, Flanigan and Fogelman (1970), however, report a negative relationship between democracy and political violence at any level (see also Adams 1970: 137 for seventy-five countries from 1946 to 1960) and at any rate of economic development. Gurr et al. (forthcoming) find significant positive relationships of anocracy[5] with their various measures of political violence, and weak negative correlations between degrees of autocracy and democracy, respectively, and their dependent variables.

> Both democratic and autocratic governments have the institutional means to "deliver" reforms, if and when they make the commitment to do so. None of these conditions is likely to be found in the typical underdeveloped, elitist country. Their rulers . . . often see conflict as a zero-sum game in which the only victory is total, political victory. [Gurr 1979: 71]

In centralistic autocracies, however, the outbreak of political violence apparently is prevented much more successfully than under any other form of government.

The structure and ethos of contemporary democratic regimes are such that they are disposed to respond to limited challenges in a conciliatory way, which reinforces the utility of protest over rebellion. On the other hand autocracies are generally disposed to rely more on coercive control, which enhances the relative utility of rebellion for challengers who are desperate enough to act at all. The nature of political regimes thus is one contextual variable which influences whether challenges take the form of protest or rebellion. [Gurr and Lichbach 1979: 160]

Gurr and Lichbach consequently conceive of the extent of protest primarily as a function of the interaction of stress with dispositions and the organizational strength of protest groups.

3. According to the findings of Hibbs (1973: 181), communist regimes are rather successful in preventing collective protests (path coefficient = −.378) as well as internal wars (path coefficient = −.279). If these forms of political dissent occur, however, turbulence usually is considerable (see the episodic revolts in communist Europe, for instance, in East Germany in 1953, in Poland in 1956 and 1970, in Hungary in 1956, and in Czechoslovakia in 1968).

Communist policy in countries external to the Russian bloc of power, however, follows different lines: "Sizable Communist parties in non-Communist nations serve to promote mass protest but have no systematic impact on the incidence of Internal War. Large-scale Communist movements are typically 'destabilizing,' but only up to a point" (Hibbs 1973: 130–131). The last result is somewhat contrary to the widespread assumption found in Kornhauser (1959: 46) and in Gurr's various writings, namely, that communist organizations are among the primary agents for organizing violent political discontent. Gurr et al. (forthcoming) report significant relationships between the size and status of the respective communist parties and all measures of conflict. In other words, whereas the sheer number of communist party members per 10,000 of population is not related to political violence, there is a clear relationship between the presence of large, illegal, or suppressed communist parties and political violence. But Gurr's empirical study of this relationship does not take account of the possibility that communist parties tend to be suppressed in countries where they are or have been engaged in violence and tolerated where they limit themselves to peaceful action. Thus a "cause" of communist violence (their illegal status) may in fact be a consequence of it.

STRUCTURAL IMBALANCES

In general terms, structural imbalances exist when states of development (or change) in one important social-structural variable are not accompanied by an equal state of development (or change) in another social-structural variable of importance. It is, of course, impossible to tell a priori which social-structural phenomenon is important and which is of less importance. In rapidly changing societies structural imbalances might occur quite frequently, and—consequently or coincidentally?—be of relatively minor importance. The notion of structural imbalance originated in structural-functional theorizing, which has always been marred by a lack of evidence for its theoretical propositions concerning the importance of various subsectors for the functioning and stability of society. These well-known problems notwithstanding, structural imbalances as explanations of macro-political and macro-structural phenomena have always drawn the attention of social scientists. This also holds true for political conflict. Four of the five structural imbalances discussed below represent differences between demands and capacities. Empirical evidence at present, however, does not corroborate most of the theoretical notions to be dealt with here. (For negative evidence on additional structural imbalances, see Hibbs 1973.)

1. The level of urbanization exceeds the level of economic development. This structural imbalance is expected to lead to discontent of large portions of the population, because the "promises" of the city are not met by equal economic capacities. Discontent in turn could manifest itself in political violence. The hypothesis is not supported in Hibbs's study (1973).

2. The level of social mobilization is greater than that of governmental performance (measured in terms of nondefense activities as a percentage of gross domestic product) or that of social welfare (measured by such variables as infant live births, caloric intake, and physicians per million population). Demands created through social mobilization are said to exceed governmental performance or social welfare, thus to create discontent and to lead to political violence. Whereas Hibbs (1973) again fails to find support for this hypothesis, Duff and McCamant (1976: 71, 79, 131; N = 20 Latin American countries) in several instances demonstrate the explanatory power of a related interaction term. Thus the *rate of increase* in social mobilization correlates consistently with political violence (*r* ranges from .30 to .44 and, in any case, higher than the correlations for level of social mobilization). Economic growth, on the other hand, has a weak negative correlation with political violence, and the excess of economic growth over the increase in social mobilization has a more strongly negative correlation (years: 1950–70, $r = -.57$). In a multi-variate analysis the latter variable turns out to be the most important one. Yet their study is open to serious criticism, the most important argument being that operationally no interaction term but rather an additive term is included in their equations (see Jacobson 1973a; N = 75 countries, period: 1961–1965, using the same inadequate measure of imbalance, for findings consistent with the hypothesis).

3. The level of education exceeds the level of economic development. Sofranko and Bealer (1972; N = 74) report that imbalance between the

educational sector and other societal sectors does not explain political violence. (They used 1955–1961 violence data from Feierabend and Feierabend 1966, and 1961–1963 violence data from Gurr with Ruttenberg 1967.)[6] Only when the imbalance among the political, the economic, the educational, the welfare, and the communication sectors (measured mostly for the end of the 1950s and the early 1960s) are taken together ("total magnitude of imbalance") does a notable relationship emerge—one that is inflated, however, due to the intercorrelations of the independent variables.

On the whole, theoretical notions much cherished in modernization literature are not supported when tested on a cross-national basis.

> However, this does not mean that *theoretically*, taken in the abstract sense, such theories are unsound. If it were possible experimentally to manipulate nations so that, for example, there was little correlation between social mobilization and social welfare, then we could observe more satisfactorily the (interactive) effects of the conjunction of high social mobilization, low social welfare, and so on, and thereby draw definitive theoretical conclusions. Yet collinearity is in itself produced by some causal process that is responsible for variables "moving together." Therefore, unless these causal processes were to be disrupted in some fundamental and improbable way, such that the variables became no longer highly correlated, we never need to know the potential consequences of such interaction effects. [Hibbs 1973: 62–63]

Perhaps there is a less "dramatic" solution to this problem than the pessimistic conclusion of Hibbs might suggest: use of improved measures instead of the typically crude measures of structural imbalance might lead to more convincing tests of these structural explanations, which remain plausible ideas after all.

4. When incorporated in more complex causal models, two imbalance terms which in bivariate analysis failed to show the alleged effect fare somewhat better. The first is based on a hypothesis of Deutsch; the second is imbedded in a series of imbalance terms within the theoretical framework of Huntington. Deutsch differentiates between an "underlying population" (total population minus mobilized population), a "mobilized population" capable of being assimilated to the dominant cultural pattern of the respective community, and a population that is mobilized yet retains its cultural distinctiveness: "The share of *mobilized* but *differentiated* persons among the total population . . . is the first crude indicator of the probable incidence and strength of national conflict" (Deutsch 1966: 130; italics added). Deutsch distinguishes between several dimensions of assimilation: "(1) language; (2) culture; (3) ethnicity with its social associations, organizational memberships and family connections; (4) aspirations; (5) capabilities; (6) attainments; (7) civic compliance; and (8) political

loyalties" (Deutsch 1974: 545). *Simultaneous* assimilation on all of these dimensions, or at least on the more important ones, will be unlikely. Rather,

> other things assumed equal, the stage of rapid social mobilization may be expected, therefore, to promote the consolidation of states whose peoples already share the same language, culture and major social institutions; while the same process may tend to strain or destroy the unity of states whose population is already divided into several groups with different languages or cultures or basic ways of life. [Deutsch 1961: 501]

"The integrative revolution does not do away with ethnocentrism; it merely modernizes it" (Geertz 1963: 154).

In Hibbs's multivariate analysis the variable "percentage of mobilized, but differentiated persons" exerts—via the intervening variable of political separatism—a strong impact on internal war. In their study of black African countries Morrison and Stevenson (1972a: 925) also report evidence that might be interpreted in favor of Deutsch's hypothesis. But they do not use a multiplicative combination of two independent variables to represent the interaction term. Rather they rely on a theoretically inappropriate additive combination. The appropriate interaction term has been used only in Hibbs's analysis, where it turns out to be a strong (indirect) predictor of internal war. We expect that this kind of structural imbalance will turn out to be one of the basic explanatory variables in comparative analyses of political violence, at least at the macro-level of analysis. The impact of this variable at the level of groups should also be studied. Such a strategy would allow for substantial statements as to the causes of protest behavior or protest readiness of groups that remain culturally distinct. In this context Gurr has suggested an interesting hypothesis: "It is highly likely that increases in economic well-being and popular political participation for majority groups in European nations exacerbate the hostilities of regional and ethnic minorities that do not have what they regard as a fair share of those benefits" (Gurr 1969: 587).

5. The following set of hypotheses draws on Huntington's theorizing on "political order in changing societies" (1968: 53–55). Huntington starts from the assumption that "social mobilization is much more destabilizing than economic development." This is due to the discrepancy between rising demands (attributed to social mobilization processes) and insufficient capabilities to fulfill these demands (economic development) which is said to be a characteristic of transitional societies. "The ability of a transitional society to satisfy these new aspirations, however, increases much more slowly than the aspirations themselves." This gap, then, is said to lead to social frustration. Depending on two intermediating conditions, namely, "opportunities for social and economic mobility and adaptable political in-

stitutions," social frustration may lead to political instability. If mobility opportunities are insufficient, people will turn to politics "to enforce [their] demands." Finally, "the political backwardness of the country in terms of political institutionalization . . . makes it difficult, if not impossible for the demands upon the government to be expressed through legitimate channels and to be moderated and aggregated within the political system," and the sharp increase in political participation gives rise to political instability. The impact of modernization thus involves the following relationships:

1. $\dfrac{\text{social mobilization}}{\text{economic development}}$ = social frustration

2. $\dfrac{\text{social frustration}}{\text{mobility opportunities}}$ = political participation

3. $\dfrac{\text{political participation}}{\text{political institutionalization}}$ = political instability.

Huntington stresses the point that it is neither the level nor the rate of political participation or political institutionalization, but rather the ratio between the two that predicts to political instability. Most important in Huntington's theorizing is his separation of socioeconomic modernization from political development, the latter manifesting itself in strong political institutions and in modern political systems (mainly a strong and adaptable party system). "Rapid increases in mobilization and participation, the principal aspects of modernization, undermine political institutions. Rapid modernization, in brief, produces not political development but political decay" (Huntington 1965: 386).

In Hibbs's study (1973) the imbalance between social mobilization (or political participation, respectively) and political institutionalization does not predict to political violence. Hibbs employs indicators of political institutionalization such as direct taxes as a percentage of general government revenue, union membership as a percentage of the nonagricultural work force (a measure which might, in fact, indicate political participation rather than political institutionalization), and age of the largest political party divided by the number of parties, whereas Huntington proposes the following four general criteria: adaptability, complexity, autonomy, and coherence (see the rather general discussion in Huntington 1968: 12–14, and see Ben-Dor 1975 for a critique). Hibbs's operationalization of political participation is open to serious criticism, as he uses electoral turnout as a measure of political participation, whereas Huntington, though not precise about this variable, seems to refer to noninstitutionalized forms of political participation. In Hibbs's final multi-equation formulation, however, a higher degree of social mobilization compared to the degree of political institutionalization increases the level of regimes' negative sanctions, including "acts of censorship against mass media, political publications . . . as well as restrictions on the political activity and participation of the general public, or specific persons, parties, and organizations" (Hibbs 1973: 89), and thus indirectly contributes to the amount of collective protest and internal war. Most other "tests" of Huntington's theory (for instance, Duvall and Welfling 1973a; N = 28 black African countries; Sanders 1973; maximum N = 136; Lehtinen 1974; N = 83; Ruhl 1975; N = 18 Latin American countries; Yough and Sigelman 1976; N = 61 underdeveloped nations; and Duff and McCamant 1976) have also failed to find (strong) support for this theory. To some extent this might be attributed to inadequate operationalizations.[7]

These discouraging results notwithstanding, Huntington's conceptualization of political instability or political decay that arises from several structural imbalances merits continued attention. There is no space for a detailed discussion here (see Zimmermann 1980 instead), but only for a few critical comments. Social frustration, for instance, may not, if proportionally greater than mobility opportunities, lead to political participation but, on the contrary, cause withdrawal. Members of the politically apathetic *Lumpenproletariat* in many underdeveloped countries seem to illustrate the point. Or to take up another point: "Demands and participation must be kept analytically separate [and also be measured separately]. . . . Increased participation need not lead to increased effective demands. There [may be] tradeoffs between participation and the satisfaction of social and economic demands" (Bienen 1974: 194). Other useful extensions are proposed by Yough and Sigelman whose analysis suggests that

> rapid social mobilization itself is far less politically destabilizing than had previously been supposed. Indeed, we would argue that Huntington and others have focused so singlemindedly on the dysfunctional aspects of rapid social change that they have overlooked the potential of such change for creating higher levels of political support. [Yough and Sigelman 1976: 229]

The authors also recommend that consideration be given to different facets of instability, violence, social mobilization, and political institutionalization. Relationships among some facets may be in line with Huntington's (one-dimensional) theoretical predictions, other facets of the same theoretical notions might operate in different ways.

One last variant of the fifth structural imbalance is introduced by Wayman (1975) who replaces social mobilization by the "relevance of modernizing cleavages." Intense modernizing (or *political*) cleavages may be caused by grievances of socially mobilized but differentiated populations. Thus Deutsch's hypothesis could be incorporated into the following reformulation of Huntington's original theory:

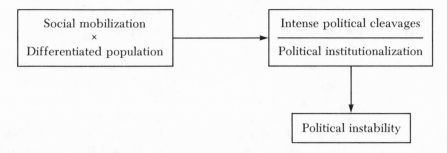

In any case, the routes and mechanisms leading eventually to political instability are not at all sufficiently specified, neither in Huntington's theory nor in any alternative formulation (for one of the most recent efforts see Linz and Stepan 1978).

COERCION

The linking of governmental coercion (repression) and violent protest provides some of the most fundamental hypotheses in research on violent political conflict. Yet most of the hypotheses have been tested unconvincingly. Coercion may be summarily defined here as force applied by the state against its population. Force denotes the actual or threatened use of violence to make a group abandon a course of action or inaction dictated by its own strong and enduring motives and wishes (drawing on the definition of Bay 1958: 93). Force, as defined here, includes both governmental uses of force (coercion) and private uses of force (violence). Much of the violence involved in protest and rebellion is in fact initiated by governments for the purpose of controlling protest and rebellion.

There are two contradictory expectations about the effects of governmental coercion on protest and rebellion: coercion either will deter them or will instigate people to higher levels of conflict behavior. The two hypotheses have been joined in a third, curvilinear hypothesis to the effect that lower levels of coercion tend to increase protest and rebellion, which reach their maximum at middle levels of coercion. Beyond this turning point, however, higher levels of coercion inhibit resistance (see Gurr 1970b: chapter 8 for case and comparative evidence favoring such a curvilinear relationship). In a more recent study (Lichbach and Gurr forthcoming) this curvilinear relationship is proposed to be inverted: the intensity of governmental coercion at time t is hypothesized to inhibit the extent of conflict at time $t + 1$, up to some threshold beyond which high levels of coercion increase the extent of future protest and rebellion. Thus there are theoretical arguments for all conceivable basic relations between governmental coercion and group protest and rebellion except for no relationship. The theoretical arguments are more complex than this summary might suggest, however, because they differ on such fundamental questions as whether coercive potential or the actual use of coercion has the stipulated effects, which aspects of conflict behavior are likely to change, and whether the effects are simultaneous or delayed.

A brief overview of some of the empirically determined relationship between coercion and political violence is given in Table 5-1; others are discussed below. As observed before in our review of cross-national research on political protest, empirical findings do not provide consistent evidence in favor of one particular hypothesis. There are, however, three general findings that seem to emerge from studies using different research designs: (1) the state's coercive capacity in general is not strongly related to magnitudes of conflict; (2) neither coercive capacity nor the state's use of coercion systematically deters conflict behavior; (3) the actual use of coercion by the state, as in the form of sanctions, is positively related to conflict behavior.

Some specific studies, findings, and methodological issues are reviewed below.

First we shall deal with some studies bearing on the impact of *coercive potential*. Several studies on the effects of coercion (for instance, Bwy 1968b) use indicators such as military expenditure as a percentage of gross domestic product or as a percentage of central government expenditure, or military manpower per population. These indicators represent coercive potential that may be much more influenced by international conditions than, for example, the indicators proposed by Hibbs, Gurr, and others: internal security forces weighted by total or adult population, and internal security forces per 1,000 sq. km. In his own study Hibbs reaches this conclusion:

> Neither the linear nor the curvilinear hypothesis is consistently supported by the empirical data. The most we can conclude, therefore, is that the strength of coercive forces available to governing elites does not seem to bear a marked curvilinear relation to mass violence, as previous analyses have suggested, and that the strength of such forces also fails to exert a substantial linear "deterrence" effect. [Hibbs 1973: 87]

Internal security forces, however, have a significant positive impact on negative sanctions, which in turn are interrelated with collective protest and internal war (see Figure 5-2 below). Thus the state's coercive capacity as such is not strongly or only indirectly related to magnitudes of conflict.

When the size of the *coercive potential* is weighted by the military's past loyalty to civilian regimes, however, Gurr finds a distinct negative relationship to conflict magnitudes, as expected. Cooper (1974: 283), however, found less consistent results in a multivariate analysis that controlled for geocultural regions and level of economic development. In his study the Latin American countries clearly stand out as a deviant case. Employing the same procedure as Gurr but using a different sample (N = 130, period: 1946–1965), Adams (1970: 147) also reports a negative relationship between the loyalty of coercive forces and violent political conflict. Yet not only the loyalty but also the "training, and technological sophistication" (Hibbs 1973: 86) of these forces should be assessed in future studies.[8]

In subsequent paragraphs the focus is not on the effects of coercive potential but almost exclusively on the consequences of *actual use of coercion*. This implies the use of a different set of indicators. The Feierabends and their co-workers, for instance, employ indicators such as censorship and lack of personal and political freedom to index actual coercion. As shown in Table 5–1, Feierabend and Feierabend (1972) and Markus and Nesvold (1972) report positive linear relationships between their measures of actual coercion and political conflict. Markus (1970: 28–30, as quoted in Markus and Nesvold 1972: 236) also finds a strong positive linear relationship between his measures of "governmental coercion" and "political instability." The same holds true when coercion and minority-related hostilities are studied, $r = .71$ (Feierabend and Feierabend 1973: 211; $N = 25$ nations, period: 1955–1959). When using negative sanctions such as acts of censorship and political restrictions as the independent variable, Hibbs (1973) also reports (significant) positive relationships with his two dimensions of mass political violence: collective protest and internal war. That neither the state's coercive capacity nor its use of coercion systematically deters conflict behavior is also one of the basic findings in the study by Gurr and Duvall (1973). "Coercive elite policies breed civil conflict more often than civil peace. Some (measures of) institutionalized coercion contribute to order, but policies as diverse as punitive acts of coercive control and maintenance of costly military establishments tend to exacerbate future conflict" (Gurr and Duvall 1973: 160). Following their data more closely they report self-canceling effects of coercion:

> Coercive capacity when used by regimes tends to have self-canceling effects on magnitude of conflict. . . . For example: government acts of coercion tend quite systematically to increase subsequent magnitude of conflict; the size of military expenditures are consistently positive correlates of conflict in our 86 countries; yet the size of internal security forces weakly inhibits conflict in all but Western nations. [Gurr and Duvall 1973: 141]

Thus, if there is one consistent result so far, it is that the use of coercion by the state, for instance, in the form of sanctions, is positively related to conflict behavior. One should add that this holds true particularly for non-communist states, whereas the deterrence model of (actual) coercion seems to work quite well in communist states (leaving out such dramatic eruptions as the East German uprising in 1953, the Hungarian revolt and the Poznan rebellion in 1956, or the massive dissent in Czechoslovakia in the first half of 1968).

Different results emerge, however, when *time lags* are taken into ac-

TABLE 5–1. Coercion and Political Violence: Some Bivariate Relationships

Author	Dependent Variable	Indicators	Independent Variable	Indicators	Number in Sample	Period	Results — *Positive Linear Relationships*
Markus and Nesvold 1972	Political instability	7-point scale	Coercion	7-point scale, from 0, denoting "civil rights present and protected" to 6, denoting "civil rights nonexistent, political opposition impossible"	10	1959–1961	γ = .62
Feierabend and Feierabend 1972	"Revolution"	Deaths from and duration of group violence (from Tanter and Midlarsky 1967)	Coercion (1948–1960)	As above	18 Latin American countries	1958–1960	r = .58
Jacobson 1973a	General conflict	Taken from Gurr 1968a	Coerciveness (early 1960s)	Size of internal security forces (from Gurr 1968a), role of the police in political activities (from Banks and Textor 1963)	75	1961–1965	p = .10 (.84 in economically developed countries)

						Curvilinear Relationships
Bwy 1968b	Anomic violence	Various indicators of internal conflicts on the basis of a factor analysis	Force (1959–1960)	Defense expenditure as percent of GNP	20 Latin American countries	1958–1960	Curvilinear relationship (but no relationship if organized violence is the dependent variable)
Gurr 1968a	Civil strife	Complex index of the pervasiveness, duration, and intensity of turmoil, conspiracy, and internal war	Military/ internal security forces	Military and internal security forces per 10,000 adults (1960)	114	1961–1965	Curvilinear relationship (being even more pronounced when leaving out countries (N = 45) with protracted political violence and those being externally threatened)
							Low-High-Medium
Markus and Nesvold 1972	Political instability (lag: 1 month)	7-point scale (see above)	Coercion	7-point scale (see above)	10	1959–1961	$\gamma = .65$

195

count. Instead of a linear positive relationship between actual coercion and political conflict, Markus and Nesvold (1972) report a curvilinear relationship when a lag of one month is incorporated into the analysis (see Table 5–1). The significance of time-lagged analyses is also stressed in the study of Anderson and Nesvold (1972; N = 22 nations), who found that in the period 1945–1958 (1) high past fluctuation in coercion, (2) high past mean coercion, (3) low past instability, (4) relatively high recent coercion, and (5) relatively low recent instability, all predicted significantly to higher levels of political violence (Anderson and Nesvold 1972: 907). In opposition to these two studies, which show at least some positive or curvilinear relationship between time-lagged measures of governmental coercion and political conflict, Hibbs reports that in the long run (lag: 10 years) there is a *negative* relationship between negative sanctions and his two measures of mass political violence (being significant only in case of internal war). Note, that, when measured simultaneously, Hibbs finds a (significant) positive relationship between negative sanctions and both collective protest and internal war.

To turn to another hypothesis, Feierabend, Nesvold, and Feierabend (1970) found cross-national evidence for a linear relationship between *fluctuations in coercion* and political violence. Markus and Nesvold (1972) also found results in support of the hypothesis that "regime coercive control varies strongly with the consistency of regime-administered negative sanctions" (Gurr 1970b: 256). Gurr mentions several reasons (1970b: 255) why the inconsistent use of force on behalf of state agents (but also on behalf of protesters: see 1970b: 260–273) leads to an increase and not a decrease in actual protests. For example, only some of the protesters are captured or punished in some other form. Nonparticipants are often indiscriminately affected by the use of coercive means leading to resentment among them, too, against such measures or against state officials directly. On the basis of learning principles and inferred expectation states, a number of possible explanations may be listed why the observed relationship between inconsistent use of coercive means and political violence is likely to hold (see also Eckstein 1965: 154): (1) fluctuations in the level of coercion may lead to a credibility gap of the regime; (2) changes in coerciveness may be exceeded by changes in expectations of the population, e.g. demands for greater liberalization; (3) a reduction in the level of repression could mean "the removal of the inhibitory mechanism, but not necessarily the removal of the instigation to violence that still may linger as the heritage of previously coercive regime" (Feierabend, Nesvold, and Feierabend 1970: 102); (4) activities that have been intermittently reinforced, e.g. protest, are especially resistant to extinction; finally, (5) occasional repressive measures may lead to very intense frustrations, thus strongly increasing the potential for protest. All of these explanations presuppose individual data or data on specific groups collected over time.

There are various dramatic historical examples that shed some light on the hypothesis mentioned (the Hungarian uprising and the Poznan rebellion in 1956, Czechoslovakia in the first half of 1968, or the Dominican Republic after the removal of the Trujillo clan—see Feierabend, Nesvold, and Feierabend 1970: 115—and most recently the fall of the Shah in Iran). This seems to be a clear vindication of Machiavelli's advice: "Undoubtedly, if high coerciveness is applied, it should be applied consistently" (Feierabend, Nesvold, and Feierabend 1970: 115). The more "successful" of the tyrants in history knew it all along.

So far only systemic coercion has been dealt with. Theoretically, however, we are more interested in finding out how "event coercion" (Anderson and Nesvold 1972: 807), the immediate use of coercion, affects ongoing episodes of conflict. In the preceding discussion coercion has been used in a more general sense, not as related to specific actions. Actually, we are interested in finding answers to both questions: (1) what consequences do specific acts of repression have; and (2) is there a general inhibiting or threatening effect that results from the existence or imminent use of a repressive potential, and, if so, how strong is this effect? Gurr et al. (forthcoming) report that there is a reciprocal relationship between governmental sanctions and political violence (see also Hibbs's causal model in Figure 5–2 below). Nesvold and Martin (1974) provide additional evidence for an interdependency between coercion and political violence. In a study of 130 nations (1955–1964) they found a positive correlation ($r = .66$) between coercion and political violence (using the operationalizations and coding procedures of Feierabend and Feierabend 1966). This relationship also holds after controlling for geocultural region, economic development, or levels of coercion (only in the case of Eastern European nations is there a slightly lower correlation, $r = .55$). Furthermore, they also found conflicts (coercion) to be persistent from one year to the following year, $r = .73$. The correlations between coercion and political violence one year later, or between political violence and coercion one year later, differed only slightly in the respective geocultural groupings.

When considering the results mentioned here, it should be kept in mind that data about coercive potentials and the ways they are applied are often error-laden (see the discussion below). Moreover, we need to know not only whether a repressive climate is created by various coercive measures of the state authorities, but also how this affects the evaluation of available resources. We need information on how "objective" data are translated into strategic operations by the parties to conflict. If this were done, the level of explanation is no longer the system level but rather the level of groups. What we are calling for here, however, is treating both aspects jointly, that is, combining system-level explanatory variables with group-level variables. We also need to know how many deaths and injuries are caused by state agents apart from other damage done (see the appropriate

coding in Gurr et al. 1978: 56–57), how this would affect the (likely) protesters and how, in turn, the state agents would react.

> A large portion of the European disturbances we have been surveying turned
> violent at exactly the moment when the authorities intervened to stop an il-
> legal but nonviolent action. This is typical of violent strikes and demonstra-
> tions. Furthermore, the great bulk of the killing and wounding in those same
> disturbances was done by troops or police rather than by insurgents or demon-
> strators. The demonstrators, on the other hand, did the bulk of the damage to
> property. [Tilly 1969: 42]

Some authors, such as Buss (1961: 31), expect attacks to be a stronger
determinant of aggression than frustration (see also Bandura 1973: 135–
136). Consequently, it will be of special importance to collect data on who
caused or provoked the outbreak of violent conflict. The distinction between four types of governmental coercion suggested by Snyder (1976:
285–288) is quite useful in the context of the preceding discussion. He differentiates between preemptive and responsive coercion, and between
violent and nonviolent means. The discussion above might easily be re-
phrased in these terms.

The learning theories from which the underlying causal explanations are
taken can be considered a repository of hypotheses (see the brief overview
in Berkowitz 1973: 116 ff.) which should be taken up in research on
political violence. For example, the analysis of so-called reinforcement
schedules—wherein one distinguishes among the frequency, intensity,
duration, consistency, contiguity or delay, and the rates of change of
rewards and punishments—easily would lead to the development of hypotheses not yet discussed in cross-national research on political violence (but
see also the hypotheses in Markus and Nesvold 1972, Anderson and
Nesvold 1972, and Nesvold and Martin 1974). Are direct or vicarious (indirect) punishments (that is, coercive acts) or rewards equally effective or
ineffective? Is there a symmetry between punishment effects and reward
effects (same slope, but different signs)? Or are vicarious punishments less
effective whereas vicarious rewards are equally effective as direct rewards? Or—even more complicating—are there additive or interactive effects between direct and vicarious forms of punishment or rewards? What
about forms of violent political protest that do not occur for some time (apparent extinction) but then, after a long hiatus, reoccur?

In sum, "there is no basis here for a 'regime coercion' variable that consistently reduces conflict magnitudes" (Gurr and Duvall 1973: 141).
Future studies should seek more precise answers to the questions whether
to use different ways of conceptualizing coercion—for instance, coercive
potential versus actual use of coercion—and whether the employment of
different indicators affect the results. Researchers should find out whether
different features of coercion tend to coincide. Moreover, in multivariate

analyses they should test for the causal impact a specific feature of coercion may have on the occurrence of other repressive features. Also, for theoretical and practical reasons, we should be mainly interested in the effects of event coercion, that is, how the actual and immediate application of state force influences the behavior of protesters. Consequently, cross-sectional aggregated data analyses of coercive potential and political violence will have to be supplemented by process-oriented longitudinal analyses of reciprocal interactions of coercion and protest under specific circumstances (see also the recent conflict models in Jackson et al. 1978). "Collective violence is not, by and large, the result of a single group's possession by an emotion, sentiment, attitude, or idea. It grows, for the most part, out of strategic *inter*action among groups" (Tilly 1978: 183; italics in original). Moreover, relationships might differ from one type of country to another (for instance, noncommunist versus communist countries where total repression seems to work quite well), and from one form of conflict behavior to another. Perhaps protesters respond differently to coercion than do rebels. Hibbs (1973), for one, reports that prior negative sanctions (1948–1957) have a strong negative impact on subsequent internal war (1958–1967; $p = .491$). In the case of collective protest, however, no such relationship holds. Rather there is a strong (simultaneous) positive relation between negative sanctions and collective protest, and vice versa. The immediate impact of negative sanctions is even greater in case of rebellion where $p = .824$, the strongest causal coefficient of all those reported by Hibbs. Thus the relationship between coercion and political conflict may very well change its sign, depending not only on the form of conflict behavior, but also on the lag in the periods of observation.

SOCIOECONOMIC INEQUALITY

"At least since Aristotle theorists have believed that political discontent and its consequences—protest, instability, violence, revolution—depend not only on the absolute level of economic well-being, but also on the distribution of wealth" (Nagel 1974: 453). Yet a high degree of socioeconomic inequality may not contribute at all to political violence, provided that a society has shared norms that justify inequality or that the repressive measures of the authorities are sufficient to keep down protests.

Two opposing hypotheses are discussed in the literature: (1) there is a positive linear relationship between the degree of socioeconomic inequality and political protest; and (2) the relationship is of a curvilinear nature.

Russett's study (1964) provides evidence for the first hypothesis. He relates inequality in land tenure (using the Gini-index) in forty-seven nations to a cumulated score of violent political deaths per million from 1950–1962 and finds a relationship of $r = .46$. When controlling for percentage of labor force in agriculture, a much stronger relationship emerges for agricultural nations ($r = .70$). The relationship is also upheld in a multiple regression analysis (N = 33) employing several other socio-economic variables (Russett et al. 1964: 321). In an analysis of the determinants of political instability (measured along three dimensions: elite instability, communal instability, and turmoil, drawing on Morrison et al. 1972: 122–124) in thirty-two black African nations during the 1960s, Barrows (1976) finds in a multiple correlation analysis that ethnic group inequality is a consistent predictor of all three of the dependent variables.

The Russett and Barrows studies employ cross-national data, as do most other studies reviewed in this chapter. An intriguing exception is a series of studies of the relationship between inequality and support for the Saigon regime in South Vietnam, all of which employ provincial-level data on land distribution, income, and government support in twenty-six provinces in 1965. The first study, by Mitchell (1968), seemed to show that poverty and high inequality led to high support for the Saigon regime. Critical reanalyses were made of Mitchell's data by Paige (1970), Paranzino (1972), and Russo (1972), advocating alternative theoretical positions and employing different methodological techniques. In general, the reanalyses are in agreement that Mitchell was wrong on both theoretical and technical grounds, and that in fact support for the Saigon government was weakest where poverty and inequality were greatest.

The last published reanalysis of the Vietnam data, by Nagel (1974), introduces a new theoretical argument and an additional data base. Nagel argues for a curvilinear relationship between inequality and discontent. He starts from Festinger's hypothesis that "the tendency to compare oneself with some other specific person decreases as the difference between his opinion or ability and one's own increases" (Festinger 1954: 120), and combines this tendency to compare with the grievance resulting from comparison. This leads to the general hypothesis that discontent due to inequality is a function of the tendency to compare multiplied by the grievance resulting from comparison. Mathematically he derives a curvilinear relationship between inequality and discontent: "discontent which, ceteris paribus, begins at zero in a perfectly egalitarian system, increases with inequality up to a maximum at some intermediate level of inequality, and then decreases again as complete inequality is approached" (Nagel 1974: 455). Yet, when relating data on inequality of land distribution in fifty-four nations (data taken from Taylor and Hudson 1972 for 1948–1967) to Gurr's three indices of conspiracy, internal war, and turmoil (1961–1965) and to four other political violence variables, the inequality measures do not show the predicted curvilinear relationship after controlling for gross national product. The latter itself consistently shows a negative relationship with the dependent variable and is the relatively more important variable.

Nagel discusses various possible explanations for his failure to find the expected relationship, such as the small number of countries—also a problem in other such studies. Apparently inequality and the level as well as the rate of economic development have to be considered simultaneously for an adequate analysis. It turns out more than once that economic growth variables are stronger predictors of political violence than inequality. On the other hand, there is persuasive theoretical reasoning for a curvilinear relationship between inequality and political violence. "Economic development increases economic inequality at the same time that social mobilization decreases the legitimacy of that inequality. Both aspects of modernization combine to produce political instability" (Huntington 1968: 58–59). Inequality should be curvilinearly related to economic development, reaching its peak at a mid-level of economic development as suggested by Olson (1963) and empirically demonstrated by Adelman and Morris (1973) and Paukert (1973) using a sample of fifty-six noncommunist states (see also the similar finding and the analysis by Ahluwalia 1976 for sixty-two countries and Ward 1978). The most serious limitation of these empirical studies is that they rely on cross-sectional data, sometimes only for the developing nations. A rigorous test of the hypothesis would require the use of longitudinal data.

The most brilliant theoretical analysis of the consequences of (income) inequality is found in Hirschman (1973). He compares the tolerance for an initially increasing inequality—others getting richer than oneself—to a traffic jam in a tunnel. If others advance, much like drivers in such a traffic jam, one expects the same for oneself. This "hope factor" leads to greater tolerance of increased inequality. If, however, there is no improvement in the situation for a person still hoping and/or if social advances lead to "discrimination against nouveaux riches," the tunnel effect levels off with time. Supporters turn into enemies of the social order. Hirschman goes on to suggest that the "tunnel effect" prevails only in ethno-culturally homogeneous societies. Note that Hirschman's thesis runs counter to Nagel's theorizing and, in fact, seems to suggest a curvilinear relationship exactly opposite in shape to that predicted by Nagel.

The most recent study (Sigelman and Simpson 1977; N = 49) bears on Hirschman's theorizing. It leads to the conclusion that, contrary to theoretical suggestions by H. T. Davis (1948) and Hirschman (1973), there is no "V-curve" relationship between economic inequality (using measures of personal income inequality taken from Paukert 1973) and political violence (1958–1967, "internal war" measure of Hibbs 1973). The inverted V-curve hypothesis of Nagel also goes unsupported. If anything, there is a moderate positive linear relationship between economic inequality and political violence, a relationship that persists if various control variables are added. Once again, economic development (affluence) proves to be a much stronger predictor of political violence than economic inequality. The results are generally consistent with Russett's early (1964) cross-national findings. A final and important point is that only cross-sectional data are used in these studies. They seem insufficient for testing a theory of dynamic interrelationships.

Altogether, the limited empirical evidence available suggests a linear positive relationship between socioeconomic inequality and political violence. There is, however, suggestive theoretical reasoning (see also Porter and Nagel 1976) for a curvilinear relationship between socioeconomic inequality and political protest that has not yet been adequately tested.

The hypotheses under review here need more precise specification in future studies. Russett and Nagel employ measures of inequality in land distribution, Barrows deals with ethnic group inequality, and Sigelman and Simpson focus on income inequality. In general, we predict stronger relationships between political conflict and inequality in the distribution of those goods that are valued relatively highly in a society. In some countries land may not be evaluated as highly as money. In others ethnic inequality may be of greater concern than income inequality (though they usually are related). Thus various facets of inequality should be tested if an adequate evaluation of the inequality variable is to be achieved. Cultural values about inequality also should be considered. In some countries inequality may be so resented that any kind of inequality contributes to political protest. In others only specific features of inequality show a relationship with the dependent variable, whereas in still other countries inequality may be so generally accepted that it is not at all related to political protest.

Furthermore, formal measures of inequality need not highly correlate with the effective degree of inequality. There are various strategies of tax avoidance and evasion to reckon with when gathering data on inequality. Data on inequality could easily become an explosive political issue. Consequently elites, especially in less egalitarian and/or more repressive societies, have an interest in not collecting or reporting the relevant data.

Finally, socioeconomic inequality must be seen in perspective to other explanatory variables, socioeconomic development and economic growth obviously being variables of major importance here.

CONFLICT TRADITIONS

Empirical evidence lends support to the biblical dictum that violence begets violence. There is, however, the danger that stable implicit (exogenous) variables (that is, variables not tested for in the model that might affect or produce correlations between prior and later measures of the same variable) and positive autocorrelated residuals (see the discussion in Hibbs 1974) contribute to positive correlations between prior and later levels of violent political conflict, thus rendering this hypothesis an extremely difficult one to test. In the study by Gurr and Duvall (1973), previous magnitudes of conflict show a positive relation to the dependent variables, being strongest in the case of turmoil and man-days of participation. The influence of past violent political conflicts is indirect and is exerted through various stress intervening variables, principally traditions (see the discussion below). Studying internal conflicts between 1948 and 1965, Gurr et al. (forthcoming) also find evidence in favor of the violence-breeds-violence hypothesis, yet with notable differentiations: conflict traditions seem to be much stronger in European and Latin countries than in neocolonial nations, where conflict patterns seem to be somewhat more erratic. Obviously, even in some of the economically more developed countries there is a culture of violent protest and rebellion stemming from historical conflicts across lines of religious, social, linguistic, and/or ethnic cleavages. In such political cultures people often "carry the burden of profound grievances throughout their lives and pass them on to their children" (Gurr 1970b: 59). Northern Ireland is an obvious European example (see Elliot and Hickie 1971, Schmitt 1974, and Lijphart 1975). Gurr et al. (forthcoming) also report that past success (defined in terms of gains by rebels) in internal wars (1850–1960) and in turmoil (1940–1960) is related to later magnitudes of the same types of conflict. In case of conspiracy positive but weaker relationships are found. The culture of violence hypothesis, whose importance has been stressed by Gurr in his theory of political violence (see Gurr 1970b: 168–177), has been empirically corroborated by himself (Gurr and Duvall 1973, Lichbach and Gurr forthcoming) and also in studies by Hibbs (1973), Cooper (1974), and by Adams (1970: 198 et passim). It also has been tested in a study of conflicts in twenty-eight black African nations by Duvall and Welfling:

> Turmoil [which is considerably underspecified in their causal model] appears to be a function of itself; that is, tumultuous African countries tend to remain tumultuous over time. . . . Internal war, however, is affected by all forms of previous conflict. No single causal mechanism predominates. Both prior internal war and turmoil are positively related to later internal war—evidence that sporadic and anomic conflict can be, in fact tends to be, translated into more organized and perhaps more deadly conflict in Africa. [Duvall and Welfling 1973a: 692]

"CLEAVAGES"

Religious, regional, ethnic, racial, linguistic, and other communal- or custom-based ties (Geertz 1963 refers to them as "primordial attachments") represent one of the most important classes of determinants of protest and turmoil, as well as of insurrection.

> Of a total of 132 contemporary states, only 12 (9.1 percent) can be described as essentially homogeneous from an ethnic viewpoint. An additional 25 states (18.9 percent of the sample) contain an ethnic group accounting for more than 90 percent of the state's total population, and in still another 25 states the largest element accounts for between 75 and 89 percent of the population. But in 31 states (23.5 percent of the total), the largest ethnic element represents

only 50 to 74 percent of the population, and in 39 cases (29.5 percent of all states) the largest group fails to account for even half of the state's population. Moreover, this portrait of ethnic diversity becomes more vivid when the number of distinct ethnic groups within states is considered. In some instances, the number of groups within a state runs into the hundreds, and in 53 states (40.2 percent of the total), the population is divided into more than *five* significant groups. [Connor 1972: 320]

Many quantitative, comparative studies provide substantial evidence that the greater the extent or intensity of cleavages between ethnic, religious, and other communal groups in a country, the greater the extent of protest and turmoil (and also rebellion). (Well-known exceptions are consociational democracies such as Switzerland and the Netherlands.) Studies which give particular attention to cleavages include Barrows (1976), Gurr and Duvall (1973), Gurr et al. (forthcoming), Hibbs (1973), Morrison and Stevenson (1972b), and Von der Mehden (1973: 173). Violent conflict along lines of cleavages is not inherently political, but it is frequently politicized as groups contend for political benefits or dominance. If one group holds disproportionate power, conflict across lines of cleavage almost invariably has political objectives.

Cleavages often are associated with conflicts that participants perceive in zero-sum terms. They can be contrasted with economic conflict, in which disputes potentially can be settled via means of bargaining, that is, contain the possibility of a solution that entails at least some gains for all of the participants. Communal conflicts are often symbolic in nature, and tend to be perceived as matters of principle, as nonnegotiable, and as touching on the identity and integrity of one's own group. They acquire zero-sum characteristics: each side automatically gets what the other loses and vice versa, thus leading to irreversible settlements (see Oberschall 1973: 50–51). The absence of cross-cutting cleavages usually entails a particularly great potential for all-out political conflicts.

OTHER BIVARIATE RELATIONSHIPS

There are a number of other variables whose relations with protest have been studied in one or a handful of quantitative comparative studies, but which are not reviewed separately here. Some of these variables are considered in the multivariate analyses, reviewed below. One of the more important variables that gets little or no attention below is legitimacy, which has been included in cross-national studies by Gurr (1968a: 1115–1116) using indirect, aggregate indicators. Valid measurement would require the collection of cross-national survey data (see Barnes, Kaase, et al. 1979). The diffusion of political violence is another such variable. Cross-national quantitative research thus far has studied only whether military coups d'état are contagious, not protest or rebellion more generally. (For a study of the diffusion of riots within a country see Midlarsky 1978). Finally, external dependence on major powers, and their political and economic penetration of dependent countries, have only begun to gain close attention as predictors of political violence and instability (see also Chapter 7 by Stohl in this *Handbook*).

SOME MULTIVARIATE ANALYSES OF CONFLICT

Detailed multivariate analyses of the correlates of protest on a cross-national base are the exception, not the rule. Here the multivariate analyses by Gurr, Hibbs, and a few other researchers are evaluated. Tilly's arguments as to the explanation of collective violence also are considered, even though his empirical evidence thus far is not grounded in detailed multivariate analyses.

There are important differences between the approaches by Gurr and Hibbs on the one hand and Tilly on the other. The approach taken by Gurr and Hibbs (and some other writers) is: (1) cross-nationally comparative; (2) concerned not with groups as the primary unit of analysis but rather with countries and their levels of conflict and instability; (3) uses mainly cross-sectional analyses; and (4) is explicitly concerned with testing hypotheses using complex statistical techniques. Gurr and Hibbs differ in several respects, however. Gurr begins with an explicit general theory, Hibbs with discrete hypotheses drawn from the literature. Thus Gurr constructs complex, composite indicators whereas Hibbs uses less aggregated indicators. Another obvious difference is that Gurr (1970b) identifies causal variables at different levels of analysis, from the social-psychological to the group to the national, whereas Hibbs (1973) is concerned mainly with the latter. Yet Gurr's measures do not directly tap the psychological-level variables, so that his approach differs from Hibbs's more in the realm of theory than in terms of empirical analysis.

Tilly's approach, on the other hand, is: (1) historically based, drawing in part on the "pre-industrial crowds" literature and more generally on European historical material; (2) is concerned primarily with the rise and decline of contending groups; (3) emphasizes group processes not psychological ones; (4) uses mainly longitudinal analyses; and (5) is, at least in comparison to Gurr and Hibbs, mainly descriptive. Many differences among these theoretical approaches, the findings, and points of criticisms reported below are due to these different foci of research.

GURR ON WHY MEN REBEL

Gurr's various multivariate analyses of civil strife and its components (Gurr 1968a, 1968b, 1969, 1970a, 1972a) will be mentioned only in passing. Also, the merits and weaknesses of his original theoretical framework (Gurr 1970b; see also 1968a), will not be placed in the foreground here (for a more detailed discussion see Zimmermann 1980: chapter 5). Rather we shall work backwards from the theoretical modifications proposed in Gurr and Duvall (1973; see also Gurr and Lichbach 1979) and briefly point to some of the advantages of the more recent formulation over his earlier work. In their major revision and extension of Gurr's original theory Gurr and Duvall (1973) follow the criticism of Abell (1971) and present their basic model of political violence in this form:

Magnitude of political violence = RD + (RD × JUST × BALANCE) + ε

where RD is relative deprivation, JUST is justification, and ε is an error term. "The term in parentheses indicates that justifications and balance have no significant effects on violent conflict independently of RD; they act rather to amplify or inhibit its effects" (Gurr and Duvall 1973: 137). Thus, in contrast to Gurr's prior quantitative analyses (for instance, Gurr 1968a), these variables are now treated methodologically as mediating conditions, as implied in Gurr's theory, and not simply in an additive manner.

Figure 5–1 shows the summary model of magnitude of political conflict as theoretically developed and empirically tested by Gurr and Duvall (1973). The parameters of the model were estimated using data for eighty-six countries; conflict was measured for the period 1961–1965, most other variables represent conditions as of 1960. Only the results related to turmoil are summarized here. Five variables explain 56 percent of the variance in magnitude of turmoil. In declining order of statistical importance they are:

strain, β = .407 (a composite indicator that incorporates measures of economic and political discrimination, political separatism, cleavages, and economic dependence)[9]

social tension, β = .359 (a multiplicative combination of indicators of strain and stress, conflict traditions, and dissident institutional support)

regime institutional support, β = − .265

conflict traditions, β = .251

economic development, β = .154

The *stress* variable is indexed by measures formerly used by Gurr (1968a) to represent short-term deprivation, plus measures of government sanctions.

Other conflict variables for which the model was estimated, with slightly different combinations of variables and somewhat higher levels of explained variance, were magnitude of rebellion (R^2 = .70), man-days of conflict (R^2 = .58), conflict deaths (R^2 = .76), and total magnitude of conflict (R^2 = .75). An indicator of external intervention was a significant explanatory factor in the equations for all facets of conflict except turmoil.

FIGURE 5–1. Revised model of conflict linkages. SOURCE: Gurr and
Duvall 1973: 149.

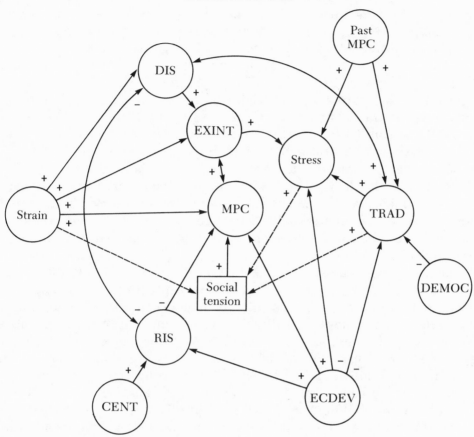

Key: MPC   = magnitude of political conflict
     EXINT   = external intervention
     DIS   = dissident institutional support
     RIS   = regime institutional support
     CENT   = autocracy or "centrism"
     ECDEV   = economic development
     DEMOC   = democracy
     TRAD   = conflict traditions

Gurr and Duvall comment, "When we compare the stress–turmoil equation with that for stress–rebellion, we are drawn to the conclusion that the
extent of foreign intervention and conflict traditions determine whether
stress leads to turmoil or to rebellion" (1973: 156).

Welfling (1975) has carried out a replication of the Gurr–Duvall approach for black African countries drawing on *Black Africa* (Morrison et

al. 1972) as a data source. Somewhat more of the variance (.51) is explained using *Black Africa's* data on conflict in place of Gurr's data ($R^2 = -.35$), which seem to be affected by error in measurement of protest. Also, in Welfling's analysis, tension has a positive sign, as might be expected on theoretical grounds, and not the negative sign which obtains when the African countries in Gurr and Duvall's data-set are analyzed separately (Welfling 1975: 883). Finally, economic development has no significance as an explanatory variable in the African context. Also of interest is the subsequent study by Gurr and Lichbach (1979), who forecast properties of conflict for ten countries (selected out of the eighty-six countries on the base of a stratified random sample) for the period 1971–1975. Parameters are estimated of a simplified variant of the model developed by Gurr and Duvall (1973), again using the 1961–1965 data. Data on the appropriate independent variables for ten countries are inserted in the equations to generate estimates of 1971–1975 conflict. These forecasted values then are compared with observed scores for the ten countries; the correspondence is fairly good.

The basic explanatory variable in Gurr's prior works is said to be relative deprivation, defined as "actor's perceptions of discrepancy between their value expectations (the goods and conditions of the life to which they believe they are justifiably entitled) and their value capabilities (the amounts of those goods and conditions that they think they are able to get and keep)" (Gurr 1968a: 1104). In later works, however, Gurr moves away from the individualistic base of his theorizing and concentrates on macro-structural conditions that are assumed to cause deprivation. Until the publication of *Why Men Rebel* in 1970 there was a distinct gap between the measures Gurr employed and his theoretical statements—the latter being derived from a combination of relative deprivation theorizing, the frustration–aggression nexus, learning principles, and such macro-structural variables as institutionalization, social and structural facilitation, and coercive potential. Yet in spite of the theoretical and operational changes introduced in his later works, the basic theoretical framework has remained the same, namely, that the relation between potential for political violence and actual political violence is mediated by a number of variables having to do with (1) beliefs and traditions about the justifiability of conflict, and (2) the balance between coercive and institutional resources of the dissidents versus the state. Depending on the relationship among these intervening variables, the potential for conflict behavior is unchanged or, more likely, enlarged, reduced, stalemated or diverted to another object. The balance of these intervening variables thus determines the outcomes with respect to political violence.

Concerning the dependent variable of interest here, political protest, only a few of Gurr's results can be considered. (In earlier works Gurr speaks of "turmoil," but later on uses "protest" to denote actions such as

riots, demonstrations, clashes, and local rebellions.) For twenty-one western societies (1961–1965) strong bivariate relationships between the institutional strength of dissidents and protest (r = .70) are reported (Gurr
1970a: 139), but not in the case of rebellion (r = .39). Thus institutionalized channels for participation in the political process (for instance,
via labor unions) do not inhibit protest but rather act as a catalyst. Three
independent variables—*relative deprivation* (indexed by aggregate measures of economic and political discrimination, potential separatism,
religious cleavages, adverse economic conditions, restrictions on political
participation, and new value-depriving policies of government), *justification* (historical extent and success of strife, governmental legitimacy), and
coercive and institutional balance—explain two thirds and more of the
variance of the various dependent variables. Interestingly enough, Gurr's
fundamental causal variable, "relative deprivation," does not do well in
explaining protest in western societies. Protest (turmoil) in this sample of
Gurr's universe of 114 countries is much better explained than in the
earlier study (Gurr 1968b). Moreover, the structure of the causal model for
explaining turmoil in western societies looks different from the model proposed for 114 countries (Gurr 1968b; Cooper 1974).

Gurr's theoretical framework has been taken up by Cooper (1974) who
proposes a new model for explaining turmoil. Whereas Gurr explains only
a quarter of the variation in turmoil in his study of 114 countries during
1961–1965 (Gurr 1968a), Cooper accounts for larger portions of the
variance when he separately analyzes nations grouped according to their
degree of modernity and along geocultural lines. In general, this procedure
increases the degree of statistical explanation achieved. The amount of
unexplained variance is further reduced when two additional variables are
introduced: interest articulation and representation of interest articulation
(indexed through the degree of polyarchy of the political system). Several
generalizations are worth noting: legitimacy is consistently and strongly
related (in the negative direction) to the dependent variable. There is considerable evidence for Gurr's culture-of-violence hypothesis in all of the
clusters except Latin America, where there is a strong reversal of the sign,
that is, past strife has a negative impact on present strife. It is noteworthy
that coercive potential (size of coercive forces, weighted by their loyalty)
inhibits protest only among the African nations, whereas in Latin American countries the partial r is a positive .41. Evidently large and loyal coercive forces in Latin America have been associated with high levels of protest. In general, coercive potential does not seem to be a decisive factor in
explaining the magnitude of protest. Finally, in western countries institutionalization lacks the negative effect it has on protest elsewhere. These
results are consistent with those reported by Gurr elsewhere, yet neither
Cooper's theoretical rationale nor his highly inferential measures are convincing. If turmoil is regarded as "situationally determined, unstructured

mass behavior" (Cooper 1974: 268), then Cooper's very indirect indicators of organizational aspects of certain demands do not make much sense as explanations of the dependent variable.

Using less aggregated measures than in his earlier study (Gurr 1970a) and a sample of thirty-eight democracies, Gurr (1972a) reports that the amount of protest is mainly determined by illegitimacy of the regime and institutional support of the dissidents. This is based on a multivariate analysis in which historical justifications (extent and success of past strife) and regime institutional support (for instance, size of progovernment labor unions, government party seats in national legislature) lose their explanatory power, as do relative deprivation and coercive potential of the dissidents. The independent variables account for 68 percent of the variance. Mediating variables like justifications and balance all in all are more important determinants of the respective forms of political violence than the deprivation variables. The greater the dissidents' control of coercive resources, for example, the greater the likelihood of rebellion (and of protest; the partial correlation coefficient is .16 versus .11 in the latter case). On the other hand, the regime's coercive potential seems to be more effective in preventing rebellion than in preventing political protest. The institutional resources of (potential) dissidents do not lead to a reduction of the protest potential but seem to be used rather as a means of voicing protest (see also Cooper 1974: 287). Looking at the impact of regime coercive control and regime institutional support, a similar conclusion is at hand: democratic societies obviously are strong enough to prevent intense and more violent forms of civil strife but show a tendency for protest to occur *in spite of* their command of considerable coercive resources. If a regime is judged as legitimate, its citizens do have clear expectations about the regime's output. If it falls behind, (milder forms of) protest behavior may result "paradoxically" because these regimes have higher overall legitimacy, compared, for example, to more coercive regimes which seem to be able to prevent most kinds of protest but are more susceptible to rebellion.

A warning should be kept in mind, however, since the interpretations given above are based on indirect measures, upon which highly inferential statements are built. The arguments concerning channels open to dissidents and some of the likely consequences thereof provide an example. The degree of institutional resources available to potential protest groups in a society is assessed on the national level, and we do not have sufficient information to ascertain whether the above statements also hold true for *specific* groups of protesters. There may be wide institutional resources available to various groups in society but not to the protesting groups, who may thus feel excluded from the political process.

Even though some of Gurr's results may be due to characteristics of the respective samples and/or to measures of independent variables, in general his theoretical model does well enough to explain large portions of the variances. Unfortunately, similar multivariate analyses using other samples, for instance, countries at a medium level of development, have not yet been reported. Altogether there seems to be considerable evidence in Gurr's studies that turmoil and protest at the aggregate level are explained only partly by relative deprivation theorizing. There does not seem to be a direct covariation between deprivation (as indirectly measured) and protest behavior. If protest behavior is to be explained, it cannot be directly accounted for by referring to a protest potential (presumably) caused by deprivation and now finding its outlet. Rather it is the *structural transformations* of protest potentials—in Gurr's terminology, the "justifications" for political protest, which include illegitimacy of the regime—that are of major importance in determining whether and how much protest behavior is to occur. The statement that the greater the amount of discontent, the greater the likelihood of violent protests does not hold, as turmoil, especially nonviolent protest, often occurs in the absence of severe deprivation. Thus one cannot infer the size of protest potentials from the degree of deprivation nor, conversely, trace protest potentials or protest behavior back to deprivations alone. Also, protest may often be used as a means of introducing certain demands into the political process and thus not only be understood as a dependent variable but also as an independent variable. By using means of (violent) protest dissidents may want to improve their bargaining position; they are not merely reacting to aversive social conditions. It is likely that elements of tactics in the use of protest, as in other forms of political violence (as well as in the processes of coalition formation) cannot be captured with aggregate measures but rather require group-level measures. "Discussions of frustration and aggression, even if preceded by a consideration of social conditions conducive to these, tell us little about the struggle for power and interaction among competing social groups which is so crucial to the occurrence, magnitude, and consequences of political violence" (G. T. Marx 1972: 129).

Most critics of Gurr's work (Freeman 1972, Cohan 1975, Tilly 1975a, Salert 1976) have focused on his overemphasis of the relative deprivation variable and the gaps of measurement incurred without considering in greater detail either the operations used or their theoretical justification. The revisions carried out in Gurr and Duvall (1973), Gurr and Lichbach (1979), and Gurr et al. (forthcoming) respond to some of the earlier criticisms. In his earlier studies Gurr uses aggregate economic, political, and social indicators for inferring psychological states of mind. As Scheuch (1966) shows in a general discussion of this and other strategies of measurement, there are always problems of analysis if the level of measurement is not identical with the level of theoretical statements. In Gurr's theory, discrepancies between expectation levels and reality are said to cause perceptions of relative deprivation which generate discontent. Gurr uses only "objective" data and does not measure subjective reactions to these circumstances. Thus there is no direct relationship between Gurr's four forms of relative deprivation (Gurr 1969: 597–605) and his later analyses. Neither expectations nor the evaluation of (one's own or the state's) capabilities to fulfill these demands, both central components of Gurr's psychological-gap hypotheses, have been directly measured in his studies. Actually, the same measures are used to make inferences as to the two components of the gap-hypotheses (i.e., expectations and capabilities). Since relative deprivation is a perceptual concept and discontent a dispositional one, they can be assessed directly only in survey-type studies. A number of such studies have been carried out and are reviewed by Muller in Chapter 2 of this *Handbook*. Their results parallel those of studies using aggregate measures of deprivation: people's beliefs, especially about the political system and its legitimacy, are usually more important than discontent in determining their willingness to take part in protest.

There are other general points of criticism which have drawn less attention in the literature. Gurr uses highly complex indices as final measures of his independent variables; the objective is to avoid idiosyncracies of specific measures by using a whole battery of indicators. This multiple-index strategy may lead to distorted results. In Gurr (1970a), for example, the coercive resources of the regime and those of the dissidents are compared with each other. The same is done for their institutional resources. The "difference" score between coercive and institutional resources (using the former two difference scores) is then inserted in the multiple regression equation. Yet two countries could have considerably different numerical values on these components while the total balance score remained the same. Obviously, theoretically important differences can be obscured through such a procedure. Gurr has abandoned this kind of summary score in later works for this and similar reasons (Gurr 1972a, Gurr and Duvall 1973).

There is another more general drawback of Gurr's use of composite indicators. If one wishes to apply the theory to public policy, one could scarcely tell agents of the state or rebels which variable would be of prime importance or what the specific impact of a distinct variable would be.

> For example, riots involve violence, whereas antigovernment demonstrations, by definition in the coding, do not. The former may call for some contingency planning involving paramilitary requirements; yet this type of preparation for and display of force utilization would be little more than inefficient "overkill" at best in the latter instance. [Chadwick and Firestone 1972: 28]

Consequently, these authors attribute "very low social utility to the findings in their present form" (1972: 28). In the end the high degree of data reduction in many of Gurr's measures may increase the amount of variance explained, but it reduces the applicability of the results in social situations. Interestingly, in later work Gurr and Duvall (1973) replace most of the complex and hard-to-interpret indicators of conflict and its causes with raw or simply transformed measures. The requirements of forecasting in Gurr and Lichbach (1979) make it necessary for the researchers to go still further in reporting equations that specify how much change in which aspect of conflict follows from a given amount of change in each raw measure of a causal variable.

There are several other theoretical issues which should be mentioned. As Tilly (1971: 419; 1975a) has pointed out, building coalitions among groups of protesters is a much neglected subject in Gurr's theory and measures, as is the role of other parties to conflict.

> An important portion of collective violence pits contenders for power against one another, rather than rebels against regimes. Gurr's scheme eliminates such conflicts in principle, while his data include them in practice. No category in the scheme, furthermore, deals with the probability or the effect of agitation, organization, mobilization, leadership, pooling of resources, development of internal communications among potential rebels. We have only the gross differences combined in Social and Structural Facilitation. [Tilly 1975a: 495]

With respect to the second point, Tilly's criticism applies only to Gurr's early theoretical writings. In chapter 9 of *Why Men Rebel* (Gurr 1970b) a number of these factors are dealt with and some are operationalized in the most recent empirical work (Gurr and Lichbach 1979, Gurr et al. forthcoming).

Lastly, and equally important, political violence is analyzed as protest against the state or its agents, even though Gurr (1970b) in his *Why Men Rebel* deals extensively with state violence as a response to or cause of dissidence (see also Gurr et al. forthcoming). Nardin (1971: 59) has reminded us that the state's role in (violent) political conflicts is "Janus-faced": on the one hand the state acts to prevent the outbreak of political violence or to keep it under control once it has occurred, on the other hand the state itself is—and increasingly so (see the results for France, Germany, and Italy in Tilly, Tilly, and Tilly 1975)—a party to conflict. A more recent example is the political scene in Northern Ireland where the intervention of British troops led to the current escalation (see, for instance, Bell 1976). Yet, rather than accepting the verdict of Nardin who criticizes Gurr for having taken over the "point of view of the authorities" (Nardin 1971: 20), one may simply state that much of the present research in political violence is rather limited in scope since the strong contribution that state violence makes to political violence is mostly excluded in these analyses (exceptions being found in Hibbs 1973; Gurr 1970b; and especially in Gurr et al. forthcoming). If one were to compare the number of victims of state violence with those affected by dissidents' use of political violence, one probably would come up with a figure for state violence several times as high as for dissidents' violence, at least for the nineteenth and twentieth century, but probably also for the periods where so-called "pre-industrial crowds" prevailed: "destruction of property, then, is a constant feature of the pre-industrial crowd; but not destruction of human lives. . . . From this balance sheet of violence and reprisal, it would appear, then, that it was authority rather than the crowd that was conspicuous for its violence to life and limb" (Rudé 1964: 255–256). Some dramatic examples of regimes' use of violence against their subjects include reigns of terror in Uganda under Idi Amin (where the number of deaths approached 300,000 according to Amnesty International), in Equatorial Guinea under Francisco Macias Nguema (claimed by his opponents to have killed about 50,000 of the country's population of 324,000—see *Newsweek*, European edition, June 20, 1977: 28); and in Cambodia by the Red Khmers (see Shawcross 1978 for a discussion of the evidence). We cited above Gurr's evidence (1979) for fifty countries in 1966–1970 where the deaths of dissidents outnumbered the deaths of regime forces by a median ratio of 7 to 3.

One theoretical response to this kind of criticism is embodied in Gurr's recent collaborative work with Lichbach, in which the extent of protest and rebellion is attributed to dissidents and intensity is said to be determined mainly by the regime's response. The variables which in Gurr's earlier work were said to determine the magnitude of civil conflict (extent plus intensity) now are modeled as causes of the extent of conflict only. The intensity of conflict is attributed to the extent and form of dissident action, to the regime's institutional strength, and to whether or not the regime has a democratic form (Gurr and Lichbach 1979, Lichbach and Gurr forthcoming).

Some of these arguments also bear on the works of other researchers who have made cross-national analyses of political violence. As Gurr, however, has been one of the pioneers of this type of research and as his works have been widely disseminated, the thrust of our critique focuses on his approach. Other issues of concern are the cross-national equivalence of indicators (for instance, on the base of his indirect indicators Gurr must attribute an equal score of legitimacy to Ethiopia, Switzerland, and Sweden) and the issue of whether requirements of measurement level necessarily have to be met. Perhaps not surprisingly, using Gurr's data and model of civil strife, Blom (1973) reports a reduction of the explained variance from 65 percent to 34 percent when a rank-ordinal measure (Kendall's tau) is used. (The *structure* of results is not changed.) What is needed, then, is more information on the robustness of various measures, that is, to what degree violations of (strong) measurement assumptions (for instance, interval-level measurement of variables) can be tolerated without leading to invalid inferences.

HIBBS ON MASS POLITICAL VIOLENCE

Hibbs (1973) analyzes the determinants of collective protest and internal war, his two dimensions of mass political violence, during 1948–1967 in 108 countries, drawing on the data collection of Taylor and Hudson (1972). The period of investigation is split into two parts, 1948–1957 (D1) and 1958–1967 (D2), allowing for specification of time-lagged effects. The dependent variable, mass political violence, denotes violent activities (1) that are aimed *against the system*, (2) that are *political*, and (3) that are *collective* in nature. ("An exception . . . is the inclusion of assassinations, which typically are not sponsored by disaffected groups," Hibbs 1973: 7.) On the basis of factor analyses the dependent variable is divided into collective protest ("riots, antigovernment demonstrations, political strikes") and internal war ("assassinations, armed attacks, deaths").[10] In addition, coups d'état and government repression (negative sanctions) are included as separate dependent variables. Coups were not included in the factor analysis because they represent elite activities and not mass activities. Here only portions of Hibbs's final causal model need interest us (see Figure 5–2).

Starting with the relations between the four simultaneously determined dependent variables, the following conclusions are reached: collective protest is more likely (p = .483—all coefficients are path coefficients) to lead to negative sanctions than is internal war (.182). Negative sanctions may be a bad policy in case of internal war, where elements of the elites have already defected. Within the block of simultaneously determined variables, two causal sequences deserve special attention: for one, the path from collective protest through negative sanctions to internal war is more important than the reverse path. That is, coercive reactions of elites to collective protests may lead to a more intense form of political violence (see C.F. Doran 1976 for some parallel results for eight Caribbean countries during 1948–1964), namely, internal war, which in turn has an impact on military coups. One should, of course, recognize that these causal sequences are highly inferential in nature, as Hibbs does not use time-series data but only cross-sectional data. Considering the inhibiting conditions, negative sanctions in D1 are of primary importance ($-$.491) for internal war. Thus, the short-term effect of political repression (negative sanctions) may be an increase in political violence. In the long run, however, there is a greater probability of a mitigating effect.[11] On the other hand, there is no such dampening effect for the dependent variable of collective protest. "These findings firmly support the proposition that 'organized' and pur-

FIGURE 5–2. Hibb's final causal model of collective protest (including relationships with internal wars and military coups). SOURCE: Hibbs 1973: 181. Reproduced by permission.

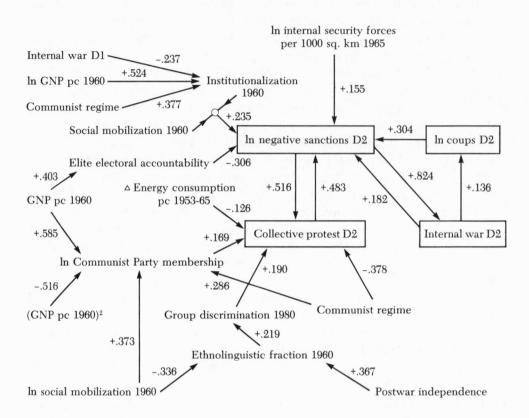

Key: ln = log-normal transformation
     D1 = first decade, 1948-57
     D2 = second decade, 1958-67
     pc = per capita
     O represents an interaction term

poseful kinds of mass violence are more easily discouraged by sustained repression than are 'spontaneous' and nonpurposeful expressions of discontent" (Hibbs 1973: 185). This interpretation is consistent with several other results (but see also footnote 11 *supra*; see Bwy 1968a for the reverse rationale).

The most important inhibiting influence is through communist regime (− .378 on collective protest and − .279 on internal war). Hibbs interprets these results by referring to the police-state climate in communist countries. (It should be pointed out that his measures are quite indirect as to this point.) The rate of economic development (indexed by "rate of change in energy consumption per capita") also inhibits collective protest (— .126). Elite electoral accountability also has a negative effect on collective protest. Assuming that elections are a means of controlling elites in democratic societies, there is at least an indirect effect (working through fewer negative sanctions, — .306) by which democratic political conditions lead to a reduction in the amount of political violence. Institutionalization tends to inhibit coups (— .171). When using institutionalization in interaction with other variables, more complex relationships emerge. If social mobilization exceeds institutionalization, a condition of major importance in Huntington's theory (see above), it turns out that this structural imbalance increases the probability of negative sanctions (.235) and, in turn, the likelihood of both forms of political violence. "This suggests that in nations where the burdens generated by social mobilization outrun the capabilities of socio-political institutions, political elites tend to resort to repression as an alternative means of social control" (Hibbs 1973: 187).

Analysis of some of the indirect effects gives the following results: gross national product per capita shows a positive relationship (.403) to elite electoral accountability (lending some credit to the hypothesis in Lipset (1959) linking economic and democratic political development) and thus indirectly leads to a reduction in negative sanctions and political violence. A similar effect is found when gross national product per capita is related to institutionalization: economically more developed nations have more stable institutions (.524) which impede the likelihood of coups (— .171) and, in combination with a comparatively lower degree of social mobilization, reduce the level of negative sanctions.

The variable of communist regime has a similar indirect influence via institutionalization (.337—but see below for a critical evaluation of this result), whereas there is a negative relationship between internal war in D1 and institutionalization (— .237). There is also a direct effect of internal war in D1 on internal war in D2 (.432). This provides strong evidence for the culture-of-violence thesis. Finally, two other determinants of collective protest, group discrimination (.190) and Communist Party membership (.169), both have positive effects. Discrimination against population segments ("the percentage of the population 'which is substantially and systematically excluded from valued economic, political, or social positions because of ethnic, religious, linguistic, or regional characteristics' " Gurr 1966: 71, quoted in Hibbs 1973: 74) thus leads to milder forms of violent protests. Depending on the elites' reactions to these protests (that is, the degree of negative sanctions), more violent protests may or may not arise. If political separatism is involved, however, the likelihood is much greater that more intense forms of political violence (internal war) will occur.

Another interesting independent variable is economic development, which leads to a reduction in political violence (through the effects on elite electoral accountability and on institutionalization). On the other hand, there is a curvilinear relationship between this explicative variable and Communist Party membership which in itself has a positive impact on collective violence (.169).

The merits of Hibbs's methodologically sophisticated approach should be apparent even from this sketch of some of his main results. We might, however, mention a few conditions neglected in this study. Hibbs points out that socioeconomic inequality is a potential causal variable left out of his equations. Furthermore, he mentions that he has neglected external interference (in political and economic terms) in internal conflict. Judging from the results of Gurr and Duvall (1973) this is a serious shortcoming. The most serious weakness, however, stems from using essentially cross-sectional data (even if several lags are incorporated into the measures) for testing causal statements. As time-series data were not available for most variables, this way of proceeding was the only viable alternative. In some cases the use of cross-sectional data may be justified.

> Short-duration time series simply cannot pick up the effects of such variables as regime type, levels of institutionalization, cultural differentiation, and democratization. These variables, which have important effects on levels of mass political violence, do not change much in the short run; and without variance, estimation precision and causal inference are not feasible. [Hibbs 1973: 201]

Yet the argument does not hold, for example, in the instance of relationships between collective protests and negative sanctions. The data source on which Hibbs relied (Taylor and Hudson 1972) provides twenty years of annual data on all conflict measures and negative sanctions for each country, which could have been analyzed to shed further light on the core relationships in his model (see Sanders 1978, 1979).

If one examines in detail the rationale for some of Hibbs's variables, a few questions remain. We doubt, for instance, that the measures of the welfare level or of the degree of institutionalization are directly applicable to communist states. (Hibbs actually adds a positive dummy term for communist regime, but this is not the point here.) In these countries the indicators of institutionalization may perhaps be better used for indexing totalitarianism. One might also wonder why "political authorities" should be "less inclined to apply 'Negative Sanctions' just because the Left has significant legislative political representation." As it turns out, they are not less inclined to do so (Hibbs 1973: 163). Furthermore, at various points indices are formed by additive combinations of various indicators without demonstrating that the procedure is theoretically or empirically justified. In addition, Sigelman and Yough point out that it is difficult to "understand how summing several raw indicators based on different metrics could conceivably preserve an 'interpretable metric'" (Sigelman and Yough 1978: 381).

Comparing the study of Hibbs with those of Gurr, a few interesting differences emerge. Many of Hibbs's statements unambiguously refer to macro-structures and not (or less so) to the behavior or reactions of smaller groups. Hibbs does not use indices as complex as those in Gurr's works. His theoretical interpretations are therefore much more easily comprehensible than those Gurr makes on the basis of abstract variables such as strain and traditions. Hibbs's strategy of incremental model specification allows him to test for various partial theories (this, to a lesser degree, also holds true for Gurr; see Gurr et al. forthcoming). However, one is impressed by the deductive reasoning found in Gurr's works, his most important weakness probably being that on the empirical level too many, often too divergent, variables are subsumed under too few theoretical concepts. It is interesting to note that Gurr and Duvall (1973; also Gurr and Lichbach 1979)—apart from incorporating some new variables—have reconstructed Gurr's theoretical model so as to be more explicit on the causal effects of specific, theoretically important variables. Hibbs's strategy clearly demonstrates how various partial theories (for instance, Huntington's hypotheses as well as Deutsch's social mobilization hypotheses) to explain political violence can be integrated and also can be more precisely tested. Hibbs may, however, be criticized for his theoretical eclecticism and for his lack of a coherent theoretical framework.

TILLY'S GROUP MOBILIZATION APPROACH

Empirical evidence and theoretical reasoning in the works of Gurr, Hibbs, Huntington, and others support the conclusion that structural conditions, that is, macro-political variables, combined with psychological deprivation variables are important for predicting civil conflict. Gurr, for one, argues that structural transformations lead to civil conflict *because* of their psychological effects. Without those transformations there is less or no motivation to collective action. Other ways of linking both theoretical streams are discussed below. The possibility of combining theories has to be borne in mind as we turn to what is perhaps the strongest attack on the relative deprivation approach, coming from Charles Tilly. On the basis of his data on collective conflict (mainly in France, 1830–1960, but also in Germany, 1830–1930, on several decades in Italy, and, more recently, in England), Tilly stresses the merits of his own group-centered approach as against deprivation and, as he calls them, "breakdown" theories.[12] Breakdown theories are said to be based on the "idea that collective violence appears as a by-product of processes of breakdown in society. Large structural rearrangements in societies—such as urbanization and industrialization—in this view tend to dissolve existing controls over antisocial behavior just as the very fact of rearrangement is subjecting many men to uncertainty and strain" (Tilly, Tilly, and Tilly 1975: 4). In general, Tilly claims breakdown theories to be invalid, while with respect to "tension release" models or deprivation models he notes that "they neglect the struggles among classes and power blocs which constitute the bulk of political conflict" (Tilly 1975a: 488).

The differences between the deprivation-frustration approach and Tilly's solidarity-resource mobilization theory have been succinctly summarized by Oberschall:

> Solidarity theorists maintain that uprooted masses do not account for most collective protest; stress that conditions that lead to violent protest are essentially the same as those that produce other forms of collective action; view all forms of collective action, including violent ones, as essentially purposeful, rational pursuits or defenses of collective interests; and note that violence is most frequently initiated and perpetrated by the agents of social control. Solidarity theorists do not minimize the effects of large-scale social changes upon the incidence and forms of social conflict, but they maintain that their impact on social conflict does not derive primarily from the production of tensions and grievances. Grievances and disaffection are a fairly permanent and recurring feature of the historical landscape. Social, economic, and political change act indirectly upon incidence and forms of conflict by changing the mobilization potential of various social formations, by changing the social milieu and ecological locus of conflict, and by changing the social control capabilities of the authorities. [Oberschall 1978a: 298]

Tilly is perhaps right with his attacks on primitive forms of breakdown and deprivation theories, yet more refined variants have been developed and tested with survey data (Muller 1975, Grofman and Muller 1973; see also Chapter 2 by Muller in this *Handbook*). On a grand historical scale and without survey data these theories will always be difficult to evaluate.

Tilly puts strong emphasis on (organized) power struggles and predicts that "collective violence tends to cluster around entries into the polity and exits from it" (Tilly 1978: 180). Yet he does not provide sufficient evidence for this basic contention. Moreover, his solidarity-resource mobilization approach is not exempted from other severe criticism (see Zimmermann 1980: chapter 8 for a more detailed account). The final causal model in Tilly, Tilly, and Tilly (1975: 244) seems to have been superimposed on the data. To give an example: the notion of power struggle is never precisely, that is, operationally, defined. Rather power is used in a general, somewhat metaphorical, sense. If Tilly objects to the ever present and applicable notion of deprivation, the same holds true for his notion of power struggles. Actually, only a very general framework is posited in which various forms of collective violence are found, forms that change over time. Tilly and his collaborators have acknowledged this themselves: "Despite a number of trials, we have not so far been able to develop a reliable procedure for enumerating contenders, measuring their mobilization, and characterizing their relationship to the existing structure of power which is truly independent of the conflicts we are attempting to explain" (Rule and Tilly 1972: 57; see also D. Snyder 1978 and the recent discussion and suggestions in Tilly 1978). What does power mean? How can it be measured? How does it affect the contending partners or the rest of the political system? How are gains and losses in power to be assessed? While making some suggestions as to how to answer these questions, Tilly's theory (1978: 115–133) is clearly underdeveloped in these respects.

A second point is related to this criticism: organizational strength, a key variable in Tilly's "mobilization–organization–power contending theory" of collective violence, is mainly assessed by the number of union members, which clearly is insufficient for indexing a theoretical variable of such importance to Tilly's causal model. As has been noted by Haupt (1977: 250), there is no further differentiation between various (forms of) organization, for instance, between unions, parties, or associations, and the specific impact these might have on the forms of collective action (but see also the study by Tilly and Lees 1974 for some noteworthy evidence in favor of Tilly's theoretical position). In any case, what is needed are indicators referring to behavioral aspects of organizational strength which are, of course, independent from the behavioral aspects that are to be explained.

A third problem is that the causal nature of the relationship between collective action and collective violence is not sufficiently specified in the theoretical model. How and when does collective action lead to collective violence? Is collective violence a last resort and/or a reaction to intensified repression by state agents? What is the causal nexus between the two variables? When elaborating a power-contending model for explaining collective violence and revolutionary activities, Tilly may perhaps have been too much influenced by French experiences, by political developments in a state whose high degree of political as well as economic and social centralization has been noted by numerous authors, Tocqueville and Marx being only the most renowned examples.

As to the individual hardship of protesters—their relative deprivation, in the sense of Gurr and Muller—there is no operationalization in the works of Tilly that comes near to a test. Following conventional usage in their study of disturbances in France from 1830 through 1968, Snyder and Tilly (1972) employ indices of food prices, of prices of manufactured goods, and of industrial production for measuring deprivation, thus running the same risks of fallacies of aggregation that imperil cross-national efforts to test deprivation theories. Although harshly put, Davies's comment is right: "Without other data, these indexes say only that there were fluctuations in food prices, manufactured goods prices, and industrial production" (Davies 1974: 608). Snyder and Tilly find only "insignificant" results when relating changes in these deprivation measures to collective violence (changes in the number of participants in disturbances), whereas their own measures of repression (excess arrests, size of national budget, man-days of detention in jail) fare considerably better, at least for the period of 1886–1939 ($R^2 = .49$). For 1830–1960 some changes in the predictive equation are introduced. R^2 drops to .17, leading the authors to conclude "that there are other variables acting on this system which we have not been able to grasp" (Snyder and Tilly 1972: 529). Their measure for indexing power struggles (elections to be held or not), however, turns out to be less powerful, although the signs are positive as predicted. They interpret their findings as being generally in favor of their power-contending model, even if the chain of inference is rather lengthy. Size of national budget is not necessarily an indicator of degree of repression used by incumbents against likely contenders. In his critique of this study, Halaby (1973) stresses the lack of correspondence between theoretical concepts and empirical measures employed, and points as well to several other methodological shortcomings. Snyder and Tilly (1973; see also Tilly, Tilly, and Tilly 1975: 81) report, however, that using real wages as a more direct measurement of deprivation also leads to insignificant results.

It is interesting to note that in his efforts to trace the rise and decline of contending groups Tilly runs the risk of committing a kind of group fallacy. His data on independent variables so far refer to macro-changes such as market penetration, urbanization, industrialization, formation of national authorities, and the nationalization of politics. Changes in the patterns of collective violence and strikes refer to group processes that are indirectly influenced by macro-changes, for instance, via processes or organization and mobilization. Yet a problem arises as to how to link processes of change at different levels of explanation within the same theoretical framework. There is a gap between the theoretical framework used, which is basically sociological and group-centered, and the measures employed, some of which refer to macro-changes and others of which acquire the status of macro-changes through the process of aggregation. Tilly speaks about three different themes he wants to interrelate: (1) the processes of state formation and industrialization; (2) conflicts between contending groups that might lead to regime changes, even in the form of revolution; and (3) groups that mobilize and participate in collective acts that may or may not be violent. His (published) data mostly refer to the third theme and cover some features of the first, but fall considerably short with respect to the second theme. Although many important theoretical suggestions derive from Tilly's skill in combining and linking these three different themes (see especially Tilly 1978: chapters 3 and 4), for purposes of developing an empirically grounded theory they must be sharply distinguished and linked in a clearer form so that operational measures can be developed.

Theories of discontent and solidarity theories need not be exclusive. "Do people respond to conflict situations voluntaristically, or as a function of their group membership? Do they participate in conflict behavior because they are innately aggressive, or frustrated, or culturally disposed to do so, or because of rationalistic calculation?" (Gurr 1978: 306). States of relative deprivation might be considered a background factor which in the presence of additional conditions leads to the formation of organizations. These in turn strengthen the solidarity among population segments that judge their state of deprivation as being intolerable and therefore call for changes. At best, deprivational states may represent a sufficient condition for protest and turmoil to occur, but certainly not a necessary condition.

> People may harbor intense grievances; yet they may possess few resources and may be vulnerable so that they can provide but negligible inputs to challengers. Others with but mild grievances, yet plentiful resources, might make substantial contributions even if they provide but a fraction of their resources to challengers. Societal breakdown is, to be sure, associated with the generation of discontent, but its main impact on conflict is by way of the costs of mobilization and collective action. Mobilizing the resources of disorganized collectivities is far costlier than doing it within solidary groups, because the latter already possess well-defined leadership and organization that can be enlisted on behalf of the challenger. [Oberschall 1978a: 306]

On the other hand, variables in solidarity theories such as organization of groups and mobilization of resources represent neither a sufficient nor a necessary condition for protest. Tilly has no explanation for why people are willing to be mobilized or why they should want to mobilize others (as to the latter, see Oberschall 1973). Some of the phenomena that are central to power contention theory are equally interpretable in terms of deprivation theory:

> Is it not possible to view losses and acquisitions of membership [in a polity] as forms of relative deprivation? Would it be unfair to say that challengers who are being denied polity membership are likely to be frustrated? Would it be inaccurate to say that members who are in the process of losing their membership are likely to perceive a gap between their desired values and declining capabilities? [Palmer and Thompson 1978: 310]

In general, we can suggest that an adequate account of protest (and rebellion) requires specification of motivational factors such as discontent and ideology as well as of mobilization factors of resource organization and power contention. The goal for future research should not be to supplant either approach but to combine them in a more fruitful way. Much of the critical cross-fire found in the literature stems from these differences in paradigms and approaches. No single approach provides a comprehensive account of civil conflict. Rather macro-structural conditions and changes stressed in the theorizing of Gurr, Tilly, Hibbs, Huntington, and others must be combined with group-level theoretical statements as suggested by

Tilly and by Gamson (1975) and finally must also be related to conditions and changes of individual deprivation, as worked out by Gurr and Muller, to name only key proponents and researchers here (see also the respective analytical suggestions in Snyder 1978).

SOME GENERAL METHODOLOGICAL ISSUES

With regard to cross-national analyses of political violence, numerous points of methological critique have already been made. There are, however, some more general questions of method still to be taken up. The first two sections here are concerned with data problems that arise in quantitative research and with some of the strategies that can be used to deal with them. Specifically, I focus on problems of collecting data on political violence and on some questions of the appropriate units and levels of analysis and measurement. The last section identifies some topics that heretofore have gotten relatively little attention in quantitative studies.

PROBLEMS OF SOURCE COVERAGE

The strongest threat to the reliability and validity of cross-national research on political violence probably arises from the limited coverage of the various new sources from which data are collected on conflict events. One should, however, not confuse the two problems dealt with here: one is whether conflict data are descriptively correct (univariate findings). The answer is, "obviously not." Yet, this need not necessarily have an effect on the second problem, the *structure* of results (bivariate or multivariate findings). Conflict analyses can still be correct, as far as the structure of relations among variables is concerned, even though they may be somewhat incorrect descriptively. This is possible if conflict data as reported in current news sources are *representative*, even though lacking in completeness or descriptive accuracy. There are two general sources of error in this respect.

1. *Not all violent political conflicts are reported.* There are two reasons for this. First, news about internal conflicts may be suppressed or distorted for political reasons. Censorship may, of course, affect other variables, too, such as those referring to the coercive capacity or acts of political systems. Second, only the most important or newsworthy events are reported, with less important conflicts being left out.

2. *Incorrect data are reported.* Information on the magnitude and other properties of violent political conflicts may be inflated or suppressed or even invented. Insufficient means of communication and/or low interest in events in some countries and regions may be responsible for this type of error.

So far we have identified only some possible sources of error. Information on how these errors affect the relationships under study would be more important, of course. Whereas random error leads to an attenuation of the respective correlations, and thus to conservative tests of the underlying hypotheses, systematic errors may either lower or inflate relationships. It could be argued, for instance, that even relatively intense conflicts are not always reported or that errors might occur in case of outliers that would not be compensated for by random error.

Whereas some researchers doing comparative studies of political violence introduce controls to test whether errors are random or whether they systematically affect their results, only a few studies have compared the coverage of various sources. Does different coverage affect the results in a random or systematic manner? C. F. Doran et al. (1973) performed one such analysis (for further studies along these lines see Scolnick 1974: 486–489). The authors applied the coding procedures of Feierabend and Feierabend (1966) to reports of conflict phenomena in thirteen Caribbean countries during 1948–1964. In addition to the Feierabends' "global" data source, *Deadline Data,* they made use of the *Hispanic-American Report.* They report, for example, that *Deadline Data* reported far fewer oppositional activities than the regional source, which in general is more detailed. Obviously, when collecting conflict data one should use more than one source to control for potential single-versus-multiple source differences and at least one regional or local source to take care of global-versus-regional differences.

A study by Hazlewood and West (1974) reports results leading to less skeptical conclusions than those of C. F. Doran et al. (but see also the criticism in Jackman and Boyd 1979). While also discovering that the regional source (*Hispanic American Review*) reported more thoroughly (years: 1955–1960, for twenty Latin American countries; indicators taken from studies by Rummel, Tanter, Feierabend and Feierabend 1966, Borock 1967, and Banks 1971) than the global sources (*New York Times Index, Deadline Data, New International Yearbook, Britannica Book of the Year, Facts on File*) Hazlewood and West nevertheless did not find distortions of *relationships* among variables. However, they tested only two hypotheses. A similar result emerges after performing factor analyses: "Despite the low bivariate correlations, the correlations between the global data and the regional data factor structures demonstrate the basic similarity of the data patterns regardless of their collection source(s)" (Hazlewood and West 1974: 330).

A similar conclusion as in Doran et al. has to be drawn if the coverage of the *New York Times*—for some researchers the best general source available—is compared to that of regional sources, as Taylor and Hudson (1972) have done. They relied mainly on the *New York Times Index,* which gives more condensed information than is found in the newspaper itself, but also used various other sources, notably the Associated Press card file for Latin America and Europe, the *Africa Diary* for African countries (apparently the only area where the *New York Times Index* falls considerably short) and the *Middle East Journal* for the Middle East. After introducing various controls as to the reliability and coverage of their various sources, they come to these general conclusions:

> First, using secondary sources tends to compensate for deficiencies and gaps in the primary source rather than to accentuate them. Second, although there is variation from country to country and from variable to variable, this variation occurs as much within a second source as between them so that the different second sources used do not constitute a barrier to cross-regional comparison. Finally, although using data from third sources would have increased the total numbers of events by perhaps as much as 15 percent, it would not have substantially altered the overall picture. [Taylor and Hudson 1972: 422]

The most recent and most ambitious test of the effects of the use of multiple sources on the analysis of political violence has been carried out by Jackman and Boyd (1979) who study the patterns of conflict in thirty black African countries. Basically, their results underscore the resumé by Taylor and Hudson (1972). In particular, Jackman and Boyd report that in comparing event counts from their data sources (*Keesing's Contemporary Archives, Facts on File,* and *African Recorder*) with data from the *World Handbook of Political and Social Indicators* (sources for Africa: *New York Times Index* and *Africa Diary*), "the benefits of reliance on multiple sources [seem to] outweigh the costs." Thus differences in source coverage may have an effect on the findings, yet "these differences [may] stem at least as much from variations across data sets in event definitions and coding procedures." To test for these explanations, which occur to them while comparing the source coverage of their three sources with that of the *World Handbook* and that of *Black Africa* (Morrison et al. 1972), Jackman and Boyd disaggregate their data on numbers of antigovernment demonstrations and political strikes by source. When testing the correlations of these two variables with measures of social mobilization and multipartyism, they find no source coverage effects in spite of the expectation that collective protest events, compared to acts of rebellion, might be underrepresented, especially in global sources. That is, the structure of multiple regression equations designed to explain numbers of conflict events is essentially the same, whichever data source is used. A second test, on the effects of differential source coverage when relating coups d'état in twenty-nine African countries to four explanatory variables, leads to essentially the same conclusion. Even though the findings of Jackman and Boyd may not hold in other contexts and for other variables, their two tests lend support to the argument "that the cost-benefit ratio from using multiple sources may be unnecessarily high." This conclusion is strengthened if one takes into consideration that African countries are primarily underreported in most of the data sources currently available.

It will be of interest to find out whether similar conclusions are reached when measures of conflict properties rather than event counts are compared in source-coverage studies. As pointed out above, Gurr argues that the "essential research question is whether it is more appropriate to measure the *properties* of conflict such as its duration, intensity, scale, and impact, either in single events or at the national level; or to concentrate on the *incidence* of conflict, i.e., on the number of distinguishable events which occur" (Gurr 1974a: 250–251). He criticizes compilers of conflict data who "repeatedly—and mistakenly, I think—. . . treat counts of conflict events as though they were conflict properties" (Gurr 1974a: 251).

UNITS AND LEVELS OF ANALYSIS

Another methodological and theoretical point deserving attention is the need to gather data that more adequately reflect on underlying theoretical questions. Many of our theoretical questions require, not cross-sectional or even time-series data, but information on sequences or processes of actions and reactions of conflicting groups. This will also have consequences for the units of analysis and inference since "the unit or units for which the longitudinal relationship is hypothesized cannot be the same as those for which the cross-sectional relationship is established" (O. D. Duncan et al. 1961: 166). In the near future this may not be possible at the broad cross-national level. Yet in more homogeneous and better reported regions efforts of this kind may lead to an enormous theoretical and practical payoff. Especially if policy implications are at stake in one way or another, sequential data are needed. Tilly (1978) has shown a viable alternative here. His detailed data on conflict in European countries seem to allow for statements on the circumstances making for either nonviolent or violent forms of protest behavior. Gamson (1975) has followed him in his investigation of the determinants of group outcomes for fifty-three "randomly" selected American protest groups between 1800 and 1945.

No longer are we concerned with patterns of political conflict that characterize different polities as such. Rather the unit of analysis changes from the national level to the group level which may lead to theoretically and empirically more fruitful statements in this area of research than are found in the present cross-national literature on political violence. It might even be suggested that only national-level conflicts such as revolutions, civil wars, and coups d'état are fruitfully studied at the national level. The group level of analysis seems more appropriate for the study of protest and localized forms of rebellion.

Empirically grounded statements referring to groups and their activities would approach the principle of direct measurement for the study of protest. They might extend to the history of groups, to their rise and decline, to processes of group mobilization (for instance, via existing core groups, quasi-groups or transitory teams; see Oberschall 1973, 1978b) and coalition formation, to the problems of organizational coordination of resources, to interactions between groups and the state, to processes of bargaining, to outcomes of group conflict, and to strategic aspects in the use of violent means. This is a perspective that so far has been largely missing from the cross-national aggregate analyses.

Group-based data should also allow for more exact measurement of the mobilization of resources (see Snyder 1978 and Tilly 1978 for some theoretical and empirical considerations). Tilly's idea of "catness" (1978: 63 ff.)—borrowed from H. White (n.d.)—seems to be a useful guideline here. As summarized by Oberschall:

> Solidary organization is a product of catness and netness, called catnet for short. Catness refers to the strength of a shared identity in a group and to the sharpness of social boundaries that comprise all those who share a common characteristic. Netness refers to the density of networks among group members that link them to each other by means of interpersonal bonds. Solidarity increased with catness. Mobilization in turn can be measured by the amount and kind of resources in a group multiplied by the probability that these will be delivered for the pursuit of group goals, when needed. [Oberschall 1978a: 308]

In sum, measures should refer to appropriate levels of theoretical inquiry: the aggregate level (nations, cities, etcetera), collectivities (groups and organizations), and/or individuals (see the discussion in Snyder 1978). If this were achieved, such theoretical issues as this could be confronted: "longitudinal data on groups and aggregate economic timeseries could indicate whether mobilization levels tend to increase in prosperous times, but *not* whether that occurs because individual members *of those groups* have more resources upon which collective claims can be made" (D. Snyder 1978: 521). Collecting data on the group level, that is, "following groups over time" (D. Snyder 1978: 519), is certainly a time-consuming undertaking. Yet in principle these data—and even data on individual perceptions (for instance, states of relative deprivation)—can be collected.

Finally, there is the issue as to which indicators should be included in the dependent variable. This is, of course, not merely a technical question but rather reflects strong differences among theoretical approaches, since the choice of the dependent variable corresponds with the unit of theoretical and empirical analysis. Thus some approaches by their very nature must produce different answers, or more appropriately put, cannot provide answers to some of the questions of interest raised. This being the case, there is no "right" or comprehensive approach to the study of civil conflict. Rather several approaches dealing with different foci of research (the national level, the group/organization level, and the individual level) must be combined to cover the lacunae of research. In short, *cross-level analysis* is called for in future studies of civil conflict if one wants to answer the question of how the conditions making for civil conflict at different levels of analysis are linked to one another. With respect to the dependent variable, the following are some of the options:

1. Obviously, if one follows the group strategy pursued by Gamson, a group's involvement in acts of political violence would be the appropriate dependent variable.

2. If the focus shifts to the outcomes of violent conflict, achievement of the pursued goals of the group becomes the appropriate explanandum.

3. There is also considerable variation (and disagreement) as to the construction and measurement of the dependent variables in aggregate measures of political violence. D. Snyder (1978: 522 ff.) has summarized some of the problems likely to be encountered, especially in the cross-national aggregate approaches to the study of violent political conflict. More generally, the task is to develop theoretically appropriate structural equation models that include multiple indicators of unmeasured variables. Whereas there are various possibilities, for instance, using event counts as in the *World Handbook* (Taylor and Hudson 1972) or constructing measures of properties as Gurr, Tilly and Snyder, and others do, the strategy pursued by Feierabend and Feierabend (1966) is the least justifiable one. They let "experts" scale the intensity of a number of categories of conflict events such as riots, mass arrests, assassinations, guerrilla warfare, civil wars, coups d'état, and—difficult to justify—other events such as general elections, resignation of cabinet officials, or peaceful demonstrations. On the basis of the scale values of such events they construct summary profiles of the "political instability" of nation–states. Obviously, correlations between the scaled instability indicators of Feierabend, Feieraband, and Nesvold (1969: 682) and the property measures of Gurr are not very helpful (see also Morrison et al. 1972: 125–126 for another such inappropriate comparison). Furthermore, "indicators of official force [such as mass arrests] should not be included in measures of collective violence and of coercion" (Snyder 1978: 523; see also the discussion in D. Snyder 1976: 288–289).[13]

TOPICS FOR FUTURE RESEARCH

Our consideration of the resource mobilization approach to protest helps identify a number of lacunae in systematic, comparative research on protest. For example, the problems of building organizations and of organization maintenance, the extent of continuity in leadership and membership structure, and the related question of goal displacement should receive more attention from scholars engaged in cross-national research on violent protest behavior (see Zald and Ash 1966 for some useful hypotheses in this respect). As several authors (Oberschall 1973, McCarthy and Zald 1977, Tilly 1978) emphasize, some of the problems of organizational coordination of resources, of division of labor, of winning a large member base, and so forth, may frequently be solved by mobilizing and combining already existing core groups.

Secondly, as the "surge and decline of collective action occurs within a system that has dynamic properties of its own," one should study "contagion effects, bandwagon effects [see the threshold models in Granovetter 1978], strategic interaction among participants, focal points, and pacesetter-follower relationships . . . in their own right" (Oberschall 1978a: 312; see also Tilly 1978: chapter 3). One has to look for "patterns of escalation and deescalation after the initiation of violence; and the interactions that produce violence in some 'intrinsically nonviolent' events and not in others" (D. Snyder 1978: 513). As Tilly argues persuasively:

> To understand and explain violent actions, you must understand nonviolent actions. Any study which treats violent events alone deals with the product of two different sets of determinants: (1) the determinants of collective action in general, whether it produces violence or not; (2) the determinants of violent outcomes to collective action. . . . [In the] first category of determinants, we find such items as the frequency of violations of established rights, the mobilization levels of different contenders for power, the current costs of different forms of action which are in the available repertoire. . . . In the second, we find the presence or absence of counterdemonstrators, the tactics of repressive forces, the length of time during which opposing parties are in direct contact with each other. . . . Each of the two sometimes changes while the other remains more or less the same: demonstrations become more frequent, although the percentage of demonstrations which produce street fighting remains the same; the authorities get tougher with strikers, although strike propensities have not altered. Either one changes the frequency of collective violence. A proper explanation of violence levels must decompose into at least these two components. [Tilly 1978: 182–183]

Research of this kind should provide answers that fill some of the black boxes in current research. At present measures of political and economic system conditions are related—via highly aggregated measures of institutional and coercive resources—to general forms and properties of protest events without showing how and why this or that type of violent or nonviolent protest event occurs. As pointed out above, cross-level analyses are called for, analyses that combine data on systemic conditions with information on processes of group mobilization and interaction with other parties to conflict. Empirical democratic theory, raising questions about how demands are raised, how they are optimally introduced into the political process, and transformed into outcomes without endangering the survival of the polity, should benefit from such research. Conflict researchers who have concentrated on "why men rebel" should not neglect the other side of the equation, "What happens when men rebel," that is, how conflict is regulated and resolved, and the eventual outcomes for the parties to conflict and for society at large.

Finally, the strategies of aggregation and disaggregation followed in cross-national research on political conflict deserve close attention. For example, a regional and time-wise disaggregation of Hibbs's data leads to results (Sanders 1978, 1979) at variance with Hibbs's results. In his recent studies Gurr followed another strategy of disaggregation, namely, to deal no longer with complex multifold measures of abstract theoretical variables but rather to use raw or simply transformed measures wherever justifiable. In our survey of theoretical variables and empirical findings in the literature it became apparent more than once that different facets of the "same" theoretical variable (for instance, socioeconomic change or socioeconomic inequality) can have quite different effects on the respective dependent variables. We need to know more about how the results are affected by the processes of aggregation and disaggregation with respect to (1) regions, subregions, and other territorial units, (2) periods of observation—including, where appropriate, time-lagged analyses, as well as (3) different aspects of the "same" theoretical variables.

CONCLUDING REMARKS: DEMOCRACY AND PROTEST

Rather than taking up again the wide variety of findings on political protest, I would like to single out two issues here. The first is the relationship between democracy and protest, which in some measure summarizes the more important findings on the determinants of protest. The argument leads, secondly, to the question of whether protest is the price democracies must pay for their long-term survival.

Are conditions of political democracy in contemporary societies a safeguard against protest, a catalyst for protest, or is there no general relationship at all to the dependent variables under review here? Obviously, the question can be answered only in contrast to other political conditions, such as autocracy. If democracy entails more political protest, is it in any way functional for the operation of democracy? Is there a "noisy and disrespectful participatory democracy" to come, as Marsh (1977: 234) predicts for Britain? Before any conclusions can be reached, the following set of conditions should be kept in mind: if dissent is constitutionally protected and institutionalized, for instance, via parliamentary mechanisms, and if disruptive protest is the principal means by which some kinds of groups organize themselves and exert coercive influence on others, there simply is no base for expecting a withering away of protest and turmoil. In the words of Eckstein and Gurr: "The risk of *chronic* low-level conflict is one of the prices democrats should expect to pay for freedom from regimentation by the state—or by authorities in other social units, whether industrial establishments, trade unions, schools and universities, or families" (Eckstein and Gurr 1975: 452; emphasis added).

Much of the evidence and speculation about the conditions of protest in democracy can be summarized in a causal model, as sketched in Figure 5-3. The main arguments underlying the linkages in the model are reviewed here.

1. Democracies provide no immediate obstacles to mobilizing groups. Liberty to do so is guaranteed by law and tradition. ("The law protects the right of dissent but grants no right to violate the law in expressing dissent," Horton and Leslie 1974: 650.)

2. High levels of wealth in western democracies facilitate group mobilization.

3. The presence of ethnic, religious, regional, racial, linguistic, or other communal minorities should affect the mobilization of groups and also have direct effects on the ultimate dependent variable, political protest.

4. Authorities in democracies usually refrain from using the full strength of coercive power at their disposal, due in part to the fact that the state as an actor often is not directly involved in conflict in democracies. Conditions (1) through (4) together facilitate the mobilization of groups. Group mobilization, in turn, increases the number of political participants which in itself should increase the likelihood of opposition.

5. Because of their values and their dependence on popular support, democratic elites fairly often respond favorably to protest, which tends to enhance future protest. This toleration of protest by incumbent elites is reciprocally related to their low use of coercive potential. (For reasons of parsimony we have omitted this double-arrow as well as other possible arrows in the model.

6. Moreover, "illegitimate policies or incumbents in otherwise highly legitimate polities are especially likely to inspire sharp protests at those policies and leaders, because they threaten people's general sense of identification with the polity" (Gurr and McClelland 1971: 32). Gurr has succinctly summarized this chain of arguments:

> Among nations generally, political groups most often mobilize people for strife. . . . Strife in the more developed and democratic nations is more often organized by legal political groups than in other nations. . . . The implications are that strife is a recurrent facet of the political process and that the effect of economic development and of political democratization is to channel it into the political process rather than to insulate politics from violence. [Gurr 1969: 586]

7. Shrinking rates of economic growth in affluent contemporary industrialized democracies also contribute to higher levels of political protest. The effect should be even stronger in case of absolute economic decline—a relationship that is not unique to democracies.

8. Finally, since democratic elites are disposed to make concessions to protest at least sometimes, rebellion becomes unnecessary for most dissidents. Also, according to Hibbs's (1973) results, low levels of coercive response make it less likely that rebellion will occur.

Autocracies—and totalitarian states even more so—are much better able than democracies to prevent the occurrence of protest. Yet there is evidence that rebellion is also inhibited by democratic political conditions

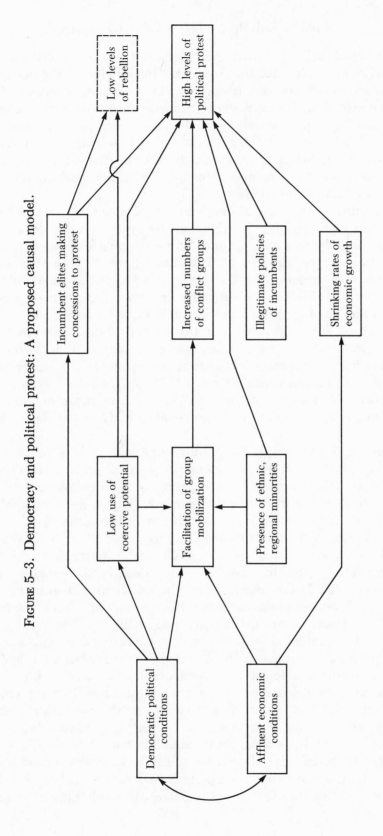

FIGURE 5-3. Democracy and political protest: A proposed causal model.

NOTE: All linkages are positive.

not just by totalitarian political order, whereas noncommunist autocracies often start to crumble once the conditions for rebellion have been met. If protest escalates to forms of internal war, for example, because authorities respond to protest with inconsistent repressive measures, autocracies are in danger of collapsing as are democracies. In "praetorian societies" (Huntington 1968) characterized by high political participation and a relatively low degree of political institutionalization, protest may well lead to military coups (see, for instance, Fossum 1967: 235; and the indirect influence via internal war in Hibbs 1973).

Taking into account the limited empirical evidence available, there hardly seems to be any justification for linking the greater occurrence of protest in some democracies to their long-term political stability, as some authors (for example, Iglitzin 1970) want to have it. There is simply too much variation among democratic countries, from relatively quiet democracies like Finland, Denmark, or Switzerland via democracies somewhat shaken by protest and turmoil to noisy participatory democracies such as Italy, France, and the United States. Perhaps Snyder's recommendation is the most sensible one here, namely, to look for "conditional theories" that specify "structural conditions . . . across which the validity of explanations varies" (Snyder 1978: 527). Claims about generally valid theories of protest will thus be dismissed in favor of more disaggregated analyses, of kinds already undertaken by Gurr (1972a), Tilly, and others.

It seems as if the long-term stability or survival of a political order depends not so much on the occurrence of political protest as on the basic legitimacy and the consistent organization of political structures. In an empirical study of persistence and change of 336 polities from 1800–1971, Gurr (1974b) comes to this major conclusion: "The more closely a polity resembles a pure democracy *or* pure autocracy, as defined here, the longer it is likely to have persisted" (Gurr 1974b: 1502; italics in original). Perhaps democratic polities that are internally consistent in the sense of Eckstein and Gurr (1975) also possess a greater reservoir of legitimacy—or in Easton's (1965) conceptualization, of "diffuse support"—and thus can survive a wide variety of protest and turmoil without severely limiting the conditions of organized dissent (for a discussion of some of the issues involved here see Zimmermann 1979). Furthermore, there are other obstacles and institutional safeguards in democracies that tend to limit the impact of protest. Dissidents' prospects are enhanced by forming coalitions among protesting groups, by sizable swings in the electorate (see Piven 1976 with respect to the United States), by getting the favorable attention of the media, and by having their demands voiced in decision-making bodies—but these are difficult to accomplish. Evidence that protest does at times have a significant impact on policies in democratic states is reviewed in Chapter 7 of this *Handbook*. But it is likely that other means of exerting political influence have higher rates of success and involve lower costs. Protest may be an efficient means to call attention to demands and problems, but it often provokes others to use their coercive power, thus worsening the protesters' situation.

It is not necessary to assume that protest is inherently successful or functional for democracies to recognize that under certain conditions it satisfies some "positive" functions (for a critique of other functional statements see Zimmermann 1980: chapter 9). "The virtue of political protest—especially in democracies—is that it can challenge consensually-arrived-at majority tyranny . . . dissent has proved itself as a powerful form of veto over dominant interests" (E. Kent 1971: 9). Protest can bring new social groups and new leaders into the political arena and thus provide a training ground for leadership in other positions. If protest and turmoil call attention to problem areas hitherto neglected and if they lead to solutions, they may be said to have a long-term beneficial effect. If (potential) dissidents gain access to institutional channels for expressing their protests, a better overall integration of the political system may result. If these channels prove to be lacking or blocked, however, the long-run future of the whole political system may be at stake because protest potential will accumulate over time to a critical level. If one were to use Hirschman's (1970) terminology, *exit* rather than *voice* may be the result. In spite of recent work by Linz (1978) on "crisis, breakdown, and reequilibration of democratic regimes," we are still far from having solid information about the conditions under which rebellious or apathetic exit rather than vociferous protest occurs.

NOTES

1. In most of these studies, P-factor analyses of the conflict variables are carried out. If one wants to characterize countries on the base of their factor scores on the respective dimensions, a Q-factor analysis has to be performed (see Banks 1972). Yet such a characterization of conflict scores of countries might also be achieved without running a factor analysis first (see Gurr's "world patterns" approach below). Also, Banks reports that "essentially similar results emerge whether variable cluster (R-mode or P-mode) or case cluster (Q-mode) techniques are employed" (Banks 1972: 507).

2. A longer period and more political units are included in Taylor and Hudson (1972), who report annual numbers of events in 136 countries for 1948 to 1967. The third edition of the *World Handbook of Political and Social Indicators* extends this data collection to 1977. Gurr's data include detailed coding of the properties of conflicts, Taylor and Hudson's data do not.

3. A class group was said to have participated in an event if it reportedly made up a substantial fraction of either the rank-and-file or the leadership of the dissident group involved.

. . . Among the "middle-class" groups are students, small businessmen and white-collar workers, and professionals—the first of these more often involved than any of the others. The "governing classes" include high officials, civil servants, and members of the military and police services—but only when they were themselves dissidents, not when acting in their official capacities. [Finally,] the "lower classes" include peasant farmers, rural and urban workers, and the unemployed, but in many events information was too imprecise for determination of just which of these groups were involved. [Gurr et al. forthcoming]

4. One might argue to the contrary that with increasing richness in a society there is more to fight about (Gurr and Duvall 1973: 158).

5. Anocracy refers to a "state . . . which has minimal functions, an uninstitutionalized pattern of political competition, and executive leaders constantly imperiled by rival leaders" (Gurr 1974b: 1487).

6. Again it seems noteworthy that similar indicators are chosen for indexing opposing theoretical concepts. For example, Duff and McCamant consider increases in education—in opposition to other authors—as an indicator of want satisfaction and not of want generation. They report consistently low negative relations to political violence, when education (percentage of children in schools) is relatively higher than the degree of mobilization (Duff and McCamant 1976: 123). Economic development should, however, be an important third variable here.

7. Discussing the implications of various techniques of standardization, Sigelman and Yough (1978: 379) point out in this context that "in sum, conclusions about the empirical validity of the overall Huntington framework and its individual predictions seem contingent upon the technique chosen, perhaps ill-advisedly, to generate composite indices." Operational shortcomings are also encountered in the ten-nation study of Schneider and Schneider (1971) who provide the strongest statistical evidence so far for Huntington's theory but deal only with a few mostly Western European nations.

8. "Moreover, the current size of these forces may in part be a *response to* the magnitude of previous mass violence, raising the problem of what causes what?" (Hibbs 1973: 86).

9. Weede (1975: 415–416), however, points out that by way of constructing their predictor variable "strain," Gurr and Duvall confound independent and dependent variables, since only correlates of internal conflict are accepted as indicators of strain and since the weight of these indicators is determined ex post facto, after regressing internal conflict on economic discrimination, political discrimination, cleavages, and economic dependence.

10. Some of the definitional ambiguities in Hibbs's study are brought up in the critique by Smaldone who notes that Hibbs's

selection of certain domestic event variables as measures of mass political violence is questionable. For example, the inclusion of *nonviolent* antigovernment demonstrations as an indicator of political violence is hardly appropriate. Additionally, assassinations are also dubious measures of *mass* political violence, especially when the assassination of opposition leaders and newspapers editors is subsumed in the definition of *antisystem* behavior. The death of persons in opposition is more likely to be regime-inspired, and more accurately indexes elite repression. Riots are also questionable indicators of mass political violence, unless they are specifically directed against the incumbent authorities. It is possible, for instance, that rioting may be more a measure of ethnic or sectarian conflict than antisystem violence. [Smaldone 1976: 153–154]

Ambiguities of this or another sort are likely to be found in most cross-national studies of political violence.

11. Tilly, Tilly, and Tilly (1975) however, contend that repression

    works in the short run. It works even better in the long run: so far as we can tell, it is not true that a population beset by consistent tyranny eventually becomes so frustrated that it will do anything to throw off the yoke; in fact, repressed populations demobilize, work through the approved channels of collective action, and seek noncollective means of accomplishing their ends. [Tilly, Tilly, and Tilly 1975: 285]

    See also Weede (1977) who performs a re-analysis of Hibbs's data, regroups the data into different periods of observation, and reports results more in favor of the Tilly et al. position. The strategy of disaggregation is also employed by Sanders (1978: 126) who reports "several significant regional effects . . . which Hibbs' analysis fails to specify." Also, he presents results not in accordance with the relationships between Hibbs's four ultimate dependent variables. Disaggregating Hibbs's data on a yearly or monthly base also leads to divergent results (Sanders 1979).

12. It should be noted that deprivation theories and breakdown theories are not necessarily the same. Tilly at various points seems to treat them as two sides of the same coin.

13. There are other serious shortcomings in the pioneering cross-national aggregate analyses of the Feierabend group, for example, the subscription to a primitive version of the frustration–aggression hypothesis, lack of fit between theoretical concepts such as political instability and the measures employed, infrequent use of control variables, arbitrary classification of nation clusters, and logical and empirical inconsistencies in the construction of their index of systemic frustration (see the discussion in Zimmermann 1980: chapter 5).

CHAPTER 6

On the Outcomes of Violent Conflict

Ted Robert Gurr

IN 1965 HARRY ECKSTEIN OBSERVED that "almost nothing careful and systematic has been written about the long-run social effects of internal wars" (1965: 136). The same observation could have been made about the outcomes of lesser conflicts like protest movements, riots, and coups d'état. About all that could be gleaned from the academic literature as of 1965 were a few items of theoretical speculation about the functions of violent conflict and a handful of case studies of the aftermaths of revolution.

In the fifteen years since 1965 a modest body of empirical findings on conflict outcomes has accumulated, most of it concerned with one of three issues: the policy impact of American protests and riots of the 1960s; the socioeconomic consequences of some twentieth-century revolutions, notably those of Mexico, Russia, Bolivia (1952), China, and Cuba; and the impact of military coups d'état on development in the Third World. Theoretically, however, the subject is almost as primitive as it ever was. No consensus can be discerned on how to conceptualize and categorize outcomes. Studies have focused variously on the fate of challenging groups,

NOTE: This chapter makes significant use of ideas and bibliographic material developed in my Fall 1978 graduate seminar on conflict theory and research at Northwestern University. I should especially like to thank Stephen C. Brooks, who surveyed the studies of riot impacts, and Kristin Bumiller, who reviewed studies of the outcomes of Latin American revolutions.

I have also benefited greatly from comments on an earlier draft of the chapter by Michael Betz, James W. Button, John M. Echols, Harry Eckstein, William A. Gamson, Mark Iris, Robert W. Jackman, Edward T. Jennings, Jr., David M. Lampton, Mark Irving Lichbach, E. Wayne Nafziger, Michael F. O'Keefe, Philippe Schmitter, Chong-Soo Tai, and Charles Tilly. It is significantly better as a consequence, though it falls short of some of their recommendations.

governmental policies toward protestors, the reallocation of public funds, the altered distribution of political power and wealth, and trajectories of national development. But nowhere is there any debate over the relative importance of these outcomes or how they relate to one another. The only general theories which purport to explain any aspect of outcomes at all are strategic ones that specify conditions under which rebels or regimes should be able to win military and political victory. Beyond that, one finds an assortment of middle-range hypotheses about how this or that aspect of one kind of open conflict influences a particular kind of outcome.

This chapter attempts to bring research on outcomes into focus. The general subject is the consequences of open, intergroup conflict character- ized by the use or explicit threat of violence (a delimitation elaborated in part II, below). Some obstacles to systematic research on the subject are reviewed in part I, an exercise that leads to a preliminary but general scheme for relating different kinds of outcomes in part II. Part III reviews current theory and research on the fate of groups in conflict, part IV surveys what is known about the consequences of protest and the policy and systemic effects of seizures of power.

I. SOME PROBLEMS OF PERSPECTIVE

Systematic research on the outcomes of conflict has been impeded by assumptions inherent in prevailing approaches to conflict that have deflected attention away from its effects. The following paragraphs sug- gest where some of the difficulties lie and what solutions to them might be available.

VIOLENT CONFLICT AS A SOCIAL PATHOLOGY

The most fundamental problems have to do with the ways in which social scientists have thought about the nature and causes of violent con- flict within the state. Most western students of conflict from Burke to Sorokin to Huntington have assumed that widespread violent conflict is in- trinsically undesirable: it occasions loss of life and destruction of property, it disrupts ordered routines of life and government, in severe form it may reverse economic progress and transform "good" government into op- pressive autocracy. It is precisely a concern for such negative consequences that has attracted many scholars to the study of riots, rebellions, and revolutions. It follows from this assumption that the outcomes of mass violence are not problematic. They are "known" to be undesirable. It also follows that the explanandum in most empirical theory about conflict is the occurrence of violent conflict per se, often indexed by reference to such noxious manifestations as the revolutionary seizure of power, the mag- nitude of disturbance, or the number of conflict deaths. These properties of conflict obviously are worth studying. But it can be surmised that a nor- mative focus of research energies on the pathological manifestations of violent conflict has deflected attention away from the careful study of outcomes.

An antidote is readily found in theoretical writings that have, emphasized some positive qualities of conflict. Lewis A. Coser's 1956 theoretical essay on *The Function of Social Conflict* derives from Georg Simmel's work the principle that "far from being necessarily dysfunctional, a certain degree of conflict is an essential element in group formation and the persistence of group life" (Coser 1956: 31). What Coser said of conflict in general is readily extended to violent conflict: identification, cohesion, and solidarity should be enhanced in groups that become engaged in violent conflict with other groups. The evidence for the proposition is not at issue here; the point is that Coser's statement of it was and is widely known among conflict researchers and should have served as an antidote to assumptions that violent conflict is necessarily pathological. Another prominent essay to the same effect was published by H. L. Nieburg in 1962; it traces the connections among law, social change, and violence. The function of law is to maintain the status quo, but the political system also is responsive to pressures to bring the law into line with social change. Violence and threat of violence are among the pressures that lead to legal change. And threats are credible to the extent that those who seek change occasionally unleash actual violence. Therefore, inasmuch as the fact of violence reinforces the effect of threat of violence, threat of violence can be a positive force for peaceful social change. Note that whereas Coser argues the functionality of (violent) conflict for groups involved in it, Nieburg specifies circumstances in which violence is healthy for an entire democratic society—if not necessarily for all its members.

A positive construction on political violence also is found in many scholarly writings on revolution and coups d'état, some of them reviewed by Bienen (1968a: chapter 3). He observes that "violence is seen as an incidental phenomenon, but not a pathological one, in much of the Marxist literature" (Bienen 1968a: 76). Some Marxists, including Engels and Lenin, thought it had positive functions as well. Engels stressed the "immense spiritual and moral regeneration" that follows from violent and victorious revolutions. Lenin's position was that "the correct and organized use of force would bring about the strengthening of class consciousness" (Bienen 1968a: 70, 71), a point similar to that made by Coser. On the other hand Lenin did not glorify violence and generally opposed its spontaneous use. Two prominent non-Marxist scholars concerned with theories of revolution who see positive consequences of revolutionary violence are Hannah Arendt and Barrington Moore. In *On Revolution*, Arendt treats violence as necessary to destroy the power of the old system and equally necessary for new political beginnings (Arendt 1963). Moore's account of the differing class alignments that have led to democratic and autocratic forms of government treats violence, and in particular the violent subordination of the peasantry, as a necessary condition of democratic society (Moore 1966). All of these writers seem to agree on a common principle, that violence is an essential but not *the* essential property of great political struggles from which are born new and better polities. Unlike Frantz Fanon (1966) or Georges Sorel (1915), they do not regard violent struggle as intrinsically desirable. Rather there are political circumstances in which it is a necessary means to desirable ends.[1]

Several scholars writing on political development in the Third World have identified some specific positive consequences of violent conflict. Sloan, in a 1971 paper, proposes that political violence in new states has the positive effects of establishing previously uncertain boundaries of political action and of defining the boundaries of emerging political communities. In the same year Popper published an essay in which he proposed that internal war may effect major transformations that stimulate political development; development will suffer only if the level of violence becomes too high. He cites five specific developmental effects:

1. internal war can stimulate development by breaking down traditional groupings such as rural villages, the old political elite, tribes, and so on, provided they are not utterly destroyed in the process

2. internal war can stimulate the creation of new social structures and compel expansion and centralization of preexisting social structures; Popper cites the war-generated growth of cities and the urban middle class in particular

3. internal war can stimulate creation of new political structures and the expansion and centralization of preexisting ones, notably political parties, the state's administrative apparatus, and security organizations

4. internal war can promote the assimilation of new technology in weaponry, transportation, communications, public administration, and the economy, with subsequent benefits in peacetime

5. internal war can stimulate other "pathologies," among which he cites hostility, propaganda, and corruption, which may have secondary developmental effects (Popper 1971: 415–417).

Popper offers scarcely any concrete examples of these developmental effects but does identify some instances of internal war, as in South Vietnam, Biafra, and Algeria, in which violence was so widespread that it was harmful for society as a whole. He particularly stresses the need for empirical research on the developmental versus pathological effects of internal wars.

There is one noteworthy difference between the arguments of Sloan and Popper, and those of Arendt, Moore, and the Marxists noted above. The developmentalists seem to assume that internal war can have positive effects irrespective of who wins, whereas scholars concerned with revolutions and modernizing coups d'état assume that the positive effects depend on who wins. At the root of the difference are contrasting standards about what kinds of effects are "positive": the developmentalists probably would answer in terms of general social and political properties of societies, the revolutionists in terms of the ascendancy of particular social groups. Since we lack a "meta-standard" according to which one or the other of these standards is better than the other, the sensible epistemological precept is to judge specific revolutions, coups, and internal wars by both standards simultaneously. But here again we confront collective ignorance: with the exception of some comparative research on coup outcomes, the theoretical arguments that violent conflict can have positive effects have inspired little more empirical research on outcome than has the contrary assumption.

CONTINGENCY VERSUS INHERENCY THEORIES
OF VIOLENT CONFLICT

In Chapter 4 of this *Handbook* Eckstein distinguishes between two classes of conflict theory: those which assume that violence is inherent in political processes and structures, and those which assume that it is contingent on special and unusual combinations of conditions. These assumptions also lead to different orientations toward outcomes. If violence is "contingent" on societal strain (C. Johnson 1966, Smelser 1963) or on social frustrations arising from depriving patterns of change (Davies 1962, Feierabend, Feierabend, and Nesvold 1969, Gurr 1970b), then the principal question is what combination of circumstances leads to violence. The most significant consequences of violence, in this research tradition, are its reciprocal effects on the conditions that generate violent conflict.

My theoretical work identifies three such feedback effects of violent conflict.

1. The occurrence of political violence enhances justifications (beliefs) that favor future political violence in two ways. The greater the extent of violence now in a society the more likely people are to accept violence as a form of conflict behavior in the future. And the greater are dissidents' gains through violence, the greater the utilitarian value violence will have in the calculations of future dissidents (Gurr 1970b: 168–177, 218–223).

2. Regimes' uses of violence in conflict situations affect the present and future conflict behavior of dissidents. One hypothesis is that the threat and severity of coercion (violence) used by regimes increases the anger of dissidents, thereby intensifying their opposition, up to some high threshold of governmental violence beyond which anger gives way to fear (Gurr 1970b: 238–251). Over the long run, the hypothesis is that when coercion is used by governments to enforce deprivations, the sense of grievance persists over time as a function of the severity of the initial deprivation (Gurr 1970b: 79–83). A general proposition about outcomes can be derived from

these two hypotheses: the greater a regime's use of violence to impose enduring deprivations on a dissident group, the greater is the potential for violent opposition by that group in the future.

3. The kinds of gains dissidents obtain through violent conflict affect the likelihood of their participation in future conflict. Material gains that are quickly consumed will lead to a recurrence of violence, whereas if "dissidents acquire through the violence the means to work constructively toward the permanent resolution of their discontent, violence has contributed to its own demise" (Gurr 1970b: 296–316, quotation 316).[2]

These hypotheses illustrate the point that "contingency" theorists are concerned with the reciprocal effects of violent conflict on the condition of future conflict. "Inherency" theorists are more likely to ask about other kinds of outcomes of violent conflict. Group mobilization theorists provide a set of examples. For these theorists, including Gamson (1975), Oberschall (1973), and Tilly (1978), violence is one of many resources that can be used in an instrumental way by groups contending for position and influence in the political system. The fundamental question in this perspective is not "why violence": the answer to that question is assumed in advance. As Tilly puts it, "collective violence has flowed regularly out of the central political processes of Western countries. People seeking to seize, hold, or realign the levers of power have continually engaged in collective violence as part of their struggles" (Tilly 1979: 83). The key question about collective violence is how its use, alone or in combination with other "resources," affects the patterns and outcomes of intergroup conflict. According to Snyder and Kelly (1976: 136), who work within this framework, these theories imply "that success of violent action depends on the power and strategies of antagonists, but this suggestion has not been empirically specified or tested." In fact, a number of specific propositions are advanced and tested by Gamson (1975) and by Snyder and Kelly (1976).

Gamson identifies a number of conditions that might influence the success of challenging groups. These include the nature of these groups' demands, their organizational characteristics, and the use of violence by or against challenging groups. Gamson's study of how these conditions have affected challenging groups in American history is reviewed in a later section. Of special relevance here is his finding that the groups that used "violence, strikes, and other constraints" (eighteen of a total of fifty-three groups studied) have had better-than-average success. His analysis does not enable us to discern the independent effects of violence on success, though, because he does not control for the effects of organizational characteristics. Most of the possible determinants of success are tested separately. Snyder and Kelly (1976) raise similar questions in a study of the success of some 6,000 Italian strikes. They make the point that "success" may be affected by contextual factors such as rates of wage changes, industrial growth, and levels of government repression, in addition to characteristics of the strike situation per se. Their results (reviewed more fully below) show that strike characteristics are more important determinants of success than context, but—unlike Gamson's findings for American groups—peaceful strikes were more likely to be successful than violent ones (Snyder and Kelly 1976: 154–158).

These two studies are of interest here for what they demonstrate about the group mobilization approach to outcomes. Both studies assume that factors other than violence influence outcomes. Snyder and Kelly's distinction between "contextual" variables and characteristics of individual strikes is a useful one, and is paralleled by Gamson's efforts to test the effects of "historical context" on the success of challenging groups. But three remarkable lacunae are common to the two studies. First, the contextual variables specified are a very limited and ad hoc collection with little bearing on the larger theoretical issues posed by group mobilization theory. Tilly in particular has emphasized the ways in which processes of urbanization and industrialization determine the identity and demands of challenging groups and the critical importance of the structure of political power for understanding how challenging and other groups act as they do (Tilly, Tilly, and Tilly 1975, Tilly 1978). Neither empirical study mentioned here systematically considers effects of such contextual factors on outcomes. Second, processes of mobilization are ignored. Oberschall (1973) and Tilly both emphasize the dynamic nature of mobilization processes: groups are not static but alter their resources, strategies, and tactics over time. Presumably the dynamics of challenging groups have as much or more to do with their successes than their static properties. Yet neither empirical study takes account of group dynamics. In fairness, Snyder and Kelly could not have done so given the nature of their sources; Gamson, on the other hand, worked with historical information suited to dynamic analysis, but only one of his independent variables, "factionalism," is coded for changes in the challenging group over time.[3] Third, neither study gives systematic attention to the characteristics of the *challenged* group, whether governments or employers. It is reasonable to suppose that the resources, interests, and dynamics of "the other party" to conflict have as much bearing on the outcomes of conflict as do characteristics of the challengers. In fact, since the challenged group is generally the more powerful one and the source of most accommodations and policy changes, it is likely to have disproportionate effects on outcomes. The only evidence on the issue in either study is Snyder and Kelly's attempt to take account of the changing legal status of strikes in Italy (1976: 140, 147).

The difference that contingency and inherency theories make for the study of outcomes can be summarized in this way. Contingency theories ask why violence occurs in politics; the outcomes of violence are not part of the answer to that question except insofar as they may affect the conditions which give rise to violent conflict in the future. Inherency theories, those concerned with group conflict, ask why and how groups fight, with what effects on their relative power and well-being. Since violence is part of the process, its effects on outcomes are sometimes considered along with others. But in neither theoretical approach are the outcomes of violent conflict per se the principal object of explanation.

ON NARROWING AND WIDENING FUNNELS OF CAUSALITY

The remedy to the obstacles considered above is quite straightforward. It is to acknowledge that the outcomes of violent conflict are problematic and intrinsically worth systematic empirical study. To act on the principle is more difficult because it poses a host of contingent conceptual and methodological problems. The model of explanation used to account for violent conflict can be thought of as a narrowing funnel of causality: there are remote and immediate causes, or preconditions and precipitants, or necessary and sufficient conditions, which are linked in a causal chain (usually but not necessarily sequential in time) that leads to a particular kind of violent process or episode. Research on outcomes, *per contra*, must begin at the narrow end of the funnel and move outward. Violent conflict has occurred; the immediate impacts may be distinct enough (does the government fall? is dissidence suppressed? are there direct concessions to dissidents?), but the effects that are more distant in time and space are much more difficult to detect in principle because they are subject to so many other influences (J. D. Powell 1976: 331 makes a similar point). The effect of the Russian Revolution of 1917 on economic productivity is a case in point (see Gerschenkron 1964, Gregory and Stuart 1974). In the short run, revolutionary policies and civil war drastically reduced industrial and agricultural production. It is equally evident that, sixty years later, the Russian economy is vastly superior and fundamentally altered. But how much of the credit is due to the revolutionary change in structure of government and control of the economy, as distinct from the inherent dynamics of industrial development, or the necessities of autonomous development in the face of external hostility, or the impact of World War II, or Russia's economic hegemony over Eastern Europe since 1945? Susan Eckstein makes a similar point in her comparative analysis of the economic effects of the Mexican Revolution of 1910-1917 and the Bolivian revolution of 1952 (S. Eckstein 1975, 1976). The positive consequences were considerably greater in Mexico than in Bolivia, but they were at least as much determined by domestic and foreign conditions as by social revolution per se. Trimberger's (1978) comparative analysis of the outcomes of four "revolutions from above" zeroes in on the attempt to attain autonomous industrial development (in Japan after 1868, Turkey after 1923, Egypt since 1952, and Peru since 1968). She identifies a number of internal and some external factors that have constrained revolutionaries in the pursuit of this goal. (The Eckstein and Trimberger studies are reviewed more fully in part IV, below.)

The fact that many variables affect the outcomes of violent conflict is not an insurmountable obstacle but rather a challenge for the theorist. One must specify just which circumstantial and intervening variables affect outcomes, so that they can be observed and their effects controlled for. The studies of Eckstein and Trimberger offer promising beginnings but are too narrow in focus to be more than suggestive about a general scheme for the analysis of the outcomes of violent conflict. In general, three things should be accomplished by an analytic scheme. First, an observable set of outcome variables must be specified. Eckstein focuses on three economic outcome variables: productivity, dependency on foreign capital, and income distribution. Trimberger is concerned with a particular constellation of these same variables, namely autonomous industrial development. There are many other outcomes equally worth studying. In the political realm, the vital outcomes include the structure of political institutions, the character and extent of political liberties, the substance of governmental policy, and the composition and rate of turnover in the political elite. (For a painstaking longitudinal study of the Mexican political elite before and after the revolution of 1910-1917 see P. H. Smith 1979). In the social realm we want to know about the effects of conflict on such variables as patterns of class stratification, the provision of education and health services, and the relative status of women and minorities.

Second, it is essential to consider what outcomes follow from different forms and properties of violent conflict. Whereas Eckstein and Trimberger are concerned with outcomes of revolutionary seizures of power, we also want to know what is likely to follow from riots and demonstrations, terrorist campaigns and rebellions. Moreover we would like to know what *features* or *properties* of conflict, not merely what forms of conflict, have a bearing on outcomes. Studies of protest movements, for example, generally treat the extent of violence used by the protesters as a major influence on how willing officials are to make concessions (see the studies reviewed in part III, below). Other aspects of violent conflict that can plausibly be argued to affect outcomes in significant ways include the numbers and social groupings of dissidents, the content and formulation of their demands, the extent to which dissidents and their opponents share common norms and values, and so forth. Third—and it is here that the analyses of Eckstein and Trimberger are of most direct help—it is necessary to specify as fully as possible the kinds of variables that influence the linkages between violent conflict and its problematic outcomes. The next section outlines a general approach, or model, for thinking about and studying the outcomes of violent political conflict. It does not purport to answer the more detailed conceptual and theoretical problems identified here, but it may help structure thinking about them and it also serves as a guide to the survey of specific studies in parts III and IV.

II. A SYNTHETIC APPROACH TO THE STUDY OF CONSEQUENCES

The foregoing review of some theoretical issues in the study of outcomes and effects of violent conflict has skirted around some basic conceptual problems which need to be aired and solved if cumulative research is to be done on the subject. Two problems are addressed here and solutions proposed for them. One concerns the kinds of conflict whose outcomes are to be assessed. The other is the relation among three different kinds of consequences—group fate, policy changes, and societal effects—and what kinds of variables, in general, are most likely to influence them.

The approach outlined here is a kind of mapping exercise, not a new departure. It is derived from, and takes into account, most tendencies in the empirical study of the consequences of conflict. Its purpose is to show how they relate to one another, not how one is intrinsically better or worse than another.

OUTCOMES OF WHAT?

What are the processes, events, or properties about whose outcomes we want to know? The answer must be precise enough so that relevant instances can be unambiguously distinguished from the larger texture of social happenings. The answer should also be broad enough to include the wide range of phenomena whose effects are in fact the subject of current research.

My proposal is that in general we want to know about the consequences of *open, intergroup conflicts characterized by the use or explicit threat of violence.* Conflict among groups contending over scarce positions and resources is a regular feature of social life. Some but not all conflicts manifest themselves in physical confrontations between contending groups, or alternatively in attacks by one party on a more or less unresisting target group. In common and scholarly language these confrontations are interpreted as "events": coups d'état, civil and guerrilla wars, rebellion, riots, terrorists campaigns, demonstrations, strikes. The central question is this: when violence is used or threatened in collective conflict situations, what consequences follow? This delimitation is more workable than asking about the outcomes of conflict in general, a topic which is probably too broad to be manageable. And it avoids the triviality of asking about the consequences of violence without reference to the circumstances in which it occurred. Attention is directed specifically to a kind of social interaction--group conflict--characterized by a readily observable, extreme form of coercion: the use or threat of deliberate physical harm. If this focus proves too restrictive for some theoretical purposes it can always be broadened. It seems better, though, to begin with a medium range of observable phenomena as the object of research.

This delimitation of the subject leaves more options open than it forecloses. For example, it is consistent with two different ways of identifying relevant conflicts for the purpose of empirical analysis. One is to begin from individual events: specific riots in particular cities, specific coups d'état or regional rebellions. The other is to focus on the larger episodes of conflict in which a series of violent and other events occur. It is the difference between studying consequences of ghetto riots in American cities on a city by city basis, or treating the net effects of the entire wave of black urban unrest from 1964 through 1969. And it is the difference between studying the effects of each major episode of rioting and demonstrations in Iran, beginning in February 1978, or analyzing the consequences of popular revolution against the Shah as a single event. Neither alternative is "better" than the other. The choice depends on the scholar's questions and chosen level of analysis. At the micro-level one wants to know how each city was affected by and responded to a riot, and what part each violent interaction played in the dynamics of a larger conflict situation. At the macro-level, one wants to know about the consequences of complex episodes of violent conflict on whole societies.

Another option left open by our delimitation is the choice among types of violent conflict whose outcomes are worth studying. The empirical literature includes comparative analyses of the consequences of strikes (for example, Shorter and Tilly 1974, Snyder and Kelly 1976); coups d'état (Dolian 1973; Jackman 1976; McKinlay and Cohan 1975, 1976; Nordlinger 1970); riots (Button 1978, Kelly and Snyder 1978, Iris 1978, C. Mueller 1978); revolutions (S. Eckstein 1976, Eisenstadt 1978, Tai 1974, Trimberger 1978); protest demonstrations (Astin et al. 1975; O'Keefe and Schumaker 1979; Schumaker 1975, 1978); and challenges in general by social movements (Gamson 1975). Each particular form of conflict poses its own research questions. And each particularistic choice is likely to overlook other questions. For example, a basic distinction is made in the literature on the causes of political violence between conflict that centers on limited issues of policy (protest, turmoil) and conflict over more fundamental issues of who rules and by what means (rebellion, revolution, internal war) (see Gurr and Duvall 1976, D. V. J. Bell 1973).[4] The issues of conflict help determine its form; they also have a profound effect on its consequences and how they are judged. So some general theory, and empirical research, is needed on what difference the *issues* of conflict make for its outcomes. (Studies which deal with this issue are reviewed in part III, below). Another basic distinction can be made between conflicts in which violence is an incidental or secondary tactic (protest campaigns, most coups, some riots) and conflict in which violence is the principal mode of interaction (civil wars, terrorist campaigns, most rebellions and revolutions, some riots). The significance of violence vis-à-vis other kinds of tactics and interactions surely affects the consequences of violent conflict. This is another fruitful but neglected subject for theory and research to which Schumaker (1978) and O'Keefe and Schumaker (1979) have opened up some promising leads. A related distinction of fundamental importance is whether conflict has a mass basis or is limited to elites. Mass violence in the forms of rebellion and revolution is likely to have more pronounced effects than the typical coup d'état.

My proposal that the subject should be the consequences of open, violent contention among groups thus does not imply that all manifestations of violent conflict ought to be lumped indistinguishably together, either theoretically or empirically. Quite the contrary: the variable forms, issues, intensities, and other properties of violent conflict comprise a set of independent variables, all of which may have some systemic consequences. The theoretical challenge is to specify how, the empirical task is to test those specifications.

To simplify somewhat a difficult task, the theoretical discussion and evaluation of evidence that follow will focus on political conflicts, that is, those conflicts in which public authorities are either active protagonists or the targets of demands for change. Evidence on the outcomes of other kinds of conflict, for example, strikes against private employers and demonstrations against university administrations, will be mentioned only in passing.

WHAT KINDS OF CONSEQUENCES? GROUP OUTCOMES
VERSUS SYSTEMIC EFFECTS

Three different kinds of outcomes of violent conflict are considered in the literature: (1) the fate of groups engaged in conflict, with considerably more attention being given to challenging or underdog groups than to challenged groups, (2) the policies adopted by advantaged groups in the face of these challenges; and (3) the extent of systemic change that follows from violent conflict, including changes in attitudes and beliefs, social and political structures, and economic production and distribution. The connections among these kinds of consequences do not get much attention, despite their obvious interdependence.

I have sketched in Figure 6–1 a process model which specifies the relationships among the consequences of violent political conflict. The central idea is that the group outcomes and the systemic effects of conflict are two different ways of looking at conflict processes that are linked by the concept of policy change. That is, the fate of challenging groups is affected and changes in social systems are effected through changes in the policies followed by powerful groups. When violent conflict takes the form of protest or resistance over limited issues, by relatively weak challenging groups,the policy changes which follow are the more or less immediate

FIGURE 6-1. Model of the policy, group, and systemic outcomes of violence political conflict.

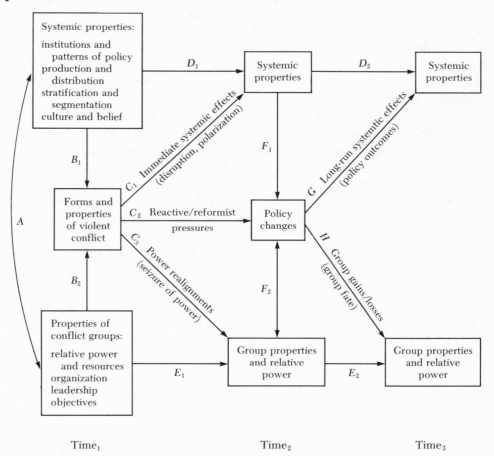

and deliberate responses of incumbent elites to the demands and threats inherent in conflict. (It is assumed that the occurrence of violent challenges and resistance represents purposeful behavior by at least one if not both parties: some group seeks some kind of change, even if it is only that the other party stop what it is doing.) Violent conflict in the form of rebellion and revolution may lead to realignments in power, the most fundamental of them being a revolutionary victory. That immediate outcome also leads to policy changes, often broad and fundamental ones. If sufficiently large and enduring, policy changes by either old or new elites can bring about gradual but substantial changes in the circumstances of particular groups and effect substantial political, economic, and social change. It is well to keep in mind that violent conflict does not necessarily have significant effects on patterns of policy; nor, if it does, are the effects necessarily favorable to the groups that initiated the conflict process; nor do policy changes necessarily lead to structural changes. The theoretical task, which awaits its Marx, or Weber, or Parsons, is to specify what kinds of violent conflict under what conditions are likely to have what kinds of outcomes.

The details of the model in Figure 6–1 are intended to represent the principal connections among the major bundles of variables that affect outcomes, some of which are well-researched, others not. Episodes of violent political conflict at time$_1$ are assumed to be a function of the properties of the socioeconomic and political system, properties that are interdependent with the properties of the groups that become parties to conflict. These complex relationships, labelled A and $B_{1,2}$, are of interest here only insofar as they affect conflict's characteristics and outcomes. It is not necessary here to make choices among the diverse etiological theories of conflict. A reasonable supposition is that B_2 is the most directly important of these linkages. Most major theories are in general agreement that the power, resources, aims, and organization of contending groups immediately determine the form and properties of violent conflict (for instance, Gurr 1970b: chapters 8-9; J. J. Johnson 1964: chapters 5, 8; Tilly 1978: chapter 4).

Three general kinds of consequences may follow immediately at Time$_2$ from violent conflict. In a direct way (C_2) conflict brings pressures to bear on those who hold power, pressures to take some mix of remedial and repressive actions. There is some theory and supporting evidence, reviewed in part III, about how some properties of protest affect officials' policy responses. And there is a substantial literature, reviewed in part IV, on governmental responses to American ghetto riots of the 1960s. Conflict may also lead to realignments in the relative power of the groups involved (C_3). The challenging group may be suppressed, its organization disbanded, and members dispersed; or, better, it may be given concessions which enable it to participate in political decisions (consultations with protest leaders, representation on councils, extension of the franchise); or in rare and dramatic instances the challenging group may seize power. There is a great deal of theoretical writing and numerous case studies about how revolutionaries can seize power (C_3) and what strategies will enable regimes to forestall them (F_2), a literature which also is reviewed in part III of this chapter.

The third class of effects of violent conflict at Time$_2$ are its immediate social and economic consequences (C_1). Depending on the intensity, duration, and locale of violent conflict, it can alter people's social concerns, increase the salience of group boundaries, contribute to the social cohesion of some groups and the disintegration of others, and disrupt existing patterns of political participation, governance, production, and distribution. These mainly negative side effects of conflict are discussed by some theorists (see part I of this chapter) but have attracted virtually no comparative study. A small exception is a handful of American public opinion studies that assess the impact of ghetto riots on attitudes about race relations and violence as a means for change (cited in part IV, below). There are also some substantial economic analyses of the impact of internal wars, including the American Civil War (Andreano 1962), the Nigerian-Biafran civil war (Nafziger 1979), and the Cuban revolution of 1959 (Lewis-Beck 1979). The literature on the disruptive effects of international war is more substantial and is reviewed by Stein and by Russett in Chapter 10 of this *Handbook.*

There are strong homeostatic forces in complex social and political systems and a comparable tendency for organized groups to persist over time irrespective of whether they are involved in open conflict. The rate of social and political change usually is glacial: it requires extraordinary events like invasion, natural disaster, fundamental technological innovation, or political revolution to set off rapid and substantial societal change. The paths marked $D_{1,2}$ in Figure 6–1 symbolize this tendency of systems to persist over time. Paths $E_{1,2}$ represent the somewhat weaker tendency of groups contending over issues of power and policy to persist, regimes presumably being somewhat more durable than challenging groups. The effect of these homeostatic forces is to inhibit policy changes in response to violent conflict (paths $F_{1,2}$) and to minimize their long-range effects.

The kind of positive policy response that does occur seldom is a simple, direct response to conflict per se. Instead it is modified to take account of other preferences (of decision makers and other powerful groups), tailored to preexisting patterns of policy, limited by scarcity of reallocable resources. In the social and economic sphere, the constraints include prevailing belief systems, rigidities in social stratification and segmentation, and limits on productivity. The position of a society in the international system may be as much or more a source of constraint than internal factors. Insofar as a society is economically and politically dependent on powerful neighbors, political allies, or the international capitalist system, policy responses to conflict may be almost entirely predetermined. In terms of the model, the constraining paths $F_{1,2}$ ordinarily will be stronger determinants of policy changes than path C_2. Yet theory and research on conflict outcomes have given them little attention. One exception is Schumaker's (1975) study of American protest groups, which demonstrates empirically that the "environment of social support" has more effect on policy responses than the characteristics and tactics of protest groups. Recent studies of revolutionary outcomes that make the same argument are S. Eckstein (1975, 1976), Skocpol (1979), and Trimberger (1978).

The ultimate impact of violent conflict on group fate and on society is assessed at $Time_3$, or more accurately at a succession of future times when the outcomes of policies can be observed. The outcomes are of two sorts: the fate of conflict groups (path H) and change in social systems (path G). Group fate is a multivariate concept that is only partially represented in studies of whether black Americans gained materially from the protests of the 1960s (Berkowitz 1974, Kelly and Snyder 1978) or whether challenging groups gained acceptance or new advantages (Gamson 1975). The counterpart to these questions is whether there are detectable changes in the characteristics of political authorities--whether their powers are enhanced, their resources diminished, their values and goals altered. The model subsumes these specific questions under the general concept of the "properties" of conflict groups--defining properties to include both the intrinsic characteristics of groups and the relationships among them. The research on the fate of conflict groups deals almost exclusively with changes in challenging groups, not with changes experienced by the challenged groups.

The societal impact of public policies in general is a popular subject in contemporary political research, especially in the United States (see for example Dolbeare 1975, Dye 1976, Lineberry 1977). The long-run effects of violent conflict, especially coups and revolutions, also are rather well-researched, though rarely analyzed using the concepts or hypotheses of policy outputs/outcomes analysis (the exceptions are to be found in studies of riot outcomes in the United States). Both the policy outcomes literature and the evidence on effects of coups and revolutions offer grounds for skepticism about the success of public policies in achieving their intended effects. John Echols has pointed out (in personal correspondence) that most of the research on the politics-policy relationship shows that patterns of political support and routine changes in political elites have little effect on the patterns or outcomes of public policy. It is reasonable to suppose, he suggests, that violent conflict provides a considerably greater impetus to change than does routine politics: the squeaky wheel presumably does get greased first. It is a hypothesis that remains to be tested. It also is likely that the contextual variables that minimize policy response to conventional politics also will operate in extreme cases: decision makers will be constrained from following through with responses to violent opposition because of competing priorities, limited resources, administrative inertia, countervailing pressures from other political groups, and so forth. In the language of our model, we expect the homeostatic effects represented by path D_2 to be stronger than the impetus to change provided by such policy changes as are made (path G). In fact they often will prevent significant policy changes from occuring at all (path C_2).

Nonetheless, policy changes following violent conflict do sometimes have substantial long-run effects on polity, economy, and society. There are well-documented studies of specific historical instances. For protest there is Rudé's analysis of eighteenth-century food riots in rural England and France. In many cases local officials responded to them in ways that alleviated the scarcities and high prices that set off the riots, and there is also evidence of changes in national policy aimed at regulating prices and ensuring safe supply of foodstuffs to the cities (Rudé 1964: chapter 16). On another continent and in another century we have Garrow's (1978) careful analysis of what followed from the 1965 protest campaign mounted by the Southern Christian Leadership Conference in Selma, Alabama. The campaign culminated in violent, nationally publicized retaliation by white Alabamans during March, acts of repression which were instrumental in convincing Congress and President Johnson of the need to pass the Voting Rights Act of 1965. Implementation of that act, in turn, fundamentally altered the political status of black Southerners.

Three "revolutionary" examples also may be cited. Beginning shortly after 1900, Indian nationalists mounted a forty-year series of challenges to colonial authority in the form of peaceful demonstrations (notably Gandhi's Satyagraha campaigns), violent clashes, and urban terrorism. The British spasmodically contracted and expanded the political rights of Indians in response to these challenges, in a process that culminated in independence (see Hula 1977: chapter 4). Second is Wilkie's (1970) analysis of halting, inconsistent, but nonetheless far-reaching efforts by Mexican leaders to bring about social change on behalf of the masses during the first forty years after that country's revolution. Finally, there is the tortuous history of the efforts of Russian revolutionaries to transform the traditional, male-dominated Islamic societies of Central Asia into modern, egalitarian societies operating on socialist principles. Massell (1974) traces in detail the trial-and-error course of policies aimed at this goal. The strategy that began to pay off in the late 1920s, after others had failed, was the creation of a set of modern institutions, parallel to those of traditional society and staffed at first by Asian women, whom the Soviets came to regard as a surrogate proletariat.

These are illustrative instances in which violent conflict has led to changes in the patterns of public policy with consequential short- and long-term effects on political, social, and economic life. Of course it was not violence per se that had these effects. In each case conflict was intense and dramatic enough to convince or compel elites to deal with the underlying social and political issues. If the same cases are viewed from the group-outcomes perspective, they are instances in which challenging groups benefited in ways that substantially altered properties of the political, social, or economic systems. As a counterpoint we note many examples of violent conflict that affect groups, and systems, for the worst: two dramatic instances from recent history are the winter of repression following the abortive Hungarian Revolution of 1956; and the end of democracy in Uruguay in 1973 as a result of a campaign to suppress the urban guerrillas who called themselves Tupamaros.

In summary, whether one approaches conflict outcomes from the point of view of the groups involved or the larger social system, the key intervening variables are the same. They are changes (or lack of changes) in the policies followed by those in power, and changes (or lack of changes) in the distribution of political power. *Policy changes* are the deliberate alterations of the laws, administrative routines, or allocations of resources by which political authorities maintain or alter the socioeconomic and political systems. Authorities who change policies in response to violent conflict in effect determine the outcomes for challenging groups and also for themselves. *Power realignments* may be either direct or indirect. *Direct changes* in the structure of power follow from violent conflict only in those uncommon instances in which dissidents seize power. More common are *indirect changes* whereby authorities alter their policies so as to accommodate or subordinate challenging groups, thereby changing power alignments in more subtle ways. From the perspective of most research on group fate, inquiry ends once the policy and power consequences of conflict for the challenging group have been assessed. From the systemic perspective, the fate of groups is peripheral to the question of what general changes in the political, economic, and social systems follow from more immediate changes in policy and structure. The approaches are complementary. Each helps clarify and answer questions of relevance to the other. Research on each of the questions presumably would be better if informed by theory and evidence developed in the other perspective. Whether or not this proves to be the case in future research, the models do help us to sort out and compare the theory and evidence in hand.

III. THEORY AND RESEARCH ON GROUP FATE

The central question in studies of group fate is whether and to what extent the challengers or underdogs in a conflict situation succeed in achieving their goals. The main lines of theoretical and empirical work on this issue are reviewed here. By reference to Figure 6–1, they are concerned mainly with paths C_2, C_3, and H—that is to say, the short-term and long-term effects of violent conflict on the properties of challenging groups. One theoretical essay, summarized immediately below, specifies some effects of violence on groups' success in general. The remainder of the relevant literature divides into two sets: studies of the success of protesters, and of combatants in internal wars.

SOME GENERAL PROPOSITIONS

In a 1973 essay (Gurr 1973) I distinguished three different objectives which led dissidents to use violence in conflict situations: defense of the status quo, the quest for reform, and revolution. One general principle applies to the outcomes of all three uses of violence in conflict: "The greater the violence used against people who believe they are in the right, the greater the likelihood of their resistance, to the extent of their capacities"

(Gurr 1973: 386). The other determinants of success are specific to the objectives sought:

   I. Violence used to maintain order or otherwise to defend a status quo is likely to succeed to the extent that:
     1. the purposes for which violence is used are generally accepted;
     2. violence is popularly accepted as a legitimate means; and
     3. those against whom violence is used are too few and powerless to increase their resistance.
  II. Violence used to persuade or coerce "powerful others" to change is likely to succeed to the extent that:
     1. the "others" accept or at least do not reject outright the desirability of the change sought;
     2. the "others" have the capacity to make the change; and
     3. the reaction of the "others" against violence does not override their willingness to change.
 III. Violence used to achieve revolutionary change is likely to succeed to the extent that:
     1. the revolutionaries overcome the resistance of their opponents, that is, win and overcome counterrevolution and passive resistance;
     2. the revolutionaries remain committed to their plans for change after gaining power; and
     3. the revolutionaries have the resources and social engineering capacities to bring about social change. [Gurr 1973: 382–392]

The propositions are illustrated by reference to the outcomes of various social movements but no attempt is made to test them. One conceptual difficulty with the propositions is that they conceive of violence as an act initiated by one party or the other to conflict rather than as an interaction. Thus it is not clear how they apply to conflict processes in which, for example, a challenging party seeking reform interacts violently with a regime seeking to maintain the status quo. Another limitation of the propositions concerns determinants of revolutionary success, which are so obvious as to appear trivial.

GROUP FATE OF PROTESTERS

Most of the empirical literature on group fate focuses on the success of protesters; the success of revolutionaries is considered in the next section. The first conceptual and methodological task in these studies is defining what constitutes "success" for protest groups. Welch points out some of the difficulties of judging the success of protest. What constitutes success varies among the leaders and followers of protest groups, third parties, and targets. Moreover, even during the course of an episode of protest there is likely to be escalation of demands and acceptable outcomes for participants (Welch 1975: 51). The most simplistic solutions have been adopted in studies of strike outcomes. The success of workers in Italian strikes studied by Snyder and Kelly is coded dichotomously (Snyder and Kelly 1976: 151); they do not specify how success or failure are defined in their sources. Shorter and Tilly's study of the magnitude and outcomes of French strikes uses a threefold classification: success, compromise, failure (Shorter and Tilly 1974: 69, 355–356). The classification is taken from the official sources on which the study is based: the authors do not define the categories nor do they assess the reliability of the data.

A more informative approach to judging success is exemplified by Gamson's study of challenging groups in American history. He defines success as having two dimensions: whether the group wins acceptance from its antagonists (as when unions secure the right to organize and bargain with employers) and whether they win new advantages (electoral success, enactment of favorable legislation, change in public beliefs) (Gamson 1975: chapter 3). Multiple categories of acceptance and advantages were used when coding information on challenging groups (1975: 173–175) but each variable was treated as a dichotomy in statistical analysis.

Another approach to assessing group fate is to ask whether challenging groups secure changes in public policy congruent with their demands. This is Schumaker's approach (1975, 1978) in a study of official responsiveness to protest in American cities in the 1960s and early 1970s. He treats policy responsiveness as a variable with five categories: repression, no response, minimal response, compromise response, or adoption of policy congruent with protesters' demands. A complementary set of categories of negative or defensive responses is proposed by Lipsky in a widely cited 1968 article. He identifies six ways in which officials ("target groups") can blunt protesters' demands: they may dispense symbolic satisfactions or token material satisfaction, make pro forma organizational changes, claim an inability to meet demands, postpone action, or publically discredit protesters (Lipsky 1968: 1152). Two other categories are added to this list by Fainstein and Fainstein (1974: 193): target groups may simply ignore protest organizations or they may give community-based protesters "the appearance of authority without its substance, thereby forcing them to discredit themselves through attempting actions that they cannot carry out." These categories, unlike those used by Schumaker, are not designed to be ranked along a continuum of responsiveness; they are simply ways of categorizing negative responses. They have been used by their authors in case studies but not in systematic comparative studies of outcomes.

The outcomes of conflict for challenging groups also can be judged by reference to changes in aggregate socioeconomic indicators. An example is Kelly and Snyder's study (1978) of the impact of riots in American cities on the economic standing and occupations of blacks. This "socioeconomic change" approach to outcomes is discussed in connection with systemic outcomes below.

Given a definition of what constitutes success for a protest group, the next step is to specify and test some of its determinants. Gamson and Schumaker both have done so, but with significant differences in their approaches. Gamson identifies a number of characteristics of protest groups that might influence their success, including the nature of their demands, their organizational characteristics, and the tactics (constraints) used by or against them. He offers no general theory or formal hypotheses but draws instead on disparate arguments in the academic literature. Most of the specific variables are listed in Table 6–1, along with summary results. The traits are listed here not in the order in which Gamson treats them, but in descending order of their importance for group success and failure, respectively. The study included a representative sample of fifty-three challenging groups in the United States which flourished at any time between 1800 and 1945. Just under half gained acceptance (47 percent) and a similar percentage (49 percent) gained new advantages.

Organizational and tactical variables predominate among the determinants of success for the protest groups studied by Gamson:large, centralized, cohesive, and bureaucratically organized groups that offered special incentives to members were highly likely to succeed. Of special relevance for our purposes is the finding that the groups that used "violence, strikes, and other constraints" (eighteen out of fifty-three) had better-than-average success, while the twenty-two groups that neither gave nor received violence had middling success. Objectives sought were somewhat less decisive: groups whose goals were limited and did not threaten their opponents' displacement tended to be more successful. Most of the conditions associated with failure are mirror images of the conditions of success. Groups that sought to displace their opponents, or had radical goals, or diffused their efforts across a multiplicity of issues were particularly likely to lose. Small, factionalized, nonbureaucratic, and decentralized groups also tended to fail. And the seven groups that were on the receiving end only of violence had virtually no success at all.

There are two significant limitations of Gamson's study. One is the scant attention given to contextual variables. Differences in success rate in different historical eras are tested, showing for example that challenging groups in wartime were more likely to gain than others. The nature of other challenging groups also is relevant to outcomes: groups that had a more radical competitor were more often successful than those with more moderate competitors. But none of the traits of opponents or political authorities are given any consideration. The second limitation is that Gamson's cross-tabular analysis does not enable us to discern the independent effects of violence (or any other single factor) on success. He neither asks nor answers the question whether the use of violent constraints, for example, added anything to the chances of success for large, bureaucratic, moderate groups, or compensated for the lack of some of those qualities.[5]

Whereas Gamson asks how a variety of traits of protest groups affects their success, Schumaker (1978) concentrates specifically on the constraints

TABLE 6.1. Traits of Fifty-three American Protest Groups Associated with Success and Failure

Group Trait	Number of Groups with Trait	Percentage that Gained Acceptance	Percentage that Gained New Advantages
1. *Traits that enhance success*			
Offer incentives for membership	11	91%	82%
Use nonviolent constraints	10	80	80
Use violent constraints	8	62	75
Bureaucratic organization	24	71	62
Do not seek antagonist's removal	37	62	68
No internal factionalism	30	57	70
Limited goals	18	56	67
Large group (over 10,000 members)	26	64	54
Centralization of power	28	54	64
Not subject to arrests	30	57	60
2. *Traits that contribute to failure*			
Receive violence, do not use it	7	14%	0%
Seek to remove antagonist	16	12	6
Focus on multiple issues	9	22	0
Subject to arrests	8	25	25
Internal factionalism	23	35	22
Nonbureaucratic organization	29	28	38
Universalistic goals	10	30	40
Decentralization of power	25	40	32
Small group (under 10,000)	27	30	44
No incentives for members except solidarity	42	36	40
Use no constraints	28	39	43
Has radical goals	35	43	40
3. *All groups*	53	47%	49%

SOURCE: Gamson 1975.

used by protesters. A five-category scale of the extent of constraints is developed (Schumaker 1978: 183). The categories are:

1. constraints avoided; protesters use private negotiations only
2. disruptive constraints avoided but protesters discredit or embarrass officials by publicizing demands

3. protesters employ nonviolent and minimally disruptive direct action tactics such as marches or rallies

4. protesters use nonviolent but disruptive or obstructive tactics such as sit-ins and boycotts

5. protesters use violence resulting in personal injury or property damage.

Working within a game-theory framework, Schumaker develops a set of two main and four subsidiary hypotheses about the effectiveness of these constraints when used by issue-specific protest groups. There are the principal hypotheses:

1. when a political conflict is confined to the protest groups and their targets (when the scope of conflict is narrow), the use of constraints will usually enhance the chances of a successful outcome for protest groups

2. when the public is involved in the resolution of a political conflict (when the scope of conflict is broad), the use of constraints will usually reduce the chances of a successful outcome for protest groups.

Given the use of constraints, public involvement is relevant to protesters' success because, at least in the American context, "the evidence clearly suggests that the public tends to view the use of constraints by protesters as illegitimate" (Schumaker 1978: 173). The argument is the same as the general principle proposed in Gurr 1973.

Schumaker's subsidiary hypotheses relate to ways in which the public becomes involved in conflict. For example, if protesters' demands imply substantial burdens on other citizens, the scope of conflict is likely to broaden and the greater will be opposition to protesters. The use of constraints by protesters is likely to be widely publicized, which also tends to enlarge the scope of conflict, while to the extent that constraints are used, public opposition will increase. Imbedded in this discussion is another subsidiary hypothesis. It is that "in a context where protest groups confront an activated and hostile public, constraint utilization may be positively related to protesters' success" (Schumaker 1978: 174). The rationale is that protesters in a "nothing to lose" situation may have so much nuisance value (or worse) to officials and the public that it is less costly to meet some of their demands than to countenance escalating violence. The implication, which Schumaker does not draw out explicitly, is that protesters who sufficiently antagonize the public by their burdensome demands and their use of constraints will reach some threshold beyond which they are increasingly likely to be successful. The argument seems to reduce to a single general proposition that the use of constraints (including violence) by protesters is curvilinearly related to success: success is greatest either when constraints are low and the scope of conflict narrow, or when constraints are so high and persistent that the public and participants are polarized.

Schumaker's hypotheses are tested using data on two samples of urban protests. Whereas Gamson's cases are historical challenging groups, Schumaker's cases are contemporary acts of protest. In one set of cases, he coded scholarly and journalistic accounts of ninety-three protests of the 1960s. In the second set, officials responded to questionnaires about how they had dealt with 119 protests in the early 1970s, and their replies were coded (for the full set of judgmental scales, see Schumaker 1978: 183). Correlation tests of the two samples gave somewhat different results, but the hypotheses received some support. Protesters got more favorable results using constraints when the scope of conflict was narrow and when the public was mostly hostile (case studies), but met less favorable responses when the scope of conflict was broad (questionnaires) and the public was mostly supportive (both samples). The correlation coefficients for all the tests were weak to moderate, however, suggesting that a number of variables other than those measured affected policy responsiveness.

In two other studies Schumaker and collaborators have examined the effectiveness of protest in very different milieus. A study by Kowalewski and Schumaker (n.d.) used specialized sources on dissident activity in the Soviet Union to gather code information on 303 instances of group protest directed at Soviet authorities, ranging from petitions by small groups to demonstrations and wildcat strikes. Violence rarely occurred in these protests and only 15 percent had positive outcomes (outcomes were coded as favorable if benefits or concessions were received and repression was low). Two factors strongly affected the outcomes: large groups were more than twice as likely to gain as small groups; and militant groups (those using disruptive tactics) were six times more likely to gain. The authors conclude that in the Soviet Union, and perhaps other hegemonic systems, force can be an effective tactic of protest as well as of control.

Quite different results are obtained by O'Keefe and Schumaker (1979) in a study of official responses to sixty protest incidents in the Philippines, Malaysa, and Thailand between 1960 and 1977, as reported in the *New York Times*. The major independent variable is a four-category scale which modifies that used by Schumaker in his American studies. The categories, by increasing degree of constraints, are: (1) public airing of grievances; (2) physical group actions; (3) obstructive group actions; and (4) violent actions. The study also takes account of four other variables that theoretically affect responses to protest: the size of the protest group, its degree of organization, the extent of change sought, and the left–right orientation of demands. The initial, exploratory analysis shows that some demands were met in 47 percent of protests, while in 33 percent the governmental response was repressive. The greater the constraints used by protesters, the more likely a repressive response. In eight of the twelve instances of violent protest the response was repressive, for example; it was positive only where the protest group was large. The other characteristics of the groups and their demands had little effect on the outcomes.

Since the Schumaker and Gamson studies are so different in research design, their results cannot be directly compared. The conceptual strength of Gamson's study is its emphasis on characteristics of protest groups; the strength of Schumaker's 1978 study is its attention to constraints and how the circumstances in which they are used affect outcomes. Gamson uses data of better quality (Schumaker's data from officials are suspect) and his analysis is more thorough, while Schumaker employs more sophisticated techniques. On one fundamental point both studies agree, however: there are specifiable circumstances under which the use of constraints, including violence, has helped American protest groups achieve their objectives. But it is not at all clear whether violence alone has positive effects. Schumaker's correlation analysis tells us nothing about whether groups that used violent constraints were more successful (under the specified conditions) than groups using nonviolent constraints. Gamson's analysis suggests that violence is almost incidental to success: only one group in his sample used violence as a primary tactic, and only six of the twenty-five "accepted" groups and five of the twenty-six "new advantages" groups used violence as an incidental tactic (Gamson 1975: 79–82). He concludes that violence is "as much a symptom of success as a cause. . . . It is the spice, not the meat and potatoes" (1975: 82). The O'Keefe and Schumaker study of protest in Southeast Asia specifically shows that violent constraints in that milieu are very likely to have negative effects except in special circumstances, namely, when the protest group is large. The Soviet study by Kowalewski and Schumaker is not directly relevant because at most the protesters were militant and did not, indeed could not, threaten coercion. In this context, militancy and group size enhanced the generally slim prospects of success. It seems clear from these diverse results that the effects of constraints generally and violence specifically on protest outcomes depends not only on group characteristics but on the political and cultural setting. What is obviously required is research in which comparable data are gathered on the relevant variables across very different kinds of societies.

There are several comparative studies of strikes which shed further light on the interaction between group characteristics, violence, and success. A study of 6,232 strikes occurring in Italy from 1878 to 1903 shows that 64 percent ended in success or compromise for the strikers (Snyder and Kelly 1976). The authors test the effects of contextual factors and characteristics of the strike situation per se on the outcomes. Context had little effect: there were slight tendencies for successes to be more common in years when wages in general were rising, and to be less common when government repression in general was high. The most relevant factors were characteristics of the strikes: large strikes were more successful than small ones, multiple-issue strikes more successful than single-issue ones, offensive ones (seeking improvements) more successful than defensive ones. Violence tended to be counterproductive: peaceful strikes were 12 percent more likely to be successful than violent ones (Snyder and Kelly 1976: 154–158). A study by Shorter and Tilly (1974) of strikes in France from 1830 to 1968 considers the effects of urban and industrial growth and organizational variables on the outcomes of strikes. The success rate of strikes tended to be slightly higher when and where strikers were numerous, while high levels of unionization contributed to compromise outcomes rather than outright success or failure (Shorter and Tilly 1974: 86–98, 295–305). Unfortunately the study does not take account of the occurrence or impact of strike violence. Neither does a more recent study by Conell (1978) of strike outcomes in late nineteenth-century Massachusetts, which shows that union sponsorship was important to the duration and success of strikes. A fourth relevant study surveys violent labor conflict in the United States through 1968. Although no quantitative analyses are offered, the evidence of many specific strikes leads the authors to conclude that "the effect of labor violence was almost always harmful to the union. There is little evidence that violence succeeded in gaining advantages for strikers" (Taft and Ross 1969: 382). The strike evidence is somewhat fragmentary but points in the same general direction, namely, that the organizational strength of striking workers contributes to their success while violence works against them.

Other empirical studies of the outcomes of group protest provide further evidence on the efficacy of militancy and violence in specific situations, but no decisive answers to the general questions raised by the preceding studies. The Tillys conclude a comparative analysis of the history of collective action in France, Italy, and Germany from 1830 to 1930 with a brief assessment of the effectiveness of violence, noting that (1) the effects of violence depend on the type of collective action and the power positions of groups involved; (2) the short-run and long-run effects differ; and (3) governmental repression works. Their elaborations on these points make them somewhat less trivial than they appear in this skeletal listing (Tilly, Tilly, and Tilly 1975: 280–285). A comparative study of school desegregation in ten American cities leads Crain to the conclusion that civil rights groups using militant tactics were less successful than groups that avoided direct action (Crain 1969: 153–159). In contrast, a careful comparative study of protest and change at American colleges and universities during 1968–1971 shows a much higher frequency of institutional change at campuses that had severe protests than at those that did not (Astin et al 1975: chapter 6). Beyond this point the evidence thins out into a variety of case studies. B. L. R. Smith (1968) comments skeptically on the effects of disruptive protest in three incidents in New York City during the 1960s. Garrow (1979) shows that the violent victimization of southern civil rights marchers was instrumental in building political support for the Voting Rights Act of 1965. Iris (1978: chapter 4) examines the responses of the Israeli government to two episodes of disruptive protest, one by poor Sephardic immigrants who called themselves Black Panthers, the other by young couples seeking housing. Statistical analysis of time-series budget data showed favorable responses on a substantial scale. But there is no cumulativeness or generalizability to these studies. They examine protests in diverse political and cultural circumstances, any combination of which may have contributed to their generally favorable outcomes.

A final comment on studies of the success of groups in conflict: none of the comparative, empirical studies cited above ask how much is gained or lost by the challenged groups. It takes only a little reflection to recognize that gains and losses in two-party conflicts are not necessarily mirror images of one another. Game theory suggests that in some real-world conflicts a gain for the challenger may be only a small loss for the target group or even have compensating gains that outweigh losses. There also are conflicts, usually the more intense and deadly ones, in which there are no winners, only groups that suffer relatively more or less. I know of no systematic studies that either assess the success of challenged groups or weigh the relative gains and losses of both parties to conflict.

REVOLUTIONARY WINNERS AND LOSERS

The question of "who wins" in revolutionary conflict poses a very different set of research problems from the literature on the success of protesters. The criteria of success are more clear-cut, there are far fewer cases, there is a great deal of prescriptive theory, but very little empirical theory or systematic evidence. John Dunn (1977: 83–97) has devoted a long essay to the question of how to judge the success of revolutionaries, in which he observes that "it is a very nice question indeed whether any professional revolutionaries ever really succeed. . . because what they do succeed in bringing about may be very different from what they had hoped" (Dunn 1977: 89). He goes on to consider alternative standards by which revolutionaries' success might be judged, including their capacity to maintain state power, enhance economic development, and bring about changes in social organization, but comes to no firm conclusion about how or even whether it is possible to judge revolutionaries' success beyond the fact of seizing power. For most revolutionaries the seizure of power is a necessary if not sufficient condition for any other kind of gain. Our subject here is theory and evidence on the conditions of revolutionary victory and defeat.

Most of the literature on the outcomes of revolutionary conflict is strategic. Theories and case studies of counterinsurgency enjoyed a brief vogue in the 1960s and are represented by Galula (1964), Pustay (1965), and R. Thompson (1966), along with many others concerned with defeating rural-based communist revolutionary movements. A history of French doctrine on how to combat revolutionary warfare is Paret (1964). A theoretically sophisticated work in this genre is Leites and Wolf's *Rebellion and Authority* (1970), which provides an analysis of ways in which both rebels and regimes can use coercion to secure civilian support for pursuing revolutionary warfare. The inspiration for contemporary theories of counterinsurgency was provided mainly by the effective suppression of communist guerrilla movements in the late 1940s and 1950s in locales such as Greece, Malaya, and the Philippines. The theories derived from such cases failed resoundingly when applied to Algeria and Vietnam (revolutionaries learn as much from their failures as regimes do from their victories), so this line of research has temporarily dried up. Its functional equivalent in the 1970s is the voluminous literature on "how to combat terrorism," which is beyond the scope of this chapter.

Counterinsurgency theory may be moribund, but not its counterpart of strategic theory on how Marxist revolutionaries can win (for a general survey see Martic 1975). There are two major tendencies in contemporary writings on the subject. The Chinese Communist victory in 1949 gave rise to one line of theorizing which stresses three factors: the necessity for building an intricate party apparatus and an interlocking set of supporting organizations, the subordination of armed struggle to political struggle, and the likelihood that protracted struggle with many setbacks is necessary for victory (Mao Tse-tung 1954, Vo-nguyen Giap 1962). Castro's success against the Batista regime in Cuba in 1959 inspired another set of theories which emphasized the primacy of the guerrilla *foco* and held out the prospect that armed struggle, once begun, could create the political conditions for victory (Guevara 1961, Debray 1967). The failure of efforts to replicate the Cuban revolution elsewhere in Latin America during the 1960s contributed to the development of a derivative set of strategies for urban guerrillas. A leading theorist is Abraham Guillen, whose 1966 book, *Strategy of the Urban Guerrilla* (in Hodges 1973) was the progenitor of the better known tactical writings of Carlos Marighella, a Brazilian revolutionary (Marighella 1970).

The strategic writings of revolutionaries and the mixed record of attempts to apply them have stimulated more dispassionate academic analyses that challenge their validity (for example, J. B. Bell 1971, C. Johnson 1973). The revolutionists are especially vulnerable to the criticism that their strategic and tactical prescriptions about how to win are generalized from particular cases where success was achieved under distinctive sociopolitical circumstances that are unlikely to be widely duplicated. Of the two models cited above, the Chinese has proven effective in Southeast Asia but neither the *foco* nor urban guerrilla strategies have brought Marxists to power anywhere in Latin America since 1959.

None of the theories about how to make or prevent revolutionary seizures of power are empirical theory in the conventional academic sense, but they differ from scientific theory in intent and usage more than in form or substance. Theorists as diverse as Guevara (1961), Vo-nguyen Giap (1962), Leites and Wolf (1970), and R. Thompson (1966) make their arguments in the form of specific cause-and-effect propositions about the conditions of success. The propositions are derived (formally by Leites and Wolf) from theoretical assumptions about revolutionary causes and processes, and each of these three theorists' propositions comprise relatively coherent, internally consistent sets. All revolutionary and counterinsurgency theories differ from empirical theory in one fundamental way: they are intended to be used, not tested. None has been tested using social scientific procedures, a liability that literally has proven fatal for many people in "field experiments."

People caught in the maelstrom of revolutionary politics may be excused for being disinterested in scientific assessment of their operating principles. It is less easy to explain why scholars have not made systematic comparative studies of the conditions of revolutionary victory and defeat. It would be an intriguing intellectual challenge to formalize the competing models of revolutionary and counterinsurgency strategy in the writings of, say, Mao and Guevara, R. Thompson, and Leites and Wolf, and test them against the contemporary record of a sample of internal wars. A representative sample including rebel victories, defeats, and no-contest decisions is needed so that empirical study will avoid the most obvious flaw of revolutionary theories: the fact that each is derived from one or a handful of cases whose outcomes the theorist hopes to duplicate.

Cases of internal war are numerous enough for a comparative study of outcomes. I have made a preliminary, unpublished study of the outcomes of all internal wars which were begun or in progress in 119 nations and colonies between 1961 and 1965. There were forty-eight distinguishable guerrilla, civil, and revolutionary wars, not counting coups, military rebellions, or isolated instances of armed resistance. By 1978 three were still major conflicts, while fragmentary accounts indicated that sporadic armed resistance continued to occur in nine other instances. Among the more or less decisively settled internal wars, nine had ended with victory or major concessions for the rebels, twenty-seven with their military defeat. If the nine continuing, low-level conflicts are counted as rebel defeats, the ratio of revolutionary success to defeat was precisely one to four.[6]

Judging victory in internal wars is a more difficult task than it might seem. The fall of Saigon signified a decisive victory for the National Liberation Front in Vietnam, and the sixteen-year rebellion of southern Sudanese came to an equally decisive end in 1972 with a negotiated compromise. The large-scale guerrilla war by Chinese communists in Malaya in the 1950s is more problematic: the government declared the emergency over in the early 1960s, even though remnants of the guerrillas still subsisted in 1978 by a kind of political banditry along the Thai-Malay border. Other "defeated" rebels, for example, the Somali tribesmen of southeastern Ethiopia, bide their time and resume hostilities later. A decade of rebellion among Kurdish tribesmen of northern Iraq seemingly ended with a settlement in 1970 (counted as a compromise in our data) that broke down several years later and ended in a crushing defeat for the Kurds in 1976–1977. An example of another kind of problematic outcome is illustrated by the Angolan war for independence from Portugal which began in 1960. Independence was gained in 1976 but the UNITA faction of the rebels did not accept the new Marxist government. In our tabulation the war is judged a rebel success and UNITA's struggle against the new government is a "new" conflict, not counted among the original sample.

The classification of immediate revolutionary outcomes is a preliminary step toward testing theories about revolutionary victory and defeat. In general the data cited above support the view that clear-cut revolutionary victories are uncommon. It also is evident that decisive outcomes are not as common in most internal wars as they have been in the best-known historical examples, for instance, France 1789 and 1848, the United States 1865, Russia 1917, China 1949, Greece 1949, Cuba 1959, Nigeria 1970, and Vietnam 1974. Dramatic victory and defeat have impressed these examples on political memory. The more numerous revolts that have ended in compromise or mutual exhaustion are less often remembered and much less studied by scholars.

The strategic writings on how to make or defeat a revolution take us to the point at which revolutionaries seize power or are so thoroughly defeated that they no longer pose a security threat. Winning may be a sufficient condition of success for incumbents, whether or not it sets new policies in motion. It is only a minimal condition of success for revolutionaries, whose policies and their outcomes are evaluated in part IV of this chapter.

IV. THEORY AND RESEARCH ON SYSTEMIC EFFECTS

Most of the research on the systemic effects of violent conflict is concerned with one of three specific types of conflict. Substantial research has been done on the consequences of protest and rebellion by blacks in the United States during the 1960s. Some of this research focuses on "group fate" questions of whether there were more substantial government responses in cities with more severe riots, but the more general question which underlies virtually all work on the question is a systemic one: did the riots of the 1960s significantly alter patterns of racial inequality in the United States? In terms of the model in Figure 6–1 above, this research is concerned with path C_2, the policy responses to riots, and G, the socioeconomic outcomes of riots and the policy responses to them. Some of them also take into account the political and socioeconomic constraints on policy responses (paths $F_{1,2}$).

Another set of studies asks whether coups d'état make any significant difference in the patterns of public policy in Third World countries.

Typically the aim is to ascertain whether social or economic development accelerates after a coup-induced change in leadership. Related to these studies in substance, if not in method, is a third set that focuses on revolutions that brought to power new leaders who were committed to implementing far-reaching societal change. These studies trace the nature and effects of revolutionary policies. By reference to the general model, studies of the consequences of both coups and revolutions deal with path C_3, the seizure of power, and its effects upon policy outputs (path F_2) and ultimate policy outcomes (path G). Research on the consequences of the violent seizure of power, revolutionary or otherwise, is reviewed in the second section of this part.

Several rather different kinds of studies of the impact of violent conflict are not considered here. There is considerable research on how internal conflict here and now affects conflict elsewhere in the future. This work falls in three distinct categories: (1) the impact of internal conflict at time$_1$ on the conditions of internal conflict at time$_2$; (2) the diffusion of one particular form of conflict across time and space; and (3) the effects of internal conflict on external conflict. Some theory and evidence on the first of these topics is cited in part I of this chapter and also in note 2. Recent examples of the rather sparse literature on the diffusion of conflict include Li and Thompson's study of "coup contagion" (1975) and Midlarsky's work on the diffusion of urban riots (1978). The extensive research on internal–external conflict linkages is reviewed by Michael Stohl in Chapter 8 of this *Handbook*.

A second general subject not reviewed here is the relation of violent conflict to the performance and stability of political systems. In this literature political violence is treated either as an aspect of political performance (the "good" political system is largely free of it; see H. Eckstein 1971) or as a manifestation of crisis that, if not dealt with effectively, will lead to fundamental change in the political system (for a recent review see Zimmermann 1979). Eventually the theoretical and empirical work on this subject should be integrated with research on the impact of specific kinds of conflict. It is too much to attempt in this chapter.

IMPACT AND OUTCOMES OF GHETTO RIOTS AND REBELLIONS

An enormous amount of research has been done on the causes, processes, and to a lesser extent the outcomes of the rioting that swept the black neighborhoods of most American cities between 1964 and 1970. According to one compilation of evidence there were some 500 such events which directly involved between a quarter and a half million people and occasioned about 240 deaths and 9,000 reported injuries (Gurr 1979: 54). They brought enormous pressures to bear on officials to quell the rioting and prevent its future reoccurrence. We are concerned here with the longer-run responses, which were of two general kinds: "law and order" policies

designed to increase social control over minorities, and reformist policies designed to alleviate, temporarily or permanently, the conditions that
were thought to be responsible for the rioting. There are upwards of
twenty empirical studies of the impacts and outcome of the riots. Most are
concerned with policy responses as manifested in new programs and increased public expenditures for existing programs. Others ask what impact
the riots had on public attitudes toward racial issues and reform—attitudes of import both to the implementation of new policies and the
nature of race relations in American society. A few deal with general improvements in the material well-being of blacks.

First we consider some theoretical issues raised by these studies. In
general, empirical research on the impact of riots has been concerned with
specific, relatively narrow hypotheses rather than general theoretical
issues. None of the hypotheses tested is derived from more general theories
about conflict outcomes. The one general theoretical issue raised in a few
studies (especially Iris 1978 and Jennings 1979) is the accuracy of the argument made by Piven and Cloward (1971) that welfare programs in the
United States are expanded to provide greater benefits during periods of
disorder and then contracted once social stability is reestablished. There is
a related but more general theoretical issue which underlies many of these
studies: whose interests are served and in what order of importance, when
democratic elites respond to disorder? With reference to the United States
the radical position is that the dominant response is coercive defense of the
status quo (see for example Rubenstein 1970, Stohl 1976). Liberal and
pluralist democratic theory would predict a reformist response to the underlying social problems (see, for example, Dahl 1967). None of the
empirical studies explicitly addresses this theoretical issue, despite its relevance to the interpretation of their findings.

The major theoretical contribution to be found in these studies is provided by Button (1978) in his conclusion to an extensive set of empirical investigations (reviewed below). He identifies five conditions under which
political violence is conducive to political and social change:

1. "when those in power have relatively plentiful public resources
   available to meet the basic demands of the partisans of violence"
2. "when the episodes of violence are not so severe or frequent as to
   cause massive societal and political instability, yet are severe enough
   to be noticed by those in political power and to threaten to escalate"
3. "when a significant number of those in political power and a portion
   of the public are generally sympathetic. . . to the goals of the
   perpetrators of violence, and when the destructive tactics employed
   are not so severe as to undermine these feelings of sympathy"
4. "when the goals or demands of those who carry out the violence are
   relatively limited, specific, and clear to those in political power"

5. "when it is utilized in conjunction with other, nonviolent, conventional strategies as means of asserting the demands of the politically powerless." [Button 1978: 174–176]

These propositions resemble those proposed by Gurr (1973) and tested by Schumaker (1975, 1978) which are reviewed above on pp. 255–260. But Button's research does not test them; rather it illustrates and suggests them.

Most of the empirical studies of riots' impact on public policy and blacks' socioeconomic status are summarized in Table 6–1.[7] They are listed in three categories: case studies of immediate responses in specific cities; comparative studies of governmental responses at city, state, and federal levels; and studies of socioeconomic changes in the status of blacks living in urban areas. One might expect that the more immediate impacts would be greatest, the more remote ones much less. In fact the results are considerably more complicated.

The first complicating factor in assessing the impact of the riots is that they coincided with an improving trend in the socioeconomic status of black Americans. The trend is clearly documented for the 1960s and early 1970s by Farley (1977) and Levitan et al. (1975), among others; more recently it has begun to reverse. It is not unreasonable to think that the riots as well as the economic boom of the 1960s affected the trend, but the empirical evidence is of little help in answering the question. A beginning point is offered by Farley and Hermalin (1972), a study not shown in Table 6–2 because not concerned directly with riot impacts. They trace the change in the status of blacks between 1960 and 1970, using nationally aggregated data, and find improvements for blacks both absolutely and relative to whites. They also comment that "our tables indicating racial differences in income and occupations suggest that blacks made particularly great advances after 1966" (Farley and Hermalin 1972: 366). The two studies that might be expected to elaborate this lead, using less aggregated data, do not provide supporting evidence. One approach is to examine changes at the neighborhood level, which Berkowitz (1974) does by looking at socioeconomic changes between 1960 and 1970 in a sample of census tracts. Ten tracts affected by riots were chosen from each of four cities (Detroit, Los Angeles, Newark, Washington) and matched with forty nonriot tracts that were also predominantly black. Changes in median family income, unemployment, white-collar job holders, and housing and family indicators were compared and showed no differential improvement for riot tracts. The only marginally significant difference was negative: income gains were slightly less in riot tracts. Another approach is to examine changes at the city level, which Kelly and Snyder (1978) do using 1960 and 1970 census data for 405 cities. They focus on changes in the median income of nonwhite families and on changing proportions of blacks in various occupational categories. They find general improvements but no statistical evidence whatsoever that the incidence of racial violence in the 405 cities studied affected the relative amount of improvement in them. The authors conclude that "all of our evidence converges on the conclusion that there is no causal relationship between racial disorders and the distribution of black socioeconomic advances in the 1960s at the local level" (Kelly and Snyder 1978: 18). In fact their study is not nearly so definitive as they imply for two reasons. They do not have annual data for the cities, many of which might show differences in the rates of improvement before and after riots; and more important, 1969 (the year of reference for 1970 census economic data) is too soon to analyze socioeconomic impacts which, if they exist at all, would more likely become visible over a longer period.

The studies of governmental policy responses have diverse research designs but yield results that are considerably more significant and positive than the census-based studies of socioeconomic improvements. The main independent variable in these studies is the occurrence of riots, but riot information is used in different ways in the research designs. Some, including the case studies and Feagin and Hahn (1973), treat the occurrence of rioting as a dichotomous variable and ask "what happens afterwards." These studies are mostly impressionistic and descriptive. All of them note substantial changes in political activities and programs following riots, but are subject to the limitation that ordinary case studies cannot definitively disentangle the local impact of riots from other factors. A second group of studies distinguishes between cities with serious riots and those with no or minor disturbances (Betz 1974, Welch 1975). Differences in policy and policy outcomes between riot and nonriot cities are attributed to the occurrence of rioting. The third group of studies takes account of the intensity, number, or other properties of riots among cities (Button 1978: c, Iris 1978: a, Mueller 1978) or among states (Colby 1975, Jennings 1979:a). This kind of research design has the advantage that it permits conclusions about the strength of association between riot properties and dimensions of policy response. The second and third groups of studies are cross-sectional: they compare a number of units at the same period, with or without time-lags between the occurrence of rioting and the measurement of policy changes. A fourth group of studies uses longitudinal analysis. The case studies noted above do so in an impressionistic way; these studies apply time-series analysis to longitudinal data. When dealing with the impact of rioting on federal policy there is no alternative to longitudinal analysis. Jennings (1979: b) affords a good example: for a twenty-nine year period, 1938–1976, he applies multiple regression analysis to determine the relative impact of unemployment and rioting on changes in welfare recipients. Even more sophisticated is the quasi-experimental analysis applied by Iris (1978) to time-series data on federal welfare and housing expenditures, and on municipal law-enforcement and recreation budgets. This type of analysis allows the researcher to tell whether the occurrence of an

TABLE 6–2. Studies of the Effects of the 1960s Urban Riots in the United States

Type of Study	Units of Analysis	Data and Methods	Findings
1. *Case studies of the impact of specific riots*			
Bullock (1969)	Watts district of Los Angeles	Unsystematic interviews, observation, descriptive	Money poured into Watts but with little or no effect on living standards
Button (1978)*	a. Dayton, OH Rochester, NY	Systematic interviews with decision makers, descriptive	Major, innovative social and housing programs in Dayton, more limited and private responses in Rochester
Locke (1969)	Detroit	Observation of political activities in six months after riot	Much organizational, political activity; open-housing policy adopted; too soon to assess real effects
C. H. Moore (1970)	Winston-Salem, NC	Systematic interviews with city leaders, black citizens	Blacks did not see riot as a demand or expect results; leaders cited positive responses
2. *Systematic comparative studies of the impact of riots on public policies*			
Betz (1974)	Riot versus nonriot cities	Comparison of percent changes in welfare expenditures before, after riots	23 riot cities show sharp increases the year after riots, 20 nonriot cities do not
Button (1978)	b. Federal government	Systematic interviews with officials, legislative analysis	Liberal, radical responses to early riots in OEO, HUD; conservative reaction to later riots

Study	Unit/Sample	Method	Findings
Colby (1975)	c. 40 riot cities	Path analysis of increases in OEO, HUD, LEAA expenditures	Riots lead to OEO increases in 1967-1969, decreases in 1970-1972; and to HUD and LEAA increases in 1970-1972
	50 states	Correlation of riots with increases in welfare rolls	The greater the riot intensity, the greater the increase in AFDC recipients and payments 1965-1969.
Feagin and Hahn (1973)	All levels of government	Assessment of others' research findings, mostly non-systematic	Limited reforms when slack resources permitted, most changes police policies
Hahn (1970)	20 riot cities	Reanalysis of Kerner Commission in-depth studies	17 of 20 cities were responsive, six of them highly so; most responsive were cities with strong elected councils, strong central governments
Iris (1978)	a. 38 cities	Quasi-experimental analysis of police, recreation budget trends 1955-1974	Police expenditures increased significantly in 20 cities, irrespective of riot severity; recreation increased in 12, mainly those with minor or no riots
	b. Federal government	Quasi-experimental analysis of welfare, housing program data trends	Most HUD increases, some AFDC increases attributed to incremental budgeting and administrative decisions unrelated to rioting
Jennings (1979)	a. 50 states	Correlation of riots with increases in welfare rolls	The greater the number of riots in a state, the greater the 1959-1970 increase in AFDC recipients

(TABLE 6–2 Continued)

Type of Study	Units of Analysis	Data and Methods	Findings
	b. Federal government	Time-series analysis of annual increases in welfare rolls	From 1938–1976 welfare increases were much more strongly related to unemployment than to number of riots
C. Mueller (1978)	77 cities	Correlational analysis of local officials' immediate responses, coded from newspapers	Riot intensity affected symbolic reassurances from officials more than long-term commitments
Welch (1975)	310 cities	Correlation analysis of budget changes 1965–1969 in riot versus nonriot cities	Riot cities received more intergovernmental funds and spent more for police and fire protection

3. Systematic studies of change in socioeconomic status of blacks

Berkowitz (1974)	riot versus nonriot census tracts in four cities	Mean changes in 1960–1970 census data on income, housing, family indicators	Riot tracts did not improve more than black nonriot tracts; a slight tendency for negative riot effects on income
Kelly and Snyder (1978)	405 cities	Correlational analysis of 1959–1969 changes in black income, occupations	Frequency and severity of riots have no effects on variation in black economic gains among cities

*Studies designated a, b, and c signify research at different levels of analysis reported in a single publication.

"interruption"—a riot or period of disorder—has a statistically significant effect on the level or trend in a dependent variable such as annual expenditures.

One other characteristic of the research designs in the quantitative studies is that most of them introduce a series of control variables that provide alternative or additive explanations for policy outcomes, for example, the size of a city's black population, the structure of municipal government, and so on. A sophisticated example is Button's path analysis of the determinants of increases in federal program expenditures in riot cities. His model of the causes of per capita increases in Office of Economic Opportunity (OEO) expenditures by city takes into account numbers of riots, numbers and rate of increase in the city's black population, the rate of increase in crime, the form of local government, and voting turnout (Button 1978: 38).

We review the main lines of research findings here; for details see the studies cited and summarized in Table 6–2. (The tactics used by police and National Guard to quell riots are part of the immediate conflict process and are not of concern here.) The first substantive responses (in point of time, not importance) are symbolic ones. Mueller (1978) finds that the immediate responses of local officials (those within the first two weeks after the onset of rioting) are of two rather distinct types: reassurances, mainly in the form of negotiations over and investigation of grievances; and long-term commitments, in the form of appointment of blacks to visible positions and promised programmatic changes. The size and intensity of rioting was more likely to increase symbolic reassurances than long-term commitments; the extent of commitments made is not well-explained in her analysis. There is also a detailed comparative study by Lipsky and Olson (1977) of riot commissions as a kind of symbolic response to riots.

A more substantial kind of policy response to rioting is to increase welfare expenditures, a response which cynics regard as "buying off the poor" and conservatives criticize as "rewarding rioters." When municipal expenditures alone are examined, riot cities on the average had no greater increases in welfare and health expenditures between 1965 and 1968–1969 than nonriot cities (Welch 1975). By contrast, all the comparative city and state studies show that expenditures and case loads of the federal Aid to Families with Dependent Children (AFDC) program increased significantly in proportion to rioting. Several of these studies (Colby 1975, Jennings 1978: a) measure rioting and AFDC increases for the same year, which raises the question of what causes what. Betz (1974) introduces time-lags between rioting and welfare increases and finds unmistakable evidence of sharp one-year welfare increases (but see the critique of his methods in Cramer and Betz 1974). These analyses all tend to support part of the Piven-Cloward thesis, cited above, about the palliative nature of welfare responses to disorder. Iris (1978: b) and Jennings (1978: b) both weigh in with important qualifications based on time-series and programmatic analysis, however. Welfare expenditures in general and AFDC in particular have grown substantially since the 1940s and Jennings's time-series analysis over the long run from 1939 to 1976 shows that unemployment was much more consequential than number of riots *at the national level* in determining annual increases. Iris's quasi-experimental analysis of national AFDC expenditures from 1955 to 1974 shows that the increases after 1967 were sharply significant. But his parallel analysis of general assistance programs, funded by state and local governments, shows that recipients and expenditures dropped substantially in the mid- to late 1960s because many were being shifted to AFDC support. Furthermore, Iris analyzed the trend in total national expenditures in welfare programs *other than* AFDC and general assistance. The only significant increase in this catch-all welfare category came in 1970, well after the climacteric of rioting. Iris concludes that the welfare response to rioting was limited largely to AFDC, and some of the apparent AFDC response was due to the shift of general-assistance recipients to AFDC support for administrative reasons (Iris 1978: chapter 7). But these results are not necessarily inconsistent with the city and state studies. The national trends are the net of much more variable state and local trends. Given an expanding federal welfare program, and bureaucratic and funding routines that provide ample scope for manipulation by local officials, we can readily account for the evidence that the most squeaky wheels (the most turbulent cities) got the most federal grease.

The urban renewal programs of the U. S. Department of Housing and Urban Development (HUD) have also gotten considerable attention in studies of riot impact, especially by Button (1978) and Iris (1978: b). Iris shows that programs planning and expenditure on HUD projects is so protracted that the increase in national-level expenditures during the later 1960s reflected decisions made well in advance of the major wave of riots. Button's analysis of HUD expenditures among forty cities leads to the statistical conclusion that neither the occurrence nor the severity of riots significantly affected per capita HUD expenditures by city in 1967–1969 but that they *did* affect 1970–1972 expenditures in a generally positive way. Moreover, Button's interviews with federal and local officials and President Lyndon Johnson's public statements all indicated that the authorities saw HUD programs in general and the Model Cities Program (enacted in 1966) in particular as major instruments for meeting the problems that underlay the ghetto riots. Case studies also show unambiguously that massive increases in HUD grants were made to a number of cities in direct response to riots, including Watts (see Bullock 1969: 51ff, Button 1978: 64), Dayton, and Rochester. The lack of consistent statistical evidence in Button's cross-city analysis and Iris's time-series analysis may be due to the variability of political and administrative time-lags between riots, planning, decisions, announced grants, and expenditures.

The most radical governmental response to poverty in the United States was the federal Antipoverty Program of 1964, whose activities were carried out through the Office of Economic Opportunity (OEO). The program was already funded and in existence before the onset of the major riots, and in Button's words OEO took a "fire-brigade" approach to them. His is the only study to focus intensively on OEO decisions and expenditures as they related to disorder. The OEO programs that responded most directly and positively to the riot were job training and community action programs—in the 1960s. By the early 1970s, a backlash had set in and OEO concentrated new funding in smaller cities which had fewer blacks and less rioting during the 1960s.

A "law 'n order" response to urban riots by federal, state, and local authorities paralleled efforts to improve the welfare, housing, and social well-being of inner-city blacks (see Feagin and Hahn 1973: chapter 5, Button 1978: chapter 4). Police quickly adopted new techniques of crowd control and made widely publicized investments in riot-control equipment. Significant federal assistance for local police became available through the Law Enforcement Assistance Administration (LEAA), which was established in 1968. Button's cross-sectional analysis of riots and LEAA funding leads him to the conclusion that "riot cities with perhaps the poorest police–black relations tended to respond directly to ghetto upheavals by obtaining significantly more LEAA funds (per capita) than other riot cities, and the expressed purpose of much of the increased funds was to arm and train their police for control of civil disorders" (Button 1978: 142). Another comparative study that shows increased expenditures on city police after riots is Welch (1975); but at the state level there was no comparable pattern of increase (Colby 1975). Police purchases of antiriot equipment in the immediate aftermath of riots does not signify that all enhanced police efforts were directed at riot control per se. Much of the new riot-related funding, especially from the LEAA, was used for community relations and other social programs. Of the riot-related appropriations of LEAA during its first year 42 percent went to police communications, 35 percent to community relations, and 23 percent to police equipment (Feagin and Hahn 1973: 232; see also Button's case studies of LEAA programs in Dayton and Rochester, Button 1978: 144–147). The results of Iris's time-series analysis of municipal budgets suggest an important qualification of these findings. Police expenditures increased in almost all cities during this period but the increase was proportional to overall increases in municipal spending; it was not significantly affected by rioting (Iris 1978: 223–226). In other words, whereas police practices and sources of funds evidently were affected by riots, trends and levels of police spending were not.

The above five paragraphs summarize the main lines of symbolic and police response to the riots. The most important result not yet considered is the evidence of systematic shifts in policy response, especially at the federal level. The skeptical point of view, represented by Feagin and Hahn's commentary on riot responses (Feagin and Hahn 1973: chapter 5), is that officials stressed the need for both control and reform but put their money on the former and gave the latter lip-service. The empirical evidence reviewed above suggests that, to the contrary, the welfare, housing, and community action responses were primary, control was secondary. This is unmistakably evident from the pattern of increase in federal funding for the major programs aimed at urban poverty: AFDC expenditures increased from $1.6 billion in 1965 to $4.9 billion in 1970; urban renewal expenditures from $0.3 billion in 1965 to $1.1 billion in 1970. Of course these were existing programs and their increases are attributable only in part to the riots. Two agencies established during the riot period as direct responses to the urban crisis were OEO, which aimed at radical socioeconomic change, and LEAA, which was concerned with social control. In 1967, OEO's second full year of operation, its outlays were $1.5 billion. In 1970, LEAA's second year, its budget was $268 million. By 1972, after three years of the Nixon Administration's more conservative policies, OEO expenditures still exceeded $1 billion while LEAA was at $700 million.

Button's study provides a context in which to interpret these budgetary figures. His evidence from interviews with federal officials, comparative analyses of riot cities, and case studies of Dayton and Rochester all document the prevalence of a moderate-to-radical reformist response to the initial riots of 1963–1966. The massive rioting of 1967–1968 pushed official and political opinion toward an emphasis on prevention along with moderate social and economic programs. The conservative emphasis on control did not reach its ascendancy until the advent of the first Nixon Administration in 1969, which continued the moderate social programs, began to cut back on OEO, and sharply increased "law and order" programs (Button 1978: chapter 5). Button's depiction of the shift in responses to riots from reform to backlash is far more consistent with the political history of the period and the empirical evidence, reviewed above, than Feagin and Hahn's more impressionistic conclusions that symbolic and control responses dominated from the outset.

There remains one major threat to the validity of Button's analysis and to the validity of most of the empirical evidence that the riots led to positive responses. The alternative explanation is that programs of socioeconomic reform were a response to the civil rights movement, which began nearly a decade before the riots and continued, albeit at a lower level, throughout the riot period. The civil rights movement unquestionably contributed to a widespread recognition that racial discrimination and inequalities were a major social problem in need of remedial public and private action. That recognition not only contributed to the passage of civil rights legislation, including the Civil Rights Acts of 1964 and 1968 and the Voting Rights Act of 1965, but underlay the Johnson Administration's design of the "Great Society" programs. Not one of the empirical studies reviewed here examines the impact of civil rights activities on social or economic programs at any level of government. One study that traces carefully the impact of civil rights campaigns is Garrow's (1979) case study which shows that the Selma, Alabama, demonstrations were instrumental to the passage of the Voting Rights Act of 1965. Only Button among the authors in Table 6–2 confronts the issue when he notes that "The early riots occurred almost simultaneously with the peaceful protest of the civil rights movement. . . . and other conventional political activities" (Button 1978: 176). We may speculate here that the riots had positive socioeconomic effects only insofar as they reinforced reformist programs which were set in motion in response to civil rights activity. The research designs used to test the impact of riots on public policy could be used as easily to assess the impact of civil rights demonstrations on city, federal policies. Another approach to this issue, using perceptual data from knowledgeable citizens, is taken in a new study by Button and Scher (forthcoming). They find that in six Florida communities the civil rights movement was perceived to have significant though not great effects on black municipal services since 1960.

What has been omitted from studies of the outcomes of the urban riots of the 1960s, aside from parallel studies of the effects of civil rights activity? Referring back to Figure 6–1, which models the full range of effects of conflict, we find that a lot has been left out. Systematic research has focused on policy responses much more than on subsequent changes in the conditions of the black and white urban poor, or the properties of political, social, and economic systems. We cited above studies that show that the relative economic status of blacks generally improved during the 1960s and early 1970s, but not in ways that could be attributed to the riots. (The more plausible hypothesis that blacks' socioeconomic gains varied among cities or states according to the intensity of civil rights activity seems not to have been tested.) There also are studies of the impact of urban riots on public opinion among blacks and whites. Presumably these attitudes are a crucial intervening variable between the occurrence of violent conflict and the formulation and implementation of public and private policies. The findings of these studies are diverse. Some show white attitudes toward blacks and their resort to violence to be unchanged after the riots (for example, Eidson 1971), others that whites became more fearful after the riots (Sears and McConahay 1973: chapter 10). Some studies of black opinion taken in the aftermath of riots show that blacks thought riots had no instrumental use (C. H. Moore 1970), others that substantial percentages of blacks were willing to use violence for social change (McCord and Howard 1968, Sears 1971). A number of studies of black opinion document their low trust in government and skepticism that positive responses could be expected (Muller 1972, Sears 1971). But none of these studies traces trends in black or white attitudes about riot-related issues over the longer run.[8]

The most challenging unanswered question is what outcomes have followed from the policy changes noted above. Welfare payments are of course a transitory response. OEO and HUD programs, and many LEAA programs, were intended to have more enduring effects on the quality of life among the urban poor. It is pretty much a commonplace that social and physical deterioration has not been arrested in the low-income areas of most cities. From the point of view of riot outcomes research, though, we would want to know whether cities and, especially, neighborhoods that had serious riots in the 1960s, and major policy innovations in response, have gotten relatively worse or better as a consequence. Berkowitz's (1974) focus on changes in census tracts is a promising approach but excludes the intervening variable of policy response. But any such studies will have to deal with the plaguing problems of the "expanding funnel of causality" mentioned in part II. There are many factors other than riots and public responses to the problems of the black poor that determine the fate of cities, and disentangling riot effects from the more fundamental and persistent effects of middle-class flight to the suburbs, shrinking job opportunities, and rising crimes may prove well-nigh impossible.

OUTCOMES OF THE SEIZURE OF POWER

On literally hundreds of occasions in the twentieth century rebels have seized power with the avowed purpose of bringing about change. In many, probably most cases the advocacy of change provided only a fig-leaf of justification for the indulgence of the new leaders' appetite for power and its perquisites.[9] In other instances their objectives of reform, national development, or revolutionary transformation were real enough but thwarted by circumstances and conditions that exceeded their grasp. And in a few dramatic instances, from Mexico to China, the seizure of power led more or less directly to fundamental and enduring change. Our review of research on the outcomes of seizure of power concentrates on systematic and comparative studies. The following diagram, derived from Figure 6–1 above, helps structure the discussion:

Most of the empirical research is concerned either with systemic effects or with policy changes. Only the case studies, and not all of them by any means, attempt to link the policies introduced by new leaders to the analysis of the outcomes of those policies. In the language of statistical models, there probably are interaction effects among the seizure of power, the nature of policy changes, and exogenous variables (such as level of development, external dependencies, and so forth) which determine whether and how the policy changes introduced by coup makers affect the social system.

The military in power. Coups d'état are relatively brief and well-orchestrated conflicts in which the military seize control of more or less intact governmental systems. There is a vast literature on the conditions under which the military are disposed to seize power and on the political role of the military in or out of power (reviewed in Zimmermann 1980: chapter 7). A significant fraction of studies asks what difference military rule makes. Studies of particular cases show that the differences can be decisive. To cite two of many well-studied instances, the Colonels' coup in Egypt in 1952 brought enduring political changes under Nasser and a succession of socioeconomic reforms that continue to the present (see Vatikiotis 1968); while Brazil's military revolution of 1964 led directly to the foundation of an authoritarian state and indirectly to a sustained economic boom (see Stepan 1973). There is also much theoretical speculation about the likely impact of military rule. On one side of what Jackman (1976: 1078) calls a "mild controversy" is the argument that the military is or can be an effective modernizing force (see Hurewitz 1969; and articles by Manfred Halpern, Lucian W. Pye, and Edward Shils in J. J. Johnson 1962). The pessimistic view is that the political skills of soldiers generally are inadequate to the tasks of mobilization and modernization (see, for example, Janowitz 1964 and Bienen 1971). Latin Americanists in particular have long been skeptical about the military in power, arguing either that they are too constrained by external dependencies or too closely aligned with the privileged class or sectoral groups to promote political mobilization or substantial reforms (see J. J. Johnson 1964, Remmer 1978). Huntington (1968: chapter 4) attempts to synthesize the two arguments by suggesting that the outcome of military rule depends on a society's level of social and economic development. In least developed countries the military can be expected to promote modernization; in more developed countries where the middle classes are a major political force, the military will tend to be conservative.

The global empirical studies that have addressed these hypotheses lead to the conclusion that military rule has weak effects, at best, on socioeconomic development. The results of four such studies are instructive. The first, by Nordlinger (1970, 1977), tested the relationship between the political strength of the military and seven indicators of economic and social change in seventy-four countries in the 1950s and early 1960s. Five of his seven measures relate to systemic effects; only two, "leadership commitment and economic development" and "change in effectiveness of tax systems" relate to policy per se. His results lead him to conclude in favor of

Huntington's hypothesis that the military promoted modernization only in the poorest countries. Taking both quantitative and case-study evidence into account, Nordlinger concludes more generally that the political and economic effects of military rule tend to be negative. A later study by Jackman (1976) reanalyzed Nordlinger's 1970 data using more appropriate techniques, with the conclusion that Nordlinger's few positive results were an artifact of inappropriate methods. Jackman also analyzed a new set of data on military rule and change in seventy-seven countries for the 1960–1970 decade, from which he concluded that "military intervention in the politics of the Third World has no unique effects on social change, regardless of either the level of economic development or geographic region" (Jackman 1976: 1096). The four change variables in this study relate to energy consumption, school enrollment, health care, and mass communications--all of them systemic effects, not measures of policy outputs per se. Two other studies by McKinlay and Cohan (1975, 1976) examine a somewhat broader set of change variables in a larger sample of 115 countries. In one study (1975) they contrast the performance of military and civilian regimes using indicators of annual rates of change from 1951 to 1970 in such variables as per capita GNP, food production, exports, primary education, and military spending and size. All but the military measures are systemic. They find that the military regimes performed somewhat better than civilian regimes in the poorest countries, while overall they had higher rates of growth in primary education. McKinlay and Cohan's second study (1976) used different data (including measures of political variables as well as socioeconimic ones) and concluded that the only sharp distinction between the two types of regimes was that the military ones had lower levels of political activity and higher levels of political change—a difference that reflects policies in a more immediate way than does economic performance.

In view of the uncertainties that lie between policy decisions and their ultimate impact on society in any and all kinds of political systems, we would expect that military regimes have considerably more potential effect on policies than on performance. Regional studies provide more evidence on this point than the global studies. The most extensive study of the subject in Latin America, by Schmitter (1971), compares both policy outputs and developmental outcomes in civilian regimes with those in military and other noncompetitive regimes. As in the global studies, he found only weak correlations between regime type and effects; more important, from our perspective, is that differences in policy proved greater than differences in outcomes. The military regimes tended to spend less on welfare, to rely more heavily on indirect taxation, and to spend less than their civilian counterparts. They also were slightly more successful in achieving economic outcomes such as lower inflation, increased foreign exchange earning, and higher economic growth. Other evidence of policy differences between military and civilian regimes in Latin America is to be found in longitudinal studies of countries that have alternated between civilian and military rule (for Brazil, see Hayes 1975; for Venezuela, see Baloyra 1974). An excellent critical survey of these studies is Remmer (1978); see also Weaver (1973).

For Africa there is a study by Dolian (1973) which focuses on the impact of coups as measured by changes in budgeted expenditures for capital investment, education, health and agricultural services, police, foreign affairs, and defense. Pre- and post-coup budget items were examined in each of eleven countries that had coups during the 1960s. The results suggest that in Africa the military pursues self-interest most of all: the percentage of defense expenditures increased substantially in all eleven countries after the coups, health and agricultural expenditures increased in three, economic development and educational expenditures increased in only two. Dolian's findings that military budgets increased following coups in Africa contrasts with McKinlay and Cohan's global results that neither military size nor expenditures are greater in military than in civilian regimes (1976: 857). A regional study of military regimes in Southeast Asia by Hoadley (1975) provides some significant contrasts to Dolian's findings. Comparative case studies of military versus civilian regimes in this region show substantial evidence of policy changes: military regimes follow more authoritarian policies, especially with respect to political liberties; are relatively successful in curbing inflation during times of peace; and are *not* likely to increase defense expenditures. Military rule in Southeast Asia did not lead to relatively greater rates of economic growth, however.

Not much is likely to be learned from further global or regional studies which examine only the systemic outcomes of military seizures of power. The results are likely to be weak and ambiguous because too many unspecified variables and interactions moderate the systemic impacts of the seizure of power. One crucial set of intervening variables is change in policies, and there evidently is much to be learned from the systematic cross-sectional and longitudinal study of policy changes introduced by new military rulers. But it probably is not enough to measure those changes using crude indicators like changes in gross budget categories. As Remmer observes, "the assumption that allocative policies provide an adequate inventory of policy outputs is theoretically unsound, particularly since common sense suggests that some of the major differences between military and civilian governments have to do with regulatory and symbolic policies" (Remmer 1978: 45). She goes on to cite the right to strike, wage and price controls, land reform, and the regulation of investment as examples of major policy variations unlikely to be reflected in budgets. A second set of intervening variables are the external and internal constraints on the implementation of public policy which affect civilian and military regimes alike. It may well be, as Schmitter comments (1975: 37), "that the

relatively constant features of ecological setting and underlying class interests. . . impose such narrow and fixed parameters upon performance
that it makes no 'real' difference if political structures are more or less centralized, more or less competitive, or more or less participatory." The implication for any and all cross-sectional studies of the outcomes of seizures
of power is that ecological, class, and other variables be entered as controls. And their effects on longitudinal analysis must also be assessed, even
if their invariance in one country makes it impossible to control for them
statistically.

Revolutionaries in power. Each revolution in western history, beginning with the French Revolution of 1789, has inspired a substantial inter-
pretative literature about its courses and consequences. The French Revolution aroused in Edmund Burke a profound skepticism which led him to
argue, among other things, that revolutions brought to power radicals who
were morally and intellectually flawed (he especially singled out lawyers)
and that such leadership led inevitably to tyrannical outcomes. (For an attempt to synthesize Burke's diverse writings on the French Revolution into
a general theory, see Freeman 1978.) In the 1930s Crane Brinton derived
from the French and other classic cases a theory of the postrevolutionary
process. The moderates ruled briefly, then lost power to extremists who
imposed a reign of terror, which gave way to Thermidor, a "convalescence
from the fever of revolution" (Brinton 1938). Another recurring scholarly
interest is whether these historical revolutions, or more recent ones, had
benefits that outweighed their costs. That is, loosely, the theme of Denis
Brogan's *The Price of Revolution* (1951). Many intriguing generalizations
can be found in this literature, some of which seem well worth testing
against the outcomes of revolutions other than those which suggested
them, tests which have yet to be accomplished.

There is also a vast descriptive literature on the formulation, implementation, and impact of policies formulated in the aftermath of specific
twentieth-century revolutions. I know of no study that pulls this information together, but the reader may get a sense of its scope and subjects from
this sketch of the research that has been done on the outcomes of the
popular revolution in Bolivia in 1952. There are three scholarly books in
English that provide general assessments of its outcomes (Malloy 1970,
1971; S. Eckstein 1976) and another which analyzes postrevolutionary
political developments (Mitchell 1978). Four works deal with agricultural
and land reform since the revolution (Flores 1954, Patch 1961, Garcia
1970, Carter 1971), another one with social mobility (Bergsten 1964). Four
other studies evaluate the success, or lack thereof, of postrevolutionary
economic policies (Zondag 1966, Thorn 1971, S. Eckstein 1975, Gomez
1976). Two studies examine U. S. policies toward and aid for the revolution (Wilkie 1969, Blasier 1971), another analyzes patterns of public expenditure since 1952 (Wilkie 1971). These are merely the published,
English-language studies identified in a brief survey. They suggest some-

thing about the amount of research done on the outcomes of better-known revolutions in Mexico, Russia, China, Cuba, and elsewhere.

An important genre of research, which is closer to our concern with systematic theory and research, offers comparative case studies and interpretations of the role revolutions play in societal development. The most influential such study has been Barrington Moore's *Social Origins of Dictatorship and Democracy* (1968), which traces the effects of different class coalitions on the course and outcomes of the English, French, Russian, and Chinese revolutions. His interest in the relations between political and economic development is shared by Kautsky in his comparative study of "modernizing revolutions" in Mexico and the Soviet Union (1975). The broadest such study is Eisenstadt's recent *Revolution and the Transformation of Societies* (1978), which offers a sociological analysis of the connections between social change and revolution in traditional, modern, and "late modern" societies. Of special concern here is chapter 8 on revolutionary patterns and outcomes. It combines conceptual analysis, propositions, observations, and brief case studies in a way that demands textual exegesis as much as summarization. The central question, for Eisenstadt, is the nature and degree of discontinuity between pre- and postrevolutionary societies. The dimensions along which discontinuity should be studied include not only class relations and modernization but the bases and symbols of legitimation, "the meanings of institutions. . . the composition of ruling groups, the degree of control and coerciveness, and the premises underlying the sociopolitical order, center–periphery relations, and the social hierarchy" (Eisenstadt 1978: 239). His propositions about the determinants of discontinuity emphasize characteristics of the revolutionary process and are illustrated by reference to the classic European and American revolutions, and the twentieth-century revolutions of Russia, Turkey, and China. An example is his proposition that the coerciveness and dislocation of postrevolutionary societies is a function of the degree of isolation of the ruling political elite from other elites, and the degree to which the former attempts to control the latter's functions and relations with other social strata. The general drift of the argument is summed up as follows:

> The ultimate outcomes of any revolution are not necessarily given in the prerevolutionary structure of the society but are the product of interaction among prerevolutionary characteristics, the forces of change--most notably, international forces--and the revolutionary process itself. Only through such interactions do coalitions of broad classes and coalitions between them and the major types of institutional entrepreneurs arise and change. [Eisenstadt 1978: 251]

The elements of a plausible and powerful theory are to be found in the book, and presumably it will have considerable influence on future case studies.

Whereas Eisenstadt is concerned with the full range of possible revolutionary outcomes, recent comparative studies by Susan Eckstein (1975, 1976) and Kay Trimberger (1978) deal with more specific and tractable economic outcomes. Eckstein proposes to account for the different economic effects of the Mexican and Bolivian revolutions. Her central thesis is that economic gains in Mexico were considerably greater because of domestic and foreign conditions that were independent of social revolution per se. "Social revolutions do not inevitably generate new economic resources, increased national economic autonomy, or egalitarian distribution of economic resources. Economic growth depends. . . also on how the powers of the state are used, and the nature of foreign investments" (S. Eckstein 1975: 59–60). The heart of her analysis is specification of how these factors affect development. In Bolivia economic growth was limited because of the inability of the Bolivian government to generate and control sufficient resources. Its failure was due to the low level of national income and technological skills, failure to secure the foreign holdings of indigenous tin barons, the need to pay heavy compensation for expropriated tin interests, and the fall in price of tin on the world market. She offers a parallel analysis of reasons for the Mexican government's relative success in restricting foreign economic intrusion, in which the key factor is the fact that the Mexican revolution created conditions favorable to the development of a domestic class of industrial capitalists, whereas the Bolivian revolution did not. Eckstein does not, however, generalize her analysis of these contingent variables beyond the Mexican and Bolivian cases. Her analysis is suggestive of what must be done in order to trace the systemic effects of revolution down an expanding funnel of causality, but only that.

A comparative historical study by Trimberger (1978) provides a more fully developed example of the kind of narrowly focused theorizing that is needed on the determinants of revolutionary outcomes. Her topic is the outcomes of "revolution from above" in Japan (1868), Turkey (1923), Egypt (1952), and Peru (1968). At their inception these conflicts were coups d'état involving high military and civil bureaucrats of the old regime, with little or no mass participation. The aims of the new rulers were essentially nationalistic: to establish a stable and powerful nation–state based on an autonomous capitalist economy. To achieve this end required, among other things, the destruction of the old economic and class order. The coup makers had the capacity to do so because, unlike most coup makers, their military and civil bureaucratic apparatus was relatively independent of the (mainly land-owning) classes which controlled the means of production. Trimberger contends that all the revolutions failed, or are failing, in their pursuit of the objective of autonomous industrial development. (Japan is an exception which she does not explain well.)

The major theoretical contribution of Trimberger's study is its specification of the conditions under which one particular outcome can be pursued and achieved. Autonomous industrial development will be sought when four conditions prevail:

> A military coup will promote revolutionary change only when a significant segment of the military bureaucracy is (a) autonomous (in recruitment and structure) from those classes which control the means of production; (b) politicized around an ideology of nation building; (c) threatened by nationalist movements from below; and (d) faced with contradictions in the international power constellation which can be exploited to increase national autonomy. [Trimberger 1978: 156]

These revolutions have all fallen short of autonomous industrial development because the revolutionary bureaucrats could not, or did not, mobilize a mass base of support. Instead they came to depend on some combination of elements of the old rural oligarchy and new capitalist classes. Some industrialization occurs under such conditions (a great deal in Japan), but it is dependent on capital from and trade with dominant capitalist economies. The result is industrialization that "will be geared to export, foster inequality, and continue poverty for the mass of the population" (Trimberger 1978: 174). Trimberger analyzes the specific sequences by which changing class alliances emerged in the four revolutionary states, but is more superficial and less convincing about the effects of dependency on the process.[10] Her general conclusion is that "relatively autonomous bureaucrats who in a crisis situation become dynamically autonomous of class forces have the capacity only to constitute themselves as a new ruling class, which in a capitalist world economy means a capitalist class" (1978: 174).

A major new study of revolutionary outcomes is Theda Skocpol's *States and Social Revolutions* (1979). She examines the processes and outcomes of revolution in France, Russia, and China, with special attention to explaining how class relationships were altered and why centralizing, bureaucratic states emerged in each society. The main causal variables in her analysis of outcomes include the socioeconomic structures of prerevolutionary society, the specific properties of the revolutionary crisis, and the nation's international situation during and after revolution. By reference to Figure 6–1, above, Skocpol's analysis focuses almost entirely on the systemic linkages. Hers is a deterministic, structural analysis that gives little attention to such voluntaristic elements as group mobilization or the intervening role of policy changes. While her analysis is in this sense a partial one, it adds the international dimension to analysis. Like Trimberger's study of *Revolution from Above* (1978), Skocpol calls our attention to the fact that the outcomes of violent conflict may be constrained by political and economic characteristics of the world system.

Moore, Eisenstadt, S. Eckstein, Trimberger, and Skocpol all offer powerful arguments about revolutionary outcomes that in principle should be susceptible to evaluation using different cases and more rigorous empirical techniques (though Skocpol [1979: 287–292] argues that the details of her theory are peculiar to France, Russia, and China and cannot be applied to other social revolutions). An example of what might be done with such arguments is Moy's (1971) use of computer simulation to evaluate Moore's and Lipset's models of democratic political development—a study only incidentally concerned with revolutionary outcomes. A number of research designs used in the comparative study of riot and coup outcomes also could be used to test specific hypotheses about revolutionary outcomes. Surprisingly, very few such studies have been attempted. Three are reviewed below, each of them a pioneering effort, all of them worth modification and application in other contexts. None of them, however, addresses general theoretical questions of the sort raised by Moore, Eisenstadt, and others. The connection between general theories about revolutionary outcomes and the use of sophisticated empirical methodologies to test them has yet to be made.

Chong-Soo Tai (1974, 1979) has applied quasi-experimental analysis to the study of policy outputs and systemic effects in six revolutions: Bolivia 1952, Cuba 1959, Egypt 1952, Iraq 1958, South Korea 1961, and Pakistan 1958. (As in Trimberger's study, some of these cases involved a military seizure of power rather than armed struggle; at best they were revolutionary in their objectives.) The quasi-experimental or interrupted time-series research design is in some respects ideally suited to the study of revolutionary outcomes: given a time-series of data on policy or systemic variables, the researcher uses statistical tests to determine whether a revolutionary seizure of power (or any other discrete "interruption") significantly affects (1) the trend in the dependent variable; (2) its absolute level; and (3) the persistence of the postrevolutionary effect over time (on the method, see Caporaso and Roos 1973). Tai examined pre–post changes in four measures of government expenditure for each of the six countries: education, public health, defense (all measured as a percent of total budget), and total expenditure. There were significant increases in trend and/or level of total expenditures in all countries except Bolivia, and decreases in defense expenditures in all except Cuba, but little change in proportional health or education expenditures. Systemic effects also were substantial in some countries. Economic performance measures showed substantial postrevolutionary increases in all countries except Bolivia and Egypt. External economic dependence (measured by concentration of export-receiving countries) declined significantly in Cuba and Iraq. Trends and levels of primary and secondary school enrollments all tended upward, the most pronounced postrevolutionary effects being in Cuba, Iraq, and Pakistan. (The fact that enrollments increased but the educational share of the budget did not illustrates Remmer's observation, above, that important changes are not necessarily reflected in budgets. Mass media expanded in most of the countries, Bolivia excepted, but only in Korea was the increase unambiguously associated with the revolution. Tai also assessed the impact of revolution on magnitudes of turmoil and internal war: turmoil declined markedly in Cuba, Egypt, and Iraq, while internal war declined in Bolivia, Cuba, and Egypt (for the obvious reason that the rebels won) but increased in Iraq (where revolution in Baghdad precipitated rebellion in the Kurdish north).

Tai's results provide a general—perhaps too general—statistical profile of dimensions of postrevolutionary change that complements what is known from case studies. Consistent with S. Eckstein's comments on Bolivia (above), Tai finds the least evidence of positive change in that country. The only significant and sustained improvement was in infant mortality—a result which one is tempted to attribute to the breakup of latifundia into individual holdings and the consequent improvement, noted in case studies, of peasants' diet. The contrast with Cuba is stark: that country experienced a general growth in government expenditure, educational enrollments, increased energy consumption, and a decline in economic dependence (for detailed studies of postrevolutionary change in Cuba, see Mesa-Lago 1971, Nelson 1972, Ritter 1974, and especially Dominguez 1978 and Lewis-Beck 1979). Tai's results also show that coups in Iraq and Pakistan had comparable effects on most of the same dimensions and more positive effects on economic performance. The similarity in the pattern of policy and systemic outcomes is quite striking in view of the differences in political styles of the three revolutions: Cuban communism, Báathist socialism in Iraq, and nonideological modernization by the military in Pakistan. In Egypt, another country ruled by military modernizers, the social impact of revolution was less than in any of the aforementioned three countries. Its major statistical effects were political and governmental, that is, declining internal conflict and increased government activity. The Korean revolution also had a substantial political impact: it put an end to a brief experiment in democracy. The only aggregate change attributable to the Korean revolution was an increase in mass media usage.

The other two studies of revolutionary outcomes examined here deal with inequalities, a perennial concern of revolutionaries and revolution watchers. The objective of redressing gross inequalities in power, income, and status is a central concern of almost all twentieth-century revolutions; a small but growing body of scholarly literature focuses on changes in inequality in postrevolutionary regimes. Lampton (1978, 1979) and Echols (1980) both do so by means of quantitative comparison, but in very different ways. Lampton's focus is on the extent and sources of inequalities in the provision of schooling and health services in China, among provinces and between urban and rural areas. The comparisons are made at several points in time—all since 1949. In a descriptive sense they show substantial discrepancies, especially between urban and rural areas, but also a shift toward equalization. Other quantitative studies also have documented the existence of substantial interregional inequalities in public expenditures and services, in both socialist and capitalist systems (Echols 1975, Zwick 1976). Lampton goes one step further and attempts to account for the differences by an examination of ecological, economic, and political factors. Whereas research in developed western systems attributes the growth and distribution of public services within nations mainly to economic variables, Lampton's results highlight the vital role of political decisions, and especially those made in Peking rather than in the provincial capitals. "The critical point," he concludes, "is that while leaders can never eliminate economic constraints, their political choices do shape the long-term structure of those constraints and, in the short run, determine how those economic variables will manifest themselves through concrete programs" (Lampton 1979: 475). From our vantage point, Lampton's work suggests several precepts. First, it demonstrates the value and feasibility of studying revolutionary effects by tracing intrasystem variations over time in policy outputs and outcomes. Moreover it shows that this can be done for a post-revolutionary society where official data are scarce. And Lampton reinforces a point we have made repeatedly about the importance of studying the two-stage sequence from revolutionary intentions to policy outputs to systemic impacts.

Echols's study (1980) deals with the much broader question of socialism's impact on racial and ethnic inequality. The question is whether minorities in the Soviet Union, Yugoslavia, Czechoslovakia, and Romania have fared better politically and materially than comparable minorities in western democracies. Examples of groups studied are Central Asians in the USSR, matched with blacks in the United States and Maoris in New Zealand; and Slovaks in Czechoslovakia matched with French-Canadians and with Scots and Welsh in Britain. Echols draws on many secondary studies for quantitative evidence about the relative status of such groups in terms of political representation, income, educational levels, and health services. Where possible, changes in group status are traced over time. The results document a general socioeconomic improvement of minorities in socialist and western democratic systems. They also show that the inequalities in socialist societies are as wide or wider than in western societies, while such trends as are discernible are divided about equally between decreasing and increasing inequalities. Echols's interpretation of socialist societies' unimpressive performance is that ethnic and racial inequalities have lower priority for socialist elites than economic growth in general and reduction of class inequalities. Other studies in fact show that socialist societies are relatively successful in reducing income inequalities across classes (Pryor 1971, Wiles 1974, Wiles and Markowski 1971).

Echols's study is not precisely a study of "revolutionary outcomes" because only in Russia and Yugoslavia did socialists come to power by revolutionary means. Moreover, he lacks data on the condition of minorities before the introduction of socialism. Nonetheless, the research design is well-suited to assessing revolutionary outcomes. It illustrates the value of using comparable developments in nonrevolutionary states as a baseline against which to judge progress in revolutionary regimes, and it also suggests that outcomes research should look at groups as well as at aggregate measures of policy and performance. And Echols's conclusions echo again a point made throughout this discussion: *the systemic outcomes of revolution depend on the policies followed by revolutionary elites.*

V. THE DESIGN OF FUTURE RESEARCH ON OUTCOMES

Let me conclude the chapter by specifying twelve criteria for good empirical research that aims at assessing the outcomes of violent conflict. The reasons for many of them should be evident from the empirical and theoretical studies reviewed above; others reflect prevailing views about the proper design of comparative research.

1. Focus on one or a few relatively narrow and precisely defined dimensions of outcomes: policies affecting welfare of the urban poor, not welfare budgets in general; types and levels of group participation in specific decision-making bodies, not general political mobilization or group acceptance; the output of heavy industry or agricultural productivity, not GNP; the income shares of specific social segments and classes, not overall inequality.

2. Take into account not only the occurrence of violent conflict but the properties of conflict and its participants: the scope and intensity of conflict, the array of group interests involved, the resources and organization of challengers. Similarly, ask whether the threat of violence in conflict has effects different from the actual use of violence.

3. Use a matching design in which changes following from violent conflict are tested against the fate of groups and the outcomes in systems that did not experience conflict; in other words, compare dissimilar cases.

4. Examine changes within particular groups and regions as well as changes at the systemic level; in other words, disaggregate.

5. Introduce control variables so as to assess the effects of ecological conditions (group and systemic resources, technological and administrative capabilities) and international factors (group alliances, foreign economic and military penetration) which may limit or enhance the prospects for change.

6. Employ multiple indicators of policy outputs, group fate, and systemic effects. Two indicators of a concept pointing in the same direction are more convincing than one. Two indicators pointing in opposite directions suggest that the theoretical map is wrong.

7. Develop coding systems to register information on theoretically im-

portant dimensions of outcomes that cannot be tapped with statistical data. It is better to approximate important variables than to measure unimportant ones precisely.

8. Examine the sequential linkages between proclaimed revolutionary intentions (or the demands of challenging groups), the shape of policy outputs, and the effects of those policies on groups and systems. It is not enough to examine policy outputs alone, or group fate alone, or systemic effects alone.

9. Measure policy outputs and systemic effects over time, either in annual time-series or in a series of cross-sections before, during, shortly after, and well after the climacteric of conflict.

10. Analyze conflict and its policy effects by testing relationships with different time-lags between the presumed cause and its hypothesized effects. It is not convincing to report a simultaneous increase in both cause and effect.

11. Use different analytic techniques to see whether they yield converging results. A theoretical argument worth keeping should be robust enough that it does not depend on the statistical methods used to test it.

12. Interpret data and findings both by reference to the theoretical model that guides the research and in the context of the specific social and historical circumstances in which conflict occurred.

Obviously no research design can satisfy all these criteria. What is needed are informed choices among design criteria and careful thought before as well as after the fact about implications of each choice. On balance, the cumulative research on a particular issue or form of conflict should collectively satisfy all the criteria. The "systemic effect" should be the gradual cumulation of definitive and generally accepted propositions about the conditions that determine whether and how riots and revolutions effect changes in policy, alter the fate of the groups involved, and reshape social systems.

NOTES

1. The same assumption is made by many who have studied military coups d'état in modernizing nations: the violent seizure of power by a military elite committed to change is likely to be better than a perpetuation of the status quo (see, for example, Huntington 1968; chapter 4, Janowitz 1964, and Trimberger 1978).

2. A number of quantitative empirical studies have attempted to test these and similar arguments about the effects of present conflict on the conditions of future conflict. Some of them are tested in the context of a larger conflict model by Gurr and Duvall (1973), while Lichbach and Gurr (forthcoming) test a variety of time-lagged relationships among the properties of conflict. Other relevant empirical work is reviewed by Zimmermann in Chapter 5 of this *Handbook*.

3. Gamson points out (personal communication) that the historical data were too sparse to provide the kind of continual record needed for dynamic analysis. His current research deals with dynamic analysis at the micro-level.

4. A recurring conceptual problem in conflict research is whether demonstrations and strikes should be regarded as part of the same general category that includes such intensely violent conflicts as insurrections and internal wars. The answer depends on the essence of conflict phenomena, which I defined in the Introduction to this *Handbook*, p. 1, as "overt, coercive interactions of contending collectivities." In my view, political demonstrations and strikes fall within this definition because they involve threats of coercion, ones which are understood by both parties: protesters, by their actions, threaten to do political or economic harm to authorities or employers, and both parties usually have at their disposal, and often resort to, means of violence. It also is evident from historical studies that strikes and demonstrations in western societies are more or less tame, ritualized derivatives of what once were quite violent and unregulated struggles (see, for example, Tilly 1978: chapters 5 and 6). On these grounds, "peaceful protest" is included within the scope of research on the outcomes of violent conflict.

5. Since Gamson has published his coded data on the fifty-three causes (1975: 176–189) they can readily be reanalyzed using regression techniques. Two such analyses have been published: one by Steedly and Foley (1979), whose findings are generally consistent with those reported by Gamson, and a second by Goldstone (1980), who comes to substantially different conclusions. Steedly and Foley conclude that "the use of violence does not greatly aid the prediction of group outcome because of the unpredictable, ambivalent reaction to violence by established groups" (1979: 1). Goldstone argues for and employs a less restrictive definition of group success than Gamson; shows that, given this definition, a protest group's goals determine its success, not its organization or tactics; and proposes that success almost always coincides with national crises. See also Gamson's rejoinder (1980).

6. The internal wars were identified from my coded data on all reported instances of civil strife in the 1960s; for a description of the data set see Gurr et al. 1978: 20–65. The cases were screened, evaluated, and background research done on their outcomes by the author working collaboratively with Barbara Gribben, Erika Gurr, Charles S. Matzke, and William Tuthill. The analysis reported here is preliminary and for some cases is based on partial and ambiguous information. There is no reason to think that more complete information or more precise guidelines will substantially alter the pattern of results, however.

7. The exceptions include preliminary papers by authors whose more recent studies are listed in Table 6–2; some case studies that comment on responses in passing; and, possibly, a handful of empirical studies that have escaped our bibliographic net.

8. There is a larger literature on public opinion about race relations and related governmental policies in the United States that I have not attempted to survey.

9. Calvert (1970) documents the occurrence of some 450 forceful seizures of power, world-wide, between 1901 and 1969. W. R. Thompson (1973) reports

a comparative analysis of the grievances of the leaders of contemporary coups d'état.

10. A flaw in Trimberger's analysis is that autonomy of industrial development is treated as a dichotomous variable: an economy is either autonomous (which is good) or dependent (which is bad), and any restriction on autonomy means failure. The overriding desirability attributed to economic autonomy is Trimberger's position, not necessarily the ultimate objective of the revolutionary bureaucrats she analyzes.

PART THREE

Theory and Research on International Conflict

CHAPTER 7

The Nexus of Civil and International Conflict

Michael Stohl

ONE OF THE MOST VENERABLE HYPOTHESES in the social science literature concerns the presumed nexus of civil conflict and international conflict. A general relationship between internal and external conflict behaviors of nations and groups is commonly asserted. Samuel Huntington, for example, suggests that "to be sure, some relationship exists between the internal and external conflicts of a state" (Huntington 1962: 40). The most commonly discussed form of the relationship is summarized by the ingroup/outgroup hypothesis. This hypothesis suggests that involvement in external conflict (usually war) increases internal cohesion and thus brings about internal peace. Thus Jean Bodin (1576) wrote that "the best way of preserving a state, and guaranteeing it against sedition, rebellion, and civil war is to keep the subjects in amity with one another, and to this end, to find an enemy against whom they can make common cause" (Bodin 1955, Mayer 1971: 141ff). In a more widely cited passage, William Graham Sumner asserted that the "relationship of comradeship and peace in the we-group and that of hostility and war towards others-groups are correlative to each other. The exigencies of war with outsiders are what makes peace inside, lest internal discord should weaken the we-group for war" (Sumner 1906: 12).

Other observers argue just as confidently that war has been associated with the occurrence of revolutions, both historically and within the mod-

Note: An earlier version of this chapter was presented to the Workshop on Social Conflict of the European Consortium for Political Research, Brussels, April 17–21, 1979. I wish to thank Ted Robert Gurr, Michael B. Nicholson, Arthur A. Stein, and Ekkart Zimmermann for their helpful criticisms of earlier drafts.

297

ern era, and thus that external conflict and violence leads to an increase, not a decrease in internal violence, and thereby to major destabilizations. Charles Tilly argues that "war bears a crucial relationship to revolution" and cites Walter Laqueur who suggests that

> war appears to have been the decisive factor in the emergence of revolutionary situations in modern times; most modern revolutions, both successful and abortive, have followed in the wake of war (the Paris Commune of 1871, the Russian Revolution of 1905, the various revolutions after the two World Wars, including the Chinese revolutions). These have occurred not only in the countries that suffered defeat. The general dislocation caused by war, the material losses and human sacrifices, create a climate conducive to radical change. A large section of the population has been armed; human life seems considerably less valuable than in peacetime. In a defeated country authority tends to disintegrate, and acute social dissatisfaction receives additional impetus from a sense of wounded national prestige (the Young Turks in 1908, Naguib and Nasser in 1952). The old leadership is discredited by defeat and thus the appeal for radical social change and national reassertion falls on fertile ground. [Laqueur 1968: 501, as quoted in Tilly 1978: 210]

Others argue that it is internal conflict or the possibility of conflict that leads to the occurrence of external conflict and war. Haas and Whiting contend that

> groups seeking self-preservation and no more, may be driven to a foreign policy of conflict--if not open war--in order to defend themselves against the onslaught of domestic rather than foreign enemies. In times of extreme domestic tensions among elites, a policy of uniting a badly divided nation against some real or alleged outside threat frequently seems useful to a ruling group. [Haas and Whiting 1956: 62]

And Cecil Rhodes, in a statement that was coincidentally self-serving, argued that "the Empire, as I have always said, is a bread and butter question. If you want to avoid civil war you must become Imperialists" (Semmel 1960: 16). Thus, although the conventional wisdom differs as to the precise nature of the relationship between internal and external conflict behavior, that collective wisdom is quite certain that the internal–external conflict nexus is an active intersect. Whereas the conventional wisdom makes intuitive sense and numerous "unique" examples may be cited to illustrate it, the scientific study of international politics has not had much success in identifying the parameters and form of this quite important relationship. In fact, the major impetus for the great majority of studies reviewed in the following pages was the finding of Rummel (1963) that there were no statistically significant relationships between measures of the two conflict spheres.

In this chapter I review these systematic studies of the internal–external conflict nexus and discuss their strengths and weaknesses. The examinations of this nexus are not limited to the direct dyadic linkage between a single nation's internal and external behaviors, but also consider the direct and indirect systemic effects of external conflict on internal political behavior. I will thus also explore the impact of international dominance and dependence and of intervention as external influences on internal political conflict. The purpose of such a review is not merely to summarize a set of empirical findings but also to map a strategy for building theory and improving method by learning from the empirical results generated thus far. In doing so I will concentrate primarily on scientific studies and their findings but will also introduce the conventional wisdom when it will contribute to furthering future research.

Why is it important to study this nexus? What does it mean that these empirical studies have not borne out the conventional wisdom? Substantively the nexus is a very important one. Scholars have often isolated themselves in narrow specialties. Students of revolutions, riots, and major popular mobilizations and protests often ignore the external behavior of nation–states. Likewise students of foreign policy and international relations often relegate internal events and conditions to positions of tertiary importance. If civil conflict and international conflict are systematically interrelated, these scholars' efforts are doomed to partiality. In this chapter I suggest that theorists of both internal and external conflict may have much more than analogies to learn from and contribute to one another.

GENERAL STUDIES OF THE NEXUS BETWEEN INTERNAL AND EXTERNAL CONFLICT

The first large-scale, data-based analysis of the internal–external conflict linkage was a by-product of the study of social relationships executed by Pitirim Sorokin. Sorokin undertook a longitudinal analysis of the ancient empires of Greece, Rome, and Byzantium and of a number of European nations over fourteen centuries (525–1927). He reported a slight tendency for internal disturbances to occur more frequently during and around years of war. However, upon closer examination he concluded that the two processes were independent of one another. Sorokin did not analyze his data with statistical methods. The conclusions were drawn by "eyeballing" differences in the curves of internal and external disturbances recorded in intervals of quarter centuries and centuries. This analysis thus does not yield discriminating results. Rather he explored gross trends for major outbreaks of internal and external violence. He stated that "so far as century periods are concerned each process has led a course independent of the other without positive or negative association" (Sorokin 1937: 488).

Raymond Cattell, conducting a research project aimed at the discovery of general cultural pattern profiles, performed factor analyses on a number of variables representing national characteristics from 1837–1937. The first two studies (Cattell 1949, Cattell 1950) analyzed data from sixty-nine nations which yielded twelve orthogonally rotated factors. The first two factors contained the variables of interest to this review. The internal and external conflict dimensions appeared to be independent of one another, except for the inclusion of secret treaties on a factor with assassinations and riots (with a relatively low loading, however). In a third study, Cattell, Bruel and Hartman (1951) dropped twenty-nine nations, whose data coverage had been considered poor, from the analysis. The forty nations that remained were chiefly comprised of the "modern industrial nations." The analysis yielded quite different findings. By limiting the sample population, Cattell found that the two processes were not as independent as the previous studies had shown. Riots, frequent involvement in war, large numbers of clashes, and two treaty variables all loaded highly on the same dimension. By limiting the study to a smaller number of similar nations, a relationship was revealed between internal and external conflict dimensions. A similar result is found in later studies that discriminate among nations and regions.

The study that generated the intensive research interest of the past fifteen years in the internal–external conflict linkage was ironically not primarily concerned with that linkage. Rummel (1976) explains that his 1963 work was a pilot study for the ongoing Dimensionality of Nations project. The original purpose of the DON project, begun with Guetzkow and Sawyer, was, first, to delineate real-world dimensions for Guetzkow's simulations and, second, to replicate Cattell's work. The conflict variables that were to become the basic data base for many of the conflict nexus researchers who followed were those selected for the pilot analysis. (Eventually there were to be 238 variables in the DON data set.)

The pilot study's legacies are numerous. Almost all subsequent studies dealing with the linkage between the internal and external behavior of nations have relied heavily on the DON project for data base, methodology, or both. Domestic and foreign conflict behavior were measured by reference to the number of discrete conflict events, or behaviors, recorded in news sources for each country. The nine measures of domestic conflict and thirteen measures of foreign conflict behavior are listed below:

Domestic Conflict Behavior Measures

  number of assassinations

  number of general strikes

  presence or absence of guerrilla warfare

  number of major government crises

  number of purges

  number of riots

  number of revolutions

number of antigovernmental demonstrations

number of people killed in all forms of domestic violence

Foreign Conflict Behavior Measures

number of antiforeign demonstrations

number of negative sanctions

number of protests

number of countries with which diplomatic relations were severed

number of ambassadors expelled or recalled

number of diplomatic officials of less than ambassador rank expelled or recalled

number of threats

presence or absence of military action

number of wars

number of troop movements

number of mobilizations

number of accusations

number of people killed in all forms of foreign conflict behavior.

These data were gathered for all nations with populations over 800,000 in the years studied. The Rummel (1963) study included data for seventy-seven nations for the period 1955–1957. Comparable data were gathered for 1958–1960 by Raymond Tanter (1966). As a result of population growth and the inclusion of newly independent nations, the Tanter study covered eighty-three nations.

The Rummel study used three separate methods in analyzing the conflict data. First, a factor analysis was performed on all twenty-two conflict variables together to see if foreign and domestic conflict variables loaded on the same factors. Second, a factor analysis was done for each of the foreign and domestic conflict variable sets separately to determine if there were different dimensions of foreign and domestic conflict. Third, the foreign and domestic conflict dimensions discovered in the second step were regressed upon one another to determine the strength and direction of the relationships among them.

The outcome of that original Rummel (1963) study has been termed "impressive and startling" (Nicholson 1971: 50). Calhoun (1978: 189–190) suggests that "the worldly but non-hellish historian might be amazed at the finding offered by Rummel." Rummel concluded that "foreign conflict behavior is generally completely unrelated to domestic conflict behavior" (Rummel 1963: 24). Tanter (1966), replicating the Rummel (1963) study with the newly collected 1958–1960 data, found a weak positive association between domestic conflict behavior and the more belligerent forms of foreign conflict behavior, although for the most part the independence of the two dimensions was reconfirmed. Subsequently, the 1955–1957 annual data were reanalyzed by Chadwick. Using a one-year time lag with the annual data, "the overall results suggest that there is a common dimension generally involving turmoil-like behavior (riots and demonstrations) and diplomatic or belligerent types of foreign conflict behavior (expelling or recalling diplomatic officials and anti-foreign demonstrations). The common dimension is lost when the annual data are aggregated" (Chadwick 1963 cited in Rummel 1969: 224–225).

Tanter (1966) also lagged the 1958–1960 data on the 1955–1957 data and found that there was a slight increase in the relationship, but only from 8.5 to 11.7 percent of the explained variance. He concluded that "there may be no simple relationship between domestic and foreign conflict behavior, but there may be a causal relationship which is being obscured by other phenomena" (Tanter 1966: 60). Perhaps more important, the Tanter study uncovered a different set of domestic conflict behavior dimensions than Rummel had found. Rummel suggested that "the domestic conflict behavior or nations varies along three uncorrelated dimensions: turmoil, revolutionary, and subversive. The foreign conflict behavior of nations varies along three uncorrelated dimensions: war, diplomatic, and belligerent" (Rummel 1963: 67). But Tanter found that the revolutionary and subversive dimensions were subsumed under one internal war dimension, while the turmoil and foreign conflict dimensions closely resembled the Rummel dimensions.

In addition to the data base and the finding that internal and external conflict dimensions of nations were unrelated, these initial studies left other legacies. The first legacy was the frequent reliance on factor analysis as a method of inquiry. It would be useful to pause and determine just what it is that factor-analytic studies can tell us. At best they can simplify vast arrays of data and tell us what covariation exists among conflict behaviors in a cross-section of nations. Obviously covariation is not causality, but with proper theoretical specification, time lags and leads may provide us with clues about directions of causality. If we keep in mind that covariations and/or causal linkages are not necessarily the same in one time period as they are in another, we may be able to make some progress. Without theoretical guidance, however, factor analysis is merely a data reduction tool. Second, the differences between the domestic conflict dimensions in the Rummel and Tanter data sets should have sensitized researchers to the possible variability of conflict dimensions across time and space. They should have become less confident in the three-factor solution to domestic conflict, which was accepted by later researchers of both internal conflict and possible linkages with external conflict (see, for example, Gurr 1970, Wilkenfeld 1968). A far more important legacy, as

Rummel (1976) recognized, was that these studies were quite atheoretic. This atheoretic approach, Rummel suggests, was an artifact of doing a pilot study. Be that as it may, a typical "theoretical" approach was adopted by Tanter (1966) and has been frequently emulated. Tanter pays homage to a number of statements of conventional wisdom (Rosecrance 1963, Haas and Whiting 1956, Q. Wright 1942) but evidences little interest in further theoretical development. The result was that for much of the work that followed ad hoc, post hoc speculations were substituted for theory building, and consequently, as we shall see below, little theoretical advance has occurred in the past fifteen years.

The empirical studies of internal–external linkages in conflict can be divided into four sets, according to their results. First are a handful of studies that demonstrate the existence of positive relationships between general dimensions of internal and external conflict. A larger group of studies shows that positive relationships are specific to particular aspects of conflict and that those relationships differ with the political and other characteristics of the nations studied. A single study reports negative relations between the two kinds of conflict, while a larger set, including the pioneering studies by Rummel (1963) and Tanter (1966), reports results that support the null hypothesis that internal and external conflict are unrelated. Each set is examined below, followed by a general interpretation.

EVIDENCE FOR A GENERAL, POSITIVE RELATIONSHIP BETWEEN INTERNAL AND EXTERNAL CONFLICT

Employing a broadly conceived measure of external aggression, Feierabend and Feierabend (1972) scaled the Rummel and Tanter 1955–1960 data on conflict behavior data and summed the results to obtain what they termed an "external aggression profile" for each nation for the entire six-year period. Using their own scale of political instability, it was found that the product moment correlation between the two scales was $r = .52$ (Feierabend and Feierabend 1972: 171), a quite high finding in the literature on the nexus. However, the method of scale construction and the inclusion of almost all foreign conflict behaviors in the indicator of external hostility makes the results difficult to interpret. They may be simply a function of the relative size of nations, on the argument that large nations are likely to have both more numerous instability events and more numerous hostile interactions with other nations than do small nations.

The early DON project data base did not include the majority of African nations, as they were not independent in 1955. Collins, employing the same general research strategy put forward by Rummel and his successors, investigated the relationship between foreign conflict behavior and domestic disorder in Africa during the period 1963–1965. In this study, the first to investigate the relationship within one geographic region, Collins reports that there were important differences between his results and earlier work: "Using seven measures of domestic and eight measures of foreign conflict behavior, cross-sectional analysis for the time period 1963–65 for thirty-three African countries demonstrated a strong basis of concomitant variation between the domestic and foreign domains" (Collins 1973: 286).

Collins posited that African states are much more subject to foreign conflict behavior motivated by domestic disorder than are more developed states. However, the size of the correlations led him to believe that foreign violence was a product of other factors as well. There was no support for the further hypothesis that official military hostility and violence were a product of domestic disorder in the preceding year. Nor was there any evidence for a causal link between the severity of foreign conflict and any patterns of domestic disorder. The clear importance of the study lay in its finding that "region" as a variable might influence the pattern of the relationship between foreign and domestic conflict. This was subsequently supported by the cluster analysis in Stohl (1970), which featured regional sociocultural groupings (see below).

Bobrow et al. (1973), in a longitudinal study primarily concerned with the impact of military assistance, also report a finding relevant to the internal–external conflict and cooperation nexus. The correlation of political strife (demands, instability, and domestic violence) with an international cooperation/conflict ratio for fifteen Asian nations from 1955–1966 produced time-series r's that were high for seven of the nations. However, because of the inclusion of both conflictual and cooperative events in the ratio measure, it is unclear whether the political strife measure was influenced more directly by cooperation or by conflict.

Following Wilkenfeld's (1969) finding that centrist nations exhibited a significant internal–external conflict linkage, Onate (1974) examined the conflict behaviors of the People's Republic of China between 1950 and 1970 as a representative "centrist" nation. Interestingly, Sorokin (1937) had cited an earlier longitudinal study by J. S. Lee (1931) which had found that internal violence in the Chinese empire had clustered before, during, and after external wars. Unfortunately, the data distribution in Onate's study was so sharply skewed that logarithmic transformation could not accomplish the objective of providing a distribution useful in statistical analysis. The raw data produced a complete lack of relationship. Onate then scaled the raw data, which unfortunately remained quite skewed. Again, no relationship was found. However, by transforming weighted raw data a moderate direct relationship between two summary dimensions of internal and external conflict dimensions was produced. Foreign conflict behavior was a better predictor of domestic conflict than was domestic conflict of foreign conflict. Onate was satisfied that no attendant loss of information occurred as a result of his transformations of the raw data, but I am not so sure. The further we move from our original data the more suspicious of our results we should become. A forthcoming analysis of the China data by Onate is likely to bring increased confidence in the findings obtained.

EVIDENCE FOR SPECIFIC POSITIVE RELATIONSHIPS BETWEEN ASPECTS OF CONFLICT

Jonathan Wilkenfeld (1968, 1969) re-evaluated the Rummel and Tanter data in "an effort to both retain and properly identify any relationships which had previously been obscured" due to the methods used to analyze the data. Consequently, he partitioned the nations into more homogeneous groups based on their political characteristics to see whether type of regime had any bearing on the relationship. The nations were divided into three groups: centrist, personalist, and polyarchic (factor names assigned by Banks and Gregg 1965). Correlations were determined for all possible pairs of domestic conflict dimensions and all foreign conflict dimensions previously determined by Rummel (1963) for the 1955–1960 data in Wilkenfeld's first study, and for all possible pairs of conflict behavior determined by Wilkenfeld's own analysis in the second study. The second study also tested the effects of time lags of one and two years.

A weakness in the first Wilkenfeld study was the use of factors that (1) did not correspond to those found in the 1958–1960 data source (see Tanter 1966), and (2) were based on factors obtained before the division of the sample into the different nation types. The second study, Wilkenfeld (1969), obtained factor scores that corresponded to the entire data set, but did not divide the sample into groups before deriving new factors. Thus equivalence was assumed across groups that were to be isolated primarily to discover if there existed within- and between-group *differences* relating to conflict variables.[1] This may very well have limited the utility of his results (see Stohl 1970 and discussion below).

The analyses did lead to some interesting conclusions. There was no significant particular relationship between any pair of internal and external conflict dimensions that held for all three types of nations. Centrist nations "exhibited a tendency for the most violent form of domestic conflict to be associated with the most violent forms of foreign conflict" (Wilkenfeld 1974: 349). Wilkenfeld posited the type of nation and the nature of the conflict as the determining factors in the relationship between internal and external conflict. Significantly, dividing the nations had finally produced some support for the conventional wisdom.

In three further studies (Zinnes and Wilkenfeld 1971, Wilkenfeld 1972, and Wilkenfeld and Zinnes 1973), Markov analysis was applied to the same Rummel–Tanter data for 1955–1960. The purpose of these investigations of stochastic processes was to determine whether foreign conflict behavior affects the changes or transitions over time between levels of domestic conflict behavior and whether the level of foreign conflict behavior can be predicted by knowledge of both domestic conflict behavior and previous foreign conflict. The analyses were conducted for all nations and also for nations grouped by political type. The factor scores obtained in the previous studies were the basic input for the Markov analysis.

The first finding of consequence was that Wilkenfeld's earlier results, that governmental structure of a state is important in predicting the relationship between domestic and foreign conflict behaviors, was sustained in all three studies. While the nature of the impact again was not consistent, some kind of impact was found in each of the studies. Predicting foreign conflict from levels of domestic conflict, Zinnes and Wilkenfeld found that "internal war affects the transitions in the levels of belligerency only for polyarchic states, while turmoil affects the transitions in the levels of belligerency only for centrist states" (Zinnes and Wilkenfeld 1971: 209–210).

Employing some additional Markov models on the same data, Wilkenfeld (1972) investigated the relationship once again. He found that foreign conflict levels were influenced by domestic conflict levels in rare instances in polyarchic states, slightly more so in centrist states (particularly with a one-year time lag) while personalist states included a few instances of "substantial" impact. Other than the influence of alternative methods, no explanation was offered for the difference in results between two studies using the same data base.

Turning the relationship around, Wilkenfeld and Zinnes (1973) explored the predictive power of foreign conflict for domestic conflict. When all nations were considered together, "the foreign conflict behavior 'war' as measured by the variables loading on this factor (military actions, wars, mobilizations and foreign killed) affects transitions in domestic conflict behavior as captured by the turmoil factor (strikes, riots, demonstrations) primarily when domestic conflict behavior is at a very high level" (Wilkenfeld and Zinnes 1973: 335). Further, dividing the nations into groups once again, they found that foreign conflict behavior affects transitions in domestic conflict primarily among the personalist and polyarchic states.

Wilkenfeld (1973) reanalyzed the data reported in Wilkenfeld, Lussier, and Tantinen (1972) and proposed a Markov process interpretation of the conflict events. Foreign conflict behavior affected transitions in domestic conflict levels in only a few cases but had its greatest impact when domestic conflict was at its lowest level.

These six studies produce interesting methodological and design perspectives. They also produce a confusing collection of often contradictory results. Wilkenfeld and Zinnes were unable to formulate a clear set of conclusions for their results. "In the writings of Wilkenfeld/Zinnes there is no attempt at a general theoretical explanation of the results they found themselves but rather much ad hoc speculation" (Zimmermann 1978: 188). In a later work (Wilkenfeld 1974), written for the purpose of drawing together his research for a textbook presentation, Wilkenfeld recognized that the results from his correlational and Markov analyses were not completely in line with one another. While correctly recognizing that the different levels of measurement involved in the two designs created difficulties, he offered no theoretically based path out of the admittedly conflicting and confusing maze that his many results constructed.

Stohl (1970) reanalyzed the Rummel (1963) data after dividing the nations into groups by political type, corresponding once again to the Banks and Gregg (1965) divisions. In support of Wilkenfeld's primary conclusion, political type of nation was found to play an important role in determining the conflict patterns within and between nations. The factor analysis of the measures of conflict behavior showed that there were different patterns of domestic and foreign conflict behavior within each of three types of political regime. Further exploration of the relationship, through regression analysis with a one-year time lag, revealed moderately strong relationships in polyarchies between diplomatic exchanges and general internal strife, and between war and internal crises. In the personalist nations, increases in foreign conflict behavior were associated with small increases in domestic conflict behavior, whereas in the centrist nations no significant relationship was discovered. It was hypothesized that the two major political factors differentiating the three groups of nations—level of social control and elites' decision latitude—could account for the differences. Thus the less the state's degree of social control and decision latitude, the higher are the associations between internal and external conflict behaviors. Stohl, following Gurr (1967), tested the effects of three additional variables by dividing the seventy-seven nations according to their sociocultural regimes, level of technological development, and size characteristics. Cluster analysis revealed that in only one of the clusters (intermediate level of technological development) were measures of domestic and foreign conflict behavior completely independent.[2] However, there was no single recognizable pattern of conflict behavior common to all the different nation clusters. It is quite clear from these comparisons that the influence of domestic and foreign conflict behavior on one another is a complex function of nations' political, social, economic, and other characteristics. Other inductive bases for grouping nations presumably would produce still different results.

A number of more recent studies of the internal–external conflict nexus has moved beyond Rummel's research design and analysis. Phillips (1973), in a study of the impact of the conflict environment of nations, used a regression analysis of the residuals in a canonical analysis of more recent DON project data. He found evidence for a relationship between internal and external violence.

The conclusion here is that nations displaying domestic violence, having a low percentage of population in agriculture, who have tended to experience unlawful changes of offices in the recent past, and have a high cost of living index, tend to send more military violence to the environment than would be expected, given normal exchange with the environment. In other words, modernizing nations experiencing inflation and internal violence possibly associated with unlawful change of leadership, are likely to respond militarily to their environment. [Phillips 1973: 143]

Phillips further suggests that most military violence is directly related to violence received, but that deviations from this pattern are related to internal violence. It should be noted that the nations Phillips is describing resemble the personalist nations that demonstrated a moderate internal–external conflict relationship in the Stohl (1970), Wilkenfeld (1972), Wilkenfeld and Zinnes (1973), and Collins (1973) studies.

Hazlewood (1973) analyzed the original Rummel and Tanter data within a general systems model. He suggests that "to the extent that internal variety is more extensive than internal constraint, the system stresses are likely to be manifested in foreign conflict behavior at a later time period" (Hazlewood 1973: 162). Employing Rummel's domestic conflict factors for 1955–1957 and Tanter's foreign conflict factors for 1958–1960 for use in subsequent canonical and path analysis, Hazlewood found that "existing internal variety (societal diversity and turmoil), even without extreme economic expansion to activate it, is strongly associated with external conflict behavior. Economic stability, societal heterogeneity, and internal turmoil predict best to war" (Hazlewood 1973: 169). However, the path analysis revealed that "the strongest path in the model relates turmoil to war for 1958–60 through prior warfare" (Hazlewood 1973: 183). This would indicate (as in Phillips 1973) that prior foreign conflict behavior was more important than domestic conflict in predicting future foreign conflict.

In a second study, Hazlewood (1975), there was an attempt to distinguish two variants of the domestic–foreign conflict linkage: diversion mechanisms and encapsulation processes. Diversion mechanisms "focus on domestic conflict as a forcing agent that predicts changes in the levels of foreign conflict" (Hazlewood 1975: 217). Encapsulation processes refer to the alternative phenomenon that increases in domestic conflict may reduce foreign conflict by focusing the attention of decision makers inward. Hazlewood was also concerned with the possibility that the Rummel-Tanter data, so heavily relied upon in previous studies, were gathered for an unrepresentative time period. He thus extended the data base to include 1955–1966 for the seventy-five nations. Unfortunately, in view of Collins's (1973) findings for African nations, Hazlewood excluded African nations from his data set since they were not included in the original data set. Despite the fact that a number of previous studies had indicated that type of nation had effects on the conflict nexus, he also chose not to divide his population into nation types for the analysis.

Since he was concerned with decision makers' manipulation of their foreign conflict behavior, Hazlewood focused solely on foreign conflict behavior sent. His results were ambiguous. Domestic conflict appeared generally more effective as a predictor of less intense rather than more intense foreign conflict. Support for neither the diversion nor the encapsulation hypothesis could be claimed without appeal to as-yet-untested exogenous variables. However, it did appear that considerably stronger relationships were found to be in the 1961–1966 data than in the 1955–1960 Rummel-Tanter data base, lending evidence to Hazlewood's suspicions concerning the original data.

A further study using these data found that contrary to previous findings, there was a weak but definable ability for domestic conflict behavior to predict to foreign conflict received more strongly than domestic conflict behavior predicted to foreign conflict behavior sent (Bergquist 1976: 264–265). Using a cross-lagged quasi-experimental design, Bergquist also found that the positive relationship between domestic and foreign conflict was strongest when low-intensity forms of conflict were involved. This reconfirmed Hazlewood's 1975 finding despite the use of a different method of analysis. As we have seen in the two separate sets of Wilkenfeld studies, change of method had previously been associated with inconsistent findings even when the same data set was used. It is comforting, given the contradictory and inconsistent findings that characterize this subfield, occasionally to find some consistency and replication of results.

EVIDENCE FOR A NEGATIVE RELATIONSHIP BETWEEN
EXTERNAL AND INTERNAL CONFLICT

Only one study reports a significant negative relationship between foreign and domestic conflict. Kegley, Richardson, and Richter (1978) used WEIS (World Events Interaction Survey) data (1966–1969) to construct measures of international conflict and Gurr's (1967) civil conflict data (1961–1965) to study almost the same seventy-three nations as Wilkenfeld's original work (1968). Foreign conflict scales were constructed by dividing conflict sent by conflict plus cooperation sent. This combination of cooperation and conflict, while common in events research, does not provide a clear measure of foreign conflict (see Aspin 1975 for a detailed critique of both this type of scale and the WEIS data generally).

Initially Kegley, Richardson and Richter tested the internal-external conflict relationship among all nations and found no meaningful relationship ($r = .02$). This, they curiously suggest, strengthens their confidence in their data and their belief "that initial findings were not merely artifacts of such things as the particular data sets or analytic techniques employed" (Kegley, Richardson, and Richter 1978: 745). Second, they divided the nations according to their degree of militarization into high, medium and low groups (based on military expenditures as a percentage of GNP) and found that for "high" militarized nations the relationship between domestic and foreign conflict is inverse ($r = -.49$). Six of these highly militarized nations had been identified by Wilkenfeld (1969) as centrist and were among the group in which he found a positive relationship. These same six nations were among the centrist nations that had evidenced no relationship in the Stohl (1970) analysis. These discrepancies in results should encourage further analysis.

EVIDENCE THAT INTERNAL AND EXTERNAL CONFLICT ARE UNRELATED

The ongoing conflict in the Middle East has produced a number of studies that have focused on the internal–external conflict nexus both for the region as a whole and for individual nations. Wilkenfeld, Lussier, and Tahtinen (1972) assessed the impact of domestic conflict levels, prior levels of participation in foreign conflict, and foreign conflict behavior received on the level of a state's current foreign conflict behavior. Daily event data for 1949–1967 for Egypt, Iraq, Israel, Jordan, Lebanon, and Syria were used in the analysis. Factor analyses performed for the six nations as a whole and for each nation individually revealed quite different factor results, indicating once again the volatility of relationships among the types of conflict behavior. The key findings in the analysis were that domestic conflict played a relatively minor role in the foreign conflict processes of each of the nations and that the Arab states appeared to operate under greater constraints from domestic and prior foreign conflict than did the Israelis. Using the same data, Wilkenfeld (1975) investigated the relationship among foreign conflict sent and foreign conflict received. He found that the effect of domestic conflict behavior on foreign conflict behavior was minimal. Only in the case of Jordan was there a significant impact of domestic conflict levels. Egypt exhibited a small impact, Israel and Syria none at all (Wilkenfeld 1975: 205).

Burrowes and Spector (1973) and T. J. Sloan (1978) have isolated Syria as a test case to investigate the general internal–external conflict nexus. Burrowes and Spector studied the period between the 1961 breakup of the United Arab Republic and the 1967 Six-Day War. Using events data for only one nation, they followed the basic strategy of Rummel (1963). The regression analyses did not indicate that domestic conflict behavior predicted to foreign conflict behavior. Time lags did not markedly improve the results. Sloan explored Syrian international conflictual and cooperative behavior between 1948 and 1973. He identified a "normal relations range" for dyadic conflict behavior and attempted to relate deviations from that range to fluctuations in domestic conflict. However, the study for the most part confirmed the lack of relationship found for the Syrian case by Burrowes and Spector. Introducing a new element into internal–external conflict studies, Sloan did find that there was some relationship between domestic conflict behaviors and external cooperative behavior during the fourteen years in his sample when Syria's domestic conflict behavior fell within the "normal relations range." While the concept of normal relations range is not without its difficulties, further refinements should prove useful.

Finally, Eberwein et al. (1978) used a data set covering 125 nations for the years 1966–1967 in an attempt to replicate the original Rummel (1963) findings. Like Rummel, they employed exploratory factor analysis and then regression analysis. In addition, they also employed confirmatory factor analysis. The exploratory factor analysis seemed to support Rummel's conclusions. Confirmatory factor analysis, however, revealed at least moderately strong relationships between the two conflict dimensions.[3] Closer analysis of the relationship through regression analysis and the examination of partial correlations indicated that this relationship could be attributed to the common influence of population and size on both conflict dimensions. This most recent study of the general relationship appears to bring us full circle to the finding of uncorrelated dimensions of internal and external conflict behavior. However, it should be noted that none of the substantive refinements demonstrated to be useful in the other studies reviewed were employed by Eberwein et al.

SUMMARY OF AGGREGATE STUDIES OF THE
INTERNAL–EXTERNAL CONFLICT NEXUS

What are we to conclude from these general studies of the nexus between internal and external conflict? Clearly the results lack consistency. No single common relationship of any kind has been found for all nations, groups of nations, or single nations over time. However, the accompanying summary (Table 7–1) reveals an interesting phenomenon. The most common form of the hypothesis in the conventional wisdom, as indicated in Table 7–1, is that foreign conflict behavior should be inversely related to domestic conflict behavior, that is, that increases in foreign conflict behavior lead to decreases in domestic conflict behavior. Yet not a single one of these general studies has found any evidence for such a relationship. The only study that reports a significant negative relationship (Kegley, Richardson, and Richter 1978) focused on domestic conflict "predicting" to foreign conflict. The result was obtained by time-lagging the data and using simple correlation analysis rather than any causal modeling procedure.

Why is it that fifteen years of quantitative research have provided no evidence for this oft-assumed relationship? The most obvious answer is that the conventional wisdom is simply incorrect. More likely, as the review by A. A. Stein (1976) indicates, the group cohesion hypothesis has not been adequately specified and tested by these general studies. Stein argues that specification of the precise form of the relationship, as well as the use of better indicators, is needed for convincing tests of the hypothesis. We will explore some evidence of this in the following section on war. In

TABLE 7-1. A Summary of General Studies of the Internal–External Conflict
Nexus

I.	Studies that find a general but positive conflict nexus relationship: Cattell, Bruel, and Hartman (1951); Chadwick (1963); Collins (1973); Feierabend and Feierabend (1972); J. S. Lee (1931); Onate (1974), and Bobrow et al. (1973).
II.	Studies that find a specific positive conflict nexus relationship: Bergquist (1976); Hazlewood (1973, 1975); Phillips (1973); Stohl (1970); Wilkenfeld (1968, 1969, 1972, 1973); Wilkenfeld and Zinnes (1973); and Zinnes and Wilkenfeld (1971).
III.	Studies that find a negative conflict nexus relationship: Kegley, Richardson, and Richter (1978).
IV.	Studies that find that there is no conflict nexus relationship: Burrowes and Spector (1973); Cattell (1949, 1950); Eberwein, et al. (1978); Rummel (1963); Sloan (1978); Sorokin (1937); Tanter (1966); Wilkenfeld (1975); and Wilkenfeld, Lussier, and Tahtinen (1972).

general it is obvious that theoretical precision has not been the norm in the
research tradition established by the Rummel (1963) and Tanter (1966)
studies.

One irate critic, Andrew Mack, suggests that these studies have been
a complete waste of time. He charges that "the studies in question are
flawed from practically every angle. The data are suspect; the methodology is used to draw conclusions unwarranted even on its own terms;
there is no theory; the assumptions about time lags are highly questionable; the behaviorist bias means that none of the really interesting
problems can be examined at all" (A. Mack 1975: 615).

The only response that Mack would find acceptable, I presume, would
be a chorus of mea culpas. The questions he raises are important, but unfortunately his charges are so exaggerated and offensive that they seem to
have been ignored by those committed to the systematic analysis of the
conflict nexus.[4] They also may have dissuaded some from pursuing further
research.

What is needed, in fact, is a carefully specified theoretical approach.
The problems that are prevalent in this literature—data sources and
coverage of events, the comparability of variables within and across nations and time periods, the choice of suitable time units and time lags, the
construction of event-based indicators, and the choice of appropriate levels
of analysis and statistical method—are problems faced by all researchers in
quantitative comparative research. Two things are required to resolve
these problems. The first is precise theoretical specification of which aspects of internal conflict affect, or are affected by, which aspects of external conflict. The second is to employ research designs using theoretically
appropriate indicators, units, time lags, and analytic methods. Were this
done, a review a few years hence will not be forced to conclude that the
continuing contradictory and conflicting results are possibly "artifactual

outcomes from specific data sets, operational techniques or statistical tools" (Zinnes 1972: 235), but rather that the general relationship does or does not hold under a specified set of conditions.

WAR AND DOMESTIC VIOLENCE

The direct relationship between political revolution and war whether as a cause or an effect, is, in fact, such a historical commonplace as to need no elaboration. [Q. Wright 1942: 257]

The causes of war have received far more attention than its consequences.[5] Perhaps this should be expected. There is no question that preventing wars is far more exciting than cleaning up after them. In this section we will examine the often neglected impact of war on domestic conflict and evaluate whether or not the historical commonplace asserted by Wright is, indeed, not in need of further elaboration.

Despite the many systematic studies of general connections between internal and external conflict, there are very few general, cross-national studies of the specific relationship between war and large-scale internal violence. Aside from the Sorokin study discussed above, I have been able to uncover only three such studies. Denton reports that in analyzing Richardson's data (1960) covering the period 1820–1949, "a general tendency is noted for peaks in civil war and peaks in general war to co-occur" (Denton 1966: 294). Denton and Phillips similarly report that between 1485 and 1940 "periods in which there is much war are quite consistently periods which exhibit a relatively high frequency of civil wars" (Denton and Phillips 1968: 192). Denton and Phillips' results were obtained by summing the number of wars and civil wars recorded for all nations in five-year periods from 1485–1940 in the data provided by Q. Wright (1942). Their analysis is, therefore, suggestive only for the international system and says nothing of the relationship between war and domestic violence in particular states. Finally, in an examination of sixty-five nations for the period 1800–1960, Flanigan and Fogelman report that "there is no general pattern of either positive or negative relationships between war and domestic violence" (Flanigan and Fogelman 1970: 5). These studies certainly do not provide a particularly auspicious beginning for theorizing about the relationship between war and domestic violence. Their approach and problems are the same as for the atheoretic general examinations of the internal–external conflict nexus reviewed above.

However, not all research on war and domestic violence has been quite so Baconian. Two quite contradictory assumptions have been suggested for researchers interested in the possible connections. As indicated earlier, one segment of the traditional literature asserts that war contributes to internal peace. Thus some researchers have sought to confirm the ingroup/outgroup hypothesis that war is inversely related to internal conflict. A second group of researchers has assumed that war has rather profound destabilizing effects on society and that mobilizations resulting from war bring with them increases in internal conflict. They have thus sought evidence of a positive relationship between the two conflict dimensions.

WAR, DOMESTIC STABILITY, AND PEACE

The gist of the ingroup/outgroup hypothesis, as stated in the quotations from Bodin and Sumner at the outset of this chapter, is that conflict with an external group minimizes conflict within the group. Arthur Stein, in an excellent review, concludes that although the hypothesis "is often assumed true and is easily illustrated, the empirical studies suggest that there are a number of intervening variables and that the hypothesis is not uniformly true" (A. A. Stein 1976: 143). Stein reviews works in psychology, sociology, anthropology, and political science and demonstrates in the process that empirical work on the hypothesis is quite rare. It certainly seems fair to conclude with Stein that many more scholars assert the ingroup/ outgroup hypothesis than actually study it in a systematic way.

A cross-national anthropological study of the hypothesis is provided by Otterbein and Otterbein (1965). Drawing upon the Human Relations Area Files and the Ethnographic Atlas, they assessed the relationship between feuding and war in a sample of fifty societies (from 1250 B.C. to 1950) and found no evidence to support the hypothesis. In a later study (Otterbein 1968), the intervening variable of political complexity was introduced. It was found that external war and internal war were not related, even for centralized political systems. Stein (1976: 148), in defense of the hypothesis, suggests that the Otterbeins' studies provide only a limited test of the hypothesis since they focus on physical violence and not on a wider measure of conflict.[6]

One of the few to contribute positive evidence on the ingroup/outgroup hypothesis was also one of the first to employ systematic and positivist empirical analysis. Durkheim, in his classic study *Suicide* (1897), had found that "wars have a restraining effect on the development of suicide. They have the same effect on robberies, frauds, abuses of confidence, etc. But one crime is an exception: homicide" (Durkheim 1951: 352). Durkheim proceeds to report large average increases in homicide in Prussia and France following their 1870 war at the same time that robberies in Prussia sank by one half. Durkheim's caveat regarding homicide has been the subject of more recent work by Archer and Gartner (1976), who examined 110 nations during this century. Comparing the homicide rates after fifty wars with changes experienced by thirty control nations, they found that most of the wars in the study were accompanied by substantial postwar increases in the rate of homicide. They argue (1) that the legitimation-of-violence interpretation, which predicts postwar increases as a result of the pervasive wartime presence of officially sanctioned killing, is the only one of seven plausible rival hypotheses not disconfirmed by the available evidence; and (2) that the ingroup/outgroup cohesion hypothesis is disconfirmed by the available evidence. There is thus only partial support for the assertion that war increases internal cohesion. Although certain indicators of societal strain and personal alienation do decrease during wartime, homicide—a quite important indicator for decline in cohesion—increases. In another such study, M. Haas (1968), studying ten European states from 1900–1960 from the causes-of-war perspective, attempted to determine the relationship between strain within a nation and military hostilities. Although the causal hypothesis was not supported, Haas did find that all three of his indicators of strain (homicide, suicide, and alcoholism) were high among the belligerent nations. Further investigations of this relationship might prove theoretically useful.[7]

Stein's suggestions as to how to improve the study of the relation of war to internal cohesion are well-grounded in the literature he reviews. He maintains that external conflict increases internal cohesion under certain conditions.

> These conditions act as intervening variables and involve, as one could have logically expected, the nature of the external conflict and the nature of the ingroup. The external conflict needs to invoke some threat, affect the entire group and all its members equally and indiscriminately, and involve a solution (or at least there must be a useful purpose in group efforts regarding the threat). The group needs to have been an ongoing one with some pre-existing cohesion or consensus, and to have a leadership that can authoritatively enforce cohesion (especially if all the members of the group do not feel the threat). The group must be able to deal with the external conflict and provide emotional comfort and support to its members. [A. A. Stein 1976: 165]

Unfortunately, no empirical research has yet followed these suggestions and to date no direct and clear support for the hypothesis has been produced in the systematic empirical literature that concerns war and domestic violence.

WAR AND CIVIL CONFLICT

While there has always been concern with the impact of war on consequent relations among nations, relatively little systematic concern has been given to the destabilizing internal effects of war. The research of Kuznets (1964), Boulding and Gleason (1965), Starr (1972), Barbera (1973), Kugler (1973), and Wheeler (1975a) has produced disagreement regarding the long-run effects of war on national economic development, power capabilities, and the pattern of social expenditures. (See the review of these and other studies by Stein and Russett in Chapter 10 of this *Handbook*.) It is not disputed, however, that there are destabilizing effects associated with the immediate occurrence of war. In addition, Tilly suggests that

> war also matters in quite a different way. By and large, wars have always provided the principal occasions on which states have increased their levies of

resources from their subject populations. Conscriptions is only the self-evident case. Demands for taxes, forced loans, food, nonmilitary labor, manufactured goods, and raw materials follow the same pattern. The increased exactions almost always meet widespread resistance, which the agents of states counter with persuasion and force. [Tilly 1978: 211]

War ought then to be associated with increases in domestic conflict. There are only a few studies that actually confront this problem with systematic data.

Tanter (1969) examined the relationship between the Vietnam war and domestic turmoil in the United States. He evaluated the impact of the escalation of U.S. force levels in Vietnam with the frequencies, rates of change, and magnitude of participation in antiwar protest, the levels of urban riots, and participation in civil rights demonstrations. He also examined the war's impact on labor strikes and levels of violent crime. His evidence, which was plotted and visually scanned rather than statistically analyzed, indicates that both the escalation of the war and the length of American participation were unrelated to urban riots, civil rights demonstrations, labor strikes, or violent crime. The initial rate of change in antiwar protests was possibly a function of troop escalation. Tanter's conclusion that "the initial escalation of the Vietnam war may be a primary cause of breakdown in social order" (1969: 539) is not justified by his evidence. In a relevant historical study Brooks (1969) has shown that protest against the Vietnam war broke with historical precedent. For the first time, students and youths were significantly in opposition. However, that does not indicate that the social order had collapsed. The fact that Tanter's other domestic conflict indicators appeared not to be correlated with the war appears to undercut his conclusion.

Stohl (1973, 1975, 1976), employing a quasi-experimental design, examined the impact of the United States' involvement in wars in the twentieth century on levels and patterns of domestic political violence. These studies break with past studies which used counts of events to examine who did what to whom in specific episodes with what issue in mind, and with what magnitude and intensity (as indexed by deaths, arrests, and duration). Unlike most previous work on civil violence, violence initiated by the state was also included. A total of 2,861 domestic violence events were identified in a systematic examination of the *New York Times* from 1890 to 1970. An interrupted time-series research design was used to determine whether nonrandom changes had taken place in the indicators of domestic political violence either at the start, during, or after the Spanish-American War, World Wars I and II, and the Korean and Vietnam wars. Significance tests measured the differences between the observed and expected characteristics of civil violence. No measure of the strength of association was used.

Assuming a group-conflict approach to politics, it was hypothesized (Stohl 1976: 64) that:

1. wartime economic mobilization brings new groups into the productive process and enhances the economic positions of these groups relative to the dominant segments, thus intensifying economic conflict and violence

2. wartime social mobility raises the status positions of underdog social groups, relative to the dominant segments, which increases the hostilities between them

3. the economic and social changes of war generate demands for the reallocation of political power and rewards, which intensify conflict and violence between top and bottom.

The quasi-experimental analysis showed that there were step-level changes in civil violence both at the start of all five wars and in the postwar periods. Unfortunately, no uniform pattern holds for any of the five wars, or for any of the different dimensions of violence. However, to varying degrees, the data generally support the contention that war is associated with increases in domestic political violence. With each of the last four wars, violence between top and bottom groups increased. World War I was found to have had the most consistent and dynamic impact on the domestic conflict variables. In general, political violence on behalf of the prevailing status quo was the variable showing the most marked increase. Thus World War I was followed by race riots in which whites attacked blacks, economic violence in which the National Guard attacked strikers on behalf of employers, and the onset of the "Red Scare" in 1919 and 1920. Since violence perpetrated by agents of the state or their supporters was seldom included in previous studies of the internal–external conflict nexus, it is possible that the strength of relationships found in those studies was underestimated.[8]

Stohl confirmed Tanter's observation that American civil rights demonstrations and urban riots did not appear to be a function of the Vietnam war and found that the incidence of social violence after the start of the Vietnam war was not influenced positively or negatively by the war. Subsequently, however, P. T. Murray (1977) has noted that of 277 serious racial riots studied for the period 1900–1975, 66 percent occurred during war years and another 12 percent within two years of the conclusion of a foreign war, a statistically significant difference if riots were evenly distributed over all years. Stohl also found that the increase noted by Tanter in violence in antiwar demonstrations until 1967 was initiated largely by prosystem agents and groups. There was thus an increase in social conflict following the onset of the war, but the original rise in violent behavior was not initiated by groups challenging the political and moral wisdom of the Vietnam policies but rather by groups defending the policies.

Some cautions about the theoretical interpretation of these results are raised by A. A. Stein.

> Stohl's positive results, however, may not disconfirm the external conflict/ internal conflict cohesion hypothesis. First, some of the wars the United States was involved in did not involve external conflict directed at the United States. Thus, while the Vietnam War is an external conflict in which the United States was involved, it is hard to argue that there was any external conflict *directed* at the United States. Second, Stohl includes governmental coercion in his definition of conflict. Thus, any internal cohesion that obtains as a function of authoritative repression would still involve conflict in Stohl's conception. [A. A. Stein 1976: 162]

Furthermore, the quasi-experimental analysis was not supplemented by others that measured the strength of association between aspects of war and civil violence. This omission is explained by the primary purpose of the study, which was to establish the necessity for including foreign conflict variables when evaluating the causes of domestic conflict;[9] the objective was not to test a general model of domestic conflict. Both the results and the lacunae of the Stohl studies suggest how much work is still undone in the study of the impact of war on domestic violence. To repeat, future research should be theoretically informed, for only by proceeding theoretically can further progress in the confirmation or disconfirmation of the competing hypotheses be accomplished.

MILITARY INTERVENTION, ECONOMIC DEPENDENCY, AND INTERNAL CONFLICT

Thus far we have discussed principally the direct relations between a nation's internal and external conflict behaviors. In this section we turn to a consideration of the conditions and impact of one nation's external intervention in another nation's domestic conflict. We will examine both behavioral and structural aspects of intervention.

Foreign intervention in internal conflict may take the direct form of overtly or covertly supplying insurgents or governments, moving troops across national boundaries, or clandestinely toppling regimes by means of "dirty tricks" including the manipulation of the media, disruption of essential services, and executive action (assassination). Structurally, intervention may be manifest in limits placed on the possibilities of independent behavior of both dependent and interdependent states. These structural limits are not necessarily the result of deliberate policy decisions but rather are often a consequence of the "normal" relations of nations within large power disparities. "Most analysts agree that interventions are the result of an interaction between circumstances at home and abroad. All the studies cited thus far mention both internal and external factors, but most of them ignore the question of when and how the two sets of factors interact" (Rosenau 1974: 173). Of the many possible permutations and combinations of internal and external factors which might determine the possibilities of intervention, a causal sequence that is a variant of the ingroup/ outgroup hypothesis is often proposed. "Frequently intransigent, promotive, and (to a much lesser extent) preservative orientations lead societies to reallocate domestic resources to foreign purposes and engage in interventionary behavior when the reallocated resources are not sufficient to bring about an adaptive solution to the perceived problem" (Rosenau 1974: 151). This corollary to the cohesion hypothesis is often referred to as "the search for external enemies" (see Simmel 1956 or Coser 1956).

FOREIGN MILITARY INTERVENTIONS AND DOMESTIC CONFLICT

Unfortunately, systematic, empirical research thus far has focused on the external determinants of interventionary behavior. Rather the main concern of researchers has been the conditions within the target or receiving nation that correlate with the occurrence of intervention. Pearson (1974a, 1974b) and Pearson and Baumann (1974) have explored much new ground in the study of intervention. In an initial study, concerned primarily with geographic proximity and the impetus to foreign military intervention in all nations from 1948 to 1967, Pearson found that "there were relatively few hostile interventions [interventions hostile from the perspective of the target government] in domestic disputes, as opposed to hostile interventions to influence targets, policies or conditions" (Pearson 1974a: 456). However, interventions in domestic disputes, when they did occur, were more frequently distant (over three thousand miles) than policy-condition interventions. All cases of distant interventions in domestic disputes were coded as friendly to the target government, and 78 percent of distant interventions to influence policies or conditions were also friendly.

In a second study, Pearson (1974b) analyzed intervention data (reported in Taylor and Hudson 1972) across an aggregate of years (1960–1967) and also by months. This allowed the investigation of domestic conflict–intervention sequences concerning two questions: (1) is violent conflict more likely than nonviolent conflict to attract foreign military intervention? and (2) are structural wars more likely than nonstructural wars to attract foreign military intervention? (Structural wars are civil conflicts concerning many substructures of a society, nonstructural wars are operationalized as coups, and other authority-centered conflicts; Pearson 1974b: 265.) J. D. Sullivan (1969) had previously examined the relationship between structural war and intervention (1948–1967) and found a positive relationship. However, as Pearson (1974a: 436 and 1974b: 266) notes, Sullivan's data set excluded a number of quite significant interventions completely and included others several times because repeated armed attacks within the same intervention were scored as independent interventions. This raised doubts about the reliability of the relationship discovered. Pearson's results, nonetheless, were consistent with Sullivan's. He found that structural wars were indeed more likely to bring intervention than nonstructural wars, and that these interventions usually favored governmental forces. Violent conflict also was more likely to attract intervention than lower levels of conflict. In general, nations with high levels of conflict were likely candidates for an intervention. A quite interesting link between intervention and domestic conflict was the finding that intervention tends to exacerbate civil conflict in the target country. Governments favored by interventions tended to repress opposition groups, who in turn raised their number of armed attacks. A direct consequence of intervention was thus increased civil violence.

In the third study (Pearson and Baumann 1974) it was found that interventions by a major power (1948–1967) were influenced by the power's appraisal of incumbent friendly regimes; the presence of the major power's economic, diplomatic, or military installations; and by the possibilities of resistance by the target government. In other words, if an intervention appeared necessary to prevent the overthrow of a friendly government with important economic, military, or diplomatic ties, intervention was more likely. In partial contrast, Odell (1974) studied 119 nations and found that instability was a more important correlate of military intervention in the 1948–1969 period than the presence of American economic interests. Given the highly aggregated nature of his data, Odell was unable to determine the directionality of relationship between intervention and instability.

A relationship between levels of instability and levels of intervention also was found in a study by Gurr and Bishop (1976). While preparing profiles of violent and nonviolent nations in the 1960s, they found that military intervention varied with levels of development as well as with internal conflict. Target nations were of the Third World; European nations rarely experienced the rebellions that might tempt other powers to intervene (Gurr and Bishop 1976: 103). Gurr (1968) and Gurr and Duvall (1973) had previously found in the development of their causal models of civil strife that the magnitude of domestic conflict was increased by external intervention.

The most recent published study on the link between intervention and domestic conflict is that of Weede (1978). He hypothesizes a "causal chain running from general societal weakness via domestic disorder to passive conflict participation, i.e. to becoming a target of military intervention" (Weede 1978: 497), which is dependent upon the nation's location within the United States' sphere of influence. Lending support to Pearson's findings for intervention in general, Weede finds that for the United States in particular, the most powerful determinant of U.S. interventions in favor of foreign governments is domestic disorder. He argues: "A causal interpretation of these correlations looks plausible: general societal weakness produces domestic disorder which in turn provokes the Free World's policemen to protect presumably status quo oriented governments from their discontented citizens and insurgents" (Weede 1978: 512).

It thus is evident that foreign military intervention affects the pattern of domestic conflict within target nations and that a fairly strong and pervasive relationship between domestic conflict and intervention exists in the post–World War II period. Pearson (1974b), Gurr and Bishop (1976), Gurr (1968), Gurr and Duvall (1973), Doran (1976), and Weede (1978) all conclude that external interventions exacerbate domestic conflict. Moreover the location of the target nation (both geographically and within the international power hierarchy) is related to the likelihood of external intervention. Thus Pearson (1974a) cites the role of geographical proximity; spheres of influence are noted by Doran (1975), Weede (1978), and Odell (1974); the likelihood of success of insurgent groups was found to be influential by Pearson and Baumann (1974); and the type of domestic conflict experienced by the target nation was correlated with interventions in the studies of Pearson (1974b) and Sullivan (1969).

DEPENDENCE, INTERDEPENDENCE, AND THE CONFLICT NEXUS

In the section on general studies of the conflict nexus, above, I noted that the correlational studies of nations grouped according to region and type found stronger relationships between internal and external conflict than when all nations were studied together (for example, Collins 1973; Wilkenfeld 1968, 1969; Stohl 1970). In this section we shall focus on the impact that properties of the international system have on the pattern and extent of domestic violence and conflict.

Kerbo (1978) has argued that because of the dominant power of the nations at the core of the internation politico-economic system and "their motivation for continued dominance of periphery, direct and international influence can be used to create the preconditions for political violence in the periphery when it is in the interests of these core actors" (Kerbo 1978: 376). To illustrate his point, Kerbo narrates the growth of political violence in Chile from 1970 to 1973 that led to the September coup that toppled Allende. Russett and his collaborators on the "Dependencia" project are attempting to investigate the relationship between conflict and coercion in dependent states by means of formal analysis of the theoretical argument developed in the "dependencia" literature and expressed in the Gurr and Duvall conclusion cited above. Briefly, that "dependencia" literature proceeds "from a structuralist paradigm which focuses on the class structure in the peripheral country, the alliance between this class structure and international capital, and the role of the state in shaping and managing the national, foreign, and class forces that propel development within countries" (Caporaso 1978: 2). Along similar lines Paige (1975) argued that the world economic system and the resultant forms of agricultural production in underdeveloped nations have had the unintended effect of promoting political violence in those countries. With this structural argument guiding their research, Russett and his collaborators on the Yale "Dependencia" project have sought to map the causes and consequences of dependence. They contend that the interaction of external dependence with latent conflict leads to escalation of the levels of violence used by both the state and its opposition (Jackson et al. 1978: 1). They have not yet systematically tested their model, but other studies help us judge whether it is correct that, as Gurr and Duvall have previously argued, "the poorer a nation, the more inviduous inequalities are supported from outside, and the more dependent on external capital and markets, the more susceptible it is to violent internal conflict" (Gurr and Duvall 1973: 161).

Midlarsky and Tanter (1967) claim to have tested the relationship between the "colonial nature of the Latin American economies" and political instability. Their sample consisted of eighteen nations for 1958–1960 (the data came from the original Tanter 1966 study). They conclude that the economic presence of the United States has a positive impact on the degree of economic development that occurs, but it also may lead to hostility towards the United States, and these two variables are positively related to the likelihood of revolutions in nondemocratic Latin American societies. Duff and McCamant (1976) rightfully suggest that severe problems with the Midlarsky and Tanter analysis and the operationalization of their independent variables should lead us to reject their results.[10] Likewise, Zimmermann (1979: 494) questions the measure of revolution used. There are thus critical shortcomings concerning measurement on both sides of the regression equation and also with the choice of regression analysis.

Duff and McCamant in turn devised their own measures of dependency, civil violence, and repression. Indicators of foreign investment, foreign trade, and foreign aid were correlated with violence and repression in the 1950s and 1960s for all Latin American nations. "The correlations between the three dependency variables and violence and repression in both the 1950's and 1960's. . . lead us to reject the proposition that any of the three forms of dependency has a direct relationship with either violence or repression" (Duff and McCamant 1976: 89). This finding is in direct contrast to a series of individual nation case studies that note the relationship between the development of authoritarian regimes and dependence.[11] Kaufman, reflecting on the experience of Latin American nations and the work of Schmitter, has argued that

> on the one hand, there is evidence that both the traditional forms of trade
> dependency and the newer forms of multinational penetration have encour-

aged and/or perpetuated highly stratified social structures characterized by extreme concentration of wealth and by the marginalization of the urban and
rural poor. . . . By encouraging a social order with so many criss-crossing
lines of cleavage, external dependency leads to the "sort of nationally
stalemated nonhegemonic class and interest structure which Karl Marx
postulated as the destructive basis for Bonapartism. [Kaufman 1976: 15]

Duff and McCamant, investigating their own data in more detail, do find
that in four nations (Cuba, Venezuela, Guatemala, and the Dominican
Republic) that experienced both high U.S. investment and economic
stagnation high levels of violence did occur. They suggest that a perhaps
more complex relationship between economic dependency and violence
than they had been able to test does indeed exist, but they are unable to offer systematic statistical evidence.

C. F. Doran (1975) studied eight Caribbean nations for the period
1948–1964. He found that the conflict dimensions of turmoil and subversion were evident in data on the Caribbean and resembled those identified
in factor analyses by Tanter (1966) and Bwy (1968b), but that the revolution factor discovered by Rummel (1963) did not appear. Searching for an
association between domestic and foreign conflict via factor scores, Doran
used the scores for the annual amounts of conflict for the entire region, not
the amount of conflict per nation at several time points. However, Doran
did not actually measure the relationship between internal instability and
United States or core state influence. Rather he noted the different patterns of domestic instability in the 1948–1960 and 1961–1964 periods
within the region as a whole, and associated these differences with Castro,
Cuba, and the resultant shifts in American policies for dealing with instability in the region. This makes for an intuitively pleasing but not a
statistically supported argument. Doran argues that the different patterns
in instability can be explained by the fact that "the United States shifted its
policy after 1960 from external defense to internal security, pouring aid into the Alliance for Progress and setting up counter-insurgency programs
throughout Latin America" (Doran 1975: 41). In a further study of the
Caribbean region, C. F. Doran (1978) employed a cross-lagged causal
model to test the relationship between instability and foreign aid in dependent nations. He found that political instability and foreign aid had a
rather strong positive correlation. He argues that instability within recipient nations pulls "foreign aid into the region and that following a one to
two year delay, aid has stimulated or 'pushed' the onset of additional
domestic political violence" (C. F. Doran 1978: 29).

Previously, Schmitter (1973) had investigated the relationship between
the allocation of aid and coercive responses to civil strife in nineteen Latin
American nations (1945–1970) and had found a weak positive association.
The strength of the relationship to be found between aid and civil strife
thus appears to vary with region and with the type of civil strife under ex-

amination. Further evidence of this variance is suggested by the results obtained by Rowe (1974). Rowe focused on the incidence of coups d'état and military assistance provided by the United States to all noncommunist aid recipients from 1948 to 1972. He reports some interesting findings. Military assistance seems to reduce the incidence of coups within already authoritarian military regimes. However, military assistance to civilian governments is associated with an increase in the incidence of coups.

The most extensive attempt to study the domestic instability–dependence relationship to date was undertaken by Eckhardt and Young (1977). They studied 114 nations in what, unfortunately, ultimately resulted in a data-reduction exercise. They used information from most major data-collection efforts of the past two decades and examined data covering much of the post-World War II era. Beginning with 212 variables, they performed a series of factor, typal, and variance analyses. Eventually, fourth-order factor analysis of a subset of fifty-one variables reduced to one quartenary factor that explained 35 percent of the total variance in the data set. The resulting factor scores then were used to develop an imperialism indicator which was employed in some further analysis.

> Factor, typal, and variance analyses all provided some support for the general hypothesis that civil conflicts were at least partly and sometimes largely functions of imperialism. Richer and more powerful nations experienced more turmoil, while poorer and less powerful nations experienced more internal war. The North–South dimension of imperialism vs. anti-imperialism explained more of the variance in civil conflicts than the East–West dimensions of capitalism vs. communism. [Eckhardt and Young 1977: 167]

The study establishes a set of covariance relations, but certainly no causal sequences can be inferred from the analyses. Naroll, in his forward to the book that reports this study, argues that the results should not be thought of as mere artifacts of systematic error in the data. In a methodological critique included as an appendix, Michik advises the reader to be wary of the results of the study, and we should be. While there may be no systematic error in the data, and Eckhardt and Young are to be commended for their scholarly integrity in including the Michik critique, we should not forget either the critique or the fact that each step in a data reduction procedure is accomplished through the elimination of information. Each step in the factor-analytic procedures leads further and further from empirical reality and concreteness. Eckhardt and Young's results, while intuitively plausible, should be approached with much care.

One final study, which differs somewhat in focus from the above but does study the indirect effects of the international system on patterns of domestic stability, is provided by C. F. Doran (1976). The nations of the European Economic Community and the Central American Common Market were examined for the period 1955–1967 using data from Taylor and Hudson (1972). Doran sought to isolate the impact of the formation and development of common markets on domestic instability. Surprisingly, he found that the formation of the markets was accompanied by increases in instability. However, the evolving markets soon experienced lower levels of turmoil than in the period immediately prior to their formation. The two common markets' experience were somewhat different. The EEC had increases in all types of instability, including elite instability, while the CACM had increases in elite instability. This led Doran to conclude that "to answer the question does integration associate with instability, one must also consider the level of modernization, the temporal phase the integration process finds itself in, and the class basis of instability" (C. F. Doran 1976: 77). Perhaps one might also investigate the level of dependence found within the market or, in light of Doran's previous work, the market's location within a particular sphere of influence.

What can we conclude about the impact of economic dependence on patterns of domestic instability and violence? While, once again, our review shows no wholly consistent relationships between different aspects of dependency and internal conflict, it is quite evident that the pattern of domestic instability is markedly influenced by a country's or region's dependence. The focus on dependence in current research on the determinants of civil strife by Gurr and Duvall, and in the empirical work being carried out in the Russett et al. "Dependencia" project, should therefore prove quite fruitful.

CONCLUSION

The two most important general conclusions we can draw from this review are, unfortunately, negative ones. First, there appears to be no single clear relationship between internal and external conflict that holds across time or space. Second, most of the conventional wisdom and theoretical speculation concerning the conflict nexus remains either unsupported by, or in direct opposition to, the systematic empirical work that has been accomplished thus far.

In the scholarly generation since Rummel (1963) concluded that no causal or correlative relationship existed between internal and external conflict, many modifications have been introduced in the data bases used, sampling of nations and time periods, research designs, and methods of analysis. And while these innovations have sometimes led to the finding of significant correlations in particular studies, the continuing lack of theoretical foundation has worked against the cumulation of evidence. Rather what has resulted is the accumulation of isolated bits of information supporting neither theoretical argument nor conventional wisdom.

What then can we do to improve the study of conflict linkages? Obviously, as a first step we require a theory-based approach. The remaining paragraphs of this chapter provide modest suggestions about the components of such a theory, identify contexts in which the theory is likely to be valid, and indicate some useful approaches to the measurement and testing of such a theory.

The construction of an adequate theory of conflict linkages is dependent upon the reciprocal development of theories of political conflict and violence in general. As previously indicated, theorists of internal and external conflict have avoided the consideration of conflict outside their particular focus when constructing their theories. The evidence we have reviewed above suggests that this has been an error and thus a hindrance to the development of conflict theory. Whatever theorists of war and civil violence do to correct this error in the future, it is essential that further research into the conflict linkage explicitly employ a causal model of political conflict and build external variables into the model (or a causal model of external conflict and build in internal variables).

The evidence indicates some promising first steps. Previous research has sensitized us to the fact that conflict linkages are contingent relationships. Whether and how external conflict affects internal conflict (and vice versa) depends on a variety of conditions such as the world region involved and the political characteristics and position of countries in the international system. Global analyses have tended to obscure these contingencies. We have seen that dependent states are more influenced by external events and more prone to external interference in their affairs than are dominant states. We thus expect relationships between internal and external conflict to be more pronounced in dependent states. We further expect that the patterns of conflict in dependent states will be significantly different from those in dominant states. For example, whereas dependent states are more likely to be the target of intervention, they are less likely to be the initiators of interventions in other states. Intervention, therefore, as a form of external conflict is likely to have quite different relationships to both prior and subsequent civil violence in dominant and dependent states.

Internal conflict patterns may be affected by external position in other ways. Dissident groups in dominant nations such as the United States are unlikely to consider the likelihood or importance of external support or intervention were they to demonstrate, riot, or be repressed. Likewise, although authorities in dominant states may consider world public opinion, they are unlikely to worry about external interference. Dissidents and authorities in dependent states would be foolish not to make such strategic judgments. Whether or not this is an important consideration for conflict linkage theorists is contingent on the adopted theoretical approach.

The resource mobilization or group conflict approach taken by Stohl (1976), for example, hypothesized that war would affect stratification patterns within nations and thus create more intense conflict between the stratified groups. Linking external variables through the specifications of a breakdown model of society, Gurr and Duvall (1973) offer alternative hypotheses which detail how external intervention exacerbates stress and strain within society. These alternative theoretical approaches identify different foci for exploring the linkage. The important point, if we are to move forward with theory building, is that with either theoretical approach one can determine whether the inclusion of external variables improves explanation. It is also possible that in our current state of theoretical development different theories may prove stronger in different contexts. The most appropriate theoretical approach might prove contingent on the type of society or historical era being studied.

The hypotheses that purport to guide linkage investigations are generally stated in the following form: external conflict in nation A at the time t caused internal conflict in nation A at time $t + 1$ (and vice versa). That is, the hypotheses are temporal and causal. Yet most tests of the linkage hypotheses have been cross-sectional and correlational. A cross-sectional test of a temporal proposition is inappropriate and the estimates provided are usable only if it is assumed that all nations travel the same time path (slope and intercept). Thus the addition of time lags to cross-sectional analyses is useful only if the dependent and independent variables can be assumed to vary in the same way over time within the cluster of nations studied. Normally, then, some form of time-series analysis is more appropriate. For example, a quasi-experimental interrupted time-series analysis (Stohl 1976) allows one to test the impact of an event or independent variable as it unravels over time. The method is limited, however, because strength of association cannot be tested. A simultaneous equation model (Gurr and Duvall 1973) makes it possible to trace time paths within a theoretical system through the use of time-lagged conflict measures. The problem of specifying the most appropriate time lags still remains, of course. Whatever time lags are chosen, each should be treated as hypothetical and its utility and validity tested in subsequent analyses.

The magnitude and intensity of conflict and other theoretically relevant variables may be assumed to affect the strength of association between internal and external conflict. Yet much of the previous research in this area has established only whether or not an event (or behavior) has occurred, and then correlated it with the occurrence of other events. This has been the case for cross-sectional as well as quasi-experimental analyses. Stohl (1976), departing from the norm, took account of the magnitude and intensity of civil violence. However, due to the limitations of the interrupted time-series design, war was treated merely as an interruption point. What limitations did that produce? As Durkheim noted eighty years ago, "while great national wars have had a strong influence on the amount of suicide in both France and Germany purely dynastic wars such as the Crimean or Italian which have not violently moved the masses, have had no appreciable effect" (Durkheim 1951: 206–207). This suggests that we would do well, when studying war's impact, to consider such properties as its length, scope, casualties, domestic popularity, and the social distance of the adversary. Likewise, there should be profit in using diverse measures of other aspects of external conflict.

Characteristics of internal conflict events should also be measured, and indicators of the role of the state in internal violence should be developed. Although rival theoretical models might consider the action of the state as indicative of breakdown, repression, or enforcement, the evidence is that external relations have influenced the role of the state in internal conflict. It would be useful to determine if the states' role is contingent on particular external variables.

The value of the preceding suggestions can be determined only by subsequent analyses. Whatever choices are made regarding the collection of data, the construction of indicators, and the method and context for testing hypotheses, it should be appreciated that the greatest profits are likely to accrue if the initial investments in each study are made in theoretical development.

NOTES

1. A basic assumption of factor analysis is that a "battery of intercorrelated variables has some common factors running through it and that the scores of an individual can be represented most economically in terms of these reference factors" (Fruchter 1954: 44). This assumes that these variables have a common interpretation within all nations studied. However, as Alker (1968: 143) and subsequent factor analyses of domestic conflict variables after Rummel and Tanter have shown, this is not necessarily the case (see, for example, Bwy 1968b). Assuming equivalence across nations may produce distorted results.

2. Cluster analysis is a simple form of correlational analysis which relates the variables into clusters such that the variables in the clusters correlate more highly with the variable in the cluster to which it is attached than to any other variable. Its primary purpose is to provide a preliminary grouping for large sets of data whose underlying dimensions are unknown (see Fruchter 1954 for a more complete explanation).

3. Confirmatory factor analysis procedures allow the investigator to fix some parameters of the model and estimate the others. The purpose is to obtain a "best fit" estimate of each parameter and an overall goodness-of-fit test for the consistency of the data with the model (see Jöreskog 1969 for a fuller explanation).

4. Stein suggests, quite correctly, that Mack's review is "marred by an unnecessary jingoistic tone and an obscurantist attack on behaviorism" (A. A. Stein 1976: 166).

5. See Chapter 10 in this *Handbook* by Bruce M. Russett and Arthur A. Stein on the outcomes and consequences of war.

6. Although not an exact test of the internal–external conflict cohesion hypothesis, Tefft and Reinhardt (1974) found that internal war was correlated with the presence of peacemaking mechanisms and external war with their absence, and that internal war was correlated, although not significantly, with stable peace and external war with no or unstable peace (Tefft and Reinhardt 1974: 167). Divale, Chambers, and Gangloff (1976) replicated these results when they introduced the intervening variable of residence type, patrilocal or matrilocal.

7. At the international level of analysis Hopmann (1967) and Holsti, Hopmann, and Sullivan (1973) tested the hypothesis that the greater the inter-alliance conflict, the greater the intra-alliance cohesion. Behavioral and attitudinal data were used to evaluate the hypothesis for the communist system (Hopmann 1967) and both NATO and the communist system (Holsti, Hopmann, and Sullivan 1973) for 1950–1965. They found that "an attitudinal component, the consensus among allies in their perception of the enemy, tended to be related to the level of threat which allies perceived to be emanating from the enemy" (Holsti, Hopmann, and Sullivan 1973: 143). The greater the conflict that existed between alliances, the greater was the resultant cooperation within them. Conversely, decreased inter-alliance conflict was associated with reduced cooperation within alliances. These findings lend support to the hypothesis in general but, of course, say nothing about the conflict nexus for nations.

8. Other studies of civil violence that neglect the external sources of behavior might also be affected. For example, Charles Tilly notes in his section on France in *The Rebellious Century* that violence among Frenchmen declined during 1870, 1914–1918, and 1940–1944 (Tilly, Tilly, and Tilly 1975: 61). He also notes that these were periods of strong repression and central control (not included in his data on collective violence). In the same work, Louise Tilly in her analysis of Italy notes that 1919, 1920, and 1921 "may well have produced the highest level of involvement in collective violence" of any three years in Italy's modern history (Tilly, Tilly, and Tilly 1975: 126) and also that after World War II, following a hiatus beginning in 1926, frequent disturbances with widespread participation resumed. Systematic inclusion of war as a variable in the Tilly model might be quite useful.

9. It is striking to note that the two most important studies of domestic conflict in the past decade ignore external violence in general and war in particular. War is mentioned in passing, of course, but the variable, war, is never included in the systematic empirical studies nor in the central theoretical statements. See Gurr, *Why Men Rebel* (1970), and Tilly, Tilly, and Tilly, *The Rebellious Century* (1975). On the other side of the relationship, J. David Singer's "correlates of war" project has thus far not considered internal conflict factors. A singular exception in the study of the causes of war is the use of the concept of "lateral pressure" in the Stanford studies (see Choucri and North 1975).

10. To derive the index that Midlarsky and Tanter call "economic presence" they multiplied United States investment per capita by proportion of total trade with the United States. First of all, there is no reason to use only U.S. invest-

ment and trade because the logic applies equally to all foreign presence. Second, investment per capita does not relate the foreign presence to the size of the economy and what results is a combination of U.S. investment and the wealth of the economy, not the importance of the foreign presence. Third, by multiplying the two figures, the distribution of the combined index becomes highly skewed, invalidating any regression analysis used on that data. [Duff and McCamant 1976: 88]

11. See, for example, Einaudi 1973, Cotler 1971, Kaufman 1976, O'Donnell 1973, and Stepan 1971.

CHAPTER 8

Why War? Evidence on the Outbreak of International Conflict

Dina A. Zinnes

THIS CHAPTER IS A STOCK-TAKING EXERCISE: what do we know about international violence based on the quantitative research efforts of the past thirty years? In one sense such an enterprise is self-justifying: international violence is a major area of concern for the field of international politics and an assessment of what we do and do not know is certainly useful as a basis for suggesting what should be done next. Although this is clearly one dimension of justification, there is a second more immediate rationale for this review.

In a provocative article, Anatol Rapoport (1976) suggests that theories or models of international politics—and therefore of such phenomena as international violence—are not possible. Unlike physics, Rapoport argues, the study of international political phenomena has uncovered no laws upon which to build theories. By "law" Rapoport means consistently observed regularities or patterns in the phenomena under study, and he cites examples from our field to show the extent to which our results appear ephemeral, transient, and sometimes contradictory. Although Rapoport suggests other reasons that international politics can never be a science like physics, the apparent absence of "laws" is the most serious charge.

Rapoport's criticism is a clear challenge to our field: is it true that after thirty years of empirical research, in which we have devoted an enormous amount of time to collecting, measuring, and summarizing observations about nation–state behavior, we cannot find any patterns, that all of our results are bits and pieces which at best contradict one another and at worst appear to be totally disjointed? Although one might not agree with Rapoport's premise that theories must be built on laws, it is nevertheless the case that if we could demonstrate the existence of such laws, they would be an invaluable asset in building theories.

Thus a second rationale for this chapter is to accept Rapoport's challenge within the subject area of international violence: what regularities can we show after thirty years of research on violent conflict among nation–states?

PROCEDURE

Before beginning, it is obvious that a few definitions are in order. How are the relevant studies to be identified?

First, it is important to emphasize that the phenomenon under study is *internation violence*. Consequently, only studies involving *nation–states* are relevant (for example, Divale et al.'s 1976 study of pre-industrial societies and similar analyses are omitted here), and of these only the ones in which violence between states is examined are reviewed here. There are a number of events-data studies that examine the general hostile behavior of nations. The only relevant portions of these studies for our purposes are those hostile behaviors that are specifically violent, that is, that involve injury or death to the citizens of one state as a consequence of the actions of another state.[1] For example, only a small portion of the work done by such researchers as Rummel are of relevance, and the hostile-interaction analyses of McClelland are not considered. Furthermore, studies that have combined general hostility and violence so that it is not possible to separate those analyses specific to violence, are also usually omitted; Pearson's (1974) analysis of intervention obviously includes some violent activities but the analyses of the violent interventions cannot be analyzed separately from interventions in general; and most of Rummel's field theory work has similar problems. Finally, the literature on international crises, particularly the work concerning the 1914 crisis, is omitted. These studies focus on the attributes of decisions during crisis periods rather than on the causes of the actual outbreak of violence. While some might feel that this narrowing of focus is unfortunate, I found it essential for the purposes of finding a reasonable starting point. Eventually we will want to incorporate these other obviously relevant pieces of information, but to do so initially is to invite chaos.

Second, it is equally important to bear in mind that the concern here is with the *outbreak* of international violence. The purpose is to attempt to discern whether there are any patterns that can be observed across studies which allow us to draw conclusions about why international violence occurs. Consequently, studies that deal with attributes of international violence, once underway, were not deemed relevant for this analysis. For example, studies of the conditions that determine victory in war (Rosen 1972), characteristics of wars (Rummel 1967, Voevodsky 1969, Kende 1971, Denton 1966, Denton and Phillips 1968), or the conditions under which wars will terminate (Klingberg 1966), were omitted from consideration. Similarly, studies that analyzed the consequences of wars (Organski 1977, Davis, Duncan, and Siverson 1978, Pelowski 1971) were also omitted. Thus this analysis is very specifically focused on the *outbreak* of international violence.

Finally, it was felt that to answer Rapoport's challenge adequately, only empirical studies could be considered. If we are to discern laws, they must be laws that have evolved from numerous observations; they cannot be simple assertions even by eminent scholars in our field. Thus the writings of political theorists, historians, and even mathematical modelers are not legitimate pieces of evidence unless they contain careful and systematic observations, collected under replicable conditions. In short, essays on why international violence occurs (for instance, Waltz 1959) are not considered.

The obvious starting point for a review such as this is Jones and Singer (1973), and this is where the first set of articles were found. However, that volume covers studies through 1969 only. All major journals in political science were searched beginning in 1970, including *American Political Science Review, American Journal of Political Science, Journal of Conflict Resolution, International Studies Quarterly, Journal of Peace Science, Journal of Peace Research, Western Political Quarterly, Peace Research Society (International) Papers, Comparative Political Studies*, and *Comparative Politics*. In addition, bibliographies in articles found in these journals were checked. Needless to say, this does not represent a complete search—interesting and relevant articles have undoubtedly appeared in journals in economics, psychology, sociology—but it does reflect time and resource limitations. It is also true that unpublished papers could not, for obvious reasons, be systemically covered.

Having delimited the subject matter and the relevant pieces of evidence, I was ready to begin. Initially it seemed that the problem was sufficiently well-specified so that the analysis would be straightforward. But as I began to compile comparative tables across different studies it became obvious that the studies were exceedingly diverse: the variables analyzed, the types of analyses performed, the criteria (r^2 or level of significance) used for judgment were so different that it was hard to see how reasonable comparisons could be made. How could a pattern be seen across such diversity?

Following a miserable night in which I dreamed of dancing correlation coefficients being chased by twisting, turning factor structures, I realized that I was approaching the problem incorrectly. What I had before me were the bits and pieces of a puzzle, but I had failed to treat them as such.

If one thought of the problem as a puzzle, then one should begin with one or two pieces and search among the remaining pieces to find something that "went with it." Each new piece should then be picked on the basis of its similarity, or correspondence, with previously "fitted" pieces. Such an approach would not be too different from looking at the problem as a detective story—something has happened, and by combining clues, certain sequences of events are ruled out and others become more plausible.

The analogy of the puzzle was also useful in suggesting a potential problem: there was no reason why it should be assumed that what I had before me were the pieces of a single puzzle. Worse, if there was more than one puzzle, it might not always be obvious which pieces went with what puzzle. Furthermore, even with all the empirical work that has been done, the chances are high that not all or even most of the pieces are curently available. So what follows is a mystery story, one possible reconstruction of what might have happened.

BEGINNING THE PUZZLE—SELECTION OF THE FIRST PIECE OF THE NATION–STATE PUZZLE

We will begin by assuming there are two puzzles. One puzzle depicts the conditions under which nation–states go to war; the other shows the conditions under which the international system is prone to war. Perhaps all the pieces fit into a single puzzle, but it is easier to proceed as if there were two sets of pieces. Since the greatest number of empirical studies have been done at the nation–state level, we will start with these analyses. The puzzle analogy suggests that the choice of an initial piece is unimportant; regardless of where one begins, the final picture should be the same. Thus the empirical studies of international violence focusing on the nation–state were canvassed to find a central, intriguing observation.

The choice fell on an observation made by Singer and Small: "most of the war in the system has been accounted for by a small fraction of nations" (Singer and Small 1972: 287). To substantiate this claim, the authors list the frequency of wars for those states most involved in the period between 1816–1965: France and England with nineteen each, Turkey with seventeen, Russia with fifteen, Sardinia with twelve, Spain with nine. Not surprisingly, most of these same states account for the greatest number of battle deaths and were involved in wars for the longest periods of time. This observation is completely consistent, though not entirely identical, with Richardson's (1960a) indication of those nations most involved in wars since 1815. The difference between the reports lies in differences of definition of war and nation–states, sources used, and time periods covered. But for our purposes these differences are not of major consequence. What is important is that these writers agree that a few states have been in most wars. An imaginative analysis of this issue by Bremer (1975) further confirms this observation.

However, we must not leap to the conclusion that international violence is perpetrated by only a select few nations—what might be termed the "bad seed" theory of war. The Singer-Small and Richardson observations must be tempered with three other observations. First, in carefully searching through his war data from 1820 to 1939, Richardson discovers that only one nation, Sweden, did not engage in any international violence. Second, this observation is substantiated by a very different analysis provided by Naroll (1969). Examining 2,000 years of history to see if he could discern what variables made wars more or less likely, Naroll concludes that "peace loving nations (defined in terms of whether they adopted a defensive or aggressive stance) are no less likely to be involved in war than warlike nations" (Naroll 1969: 152). Third, Richardson divides the historical period from 1820 to 1939 into six twenty-year periods and in each period counts the number of new belligerents that participate in wars. By dividing the number of new belligerents by the total number of belligerents in each period, he obtains a proportion that he can now observe from period to period. Intriguingly this proportion does not dwindle to zero, as would have to be the case if the "bad seed" theory were correct—once the bad seeds were counted in the first period they would drop out of the numerator for the next period and thus one would expect the fraction to go to zero. On the contrary, the proportions stay about the same (after an initial high value due to the fact that all belligerents were "new" in the first observation period): .73, .37, .42, .34, .24, .37.

If we combine these latter points with the initial observation made both by Singer and Small and by Richardson, it would seem that we must arrive at the following general observation. International violence is a widespread phenomenon not confined to just a few states; at one time or another almost all states have engaged in this type of activity. However, some nations seem more prone to engage in this type of behavior than others. This would seem to be the first piece of the puzzle: why are some states more war-prone?

A possible answer to this query is that there is a characteristic or attribute that makes a nation prone to war. Although all nations have this quality, some have more of it than others. But if we adopt this line of reasoning, then we must bear in mind the previously cited Singer-Small and Richardson observations. These observations had an implicit time dimension: it was not just that some nations were engaged in more wars than others, it was through 150 years of history that some nations were involved in more wars. Furthermore, we can turn Richardson's "new belligerent" analysis around and note that not only does this ratio not dwindle to zero over the six periods, but it also does not increase to one, which would be the case if only new belligerents fought in each period. This suggests that while each period sees some new nations fighting, it is also the case that old belligerents continue to fight. If there are attributes that make nations war-prone, it is plausible that these attributes do not change dramatically with time, since some nations are consistently more prone to violence than others. Such a conclusion would be consistent with another study by Singer and Small (1966). Although the initial purpose of this study was to examine the relationship between alliances and measures of war, the authors discover that high correlations between these variables are wiped out when nations' length of membership in the international system (system tenure) is considered. More specific to our present concern, they find high correlations between system tenure and war-proneness: nations that are in the system for a long period of time tend to engage in many wars. We will begin our search by examining national attributes that do not change drastically over time.

FITTING OTHER PIECES—
THE SEARCH FOR THE MISSING ATTRIBUTE

One of the most extensive studies of the attributes of nations was done by Rummel (1968). Looking cross-sectionally at all states in the mid-1950s, Rummel correlates 235 different attributes of nations with thirteen measures of foreign conflict behavior. One of these foreign conflict measures is the frequency of war. What is striking about these results is the almost total absence of any relationship (r is less than .3 and not significant) between war and its major potential determinants.[2] For example, Rummel uses a large number of variables to tap basic concepts in demography, economics, geography, culture, political system, and values. With a few exceptions there is no covariation.[3] If we consider the variable "military acts," which by Rummel's definition (1963: 27) reflects international violence at a somewhat lower level than war, we obtain a comparable result: there are still no variables within the major categories cited above that produce correlations of at least .3 (that is, explain a minimum of 9 percent of the variance) and that are statistically significant at the .05 level. One interesting exception to this is the proportion of Muslims in a country's population, which correlates .38 and is statistically significant. Finally, one additional measure of international violence might be considered: Rummel's variable "number killed in foreign violence." The difficulty with this variable is that it includes the number killed on all sides of a conflict and is thus not a measure of one nation's level of international violence. Nevertheless, this variable confirms the previous results: with a few odd exceptions, no significant correlations of .3 or larger appear with any of the main attribute variables.

Rummel's study covers only a few years and is thus necessarily biased by the events and circumstances of the mid-1950s. But we cannot easily dismiss the results on these grounds for they are confirmed by a variety of other analyses. In an earlier study, Rummel (1964) provided a series of multiple correlations between foreign-conflict variables and a series of dimensions of nations previously obtained in a study by Berry (1961). Berry's study was a factor analysis of a large number of attributes of nations by which he identified four main dimensions: technology, demography, size, and income. It is the factor scores on these four dimensions that Rummel correlates (together with several variables from his own work, which will be discussed later) with the same three variables of war, military action, and number of foreign killed. Once again, the partial correlations between "war" and these dimensions are extremely low and not statistically significant. "Military action" and "number killed in foreign violence" each produce one partial correlation that is statistically significant but they are too weak ($-.26$ and $-.25$ respectively) to be considered seriously.

Using data that overlap Rummel's but include data from Tanter (1966) and Banks and Textor (1963), M. Haas provides a series of additional analyses. In the first of these studies, Haas (1965) shows, via simple chi-square analyses, that there is essentially no relationship between type of regime, level of development, degree of urbanization, or population density and foreign conflict behavior. These results are further supported by a considerably more extensive set of correlations reported in the second study (M. Haas 1974). Based on essentially the same data, Haas correlates a large number of independent variables against the dependent variable of war frequency. The independent variables include such indicators of growth and development as GNP, population, electricity production, telephones per capita, urbanization, level of education, and agricultural work force, in addition to measures of government instability and crises. It is also important to note that Haas examined *changes* in the levels of some of these variables; for example, he correlated the *change* in national income with war frequency. Yet the results are the same: there are no correlations between any of these variables and war frequency that reach .3.

The two Rummel and the two Haas studies are essentially cross-sectional, and one might wonder if the findings of these analyses are specific to the period of time examined. But this is not the case. There are six additional longitudinal studies that lend support to what we have seen so far. Using an analysis of covariance design, Bremer, Singer, and Luterbacher (1973) examined the relationship between population density and changes in population density and war participation for European nations between 1816 and 1965. Using various measures of population density (crowding) and different indices to capture the war-proneness of a nation, they were unable to find any relationship between "how crowded a nation was . . . [and] its war participation, controlling for nation-specific differences such as culture" (Bremer, Singer, and Luterbacher 1973: 345). Similar results were obtained when the analyses were done separately for nations that initiated wars and nations that were simply defenders in wars. A second study (Small and Singer 1976) considers the war-proneness of democratic regimes from 1816 to 1965. These researchers find no detectable difference between democracies and nondemocracies for these years either in terms of participation or war initiation. In a third longitudinal study, M. Haas (1968) analyzes ten western countries (Australia, Finland, France, Germany, Great Britain, Norway, Spain, Switzerland, the United States, and Japan) from 1900 to 1960. Correlating war frequency with level of industrialization (measured by per capita production of electricity) within each country through time, he found that none of the correlations was statistically significant. When level of industrialization was compared with a scale of a state's war aggressiveness (experts were asked to rate the states), the results were still not significant.

Two studies done by Ray (1974, 1978) provide still more support. Ten states similar to those studied by Haas (Great Britain, France, Spain, Germany, Australia, Russia, Turkey, Italy, Poland, and Rumania) were examined from 1816 and 1970. The 1974 study considers the relationship between "status inconsistency" and several measures of war involvement.[4] "Status inconsistency" is an index that compares various measures of a nation's power (for example, population, iron and steel production, military expenditures) with the diplomatic status accorded it by other nations (measured by the percentage of states that send diplomatic missions). The concept "status inconsistency" comes from the sociological literature, where it refers to individuals, while in Ray's study it denotes the discrepancy between a nation's actual power capacity and its perceived importance by others. Thus "status inconsistency" is a somewhat different attribute measure but not completely unrelated to those seen above, since it takes account of a state's resources relative to its international position. Although Ray's measure of war involvement differs from the variable "war frequency" used in the previous studies—Ray considers the number of months a nation was involved in a war and the number of deaths it suffered—his results are, nevertheless, consistent with what has been seen so far. Correlating through time for each of the nations considered, he finds that there is no relationship between status inconsistency and war involvement. In a more recent paper Ray (1978) explores a corollary hypothesis: the relationship between status inconsistency and war initiation. The results are still null.

A sixth longitudinal analysis is provided by Gochman (1975a), who reports several results of interest. Like Ray, Gochman concerns himself with status inconsistency. There are, however, two differences between the two studies. Gochman uses a different scaling procedure to combine the six capability dimensions before he compares capabilities and diplomatic recognition in the measurement of status inconsistency, and his analysis consists of a simple contingency table which compares conflict involvement with over- or underrecognition. These differences notwithstanding, Gochman's results conform to Ray's—no relationship is found. In addition, Gochman examines the six capability measures separately against conflict involvement and again finds no association. Modified multivariate hypotheses in which conflict involvement is predicted on the basis of changes in capabilities, previous war involvements, an index measuring economic and military cross-pressures, and an index measuring system polarity—all weighted in terms of status inconsistency or power— do not fare any better. There is one exception to Gochman's largely null findings. For certain states in the twentieth century (France, Germany, Austria, Japan) good predictions are obtained when the above four variables are not weighted by the status or capability measures.[5]

In brief, ten studies—four cross-sectional and six longitudinal—suggest that a variety of variables that change slowly with respect to time are not related to war propensity. But the consistency of this evidence is counteracted by one final study that must be considered. The design of the study is neither longitudinal nor cross-sectional; instead it examines typical or average states. Stuckey and Singer (1973) investigate the relationship between capability or power indicators and the war behavior of nations for the period between 1820 to 1964 in the following fashion. Using the same six dimensions described previously (population, urban population, iron/ steel production, fuel consumption, military personnel, and military expenditures), these researchers construct three indices. The first, known as the composite index, calculates each nation's percentage share of a given dimension (for example, a nation's percentage share of population size with respect to all other nations in the international system) and then averages these percentage shares across the six dimensions to give each nation a composite index score. The second index focuses on the military-industrial capacity of a nation and calculates a nation's deviation from the mean on three dimensions—iron/steel production, fuel consumption, and military expenditures—and then averages these three deviations to produce for each nation a single military-industrial score. The third index is a measure of a nation's industrialization and is determined by dividing the two industrialization dimensions by population, transforming these values to z scores, and by averaging the two to produce a single score for each nation. Calculations are performed for five-year periods, so that every nation has a score on each of the three indices every five years; for every five-year period and each of the three indices, the authors rank-order all nations. The dependent variable, war experiences, is measured using frequency counts, numbers of months involved, and numbers killed. The "average war experience" along each of these variables is then calculated for each of the ranks; for example, the average number of wars engaged in by all those nations ranked 1, ranked 2, etcetera, on the composite index. Rank-order correlations are then calculated between the ranks and the "average war experience." As can be seen, this study is not cross-sectional in the typical sense since it does not examine specific nations, and whereas the data are drawn from a long time span, the analysis itself is not longitudinal.

This more detailed description of the Stuckey-Singer study has been provided because their findings are partially at variance with what we have seen thus far. The industrialization index is generally a poor predictor with respect to any of the "war experience" measures and thus conforms to the results of the studies cited above. The military-industrial index does somewhat better and is a particularly good predictor of war experience in the nineteenth century. The composite index is best, however, in that it produces uniformly high correlations for all time periods and all war experience measures. Let us examine these results more carefully.

Since the industrialization index is a poor predictor and since the military-industrial index is composed of two of the same industrial measures, it is probably reasonable to conclude that the results for the military-industrial index are principally a function of the military measure. The military measure in this case is military expenditures. If this reasoning is valid, the good correlations for the nineteenth century between the military-industrial index and war experiences implies that nations with high military expenditures tend also to be involved in many wars. We will want to return to this result in another context. The results for the composite index are somewhat more difficult to interpret. On the one hand, using the same reasoning as before, one could argue that the high correlations in this case must be due to the demographic and military measures since the two industrial measures did poorly previously. However, this line of argument may not be valid since the composite index is calculated in a fashion very different from the other two. While the other measures are based on mean deviations, the composite index takes account of percentage shares. Thus it is unclear whether the correlations are due to measurement techniques or to the particular variables used. In any case, the results are in direct contrast to those seen thus far. For whichever reason, the composite index appears to be an excellent predictor of a nation's war behavior.

So where are we? Having followed what appeared to be a lead in Singer-Small and Richardson, we began a search for possible attributes that might account for the fact that some nations were involved in more wars than others. The initial query was with respect to variables that tend to change slowly over time, thus allowing us to account for the fact that those nations that get involved in many wars do so consistently through time. But the pieces of the puzzle that we have available at this time suggest that this lead was wrong. With one exception (Stuckey and Singer

1973), we have yet to find any meaningful relationship between major variables such as power, regime type, size, or development and war-proneness. So let us reconsider one of our leads. If we suppose that the missing attribute does not change slowly with time, there are still conditions under which the Singer-Small and Richardson observations would hold. For example, if high values on the missing attribute(s) produces war-proneness, then it might be the case that those nations most frequently observed to be in wars are those which have the greatest degree of oscillation of this attribute. If the attribute fluctuates frequently, nations having the greatest number of oscillations would be the ones to engage in the most wars.

Obviously the identification of those attributes most likely to change rapidly with time represents a subjective assessment. But let us see where this takes us. We return again to a Rummel study (1963, also contained in 1968), which treats an attribute that presumably fluctuates through time, namely internal conflict behavior. The 1963 study was initially an attempt to compare measures of domestic conflict like strikes, government crises, and riots with measures of foreign conflict behavior including, as we saw above, at least three variables that tap different aspects of involvement in international violence. After factor-analyzing domestic conflict and foreign conflict variables separately to demonstrate that these two sets of variables each contain high intercorrelations, Rummel then factors all measures of conflict together and finds no relationship between the domestic conflict variables and foreign conflict variables. Indeed if we look more carefully at the bivariate correlations between his nine measures of domestic conflict and war, we find that no correlations are above .3 and none are statistically significant. When we further consider "military acts" and "foreign killed," we pick up one correlation in the .3 range between "purges" and these two variables. Finally, when Rummel correlates the three domestic factor dimensions with the "war" dimension which contains the three main international violence variables, he finds a small multiple r of .26. Thus, with the one intriguing exception of purges, this study suggests that measures of internal disruption do not appear to predict the international violence behavior of states.

These results are confirmed in a replication study done by Tanter (1966). While Rummel's study was for the years 1955–1957 (values of the variables were aggregated for the three years for each country) for seventy-seven nations, Tanter considered the period from 1958 to 1960 for eighty-three nations. The factor-analytic results were roughly comparable to those obtained by Rummel, and, more pointedly, the correlations between each of the internal conflict measures and the frequency-of-war variable were again essentially nonexistent. Correlations with "military action" were also near zero but two correlations in the .3 range did appear between both "assassinations" and "government crises" and "foreign killed." Finally, a multiple regression of several of the domestic conflict variables and the war dimension failed to produce a correlation above .3.

Collins (1973) provides additional evidence along these lines. In a study very similar to the ones done by Rummel and Tanter, Collins analyzes thirty-three independent African states using data for the period from 1963 to 1965. Whereas his variables correspond roughly to those used by Rummel and Tanter, the types of countries being examined and the sources used made it necessary to use slightly different measures of domestic conflict.[6] Nevertheless, the results are largely the same. Measures of political clashes, subversion, elite instability, and political arrests were not correlated with either measure of involvement in international violence. There were, however, two interesting exceptions to this absence of correlation: revolutions did significantly correlate with "military violence" at .39 and domestic suppression did correlate significantly with number killed, r = .36.

Haas's study (1974), discussed previously, provides further support, though here one might question the categorization of the variables used as "fluctuating." In any case, the results are equally negligible. Correlations between war frequency (again done through time, by country) or the war aggressiveness scale and unemployment rates, suicides, homicides, and alcoholism are all extremely low.

Finally, in a somewhat different type of analysis, Zinnes and Wilkenfeld (1971) also find that domestic conflict is not related to international violence. Using the results of a factor analysis of both the Rummel and Tanter data, they constructed a series of transition matrices between levels of domestic conflict, as measured by the two factors of internal war and turmoil, and the levels of foreign conflict behavior, as measured by the dimensions of war, belligerency, and diplomacy. For our purposes only the war dimension is relevant. By holding the transition between amount of war constant, that is, by considering only transitions between no war and some war in a subsequent time period, the effects on this transition of the two domestic conflict dimensions could be examined. It was found that the domestic conflict dimensions did not influence the transitions on the war dimension.

In short, the evidence thus far would seem to imply that we have once again come up against a dead end. But not entirely. There is a series of studies that at least initially seems to contradict the above results but, when considered more carefully, in fact suggests yet another line of attack. Provoked by the Rummel and Tanter results, Wilkenfeld (1968, 1973a) replicated these analyses for groups of states categorized essentially by government type. In some groups he found significant positive correlations between domestic confict and foreign conflict. For our purposes the important relationships are the correlations between each of the domestic conflict factors and the war dimension. Using factor scores for the nations, Wilkenfeld finds that the "revolutionary" variable correlates significantly, $r = .55$, with the "war" variable for centrist (authoritarian) countries and that the "turmoil" variable correlates significantly with the "war" variable for polyarchic (democratic) nations, $r = .39$. In short, if we take into account the structure of governments, it would appear that certain types of internal disruption are related to the international violence behavior of a nation—though the direction of the causal connection is not clear.

Another intriguing result in this regard is found in Hazelwood (1973b). This study provides a considerably more complex statistical analysis than has been seen thus far, but by examining what are essentially regression coefficients we can discern at least one result of relevance. In his first canonical correlation, Hazelwood finds that population diversity and ethnic diversity together with Rummel's dimension of turmoil relate very strongly with Rummel's war dimension. This is particularly interesting if we recall one tiny piece of evidence seen earlier: in the 1968 Rummel study a significant correlation of .38 was found between proportion of the population that was Muslim and "military action." If that independent variable in Rummel's analysis is interpreted as a measure of population diversity, it seems consistent with Hazelwood's results. Thus we see, as in the Wilkenfeld study, that when several variables are combined, some relationships do appear.

A third study of interest is by Bobrow et al. (1973). Although their principal interest is the impact of military assistance, they report one analysis relevant in this context. Looking at fifteen Asian nations from 1955–1966, these researchers correlate a variable denoted "political strife" with another variable labeled the "international cooperation/conflict ratio" for each nation over time. "Political strife" is composed of demands, instability, and domestic violence and thus overlaps the domestic conflict variables considered above, but also includes additional properties. Although the cooperation/conflict ratio is not an exact measure of international violence, it does include violent behaviors. In the last series of analyses reported in this paper, one finds that the r's between "political strife" and the cooperation/conflict ratio are very high for seven of the fifteen countries. Some correlations exceed .8, indicating that the more internal strife the greater a nation's external conflict behavior.

If we compare these three studies, we see that each suggests that a relationship exists between variables that measure internal conflict and variables that measure violent international behavior *when the internal conflict measures are taken together with other attributes* of nations, such as governmental structure (Wilkenfeld), population diversity (Hazelwood), or demands and instability (Bobrow et al.). Looking back at our first line of attack, we now see that our initial lead may have taken us nowhere because we did not consider the interaction of time-stable variables with factors that fluctuate more readily. Thus governmental structure or population diversity, as more stable attributes of nations, have to be combined with variables like internal disruption before we are able to predict whether a nation is prone to war.

Although considerably more difficult to compare, because the analyses are so different, the results reported by Choucri and North (1975) appear to provide yet another clue. Looking at the major countries (Britain, France, Germany, Italy, Russia, Austria) involved in World War I, these researchers examined the thirty-five-year-period from 1871 to 1914. They present a model composed of a series of simultaneous equations that link a variety of variables, through various paths, to violent behavior. This system of simultaneous equations is fitted to each of the six countries separately. Since the results do in fact differ from case to case, it is somewhat difficult to draw general conclusions. Furthermore, violence is not directly linked in the model to variables comparable to those seen in the three preceding studies. Nevertheless, there are cases in which the variables "population density" and "national income per capita" do affect violence indirectly by affecting colonial area, military expenditures, and alliances. Thus, whereas Rummel found no relationships between measures like population density and international violence, Choucri and North suggest that such links can be found if indirect relationships are postulated and examined through time.

ANOTHER PERSPECTIVE ON THE NATION–STATE PUZZLE

Let us move now from this corner of the puzzle to a different corner. Another intriguing observation about international violence is the consistent correlation found between defense expenditures and international violence. Such a result might appear trivial until one considers the implications with respect to deterrence theory or the typical arguments made in favor of defense expenditures. If increases in defense expenditures are positively correlated with an increase in war participation, then the path to peace is surely disarmament. This would seem to be the implication of a large number of studies. Choucri and North (1975) find a relationship between defense expenditure and violence, both directly and indirectly through the medium of alliances, for almost all of their six cases. In Rummel's study of 235 variables (1968) a variety of indicators of defense expenditures (defense expenditures relative to population, government expenditures and GNP, and size of military) all have significant correlations in the range of .35 with at least one of three violence variables. Similar results are obtained by M. Haas (1974). In addition, Naroll's (1969) study of 2,000 years of history allows him to conclude that "armament tends to make war more likely," and Richardson's analyses of the cost of defense per population and the number killed in wars produced a significant, though rather low, correlation. Further, Weede (1970) finds a significant correlation of .47 over fifty-nine nations (1955–1960) between violent foreign conflict and a variable combining military personnel per population and defense expenditures as a proportion of GNP. It will be recalled that in the Stuckey-Singer analysis (1973) the military-industrial index was found to be positively related to a nation's war behavior. Sylvan (1976) examined fifteen Asian countries between 1956 and 1970 using a quasi-experimental design. Countries were divided into experimental and control groups on the basis of the amount of external military aid each received relative to military expenditures. The experimental group consisted of those nations in which this ratio exceeded one, the control group was composed of those in which the ratio was less than one. Sylvan constructed an index that compared a variety of cooperative actions with conflictful behaviors, one component of conflict behavior being international violence. Plotting this ratio through time, he is able to show that following military assistance, the experimental group evidences a sharp increase in its conflictful behavior when contrasted with the control group. Newcombe (1969, 1973) suggests that a relationship exists between a "tension" ratio and the frequency of war. The tension ratio is constructed by comparing actual defense expenditures with "predicted" defense expenditures, where the latter are determined from a regression of defense expenditures on GNP. Thus the tension ratio indicates whether a nation is over- or underdefensive when compared to all nations in the system. Finally, Wallace (1977) shows that serious disputes between nations engaged in an arms race have a significantly greater probability of resulting in all-out war than those exhibiting more normal patterns of competition.

In short, we have a set of results over a variety of time periods and nations that consistently indicate that the more armaments the greater the likelihood that a nation will behave violently. But what do these results say with respect to our previous analysis? With respect to our previous categorizations of slow- and fast-changing variables, one might argue that defense expenditures fit the latter category, that is, they resemble the variable "internal disruption" more than the variable "geographical size." Yet unlike the other "fast-changing" variables that have been examined, defense expenditures are *responses* to environmental conditions. Nations usually arm not as a function of internal problems (though there are obviously some conditions under which this occurs) but in response to what is happening externally. Indeed, recent studies of arms races largely support this stimulus–response supposition (see Rattinger 1975, 1976; Hollist 1977a, 1977b; Zinnes and Gillespie 1973). Consequently, the observed relationship between defense expenditure indices and international violence could be a clue pointing in a different direction: perhaps we have focused too narrowly on the attributes of nations and have ignored too long the environmental conditions that surround nations. Perhaps countries that have been involved in wars most frequently are situated in very special environments. The question then is not what attributes make a nation violence-prone, but what environmental circumstances provoke violent behavior.

There is another piece of evidence that directs our attention to the environment. The most striking results in the Rummel (1963) and Tanter (1966) analyses are the highly significant correlations, in both data sets, among measures of foreign conflict behavior. Thus both Rummel and Tanter find strong correlations between such measures as threats, accusations, diplomatic protests, severance of diplomatic relations, and the three measures of international violence (r's in the .6 range). This suggests that when nations react with violent behavior, such reactions are accompanied by a variety of other forms of hostile behavior which also reflect environmental provocation. Since it seems unlikely that a nation would threaten or protest in the absence of changes in its environment, the implication is strong that violence is a reaction, a response to external stimuli.

One might speculate, on the contrary, that the Rummel-Tanter foreign conflict measures are simply indicators of internally generated behavior, unrelated to external provocations. The fact that other measures of foreign conflict behavior correlate with frequency of war or military actions might simply be an indication that a nation is consistent in generating belligerent kinds of foreign policy. But empirically this is not the case, as can be seen in a study by Terrell (1972). Examining seventy-five countries for the period of 1955–1960, Terrell factor-analyzes eighteen variables measuring different facets of international involvement and obtains four factors which he interprets as political (number of embassies in other countries, number of treaties, number of memberships in international organizations [IOs], number of representatives at United Nations), economic (exports/GNP, trade/GNP), social (visitors/population, foreign mail/population), and military (number military treaties/total treaties, military aid from United States). Correlating factor scores on these four dimensions with the Rummel "war" dimension, Terrell finds that none of the correlations are greater than .28—though the economic and social factors do produce significant negative correlations. Thus it would appear that a difference does exist between those behavioral variables reviewed above that measure a form of *interaction* with the environment, and Terrell's variables which might be considered as simply measuring externally directed behavior (for instance, the number of embassies, or representatives at the United Nations).

Thus we have two pieces of evidence: significant correlations between international violence on the one hand and defense expenditures and other forms of hostile behavior on the other. Are there other indications that international violence is a function of external stimuli? Surprisingly, there are rather few empirical studies of hostile interactions involving violence.

However, there is one of direct relevance and three others that shed some light in this direction.

Although Milstein's (1972) principal interest was in tracing the impact of American and Soviet influence on the Arab-Israeli conflict, his initial analyses provide us with some important information about interaction patterns with respect to violence. Milstein examines the period between 1948 and 1969, using a content analysis of newspapers to count the number of weeks each side engaged in various types of violent actions (encounters between government forces, encounters between guerrilla forces, attacks on civilians, attacks on installations, mobilizations, troop movements, declarations of emergencies, alerts). He then correlates the activities of each of the Arab countries (Egypt, Jordan, Iraq, Saudi Arabia, Syria, and Lebanon) with Israel within each action type and for different time lags. For example, he correlates Egypt's attacks on Israeli civilians with Israel's attacks on Egypt's civilians. Not all pairs of countries for all action types produce high correlations, but encounters between government forces and guerrilla encounters produce consistently high r's (between .56 and .82) between Egypt and Israel and between Jordan and Israel.

The evidence from the other studies is less direct, though these studies do imply that violence is at least in part a function of interactions between nations. Richardson (1960b) constructs a histogram showing how many dyads of nations had how many years of peace. Inspection of this histogram shows it to be monotonically decreasing, almost as if it could be described by a geometric progression. Richardson concludes from this histogram that "this decreasing frequency of retaliations . . . as the interval of peace increased is what we should expect if a slow process of forgetting and forgiving went on" (Richardson 1960b: 200). Or to state it somewhat differently: the longer peace exists between two enemies, the less likely they will fight each other again.

In another analysis, Richardson compares allies and enemies across the two world wars and finds that if two nations fought against one another in the first war, they were more likely to fight each other in the second. This result was also confirmed by Starr (1974) in a more extended analysis of the changes between friendship and enmity across successive wars: those who were enemies before had a greater probability of being enemies in a subsequent war.

Thus the environment and, more specifically, the inputs and provocations from the environment are important in shaping and determining the violent behavior of nations. But to this point we have been considering the environment as a stimulus or pinprick that forces a nation to respond. However, the environment could shape the behavior of a nation in a more passive way. Are there any studies that examine the impact of external environmental conditions on violent behavior?

A series of studies sheds some light on the relevance of external conditions by focusing on the relationship between borders and international conflict. While one might argue that borders, like geographical size or GNP, are an attribute of a state, borders are unlike other attributes because they signify contact with the external environment. In an initial study done by Richardson (1960a) the number of wars experienced by thirty-three states was correlated with the number of bordering foreign states. A statistically significant $r = .77$ was obtained. This result was later confirmed by Midlarsky (1975) when he correlated the log of the number of borders of each of the nonisland nation central powers (as reported by Richardson) with the number of wars in which each participated from 1820 to 1945 (using the Correlates of War data): $r = .84$. These findings are supported by a study by Weede (1970) in which contiguity in a dyad and violent conflict between the members of the dyad correlated .48 (N = 59, for 1955–1960).

In a considerably more extensive project, Starr and Most (1976) collected data on national borders between 1946 and 1965, paying special attention to the definition of an international border and to classifying types of borders. Correlating the total number of borders with the number of new war participations over different data sets (using Correlates of War and Stockholm International Peace Research data), these researchers obtained results comparable to those reported by Richardson and Midlarsky. However, in their second study Starr and Most (1977) point out that the strength of the correlation coefficient is affected by changing the time period over which the data are aggregated and by taking into account the type of border. An important conclusion is that during this postwar period, colonial borders had a stronger relationship with new war participations than did other types of borders. A second analysis is also of interest. Examination of the transition from peace to war over a five-year period showed that if a nation had a warring nation on its border, its chances of moving from peace to war during the five years was enhanced.

While not directly examining the impact of borders, Garnham (1976a) explores a related hypothesis: "War is more probable between relatively proximate pairs of nation-states and less probable between relatively distant pairs." Looking at all dyadic wars (wars involving only two nations) between 1816 and 1965, Garnham compared the distance between the nation–state capitals of these belligerents with the distance between capitals for comparable pairs of nonbelligerent states. The nonbelligerent dyads were matched with the belligerent dyads on the basis of population to make the two sets of dyads (belligerent and nonbelligerent) comparable. The analysis showed that the belligerent dyads were more likely to be proximate than comparable nonbelligerent pairs.

Finally, in a very different type of analysis, Wesley (1969) suggests that numbers of borders might be a very imprecise measure of geographical contact or opportunity for war. Therefore, he proposes the use of the length of frontiers measured in population units (his measure of geographical opportunity for war is a combination of frontier length and population size). He argues that war dead are generated at a rate proportional to geographical opportunity and shows, using Richardson's data on wars from 1820 to 1945, that with a proper choice of constants, the geographical opportunity index provides a very accurate prediction of the number of war dead.

These studies suggest that the environment has an important bearing on the violent behavior of nations: border contact with other nations increases a nation's chances of becoming violent, having a warring nation on one's border enhances a nation's inclination to violence, proximity increases the probability that two nations will fight (familiarity breeds contempt?), and proximity in combination with population determines war casualties. In short, contact and contiguity appear to be relevant factors in predicting international violence. Are there other environmental factors of relevance? Three studies have examined the importance of relative power as a factor in determining violence. In the first of these, already cited above (Garnham 1976a), the relative power of belligerent nation pairs in dyadic wars is compared with the relative power of nonbelligerent nation pairs, using four different power indicators. Garnham finds that when power is measured using population, it is more likely that equally powerful nations will fight than nations of disparate power. For the remaining three power indicators—geographical size, fuel consumption, and steel production—he finds that nonwar dyads are "as similar or more similar than the war dyads," that is, nations equal in power along these dimensions are not more likely to engage in war.

While the remaining two studies are also concerned with power relationships between belligerent nations, they combine this interest with a study of contiguity. Weede (1976) focuses specifically on Asian countries for the period between 1950–1969. He forms all possible dyads between these countries, separating those dyads that are contiguous and adding to these contiguous dyads all other contiguous dyads involving one Asian and one non-Asian country. Weede's interest lies in the power relationship between contiguous dyads: is a contiguous dyad involving one nation with overwhelming power more or less likely to become involved in a war than a contiguous dyad in which the two nations are equal in power? A nation with preponderant power is defined as one having ten times the GNP of another nation. Weede shows through a variety of analyses that war is considerably less likely in the presence of preponderant power.

These results are supported by a very similar study done by Garnham (1976b). Although the basic question posed by Garnham is almost identical to that posed by Weede, the research design is different. Garnham selects his cases for analysis by considering all states that experienced lethal international violence during the period 1969–1973. He finds sixteen conflicts involving twenty-four nations. For each of the twenty-four nations he identifies all contiguous states. Thus he has, in effect, sixteen cases of contiguous states that engaged in violence. By examining borders, he finds another sixty-two contiguous dyads which did not engage in violence. The question then is whether a difference can be found between these two sets of dyads on the basis of power differences. Garnham proposes six different variables to measure power: geographical area, population, GNP, kilowatt-hours, military manpower, and defense expenditures. Using both pattern recognition and discriminate function analysis, he finds that violent conflict is more likely between contiguous nation states having approximately equal power.

Thus these two studies not only confirm the importance of the external environment, they imply that amount of contact should be considered in conjunction with the quality of the contact. If a tiny nation is surrounded by five large nations, that is, shares frontiers with five other countries, the Richardson analysis would suggest that this nation has a high propensity to go to war. But the Weede and Garnham studies temper this prediction by suggesting that the relative powers of the contiguous neighbors will make this tiny nation less prone to violence. Of course, the interesting and as yet unanswered question is how these variables interact to shape violent conflict: what is the interrelationship between frontiers, contiguity, power, and international violence?

This ends the construction of the first, "nation–state" puzzle. The picture is far from complete but we have run out of pieces. While there are undoubtedly studies that we have missed, the above construction includes most of what currently exists in the published literature. Seen from the nation–state perspective, the contours of the puzzle look somewhat as follows. Neither slow-changing nor fast-changing attributes of nations by themselves appear to be directly related to a nation's war behavior. When considered in combination, however, these attributes can predict some violent behavior of nations. But looking at the puzzle from a different corner we have seen even stronger evidence to suggest that the environment is a critical ingredient for understanding the violent activities of states. The considerable array of studies that link defense expenditures to war behavior, combined with the number of studies that show a relationship between provocations from other states, proximity, and power differentials strongly argue for a greater concentration in future research on the environmental determinants of international violence.

Having gone as far as is possible at the nation–state level, we shift our focus to the systemic puzzle. Perhaps there is only one puzzle, but I will begin with the simpler assumption that there are two puzzles. We will want to bear in mind the results obtained for the nation-state puzzle: are there comparable patterns at the systemic level?

THE SYSTEMIC PUZZLE

The systemic studies to be considered are based on aggregations of the attributes and behaviors of nations in the international system for specified periods of time. For example, a typical systemic study might develop an annually measured index of polarity, based on the number and patterns of alliances in the world, and correlate this time-series variable with the number of wars occurring each year. Two observations: first, few studies examine international violence at the systemic level, compared to the number of studies at the nation-state level. Second, most of the systemic studies have been done by individuals associated with the Correlates of War (COW) project directed by J. David Singer. Thus this part of the review will be briefer and will be mainly devoted to COW-related papers.

Our investigation of the nation–state puzzle led to an initial consideration of national attributes that might be responsible for warlike behavior. With few exceptions, we were unable to find any relationships. Thus an obvious query at the systemic level is whether a similar pattern exists: are there relationships between certain systemic configurations and the amount or characteristics of war within the system? As was true with the nation–state puzzle, this question can be examined in terms of two types of attributes, systemic attributes that change relatively slowly and those that change rapidly.

The most salient slow-changing attributes examined within the context of the nation–state puzzle were indices of the capability or "power" of nations. The comparable systemic attributes would be the distributions of such capabilities across system members. Two sets of studies are relevant. The first set, composed of two articles, traces the impact of distribution capability indices, that reflect the degree of dispersion or concentration of power within the system. Singer, Bremer, and Stuckey (1972) construct an index designated CON which was designed to capture the extent to which the six capability dimensions treated in other COW studies are disproportionately distributed among the system's members.[7] The correlation between CON and nation-months spent in warfare for the total span of years examined, 1820–1965, is very low, but they find a high $r = .81$ for the nineteenth century. Thus for the nineteenth century it appears that the more concentrated the capabilities, the greater the amount of warfare. Subsequent multiple correlations, involving, in addition to CON, changes in CON and another distributional index, confirm that CON is the strongest correlate of the nation-months-of-war measure. The second article (Wallace 1972b) examines the relationship between changes in total population and military personnel as the capability indices, and battle deaths as a measure of the dependent variable, "war." Wallace's study shows that if capability distribution is measured in terms of the standard deviation of the distribution of change in either total population or military personnel, there are essentially no correlations between these measures and battle-connected deaths, regardless of the period examined.

The second set of studies focuses on capabilities in an indirect fashion. The four studies in this group examine the relationship between the distribution of "status inconsistency" throughout the system and various measures of the amount of war in the system. The measures of status inconsistency, as was true in the case of the nation–state discussion, are constructed by making comparisons between capability measures and a nation's diplomatic score (the number of embassies established within that state), and then summing over all nations to produce a systemic indicator of status inconsistency. In the first of these studies, Wallace (1971) computes rank-order correlations between each of four status inconsistency measures (total population, urban population, military personnel, and iron and steel production, each compared with the diplomatic score) and two "war" measures, battle deaths and nation-months. The correlations, calculated for various historical periods and four different lags (no lag, five years, ten years, and fifteen years), are generally low but they strengthen as the lags are increased. The best correlations are obtained for the fifteen-year lag condition and for those status inconsistency measures using total population and military personnel. These correlations range from .3 to .53. In the second study Wallace (1972b) uses Pearson product-moment correlations and finds that the correlations with status inconsistency as measured by total population and military personnel (the two better indicators in the previous study), produce correlations with battle deaths in the range of about .45, without lags.[8]

In the third study Wallace (1973b) gives the Pearson correlations between the two measures of war (battle deaths and nation-months) and the four measures of status inconsistency used in the first study, for all the different lag conditions and for the various historical periods. As one might anticipate, the results for the no-lag condition are identical with those seen in the second article, that is, correlations of reasonably high magnitude (in the range of .45) are obtained for status inconsistency and battle deaths under the no-lag condition for the entire historical period. However, it is also the case that one of the findings of the first study is supported in this analysis: as the lags are increased, is it generally the case that the correlations increase, and the best results are obtained for the fifteen-year lags.

Taken together, these studies suggest that as status inconsistency increases within the international system, the amount of war in the system, as measured by battle deaths and nation-months, subsequently increases. These results gain additional support from a study done by East (1972). East uses the Spearman rho between GNP and diplomatic status, and between defense expenditures and diplomatic status, to obtain two indicators of systemic status inconsistency. The larger the value of a positive rho, the less status-discrepant the system. Thus East predicts that international violence will be inversely correlated with the value of the Spearman rho. Using two different measures of international violence, one obtained from COW and the other from the Office of Naval Research, East finds significant Pearson correlation values for the period of 1948–1964. Using the COW data, he finds correlations in the range of $-.3$ to $-.48$ (depending on the different ways in which the diplomatic indicator or the violence indicators are aggregated). The results for the ONR data are more diverse, ranging from essentially no correlation to correlations of $-.7$ depending on the type of aggregation procedure used.

In general, then, systemic status inconsistency appears to be a better predictor of the amount of systemic war than simple indicators of capability distribution. Furthermore, unlike the nation–state puzzle, status inconsistency at the systemic level seems to bear a significant relationship to systemic war. This conclusion can perhaps be seen more clearly by looking at Table 8–1, which provides a comparative summary of the studies. The columns of the table give the different measures of war used and the typical time segments used in the analyses, though it should be noted that studies differ in how the nineteenth and twentieth centuries are distinguished. The slash between the two numbers given for the Wallace studies indicates the no-lag and fifteen-year lag conditions, respectively. The results are not overwhelming but a comparison of the capability measures with the status inconsistency measures, particularly under the fifteen-year lag condition, suggests that the latter is a somewhat better predictor of war though this clearly depends on the measure of status inconsistency chosen and the time period examined.

We turn next to the second type of systemic attributes—attributes that arguably change more rapidly with time. The principal "rapidly changing attribute" that has been examined at the systemic level is alliance structure, as seen from three different perspectives: (1) simple measures of alliance aggregation (number of nations in types of alliances); (2) polarity indices that measure the extent of systemic cleavage; and (3) a measure of membership in international organizations. A comparison of the results of these studies is provided in Table 8–2. The columns give the three main measures of "war" and the various time segments, while the rows group together studies on the basis of the three different perspectives on alliance structure: aggregation, polarity, and membership in international organizations (IOs). The reader should note that the measurement of independent variables differs among studies, especially for polarity.

A perusal of the table with respect to alliance aggregation shows that it is a good predictor only of nation-months of war and battle deaths for the twentieth century. The results for polarity are considerably more difficult

TABLE 8–1. Distribution of Capabilities in the International System as Predictors of War

Measures of Distribution of Capabilities	War Frequency, 20th century	Nation-Months of War			Battle Deaths		
		Total	19th century	20th century	Total	19th century	20th century
Capabilities							
Singer, Bremer, Stuckey (1972)							
power concentration index (CON)		–.10	.81	–.23			
Δpower concentration index (ΔCON)		–.38	.19	–.41			
nation ranking index (MOVE)		.34	.19	–.41			
Wallace (1972)							
σΔtotal population					.11		.34 (1850–1964)
σΔmilitary personnel					.16		.18

Status Inconsistency

Wallace (1972, 1973)

total population v. DS	.31/.53	.16/.63	.46/.43	.28/.36
urban population v. DS	.22/.37	−.13/.34	.34/.27	.05/.14
military personnel v. DS	.37/.39	.31/.53	.45/.28	.37/.15
iron/steel production v. DS	.00/.53	−.28/.12	.05/.42	−.29/−.02
Δtotal population v. DS	−.06/.07	−.25/−.11	.10/.02	−.12/−.12
Δurban population v. DS	.14/.47	−.07/.17	.03/.18	−.07/−.12
Δmilitary personnel v. DS	.27/.16	.10/−.26	.17/.25	.20/−.09
Δiron/steel production v. DS	.08/.67	−.20/.58	.16/.50	−.12/.48

East (1972)

$\rho_{GNP \text{ v. } DS}$ −.482 (.299)

$\rho_{defense\ expenditure \text{ v. } DS}$ −.464 (−.703)

NOTE: Δ = rate of change in   DS = diplomacy score   All values shown are Pearson product-moment correlations; significance levels are not reported by the authors. The Wallace (1971) study, cited in the text, is not included because the analysis was somewhat different. See text for further elaboration.

TABLE 8–2. Alliance Aggregation, Polarity, and IO Memberships as Predictors of War

	Measures of Warfare								
	War Frequency			Nation-Months of War			Battle Deaths		
	Total	19th century	20th century	Total	19th century	20th century	Total	19th century	20th century
Alliance Aggregation									
Singer and Small (1968) percent all nations in any alliance	.07 (.19)	-.00 (-.05)	.18 (.25)	.30 (.33)	-.16 (-.19)	.53 (.45)	.34 (.35)	-.27 (-.45)	.56 (.50)
Wallace (1972) alliance aggregation				.32					.34 (1850–1964)
Polarity									
Singer and Small (1968) bipolarity	.01 (.16)	-.12 (-.06)	.26 (.02)	.13 (.16)	-.23 (-.14)	.28 (.27)	.19 (.18)	-.28 (-.30)	.31 (.32)
Wallace (1973) bipolarity (weighted) interstate				-.30	-.15	-.35	-.41	-.28	-.46

Wallace (1973)						
cross-cutting	−.31	−.06	−.38	−.39	−.10	−.43
Bueno de Mesquita (1975)						
bipolarity	.32					
Δbipolarity	.52					
tightness	.11					
Δtightness	.73					
Haas (1974: 378)						
percent of poles .58	.26 (.60)					
Organization Membership						
Singer and Wallace (1970)						
number of IO's −.06	.26			.22		
simple memberships −.08	.23			.20		
weighted memberships −.07	.27			.23		
percent change in weighted memberships −.19	−.04			.03		

NOTE: Values in parentheses are for the central system. Authors do not report significance levels.

to summarize in a meaningful fashion. The contradictory results in this section indicate that the different measures being used do not all reflect comparable aspects of systemic polarity. For example, Singer and Small's (1968) bipolarity index has almost no predictive power with respect to the frequency of war in the system yet M. Haas (1974) finds a respectable correlation between the number of poles and war frequency. The picture is even more confusing in the second and third columns. If we compare the nation-months-of-war measure for the total period, we find that Singer and Small (1968), Bueno de Mesquita (1975a), and M. Haas (1974) obtain positive correlations, albeit of different magnitudes, whereas Wallace's (1973) bipolarity and cross-cutting measures produce negative correlations. A similar contrast between Singer and Small (1968) and Wallace (1973) is seen for the battle deaths measure. These tantalizing contrasts preclude the drawing of conclusions and strongly suggest the need for a careful examination and comparison of the different measures used, an analysis beyond the scope of this chapter. Such an analysis should probably also take into account the fact that the largest correlations in Table 8–2 are obtained by Bueno de Mesquita's indicators of bipolarity change. It is particularily intriguing to find that whereas Bueno de Mesquita's index of the tightness of poles has a very weak correlation with war months, changes in this same index produce the strongest correlation in the table.

Finally, it should be noted that Wallace's (1973) study includes a set of analyses not shown in Table 8–2. At the conclusion of his article Wallace presents a series of curvilinear regressions. For the total period examined the r^2 (not r) values jump to .61 and .77, allowing Wallace to conclude that war is more probable both at very low and at very high levels of polarization, while the chances of war are minimized when the alliance configuration is moderately polarized. While one might want to quibble with the translation of the war measures into "probability of war," the results are certainly intriguing.

The last set of analyses in Table 8–2, those concerned with IO membership, are more clear-cut, if less exciting. Singer and Wallace's (1970) results indicate that IO membership has little to do with war activity. Interestingly, these authors find that if the correlations are lagged in reverse, so that war becomes the independent variable, considerably better relationships are obtained. However, our focus on the causes rather than consequences of war places these analyses outside of the present puzzle.

The pieces of the systemic puzzle are few and ambiguous. The indices of capability distribution are generally poor predictors of the amount of international violence in the system and yet indices of systemic status inconsistency, which contain capability measures, do predict, under certain conditions, some aspects of international violence. It is still more perplexing to recall that status inconsistency measures at the nation–state level were typically inconsequential in predicting the violent behavior of nations. Why should aggregate measures have greater predictive power than the nation–state measures? The results pertaining to alliance structure are even more confusing. Only under very special conditions are any reasonable correlations obtained between alliances and amounts of war. More significantly, exceedingly discrepant results are found for different measures of systemic polarity—discrepant not only in terms of magnitude but also of direction. One can only conclude that the systemic picture, in contrast to the nation–state puzzle, is blurred and sketchy.

CONCLUSION: WAS RAPOPORT RIGHT?

So what can we say on the basis of this review? First, it is clear from the two partially constructed pictures that it is too early to draw conclusions about one versus two puzzles. In fact, the contradictory results obtained for the status inconsistency measures from the nation–state to the systemic puzzle implies that for the time being two puzzles are required. Second, it is also obvious that the systemic puzzle is far and away the greater mystery of the two. Indeed, it is difficult to draw any meaningful conclusions about the systemic puzzle at this stage of research.

On the other hand, the nation-state puzzle has begun to take shape. This partially completed puzzle suggests that no single attribute makes a nation prone to war. However, a combination of two general types of variables—those that change slowly (governmental structure, level of development, amount of resources) and fast-changing ones (unemployment, civil strife, suicide rates)—does seem to discriminate between nations that become heavily involved in war and those that do not. If we combine measures of internal strife with such factors as governmental structure and population diversity, we begin to be able to predict international violence. Perhaps of greater significance, the nation–state puzzle has shown that we must not become obsessed with attributes of nations to the exclusion of environmental factors. We must take account of the fact that nations react to inputs from an external environment. Analyses of defense expenditures and other aspects of hostile foreign behavior, reinforced by an analysis of the violent interactions of nations in the Middle East conflict, indicate that the violent behavior of a nation is related to the stimuli it receives. We must think more generally of the external conditions that surround a nation and constrain or make more plausible the use of warfare. Contiguity and power relationships clearly are conditions of this sort and the results thus far suggest that these have a decided impact on violence.

Our conclusions are far from earth-shaking. Even at the nation–state level the mystery is a long way from being solved. Indeed, we seem to have two distinct parts of a puzzle that obviously do not fit together—attributes and environment. Thus in one sense we have not been successful in answering Rapoport's challenge. We cannot say that there is overwhelming evidence to suggest that x and y predict z. On the other hand, the situation is not as bleak as Rapoport and others might lead us to believe. Perhaps the most encouraging conclusion of this review is that it is possible to construct at least a partial picture: a number of the pieces *do* fit together. We are not working in a vacuum, producing studies that have no relationship to one another. It is intriguing and encouraging to discover that despite some problems of noncomparability in measurement, methods, and occasionally in results, it is nevertheless possible to see an accumulation of reinforcing results.

My answer to Rapoport then is that while we surely do not have laws, the empirical findings that have been produced, and are being produced, appear to be moving us slowly toward lawlike generalizations.

NOTES

1. It should be noted that the definition of internation violence differs from study to study and that our examination will incorporate all levels of violence from border clashes to major wars.

2. Throughout this discussion we will require that $r \leq .3$ and/or be statistically significant in order to draw any conclusion about support for a hypothesis. If $r = .3$, then $r^2 = .09$, that is, the amount of variance explained is roughly 10 percent. This would seem to be a minimal criterion for concluding that a hypothesis is supported.

3. The exceptions include number of marriages per population, length of railroad tracks, and number of foreign students in a country. Each of these variables correlates significantly, $r \leq .3$, with wars. However, it is difficult to interpret these results.

4. See Bueno de Mesquita, Chapter 9 of this *Handbook*, for a discussion of status inconsistency theory.

5. Although the Haas, Ray, and Gochman studies do raise questions about the validity of using Pearson-product correlations in time-series data, the correspondence between these results and those found in the other studies seems to suggest that if the latter analyses were redone with proper corrections, the results probably would not be dramatically different.

6. For a full review of these and related studies, see Chapter 7 in this *Handbook*.

7. This measure is comparable to a GINI index of inequality but avoids some of the disadvantages of GINI.

8. The puzzling discrepancy between the results of the two studies—the weak rank-order correlations for the zero-lag condition in the first study and the reasonably high Pearson product-moment correlation in the second study—could be attributed to the use of somewhat different aggregation procedures which are not entirely clear from the articles, or possibly to the different correlation procedures used.

CHAPTER 9

Theories of International Conflict: An Analysis and an Appraisal

Bruce Bueno de Mesquita

DESPITE THE EFFORTS OF SUCH INTELLECTUAL GIANTS as Kant, Spinoza, Rousseau, and others, we know little more about the general sources of international conflict today than was known to Thucydides more than two millennia ago. The failure to identify a generally accepted theory of international conflict has led some to conclude that scientific explanations of such conflicts are not possible (Aron 1960, Rapoport 1976). The empirical record does not provide much encouragement for those who reject that conclusion. Still, I assume—as an article of faith—that international conflict is susceptible to rigorous, scientific theorizing. In the pages that follow I will try to clarify what is meant by scientific theorizing, and I will then apply that meaning to a portion of the contemporary literature concerned with international conflict, especially in the form of war.

Among the issues I focus on are the functions of deduction and induction in research on international conflict, the general failure to establish criteria for falsification or verification of theories and their attendant propositions, and the general tenacity with which we continue to cling to ideas despite repeated demonstrations that they are based on flawed logic or are inconsistent with the events they are alleged to explain. I include a rather lengthy discussion of Arrow's impossibility theorem—a subject

NOTE: I wish to thank Bruce Berkowitz, Ted Robert Gurr, Chung Hsiou Huang, Jacek Kugler, Philip Schrodt, Walter Petersen, and Dina A. Zinnes for their many insightful comments on earlier drafts. Of course I accept full responsibility for any errors.

almost never dealt with by students of international conflict—because Arrow's theorem draws our attention to the potential pitfalls of treating such social aggregates as nations as if they are purposive, unitary actors. In particular, Arrow's research on social choice highlights the importance of making explicit the particular assumptions one uses, especially when treating nations as goal-seeking actors.

After delineating my criteria for theory building, I examine some of the most prominent themes concerned with international conflict, including the balance-of-power theory, the power transition theory, theories of polarity, status inconsistency, arms races, deterrence, and the linkage between domestic and foreign violence. Two important themes are not discussed. The extensive literature on imperialism and international conflict is left out because others—most recently, Waltz (1975)—have dealt with its theoretical shortcomings in an exceptionally clear manner. The increasingly significant literature on dependency and international conflict is excluded because the nonideological, serious exploration of its central propositions is in its infancy.

THEORY, METHOD, AND DATA: THE RESEARCHERS' TRILOGY

Although a generally acceptable theory (or theories) of conflict is yet to be found, one should not conclude that all the research in this field has taken us nowhere. The largely inductive orientation of most international relations research of the past thirty years, reviewed by Zinnes in Chapter 8 of this *Handbook*, has yielded many potentially important hypotheses, while the recent trend toward more deductive research is providing the foundation to assess the logical plausibility of many hypotheses. Indeed, for those willing to accept logical inconsistency as the grounds on which a theory— or explanation of relations among variables—may be falsified, researchers have provided sufficient information to falsify a very large body of would-be theories. Unfortunately, the urge for positive findings has led to inadequate assessments of the internal, logical structure of the "theories" from which many prevalent hypotheses might be derived. Furthermore, even where substantial empirical, as well as logical, evidence has been amassed to cast grave doubts upon a hypothesis, there is a tendency to cling tenaciously to the belief that the hypothesis can somehow be salvaged. Indeed, some "theories"—such as the balance of power—survive despite their seemingly fatal flaws. Claude (1962), for instance, notes the many mutually incompatible meanings given the balance of power in the writings of a single individual, while Riker (1962) identifies logical inconsistencies among a set of six widely accepted rules (proposed by Kaplan 1957) that are supposed to lead to a balance of power. There seems even to be confusion as to what could, in principle, be falsifying evidence. This should alarm us as researchers since it implies that we lack accepted standards for assessing research. It should also alarm us as citizens since some of our hypotheses, especially those from the balance-of-power "theory," are frequently cited by policy makers as the justification or rationale for their behavior. If the hypotheses of balance-of-power theorists are internally inconsistent, and hence incapable of derivation from their assumptions, then policies based on the balance of power are not likely to lead systematically to the outcomes that one expects.

What might be a reasonable set of standards for falsification? The question is almost rhetorical. As a philosophical or epistemological question, there is probably very little disagreement among students of international conflict. As a behavioral question, on the other hand, differences seem to abound. At least one possible source of confusion revolves around the notions of falsification and verification. Waltz (1975), using theory to mean the explanation of relations among variables—exactly the meaning I am using—says: "Theories, though not divorced from the world of experiment and observation, are only indirectly connected with it. Thus the well-known statement that theories can never be proved true." Yet, theories must either be logically true or logically false. And at least in principle, we can know with certainty which of these conditions obtains. The truth of a theory resides in whether or not its conclusions (that is, theorems) can be arrived at without faulty logic. *If a deduction follows logically from a set of assumptions then that deduction is necessarily true under the precise conditions assumed in the theory.* The truthfulness of the deduced relationship among variables, given the assumptions of the theory, is not an empirical question. Consequently, the deduction need not be subject to empirical evaluation to determine its truthfulness. But when one studies data that approximate, but do not comply precisely, with the assumptions of one's theories, then empiricism becomes crucial. For *it is only by observation that one can determine whether a theory's generalizations are useful explanations of reality.*

The purpose of theory, of course, is not to replicate reality, but rather to provide an explanation of real events. Axioms and assumptions provide a basis for simplifying and organizing reality by delineating the precise conditions about which one is theorizing. As such, it is as inappropriate to speak of assumptions being true or false as it is to speak about a theory being empirically (as apposed to logically) true or false. Assumptions, like the theories based on them, are neither! Assumptions define the constrained conditions under which the subsequent deductions—if made correctly—are necessarily true.[1] Since reality is rarely, if ever, as simple or as organized as a theory, the theorist's problem is to arrive at deductions that are based on sufficiently "realistic" assumptions so that his/her deductions explain a significant class of "real world" events. The empiricist's problem is to construct tests that approximate as closely as possible the requirements of the theory, without excluding so many events of interest as to make the theory trivial. It is, in my estimation, the purpose of empirical tests to determine if a theory, though logically true, is informative or trivial. Thus a theory with antecedent conditions that are not even approximated in reality—or that are actually incompatible with reality—may be logically true, but it is useless as an explanation of relationships between variables in reality. The degree to which the constraining assumptions of a theory are helpful in explaining reality is, of course, a subjective issue which must be resolved by each researcher. Still, certain lessons can be extracted from a consideration of the nexus between theory and reality. The most relevant of those lessons for this chapter concerns the connections between theory, method, and data.

Data provide the facts, or summary of reality, that theories attempt to explain. Method provides the analytic tools by which one evaluates the extent to which reality conforms to the expectations of one's theories. That is, method applied to data allows one to ascertain if a theory, though logically true, is trivial. Before that evaluation can be made, however, the researcher must have selected the appropriate data and method for evaluating the usefulness of his or her theory. And those selections are dictated by the requirements of the theory. This is a point that, though seemingly obvious, has been obscured during the past two decades of research on international conflicts.

At least since the 1950s, students of conflict have debated the merits of quantification and nonquantification. The debate has largely centered on whether quantification or nonquantification provides greater precision, validity, reproduceability, and generalizability. These may, however, be entirely false issues, serving only to distract attention from fundamental theoretical questions. The debate presumes that some methods are inherently superior to others. In fact, since methods are tools for evaluating the empirical usefulness of a theory, their selection must be guided by the requirements and limitations of one's theory (and data). In that sense, nonstatistical case studies are not inherently inferior to the evaluation of a large sample through the use of inferential statistics. Instead, case studies are the preferred method, given certain types of hypotheses, while inferential statistics are preferred for other types of hypotheses. In particular, if one deduces (or simply posits) a hypothesis that identifies either necessary or sufficient conditions, then a single case involving *appropriate data* is all that is needed to reveal either a flaw in the derivation of the hypothesis or the triviality of the theory, given its constraining assumptions (H. Eckstein 1975). Given the common situation in which no case complies precisely with the assumptions of the theory, the evaluation of many cases is preferred to a single case. With many cases, statistical analysis provides an efficient means of evaluating a hypothesis. Other methods may be equally rigorous (or lacking in rigor), but statistical analysis provides two critical advantages. First, statistical analysis is built upon statistical theory. This means that the methodological assumptions of the researcher's analytic technique are completely explicit, thus facilitating our evaluation of the appropriateness of the technique used. Second, inferential statistics, because of its reliance on probability theory, and the attendant restrictions on degrees of freedom, encourages parsimony. Put somewhat differently, quantification insures an explicitness about one's methodology that leaves one open to precise and specific criticism. Less explicit methods—and nonquantitative studies need not be less explicit—encourage confusion and uncertainty about the meaning of findings or about the appropriateness of the tests employed for the question at hand.

Accompanying the potential clarity and explicitness of quantitative methods are some grave pitfalls. The fact that a powerful statistical theory can be marshaled to analyze one's data is not, of course, a substitute for theorizing about the substantive problem one intends to investigate. There is some danger of mistaking the sophistication of a statistical procedure for the elegance of a theory. Some of the applications of factor analysis in the study of international conflict, for instance, have contributed complexity and obscurity rather than parsimony and clarity. Yet even in these cases one should not overlook the inherent advantage of being able to pinpoint precisely how a misused or overinterpreted technique has been abused. The very fact that we can, on occasion, identify the proverbial "garbage in–garbage out" syndrome indicates the critical facility afforded those familiar with statistical theory.

Quantitative analysis often is criticized for the degree to which its adherents test "trivial" questions. The argument is sometimes made that those things that really count can not be counted. Whereas some quantitative research—and nonquantitative research as well—has certainly been "trivial," there is little reason to believe that this is a problem inherent in quantitative analysis. Many applications of statistical techniques have yielded little of consequence, but there appears to be no compelling reason to think that this is a result of the methodology rather than an inadequacy of the methodologist.

ARROW'S PARADOX: CAN WE ASSUME STATES ARE PURPOSIVE ACTORS?

Closely related to the trilogy of theory, method, and data is the selection of the researcher's unit of analysis, and the delineation of assumptions about the factors guiding that unit's behavior (if the unit is treated as a behaving entity). Balance-of-power theorists, for instance, choose the nation–state as their unit of analysis and treat it as if it were a purposive, unitary actor. Yet they do not explain whether the "actor" is everyone in the nation, everyone in the government, all senior decision makers, the head of state, or some other group or individual. Only some of these assumptions are logically compatible with the assumption that the "nation" behaves purposively. Similarly, those who speak of a nation's status inconsistency, or national perceptions of threat arising from the arms procurement policies of an adversary, can treat national behavior as if it is purposive, goal-seeking behavior only if they are willing to make certain explicit and highly restrictive assumptions about the process by which major foreign policy decisions are made. Arrow's impossibility theorem (1951) is the central theoretical contribution to our understanding of the limits that must be imposed if one is to treat any social aggregate as if it is purposive. Consequently, I turn now to an exploration of the impossibility theorem.

Those who choose to view nations as purposive, goal-seeking, unitary actors—and included in this group are all those who study nations as their unit of analysis—implicitly assume that the internal rules of foreign policy decision making contain some meaningful ways of converting the policy preferences of relevant individuals into a responsive national policy. In public choice terms, those who take this position assume that it is always possible to construct a meaningful social welfare function. Yet Arrow's impossibility theorem provides a logical proof that, given a set of reasonable assumptions about decision making, only a decision rule requiring unanimity or dictatorial decision making can be assured of producing purposive decisions that are responsive to the preferences of the relevant set of decision makers. Sen (1970) showed that by altering some of Arrow's conditions it was possible to produce a social choice that was responsive and purposive without restricting decision making to dictatorship or unanimity. Sen's proof depends on restricting the set of socially tenable policy positions to a considerably smaller number than the set of logically possible policy preference orderings.[2]

Arrow's impossibility theorem has been very influential among students of social choice theory, especially as applied to voting behavior. One might conclude from these applications that Arrow's warning—that all rules (except dictatorship or unanimity) for aggregating individual preferences into a social choice are manipulable—is applicable only to formal voting. In fact, Arrow's proof applies to all means of making choices on behalf of a group, hence it is of central relevance for students of foreign policy and international relations. It is applicable to all studies concerned with assessing the national interest or character (Morgenthau 1973), national satisfaction or dissatisfaction (Organski 1968, Organski and Kugler 1980, Garnham 1976b, Weede 1976), national feelings of status inconsistency or relative deprivation (Ray 1979, Gochman 1975, Wallace 1973, Galtung 1964, Gurr 1970b, Midlarsky 1975), and the like. One may object that despite the degree to which international relations scholars committed to the nation–state as their unit of analysis have ignored the problems discussed in the social choice literature, their research has continued uninterrupted.

Yet, even a cursory examination of the empirical record of their research will suggest that very few clear patterns of national behavior have e-merged (see Chapter 8 by Zinnes in this *Handbook*). Why should this be so?

If foreign policy decisions are not made by a dictator, are not un-animous, and are not chosen from among a significantly restricted set of options, then there is no reason to expect them to reflect anything other than the distribution of manipulative skills among the relevant decision makers. Consequently, if we do not assume that one of the three rules for aggregating preferences mentioned above holds, we can not logically assume that the nation is a purposive unitary actor. If we wish to assume the nation is a unitary actor, we should be explicit about our underlying assumptions. Assuming dictatorial decision making leads to very different theoretical expectations from what one would derive by assuming unanim-ity which, in turn, yields expectations different from what Sen calls value and extremal restrictiveness. For instance, the assumption that certain preference orderings are behaviorally unacceptable—though logically pos-sible—greatly reduces one's ability to account for dramatic foreign policy shifts. Yet such shifts might readily be accounted for if one assumes that a gatekeeping "dictator" has final authority for all decisions. Can one ac-count for the American swing toward China in the 1970s and away from Taiwan, or the American swing toward the Soviet Union in the 1940s while at the same time asserting—as might have seemed reasonable to some researchers—that it was politically unacceptable for American leaders to prefer communists to anticommunists? That is, Sen's conditions prevent socially intransitive preference orderings (and the nonsensical policies that may emerge from such intransitivities) at the price of reduc-ing the degree of expected flux in policy. Unanimity as a decision rule prevents social intransitivities in the formation of foreign policy, but at the price of assuming that no decisions are controversial. Anyone who lived through the Vietnam war period knows that American policy was con-troversial even among some of the senior American foreign policy decision makers. Dictatorship too prevents the possibility of nonsensical policies resulting from social intransitivities, but at the price of assuming there are no competing, legitimate centers of foreign policy decision making.

The lesson to be extracted from the above discussion is, I believe, that those who pursue the nation–state (or any other collectivity, including alliances, supranational organizations, and the like) as the key unit of analysis in studying international conflict must be careful to consider the implications of their assumption of attributing purposiveness to national policies. Furthermore, they must be aware that alternative assumptions about the process of decision making can have important logical and behavioral implications for the hypotheses they formulate or test.

When one focuses on individuals and their efforts to translate their own preferences into national policy, then the danger of falling into Arrow's paradox is almost nil. That is not to say that international relations must be or should be studied from the perspective of individuals. As we have seen, given appropriate assumptions, nations, alliances, and systems may be viewed as purposive. Even when such assumptions are unacceptable, such collectivities as nations or alliances are relevant as entities endowed with attributes that may constrain the alternatives open to decision makers. By understanding how such attributes as bipolarity or multipolarity, tightness or looseness of alliances, wealth or poverty, largeness or smallness of nations, and the like affect the feasibility of alternatives, one may learn a great deal about the options that particular decision makers in particular places at particular times can or cannot choose. If one ignores these constraints, proceeding directly to an examination of decision makers, the road toward the elimination of seemingly plausible hypotheses will be a long and arduous one. The careful combination of theorizing about individuals, coupled with theoretical sensitivity to the conditions under which choices are made, seems to me at least to be the most efficient path toward meaningful generalizations about international conflict. With these thoughts in mind, I turn now to an examination of some of the major themes in international relations research. I do so with the awareness that few of these themes satisfy my rather strict requirements for a theory. Perhaps only some of the research on arms races and on deterrence qualify as theories of international conflict by the requirements I have suggested here. Nevertheless, I will examine such topics as the balance-of-power theory, the power transition theory, and others. These subjects represent the principal concerns of students of international conflict. Whenever possible, I will apply my notion of theory to the main hypotheses, propositions, and hunches that emerge from these themes. I hope that exercise will help reveal the strengths and weaknesses in our current understanding of international conflict and will point in one potentially fruitful direction for future research.

BALANCE-OF-POWER THEORIES

Probably the hoariest and most influential attempt at theory-building in international relations concerns the balance of power. Presidents refer to the importance of maintaining the balance of power as a justification for their responses to international crises and demands, journalists cite it as a governing force in the conduct of foreign policy, and scholars attribute changes in the peace and stability of the international system to its ebb and flow. Yet the concept itself is assigned a wide number of meanings, including an equal distribution of power among all nations, an equal distribution among relevant nations, an equal distribution among coalitions of nations, and an unequal distribution favoring one coalition or nation. It is sometimes described as a goal to be attained, especially by policy makers, and at other times it is described as the consequence of particular goals and strategies. E. Haas (1953), Claude (1962), Zinnes (1967), and others note that the balance of power has been used to describe a system, a policy, and a situation. The imprecise use of the phrase "the balance-of-power theory" has led to considerable confusion. There is an unfortunate tendency to label almost all theories about power and international conflict as balance-of-power theories, rendering the term all but meaningless.

The ambiguity surrounding the meaning of "the balance-of-power theory" is, indeed, one reason that almost any empirical result can be shown to support, or contradict, the balance-of-power theory in some guise. The set of meanings attributed to the family of theories called the balance-of-power theory is clearly delineated by Zinnes (1967), who identifies six principal variants. Letting A, B, C, D, and E be all the nations in the international system, the six balance-of-power systems identified by Zinnes are:

1. $A = B = C = D = E$
2. $A + B = C + D + E$
3. $A + B = C + D$; E is nonaligned
4. $A + B < C + D$; E is capable of joining either alliance, so that $A + B + E > C + D$, and $A + B < C + D + E$
5. $\sum_{i=j} x_i > x_j$
6. $\sum_{i \neq j} x_i > x_j$.

In the first system each state's power is equal to that of each other state, whereas the second system consists of two coalitions, each of which is equal to the other in power. The third and fourth systems are variations that include a potentially pivotal "balancer" state (E). The fifth system is a collective security system such as was envisaged by Woodrow Wilson, while the sixth variant depicts a system with a preponderant state (j) that can be defeated only by the combined power of all other states.

In this section I examine the most prominent versions of the balance-of-power theory, which I believe are those including coalitions and excluding, in the first instance, a pivotal balancer state, and including such a state in the second instance. I will also consider, albeit briefly, the view of the balance-of-power theory that proposes that the presence of a preponderantly powerful state tends to discourage war. Much of what is relevant about this focus is incorporated in the discussion of the power transition theory, which shares the hypothesis that a roughly equal distribution of power encourages war.

Most versions of the balance-of-power theory either implicitly or explicitly make the following assumptions:

1. states prefer expanding their power to maintaining their power, and prefer maintaining their power to losing power

2. states will act to prevent other states from expanding in power at their expense

3. war, alliances, and diplomacy are the central vehicles by which the power distribution among states is changed.

From these assumptions, balance-of-power theorists generally attempt to derive the following four key balance-of-power hypotheses:

1. alliances are temporary

2. alliances are nonideological

3. the sovereignty of small (essential) states is assured by each nation's quest for power

4. systems in which power is roughly equally distributed among coalitions of nations (or individual nations) tend to experience less war than systems where power is "out of balance."

The derivation of the first three hypotheses depends upon each state's need to keep open its strategic options for augmenting its power in the future. The final hypothesis depends on the notion that an equal distribution of power makes victory in war too uncertain to warrant risking the initiation of a war. Let us now examine the underlying logic of these propositions in greater detail.

The sources of any shortcomings in the balance-of-power theory presumably lie, as suggested at the beginning of this chapter, either in making overly restrictive, trivializing assumptions or in making logically inconsistent assumptions. Indeed, Organski points out one assumption that probably makes the theory empirically trivial. He notes that balance-of-power theorists ignore internal development through industrialization as an important source of power. The theory, instead, focuses exclusively on external means of increasing a nation's power. Such a focus is most appropriate in describing power relationships before the industrial revolution created radically different growth rates among nations. Once differences in rates of growth raised the possibility of seemingly weak states rising to challenge more powerful nations, the need to rely on "outside" help—which is so central to all balance-of-power theories—in planning and waging war declined drastically, thus altering a fundamental tenet of the balance-of-power theory. Where the industrial revolution is not firmly entrenched (for example, in parts of the Third World), the fact that the balance-of-power theory overlooks differential growth rates is not critical, but in the industrialized world, and in relations between industrialized and nonindustrialized nations, the balance-of-power theory's exclusive reliance on external means of supplementing national power renders the theory's alliance hypotheses empirically trivial. Why is that?

According to most balance-of-power theorists, power is acquired by (1) the addition of territory; (2) the erection of buffer states; (3) undermining the enemy's strength; and most importantly (4) forming alliances (Hartmann 1978). The proposition that the balance of power protects the sovereignty of small nations (Gulick 1955, Morgenthau 1973, Kaplan 1957) is critically dependent on their importance as potential buffers or allies. For a nation whose power is increasing primarily through internal development, the strategy of alliance formation and the establishment of buffers is relatively unimportant. Consequently, at least in some cases, such nations would not care about protecting the sovereignty of small nations. Hence, if Organski's observation is heeded, one must dismiss as a necessary consequence of the desire to maximize power that one must protect the independence of small nations. Similarly, if power is acquired through internal means, some nations can afford the luxury of ideological alliances. Such alliances are likely to survive considerably longer than those motivated solely by a quest for power, thereby rendering the two alliance-related hypotheses of the balance-of-power theory empirically trivial.

The theory's failure to take internal development into account has an additional implicit consequence that should be considered. Except for the unusual circumstance when opposed nations are equal in power, as in Zinnes's first system, alliances are essential within the balance-of-power framework for protecting the sovereignty of those weak states threatened by an expansionist adversary. In order to thwart the expansionist desires of the adversary and to prevent the possibility of its becoming so powerful that it can defeat any coalition, other states must come to the aid of the expansionist's intended victim. In other words, the balance-of-power theory implies that most wars are multilateral. Yet about 60 percent of the interstate wars since the Congress of Vienna have been bilateral, indicating that the balance-of-power theory does not adequately explain the failure of third party nations to protect weak states from the power-seeking policies of their adversaries (Singer and Small 1972).

What about the key proposition that the balance of power tends to lead to peace? A number of researchers have marshaled empirical evidence that suggests that this proposition is false. Singer, Bremer, and Stuckey (1972), for instance, note that major-power wars tend to follow periods of relative equality in the distribution of power in the twentieth century. Stoessinger (1973), referring to the balance-of-power theory in terms of the view that peace is insured by an equal distribution of power, reminds us that the Pax Romana was guaranteed by the overwhelming preponderance of power in the hands of ancient Rome. In much the same way, he argues that the relative peace that prevailed in Europe during the post-Napoleonic nineteenth century can be attributed to the preponderant major-power concert produced by the Congress system. Indeed, Stoessinger concludes that "the evidence seems to point to the fact that the long-alleged causal relationship between equilibrium and the attainment of peace simply does not exist" (Stoessinger 1973: 183). Although some evidence contradicts Stoessinger's interpretation of the structure of the European "balance of power" during the nineteenth century (Singer, Bremer, and Stuckey 1972), his generalization appears to be true for the twentieth century (Singer, Bremer, and Stuckey 1972), and may be true for the entire post-Napoleonic period (Organski and Kugler 1980). The question at hand, then, is what theoretical explanation can be offered for the apparent failures of the balance-of-power theory (when conceived in terms of Zinnes's first two systems), at least as an explanation of the occurrence of war or peace?

First of all, it should be made clear that it does not seem possible to deduce anything about the likelihood of war or peace from the explicit assumptions generally made by balance-of-power theorists. The general argument is that if a state or group of states begins to preponderate over others, then the others will pool their power in a coalition large enough to redress the balance, restoring the semblance of equality or shifting the movement toward preponderance in their own favor. If they do the latter, as one would expect if each state is trying to maximize its individual power, then those outside the coalition, and perhaps some within the coalition, will group together to again redress the balance. If the effort is unsuccessful, the system will move further out of balance. As this happens, new alignment patterns emerge to help some states gain an advantage over others, including their erstwhile allies. This, of course, drives those allies into new countercoalitions.

Over the long run one of two consequences comes about. Either one state succeeds in being in so many winning coalitions that it becomes stronger than the combined strength of all other states or no state becomes that powerful. In the latter case no actor can be sure of forming a coalition that cannot be countered, and so the system is roughly in balance (Zinnes, Gillespie, and Tahim 1978). In the former case, a single state is dominant and, so long as it remains internally cohesive, cannot be defeated so that a balance of power is not possible. As with the free market, a monopoly of power is seen as unlikely, hence the notion that each state pursuing its own interest will lead to a balance of power.

Whereas the balance-of-power argument may seem reasonable, and whereas it provides a reason to believe that alliances are temporary, short-lived, and nonideological (Morgenthau 1973, McGowan and Rood 1975), it does not provide a basis for believing that a balance of power leads to peace. On the contrary, *when the system begins to shift away from a balance, war can be one of the strategies used to eliminate the threat of preponderance. Similarly, the assumption that each state is trying to max-*

imize its power implicitly allows the possibility that they will do so by waging war, regardless of the distribution of power.

The hypothesis that the balance of power leads to peace requires the added assumption that "a state will not go to war . . . if it perceives its power (or the power of its coalition) as 'significantly' less than that of the enemy at the time that such a decision must be made" (Zinnes, North, and Koch 1961). Others state the assumption more boldly, claiming that nations wage war only when the expectation is that they will win. The former assumption indicates that at least with regard to war, there are no risk-acceptant decision makers, while the latter assumption indicates that there are neither risk-acceptant nor risk-neutral decision makers.

Risk-taking orientations clearly vary across individuals and circumstances. Some prefer the gamble of a long shot whereas others fear even the slightest risk of defeat. Only if decision makers are risk-avoidant can one conclude that no war occurs when there is a complete balance of power, with its implication that each side in a war would have an a priori equal probability of winning or losing. If risk-taking in foreign policy is a variable and not a constant (Bueno de Mesquita 1978), then the deduction that peace follows from the balance of power may be empirically trivial since a crucial assumption is not even approximately satisfied in reality. On the other hand, even if risk-taking is a constant, the peace hypothesis still cannot be deduced from the balance-of-power theory. This is so because it hinges on the coexistence of logically incompatible assumptions.

The fundamental assumption of the balance-of-power theory is that at least some states are expansionist. This has important implications concerning risk-taking that must now be explored. According to the theory, when a state expands its power, other states become alerted to the threat that the newly expanded state represents. If necessary, they form alliances to prevent any further expansion and, if possible, strip the expansionist state of its newly acquired power. Thus the very fact that a state tries to expand means that it accepts the risk of becoming the target of hostility from other states. If every state chose to maintain its position, then (1) no balance of power would result (unless by chance the states were "in balance" when they adopted their respective maintenance goals) and (2) no state would be in danger of becoming the target of the power-related hostilities of others. Thus expansionist states are the sole source of such hostilities, some of which are aimed against them. When a nation is confronted with a coalition of nations whose purpose is to strip this nation of some of its power there is always some probability that the coalition will succeed. This success, in turn, can be expected to mean a decline in the nation's power from its current level. Furthermore, if the adversaries also are expansionist, there is a real possibility that the decline will leave less power for the loser than it had before it began its expansionist policy. Hence expansionist states have some probability of gaining and some probability of losing power. The latter probability presumably increases with each success they have since, as a state approaches preponderance, the incentive for other states to form an effective countercoalition steadily increases. Losing power is clearly less desirable for them than maintaining their current level of power. If they did not try to expand, according to the balance-of-power theory, they would not experience the risk of becoming the target of an overwhelming countercoalition. They also would be in less danger of defeat by an expansionist state since a threat against them would provide the basis for the formation of a coalition against the expansionist. In other words, the adoption of an expansionist strategy means, within the balance-of-power framework, that the expansionist state is increasing its probability of losing power over that probability for a maintainer state. Thus, expansionist states can be, and often are, risk-acceptant.

We saw earlier that the peace hypothesis of the balance of power depends on the assumption that no state follows a risk-acceptant foreign policy. We have just seen that according to the theory expansionist states can be risk-acceptant. Thus the theory simultaneously assumes that no states are risk-acceptant and that some states may be risk-acceptant. That is a logical impossibility. It is no wonder that Stoessinger and others find little or no empirical relationship between the distribution of power in the international system or subsystems and the likelihood of war.

BALANCE-OF-POWER THEORY WITH
A BALANCER STATE

An alternative view of the balance of power contends that

> In the anarchic world of nation–states, each protagonist sought to maximize his safety through the enhancement of his power. In this competition, the quest for safety expressed itself chiefly in a search for allies. The safety of all was assured only if no one nation or group of nations was permitted to achieve a preponderance of power—if, in other words, a rough balance was achieved. Whenever the system threatened to break down, a "balancer" would ally himself with the weaker group of nations and thus restore the unstable equilibrium known as the "balance of power." [Stoessinger 1973: 180]

Morgenthau describes the balancer as motivated solely by the desire to maintain the system:

> Regardless of the concrete policies the balance will serve. In consequence, the holder of the balance will throw its weight at one time in this scale, at another time in the other scale, guided only by one consideration—the relative position of the scales. . . . The balancer is in a position of "splendid isolation." It is isolated by its own choice: for, while the two scales of the balance must vie with each other to add its weight to theirs in order to gain the overweight necessary for success, it must refuse to enter into permanent ties with either side. [Morgenthau 1973: 193–194]

The introduction of a balancer state into the theory greatly complicates the system without resolving any of the ·logical flaws noted earlier. Instead, the notion of the balancer adds further problems to the logic of the balance-of-power theory. Note that the balancer's interests are intimately tied to preserving the balance of power. No other state holds this interest, preferring instead to upset the balance in its favor. In itself, this difference in preference is not problematic. It does, however, mean that the earlier risk-taking argument can be greatly strengthened. Earlier I claimed that foreign policy decisions in expansionist states can be risk-acceptant. The balancer argument implies that some expansionist states *must* have risk-acceptant foreign policies. To see why we must first explore the power of the balancer.

How powerful must the balancer be? A state that is weaker than either contending expansionist coalition cannot be the balancer. This is so because one could then conceive of either (or both) of the contending coalitions turning their expansionist desires in its direction and defeating it. The balancer's preservation would then depend on some other state or coalition intervening on its behalf, making that other actor the actual balancer. Thus the balancer must be at least as powerful as any likely combination of states. Only then is its ability to defend the "balance of power" assured.[3]

Because of the balancer's commitment to the preservation of a more or less balanced system (and it must have such a commitment to distinguish it from other powerful states), balancer theorists stipulate that it always joins the weaker side if the balance of power is threatened. This means that its behavior is highly predictable. Yet, according to balancer theorists, conflicts requiring the intervention of the balancer do arise, even though the decision makers in other states—being at least as well informed as we are—can readily know that expansionist actions generally lead to their defeat following the decisive intervention of the balancer state. Clearly, acts of aggression or other efforts at expansion represent a willingness to accept extraordinary risks, thus revealing that expansionist states are necessarily risk-acceptant. The balancer notion actually suggests a system in which there may be a rough equality of power among many states or coalitions in the international system, but in which the fundamental characteristic of the system is the preponderance of a single benevolent balancer state. In that sense, the notion of a balancer is contrary to the realist, power-politics orientation that gave credence to the balancer variation of the balance-of-power theory in the first place.

The balancer view of the balance-of-power theory, as I have noted, implicitly assumes that the balancer is a preponderant state. What can be said of the general proposition that peace tends to follow from a very unequal distribution of power brought about by the presence of a preponderant nation? It will be recalled that Singer, Bremer, and Stuckey (1972) marshal some evidence from twentieth-century wars involving major powers to support this proposition. However, they also find it unsupported in the nineteenth century. In an analysis of inequalities in the distribution of power among coalitions of nations, I found no support for this proposition for the period from 1895 through 1965 (Bueno de Mesquita 1975a). The notion that a preponderant state brings stability to the international system depends on the additional assumption that it acts as a "benevolent dictator." Since no combination of forces can stop a preponderant state from seizing any resources or territory it desires, international peace depends on the leadership of the preponderant nation not following the *Realpolitik* dictum that more power is better than less power.

THE POWER TRANSITION THEORY

Organski's critique of the balance-of-power theory (1968) as being inattentive to the role of internal development in power politics led him to propose an alternative theory. According to Organski, the balance-of-power theory might have been useful for accounting for war and peace between states before the industrial revolution, but it is incapable of explaining war and peace in the present period of transitional growth in power. His alternative, the power transition theory, may be summarized as follows:

> Two characteristics—the shifts in power due to industrialization and the ties between nations—provide the basis for a recurring pattern that can be traced in recent international events. The most powerful nation in the world customarily heads an international order that includes other major nations (the powerful and satisfied) and also some minor nations and dependencies (the weak and satisfied and the weak and dissatisfied). As long as the satisfied nations enjoy a large preponderance of power over the rest of the world, peace is guaranteed. However, as new nations industrialize, the old leader is challenged. . . . Such a challenge usually results in war, although it is possible for world leadership to be transferred from one nation to another without a conflict. Certainly the major wars of recent history have all been wars involving the dominant nation and its allies against a challenger who has recently risen in power thanks to industrialization. [Organski 1968: 376]

The power transition theory differs from the balance-of-power theory in fundamental ways. The power transition theory leads to the conclusion that major war is most likely when power is approximately equally distributed among the most powerful states, and is least likely when there is a large inequality in the power of the dominant state and its would-be challengers. The argument is that when a large preponderance exists the dominant state feels no threat and, hence, has no reason to wage war, while the weaker states are dissatisfied and do have a reason to wage war, but lack the wherewithal to do so.

The power transition theory, unlike theories of the balance of power, does not purport to be a general theory of war. Instead, its purpose is to explain those few, but cataclysmic, wars between the most powerful and next most powerful nations in the relevant international system. Organski and Kugler (1970), for instance, identify five wars suitable for analysis within the power transition framework. These are the Napoleonic wars, the Franco-Prussian war, the Russo-Japanese war (of 1904), and World Wars I and II. Both Garnham (1976b) and Weede (1976) define the relevant set of wars somewhat more broadly to include major regional conflicts.

The three central hypotheses about these major wars are: (1) the weaker challenger state initiates a transition war against the stronger dominant state; (2) when the challenger state is a member of the dominant nation's coalition (that is, the challenger is strong and satisfied), the power transition occurs peacefully; and (3) "alliances should not play a major role in the initiation of war" (Organski and Kugler 1979).

If we assume that the third hypothesis is correct, then power transition wars generally are bilateral. Like Organski and Kugler, I have no data with which to assess the Napoleonic wars, but the other four major wars are readily examined in light of the power transition theory's three key hypotheses. At first blush it does appear that the power transition theory is supported. In terms of absolute national capabilities, Germany might have been weaker than its adversaries at the outset of both World Wars, while Japan appears to have been weaker than Russia in 1904. The Franco-Prussian War is less clear-cut, with both the relative strength of the two sides and the identity of the initiator open to question. On the question of relative power, France was widely believed to be the stronger of the two sides and, indeed, much of the available evidence supported that view. The surprising swiftness with which Prussia defeated France, however, clearly reveals that Prussia, not France, was the stronger side. As for the initiation of the war, Bismarck is frequently credited with trapping the French into attacking, thus suggesting that it was he, and not Napoleon III, who was the actual aggressor. The inflammatory editing of the Ems telegram by Bismarck is often cited in support of this viewpoint. Others, however, contend that Bismarck did not plan on war, though he was prepared to fight, while Napoleon III was merely waiting for an excuse to attack Prussia (A. J. P. Taylor 1954). Thus evidence can be marshaled to support or contradict the power transition theory's first hypothesis as it applies to the Franco-Prussian war.

Beyond the first blush, all five major wars appear inconsistent with the power transition theory's hypotheses. Of the five wars only two actually were bilateral conflicts, and even in these two cases, the attacker believed support would be forthcoming. Napoleon III is known to have expected some support from Britain and Russia, as well as from the military intervention of Italy and Austria-Hungary against Germany. With such support, France's attack of Prussia would probably have led to victory.

Without such support, the French were still in a position to believe that they had the superior capabilities and would, therefore, defeat Prussia. Napoleon's expectations of aid, though sincere, were probably unrealistic (Altfeld and Bueno de Mesquita 1979). None of the nations in question had explicitly committed themselves to armed intervention in a war with Prussia.

The other major bilateral war—the Russo-Japanese war of 1904—seems to me to contradict the power transition theory on two grounds. First, although Japan's absolute power base was certainly smaller than Russia's, this is not an accurate portrayal of the resources each side could actually bring to bear in the war. The Japanese had only to deliver a blow against Russian holdings in Asia, with Port Arthur the scene of Japan's first attack. This was only about a two-day journey by sea for the Japanese. For the Russians, with their power concentrated thousands of miles away in Europe, with the transsiberian railway as yet unfinished and inadequate for the task facing the Russians, and with the long-standing Russian aspiration for a warm-water port as yet unfulfilled, there was little they could do to mobilize their national capabilities against the Japanese. Russia simply was not as strong as Japan in Asia, thus contradicting the first hypothesis of the power transition theory (Blainey 1973, Bueno de Mesquita 1980).

Beyond the relative strength of the two sides in this "long distance" war is the question of whether the Russians or Japanese might have believed the conflict would become multilateral. Here again the evidence seems to contradict the power transition theory. It simply is not the case that alliances played only a minor role in the initiation of this war. When the war broke out, Britain and Japan were committed to each other's defense under certain contingencies. The French and Russians also shared a military agreement with each other. The Russians certainly could not have ignored the possibility of fighting a two-front war, with the Japanese as their opponent in Asia and the British opposed to them in Europe. Indeed, the British Foreign Secretary indicated that a war between Japan and Russia might draw Britain in, and the British government on the eve of the war "confirmed that she would fulfill her obligations under the alliance" (Nish 1966: 275). Britain's decision to remain out of the war was affected both by concern over the possible spread of the conflict into a general war among the European powers, and by the quick successes of the Japanese against the Russians. Nevertheless, contrary to the expectations of the power transition theory, alliances were not seen as unimportant in the calculations leading up to the outbreak of the Russo-Japanese war.

The importance of alliances to the conclusion of World Wars I and II and the Napoleonic wars hardly needs mention. Each of these were long wars in which the relative power of the aggressor and its victim was not, by itself, central to the outcome. Instead, it was the array of forces on each side that ultimately determined who would be victorious and who would be defeated. Although the aggressors could, conceivably, have consistently miscalculated what the expected behavior of other nations would be, that they did make such calculations is well documented. Hitler, for instance, believed the British and French would not intervene over the invasion of Poland because the British and French would have faced what Hitler thought were insurmountable odds, at least in the short run (Speer 1971). According to Speer, Hitler believed that Germany was stronger rather than weaker than its potential adversaries in 1939, though he recognizes that Germany's power advantage was temporary. Apparently Hitler recognized the likelihood of a "power transition" and chose to act before Germany was less likely to win (Speer 1971: 225). Hitler also clearly believed that the war had the potential to become multilateral, indicating that alliance considerations were important to him. Yet the power transition theory explicitly states that alliances should be relatively unimportant in major-power wars.

The apparent empirical shortcomings of the first and third hypotheses of the power transition theory result, I believe, from overly restrictive assumptions in the theory. In particular, the power transition theory swings too far in its focus on internal development as the principal source of changes in power. Although Organski was apparently correct in challenging the balance of power's reliance on external means of supplementing national power, this is not equivalent to the virtual dismissal of such power strategies as alliance formation. Once alliances are recognized as a legitimate—and frequently used—vehicle for augmenting national power, the alliance hypothesis of the power transition theory loses its logical foundation.

The first hypothesis that states that power transition wars are initiated by the weaker challenger state can be true only if the leaders of such states are willing to accept a very high risk of defeat. If stronger and weaker have any real meaning, then the weaker state—without any expectation of aid from its allies according to the theory—must fight a stronger adversary (who might, potentially, be assisted by its strong, satisfied allies). The challenger is almost certain to lose, unless the power transition has already taken place and it has become the stronger state. Indeed, it is irrational for a weak state to initiate a war against a stronger state when the war is expected to be bilateral and the goal is to win even if the key decision makers are risk-acceptant (Bueno de Mesquita 1980).

The second hypothesis of the power transition theory stipulates that a peaceful transition is possible. According to the theory, the state that is dominant at any given point in time is satisfied with the current world order because it used its power to establish the "rules of the game" to its own liking. In order to enforce those rules, it—together with those allies that share its satisfaction—must be more powerful than the power of all other states combined. Furthermore, the satisfied states must not be motivated primarily—or perhaps at all—by the desire to dominate and control world politics, but rather by the desire to realize more tangible goals. Why must this be so? Organski indicates that a "peaceful adjustment is possible in the case of a challenger who is willing to continue the existing international order and abide by its rules" (Organski 1968: 375). Of course, when such a "changing of the guard" takes place, even with the existing "rules of the game" being preserved intact, one fundamental change must occur. A state that had been dominant willingly steps aside to become a lesser power, while a formerly lesser power replaces it at the helm of the international system. Thus the previously dominant state is unconcerned by its loss in prestige, its relative drop in power, or the risk that the new dominant state might change the rules later when the currently dominant state is no longer able to challenge the changes successfully. The erstwhile dominant state peacefully surrenders its position because its primary objective is simply to preserve for the moment the "rules of the game" it established, and those rules, which identify roles to be played, do not identify the actors who must fill the critical roles in world politics.

The assumption that the dominant state is not motivated by a strong desire to preserve its prestige and relative power advantage greatly limits the domain of nations and situations that might be explained by the power transition theory. Such wars as the Seven Weeks war, which was fought in part to determine whether Prussia would come to dominate the German states or whether Austria-Hungary would continue to do so do not fall under the rubric of power transition because the dominant state in that system—Austria-Hungary—and its challenger—Prussia—did not differ very much on the "rules of the game" but rather on the question of which state was superior.

Unlike the various balance-of-power theories, the power transition theory does not appear to contain any internal inconsistencies and thus is not theoretically false. However, the implicit assumption that actors are risk-acceptant, which is required to deduce that transition wars are initiated by the weaker challenger is a restrictive assumption that greatly reduces the "realism" of the theory's hypotheses. Still, under appropriate conditions, the power transition theory may provide helpful insights into some cataclysmic major wars. One can only hope that further developments will lead to the incorporation of those critical wars into a more general theory that does not exclude so many other events or that is not restricted to conflict between states that have not yet reached the stage of power maturity.

POLARIZATION AND WAR

The apparent division of the international system into two contending poles during the cold war stimulated considerable interest in the relationship between the polarization of interests and the instability of the international community. Two aspects of such polarization, or division of interests, continue to attract attention. First is the number of poles, or coalitions of nations, in the system. Second are the characteristics of the bonds linking nations to one another, both within and across poles. Studies concerned with the number of poles (Waltz 1964, Deutsch and Singer 1964, Rosecrance 1966) focus on the bipolarity or multipolarity of the international system, whereas studies concerned with the bonds between nations focus on the tightness or looseness and discreteness or interactiveness of the system's poles (Kaplan 1957; Bueno de Mesquita 1975a, 1978). The literature concerning each of these attributes is filled with contradictory hypotheses that stem from alternative assumptions about decision making in the international arena. Yet there is also a core of important assumptions that are largely accepted by theorists concerned with polarity and war. Let us look at the various assumptions and hypotheses in terms of their logical consistency and empirical relevance.

Several assumptions, whether explicit or implicit, appear to be commonly held by researchers concerned with polarity and war. First, it is generally agreed that when nations join military alliances, or in some other way link their foreign policies to those of other nations, they restrict their decision-making options. This assumption of reduced autonomy is essential to the pursuit of any investigation of polarity since the significance of a bloc of nations rests in the presumed unity of action—or unanimity of preferences—by its members, at least in the face of some specified contingency. In other words, decision making on critical war or peace decisions is assumed to be free of the social intransitivities likely to lead to paradoxical policy choices (Allison and Halperin 1972, Altfeld and Bueno de Mesquita 1979).

Second, it is generally agreed that the level of uncertainty about the consequences of particular actions in the international arena increases as the number of autonomous actors—or poles—increases (Waltz 1964, Deutsch and Singer 1964). The reasoning underlying this assumption is quite straightforward. As the number of autonomous actors increases, the potential sources of important information also increases, probably at a faster rate than the expansion in decision maker ability to analyze and interpret the information. Consequently, in any given short period of time decision makers know the content of a smaller percentage of the information circulating in the system than they would have known if there were fewer sources of information; hence the increase in the variance in their probability estimates concerning the consequences of their actions. It is the magnitude of that variance that characterizes uncertainty.

The fundamental source of difference among theorists in this area concerns the implications of bipolarity or multipolarity—and the attendant uncertainty—for international stability and peace. Deutsch and Singer (1964) contend that multipolar structures produce greater stability than bipolar structures for two reasons. First, multipolarity is conducive to pluralist cross-cutting pressures whereas bipolarity is conducive to reinforcing antagonisms. They contend that "the argument is nothing more than a special case of the widely employed pluralism model . . . and it stands in contrast to the self-aggravating system as seen in forest fires, compound interest, nuclear fission, runaway inflation or deflation, and drug addiction." Why the pluralist view is more appropriate than the assumption that the polarization of interests is self-aggravating is not demonstrated, but rather asserted.

Second, Deutsch and Singer propose that the uncertainty produced by multipolarity is stabilizing because

> it is generally recognized that below a certain signal-to-noise ratio, the signal is essentially undetectable. . . . Each state in this case would have to treat the message from its most prominent adversary of the moment as the signal relevant to this incipient conflict in or before its early stage of escalation; and it' would tend to treat all other messages, concerning all other pairs of states, as noise of relatively little relevance to this particular conflict. [Deutsch and Singer 1964: 398]

Underlying this argument are two somewhat troubling assumptions. First, it is assumed that the information lost through noise was disproportionately likely to be destabilizing, while the possibility that the lost information contained positive content that might have lowered tensions rather than raised them is ignored. Certainly studies of the outbreak of World War I suggest that such positive information was lost in the welter of signals being received by the various actors (Holsti, North, and Brody 1968, Zinnes 1968). Second, it is assumed that states will not take advantage of the uncertainties of the moment to press their own advantage, even if doing so involves acting under conditions that are relatively favorable for them. That is, there may be states that are incapable of achieving success against some well-informed adversary, but capable of achieving gains if the adversary is sufficiently ill-informed or befuddled by a high level of noise so that it is unlikely to react adequately. This point—which bears directly on the issue of risk-taking raised earlier—will be returned to shortly.

While Deutsch and Singer (1964) are content to assume that uncertainty encourages restrained, cautious decision making, Waltz (1964) argues the opposite. In his judgment, the uncertainties brought on by multipolarization increase the likelihood of miscalculation, misjudgment, or misperception, each of which may result in destabilizing actions. But why should uncertainty encourage miscalculated behavior that can lead to war? It should not unless one makes the additional assumption that decision makers are willing to take the risk of departing from their current pattern of actions and undertake decisions with unknown or very uncertain consequences.

That is, one must assume that decision makers under uncertainty are risk-acceptant to provide a logical basis for concluding that uncertainty increases the likelihood of war.

Waltz's contention that multipolarity tends to lead to war, and Deutsch and Singer's conclusion that multipolarity tends to lead to peace each are dependent on alternative assumptions about risk-taking under uncertainty. Whereas Waltz seems to believe that decision makers under uncertainty generally derive some utility from taking risks, Deutsch and Singer believe decision makers derive some utility from avoiding risks. It seems very unlikely, though logically possible, that risk-taking orientations under uncertainty are homogeneously distributed among decision makers. Certainly Chamberlain and Hitler were very different on this score, as perhaps were Napoleon and Wellington (Keegan 1976). If decision making under uncertainty is neither generally risk-acceptant nor risk-avoidant, then there is no basis for believing that either bipolarity or multipolarity is more conducive to peace and stability. Indeed, if risk-taking is not homogeneously distributed, then there is no reason to believe that there is any system-wide relationship between the number of poles and the likelihood of war (Bueno de Mesquita 1978).

Closely associated with the polarity of the international system is the degree to which nations around the same pole share similar foreign policy objectives and the degree to which nations at different poles have dissimilar objectives. When nations in different blocs share some common goals, one might assume that they will develop commitments between them that help draw their respective blocs closer together, thereby reducing the discrepancy in each other's objectives. This is, in somewhat simplified terms, the argument for détente. The increased commonality of interests among adversaries produced by détente was often cited by Richard Nixon and Henry Kissenger as a vehicle for reducing the probability of war among the superpowers. Whether the association between détente and war or peace actually exists depends on whether the apparent commonality of interests inhibits warlike decisions. If, as was argued for uncertainty, the apparent increase in shared interests has different effects on different decision makers, détente should bear no systematic relationship to war (Bueno de Mesquita 1978, Bueno de Mesquita 1980).

As with the number of poles and the degree of interbloc interactions, there are several hypotheses that relate the level of intrabloc commitments—or tightness—to the probability of war. The most commonly held position may be characterized as follows. When all the members of a bloc are substantially committed to each other, it is difficult for any one member to venture on an independent foreign policy course that involves commitments to nations outside the bloc. From this assumption follows the hypothesis that the more tight-knit the commitments within a bloc, the lower the probability that friendly cross-cutting, interbloc relations will develop. If hostile sentiments between blocs are not mitigated by friendly interactions between individual members of different blocs, then the greater the tightness of commitments within blocs, the higher the probability of war between blocs (Kaplan 1957).

The conclusion that tightness increases the likelihood of war is related closely, though not explicitly, to the uncertainty–risk-taking relationship discussed in the context of the number of poles in the system. Tight blocs contain relatively unambiguous commitments among their members and, consequently, alleviate uncertainty about contingent behavior. Loose blocs, conversely, possess a high level of uncertainty. If risk-taking under uncertainty is uniformly distributed, tightness may either, as Kaplan suggests, increase the likelihood of war or it may produce cautious behavior that decreases the probability of war. But if, as I have argued elsewhere, risk-taking varies from decision maker to decision maker, tightness should be unrelated to the probability of war—a hypothesis supported by the available evidence (Bueno de Mesquita 1978).

In the case of hypotheses concerned with the various components of systemic polarity, it appears that several logically consistent arguments have been proposed that are mutually contradictory. The unspoken assumption that generally provides the basis for the competing hypotheses is that risk-taking orientations under uncertainty are homogeneously distributed. If risk-taking varies across decision makers and circumstances, most current hypotheses about polarity and war are relatively uninformative.

WAR AND STATUS INCONSISTENCY

During the past decade or so psychological explanations of war have achieved some prominence and received some empirical attention. Among the topics that have been investigated is relative deprivation, in the guise of status inconsistency (Galtung 1964, Wallace 1973b, Midlarsky 1975, Ray 1979).

According to some,

> status inconsistency creates dissatisfaction within a nation because, from its point of view, it violates the crucial system norm that nations receive rewards in proportion to their position on the pecking order. . . . [T]he frustration thus engendered, coupled with the leverage possessed by such a nation in having at least one high status, create both the motive and the opportunity for increasingly aggressive international behavior, resulting in war if the discrepancy remains uncorrected. [Wallace 1972b: 53–54]

The hypothesis, then, is that status inconsistent nations are more likely to try to redress their grievances through war than status consistent nations. Three critical assumptions from which the hypothesis is derived are (1) there are rewards to be allocated—rather than taken—in the system;

(2) the rewards are allocated according to some status-related rule that fixes each nation's share as a monotonic function of national rank (presumably on either the dimension of achieved status or that of ascribed status); and (3) a nation's failure to receive a share of rewards commensurate with its expectations breeds frustration that leads to aggression (Wallace 1972b).

The hypothesis is a logical consequence of the assumptions just enumerated. Yet the empirical "fit" between the war-proneness of individual nations—the unit whose behavior is supposed to be explained by the hypothesis—and their status inconsistency is surprisingly weak (see Chapter 8 of this *Handbook*). Why should this be so? One possible explanation is that the relevant variables have not been measured adequately. The long history of debate over what is meant by power—or achieved status—certainly implies that this crucial component of the hypothesis is not easily measured. Still, among quantitative researchers at least, there appears to be some convergence, if not consensus, on the apparent validity of several indicators of national power. Indeed, these indicators have produced some promising results when applied to other power-related hypotheses, thereby suggesting that they do have some validity. The measure of ascribed status most frequently used is the diplomatic importance score for each nation (Singer and Small 1966a). Although less well-developed than many indicators of achieved status, the diplomatic importance data seem to fit with many researchers' intuitive judgment of the ascribed status of at least many nations across a fairly long time span, and there is no reason to doubt that the indicator is at least somewhat correlated with the theoretical concept of ascribed status. Still, it is possible that there is enough noise in each of the relevant indicators to mask the true relationship between status inconsistency and aggressive behavior. But even if the measurement and specification problems inherent in the hypothesis were overcome, one might still expect a poor empirical fit. I believe this to be true because of the nature of the assumptions from which the status inconsistency hypothesis is derived.

Although the proposition under examination is certainly capable of logical deduction, and hence is plausible, it seems to me that between the assumptions leading to the deduction and the real-life situation of decision makers there lies a world of difference. The first two assumptions describe a world in which orderly rules govern the distribution of rewards. The third assumption describes the expected reaction of any nation that finds the rules unfair. Arrow's impossibility theorem (1951) proves that no decision-making rules, other than unanimity or dictatorship, guarantee that decisions represent the "collective will" or "social norm" of a country. It seems unlikely that a system-wide rule or social norm exists governing the allocation of valued, scarce rewards. Indeed, if decision makers are trying to maximize their own nation's status—as is implied by most discussions of status inconsistency—we may be certain that no rule that fixes rewards as a proportion of one's position in the pecking order could achieve anything approaching consensus without at least some actors behaving contrary to their own interests (Bueno de Mesquita 1975b, Bueno de Mesquita 1979). Hence the first two assumptions of the status inconsistency argument are about a world in which at least some actors do not care about their relative status or status inconsistency, thus contradicting the generality of the hypothesis. To be informative, then, the hypothesis must include that some status inconsistent nations are likely to be driven to aggressive behavior, whereas others are not. But how are we to know which decision makers will wage war to redress their status inconsistency and which will use other strategies, such as alliance formation, internal development, or exhortations to do better to redress their grievances? And which will care so little, or will be so ineffective, that they will do futile things or do nothing? The theory of status inconsistency is not well enough developed to answer these questions. Of course, including nations prone to strategies other than war in one's analyses will lead to a poor empirical "fit." This is what we expect (and find) with tests based on the inadequately specified hypothesis of the status inconsistenty literature.

Even if the first two assumptions did not severely restrict the usefulness of the hypothesis, a serious problem would remain. The third assumption implies that decision makers believe war is an effective means of acquiring increased achieved or ascribed status. This is an empirical question which has been studied only modestly (see the review by Stein and Russett in Chapter 10 of this *Handbook*). Still, the evidence is instructive. Organski and Kugler (1977) report that the postwar growth in power or achieved status of the victors in World Wars I and II fall below prewar expectations, while the growth in power of the vanquished quickly rises to or surpasses the prewar forecasts. Certainly this suggests that growth in achieved status is not assured by victory. Even a cursory examination of the ascribed status data indicates that victory also does not assure a rise in a nation's score on that dimension. The Japanese defeat of Russia in 1904, for instance, yielded little or no change in Japan's diplomatic importance score, even though this war would appear to fit the logic of the status inconsistency hypothesis as well or better than any other war. Thus the empirical premise on which the presumption that war is the vehicle for redressing one's status inconsistency is based appears to be false.

ARMS RACE MODELS

In the wake of World War I, Lewis Fry Richardson began constructing what is probably the first mathematical model in political science. Richardson's arms race model specified that as a nation's own stock of weapons grew there would be a depressing impact on current arms production, whereas as a nation's adversary's arms stock grew there would be an inflating effect on arms production, with the actual level of such production depending on the magnitude of the "fatigue and expense" coefficient compared to the "defense" coefficient (1960a). The general structure of the basic Richardson models is depicted in two equations:

$$dx/dt = ky - Ax + g$$

$$dy/dt = iy - Bx + h,$$

with x being the amount of armaments currently held by one side, and y the amount currently held by the other side. k and i are x and y's "defense" coefficients, while A and B are their respective "expense and fatigue" coefficients. g and h are the "feelings" of the two sides, while dx/dt and dy/dt are the rates at which each side arms in response to the arms expenditures of the other side (x and i), the domestic impact of previous arms expenditures (A and B), and general feelings (g and h).

Richardson-type models are generally successful at accounting for variations in arms expenditures, but they have been studied only modestly as potential tools for explaining the occurrence of international conflict. In general some modest empirical support is found for the proposition that arms levels and arms production are associated with the incidence of international violence (Rummel 1968, Naroll 1969, Newcombe and Wert 1973), but there is also some empirical evidence that suggests that the presence of substantial armaments deters aggression (Russett 1963). Continued interest in the Richardson arms race models has yielded several attempts to modify their basic structure (Smoker 1964, McGuire 1965, Intriligator 1969, Brito 1972, Simaan and Cruz 1973, Gillespie et al. 1977, Gillespie, Zinnes, and Rubison 1978, Boulding 1962).

Early criticism of Richardson's work focused on the fact that the arms race, as conceived by Richardson, did not include a decision-making calculus. Richardson's "mediated" stimulus-response structure portrayed a process of semi-automatic "standard operating responses" to changes in the armaments level of one's adversaries. The fatigue and defense coefficients were not really conceptualized either as reflecting a political decision-making process or as resulting from purposive, goal-seeking behavior (Rapoport 1957, Alker 1968b). Brito and Intriligator (1973) and Simaan and Cruz (1973) have pioneered in reformulating Richardson's original arms race models to include national goal-seeking behavior. More recently, Gillespie et al. (1977) have extended this work to incorporate specific goals drawn from the balance-of-power literature. These efforts have proved fruitful in providing excellent approximations of arms expenditures in a number of countries, but they still do not provide an adequate basis for hypothesizing about the linkage between the presence or intensity of an arms race and the likelihood of conflict. Still, using optimal control theory, Gillespie et al. (1977) are able to deduce some provocative implications about the expected stability of particular pairs of nations given particular combinations of optimizing strategies.

Most recent criticism of the arms race literature draws attention to its apolitical nature. Gillespie, Zinnes, and Rubison (1978), for instance, argue that arms race modelers have been inattentive to the cumulative effect on decision making of alternative arms expenditure histories. Incorporating a cumulative memory coefficient into the model—to make it more reflective of strategic, political decision making—they find that it improves the model's ability to account for fluctuations in arms expenditures. Others, however, feel that the very concept of arms expenditures as a principally foreign policy process is incorrect. Largely in response to the success of research on the budgetary process, some have suggested that arms expenditures are more responsive to internal incremental processes of budgetary allocations, while others suggest that arms production is a function both of incrementalist decision making and of concern for the weapons production of one's adversary (Lapp 1968, Wohlstetter 1974, Ostrom 1977, Organski and Kugler 1980).

Allison (1971), Halperin (1974), and others suggest that neither the arms race models nor the incrementalist models are adequate for accounting for weapons expenditures and production. Instead, they suggest that weapons decisions, like so many other governmental decisions, are the result of bureaucratic bargaining, vote trading, coalition formation, and compromise, all motivated by individuals' desires to maximize their own career development or policy preferences. That is, these researchers have accepted a more or less individualist, rational-choice perspective that emerges as a natural implication of Arrow's impossibility theorem. Thus once decision makers recognize that they can manipulate decision making rules, they will do so in such ways as will advance their interests. The policy of arms production and expenditures is arrived at not by identifying the option that insures the "collective welfare" (which, in any event, is almost certainly defined differently by different factions, or coalitions, in the society), but rather by identifying the alternative that provides a compromise solution to the competing interests vying for control over the decision. Such a view, which seems compelling to this author at least, unfortunately is not readily amenable to empirical examination. It requires knowing (1) who the relevant decision makers, advisers, and other interested parties are to each decision; (2) what their preference orderings are on the alternative ways for providing security against outside aggression; and (3) what are their cardinal utilities for each of the alternatives, as well as for different degrees of national security. Point (3), of course, is almost impossible to measure.

Some recent studies that share a concern for finding empirically viable means of examining the implications of individual utility-maximization models of conflict decision making suggest that indicators of preference orderings and even of utility may be constructed (Lucier 1978, Altfeld 1979, Altfeld and Bueno de Mesquita 1979, Bueno de Mesquita 1980). Lucier's recent work on arms race models suggests that the degree to which arms production is responsive to the arms production of an adversary is a critical policy decision that reflects the preferences of the particular decision makers in power at a given time. He argues, therefore, that a flaw in the application of Richardson-like models is that stockpiles are assumed to be variables, but the "fatigue" and "defense" coefficients are assumed to be constants within nations. Lucier obtains a substantial empirical fit, not only for arms production but also for levels of international tension, by permitting those coefficients to vary from regime to regime or administration to administration. In this way he captures some of the variation in preference ordering from one set of leaders to another.

DETERRENCE AND INTERNATIONAL CONFLICT

Closely associated with research on arms races and international conflict are studies of the deterrent effect of weapons development and deployment. Although theories about deterrence have existed for hundreds of years, my concern here is primarily with the theory of strategic nuclear deterrence as it has evolved during the past thirty years.

Deterrence may be defined as "the persuasion of one's opponent that the costs and/or risks of a given course of action he might take outweigh its benefits" (George and Smoke 1974: 11). In the case of nuclear deterrence Schelling (1960) contends that the key to deterrence is the ability to make a credible, intense threat. If one's adversary, for instance, is convinced that a first strike will yield a credible threat that the victim will annihilate the aggressor's civilian population and/or its economic base, then the aggressor will presumably be deterred from attacking in the first place. McGuire (1965), Ellsberg (1969), Schelling (1966) and others sometimes equate the concept of an intense, credible threat with the "survivability" of one's missiles or with the related notion of assured destruction.

Broadly speaking, strategic nuclear deterrence depends on the ability to survive a first strike with a sufficient capability so that one's adversary is assured that even a successful counterforce strike would leave him open to certain destruction. Several interesting implications arise. In order to assure international stability (and the absence of nuclear war, if not the presence of positive peace), one should avoid the development of technologies or strategies that insure the successful defense of one's civilian population. Civil defense measures, for instance, if effective, are likely to be viewed as provocative by one's adversary. This is so because any development that jeopardizes the adversary's ability to impose unacceptable costs in a second strike encourages him to believe that a first strike is being planned against him. Such a belief, of course, raises the probability of his launching a pre-emptive first strike. By the same logic, such defense technologies as ABM's are viewed as destabilizing. That, of course, is why ABM's were banned under the SALT I agreement.

While the theory indicates that too good a defense is destabilizing it does not lead to the conclusion that the best defense is a good offense. Indeed, the exclusive development of offensive, first-strike weapons is surely as destabilizing as the development of measures that prevent assured destruction. Rather deterrence theory portrays security as emerging from a mix of first-strike and second-strike capabilities. Paradoxically, even though such mixes enhance security and stability, they also may increase potentially destabilizing uncertainties about the intentions of one's foe. Recognizing the danger such uncertainty can entail, both Ellsberg (1969) and McGuire (1965) argue for the rationality of enemies exchanging some relevant national secrets.

The deterrence literature, more so than any other body of research concerned with international conflict, is almost exclusively theoretical, and often follows the method of deductive—sometimes mathematical—logic. The fortunate absence of empirical cases, coupled with the practical necessity of understanding how to prevent nuclear war has made rigorous theoretical development in this area absolutely critical. The literature has developed in two not completely exclusive directions. Some have approached deterrence in a fairly formal deductive vein (Morgenstern 1959, Schelling 1960, Rapoport 1960, Rapoport 1967, Ellsberg 1969), whereas others take a less formally deductive view (Wohlstetter 1959, Kahn 1960, G. Snyder 1961, Singer 1962, George and Smoke 1974). Whichever approach is taken, the implications and refinements are generally consistent with the brief summary in the preceding paragraph. Before I turn to an evaluation of the deterrence argument, let me state that the issue is not the logical truthfulness of theories of deterrence, but rather the empirical usefulness of deductions about deterrence.

The deterrence literature has been seriously criticized from a variety of perspectives. Among the most compelling criticisms are those related to the inherent limitations of some of the games that are alleged to capture the critical elements of a deterrence situation. Schelling (1960) was perhaps the first to note that deterrence situations are akin to non–zero-sum games. With the overwhelming preponderance of nuclear capabilities in the hands of two states, deterrence has generally been characterized as either a prisoner's dilemma or a game of chicken (K. W. Deutsch 1968, Riker and Ordeshook 1973, M. Sullivan 1976). The characteristics of each of these games is portrayed in Figures 9–1 and 9–2. As is well known, the prisoner's dilemma when played once possesses an equilibrium pair of strategies, with the minimax solution being jointly competitive behavior.[4] The game

FIGURE 9–1. Prisoner's dilemma.

ACTOR B

	Strategy b1		Strategy b2	
Strategy a1	–5	–5	–20	10
Strategy a2	10	–20	–10	–10

ACTOR A

NOTE: A's expected payoff is listed to the left of B's expected payoff.

of chicken—which seems to characterize the policy of brinkmanship—does not have a single minimax solution. Instead, there are two noninterchangeable equilibrium pairs, (a1,b2) and (a2,b1). This means that a player willing to behave recklessly and appear irrational may be able to force his opponent into succumbing to his threats, thereby achieving great gains that may render the opponent impotent. But if each player perceives

FIGURE 9–2. Game of chicken.

ACTOR B

	Strategy b1		Strategy b2	
Strategy a1	10	10	5	20
Strategy a2	20	5	–10	–10

ACTOR A

NOTE: A's expected payoff is listed to the left of B's expected payoff.

the benefits of seeming reckless and irrational—and behaves consistent with that perception—then both may be brought to total ruin (Schelling 1960). In the case of chicken, or the strategy of brinkmanship, then, no stable outcome can be assured. In the case of the prisoner's dilemma, stability depends on a single play of the game. Once the game is played repeatedly—as it obviously must be in reality—each player has incentives to abandon his pure strategy. In particular, both players are better off with the payoff from (a1,b1) than they are from (a2,b2), but A is best off with (a2,b1) whereas B is best off with (a1,b2). Thus each player has incentives to play a mixed strategy once the players have enough experience to calculate each other's likely mix of cooperative and competitive strategies. The iterative, mixed strategy version of the prisoner's dilemma—which more closely approximates conditions in reality than does a single episode of the game—does not possess an easily found stable outcome. In other words, even the seemingly more stable conditions of the prisoner's dilemma may lead to the same dangerous uncertainties that are created by the brinkmanship strategy portrayed in the game of chicken.

When the game of chicken is played iteratively—as might happen if a nation provoked one crisis after another (as perhaps the Soviets did during the heyday of Berlin crises)—then the likelihood of disaster increases rapidly. Consider a scenario in which one nation behaves in a seemingly reckless manner—hoping to compel its adversary to capitulate to its demands—while it expects its adversary to behave responsibly and back down with a probability of .90. With the first seemingly reckless act, the initiator of the crisis is almost certain to get his way. With the second act there is a .19 chance that he will not have gotten his way during one of the two crises. By the seventh crisis, the chances of his having succeeded each time is less than fifty-fifty, and so on. That is, across time, the reckless strategy (even barring learning and so forth) is less and less likely to end without a disaster (K. W. Deutsch 1968).

The problem of finding a stable minimax solution to deterrence games is, unfortunately, considerably more problematic than one might think even from the pessimistic discussion of chicken and the prisoner's dilemma. Game theoretic approaches uniformly study deterrence as if it were similar to a non–zero-sum finite game. However, even though there are upper and lower bounds to the payoffs that one might receive in a deterrent situation, the set of possible payoffs is probably continuous within those boundaries. In other words, deterrence is not like a finite (or matrix) game such as the prisoner's dilemma, but rather is more accurately conceived of as a bounded, infinite non–zero-sum game. Riker and Ordeshook (1973) note that "we encounter considerable difficulty defining solutions for infinite games; and so we may safely assume that knowing that an equilibrium exists for infinite games with continuous payoffs does not tell us very much about the choices of decision makers" (Riker and Ordeshook 1973: 228). In other words, each side in such a game of deterrence is unable to identify the best strategic response to the expected behavior of the adversary because it is extremely difficult to anticipate the adversary's behavior. This opens the possibility for one side or the other to obtain a sufficient advantage to provoke a nuclear war. Indeed, one implication that may be drawn from the theory of bounded, infinite, non–zero-sum games is that efforts to set limits on arms can backfire, creating more tension and raising the probability of war. This is a conclusion also reached from an expected utility approach to deterrence, as evidenced by McGuire's observation that "it is easy to imagine disarmament arrangements from which both sides could suffer. One example would be an agreement to limit numbers of missiles with no limitations on warheads technology" (McGuire 1965: 26).

Rational choice approaches to deterrence ignore not only the likelihood that the payoffs from threats or deterrence are continuous (though bounded), but also the possibility that different maximization rules govern the behavior of different decision makers. Consider, for instance, the possibility that one side follows a minimax strategy, whereas decisions taken on the other side follow a minimax regret strategy. In some situations, the minimax strategy and minimax regret strategy are the same, but in other situations they are very different. When they are different, it may be impossible to identify a set of strategic moves that yield a stable deterrent outcome. This possibility is further reinforced as we expand the number of alternative, rational-maximizing, or satisficing-decision rules that might be applied to any rational decision-making situation. It is also reinforced as the setting changes from a two-player situation to one in which there are several potential sources of nuclear threat. In reality it is more likely that different decision makers employ different decision rules than that they all employ the minimax rule, and it is increasingly likely that the American and Soviet duopoly of nuclear power will be broken. Hence the likelihood of finding stable deterrent solutions within the confines of current deterrence theory is probably low and decreasing. Yet if we assume that decision making is irrational—the only alternative to assuming rationality—then identifying stable deterrent strategies is even more unlikely.

EFFECTS OF DOMESTIC CONFLICT ON FOREIGN CONFLICT

Arms race models are "stimulus-response" models sensitive to conflictual developments beyond the boundaries of the responding nation. Other stimulus-response models focus on internal, domestic stimuli of foreign conflict behavior. Most notable is the proposition that national leaders use foreign conflict as a vehicle for distracting attention away from domestic conflict (Rummel 1963, Tanter 1966, Zinnes and Wilkenfeld 1971,

Wilkenfeld 1973b, Dehio 1962, Fried, Harris, and Murphy 1968). When the hypothesis is stated in such bold, general terms there is little reason to expect it to be true. Blainey, for instance, maintains:

> Scapegoat interpretations of war seem plausible but are probably erroneous. They rely on dubious assumptions. They usually assume that peace is a newsless limbo which requires little explanation. They usually assume that a troubled nation will seize on an enemy, large or small, near or far; but this assumption is not easy to accept. They assume that one nation can be blamed for a war, and yet war is a relationship between at least two nations and cannot be explained by examining one nation in isolation. Even if, on the contrary, wars can be logically blamed on one nation, scapegoat theory is still misleading: it assumes that the strife-torn nations initiate the fighting, but in fact the fighting in most of the relevant wars between 1815 and 1939 was not initiated by the strife-torn nation. [Blainey 1973: 81–82]

Indeed, the empirical evidence concerning the linkage between domestic and foreign conflict offers only modest support for the proposition, and then only under very constrained circumstances (see Stohl, Chapter 7 of this *Handbook*, for a review of the evidence).

The domestic–foreign conflict proposition fails to isolate those circumstances in which generating foreign conflict is likely to distract attention from domestic unrest from those in which foreign conflict might exacerbate such unrest. Would the war in Vietnam have stirred an outcry of opposition in the United States if there were not already great divisions in the society stemming from the civil rights movement, urban riots, the war on poverty, and the like? We cannot answer this question, but the very fact that the war might plausibly be seen as an event that heated up the already high level of domestic discontent suggests that foreign conflict does not always mitigate domestic conflict. One might further inquire whether all types of foreign conflict are theoretically appropriate distractions for all types of domestic conflict. Presumably there is some calculation of the costs and benefits of one type of conflict as compared to another, and especially of the likelihood of succeeding in checking domestic unrest by initiating a foreign problem, as compared to the risk of pursuing a domestic response to the domestic conflict. To see this more clearly, I construct a simple expected-utility model of the type a rational utility maximizer might use in deciding whether a foreign conflict response to a domestic problem is likely to be effective. In the expected-utility model, the decision maker attempts to find the strategy for resolving a domestic conflict that leaves him/her best off. Two sets of strategies may be used (though for simplicity's sake I treat them each as if they were one-member sets). F is the strategy of using a foreign conflict response to the domestic unrest, while D is the strategy of using a domestic response to the same domestic unrest. P is the probability of F succeeding ($1 - P$ being the probability of F failing), while Q is the probability of D succeeding (and $1 - Q$ is the probability of D failing). Each strategy, of course, has a cost and a benefit associated with it. If the domestic conflict is satisfactorily resolved (regardless by which strategy), the decision maker derives B benefits, while B' benefits are derived from failure. (B' will almost certainly be 0, but for the moment let us assume its value is unknown.) Finally, the cost of F is C, while the cost of D is K. With $E(F)$ and $E(D)$ being the expected utility associated with each strategy, we may say that:

$$E(F) = (PB + (1-P)(B')) - C = PB + B' \, PB' - C \tag{1}$$

$$E(D) = (QB + (1-Q)(B')) - K = QB + B' - QB' - K \tag{2}$$

If $EF > E(D)$, then a foreign conflict response is preferred to a domestic response. If $E(F) < E(D)$, then a domestic response is preferred, and if $E(F) = E(D)$, the decision maker is indifferent as to the two strategies. If the utility of failure (B') is zero, then equations (1) and (2) reduce to:

$$E(F) = PB - C \tag{3}$$

$$E(D) = QB - K \tag{4}$$

Whether B' is or is not zero, there are a great many circumstances in which $E(D) > E(F)$, making a foreign conflict response to a domestic conflict irrational under those circumstances. The poor empirical fit reported by Rummel (1963), Tanter (1966), and others may now be understood clearly. The hypothesis is true only if the net expected benefits of using a foreign conflict strategy outstrip the net expected benefits from the alternative(s). Knowing that, we may begin to anticipate the circumstances that are theoretically likely to reveal an association between domestic and foreign conflict.

One circumstance that favors a foreign conflict response to domestic unrest arises when the cost of the foreign response is minimized. As C approaches 0, the likelihood (though still a probability and not a certainty) that $E(F) > E(D)$ increases. Therefore, all other things being equal, a modest foreign policy response is more likely to achieve the desired outcome than a severe foreign policy response. Indeed, two studies, each with quite separate purposes, support this deduction. Wilkenfeld, studying the association between domestic and foreign conflict for different regime types, reports that "for the personal ruler, relatively free to make foreign policy decisions and alter them, the prospect of diverting attention from his deteriorating domestic situation by engaging in a mild form of foreign conflict is a tempting policy alternative and one not difficult to pursue" (Wilkenfeld 1973b: 298). John Mueller reports in his study of the popularity of American presidents that the more opportunities they have had to make domestic policy decisions, the less popular they become. Similarly, the longer they engage the nation in war, the less popular they become. However, short-run foreign policy initiatives create a "rally round the flag" effect that enhance the president's popularity (J. E. Mueller 1970). Given the expected-utility model, these two inductive studies may now be linked together, making cumulative, seemingly unrelated findings. By specifying a process that relates domestic and foreign conflict in an explicit and logical fashion, I have provided a simple explanation for the failure of so many to find a general association between domestic and foreign conflict. At the same time, I have provided a basis for conducting future empirical research based on the variability in P, Q, B, and B', as well as in C and K. As with the status inconsistency model (which also could be specified more clearly with a model like an expected-utility model), it is now clear that most work on the foreign–domestic conflict proposition has left out important variables and has inadequately made clear the domain of circumstances under which the proposition is expected to be true.

CONCLUSIONS

Several of the dominant research themes in international relations have formed the focus of this chapter. My purpose has been twofold. First, I have examined some of the most central efforts to theorize about international conflict, and have found that too often we do not bring as much rigor to our theorizing as we do to our data analysis. Second, I have tried to draw attention to some general theoretical issues that bear on our research too infrequently.

There has been considerable debate over the advantages of one research strategy versus another. In many instances this debate has played a valuable role in raising our awareness of the potential pitfalls inherent in the research designs and strategies we use. Certainly the quality of data analysis has improved dramatically. Whether there has been a concomitant improvement in our knowledge about international conflict is a different matter. As other chapters in this and other collections (Greenstein and Polsby 1975) suggest, there has been little movement toward cumulative knowledge or toward widely accepted generalizations about international conflict. A review of this essay suggests that it is partly due to our failure to develop rigorous and explicit methods of theorizing. Whether our approach is primarily inductive or deductive, statistical or nonstatistical, we should be able to agree that any series of observations that cannot be explained by a set of internally consistent statements must be spurious. Any hypothesis incapable of derivation from a consistent set of assumptions must be false. That is not to say that we must agree on assumptions or theoretical paradigms, but merely to suggest that whatever strategy of theorizing we use must conform to the rules of logic. This seems so obvious a point that one must wonder at its need to be stated. Yet we must not forget that compelling logical critiques of many aspects of the balance-of-power theory have failed to dissuade researchers. Indeed, few researchers have even felt obliged to respond to these critiques either by showing flaws in the critiques' logic or by improving the balance-of-power "theory" by repairing some of the logical damage.

Perhaps the single most important source of theoretical confusion in the study of international conflict lies in the much discussed "levels of analysis" problem (Singer 1961). One aspect of the levels of analysis problem that has received too little attention is the personification of social collectivities from interest groups to the international system. Ultimately, only individual human beings, acting alone, in response to others, or in conjunction with others, are capable of making decisions. Attributing decision-making characteristics to collectivities places the researcher in serious danger of making theoretically nonsensical and behaviorally spurious statements about such cognitive or affective characteristics as goals, preferences, motivations, and strategies. One may speak of the state as if it were a unitary actor, but without appropriate constraining assumptions such an approach is unlikely to be fruitful. Social collectivities, on the other hand, are an invaluable focus for those trying to identify the environmental constraints that restrict or shape decision maker options. Thus nations do not seek power, individuals do, but national resources influence whether the quest for power is pursued through internal development, through the use of diplomacy, through the use of military might, or through some combination of these. By observing the distinction between environmental constraints on decisions and the decisions themselves we are likely to construct more meaningful and useful theories. By applying the same rigor to the construction of testable propositions that we now apply to the construction of our tests, we are less likely to pursue ad hoc hypotheses that are logically implausible and more likely to discover the behavioral regularities and environmental constraints that I assumed at the outset govern international conflict.

NOTES

1. Of course, it makes no difference whether a hypothesis is actually deduced or induced. It is critical, however, that a hypothesis can be, in principle, logically deduced. If a hypothesis, or an empirical generalization cannot be supplied with a logical foundation, it must be spurious.
2. Others besides Sen have identified conditions that make it possible for groups to hold socially transitive preference orderings. Each such condition avoids Arrow's paradox by assuming that one of Arrow's conditions does not hold. Although it is reasonable to believe that many of Arrow's assumptions are violated at any given time in reality, the problem with each such solution is that there rarely is any way to know in advance which conditions will be

violated. Hence it is risky to suppose that such assumptions solve Arrow's paradox, especially under such stressful conditions as exist when foreign policy is being made in the face of international conflict.

3. In the limit, of course, this means that the balancer must be more powerful than all other states put together. This is so because no combination of states can be ruled out by balance-of-power theorists, especially since they subscribe to the contention that alliances are nonideological.

   In the discussion of the balance of power, as well as throughout this essay, the reader should bear in mind that references to states as purposive actors, such as when I say "the state pursues an expansionist policy" are shorthand for "the policy selected by the key foreign policy decision makers is . . . ."

4. The minimax (or maximin) strategy is that strategy that minimizes a player's maximum loss (or maximizes a player's minimum gain). The minimax regret strategy follows the same logic as the minimax strategy except that the player reconstructs the "payoff matrix" to reflect his level of regret, with regret determined by the difference between what he would have gotten had he known the true state of nature (that is, his opponent's strategic choice) and what he gets by choosing a strategy under uncertainty. While a minimax strategist chooses from the original payoff matrix of the decision game he is involved in, the minimax regretter chooses the minimax strategy from the payoff matrix after it is reconstructed to reflect regret (or opportunity costs).

CHAPTER 10

Evaluating War: Outcomes and Consequences

Arthur A. Stein and Bruce M. Russett

WAR IS A MAJOR AGENT OF CHANGE and a neglected one. Though war has been studied in a variety of contexts, its role as an independent variable has been curiously ignored. Historians, for example, generally focus on the origins of war or on the diplomacy of wartime and the immediate postwar period. Yet, in the words of one historian, war must be studied "in the framework of economic, social and cultural history as well" (Hans Delbrück, quoted in Michael Howard 1976: x).

Much the same is true of social scientists. Traditionally, the causes and consequences of war have been the central concerns of students of international politics, and major concerns in other disciplines as well. But in recent years social scientists have paid relatively little attention to war's effects. With the end of World War II and the onset of the Cold War, the focus of scholarly concern shifted to the prevention of war. Thus the new behavioral, theoretically oriented discipline of international relations was concerned at its birth with war causation, deterrence, strategic stability, crisis, and crisis management—with the causes rather than the effects of war. As a review of studies published during the first decade of the *Journal of Conflict Resolution* concluded, "for most JCR contributors, once a war happens, it ceases to be interesting" (Converse 1968: 476–477). Yet the consequences of war have received more attention than the consequences of less extreme forms of international conflict. Whereas the discussion that

NOTE: The authors acknowledge the assistance of Amy Davis, Robert Jervis, Stephen Krasner, and especially Ted Robert Gurr. Arthur Stein acknowledges the financial assistance provided by the Academic Senate of the University of California, Los Angeles.

follows concerns international conflict generally, most references and discussion will use examples provided by war.

Scholars and policy makers alike have good reason to learn more about the effects of war and other forms of international conflict. First, if, as Clausewitz suggested, "war is nothing but a continuation of political intercourse with a mixture of other means," we should evaluate war much as we evaluate those other means. Wars occur frequently and can have massive effects on individuals, groups, nations, and international systems. Thus knowledge of the likely consequences of conflict is necessary for those who would use rational-choice models of conflict initiation. Too often, the analysis of costs, by both scholars and policy makers, involves only those costs that are perceived to accompany cooperation. Similarly, the calculation of benefits is concerned only with those assumed to follow from a successful strategy of coercion or defection from cooperation. Any such logical calculus should include the calculation of all consequences, desired and undesired, and this requires an evaluation of international conflict as a public policy. Scholars and policy makers should therefore ascertain whether a policy of international conflict has accomplished (or is likely to accomplish) its intended goals. This in turn requires an evaluation of costs typically unanticipated or uncalculated (Claude 1975). Indeed, one scholar's list of the seven factors that strongly influence national leaders in decisions on whether to go to war includes "knowledge or forgetfulness of the realities and sufferings of war" (Blainey 1973: 246). Note that the author assumes forgetfulness to be as important as knowledge, and the relevant knowledge to be only of suffering in general rather than of more specific consequences.

Second, to the degree that war's consequences are themselves determinants of subsequent international conflicts, an understanding of these consequences is central to a correct specification of the simultaneous casual relationships that lead to war. One review of the anthropological literature on war divides studies into sixteen categories and suggests that these actually comprise eight pairs, where "for each pair, the variable that is responsible for warfare is essentially the same variable that is affected by warfare" (Otterbein 1973: 927). Finally, and most simply, if war is a major agent of social change, as is generally acknowledged, it should be studied in order to obtain an adequate and complete understanding of social change itself.

War's consequences, as will be seen below, are evident at all levels of analysis; war affects individuals, groups, nations, and international systems.[1] At each level of analysis, however, war's consequences vary, and these variations can be characterized in a number of ways.

1. Timing of impact. Some consequences, as for social cohesion, may be felt immediately, whereas others may not be felt until long after a conflict is over. The consequences of a chosen method of wartime financing, for

example, may not be fully felt until generations after the war is over. National leaders can force future generations to bear some of the costs of their decisions. Indeed, it has been estimated that most of the monetary cost of America's wars has been borne after the wars have been over (Clayton 1969; U.S. Congress, Joint Economic Committee 1969).

2. Duration. Some effects persist; others are ephemeral. The effects of wartime mobilization on domestic labor, on employment levels, and on the utilization of normally unused labor supplies, for example, are contemporaneous, that is, they are typically felt only during the war itself. Other effects that occur as a result of war are transitory; they are experienced during the war and immediately after the war. A recent study of the effects of war on production suggests that even war losers return within years to the level of production that would have been predicted from extrapolations of prewar trends (Organski and Kugler 1977). Still other effects are permanent. Death is certainly a permanent effect, as are certain injuries. Wartime mobilization typically leads to accelerated technological diffusion, a process that may stabilize after the conflict is over but certainly will not be reversed; there is no return to a prewar state of technology. Similar differences in duration are evident in consequences that occur only after wars end. Some, such as postwar baby booms, are temporary. Others, such as the disappearance of actors from the international system, are permanent.

3. The ways in which wars affect individuals, groups, nations, and international systems can also be categorized. Wars often work changes in the capabilities of actors. The destruction of productive facilities, increased productivity, and technological diffusion, for example, all involve changes in the capabilities of nations and thus in the structure of the international system. Alternatively, wars may change actors' choices, as, for example, when individuals' war experiences shift their evaluation of costs and benefits; war-weariness is one such effect. Finally, wars may entail structural changes for actors, unchosen shifts in the context or environment within which they act. Conscription is probably the most common such wartime experience. Other examples are forced evacuations and ostracism of minority groups.

4. In addition to categorizing the effects of war, whether by type, timing, or duration, it is important to classify wars themselves, for variations in their characteristics determine which consequences occur and to what degree. International conflicts, including wars, vary in intensity and extensity. Some wars last years, even decades; others last only a few days. Some wars involve two nations; others are labeled "world wars." Sometimes fighting is limited; in other cases the scope and degree of destruction is much greater. Typically, it is assumed that larger wars are likely to manifest more consequences and effect more long-term changes.

5. There is also variation in the degree of threat to the warring states. In

some wars, all belligerents feel threatened; in others, an aggressor revisionist state threatens status quo states; and at other times none of the belligerents may be or perceive themselves to be seriously threatened. Indeed, the existence of external threat is an intervening variable in the social-psychological literature that posits a relationship between external conflict and changes in internal cohesion (A. A. Stein 1976).

6. There are also differences in the ways nations wage war. In some cases, states can wage war without extensively mobilizing the society; in other cases, the state mobilizes the entire society for the war effort. Many of the domestic effects of war are indeed a function of the extent of wartime mobilization (A. A. Stein 1980).

7. A conflict's course, and especially its conclusion, can also be important determinants of change. For the participants, wars are resolved by victory, defeat, or compromise (or degrees of these), and each has a different impact. Defeat, for example, typically leads to a regime change in the defeated state.

8. Finally, the prewar attributes of actors may also determine the ways in which those actors are affected by war. The effect of war on a nation's capability, for example, may be a function not only of the characteristics of that war but also of the characteristics of the nation itself. Thus the effects of war on national capabilities may be different for major and minor powers (Wheeler 1975d).

These categorizations of causes and effects suggest the existence of a wide variety of specific consequences occurring in a wide range of wartime and postwar contexts. Many of these can be illustrated. Yet the paucity of sound empirical studies of wars' effects is such that many of their complexities and subtleties cannot be evaluated.

OUTCOMES OF INTERNATIONAL CONFLICTS

The outcomes of international conflicts vary. Outright victory and defeat are the two most obvious, but others, such as compromise and stalemate, can also be identified.[2] Further, if victory and defeat are assessed by reference to the objectives of the participants, a war's end may find all parties feeling victorious or defeated. On the other hand, a war's outcome may not even involve a resolution of the issues that were originally cited to justify the conflict. Unfortunately, scholars are less subtle in describing the outcomes of wars and other international conflicts than we might wish. Victory and defeat remain the predominant descriptions of a nation's status at the end of a war, and careful distinctions are rarely made. Thus, despite emphasis on the importance of subtlety and careful distinction, a number of scholars have proceeded to label France, Italy, and Poland, as well as the United States, winners of World War II (Singer and Small

1972; see also Organski and Kugler 1977). Similarly, those who have attempted to "predict" the outcomes of past wars also have used a simple dichotomy.

The early empirical attempts to predict war outcomes focused on the most easily quantifiable component: battle deaths. It was hypothesized that some relationship existed between battle casualties—or population losses, or relative population losses—and the outcome of war. Richardson, for example, searched for a threshold for population losses and assumed that "defeat would usually occur when the less populous side had lost in dead some number between 0.05 and 5 percent of its population" (Richardson 1960b: 299). Klingberg found that "there is some evidence that nations in modern times will tend to surrender before they have suffered population losses greater than three or four percent" (Klingberg 1966: 168). Rosen tested Richardson's hypothesis and found that "in only 2 of 77 cases did states suffer more than 5 percent population loss in battle before yielding," but "on the other hand, his [Richardson's] lower limit is definitely disconfirmed: in 23 of 77 cases the defeated party lost less than 0.05 per cent of its population in battle deaths" (Rosen 1972: 179).

Not only has no general relationship between fatalities and victory or defeat been found (Klingberg 1966, Singer and Small 1972), but also there has been no scholarly consensus on the narrower issue of predicting duration or point of termination on the basis of battle deaths, regardless of whether those deaths are suffered by winner and/or loser and without attempting to predict victor or vanquished (Weiss 1963; Horvath 1968; Voevodsky 1969, 1972; Singer and Small 1972).

These works, which attempt to predict war's outcome by reference to battle deaths, focus on the loser and on the point at which costs lead a nation to give up; in other words, they assume the loser's role to be decisive in terminating war (Coser 1961).

There is an alternative approach, however, that focuses on the relative strength and power of the warring parties. One recent study of seemingly aberrant cases, four post–World War II international conflicts in which the apparently weaker power won, uses a refined measure of power that combines gross national product, tax effort, and foreign aid received to establish that the superior power was in fact victorious in the cases they describe (Organski and Kugler 1978).[3] To explain the outcome of these wars does not require reference to other factors, they argue, but requires an accurate measure of power that includes governmental extraction capacity.

A cross-cultural study of war in fifty primitive societies from all over the globe, in which each society represents a different culture, suggests that quite different factors are determinative (Otterbein 1970). In this study, military success is defined as the expansion of territorial borders (very much like Organski and Kugler 1977; compare with the procedure used by Singer and Small 1972), and explained by the degree of military sophistication. The study shows a significant positive correlation between military sophistication and military success. On the other hand, there is no significant correlation between political centralization, a variable which would seem to be related to Organski and Kugler's (1978) extraction capacity, and military success. Indeed, when Otterbein (1970) controls for political centralization, the significant positive relationship between military sophistication and military success is unaffected, and no significant relationship emerges between political centralization and military success even when controlling for military sophistication. Clearly, military sophistication and the strength it imparts, and not political centralization, explain military success in this particular sample of primitive wars.

The work of Steven Rosen (1970, 1972) explicitly interrelates two dimensions of state power: strength and cost-tolerance. Rosen argues that the power of a state involves not only its ability to harm (its strength) but also its willingness to suffer (its cost-tolerance). Thus the superior military or material strength of one nation may be offset by the superior cost-tolerance of the other, weaker nation with which it is at war. Rosen partially tests this theory in an analysis of seventy-seven wars during the last two centuries (Rosen 1972). In a comparison of warring nations (or coalitions), he finds that greater strength (as measured by governmental revenue) predicts the winner 79 percent of the time. The side that lost a lower percentage of its population in battle won 75 percent of the time, and the side that lost a lower absolute number of lives in battle won 55 percent of the time, while the party with both greater revenues and a lower relative loss of population in battle won fully 84 percent of the time. On the other hand, there were times that the seemingly weaker side was victorious. One-fifth of the wars Rosen studies were won by the weaker power (that is, the side with less government revenue) and 45 percent were won by those suffering a greater absolute loss of lives in battle. Even those nations suffering a relatively greater population loss won, albeit less often (25 percent of the time). Thus it seems that in a minority of cases, superior cost-tolerance can compensate for relative material weakness and result in military victory for the apparently weaker side.

In most cases, wars' outcomes are determined by the strengths of the belligerents, with the superior side winning. Sometimes that superior strength is provided by greater military sophistication, in which case the militarily more sophisticated side will be victorious. When there is no such asymmetry in the levels of military sophistication, the side that mobilizes more resources and inflicts greater damage will win. Occasionally, however, a superior ability to tolerate harm and suffering can compensate for inferior strength and result in military victory.

WAR AND INDIVIDUALS

Individuals are clearly affected by international conflict, especially war. Some individuals die in war. Others suffer permanently debilitating injuries. Families experience the premature death of a relative. Politically, the most salient effect of war on individuals is on images and attitudes.[4] Individuals are most directly affected by firsthand experiences. Decision makers, for example, are often influenced by their wartime experiences as they continue to grapple with similar issues after a war's end. It is now a commonplace that "the impact of the two world wars on later perceptions show that as generals are prepared to fight the last war, diplomats are prepared to avoid it" (Jervis 1976: 267). Political leaders learn from history (May 1973, Jervis 1976: chapter 6), and it is the last major war that has the greatest impact on them (Jervis 1976: 261).

Although it is possible to illustrate the impact of historical conflicts, it is much more difficult to validate the causal propositions concerning the effects of war on individuals' images and attitudes. There are alternative explanations of behavior that do not include historical experience as a determinant, and it is often possible to offer an alternative explanation for those cases in which the impact of history is claimed to be important. It may be, for example, that historical analogies often are offered as rationalizations for behavior that was not in fact influenced by those historical experiences.

Wars do not affect only those who participate directly. Indeed, "events that are terribly important for the nation (e.g. wars) can have so great an impact that the perceptual predispositions of those who did not participate in the making of the policy will be affected almost as much as those who did" (Jervis 1976: 239). The very "dramatic and pervasive nature of a war and its consequences, the experiences associated with it—the diplomacy that preceded it, the methods of fighting it, the alliances that were formed, and the way the war was terminated—will deeply influence the perceptual predispositions of most citizens" (Jervis 1976: 266). In the case of major wars, anyone who is aware of the conflict can perhaps be considered a direct participant, and policy makers who were old enough to remember the last major war can be assumed to have been affected by it (Jervis 1976: 266).

Wars can thus affect entire generations of individuals, and there is quite extensive evidence that generational attitudinal changes persist long after the original stimulus is gone (Mannheim 1952, Bobrow and Cutler 1967, Spitzer 1973). Such generational effects have led many scholars to search for periodicity in the occurrence of war (J. S. Lee 1931, Moyal 1949, Toynbee 1954, Richardson 1960b, Sorokin 1962, Q. Wright 1965, Denton 1966, Denton and Phillips 1968, Denton 1969, Dewey 1971, Singer and Small 1972, Small and Singer 1979; for a thorough review of this literature, see Beer 1979). Some suggest that war generations become war-weary; that those who remember war's dislocations and suffering wish not to experience them again. As one scholar characterizes war, it is a disease, and all those who have suffered its ravages are provided with an immunity against future infection (Richardson 1960a: 232–236). According to those who posit the existence of war-weariness, future wars begin because memories fade; they are started by a new generation too young to remember or to have lived through the last war (Blainey 1973: 246). Yet the occurrence of World War II so soon after the World War I presents a problem for the war-weariness hypothesis, which one cycle theorist deals with by arguing that World War II was "manifestly something contrary to human nature" (Toynbee 1954: 326).[5]

The most recent empirical investigation of cycles in the occurrence of war (Singer and Cusack 1980) concludes that there is no convincing evidence to support most cyclical interpretations. The authors do find some evidence for the proposition that for major powers defeated in war, the greater the cost of *that* war in battle deaths, the longer is the interval to the *next* war—but that the longer that interval, the more intense the next war is likely to be.

Such theories of cyclical behavior have been applied not only to war's occurrence but also to foreign policy more generally. Numerous scholars have argued that cycles exist in American public opinion concerning foreign policy, as well as in the actual course of American foreign policy, which, they suggest, shifts between extremes of international involvement and isolationism. These shifts between isolation and involvement are often related to war experiences (Klingberg 1952, Perkins 1968, Hoffmann 1968, Roskin 1974, Russett 1975, Russett and Hanson 1975, Russett and Nincic 1976, Klingberg 1979). It is often argued that the dissatisfactions stemming from American experiences in World War I led to the isolationism of the interwar years and to the retrospective belief of many Americans that the nation's involvement in the war had been a great mistake. The experience of World War II, on the other hand, led to a commitment to prevent the next great war through greater involvement in international affairs. Many now suggest that the Vietnam experience may lead to a new isolationism, to a rejection of the involvement and interventionism that followed World War II. "Each elite American generation comes to favor one of these orientations by living through the catastrophe brought on by the application *ad absurdum* of the opposite paradigm at the hands of the previous elite generation" (Roskin 1974: 563). Typically, these catastrophes are wars, which thus play a central role in the American oscillation between extreme involvement and isolation.

While scholars tend to agree that wars may broadly affect generational attitudes toward war itself as well as more general perceptual orientations, they disagree on the degree of specificity of attitude changes. A survey in

1976 of Americans in "leadership" positions focused on detailed attitudes toward the Vietnam war and on the lessons and prescriptions that people derived from it. In their reports of this study, Holsti and Rosenau (1979, 1980) contend, and demonstrate with the aggregate results of a survey, that there were several different belief systems, each widely held, concerning the American experience in the Vietnam war. Briefly, they divide American leaders according to their positions on Vietnam early in the war and again in the war's late stages, thereby distinguishing consistent supporters and consistent opponents, converts (in both directions), and several types of "ambivalents." Individuals within each group, they show, shared particular views about the reasons for the American failure and drew similar lessons from the experience. But between groups there were very sharp cleavages, with each group believing the war had very different consequences for the United States and the world system, and drawing very different lessons.

> While there is general agreement that Americans *should* learn from past mistakes, this consensus breaks down once attention focuses on specific substantive lessons. Disagreement pervades all levels of thinking about how the lessons of Vietnam should guide the future conduct of American foreign policy, from the broadest questions of "grand design" through "grand strategy" and "tactics." [Holsti and Rosenau 1979: 49]

The authors note that we do not have available the sort of controlled experiment that would make it certain that it was the war, rather than other international or domestic events, that produced this fragmentation of belief systems. Nevertheless it does appear that the "lessons" learned varied to the extent that original attitudes toward the war varied during its course. In situations where varying attitudes toward war involvement exist, individuals are likely to assimilate events to their pre-existing beliefs, which may vary by class, occupation, or ethnic group as well as by age.

An examination of mass opinion surveyed at different times from 1973 to 1978 (Kriesberg and Klein 1980) indicates that whereas age and war generation were important discriminators of opinions favoring or opposing military spending in 1973 and 1975, by 1978 the power of these variables to discriminate attitudes had declined significantly. They suggest that the impact of the Vietnam war on mass attitudes was fading rapidly, being replaced by general increases in conservatism and anti-Soviet sentiment. Thus while wars may affect the attitudes held by whole generations, it is clear that the effect does fade over time, and that we know little about the determinants of the "half-life" of such attitude changes.

Wars affect individuals' political attitudes and, most important, their attitudes toward war itself. Thus one effect of past wars is that they determine aspects of future wars. The timing and conditions of future wars are sown by past wars. Although not prevented, subsequent wars are different, yet the statement "Those who remember the past are condemned to make the opposite mistake" (Jervis 1976: 275) probably is still too simple.

WAR AND SOCIETY

Most literature on the consequences of war is devoted to war's effects on individual societies. Typically, these works focus on war and the state, war and the economy, or war and social cohesion. Discussions of each of these follow.

WAR AND THE STATE

War is generally recognized as a determinant of the origins, development, consolidation, and viability of the state. There are two general explanations of state origins, and in both, war plays a major role.[6] The first group of theorists stresses the importance of conflict and the coercive nature of state origins. They all argue that increased political centralization and the state itself emerged from competition, conquest, and coercion, although some emphasize intersocietal conflict and conquest while others point to intrasocietal conflict.

A somewhat different explanation is that centralized political coordination emerged not from competition and coercion but from voluntarism and integration. Briefly, this set of theories stresses the importance of centralized political control as the only means by which societies can meet certain demands and fulfill certain needs. One of the most basic of the benefits provided by central governments is security, and some theorists suggest that the state arose precisely because of the threat posed by war. In other words, the state is a political organization that provides collective goods, including protection (Lane 1958). It provides security from internal dissension by "producing" justice and provides protection against external threats by "producing" defense (Ames and Rapp 1977; see also Lane 1942). Communities with central governments are created in order to transcend the anarchic state of nature that is characterized by conflict among all individuals because governments are the only agents that can provide internal peace, limit armed conflict to confrontations with outsiders, and limit the degree of danger such external conflicts pose. Thus the threat of war makes the state, which may then make wars.

Despite problems with both sets of arguments,

> there is little question that, in one way or another, war played a decisive role in the rise of the state. Historical or archeological evidence of war is found in the early stages of state formation in Mesopotamia, Egypt, India, China, Japan, Greece, Rome, northern Europe, central Africa, Polynesia, Middle America, Peru, and Colombia, to name only the most prominent examples. [Carneiro, 1970: 734; also Wesson 1967]

Success in war is one of the general conditions that predicts state-making (Tilly 1975a: 40). War is clearly a mechanism of state formation, and whether voluntaristic or coercive, extends the area of "peace."

An extension of these arguments is the claim that war is important in determining the size of the state (that is, territory encompassed). If states are envisaged as "firms" that provide the "public good" of "protection," then "economies of scale" may exist that suggest a range of optimal state size. Changes in military technology, for example, can alter the range of optimal state size and thus explain the consolidation of political and military power in Europe in the early modern period (Bean 1973, Morton 1969). The increased effectiveness of the infantry resulted in a rise in the size of armies, and involved "a shift in the production function of defense so that the minimum efficient size of state was increased and the centralized state was given a greater advantage over the decentralized state" (Bean 1973: 220). In other words, changes in the art of war can change the advantages and disadvantages of scale and thus lead to changes in the amount of territory controlled by the state. In this way, war becomes responsible not only for the rise of the state but for its growth and development as well. Indeed, since neolithic times the typical size of political units, whether states or empires, has shown a long-term tendency to increase (Hart 1948, Naroll 1967, Taagepara 1968, Marano 1973, Ogburn 1964, Carneiro 1978).

The occurrence of war and changes in the art of war are responsible not only for increasing the size of the territory that states encompass, but also for increases in the scope of the state. War preparation and direction are tasks reserved to the central state apparatus which require the extraction and utilization of resources. Governments expend more resources during war than they do in peacetime, and wars thus act as a persistent stimulus to increase the fiscal burden (Tilly 1975a: 54; Ardant 1975). Large wartime increases in state expenditures are followed by some postwar shrinkage, but to a plateau higher than the prewar level. This has been dubbed the "displacement effect" (Peacock and Wiseman 1961). Postwar governmental expenditures exceed prewar ones, and the difference cannot be fully accounted for by increased war-related costs such as pensions and debts. War thus acts as a major determinant of net increases in the size of the state, where size refers to relative proportion of national product expended by the government (Peacock and Wiseman 1961, Kendrick 1955, Fabricant 1949, Musgrave and Culbertson 1953, Pryor 1968). There also is evidence that military expenditures and/or the size of national armed forces remain at a postwar plateau that is higher than the prewar level. This so-called "ratchet effect" is reported for United States wars by Russett (1970: 2–5), but does not apply to the post–Vietnam war period (A. A. Stein 1980).

The existence of a war-induced displacement effect is not questioned, but the explanation for it is a matter of some dispute. Peacock and Wiseman (1961) attribute the growth in government expenditures to increased popular tolerance of added taxation in wartime, a tolerance that spills over into the postwar period. Critics have pointed out that war need not be financed by added taxation and extraction (Pryor 1968, Hamilton 1977, M. A. Robinson 1955, Friedman 1952).[7] Yet the historical record reveals that war has played a central role in the development of Western European systems of taxation and of specific taxes as well (Ames and Rapp 1977, Tilly 1975a: 42). Indeed, not only are there often wartime increases in taxation, but there is a generally greater reliance on direct taxation for increased extraction; thus the proportion of direct taxes to indirect taxes increases in wartime (A. A. Stein 1980).

As important as the financial growth of the state resulting from war is the attendant relative growth of state powers. The state is a monopoly supplier of defense and is thus the coordinator of societal activities in the war effort. The scope of state control increases as the central state becomes involved in activities it has previously not attempted to regulate. As a monopoly, the state can affect the extent to which monopolies prevail in other fields of production (Lane 1958: 416). Wartime increases in the size of the central government thus involve an increase in governmental concentration relative to the size of local governments (Peacock and Wiseman 1961, A. A. Stein 1980). In addition, the increased size of government may potentially lead to increased concentration in other areas as the central government expands the scope of its control. An analysis of ten centuries of European history that compares historical epochs alternatively characterized as "laisser-faire" and "public control" concludes that "during periods of laisser-faire, the incidence of wars appears to decline and it increases during periods classified as government control" (Crowley 1971: 41; also see Marr 1974).[8]

War is thus linked to the origins, development, consolidation, absolute growth, and relative growth of the state. As Charles Tilly suggests in his introduction to a collection of essays on *The Formation of States in Western Europe*, "war made the state, and the state made war," and "preparation for war has been the great state building activity" (Tilly 1975a: 42, 74).

Yet war has destroyed states as well as built them. For many states, a defeat in war has meant their complete disappearance, as is discussed below. Victors rarely change regimes as a result of their participation in war, but defeat in sustained war between major powers since 1850 has almost invariably meant such a change (see Table 10–1). Indeed, the application of evolutionary models suggests that success or failure in wartime determines processes of societal selection, a social survival of the "fittest" (Otterbein 1973: 943–944). In other words, *inter*societal selection operates through the rise and fall of states, and *intra*societal selection through the strengthening or collapse of domestic regimes.

TABLE 10.1. Regime Change and the Outcomes of Sustained War between Major Powers

	Winners	Losers
Regime change	0	9
No regime change	10	0
*The Major-Power Wars**	*Winner(s)*	*Loser(s)*
Franco-Prussian	Prussia	France
Russo-Japanese	Japan	Russia†
World War I	Great Britain	Germany
	France	Austria-Hungary
	United States	Russia
	Italy	
	Japan	
World War II	United States	Germany
	U.S.S.R.	Japan
	Great Britain	Italy
		France

* Wars in which there was a clear loser (that is, a nation that surrendered, was occupied, or lost territory).
† Classified as a regime change because of the Revolution of 1905, the writing of a new constitution, and the czar's being forced to establish a Duma. This is a marginal case since the chief of state (the czar) did not change.

WAR AND THE ECONOMY

The relationship between war and progress, especially economic progress, has been the subject of much debate. To some, war is the engine that propels such economic change, indeed, that drives civilization itself. To others, however, war is the antithesis of all that they believe economic progress to represent (Russell 1936, D. Dunn 1974, Deane 1975, Winter 1975). Unfortunately, the arguments in this debate are clouded by moral judgments and definitional imprecision. Progress, along with certain other concepts, is such a vague explanandum that many scholars have abandoned it altogether. For in using it, "we attempt to explain so much that we end up explaining nothing" (Tilly 1975b: 617). By disaggregating the elements of the debate, however, it becomes much easier to get a handle on the problem of the actual relationship between war and economic progress.

Those who posit that war hinders economic growth argue that the main direct economic effect of war is destruction (Marwick 1968, 1974; C. W. Wright 1943): people are killed and productive facilities destroyed. In addition to such outright destruction, there is a wartime loss of production due to the transfer of facilities from the production of peacetime goods to the production of equipment that consumes rather than reproduces capital.[9] Variation in the degree of all of these wartime losses of human and physical capital partially determines differences in the amount of lost potential production.

Labor and capital are not the only factors of production that can be destroyed in war, for the advanced technology of modern warfare can make possible the physical destruction of the land as well. The environmental effects of the American devastation of Indochina are severe and long-lasting, and clearly affect the prospects of future economic progress there (Westing and Pfeiffer 1972, Neilands et al. 1972, Stockholm International Peace Research Institute 1976). Certainly the effects of the wartime use of nuclear weapons would affect economic recovery, if recovery would in fact be possible (Dentler and Cutright 1963, National Academy of Sciences 1975).

War also adversely affects the economy in less direct ways. The wartime destruction of capital, for example, is not only direct, but indirect, via inflation and debt or the sale of foreign investments to finance the import of war materiel. In addition, the wartime disruption of international trade harms economic welfare by diverting economic resources from their most efficient uses. Finally, some scholars argue that the increased governmental control of wartime destroys individual initiative, which in turn retards economic progress (C. W. Wright 1943: 14).

Others, however, argue that war can serve to stimulate economic growth. Proponents of the view that war plays a constructive role in economic development point to a largely different set of factors. First, they emphasize that war leads to the utilization of unused capacity and brings underutilized factors into the production process. There is, for example, increased participation in the labor force by women and minorities in heterogeneous societies during wartime (A. A. Stein 1980). Similarly, wartime mobilization once served to draw peripheral geographical areas into a national market (Tilly 1975a: 73). In addition, wartime increases in demand and resource coordination can lead to a more efficient utilization of factors of production by increasing concentration and scale and thus increasing productivity as well. Indeed, wartime mobilization leads to increased technological innovation and, more importantly, to technological diffusion, both of which promote growth.[10] In a variety of ways, war also involves a redistribution of wealth and income, and this too promotes growth (C. W. Wright 1943, A. A. Stein 1980). Finally, the disruption of international trade leads to substitution for imported raw materials and to the development and protection of infant industries producing previously imported goods. This too is beneficial to future growth. Biersteker (1979) discusses the experience of Biafra during the Nigerian civil war.

Historical attempts to disentangle the argument between those who claim that war promotes economic growth and those who see only its destructive capabilities have not been very successful. Whereas it has been possible to refute some of the more extreme arguments,[11] it remains the case that examples of war as both growth-promoting and -retarding abound (Wheeler 1975d; see also Lane 1942). Again, disaggregating the arguments rather than discussing war and economic progress more generally, is essential to understanding the economic effects of war. Unfortunately, a problem remains in that these two schools rarely address one another directly; their only direct disagreements concern the relationship between war and technological innovation and the effects of the disruption of international trade. Even should these direct disagreements be resolved empirically, we would not be much closer to a true evaluation of war's economic effects, for the two camps place their primary emphases on different factors. The destructivists point to capital destruction, an effect of war that cannot be disputed. The constructivists, on the other hand, focus on the increased demand and productivity generated by war, an effect that also clearly occurs. In other words, war both promotes and retards growth, and we can make and validate hypotheses about specific positive and negative effects of war. Moreover, the variable properties of war itself affect the degree of positive and negative consequences. To try to step back and reaggregate these diverse and divergent consequences into an overall assessment of war's effects on economic progress would require the evaluation of counterfactual arguments and would require extensive empirical work in order to specify intervening conditions.

WAR AND SOCIAL COHESION

It is often assumed that war increases the internal cohesion of the warring state. The belief in this relationship is so strong that it has frequently been suggested that insecure political elites sometimes initiate war in order to increase domestic unity and secure their positions (Rosecrance 1963).[12] Yet the opposite claim, that war leads to social disorganization and internal dissension, even to revolution, has also been mentioned, although less often.

A review of the theoretical and empirical work on this problem suggests that both arguments have validity (A. A. Stein 1976, 1980; see also Stohl, Chapter 7 of this *Handbook*). The contradiction arises from static analyses of the relationship between war and cohesion. A dynamic analysis, on the other hand, suggests that a more complex relationship in fact exists. War can indeed increase internal cohesion, but only under a variety of specific conditions, including the existence of an external threat to the society. Where no such threat exists, cohesion does not increase.

In addition, the very process of waging war serves to decrease societal cohesion, regardless of any original increases in cohesion that may be engendered by the existence of an external threat (A. A. Stein 1980). The increased governmental extraction that accompanies war (that is, the process of mobilization) leads to a decrease in social cohesion. Historically, "the most serious and persistent precipitant of violent conflicts between European state-makers and the populations they attempted to rule were attempts to collect taxes" (Tilly 1975a: 54; Ardant 1975). Since increased extraction, including even the creation of new taxes, is a hallmark of war, it is not surprising that there is a "tendency of revolutions to occur in conjunction with the preparation and the termination of war" (Tilly 1975a: 74, Skocpol 1976).[13] In other words, the very process of providing community defense during wartime leads to a decrease in cohesion even when there exists an external threat to that community.

The net effect of a war on social cohesion thus depends on the character of that war. When an external threat exists, there is an initial increase in social cohesion following the onset of war. The wartime mobilization process, however, tends independently to decrease the level of social cohesion. The existence of the external threat may have an additional mitigating effect in that marginal decreases in the level of cohesion per unit of mobilization may be less than they would be during an otherwise similar but a nonthreatening war. When no external threat exists, mobilization will immediately lead to a decrease in the level of social cohesion (A. A. Stein 1980).[14]

WAR AND THE INTERNATIONAL SYSTEM

"From the point of view of the international system . . . war appears as a basic determinants of the shape the system assumes at any one time" (Bull 1973: 119). Indeed war may be the characteristic condition of the state system (Tilly 1975a: 52; see also Finer 1975). Most fundamentally, wars affect the distribution of power in the international system and they do so in a number of wars.

> It is war . . . that help[s] to determine whether particular states survive or are eliminated, whether their futures remain the same or are changes, whether their people are ruled by one government or another . . . whether there is a balance of power in the international system or one state becomes proponderant. [Bull 1973: 118]

This argument, that wars play a major role in the distribution of power, is a central one. Modelski, arguing in support of this conventional wisdom, argues that war justifies and legitimizes the international status system and, indeed, that "war 'causes' the Great Powers" (Modelski 1972a: 48).[15] He has shown, for example, that the outcomes of most wars in the last five centuries have involved the rise of a new great power or the decline of an old one (Modelski 1972a: 51, 1972b: 292, 1978a: 48). More recently, Modelski (1978b) argues that in modern times a succession of world powers have shaped the political system, and that these powers and the constitution of the global political system are determined by global wars.

Modelski further demonstrates the importance of war by compiling a list of the great powers that existed between 1815 and 1970. The criteria for inclusion are formal ones: participation in the Concert of Europe, permanent membership in the Council of the League of Nations, and permanent membership in the Security Council of the United Nations (Modelski 1972b: 144). Four of the nine nations that he lists actually lost their great power status during this period, all as a result of war (Austria-Hungary in 1918, Italy in 1943, Germany and Japan in 1945). This finding is mirrored by Singer and Small's (1972: 24–26) categorization of major powers and by Kohler's (1975: 57) classification of imperial leaders, both of which show that states that have lost their positions as great powers or as imperial leaders have done so as a result of wars. Clearly, wars can lead to the loss of great-power status and to the dissolution of empires.

The degree of such war-effected change is a function not only of the course and termination point of the war, but of the assimilative process of the postconfrontation period. Charles Doran (1971) studies the process of assimilation that follows a thwarted bid for hegemony by one or more states, and defines assimilation as a collective process "in which a defeated aggressor state comes to reject . . . its status of belligerency, at least with respect to former issues and opponents" (C. R. Doran 1971: 24), and in which the other major powers accept a new role for the defeated state in the postwar international system. He argues that one of three possible outcomes—overassimilation, underassimilation, or controlled assimilation—will follow such an unsuccessful bid for hegemony. The outcome may entail the disappearance, completely or from great-power status, of the defeated aspiring hegemon (overassimilation), the assertion of a new hegemonic attempt by the underassimilated aspiring hegemon (underassimilation), or the establishment of a stable international order without the overt or covert instabilities entailed in the other two outcomes (controlled assimilation). Doran argues that assimilation is a function of interactor systemic changes (which include the material changes wrought in wartime and the postwar adjustive actions taken by the winners and losers), of intra-actor organic changes (including relative development and growth rates), and of changes in the character of the regimes.[16]

This impact of war on the great powers also affects subsequent war. Modelski (1972a, 1972b, 1978a) argues that war is a great power activity and that wars disproportionately involve great powers—points well-established in the literature (Russett and Monsen 1975, Stuckey and Singer 1973, Weede 1970). Thus the dissolution and creation of great powers in the wake of global war can affect the prospects for future war, its time of occurrence, and its scope. In addition, Kohler (1975) argues that imperial states do become more peaceful (that is, are involved in fewer wars) after they lose their empires.

Two recent empirical studies concerned with wars' effects on national power and the distribution of power in the international system challenge this conventional wisdom. Henry Barbera (1973), the author of one such study, couches his argument not in terms of power but of development, and uses as his indicator of development the number of telephones per capita. He finds that the occurrence of the two world wars of the twentieth century had little effect on various aspects of the international hierarchy of development. Barbera controls for prewar levels of development and for the nature and degree of participation in war, and rarely finds the wars to have had much effect at all, especially on the developed nations. He does not distinguish between winners and losers, but instead contrasts nations by the duration of their participation (number of years) and by whether or not they were occupied, and finds little difference across these groups.

The second recent empirical study, that of Organski and Kugler (1977), concludes that the occurrence and outcome of war make very little difference for national power. By comparing the actual gross national products of belligerent nations following the two world wars of the twentieth century with the expected GNPs for those nations as extrapolated from prewar data, the authors conclude that in the long run wars make no difference. The power levels of winners and of neutrals are affected only marginally; defeated nations suffer only short-term losses and return to their expected position in fifteen to twenty years. In other words, "the power distribution in the system [soon] returns to levels anticipated had the war not occurred" (Organski and Kugler 1977: 1365).

Unfortunately, the conclusions of the latter study are questionable. The steps taken in order to assure intertemporally comparable units limit the value of the findings. To assure comparability, for example, certain nations were dropped from the study. Austria could not be included since the Austro-Hungarian Empire was dismembered, and Austria was absorbed by Germany prior to the outbreak of World War II—clearly a loss of national power. On the other hand, nations that underwent territorial or governmental changes, such as Germany, were retained in the study, but their 1970 boundaries were used throughout in order to insure comparability. Thus only West Germany is actually included and yearly estimates were made for what would have been West Germany's GNP in the years prior to 1945. East Germany, though the most prosperous of the East European states, is poorer than West Germany and would not compare so well with the extrapolated prewar trend. Such exclusions for the sake of insuring comparability have the effect of tipping the evidence in favor of the authors' hypothesis.

In the end, the study's findings show only that several particular pieces of terrority and their resident populations recovered their material capacity to produce, and returned in fifteen or twenty years to the level that they would have been expected to reach if no war had occurred. This "phoenix factor" is an important finding, but it should not be confused with an argument that the power of the state returns to its former level. Some of the states in question (Austria, Hungary, West and East Germany) are in fact significantly smaller than their predecessors. The "births" and "deaths" of states are themselves an effect of war (Modelski 1972b). General wars have often been the principal means of boundary realignment in the international system (Tilly 1975a: p. 52; see also Finer 1975). The effects of the final solution to the German problem in the twentieth century, that of division, can hardly be ignored. Moreover, the nature of the government, its orientation, and whether it does or does not maintain an army, are also excluded from Organski and Kugler's purview. Yet this is one of the determinants of the assimilation process discussed by Doran, and as has been argued above, defeat in sustained wars usually involves a regime change in the defeated nation.

It is important to confront—as Organski and Kugler do—the argument that postwar American aid may have been responsible for the recovery rates of both defeated and victorious states following World War II. C. R. Doran (1971) argues, after all, that the postwar adjustment decisions made by the victors are a determinant of the assimilation process. Organski and Kugler's procedure is to correlate the annual recovery rate (changes in relative growth) with American foreign aid (using various lags). Correlating total aid by year with annual growth rates for all recipient states grouped together, they find no significant relationship between high-aid years and subsequent high growth. Furthermore, they note that there was a perfect inverse relationship between the total amount of aid received by each of the five major recipient states and the states' growth rates. Nevertheless, the matter is not completely settled, because this kind of empirical test misses the subtle examples provided by Doran of the range of assimilative techniques available to the victorious powers, specifically those made available after World War II. The forms of actual assistance varied; for example, the greatest American assistance to Japan came not in the form of direct aid, but from allowing the Japanese to undervalue the yen systematically and so enjoy export-led growth. The postwar decisions made by the victors do matter in the postwar assimilation process.

Wars affect the international system not only by affecting the number of great powers, but also by affecting the total number of actors in the international system. "Most of the political units which disappeared perished in war," which in Europe meant that "the thousand state-like units spattering the political map of fourteenth-century Europe dwindled to fewer than thirty by World War I," and that "war [thus] shaped and reshaped the European state system" (Tilly 1975a: 42, 76, 75). The historical increase in the size of political units discussed above implies a decrease in the number of autonomous political units. Indeed, the twelve millennia since neolithic times have witnessed a long-term decrease in the number of autonomous political units, a political evolution that, according to one author, has been driven by war (Carneiro 1978).

In addition, war has been responsible not only for the disappearance of states but also for the appearance of new ones. "There have been three main waves of new state making since the late eighteenth century," and "each wave has come with the collapse of empires" (Lyon 1973: 26–27). Two of the three waves are directly related to war: both world wars in the twentieth century involved the creation of large numbers of states as the wars led to the collapse of empires with major consequences for international order. Twenty new nation–states joined the interstate system between 1918 and 1922, and another fourteen came into being in the years from 1944 to 1949.[17]

Clearly, wars profoundly affect the international system. Their consequences for nation–states, especially those effects involving states' capabilities and choices, have international repercussions. More directly, wars can fundamentally change the international system by affecting the number of actors in the system and their relative power.

CONCLUSION

Destruction is a part of war, perhaps its most salient feature. War kills people, destroys capital, and damages the land. War can also destroy the political and economic institutions, both domestic and international, that organize and sustain societal activity.

Yet war also has a rejuvenating character. The demands of war and wartime mobilization, whether for increased production or greater social coordination, are generated in a context that rewards successful adaptation and makes rapid change possible.

Wars affect bystanders as well as participants. The systemic changes wrought by war, for example, affect all nations in the system, regardless of whether they actually participated.

Different perceptions of the long-term effects of war are at the heart of many of the literature's key debates. There is no question but that numerous effects occur during wartime. People die; nations are victorious and are defeated; indeed, nations die and are born. The long-term consequences are more elusive, however. All people die eventually, so it is possible to argue that war only hastens a certain fate. Thus the critical question is whether war creates fundamental transformations or whether it acts merely as an evolutionary stimulant, reinforcing extant trends and speeding the emergence of already inevitable occurrences. In other words, do wars involve real discontinuities in historical development or do they simply cause ripples in a basically continuous process of a development that is fueled by other determinants? Unfortunately, the currently available empirical work is hardly adequate to the task of determining if wars affect, for example, the course of economic development or if they effect changes in the international balance of power, or if wars merely lead to short-term distractions from long-term dynamics. The characteristics of both wars and the nations engaged in them are important in this regard, and this potential relationship certainly deserves more systematic study.

The greatest single weakness in the literature on the various effects of war, whether on the international system, the state, or the individual, is its paucity. Despite the existence of numerous references to and examples of war's consequences, it is not even possible to illustrate all of the possible combinations discussed in the introduction. To limit this discussion to those works that offer adequate empirical validations of the various propositions concerning war's effects would only emphasize this problem, for much of the work on the consequences of war is hazy and impressionistic. Too often, too little is known even to unravel the most basic of the scholarly disagreements that exist in this literature.

A second problem with this literature is that it does not constitute a sufficient base for the study of war as a public policy. If wars represent purposive behavior, as is generally assumed, then discussions of their effects should both evaluate war's utility in achieving desired outcomes (intended consequences) and assess its unintended and often unanticipated consequences. For the most part, scholars do a better job with the latter; most of the effects they discuss are not those that constitute reasons for going to war in the first place. Knowledge of these side-effects may nonetheless be quite basic to a rational decision on the question of whether or not a nation should fight. In addition, such knowledge becomes very useful once the decision to go to war has been made, for many of these effects are consequences of the mobilization that must then be planned. Thus it would be more useful if these discussions were more conscious of war's side-effects as being unintended consequences of deliberate policy rather than treating them as interesting but inevitable wartime and postwar occurrences.

More striking, however, is that war's intended consequences are virtually ignored. It should be relatively easy, for example, to determine if a nation accomplishes what it set out to do by going to war—to acquire territory, prevent territorial loss, or some other goal. Yet so basic a determination has not been systematically made, perhaps because it is so obvious as to be completely overlooked. Scholars never fail to label warring nations as winners or losers, but they almost always fail to mention whether these nations achieved what they desired by going to war in the first place.

War is a public policy with enormous effects. Yet it is the least evaluated of public policies, when it should perhaps be the most carefully assessed. Scholars and politicians alike have failed to assess war's effectiveness and war's effects. Politicians may perhaps have reasons for wishing to avoid such evaluations, especially public ones. Scholars have no excuse.

NOTES

1. For bibliographies of the effects of war, see Marwick (1974), K. L. Nelson (1971), Stein (1976, 1980), Winter (1975b), *War and Society Newsletter* (1973–present).

2. One political scientist has in fact proposed a six-part typology of conflict resolution, suggesting a fair degree of subtlety in the range of conflict's outcomes (K. J. Holsti 1966, 1977).

3. Organski and Kugler (1978) analyze six post–World War II international conflicts, counting three Arab-Israeli wars as one international conflict.

4. There are other effects of war which are not reviewed here. There is a very large literature dealing, for example, with psychological reactions to combat and stress (see the discussion and references in Williams and Tarr 1974: 214–221 and in Lang 1972: 53–82, 201–204). It includes studies of postwar repercussions for soldiers (Lifton 1973, Helmer 1974), and psychological effects endured by those interned in concentration camps, prisoners of war, and noncombatants who survive large-scale countercity attacks (Bettelheim 1960, Lifton 1976). For a discussion of other human costs of war, see note 9 below.

5. Some argue that the experience of twentieth-century wars has led to the rise of a quite modern attitude of "rejection of the concept of war as a means of resolving international disputes" (Brodie 1973: 274). This is not to say that distaste for war is anything new, for study of the intellectual history of war-weariness and war cycles should "disabuse [one] of the notion that a feeling of distaste for war and of repudiation of its awful characteristics and consequences is a uniquely recent development" (Brodie 1973: 230). According to some, however, the movement toward a rejection of the legitimacy of war, a phenomenon that is in evidence in those areas that have experienced the ravages of war in this century most, *is* new. Adda Bozeman (1976a, 1976b) in fact argues that this twentieth-century attitude may be a western phenomenon that is not paralleled elsewhere.

6. For a general discussion of the systemic sources of domestic politics, see Gourevitch (1978). Reviews of the literature on state origins can be found in R. Cohen (1978), Service (1975, 1978), Fried (1978), H. T. Wright (1978), and Carneiro (1970). The views of social Darwinists are briefly summarized by Naroll and Divale (1976: 100–101). A classic statement of conquest theory is by Gumplowicz (1963, reprint of translation of 1905 revision of 1885 original). Conquest theories are examined critically by R. Holsti (1913), W. C. MacLeod (1924, 1931), and Lowie (1927).

7. Modern governments need not extract additional taxes to pay for war because they can simply print more money and generate inflation—an indirect means of taxation. In general, however, wars are never financed solely by inflation, but by at least some increase in taxation. Further, large governments that control a sizable portion of the social product can simply transfer already extracted resources for use in waging war. In such cases, war's end may bring a "negative displacement effect" in that the postwar proportion of social product expended by the state is smaller than that expended prior to the war (A. A. Stein 1980). Waging a war without mobilizing extra resources may lead to

a postwar shrinkage of government since there is often a popular expectation that a reduction in government size will follow the war. When war is fought without the mobilization of extra resources, it can only be accomplished by a net decline in other governmental expenditures.

8. Specific economic and political manifestations of increased state control are widely discussed (Corwin 1947, Fraser 1973, Hurwitz 1949, Lerner 1940, Mowry 1941, Polenberg 1972, Swisher 1940, Satow 1972, Stohl 1976).

9. Numerous attempts to calculate the human capital losses of war are summarized by Kiker and Cochrane (1973). The specific costs to the United States are discussed in C. W. Wright (1943), and long-term demographic effects are discussed by Hulse (1961) and Otterbein (1973), as well as in some of the essays in Fried, Harris, and Murphy (1968). The human capital losses of war need not only involve actual wartime casualties. The economic and social ravages of war can affect health with consequent losses in human capital. For example, the infant mortality rate in Germany from 1945 to 1949 was much higher than that recorded for 1935 to 1939. If we treat those "excess" infant deaths as caused by disruption resulting from the war, they amount to over 130,000 war-caused deaths. And of course Germany by no means represents the worst case from World War II, only the easiest to document (data from *U.N. Demographic Yearbook* 1966: 292). Increased incidence of birth defects, child mortality, and cancer as a result of war and the weapons used against civilian populations can have even longer-term effects.

Arguments against viewing wartime casualties as losses all come from nineteenth-century perspectives on evolution (Russell 1972, reprint of 1936 original; D. Dunn 1974). Similarly, the cost entailed in the destruction of physical capital can also be disputed (see the discussion below of Organski and Kugler 1977). Indeed, some argue that the relative economic advantage currently possessed by Japan and West Germany is due to the destruction of their physical plants during World War II. This destruction allowed them to completely rebuild and they therefore possess a production infrastructure that is younger and more modern than that possessed by the victorious nations of World War II.

10. The impact of war on scientific and technological development is greatly debated and difficult to disentangle (Russell 1972, reprint of 1936 original; Nef 1950; Morton 1969; MacLeod and MacLeod 1975; Price 1961: 103–105; Rosenberg 1969; Simonton 1976). On the whole, however, it appears that war has little systematic effect on the overall level or rate of scientific development.

11. One of the more extreme arguments is made by Sombart, who claims that the economic stimulus of war was central to the development of capitalism. This position was attacked by Nef (1950), and their debate is reviewed by D. Dunn (1974) and Winter (1975a).

12. Of course this is an old hypothesis. For some older references to it, see the citations in Rummel (1963) and Tanter (1966). Despite many subsequent analyses, the evidence remains ambiguous; see Stohl's essay in this volume for a full review.

13. There are also, of course, nonrevolutionary manifestations of decreased cohesion (Brooks 1969; J. E. Mueller 1971, 1973; Perkins 1971; E. H. Powell

1970; Schaich 1975; Stohl 1973, 1975, 1976; Tanter 1969). Indeed, such manifestations need not always involve political acts. For an extended discussion of the various manifestations of decreased cohesion and their interrelationships, see A. A. Stein (1980).

14. Changes in cohesion can also be effected by wartime changes in the state and economy. Such feedback effects of these other war-related changes on domestic cohesion are rarely treated, though it is clear that the net effect of war is decreased cohesion as a function of mobilization (A. A. Stein 1980). The impact of differential war outcomes (victory or defeat), is also rarely treated, but there is some reason to expect decreased cohesion in either case (Stohl 1976) and greater decreases in losing nations.

15. Similarly, Modelski has argued elsewhere (1978b) that because the nation–state has proved to be the most effective unit of political organization for waging war, it has been for some time the basic unit of world order.

16. The long-term societal effects of war may also be affected by whether the outcome results in a plural international system or in a universal empire. Wesson (1976, 1978) argues that these different systems have different implications for domestic political rule and for the prospects for societal innovation or decay.

17. Calculated using data from Singer and Small (1972: 24–29; see also Albertini 1969). The most recent phase of state-creation since 1960 (more than sixty new states) is more distant in time from World War II, but stems from a collapse of empires that is arguably still a result of that war.

PART FOUR

Practical Implications
of Conflict Research

CHAPTER 11

Political Stability
and Conflict Management

Dennis C. Pirages

THIS CHAPTER APPROACHES CONFLICT from a perspective different from others in this volume. Other chapters focus on definitions, causes, and correlates of various types of political conflict and violence; in other words, on questions of why people rebel. This chapter is more conceptual and focuses on the less studied but equally important causes and correlates of political stability and the dynamics of conflict management. The emphasis here is on why people don't rebel most of the time.

It is somewhat ironic that relatively few comprehensive studies of the persistence of peace and stability within societies have been done in political science. An emphasis on violence and bloodshed gives testimony to scholarly preoccupation with various kinds of social pathologies rather than with what could be defined as positive standards of societal health. Since there are only a few general political theories of stability, an analysis of relevant propositions must borrow from work in diverse disciplines which has been done at different levels of analysis. In the available space there is no possibility of covering all of the relevant literature, but I have made an attempt to select priority areas and to reference the studies containing the most relevant conceptual and propositional inventories.

One source of information about stability is obviously the literature on political conflict. If the causes and correlates of violence are accurately identified, presumably stability is promoted by doing away with them. But this literature rarely makes the leap from identification of causes of violence to suggestions for remedies. There are some relevant insights in the nascent field of peace research. But most of these studies cluster under the heading of conflict resolution and deal with individuals, small groups, or international actors. Only limited attention is paid to conflict resolution within nation–states. Numerous propositions that have some relevance to the study of political stability can be deduced from social psychology, general systems theory, and organizational theory.

The focus of this chapter, political stability and conflict management, raises some important ethical questions, arising from an almost universal condemnation of tangible strife, violence, and bloodshed. People prefer to live in peaceful and stable societies. They often fail to recognize that conflict may be the only means available to change established political rules and they are reluctant to look at evidence that stability sometimes depends upon repression. Within apparently stable and peaceful societies it is possible to find structural violence in the form of institutional repression of individual aspirations (see Galtung 1969). At the outset it is thus necessary at least to pose the important and controversial question of whether peace and stability should be considered ends in themselves.

This ethical question cannot possibly be resolved within the confines of this chapter. The only assumption made here is that the empirical and scientific study of conflict management and of conditions promoting political stability is intrinsically worthwhile. In the political world, authorities use stability-inducing tactics on a daily basis. This clarification of management techniques that are, or could be, used might possibly increase the control of authoritarian leaders over their societies. But such knowledge can also be used by those who might be considered the oppressed. They could increase their sophistication about and resistance to the techniques that they abhor.

In what follows, political stability and conflict management are analyzed from two different perspectives. The *structural* conditions that increase or decrease stability within relevant social units are analyzed in the first section. These represent constraints within which authorities must operate. Conflict management as a *process* is discussed in the second section. These management techniques can be employed by authorities who may or may not make wise or ethical decisions regarding their use.

THE CONTROL PERSPECTIVE

All societies are characterized by asymmetric relationships among the people who comprise them. There are at least four major sources of these asymmetries:

1. natural capabilities of people are unequally distributed because of biological, social, and cultural mechanisms
2. access to resources is not uniform for all members of the social unit

3. the distribution of property rights and positions among members provides differential control possibilities

4. social exchange, conflict, and population shifts result in differences in resource control and action possibilities (Baumgartner et al. 1976: 226).

Maintaining asymmetric social structures over time creates potential problems of conflict management. Not all asymmetries lead to conflict nor are all asymmetries appropriately classified as political. Eckstein and Gurr (1975: 15–23) suggest that there are three criteria for defining politically relevant asymmetries. Asymmetric relationships must exist among people acting in their capacities (roles) as members of a social unit. They must occur among hierarchically ordered segments or members of a social unit and affect relations among them. And these asymmetric relations must be concerned with the direction of the social unit. Within asymmetric social units, political authorities (superordinates) issue directives to subordinates relating to the persistence of the unit.

The evolution of these asymmetries and hierarchies in human social units might be a critical component of human success in the evolutionary struggle with other species. Willhoite (1976) has taken the position that dominance–deference hierarchies are part of human biological nature. Supporting his contention by reference to studies of primate political behavior, Willhoite sees stratification of political authority, power, and influence to be intrinsic in all social units. There are also logical reasons for the pervasiveness of asymmetries and hierarchies in human societies. Collective survival of large social units requires concentration of decision-making capability in the hands of a few authorities. Concentration of power facilitates timely decision making, gives social units flexibility, permits rapid responses to external challenges from nature and from other social units, and permits those units possessing well-organized authority systems to prevail over poorly organized ones.

Since asymmetry, hierarchy, and political authority are universally found within persisting human social units, the nature of relationships between superordinates and subordinates is of central interest in political research. There are at least two useful perspectives from which hierarchies and relations within them can be analyzed: from the bottom up or the top down. The former view takes the vantage point of subordinates or potential partisans who attempt to influence authorities to act in their favor. The alternative view stresses the perspective from the top down, focusing on the processes by which authorities attempt to achieve collective goals while protecting their positions and maintaining citizen compliance with their decisions (see Gamson 1968: 2–19; Converse 1968). Since the maintenance of stability and management of conflict—both central tasks for authorities—are the focus of this chapter, the control or top–down perspective is the more fruitful one and shapes the analysis that follows.

THE NATURE OF CONFLICT

Conflict is a concept that has been defined very differently by different scholars. The major disagreement is over the breadth of the concept. At one extreme the contention is that conflict should be used to describe all forms of antagonistic struggle, manifest or latent. Others suggest a narrower definition, that conflict must be overt and visible (see Fink 1968: 431–453). Since it is impossible to resolve this definitional question easily, a narrow definition of conflict is chosen here.

Mack and Snyder (1957) define conflict by distinguishing it from competition. Social units are governed by sets of rules or directives that guide interactions among members. Advancement within the social hierarchy is an aspiration of most individuals. According to Mack and Snyder, as long as this striving and maneuvering takes place according to established rules, it can be considered peaceful competition rather than malignant conflict. But the rules themselves are sometimes in question. Not all subordinates accept the rules by which the game is played. When members of a social unit go beyond the rules and attempt to "destroy, injure, thwart, or otherwise control another party or parties" (Mack and Snyder 1957: 218) a situation of conflict is said to exist.

There is, of course, a value assumption in choosing to organize the data around this narrow definition of conflict. The assumption is that most of the time rules should be followed since the violence and bloodshed associated with not following them is likely to be a social evil that is greater than the evil inherent in following them. It should be kept in mind, however, that sometimes breaking rules is not only functional for a social unit but also necessary for the unit's survival.

Authorities in all social units are faced with problems of scarcity. Human beings, like other species, tend to increase their numbers and wants until they approach the limits of environmental capacity to sustain them (see Pirages 1978a: 14–15). Mack and Snyder (1957: 218) argue that conflict arises from "position scarcity" and "resource scarcity." There are only a limited number of positions of real power in any social hierarchy and no more than one individual can occupy each one. Similarly, there are few examples of social units in which the supply of desired objects is so great that all parties can satiate their wants. Position and resource scarcity, and the dissatisfaction that arises from them, is thus a central problem for political authorities.

Social units are governed by authoritative sets of rules and directives issued by superordinates (political elites). Loyal citizens (subordinates) agree to be bound by these rules in their quest for scarce positions or resources. Political stability exists when striving for scarce positions and resources takes place according to these "established rules that strictly limit what competitors can do to each other in the course of striving" (Mack and Snyder 1957: 217). Competition restricted to prescribed systems of rules is a desirable state of affairs, and certain types of competition (for instance, for political office) could be considered essential to the continued survival of relevant social units. It is only when relevant actors regularly engage in behavior falling outside the bounds of accepted rules that conflict, violence, and injury result for parties involved.

Political scientists have attempted to define the business of politics in more than a hundred ways. In many respects the definition offered by Easton (1965a: chapter 4) is most useful. For Easton, political processes are concerned with the authoritative allocation of values for a social unit. Values thus allocated by authorities may range from those that are very concrete (taxation) to those that are very abstract (presidential medals). The allocation process within a social hierarchy is one that is closely tied to potential conflict as subordinates attempt to improve their situation. Authorities must use resources at their command to maintain order among the potential combatants as well as to retain their own positions at the top of the hierarchy.

One of the generalizations about political behavior that seems to hold true over time and across cultures is that authorities or superordinates rarely retire voluntarily once they have assumed positions of leadership. This propensity is most obvious in more authoritarian political systems where there are few rules restricting tenure in high office. Only rarely do dictators leave office in positions other than prone. The cases of leaders such as Joseph Stalin, Mao Tse-tung, Francisco Franco, Fidel Castro, and Ferdinand Marcos illustrate this tendency to cling to power as long as possible. In more liberal political systems such tendencies are checked by law. But even in these political systems ruling political parties attempt to maintain control and incumbents are simply recycled within party hierarchies—witness the careers of Winston Churchill, Charles DeGaulle, or Franklin Roosevelt. Whatever the nature of the representational system and whatever the motives of political leaders, most incumbents in political office use resources at their command to control "vertical" conflicts, that is, pressures from subordinates that present threats to their persistence in office (see Gamson 1968: 111–113).

Management of vertical conflict related to the allocation of privilege within an established hierarchy is only one aspect of conflict management; it is also necessary for authorities to restrict conflict among subordinates. This horizontal conflict can spread rapidly and eventually become as much of a threat to stability as the more direct vertical striving to replace authorities.

BASIC LIMITS—A SOCIOECOLOGICAL PERSPECTIVE

All authority systems operate within a set of constraints determined by physical and social environments. The physical environment in which social units are embedded determines the maximum size of the available resource base. Resources comprise anything needed by organisms to increase the rate of energy conversion (Watt 1973: 20). Another way of putting this is that resources, particularly energy, are essential to growth in population size and well-being. The resources that human beings need and that are allocated by political processes are basically the same that other species need: minerals, land, water, energy, food, air. Resource bases expand and contract over time as a result of changes in the physical environment, technological innovations, and other human activities. Thus the amount of resources available for allocation by political authorities and, indirectly, for managing conflict and maintaining stability fluctuates with these expansions and contractions. There is historical evidence that these types of fluctuations have had a dramatic impact on well-being both within and between nations (see Wallerstein 1974: 39–48, MacNeil 1976, Ladurie 1971).

Populations of all species, including Homo sapiens, tend to expand until a resource needed for survival is in short supply. Thus human history has been characterized by perpetual cyclical resource shortages as populations, living standards, and expectations have increased when resources were abundant and have been savagely cut back when resources have been reduced by famine, plague, and warfare. As resources available for allocation have fluctuated over time, so have the fortunes of political authorities. And those cyclical fluctuations are destined to remain a factor that limits political stability, unless and until planning efforts lead to population and production policies which guarantee enough long-term "resource slack" to compensate for the downturns in these natural cycles.

Until very recently an ecological perspective on political stability has been absent from the literature. Some work in international relations took notice of "geopolitics" as an important set of variables, but the impact of ecological thinking in conflict–stability theory was almost completely lacking. Contemporary academic and political perspectives have been shaped by the luxury of more than three centuries of continued growth. Scarcity has not been perceived as a political problem in need of solution, given the wonders bequeathed by new technologies. But most of this technological innovation centered on using fossil fuels which now, in relation to demand, seem in very short supply. In the last decade changing perceptions of technology and "ecological scarcity" have begun to thrust technology, populations, and resources into new prominence as variables that determine underlying patterns of conflict and stability (see Ophuls 1977: 9).

The ecological perspective on politics has inspired a number of relevant propositions that have been tested in international relations. Choucri (1974) has done an exhaustive inventory of propositions linking population and violence. Whereas most of her propositions are applicable most directly to relations among nations, many of them can be translated into testable propositions related to political stability within nations. Choucri and North (1975) have used the term "lateral pressures" to refer to the dynamics of international conflict that result from population growth in confined geographical territories combined with increased technological capabilities. Whereas they have tested a number of hypotheses using data on historical conflicts between nations, adaptations of these propositions are certainly relevant to struggles for resources within social units.

Political institutions and authority relationships evolve within the constraints set by technology, the social environment, and the physical environment (see Boulding 1978: chapter 1). Democratic authority relationships in large political units rarely existed before the Industrial Revolution, and political stability was typically insured by force rather than by consent. In a sense, mass democracy combined with political stability represents a political adaptation to the abundance of the industrial epoch. Most subordinates in industrial societies feel that they can play a role in determining their own fate. Given the relative abundance of the industrial period, authorities have been able to respond by permitting significant participation in collective decision making. Many scholars now point out that for a number of reasons the era of industrial abundance is ending and that new political institutions capable of controlling serious conflict will be required (see Renshaw 1976, Harmon 1976, Stavrianos 1976, Giarini and Loubergé 1978).

The most thorough analysis of the implications of slowed growth and ecological scarcity on the future of political stability has been done by Ophuls (1977). He argues that the largess of the Industrial Revolution has permitted the evolution of "non-politics" in highly industrialized societies. Few tough decisions have been necessary during the growth period, and political institutions are now ill-equipped to deal with scarcity problems (chapter 6). In a future of increasing scarcity and unrest, the collective good must be given increasing priority and the community must have sufficient means to enforce its demands on individuals (Ophuls 1977: 226). The implications of Ophuls's arguments are far-reaching, but one of them certainly is that democratic stability will come increasingly under attack during the impending transition that he foresees.

In addition to constraints inherent in the physical environment, there are important social and psychological processes that have typified the Industrial Revolution and its aftermath. A universal revolution of rising expectations and its related pressures on political authorities is one of them. Human beings now anchor their expectations in relation to what they perceive others in similar circumstances and of similar abilities to have

(Festinger 1954). Human satisfaction and human deprivation are better addressed as relative satisfaction and relative deprivation (Gurr 1970). Most people no longer are objectively content with their share of social resources but rate themselves in relation to others and hope to keep ahead of them (see Hirsch 1978). Thus it is likely that, if predictions of slower economic growth are valid, the evolutionary process of bringing human expectations into line with environmental constraints will lead to significant future political instability.

TECHNOLOGY, MODERNIZATION, AND STABILITY

Technological innovations have done much to destabilize traditional societies, shape social hierarchies, change authority patterns, and enhance state power. The impact of technology is seen in the large-scale transformation of societies accompanying the Industrial Revolution. The political impact of technological innovations has been considerable. Before the onset of the Industrial Revolution a traditional type of political stability was common among most of the world's political units. Subordinates were compliant and accepted harsh authority and great inequality because of the strong hold of tradition on the pre-industrial mentality. But the Industrial Revolution changed all that. The application of new technologies created new resources on an unprecedented scale. This burst of human creativity was accompanied by citizen demands for new political, social, and economic rights. These new demands could be managed only by authorities whose power was increasing apace with industrial progress. As the Industrial Revolution unfolded, a new type of stability, based on increased state power and resources, supplanted the traditional stability of the pre-industrial world.

Since the Industrial Revolution has been central in the development of the modern nation–state there is a substantial literature linking its manifestations with changing authority patterns, conflict management, and sociopolitical stability. The political component of the Industrial Revolution is referred to as political development, but there is little scholarly agreement on a precise definition. Political development has been defined as the creation of democratic authority patterns, greater national integration, increased political participation, greater institutional rationalization, and so forth (Packenham 1964, Almond and Verba 1963, Cutright 1963).

There are problems with many of the propositions that have been generated by these types of approaches to political development. The nature of the causal variables has often been inadequately specified. It is generally unclear whether levels of industrialization lead to specified outcomes or whether it is rates of change in available resources and positions that are most important. The aspects of political development that have been studied are often measured by flawed indicators, and little notice is given to break points on the modernization scale. Propositions that might hold for less industrialized countries often do not hold for those that are more highly developed. This section deals with the literature linking technology and political stability, and examines some commonly accepted propositions relating industrialization and political stability.

L. Hurwitz (1972) has summarized scholarly attempts to define stability and found five different concepts of political stability in the contemporary literature. The most obvious approach is to define political stability as absence of domestic conflict and violent behavior (see Russett 1964: 97–100; Feierabend and Feierabend 1966). But such an obvious and simple concept is beset with problems. Not only is measurement of conflict and violence difficult, but conceptualizing stability as the absence of violence also adds little to our theoretical understanding. There may well be two aspects of such stability that are worth studying, consensual and autocratic stability. In the case of the former, violence and conflict may be minimized through consent of the governed while in the latter case conflict is minimized through the constant application of coercion to those disposed to resist. From a western normative perspective, consensual stability is the preferred state of affairs; it is the type of stability that has been studied most often. Autocratic stability leads to the repression of conflict, which can then suddenly and unexpectedly explode.

Another basic approach to political stability equates it with the absence of systemic transformation. Hurwitz suggests two different types of such stability, longevity of governments and absence of structural change. According to these definitions a political system is stable if it is characterized by governments of great duration. But longevity in office can result as easily from obstinacy on the part of incumbents as from popular support. Political systems are also considered stable if they avoid changes in their basic configurations over the years. This definition suffers from a measurement problem, namely how to measure degree of reconfiguration (for an empirical solution see Gurr 1974b), and from the bias toward longevity mentioned above (see Russett 1964: 97–100; Taylor and Herman 1971).

The two other approaches outlined by L. Hurwitz consider stability as existence of a legitimate constitutional order and stability as a multifaceted societal attribute. The major problem with the former definition is that there is little agreement on what constitutes legitimacy or how to measure it. But legitimacy does have the virtue of being a positive and desirable phenomenon rather than simply the absence of negative ones (see Lipset 1959). Stability as a multifaceted societal attribute concentrates on system stability as a whole rather than on a single dimension. The difficulties with it lie in problems of quantification and aggregation. Its distinct advantages lie in the recognition that stability is too complex to be reduced to isolated variables (see H. Eckstein 1966).

As this inventory of definitions and approaches would suggest, the propositions linking technology-induced modernization and political stability contain a wide variety of definitions of both development and stability. In addition, many who have worked in this area unfortunately are best characterized as linear thinkers. Within this perspective, the social world shaped by technology is moving in one direction. The future of modernizing countries can be inferred by extrapolating data on modernization during the last 200 years. In effect, the political future is seen as a continuation with variation of historical trends. This perspective may be contrasted with that of the cyclical or relational thinkers who work with a much longer view of history and who recognize that all great empires have risen and fallen and that political systems can decay as well as develop.

THE LINEAR TRADITION

This extensive research tradition links modernization and sociopolitical stability in national social units. The most common method of inquiry has been cross-national analysis, relating various indices of modernization with selected aspects of political development and stability. These studies have been buttressed by longitudinal analyses of political development in response to modernization over time in selected countries. Thus within this research paradigm data are gathered by comparing contemporary nations at different levels of development and by looking at historical processes of change. It is assumed that industrialization–modernization is a force that drives sociopolitical development down a single path that should lead to "democratic stability."

Seymour Martin Lipset was one of the first to analyze these relationships using cross-national data (Lipset 1959). His early studies seem crude and his concepts somewhat unclear, but they were responsible for spawning a series of follow-up studies in the linear tradition. Lipset was concerned with identifying the structural requisites for democracy and stability. It seems implicit in his work that the two are closely related, and he has made little attempt to differentiate between them. Working backward from his dependent to independent variables, Lipset proceeded by dividing his sample of countries into four categories based upon authority systems and levels of stability: European and English-speaking stable democracies, European and English-speaking unstable democracies and dictatorships, Latin American democracies and unstable dictatorships, and Latin American stable dictatorships. He then gathered socioeconomic data for these countries on urbanization, education, wealth, and industrialization. He found striking socioeconomic differences among his categories of political systems. In the European and English-speaking democracies, for example, he found 205 telephones, 350 radios, and 341 newspaper copies per 1,000 persons. This contrasted sharply with 58 telephones, 160 radios, and 167 newspaper copies per 1,000 persons in European and English-speaking unstable democracies and dictatorships.

Similar results were found when he related democratic stability to his other three categories of socioeconomic data. All of these differences were much more pronounced when European and English-speaking democracies were compared with Latin American dictatorships.

Lipset explains his findings by specifying a series of mediating variables such as increasing individual income, security, education, and formation of interest groups, that seem to be an integral part of the modernization process. The wealthier a society the more widely income can be distributed and the less the gaps between rich and poor. Thus in affluent societies there is less likelihood of mass dissatisfaction and violent actions by dissatisfied persons. More highly educated and economically secure individuals are less likely to risk their stake in the system by violent actions outside of the rules prescribed by governments (Lipset 1960). Lipset's economic determinism has been supported by several other studies (see Almond and Coleman 1960: 532–576, Deutsch 1960, Cutright 1963). In retrospect, however, Lipset's analysis relates to a very narrow span of time in which rapid economic growth was creating resources and positions at an unprecedented rate. His explanations are of a static nature and he never clearly confronts the question of levels versus rates of economic development as explanatory variables (see Olson 1963).

Sociologist Phillips Cutright more carefully defines national political development as the presence of more complex and specialized national political institutions (Cutright 1963). Such institutions, he reasons, should be closely related to political stability. He defines stability by reference to variables such as rule by chief executives who are elected to office by competitive and open elections, and parliaments in which minority parties exist and control at least 30 percent of the vote. Cutright finds a close relationship between his indicators of political stability and four indicators of socioeconomic development: communication, urbanization, education, and labor force distribution. The closest relationship exists between indicators of communications development and political stability. In general, those countries having highly developed educational, communications, and economic systems are found to be more stable.

These and other linear studies linking modernization and political development ignore several anomalies in the data. It is difficult to explain apparently increased instability and autocratic authority structures in the less developed countries that currently are modernizing. Furthermore, recent data indicate increased instability in some highly industrialized countries based upon ethnicity and demands for regional autonomy (Heisler 1977). In addition, studies focusing on democratic stability have been unable to explain the persistence of nonresponsive and potentially unstable regimes in the Soviet Union, East Germany, Czechoslovakia, and Poland, all industrialized countries that seemingly have not followed the "prescribed" developmental path. Neubauer (1967) has given a more sophisticated interpretation to the Lipset-Cutright propositions by introducing a "threshold" concept into the analyses. Working with his own indicators of democratic development, Neubauer finds that above a certain high threshold of industrialization there is no clear relationship between his index of democratic development (stability) and various indicators of levels of socioeconomic development. In other words, once a country reaches a certain point in industrial sophistication the relationship between modernization and democratic political development breaks down.

L. Hurwitz (1972) has focused directly on stability in countries above Neubauer's threshold. He concentrates on twenty industrialized democracies in attempting to account for real differences in their levels of political stability. His index of democratic political stability consists of measures of persistence of patterns and of legitimacy–system support. In this respect it is a multifaceted index that combines attributes used in other linear studies (see L. Hurwitz 1971). Using these data, he tests many "traditional" attempts to explain stability structurally, including theories employing economic development, religion, party systems, cultural homogeneity, and democratic attainment as key explanatory variables. For countries above the Neubauer threshold he finds that the traditional theories do not explain as much of the variance in stability as might be expected. The strongest relationship exists between party systems and stability: the greater the number of parties, the lower the stability rating. Weaker relationships that run in the expected direction are found between cultural homogeneity and stability, and levels of economic attainment and stability. The biggest surprise is that there is a negative relationship between democracy and stability. Higher levels of democratic performance are weakly associated with greater instability, at least for this sample of twenty countries. Hurwitz argues that there is not necessarily a causal relationship between democracy and instability but rather that democracies are more permissive than their less democratic counterparts in giving vent to antisystem forces that exist in all political systems.

Although neither Neubauer nor Hurwitz deals with it, a similar threshold exists at the other end of the modernization continuum. As the least industrial countries begin to industrialize, "social mobilization" processes erode major clusters of old social, economic, and psychological commitments and make people available for new patterns of socialization and behavior (Deutsch 1961). This erosion process is associated with increased instability and more authoritarian political patterns until such developing nations cross a threshold where enough managerial resources and capability are available to move toward more stable and consensual forms of government (see R. Clark 1974: chapter 5).

In conclusion, several critical observations about the linear perspective on modernization and stability are in order. There is a strong and unexplained bias toward defining democracy as political stability. The two concepts are quite distinct and a more objective view would stress that there is more than one path to stability. The Industrial Revolution has led to unparalleled levels of production of resources and positions and thus to unprecedented state power. This power can be used to build consensus in a liberal democratic setting or it can be used to create mechanisms of control in a more authoritarian setting. None of the linear thinkers deals with the socialist anomaly, namely, that highly industrialized and apparently stable state socialist countries have not developed liberal democratic political institutions.

In addition, none of these studies conceptualizes and operationalizes the key variables in a wholly satisfactory manner, and there is little continuity in measurement. Each study concentrates on a piece of the whole puzzle and no synthetic overview has yet been done. Most of these studies are characterized by a static view of the industrial world and a linear perspective on change. The links between technology and availability of resources, on the one hand, and authority systems and political stability, on the other, has been investigated inadequately. And all of these studies suffer from lack of a broad historical perspective. The concepts used and the dynamics explained are those of the recent period of rapid growth in technology and resources. Many critics have argued that industrial countries are moving into an era in which these old relationships may no longer apply (Ophuls 1977; Renshaw 1976; Jackson 1979; Pirages 1977, 1978a; deSchweinitz 1964; Harmon 1976).

THE CYCLICAL PERSPECTIVE

The linear perspective on political development and stability is not informed by an adequate long-term view of world history. The Industrial Revolution and the modernization associated with it represents a short interval in human experience. Over the longer run, great civilizations, empires, and lesser polities have risen and fallen with great regularity (see Wesson 1967, 1978). It is only our industrial myopia that keeps us from seeing the world industrial empire as but another example of civilization that has just experienced a prolonged period of ascendance. A cyclical view recognizes that what ascends can also decline. And there are disturbing indications that some decline in industrial civilization could be upon us. If this is the case, the political institutions and relationships associated with ascendance may not resemble those associated with decline.

On a less grand scale one does not have to accept arguments about the future decline of western civilization to appreciate the virtues of the cyclical or relational perspective on political development and stability. Recent history has also witnessed the rise and fall of many national political units and certainly exhibits few linear long-term trends. Huntington (1968) has introduced the concept of cycles into the contemporary literature on political development. He sees political development as resulting from a balanced relationship between social mobilization and political institutionalization. Political stability comes from offsetting the growth of individual and group demands for resources and participation, with increased capabilities of political institutions to control and respond. Instability results from imbalance in the relationship between demands of an ethnic, religious, economic, territorial, or social nature and the capacity of political incumbents and institutions to absorb and satisfy them (Huntington 1968: 4–11).

Huntington observes that a political community depends on the strength of political organizations and procedures in a society, which in turn is related to the scope of support for them and their level of institutionalization. Institutionalization is defined along four dimensions: adaptability–rigidity, complexity–simplicity, autonomy–subordination, and coherence–disunity. A high level of institutionalization is indicated by adaptability, complexity, autonomy, and coherence in political organization. Adaptability is the capacity to adjust to new and different challenges. Complexity refers to the multiplication and differentiation of subunits within a political system. Autonomy signifies the separation of political institutions from the control of specific social groups. Coherence refers to the unity of those participating in the political organization and the level of consensus found in it (Huntington 1968: 12–24).

Huntington focuses his efforts on the less developed countries and argues that economic change can produce political decay as well as political development. The decay in political institutions has been largely overlooked in most of the literature on modernization. According to Huntington, the extent to which political decay takes place during modernization depends on the strength of its traditional political institutions. Huntington does not apply his analysis to more highly developed countries, but it would seem possible that political decay can take place in industrialized societies as well. Economic change can present new challenges to political institutions. Adaptable institutions can become rigid over time and may be unable to adjust to new demands, or autonomous political institutions may be captured by various groups. Thus political development and political decay are dynamic, cyclical processes, and this perspective is applicable to the developed as well as the developing political systems.

Gurr (1974b) adds historical insight to the cyclical perspective. His premise is that patterns of authority relations are one of the most important features of political systems. A stable political system is one in which authority patterns remain similar over time. Durable political systems are those that persist for long periods of time and that are adaptable, demonstrating a capacity for undergoing gradual change. He uses the eighty-two nations that Singer and Small (1966a) identified as members of the international system at any time between 1817 and 1940. From this initial universe Gurr works backward to 1800 and forward to 1970 and identifies

294 discrete historical political systems not terminated by outside intervention that existed in these eighty-two countries during the expanded historical period. He finds that the median polity lifespan was only twelve years.

Gurr uses data on these historical polities to test several propositions about the conditions leading to political adaptability and persistence. Persistence is the number of years a polity lasts without an abrupt, major change of pattern. Adaptability is a more complex measure of gradual and minor changes in a political system. The propositions he tests are the following:

1. persistence and adaptability tend to be greater in polities of high directiveness and complexity
2. persistence and adaptability tend to be enhanced most by democratic authority traits, less by autocratic traits and least by anocratic traits
3. persistence and adaptability tend to be greater in polities with *consistently* democratic and autocratic authority patterns than in polities with mixed or anocratic authority patterns.

His data indicate that the first two hypotheses receive little support in this sample of political systems. The more complex and directive political systems do not necessarily persist longer. This relationship holds true only for the European and contemporary subsamples, where it is positive but weak. Surprisingly, the relationship between democracy and persistence also holds up only within the European subsample; in the nineteenth century autocracies were the most persistent. The third hypothesis linking durability with consistency, however, seems to be validated by the data. Highly coherent polities have higher mean durability scores than incoherent and anocratic polities, both for the whole sample and for each subsample.

Gurr concludes by speculating about long-term trends suggested by the data. He notes that the nineteenth and twentieth centuries have been times of political experimentation, and the political systems that survived this "trial and error" process now have a much greater chance of remaining stable. He argues that the most durable political systems are "now those which have responded to the stress of socioeconomic change by assuming the task of managing it" (Gurr 1974b: 1503). This can be done directly, by state control of institutions of socialization and production, or indirectly, by regulation and support of quasi-autonomous institutions. In other words, Gurr, like Huntington, emphasizes the evolving ability of some systems to cope managerially with the stress of change. There are many roads to stability and many roads to decline, but it cannot be claimed that stability as an end is necessarily more important than the means by which it is attained.

Additional support is given to Gurr's speculation by Pirages (1972). In a study of modernization and political stability in a socialist country (Poland) he finds that state control of economic rewards is one of the most important factors in maintaining stability. Although meaningful political participation is somewhat restricted within a system that is basically controlled by one party, it does not seem to be a priority concern among people who perceive that their basic economic needs are being met. In addition, however, state control of mass media, education, youth organizations, and so on, gives authorities significant power to maintain control without the direct use of force.

Gurr's suggestion that consistent authority patterns within a social unit are an important correlate of political stability coincides with a theoretical argument by H. Eckstein (1969). Eckstein identifies congruence and consonance of authority patterns within social units as key variables influencing political stability and governmental performance. Congruence refers to the similarity of authority patterns in different social units. The greater the level of congruence between political authority patterns and those in adjacent sectors of society, the higher the level of overall government performance and the more durable governments are expected to be. Consonance refers to the matching of patterns along a vertical dimension of authority. It is maximized when the attitudes and behaviors of superordinates and subordinates are similar and when attitudes toward authority in a social unit are distributed consistently. In general, the more consonance within the authority patterns of government and related social units, such as political parties, the higher the level of government stability and performance.

Eckstein makes an argument, similar to that made by Etzioni (1961; see below), that incongruent and dissonant authority patterns tend to change toward congruent and consonant ones over time. Indeed, this dynamic element of authority patterns is the focus of political engineering. The various segments of society to which Eckstein refers are not isolated and authority patterns in one segment feed back into others. Thus the political segment (authorities) can take the lead in establishing preferred authority patterns in other segments or its own patterns can be modified in response to those that exist within these segments. In the end, it is the human element—the expectations, terminal values, ideals, and ethical perspectives of human beings—that establishes the parameters within which authority patterns persist or decay. The trend for most of the Industrial Revolution has been toward congruence, accompanied by a widening of democratic authority patterns across all social segments. This in turn has been related to the "system slack" or abundance inherent in the dynamic growth of positions and resources that has followed from industrialization. As mentioned above, however, there are serious questions about the persistence of this trend once economic growth slows in advanced industrial societies and competition for perceived scarce resources and positions intensifies.

CONFLICT MANAGEMENT: BASIC STRATEGIES

The physical environment in which social units operate, the levels and rates of socioeconomic development attained by units, the nature of asymmetries within them, the expectations of the members of the units, and the positions and resources available for allocation by superordinates—all are important factors in determining political stability. But these structural factors only partially explain the success, or lack of it, experienced by superordinates in managing conflict and preserving stability. Some superordinates (political elites) perform better than others in responding to and controlling potentially serious conflicts. Conflict management is an active process, and there are many strategies, skills, and procedures that can be employed to contain conflicts once they are set in motion.

Several attempts have been made to analyze and clarify general strategies that can be employed by superordinates to gain compliance from subordinates. These typologies are useful in understanding the types of "currencies" that can be earned, stored, and spent by political authorities in maintaining stability. The observations from which these more general propositions have been derived come from a variety of disciplinary perspectives, including organization theory, systems analysis, psychology, and political science. There is a remarkable convergence of concepts in the work that has been done in power-compliance relationships in these different fields.

Subordinate compliance is essential to the maintenance of asymmetries within social units. According to Etzioni (1961: 3–4) compliance refers both to a relationship in which an actor behaves in accordance with a directive supported by another actor's power, and to the orientation of the subordinated actor to the power applied. Superordinates in social units possess the power to induce others to obey their orders about the direction of the social unit. Subordinate orientations to these directives can range from positive commitment to alienation. Etzioni focuses on organizations as his units of analysis, but the power-compliance typology that he derives from his observations is particularly relevant to political relations within national social units. He suggests three types of power that superordinates can exercise in gaining compliance from subordinates: coercive, remunerative, and normative. These are matched by three possible kinds of involvement by subordinates: alienative, calculative, and moral. Using coercive power leads most frequently to alienation, remunerative power elicits calculative involvement, and normative power can lead to moral involvement (Etzioni 1961: 4–11).

Development and application of normative power is a preferred management strategy since it requires few resources and leads to or maintains moral involvement among committed subordinates. But when subordinates are only mildly committed or when they are alienated the application of normative power is likely to be ineffective. "Normative power rests on the allocation and manipulation of symbolic rewards and deprivations; . . . manipulation of mass media, allocation of esteem and prestige symbols, administration of ritual, and influence over the distribution of 'acceptance' and 'positive response' " (Etzioni 1961: 5). Thus Etzioni identifies two aspects of normative power: the first is based upon the manipulation of symbols that are linked to superordinate goals or beliefs, the second is based upon allocation of acceptance and positive response.

Remunerative power is based on "control over material resources and rewards" (Etzioni 1961: 5). Such power depends upon the ability of authorities to induce the economy to produce such rewards and to allocate positions effectively. Thus ability to use this form of power is closely linked to economic expansion. The greater the growth in resources and positions, the greater the potential for remuneration as a managerial strategy. But remunerative power has drawbacks because economic performance is not always within the control of political leaders. Poor harvests, shortages of fuels or minerals, global depressions, or general strikes by workers can severely contract the resource base that underlies the application of remunerative power within national units.

Coercive power rests on the application of "physical sanctions such as infliction of pain, deformity, or death" (Etzioni 1961: 5). Coercive power is potentially destructive of authority and is expensive to employ; superordinates normally use it only when there is no other recourse, since its application has an adverse effect on the morale of the social unit. Thus coercive power is likely to be used in revolutionary situations when newly established governments have little normative or remunerative power.

Aside from his very useful typology, Etzioni develops several propositions that can be applied to the study of conflict management and political stability. He suggests that compliance relationships can be either congruent or incongruent. Congruent compliance relations include the use of coercive power in dealing with alienated subordinates, the use of remunerative power in dealing with those who are calculatively involved, and the use of normative power in dealing with those who are morally involved or committed. Congruent compliance relationships are more effective than incongruent ones, and organizations tend to shift their compliance structures from less to more congruent types over time (Etzioni 1961: 14). Although this proposition has not been empirically tested, it does suggest that political compliance relationships will be more stable and effective to the extent that the types of power exercised by superordinates match the types of involvement by subordinates. Etzioni also suggests that modern political democracies rely more on utilitarian control in their organizational infrastructure than do traditional or transitional political systems and that "totalitarian" political systems would have a much higher tolerance for coercion than do democracies (1961: 312). These propositions are similar to H. Eckstein's congruence and consonance arguments, discussed above.

Kelman (1961: 59) distinguishes three similar processes that lead individuals to accept what he refers to as influence. Working in an experimental communications research setting, Kelman finds that individuals accept influence because of compliance (seeking of rewards and avoidance of punishment), identification (adoption of desired behavior because of desires for satisfying group or personal relationship), and internalization (accepting of influence on the grounds that the induced behavior is intrinsically rewarding). On the basis of his limited data, Kelman suggests that people's attitudes toward their governments (superordinates) might be categorized in similar terms. Some subordinates accept political systems because of compliance, fear of social ostracism, or persecution. Others may base their attitudes toward government on identification, their relationship to political institutions being an essential part of their identity. A third group of individuals may see their country's form of government as being fully congruent and integrated with their own value systems. The conditions under which people's political attitudes can be expected to change are related to the motivational processes that underlie them.

Baumgartner, Buckley, and Burns (1975) see the exercise of political power as oriented toward the structuring of asymmetries within social units. They use the term "relational control" to refer to attempts by groups "to promote, ensure, or stabilize their advantage or dominance over others." The typology of control techniques that they develop is similar to that used by Etzioni. They distinguish three bases of relational control with respect to human systems of interaction: control of action opportunities, control of differential payoffs or outcomes of interaction, and control of cultural orientations and ideology (Baumgartner, Buckley, and Burns 1975: 418). These correspond very closely to Etzioni's three types of power: coercive power, remunerative power, and normative power. Action possibilities within a social unit may be structured so that subordinates have restricted possibilities to communicate, combine, or cooperate. Similarly, outcome structures can be changed to promote certain actions and discourage others through differential payoffs. Finally, actors' basic attitudes and orientations toward each other or toward political authorities can be affected by ideologies, control of communications media, ritual, or myth (1975: 419–423).

Superordinates are faced with a dilemma because the tasks that must be performed in a society require cooperation, whereas management of conflict-related asymmetries is easiest when individuals are atomized.

Baumgartner, Buckley, and Burns suggest that rulers have developed five strategies that enable them to increase cooperation among subordinates while remaining firmly in control:

1. the associations among subordinates may be structured and limited to certain specified domains

2. rewards may be used to create status and wage hierarchies that inhibit political coordination while encouraging cooperation in production

3. talented individuals who might provide opposition can be coopted into the managerial ranks

4. religious and ideological specialists may be used to influence socialization processes in directions that stress subordination and obedience to authority

5. laws can be drafted to limit the collective action of subordinates (Baumgartner, Buckley, and Burns 1975: 425).

Gamson (1968) has worked more directly with political relationships and has made a distinction between the efficiency of political leaders in achieving collective goals and their bias in handling conflicts of interest. "Potential partisans" (politically active subordinates) may become dissatisfied on either account. He identifies two basic types of strategies that can be used by superordinates to manage the discontent which inevitably results from allocation decisions. The first and more democratic method is to monitor public opinion and alter decisions in conformity with the demands of politically powerful partisans. Gamson suggests that this strategy relieves pressure best when partisans controlling the greatest amount of resources feel the least discontent. The risk in employing this strategy is that such responses to demands can be seen as satisfying individual interests at the expense of the attainment of the collective good.

The second strategy for managing discontent is called social control and can be used to contain partisan influence at its source. There are three components in Gamson's social control strategy. Authorities can regulate the access of potential partisans to resources and restrict their abilities to influence decision makers. Authorities can reward or punish potential partisans on the basis of the latter's attempts to influence. And authorities can attempt to control attitudes toward political objects among political partisans (Gamson 1968: 116–117).

Authorities control partisan access to the units they govern. This insulation from potentially disruptive forces takes the form of limiting partisan entry into the social unit, selectively limiting access to important positions within the unit, or selectively exiling troublesome members of the unit. In the case of national social units there is less control over entry and exit than there is in voluntary associations, but selective immigration policies, restrictions on voting rights, and loss of citizenship for certain types of offenses can be used to control troublesome elements. Furthermore, redefinition of the boundaries of a national unit can be used to exclude unwanted elements from national political processes. Subnational units can exclude unwanted groups from membership by "gerrymandering," altering the boundaries of voting units so that unwanted individuals are placed in other jurisdictions.

Social units have systems of sanctions by which members are rewarded and punished for their actions. Authorities can control these sanctions and use social resources to reward the good citizen and punish the deviant. Irresponsible or uncooperative partisans holding political resources can be stripped of them or removed from positions of power. Those who are cooperative can be rewarded by promotion to more significant positions (Gamson 1968: 122–125).

Gamson identifies several aspects of persuasion, a strategy that attempts to control the desire rather than the ability to influence. Persuasion includes all of the techniques used to control the orientations of potential partisans without actually altering their objective situation. Authorities can control information both by withholding evidence of failures and by emphasizing successes. They can surround themselves with the trappings of omniscience in order to create the impression that they possess privileged insight or information not available to the potential partisan. Conversely, authorities might encourage identification with them and their causes in order to minimize suspicions and maximize trust. This can include the use of political socialization techniques to build new images of the authorities and their causes or actual processes (see Renshon 1977). Finally, potential partisans can be persuaded to honor decisions of authorities by invoking their patriotism or sense of duty. When regime legitimacy is high the opportunities to use such appeals is much greater than when legitimacy is under attack (Gamson 1968: 125–143).

MANAGING VERTICAL TENSIONS

An authority pattern is "a set of asymmetric relations among hierarchically ordered members of a social unit that involves the direction of the unit" (Eckstein and Gurr 1975: 22). The superordinates in these relationships issue directives with which subordinates are expected to comply. In societies pervaded by the egalitarian ethos, which includes most contemporary western societies and many others, people normally do not like to think of themselves as subordinates along any social dimension. Thus asymmetric political processes by their nature create friction between superordinates and subordinates. Furthermore, whether or not they have egalitarian values, not all subordinates can be expected to accept the substance of superordinates' directives. Therefore, there arises in all political systems the recurring problem of keeping subordinates from actively resisting the established hierarchy. If relationships with subordinates are not carefully managed, today's subordinates could be tomorrow's superordinates.

APATHY AND QUIESCENCE

Although unacceptable to democratic values, a key managerial strategy is to keep subordinates from actually participating in politics. If all subordinates (citizens) actively participated in politics all of the time, most authority systems would be constantly in disarray as authorities found themselves incapable of responding to citizen demands. Superordinates do not necessarily require but certainly profit from high levels of citizen apathy. Particularly in democratic authority structures, active political participation is considered by subordinates to be one of the privileges of citizenship. But even in these systems not all people actively involve themselves in politics for reasons ranging from feelings of powerlessness (lack of political efficacy) to preoccupation with matters of everyday life. In their study of five industrial democracies Almond and Verba report that a significant portion of the populations surveyed never talk about politics, do not follow accounts of political affairs, and do not believe that they can influence national governments. This apathy is most pronounced in Italy and Mexico, where more than one-half of the sample report such behavior and beliefs, and least pronounced in the United States (see Almond and Verba 1965: chapters 2, 3, 6).

Apathy as an aspect of conflict management raises a critical ethical point. It is in the interest of ruling authorities to cultivate apathy whereas it often can be in the interest of the masses or subordinates to combat it. Robert Dahl suggests the possibility that good performance on the part of political authorities may give citizens the perception that the elites are making valid, rightful, and intelligent decisions. This could lead to situations that might be mistaken for citizen apathy. He suggests three classes of reasons why citizens may comply with authority and remain inactive in political affairs. Dahl calls them criteria for authority. They are the criterion of personal choice, the criterion of competence, and the criterion of economy. Citizens may be passive because decisions taken by ruling political elites may correspond with their own political choices. Second, they may defer to authorities because the authorities are viewed as more competent—which may well be the case. Finally, decisions and directions of authorities may be viewed as less than perfect, but supportable on the grounds that delegating decision-making power to them economizes on time, attention, and energy (Dahl 1970: 8ff.). Thus Dahl suggests an ethical tension between political participation as a goal in an ideal polity and the efforts of authorities to minimize activism through good performance. It is clear, however, that significant apathy derived from the triple criteria of choice, competence, and economy is an important factor in maintaining political stability.

Edelman (1964) substitutes the term "quiescence" for apathy, arguing that the former is the result of an active process in a political context whereas the latter connotes a mental state. He claims that political leaders create quiescence through manipulation of symbols. In politics there are often diffuse but intense subordinate demands that some issue or social ill be dealt with. The passage of legislation gives symbolic reassurance that something has been done and reduces political activity as larger diffuse groups lapse into political quiescence. But the administrative reality or the ultimate impact of the legislation is likely to be the concern only of an interested, small, and highly organized group that will be directly affected. Edelman formulates three hypotheses relating symbolic reassurance and political quiescence:

1. the demands of large, diffuse, organized groups of subordinates for resources and positions are less satiable than are their interests in being symbolically reassured

2. interest in symbolic reassurance is highest when the economic situation of a large subordinate group is threatened and it is too poorly organized to further its own interests

3. lack of organization, interest in symbolic reassurance, and quiescence by some groups is critical to the ability of more tightly organized groups to use political agencies to make good their claims (Edelman 1964: chapter 2).

Thus symbolic reassurance is an important tactic for authorities in managing countless potentially conflicting demands for positions and resources. This strategy works best when dealing with large, diffuse, threatened, and disorganized groups. Moreover, cultivating quiescence among some groups is essential if the concrete demands of other groups are to be met.

STRUCTURING HIERARCHIES

The structure of social hierarchies can be manipulated in order to maintain stability. All societies are characterized by differing degrees of grouping among subordinates. These groups can be based upon primary affiliations, such as family and friendship groups, or upon secondary affiliations such as association memberships or social class. Manipulation of the social hierarchy by selectively creating and nurturing such groups and by exploiting the cleavages that may exist among them is another means of maintaining political stability.

Kornhauser (1959: 77-78) uses the term "mass society" to describe social units in which there is minimal group infrastructure mediating between lower participants and ruling political elites. Polities without such buffering groups are characterized by persistent threats of mass violence because authorities are directly exposed to the demands of subordinate masses. In such structures there are no secondary authorities sharing power. Subordinates in mass societies, according to Kornhauser, can become more easily devoted to fanatical causes because of the lack of significant ties with moderating groups. When strong mediating structures exist in a hierarchy, overlapping group memberships can keep the concerns of any one group from dominating all aspects of members' lives.

If authorities can maintain subordinate membership in and loyalty to many groups, the pressures that magnify political conflicts can be reduced. This works in two different ways. Individuals develop loyalties to groups of which they are members because they want to be accepted by others, want to help in attaining group goals, want the group to persist, and find the group useful in validating their opinions and providing information about reality (Kiesler and Kiesler 1969: 33). On the other hand, groups can survive only when compromises take place within them since group members come to the group setting with conflicting perspectives and loyalties. The success of any one group depends "upon the incorporation or accommodation of the conflicting loyalties of any significant segments of the group, an accommodation that may result in altering the original (group) claims" (Truman 1951: 509). Extreme actions by both individuals and groups are tempered by the compromises inherent in multiple group membership.

An obvious manifestation of group pressures on individual behavior has been documented in the literature on voting behavior. When individuals belong to several groups having different perspectives, the individual is subject to cross-pressures. Cross-pressures are related to Festinger's concept of cognitive dissonance. People want to do what they feel to be right but have difficulty in acting decisively when they get conflicting signals from several different sources (see Festinger 1957). Lipset reports that such cross-pressures were manifested in German elections when individuals belonging to several groups backing different political parties invalidated their votes by voting for more than one party on the ballots (Lipset 1960: 213). Individuals exposed to cross-pressures may lose interest in political campaigns, refuse to vote, delay voting decisions, change voting intentions frequently, or intentionally void ballots (see Lazarsfeld, Berelson, and Gaudet 1944). The same cross-pressures that keep people from voting decisively in elections can also keep individuals from engaging in destabilizing and extremist political activities.

A closely related proposition concerns convergence between issue cleavages and membership in various reference groups. All societies experience some types of basic issue disagreements or cleavages in the social fabric. When one or a small number of important and related cleavages cut through society congruent with ethnic, social, class, regional, occupational, or religious distinctions, the basic social contract holding societies togetner is likely to be called into question. But when basic disagreements and issue cleavages cross-cut these different distinctions they are likely to be softened or canceled out by multiple affiliations (Coser 1956: 77ff). When lines of cleavage converge with individual patterns of group membership, individuals can be mobilized for decisive action. When lines of cleavage are not convergent with affiliations, it is more difficult to mobilize people for decisive action.

In summarizing the implications of cross-pressures for democratic stability, Taylor and Rae (1969: 544) suggest that "if a society is either too homogeneous or too heterogeneous over racial, linguistic, and religious cleavages, then democratic political organization is not likely to be stable." If there is insufficient cross-cutting between politically relevant cleavages, stability is likely to give way to radical politics. On the other hand, a society can be so heterogeneous or disordered across its relevant cleavages that anarchy results. The ideal pluralist democratic society is one in which there is a balance of homogeneity and heterogeneity. It is difficult, however, to operationalize such a vague nation in cross-national studies (see also Nordlinger 1977, Enloe 1972).

AGENDA CONTROL

Political systems are concerned with the direction of social units, including their definition of goals and regulation of conduct of members. Some consensus on common goals among members of a political community is necessary if stability is to be maintained. Political issues rise out of dissensus among members of a political community. If authorities can process these issues smoothly, most subordinates are likely to play by the rules and restrict themselves to sanctioned competition. When issues proliferate and cannot be processed smoothly by authorities, conflict is a likely result (see Spiro 1962).

Downs (1957: 66–68) distinguishes between consensus of intensities and consensus of views. Consensus of intensities refers to general community agreement among subordinates and between superordinates and subordinates upon the agenda of issues considered most important; consensus of views refers to policies to be followed in any particular issue area. Although it may seem paradoxical, political communities require both consensus and dissensus if they are to flourish over time: consensus on the shape of the issue agenda (intensities) and dissensus over policies (views) in particular issue areas. If there is no consensus on the shape of the issue agenda there are obviously few shared goals and little possibility for enduring political community. If there is no dissensus over policies there is no politics, a situation that might exist in some monastic orders but not in other political communities. In some political systems an *apparent* absence of dissensus of views could be a result of coercion and intimidation and a prelude to political violence.

Authorities strive to maintain consensus by controlling, whenever possible, the shape and content of the issue agenda. All political authorities have a limited capacity to deal with issues. This capacity is determined by the political culture within which the authorities operate, the types of demands with which they must cope, the resources available to meet these demands, and the nature of the political institutions that process the issues. There is limited capacity to process issues when there are billions of potential issues that can produce conflict. Conflict management involves the reduction of the issues on the agenda to a manageable number.

There are a number of ways that agendas can be controlled. The first is through nondecision. Private conflicts and issues are placed on the public agenda because someone wishes to alter existing relationships among private interests (Schattschneider 1960: 38). There can be countless numbers of such private issues and conflicts qualifying for public attention. Conflict is avoided through the establishment of priorities, thus keeping the agenda as narrow as possible. Bachrach and Baratz refer to the ability of authorities to keep potential issues from reaching public attention as "the second face of power" (Bachrach and Baratz 1962: 949). It is in their interest to use control over agendas to keep potentially explosive issues from surfacing.

Schattschneider (1960: 72–74) mentions several ways in which agendas can be controlled. Primary among these is displacement of less manageable with more manageable conflicts. Those issues that might become politically most troublesome can be avoided by focusing public attention on other issues that are less likely to be divisive. In the process, strong and dangerous alignments of proponents and opponents may be destroyed as the "power of irrelevance . . . transmutes one conflict into another and turns existing alignments inside out" Schattschneider 1960: 74). The agenda of issues also can be managed by focusing attention on procedures rather than on substance. This strategy relies on concentrating subordinate attention on procedural issues rather than on those of substance. Thus emphasis on institutions, power, safeguards, rights, and other procedural guarantees can deflect attention from issues of substance.

Finally, Schattschneider (1960: chapter 1) suggests that authorities might localize and control serious agenda items before these potential conflicts have an opportunity to spread. The seriousness of conflict is determined by the scope of its contagion—the extent to which indirectly affected citizens become involved in it. Since the strength of contestants is pretty well known in advance in conflicts of smaller scale, it is in the interest of the weaker parties to enlist outsiders in the cause. Conflict management strategy would suggest using every opportunity to insulate the dispute from outsiders in order to limit its scope. One way of decreasing the seriousness of such conflict is to remove it from a national political agenda by relegating it to the agenda of a subordinate political unit. When issues become localized in this way, the potential for mobilizing a powerful constituency is much diminished. In the United States, the separation of powers, whereby certain whole categories of issues are reserved to the states rather than the federal government, is an example of conflict localization.

RESOLVING HORIZONTAL CONFLICTS

Suppression of potential violence of a vertical nature between superordinates and subordinates is one essential component of conflict management. But subordinates and subordinate groups also violate accepted rules in their horizontal interactions with each other. While a certain amount of such conflict can be tolerated or can even be functional for social stability, authorities must monitor it carefully to keep it from spreading both horizontally and vertically. Thus a second essential aspect of conflict management is the resolution of serious disputes among subordinates.

The literature on conflict resolution is simultaneously vast and underdeveloped. Relevant studies have been done in many disciplines and on several levels of analysis. But there is a paucity of studies linking conflict resolution to the stability of political systems. In the following sections an attempt is made to select some of the politically most relevant themes and studies from a wide variety of disciplines, ranging from organizational theory to peace research. The studies cited provide points of entry into a much wider literature that has been omitted here because of considerations of space.

Morton Deutsch (1973) has examined a large number of propositions about factors that influence the resolution of conflict. Surveying the existing literature and working experimentally in a laboratory setting, Deutsch identifies three factors that seem to determine the outcomes of conflicts once they are set in motion. The first factor is the nature of the conflict, including its size, the centrality of the issues, the number and interdependence of the issues, and consciousness of the issues by the parties involved. The second factor is the characteristics of the parties to conflict and includes such factors as their number, personality characteristics, beliefs, and estimates of success. The final factor that influences the course of a conflict concerns the types of institutions available to regulate it and the willingness and ability of the parties involved to accept the outcome of regulation.

THE NATURE OF CONFLICTS

The size of conflicts is one of the most important variables in determining the potential for their resolution. "A conflict may be big because the participants perceive themselves to have important interests that are in opposition to one another, or it may be large, despite the congruence of their

interests, because they have opposing views on how to pursue their important mutual interests" (M. Deutsch 1973: 869). Large conflicts can be reduced in size by diminishing participant perceptions of differing interests
or by shrinking the perceived importance of what is at stake. Issue rigidity
and centrality are also critical to the resolution of disputes. Issues that are
perceived to be important to subordinate well-being and that do not lend
themselves to many satisfactory alternatives for achieving desired outcomes are less likely to be resolved than are those characterized by less centrality and rigidity. The number and interdependence of the issues involved are also critical. If a single conflict can be broken down into several
subissues there can be victories for all sides in a dispute. If it cannot be
broken down, a winner-take-all atmosphere is likely to chill prospects for
solution. Thus conflicts can best be managed when the size can be
diminished, when the issues can be made to appear less central, when
many paths to a resolution can be taken, and when issues can be broken
down into many subissues (M. Deutsch 1973: 369–373).

Conflicts among subordinates, when not promptly dealt with, are contagious and tend to escalate rapidly. Schattschneider (1960: 2) makes a
distinction between the immediate combatants in conflicts and the audience to which they can expand. The outcome of conflicts is frequently
determined by the extent to which the audience becomes involved in them.
He refers to this as the "scope of contagion." Similarly, Coleman suggests a
"Gresham's law of conflict," according to which the harmful and dangerous elements in a dispute tend to drive out the positive ones over time (Coleman 1957: 14). M. Deutsch (1973: 352) identifies three interrelated processes that escalate conflict. They include competitive pressures involved
in the attempt to win the conflict, misconceptions and biased perceptions
on the part of the combatants, and commitments that arise out of pressures
for cognitive and social consistency.

Disputes tend to expand when the parties involved are of much different
strengths. Weaker parties can augment their strength by defining the core
of a dispute so that it involves a larger share of an audience or by linking
core issues with others that have more audience appeal. Once disputes
begin to escalate sharply, it is necessary for each party to recruit from
a wider audience in an attempt to reach the original goals (see Schattschneider 1960: chapter 1).

Conflict resolution requires employment of strategies designed to check
the tendency to escalate. The most obvious requisite for successful conflict
management is to address nascent conflicts promptly so that there is little
time for the parties involved to take their case to a larger audience. In addition, since large disputes that are difficult to settle tend to drive out
smaller ones that can be settled more easily, it is imperative to break large
disputes down into component parts whenever possible. Fisher (1969: 159)
calls this process "fractionation." He identifies five variables that can be

manipulated by fractionating processes. They include the number of parties involved, physical issues, issues of principle, the substantive precedents established by a settlement, and its procedural precedents. Conflicts can best be contained by confining them to the smallest number and to the least powerful combatants. The natural tendency is for subordinates involved in a dispute to attempt to bring others—groups, organizations, or even nations—into the dispute on their side. Successful fractionation requires countering this tendency by scaling down the numbers and power of the contending parties. Disputes are more easily reconciled, for example, if individuals rather than organizations, or subnational units rather than national units, are defined as the key parties in a dispute (Fisher 1964: 159–160).

Issues also have an optimal content that makes them easier to resolve. Issues that are defined too broadly may never be resolved, and in most cases pressures to decouple can be applied by authorities. Issues that are defined too narrowly may leave no room for compromise. No two individuals can occupy the same position at the same time, and finite resources desired by many parties cannot be expanded upon command. This problem of narrow issue definition can be dealt with in several ways. Time can be introduced as a variable, adding a new dimension to a conflict. In Colombia, for example, two violently combative political parties have averted serious bloodshed since the late 1950s by agreeing to rotate control of the executive at fixed intervals. Issues may also be broadened by redefining the matter that is under dispute, making additional aspects of it subject to negotiation and compromise. The welfare of dissidents in the Soviet Union either can be defined solely as an issue of human rights or it can be broadened by placing it on a longer agenda of East–West relations. Finally, an agenda can be expanded by "coupling" issues, bringing together apparently different disputes that involve the original parties, thus increasing the items available for a negotiated settlement even though the only thing the issues have in common is that the same parties are involved (Fisher 1971: 160–162).

Principles and precedents are also important in determining the likelihood of a dispute being settled. When disputes are defined as matters of principle, or if precedents are perceived to be set, it is much more difficult to reconcile divergent points of view. Principles are best dealt with by separating them from the issues under discussion. It is necessary to get all parties to recognize the legitimacy of the other principles involved or to accept that the principles might not be applicable to the issues in dispute. Parties to a dispute also are concerned about substantive and procedural precedents that could be established by a settlement. Most conflicts can be resolved more easily when a clear statement by parties involved indicates that the settlement is considered by both to be a unique case (Fisher 1971: 163–165).

CHARACTERISTICS OF PARTIES TO CONFLICT

There has not been a great deal of research on the personality determinants of conflict resolution (see Terhune 1970). There have been, however, significant studies made of the role of third parties. In a sense, authorities in social units often act as third parties either directly, in the role of mediators, or indirectly, through legislative mandates. The question for authorities is one of deciding when to intervene in disputes and when to remain aloof, what types of conflict resolution processes to suggest, and when to increase or decrease tension among disputants.

Latour (1976) has investigated the preferences for various types of conflict resolution processes among disputants under different sets of constraints in a laboratory setting. They have suggested a continuum of conflict resolution methods ranging from autocratic resolution through arbitration, moot mediation, and direct bargaining. At the autocratic end of the continuum, third parties are very active in the resolution of conflict whereas at the other end there is no role for third parties. The authors identify three variables that they suspect influence the effectiveness and choice of conflict resolution approaches. These are temporal urgency, existence of standards or rules governing the situation, and outcome correspondence. Temporal urgency refers to the amount of time that disputants feel is available to resolve the dispute or to the seriousness of the situation. The expectation is that when time is perceived to be short, disputants are more likely to restrict their own participation and relinquish more control to third parties or authorities. Where adequate time is perceived to be available, however, disputants can be expected to reserve a greater role for themselves. Where standards applicable to the dispute exist, the expectation is that more parsimonious and autocratic methods of decision making will be preferred. Outcome correspondence refers to the extent to which the parties involved will share gains or losses resulting from their interaction. The authors hedge on this prediction and suggest reasons that disputants might prefer either autocratic or participatory resolution of conflicts when there is correspondence of outcomes.

The empirical results of the study indicate that there is little preference for bargaining as a method of resolving disputes. Most subjects display a general preference for the intervention of a third party. But preferences move more strongly toward third-party participation when (1) outcomes are perceived to be noncorrespondent; (2) there is an available standard that is applicable to the case; and (3) time is perceived to be pressing. Although these experimental results are interesting, the study is limited to the laboratory. There is little indication of what this suggests for the intervention of authorities in conflicts among subordinates. The linkage between the laboratory setting and real-world conflicts, where the stakes may be perceived by participants to be considerably higher, has not been made.

Walton (1969) has studied conflict and conflict management in various different organizational settings. He points out that conflict, moving beyond accepted rules in dealing with others, is not always destructive. A moderate level of conflict may have constructive consequences such as increasing the level of motivation, increasing individual innovation, and better defining the role of an individual.

Walton also has investigated the role that third-party mediation can play in resolving organizational disputes. In general, he finds that there are five role attributes that are optimal for identifying third parties:

1. high professional expertise regarding social processes
2. low power over the fate of the principals
3. high control over the confrontation setting and processes
4. moderate knowledge about the principles, issues, and background factors
5. neutrality or balance with respect to substantive outcome, personal relationships, and conflict resolution methodology (Walton 1969: 150).

The extent to which these principles apply to the posture assumed by authorities in their more general conflict management role is unclear, but at least the principles seem applicable where government agencies get directly involved in providing mediators for disputes among subordinates.

Fisher (1972) has completed an exhaustive literature survey of the roles that can be played by third parties in consultation situations. Meyer (1960) has examined the role that is played by mediators in collective bargaining. N. Schwartz (1969–1970) has focused more directly on social conflict situations and the question of selecting a mediator. Working from an anthropological perspective and using a Guatemalan village as a case study, he finds that the most effective mediator is a person whose reputation and behavior would make the person unacceptable for membership in the contending groups. A mediator who is not a threat to the parties involved can often perform "improper" functions that are necessary to break an impasse. This finding is similar to the point made by Walton and would seem to indicate that intervention by highly visible government authorities may not be optimal for conflict resolution among subordinates.

There is also a significant literature dealing with third parties and conflict resolution in international affairs. However, its applicability to the types of disputes discussed here is questionable, particularly because the power configurations in national political systems are very different from those in international disputes. Young (1967) has investigated the role of third parties in international crises with particular attention paid to the role of the U. N. Secretary General in superpower conflicts. Ott (1972) has investigated two international situations where third-party mediation was a significant factor in the resolution of the disputes. Although his empirical data are related to only two cases of confrontation, Malaysia–Indonesia in 1963–1966 and the Sabah dispute of 1961–1966 between Malaysia and the Philippines, he suggests five factors that facilitate successful international third-party mediation. These include: (1) an even distribution of power among the parties to a dispute; (2) an absence of vital security issues; (3) a perceived high and rising price for nonsettlement of the dispute; (4) an absence of personality conflicts or negotiating positions struck for mainly political purposes; and (5) well-timed initiatives by a skilled mediator (Ott 1972: 616). Ott finds that in these situations the skill of the mediator is probably less important than the other four factors that he has identified.

INSTITUTIONALIZATION AND REGULATION

Factors that affect the institutionalization and regulation of conflict are perhaps of greatest interest to political scientists. The first important principle is that participants in a dispute must be organized internally and have control of their component groups and individuals if conflicts are to be resolved systematically (Dahrendorf 1959: 226). In other words, parties to negotiations must be able to deliver regularly on the promises that they make. In addition, for optimal conflict regulation to develop, each party to a conflict must recognize the legitimacy of the other parties and be willing to accept outcomes. Conflicts are more likely to be regulated if there are institutional precedents to be cited. And finally, conflicts are more likely to be resolved if all sides perceive themselves to be part of a common community (M. Deutsch 1973: 377–378).

Where rules are applicable to a potential conflict situation, M. Deutsch suggests that the rules (or laws) are most likely to be followed when:

1. the rules are known by all parties
2. the rules are clear, unambiguous, and consistent
3. the rules are perceived to be unbiased
4. there is confidence that others adhere to the rules
5. violators can be quickly found out
6. there is social approval for adherence to the rules
7. adherence to the rules has been rewarded in the past
8. the adversaries would like to employ rules in the future (M. Deutsch 1973: 379–380).

Conflicts are less likely to develop in social units where there are rules applicable to disputes and where the above conditions exist.

Although it may seem to be a bit of a paradox, conflict itself can be an important element in long-term institutional stability. Periodic conflict may be essential as a safety valve. Short bursts of instability may relieve tensions that accumulate in stable societies. Furthermore, periodic disruptive conflict represents a way for newly emergent groups to challenge established social hierarchies and change oppressive rules. Repeated violent incidents can lead to institutionalized conflict resolution where none has previously existed (Gurr 1976).

Coser (1956) has outlined a number of propositions from sociological theory that illustrate aspects of conflict that promote stability. He points out that highly integrated relationships permit the manifestation of types of conflict that would never take place under less secure circumstances. In other words, apparent absence of conflict in a social unit cannot necessarily be taken as a sign of group cohesion. In fact, he argues that conflict may well be essential to forge group consciousness and cohesiveness (Coser 1956: 33–35). Coser also asserts that an outside threat or conflict with another social unit can promote internal cohesion. A state of conflict with a common enemy, so the argument goes, will cause members of a social unit to pull more tightly together and overcome internal disunity. This particular assertion must be taken with caution since the empirical evidence indicates no such clear linkage between external conflict and internal cohesion in national political units (see Chapter 7 of this *Handbook*).

PEACEFUL APPROACHES TO CHANGE

Although little systematic research has been done so far, the study of peaceful societies and cooperative approaches to conflict resolution promises to yield new propositions about political stability. M. Deutsch (1973: 20) makes an important basic distinction between cooperative and competitive processes of conflict resolution. A cooperative situation is characterized by "promotive interdependence." The goals of participants are "so linked that any participant can attain his or her goal if, and only if, the others with whom he or she is linked can attain their goals." A competitive situation is characterized by "contrient interdependence" within which goals of participants "are so linked together that there is a negative correlation between their goal attainments."

The initial postures of parties in conflict can initiate self-reinforcing competitive or cooperative spirals. Deutsch formulates this tendency into a "crude law of social relations" which states that "the characteristic processes and effects elicited by a given type of social relationship (cooperative or competitive) tend also to elicit that type of social relationship" (M. Deutsch 1973: 365). In other words, the perspectives and strategies employed by one party in a dispute are reflected by the opposition and shape the final outcome. This tendency for the actions of one party to be "mirrored" by the actions of other parties has been noted as a central characteristic of United States–Soviet relations during the Cold War (Triska and Finley 1965).

Attempts to manage conflict are likely to be more successful when a co-operative atmosphere develops from the beginning. A cooperative perspective is characterized by open and honest communication of relevant information among participants, increased sensitivity to similarities and common interests, and development of trust. Cooperation facilitates recognition of the legitimacy of each other's interests and of the necessity of finding a solution that is responsive to the needs of all parties. A competitive process, by contrast, is characterized by lack of or misleading communication, increased sensitivity to differences instead of similarities, suspicion of and hostile attitudes toward the other parties, and a tendency toward unilateral imposition of solutions (M. Deutsch 1973: 29–30). By the time most conflicts surface, there already is a history of competition and aggression between the parties involved. Conflicts can be resolved most effectively if self-reinforcing negative spirals can be broken and replaced by a positive and cooperative perspective.

Janis and Katz (1959: 85) lament the paucity of research dealing with positive psychological forces in human conduct such as ethical principles and social norms that promote peace and stability, a condition that still persists. They argue that the means, peaceful or violent, employed in any confrontation, struggle, or negotiation determine the ends. Use of violent means to attain peaceful ends increases the probability that such violent means will be used again in similar situations and decreases the probability that stability ultimately will be achieved. Even when violence is socially sanctioned, those using violent means may still react with some degree of guilt due to early internalization of nonviolent values. Guilt reactions may lead to unwarranted fears of punishment, preoccupation with questions about correctness of violent actions, and affective problems related to guilt, all of which would tend to escalate hostilities. Furthermore, participation in group-sanctioned violent actions may lessen individual and collective superego control and lead to more extreme forms of violence. Finally, a social contagion effect may be noted among followers when group leaders engage in violent conduct (Janis and Katz 1959: 92–93).

On the other hand, Janis and Katz suggest that there may be many positive psychological results from nonviolence. Individuals may undergo relearning and discover that acting in a nonviolent manner does not lead enemies to take advantage. A reduction in emotional tension may occur as anxieties regarding nonviolent approaches prove unfounded. And last, internal efforts to justify friendly treatment of potential enemies can lead to cognitive restructuring including reduced hostility toward rival groups and more favorable evaluations of the use of positive approaches to conflict resolution in general (Janis and Katz 1959: 94–95).

Another method of gaining understanding of cooperative approaches is to study the writings and experiences of practitioners of nonviolence. Naess (1958) has attempted to systematize hypotheses deduced from the philosophical approach and actions of Mahatma Gandhi, one of the foremost proponents of nonviolent approaches to change. Naess derives interrelated propositions that are too numerous to be detailed here. The hypotheses relate to three issues: management of confrontations, building cooperation, and opening communication. The primary strategy in Gandhi's peaceful confrontation ethics was to act in struggle in a manner conducive to the reduction of violence in the long term. In selecting strategies Gandhi stressed, as does Deutsch, that it is means that determine ends. It is better not to violate rules, if possible, and to resist passively when it is not possible. In creating programs and in approaching confrontations it is important to stress constructive and positive elements while avoiding negative and punitive ones. Violence and attempts to deal from positions of strength are seen as likely to increase rather than reduce violence (Naess 1958: 142–144).

Peaceful resolution of disputes and maintenance of stability requires trust and cooperation among the parties involved. Trust can be built by stressing goals common to those involved and by treating opponents with respect. According to Naess, participants in confrontations or negotiations should avoid humiliating or provoking opponents. Peaceful resolution of disputes also is facilitated by accurate communication of as much information as possible. Secrecy and distortion should be avoided. Opponents should be apprised of all aspects of the case to be made and objectives should never be changed during the course of negotiations. Secret moves should be avoided on the grounds that they create mistrust (Naess 1958: 145–147).

One of the problems with propositions deduced from Gandhi's philosophy is that most of them remain untested in a wide range of confrontation situations. It is unclear, for example, whether Gandhi's successes were peculiar to the Indian political culture and situation in which there were many shared peaceful norms among disputants or whether they have more universal applicability. An analysis of Gandhi's theory of satyagraha, nonviolent resistance, as a two-party game, reveals many limiting conditions and several inconsistencies in his approach (Klitgaard 1971). For example, in order for the strategy to succeed, Klitgaard points out, one's opponent must be a utility maximizer and not an absolutist and there must be substantial potential sympathy for the plight of the protester. Furthermore, although the philosophy is nonviolent, violence always seems to follow supposedly nonviolent rule violations. Thus, whereas peaceful approaches to conflict may be useful, much more information about their applicability to different situations must be gathered and propositions deduced from them must be tested much more thoroughly.

Fabbro (1978) and J. Steiner (1969) adopt different approaches to the study of peaceful reconciliation of disputes. Fabbro has examined anthropological data for seven types of apparently nonviolent societies and attempted to isolate social and environmental factors that might be responsible. He finds that in none of the groups there is a large economic surplus and what surplus there may be is distributed equitably. All of the peaceful societies are small, which facilitates egalitarian decision making and processes of social control.

Steiner explores the Swiss example, a country that has regulated its political conflicts with very little violence for a long time. He tests sixteen hypotheses about conflict derived from the literature and finds that few of them are thrown into doubt. But six new propositions relating conflict regulation and stability are suggested by the Swiss example. In general, there will be little violence if elites from different subcultures interact relatively often in informal settings, if they interact out of public sight, if political decision-making processes move relatively slowly, if there is little room for innovation in political decision making, if political role-holders seldom change, and if political leaders have relatively little visibility (J. Steiner 1969: 297).

In summary, it would seem that much more is to be learned about the management and resolution of conflict by studying peaceful approaches to change and peaceful societies. The existing data are sparse and propositions have not been widely tested. More data must be collected and the kinds of propositions cited here must be tested in many cultural settings. Comparisons between peaceful and violent societies having similar social hierarchies might also be useful. This type of information should not only increase our understanding of how some societies have achieved peace and stability but may also contribute to the construction of more peaceful societies in the future.

CHAPTER 12

Theory and Practice
in Conflict Research

Terry Nardin

INSOFAR AS IT DRAWS UPON the stock of ideas and methods that constitutes the social sciences, the effort to understand human conflict encounters the same issues of conceptualization, explanation, and objectivity that arise in connection with the social sciences generally. To consider these issues is to reflect upon the presuppositions of social inquiry, including those aspects of it that raise questions of "value," and thus have practical as well as theoretical implications. Sometimes our interest focuses on the implications of the practical aspects of social science for inquiry itself (as, for example, when we are concerned with how inquiry may be affected by the moral commitments of the researcher). At other times, we are interested in the implications of social science outside its own sphere (for example, when we wonder whether a certain explanation does not commit us to a particular political position). To give thought to the relation between theory and practice is thus both to consider the implications of practical concerns for the adequacy of theoretical understanding and to consider the consequences of how people understand the social world for their conduct in it.

That theorizing is tied to practical concerns is nowhere more apparent than in relation to political conflict, where the attempt to understand has long been motivated by the desire to avoid, bring about, or otherwise influence wars, revolutions, and other human struggles. The task of this chapter is to consider one version of the charge that the social sciences have been distorted by political concerns and that politics has in turn been corrupted by this distorted understanding: the charge is that there is a close and mutually reinforcing relationship between empirical conflict theory and the perpetuation of coercive and dehumanizing forms of political life.

THE IDENTITY OF CONFLICT RESEARCH

"Conflict research" is a vague expression, and before we can profitably consider the activity to which it refers from the perspective of the relationship of theory to practice, we need to clarify how the expression is best used. A denotatively precise although perhaps excessively narrow definition of "conflict research" might refer to the scholarship represented by the studies relied upon in the preceding chapters of this *Handbook*. If we take such a definition as our point of departure, how might this branch of inquiry be characterized?

On the whole, the research arrayed here reflects a commitment to a certain style of theorizing. We are dealing with a body of scholarship that is self-consciously scientific in seeking to account for the phenomena of conflict in terms of intellectual constructs whose descriptive and explanatory adequacy is to be tested by the methods of controlled observation. It is also self-consciously empiricist in being preoccupied with observables and in its tendency to equate theory with empirical generalization. Conflict theory as it appears here reflects the complexity of experience as embodied in data assembled by the observer. It seeks to disentangle this complexity by charting the regularities they display, in contrast with research guided by what might be called the "formalist" program of revealing the logical structure of experience (Diesing 1971: chapter 9). The formalist is concerned with exploring the implications of a number of purposely abstract assumptions from which it is possible to generate a body of deductively related theorems. The theories of the empiricist, on the other hand, typically comprise a list of inductively related propositions which, although formulated in a common vocabulary, do not constitute a single deductive system. Scholars like Anatol Rapoport or Kenneth Boulding whose characteristic thinking is in the formal mode would certainly seem to be engaged in "conflict research," but their style does not characterize this *Handbook*.

Empirical conflict theory tends to focus on overt and measurable conflict behavior: to study incidents of physical violence, for example, rather than the conceptual and institutional context of such incidents (E. P. Thompson 1963: 9–11). This surely reflects the empiricist conviction about the importance of observables. Quantitative data on strikes, riots, arrests, and coups d'état are easier to understand, appear more objective, and are thought to be more suited to cross-cultural comparison than data on perceptions, intentions, or other aspects of conflict as understood from the internal point of view of the participant. The argument that human behavior cannot be adequately described without referring to the cultural circumstances within which it occurs—that is, in relation to ideas—and that the explanation of conflict therefore requires the theorist to interpret the significance of behavior within these cultural circumstances, has had little apparent impact on conflict research.[1] The usual solution of the empirical theorist to the problem of how to index the concept of "violence" and turn it into a variable is to exclude the understanding, the ideas, of those whose conduct is being studied. "The trouble with letting much depend on intentions," says historian Charles Tilly, "is that intentions are mixed and hard to discern" (Tilly 1978: 175). The remedy is to attempt to limit the definition of "violence" to what can be conceptualized entirely from the external point of view of the observer. Tilly, for example, suggests that "violence" is best defined as "any observable interaction in the course of which persons or objects are seized or physically damaged in spite of resistance" (Tilly 1978: 176). This way of attempting to solve the problem is highly characteristic of the empirical theorist. But from the perspective of a concern with understanding the significance of particular incidents of seizure or physical damage, in a particular historical situation, such a solution is unhelpful.

Another characteristic of empirical conflict research is the attitude of its practitioners toward the relationship of theory and practice. Conflict research reflects a commitment to what is regarded as theoretical illumination, but it is also practically motivated. Like many other branches of inquiry, it is the offspring of a wish to ameliorate the human condition. The hope of the conflict theorist is to discover the knowledge that would allow society to so arrange human affairs that the harmful aspects of conflict are avoided. But although the motive for theorizing is predominantly practical, theory and practice as modes of activity are held to be distinct. Nevertheless, the theory required for practical purposes is the same theory sought by the impartial discoverer of knowledge. A product of the activity of scientific inquiry rather than the reasonings of everyday life, it constitutes a form of rationality more disciplined than common sense. Practice, in turn, is understood as action to realize values, which are not themselves determined by theoretical reflection, through the technical application of the knowledge embodied in an adequate theory. There is nothing in this understanding of the relationship of theory and practice that commits the empirical theorist to any particular set of values or policies. Conflict theory may suggest to authorities the practical means to suppress political resistance, but it is equally capable of instructing the revolutionary or reformer.

These assumptions concerning the nature of theory and its relationship to practical concerns have been attacked, not only on epistemological grounds, but also as reflecting a morally defective understanding of both science and politics. Before considering these charges, however, we should ask whether it makes sense to limit the scope of the discussion by identifying "conflict research" with the work of the empirical theorists. I think it does, not only because the style of inquiry identified here has a certain unity that distinguishes it from research guided by phenomenological, hermeneutic, or other interpretive methodologies, but also because it is just this sort of conflict research that has been the main target of practically motivated criticism. And where empirical research on conflict has transformed itself into something more broadly conceived—as has happened within what is called "peace research" in Europe—it has been under the impact of such criticism that the change has taken place. What I attempt to do here is to sketch what I see as some of the basic issues in the clash between the empirical theorizing that constitutes conflict and peace research in the narrow sense, and the criticism of this approach which is motivated by a wish to restructure conflict and peace research along other lines. The task is a difficult one, for the issues raised echo those that have arisen outside conflict research and that have ramifications extending far beyond its limited horizon. Something of this broader intellectual context must be understood if the significance of the practically inspired criticism of conflict research is to be appreciated.

PRACTICAL CRITICISM OF CONFLICT RESEARCH

Our habit of referring to the criticism of a doctrine, theory, or school of thought as a "critique" derives from Kant's use of the term in *The Critique of Pure Reason* and the other works of his critical philosophy. To engage in the activity of critique in Kant's sense is to explore the presuppositions of a mode of thought. The purpose of critique is to establish the basis of scientific and other forms of reason. Science, for example, presupposes both a reality outside the observer and certain basic concepts—space, time, and causality—in terms of which that reality can be made intelligible, something more than a chaos of sense impressions. To engage in critique is thus to probe the assumptions of knowledge and experience in their most general forms. It is to be distinguished from the examination of the arguments of "books and systems." However, their consideration (which Kant calls "dialectic") constitutes a subsidiary part of the activity of critique, because such arguments may contain errors of reasoning that interfere with our understanding of experience and of the world itself. These ideas and their associated terminology were passed on through Hegel to Marx and the Marxist tradition, and are echoed in the controversies of our own time concerning the nature and possibility of a science of human behavior. Because we have inherited the notion of critique largely by way of Marxism, its main application at present is in the so-called "radical critique" of disciplines such as economics, sociology, and peace research.

Clearly, however, something has been lost. Whereas "critique" originally stood for the unconditioned exploration of the most fundamental modes of thought, it has come to mean the evaluation of any set of ideas, however limited; it has been edged aside by "dialectic" or the criticism of errors, especially those of "ideology." Critique is thus in danger of being debased to the level of mere fault-finding. I emphasize the distance between the Kantian and radical conceptions of critique not merely to point out certain limitations of the latter, but also to suggest the direction that the activity of critique in the social sciences should take if it is to be of use to us in understanding the premises—and implications—of our own activity as social scientists. At the moment, talk of critique is often more pretension.

Ideas can be criticized, in the various senses of that term, from a variety of perspectives. In speaking of "practical" criticism, I mean to focus attention on those examinations of empirical theory that are motivated by a concern with its implications for the conduct of human affairs, especially politics. The traditional name for this world of human and political activity is "practice," although, as we shall see, it is in some ways an unfortunate one. To examine something from the point of view of practice is to consider how it may assist or hinder the realization of human purposes. Practical criticism of an idea may thus be distinguished from the purely theoretical in that the latter is an enterprise guided only by the standard of truth, whereas the former is concerned with evaluating human consequences. The two often go together, of course; we may question an idea because we doubt the adequacy of the understanding it confers *and* because we dislike its practical implications. Theoretical criticism of ideas about human conflict, for example, is often motivated by practical concerns such as the desire to influence conflicts or to point out the moral implications of adopting a certain understanding of their causes. We are concerned here, then, not with all of the questions that might be raised about conflict research on theoretical grounds, but only with those questions that, in addition to being theoretical, are also directly inspired by a wish to alter the relationship between conflict research and the world of practice.

THE RADICAL CRITIQUE

In the 1960s each of the social science disciplines experienced a wave of criticism set in motion largely by political events. Much of the resulting discussion, with its emphasis on relevance, militant theory, and the corruption of social scientists by their military and industrial paymasters, is now a historical relic. Underlying the rhetoric of these controversies, however, were some questions of fundamental significance concerning the social place and consequences of the social sciences. These questions about conflict research were raised in connection with the strategic studies underlying the balance of terror, with the analyses of some then prominent theoretical treatments of revolutions and social change, with the sponsorship by the United States Army of research on revolutions on Project Camelot (and counterinsurgency research generally), with the reports of the various American investigatory commissions looking into the matter of civil disorders, and with the emerging discipline of peace research. Because the issues, insofar as they concern research on conflict, were most fully debated in the last context, I will concentrate on it.[2]

The initial focus of peace research during its development as a self-conscious discipline during the 1950s and 1960s was on international war, especially nuclear war between the superpowers. In contrast to cold-war thinking, according to which the danger of nuclear war could be attributed to Soviet belligerence, peace research reflected the view, common among scholars of international relations, that the danger of war could be traced to the insecurities of a situation in which armed adversaries confronted one another in an atmosphere of mistrust and misperception. In order to achieve peace, it would be necessary to put an end to this insecurity, and this in turn was thought to require correction of the images of hostility through which the powers interpreted each other's policies. There was thus much interest in the importance of undistorted communication, together with a continuing interest in disarmament, arms control, and the strengthening of supranational institutions.

The turbulence of the 1960s provoked a shift of concern within peace research from international conflict to the issues of internal political controversy: protest, repression, social change, and revolutionary warfare. In its search for a remedy for international conflict, peace research had tended to look toward the development of an international authority of some kind, one capable of impartially performing the functions of inspection, verification, and peacekeeping required to maintain order in a partially disarmed but still unstable international system. The real problems of controlling international aggression and of moving the system to a less anarchic condition distracted attention from the largely academic problem of controlling an international authority and insuring its impartiality. In the domestic context, however, the possibility of the misuse of public authority was increasingly apparent, and the distinction between a publicly authorized and legitimate use of force and illegitimate private violence was increasingly perceived as masking the fact that powerful factions were using the apparatus of government to promote their own private ends (Garver 1968, Wolff 1969). Hence the whole enterprise of seeking peace through the strengthening of central institutions and through the suppression of violence came to be seen as suspect.

The consequences for peace research were devastating. The consensus on which its approach had been based dissolved under the accusation that beneath its pretensions of generating knowledge about peace could be discerned a commitment to the preservation of the existing order (Schmid 1968). Peace research, the radical critics asserted, had succumbed to the invitation of the ruling elites to join them in the practical enterprise "of maintaining power, of freezing the status quo, of manipulating the underdog so that he does not take up arms against the topdog," and was thus in danger of becoming "a conservative force in politics" (Galtung 1969: 2–3). Different critics, to be sure, offered different explanations for the developments, which in turn implied different remedies. For some, the problem was merely one of misapplication of social science theory and methods to the wrong political ends, in an unscientific manner at that (Olsen and Jarvad 1970). Others suggested that the source of the practical distortion of peace research was to be found in the fact that it sought to combine the methods of American social science with the politics of the peace movement (Schmid 1970). Both of these modes of activity were said to share a view of conflict as a sort of irrationality that dispassionate inquiry could dispel, whereas, in truth, conflict is best understood as reflecting real differences rooted in the structure of society. "On the basis of this ideology, the knowledge and skills of neopositivist social science were to be turned into a technology for peace" (Schmid 1970: 22). Because the technological knowledge and policy advice provided by peace research can be applied only by those with the power to put it into practice, the governing elites, peace research finds itself in their service. The military, government, and corporate management in turn constitute the chief source of the demand for the results of peace research and are therefore its main sponsors. Because it is committed to the ideal of scientific objectivity, peace research attempts to avoid the corruption inherent in this situation by adopting the perspective of the system as a whole, rather than that of the parties to conflicts within the system. But to the extent that peace research is taken in by the claim of the powerful that they represent the system as a whole, this attempt at impartiality must fail.

From the standpoint of the radical critic, the empiricist premises of peace research virtually guarantee this failure. Because it is empiricist, it can think of objectivity in no other terms but those of intersubjective agreement, and this means that consensus becomes the criterion of truth (Schmid 1970: 59–60). But this consensus is not impartial, rather it reflects the ruling ideology. This analysis would appear to set the stage for a demand for "critical theory" along Marxist lines, and such a demand was in fact forthcoming. Thus it was argued (Dencik 1970) that in its concern with promoting peace—understood as the absence of overt hostility— peace research had concerned itself with the mere symptoms of conflict. By ignoring the underlying conflicts of interest between incumbent governments and revolutionary movements, or between the advanced capitalist states and the less developed Third World—both ultimately class conflicts—peace research was allowing itself to be guided by an interest in pacification, rather than by a concern with the redistribution of wealth and power. To achieve these objectives would require a revolutionary transformation of existing societies and of the international system. This in turn would require that conflicts of interest, which are likely to be hidden because of "false consciousness" and thus are merely latent, be made manifest through the critique of ideology. True peace requires not the amelioration of the symptoms of conflict but the reduction of real conflicts of interest that exist, whether or not they are perceived, in the relations between social classes or between more and less developed societies. The practical vocation of peace research is to clarify these conflicts, thereby showing the way to peace by helping to bring about the sort of revolutionary change that might result in a form of society in which conflicts of interest do not exist.

The initial result of such criticism was to divide the community of peace researchers along political—but not, in fact, along methodological—lines. Similar divisions were appearing in other social science disciplines. Theories of conflict (such as those based on Parsonian functionalism, on the sociological tradition concerned with crowd psychology, mass society, and collective behavior, on a generation of research within political science on political development, and on the social psychology of aggression) were subjected to repeated and probing criticism inspired by the insight that to some extent these theories reflected the same assumptions about conflict as those of the political authorities, editorialists, and others who were demanding the repression of protest and a return to order as they understood it. Although they could not be described as Marxist—in contrast to the European critics of peace research, many of whom did in fact regard themselves as Marxists—the American critics of conflict research (such as Horowitz 1967, Skolnick 1969, Nardin 1971, and Wolin 1973) were recognizably engaged in a form of practical criticism that has its roots in Marxist critical theory. Its characteristic features include a view of social science as containing implicit justifications for particular policies as well as explanations of social phenomena, an effort to "unmask" the pretensions to scientific objectivity and political neutrality, and finally the attempt to suggest an alternative approach to theory which would not only avoid the theoretical blunders that had been identified, but would provide the foundations for more defensible public policy.

SOME LIMITATIONS OF THE RADICAL CRITIQUE

The themes raised by the criticism of peace and conflict research by about 1970 ushered in a period of active inquiry into "structures" of international domination, dependency, and imperialism.[3] The radical critique itself, however, appears to be a spent force. It remains important nevertheless to consider some of the difficulties encountered by the first wave of practical criticism, because they seem to arise wherever empirical theory is criticized from the practical standpoint and because they are, I shall argue, extremely difficult to overcome. Three points particularly need to be made.

First, insofar as it attacks the epistemological premises of empirical theory, the radical critique as it has so far been developed in the literature of peace research really has nothing different to offer. It is usual for the critic to charge that empirical conflict theories mask hidden interests and thus betray their own commitment to value-freedom, scientific objectivity, political neutrality, and the other shibboleths of "positivism." This in itself entails no inherent difficulties, but if the criticism is taken further in the direction of adopting the premises of the Marxist critique of ideology, it runs the danger of self-contradiction. For it is part of the Marxist analysis to argue that because all knowledge is affected by the social circumstances under which it is produced, the claims of social science to objectivity and value-freedom are necessary illusory. The radical critic thus claims that the theories of empirical social science concerning conflict and peace constitute a distorted understanding of those matters rather than genuine knowledge. But this claim as formulated implies that there in fact exists genuine or objective knowledge, in comparison with which the conclusions of the empirical theorist can be seen to be distorted and illusory. A critique of ideology made in this fashion, without qualification, implies that the standpoint from which the criticism is made is itself objective rather than ideological. The result is what Alasdair MacIntyre (1973: 322) has called "epistemological self-righteousness," a confidence that the critic of positivism has been able to avoid the ideological distortion that is said to limit the positivist program for generating objective scientific knowledge. The radical critic thus often turns out to be working with a simplistic version of the epistemological premises that characterize all scientific inquiry, namely, the elimination of error in the search for knowledge. Only when "critical theory" abandons the illusion of truths that are "objective" in some final or absolute sense and opens itself to criticism and revision can it avoid becoming an obstacle to the search for scientific understanding. The danger of epistemological self-righteousness in the radical critic is most apparent when criticism of critical theory is rejected as "ideology." In that case, the claims of critical theory become mere dogma—a point that is amply illustrated by the history of Marxism and psychoanalysis, both of which display similar tendencies to insulate themselves from critical scrutiny.

Second, the radical critique on the whole offers no new understanding of the relationship between theory and practice. In one form it urges a rededication of peace research to the ideal of science. Schmid (1970: 69), for example, appears to advocate a separation of theory and practice, arguing that peace researchers should purge their concepts and theories of ideological contamination and thus attempt "to move from the level of ideology to the level of science." The object of peace research should once again become understanding, not success in the achievement of practical ends; pursuit of the latter is best left to the politician and the political activist. Those engaged in peace research who have strong "political feelings" are free to join the political struggle to promote what they believe to be right. Such a view presupposes the same distinction between fact and value, empirical theory and political practice, that is central to the empiricist approach, according to which the roles of scientist and citizen are separate even though the individual may participate in each. I think, for reasons given further on, that Schmid's view is largely correct. Another, more activist version of the radical position wants to apply theory on behalf of the oppressed. Its advocates argue that revolutionary change is required in order to realize "true" peace (Dencik 1970: 88, Carroll 1972: 600, Wallace 1972a: 39). This argument offers no challenge, in contrast to the earlier and more sophisticated versions of the Marxist critique of empirical theory (discussed below), to the empirical theorists' distinction between empirical theory and political practice and their assumption that good theory is required for competent practice. This radical critique has been limited to questioning the uses to which empirical theory has been put, and to suggesting that justice requires that peace research be made to serve the victims rather than the holders of power. If the empirical theorists' approach to political practice constitutes "technological rationality" and ends in a "manipulative" approach to social change, as those within the Marxist tradition have argued, it is hard to see how the idea of radical social science as empirical social science put to the service of the revolutionary can escape the charge. The radical critics of peace and conflict research have failed to exploit even the resources for dealing with this problem made available by the broader tradition of critical theory.

Finally, although the radical critique makes a contribution in pointing out how the practical concerns of the empirical theorists distort empirical conflict research, it allows its own practical concerns to distort its own theorizing. This is perhaps best illustrated by the enthusiasm with which the concept of "structural violence" was adopted by those who were unhappy with the empiricist's tendency to identify violence with direct physical injury. This narrow conception of violence seemed to focus the spotlight of blame on the acts of protesters and insurgents while neglecting the harm inflicted by institutions. If "peace" means "absence of violence," it was argued, then peace research should not define violence narrowly as direct physical injury (Galtung 1969: 168). The realization that the various sorts of deprivation and suffering that have long been identified as social injustice are in fact a form of violence has the happy consequence of giving "peace" the meaning of overcoming social injustice as well as putting an end to the physical destruction of armed conflict. The final stage of this semantic game was to argue that peace research might without contradiction support armed struggles, including wars of national liberation, whose aim was to put an end to social injustice ("structural violence") and thus establish true peace. This sort of thinking reflected a twofold practical concern: to produce a justification for wars of national liberation within the existing conceptual framework of peace research (this seems to be Dencik's main concern) and to patch over the dissension within peace research between the radicals and those whose work had been attacked, by broadening the definition of peace in such a way as to permit those with diverse political views to cooperate within the framework of "peace research" (Galtung's goal). The theory generated by the radical critique thus reflects the practical concerns of the peace research movement itself.

Reading over the literature produced by these controversies, one is forced to conclude that the hard questions concerning the practical implications of empirical theory have not been adequately considered by either the radical critics or those engaged in empirical peace and conflict research. It is true that the question of whether or not peace research can be "applied" has been canvassed in the journals (Rapoport 1970, Kent 1971, Stohl and Chamberlain 1972). But the specific question of the applicability of empirical *theory* (as opposed to methods, skills, and information) is neglected. To make headway on this issue would require not only a re-examination of our understanding of empirical theory, but also an inquiry into the characteristics of practical activity and, above all, political activity. The question then becomes, given the diverse character of practical activity, what sorts of knowledge are appropriate? What, given various understandings of practice, is the relevance of "empirical theory?" And, perhaps most important, what are the moral implications of the search for practically relevant theory?

PRACTICAL CRITICISM OF EMPIRICAL SOCIAL AND POLITICAL THEORY

These are questions that have been addressed in the larger debate concerning empirical theory, even though they have been neglected in the radical criticism of conflict research. From the perspective of practical concerns, empirical social and political theory has experienced a double challenge. It has, first of all, been questioned on the grounds of moral impoverishment, of supporting practical action with undesirable consequences for society and politics. Empirical theory, it is argued, reflects an instrumentalist conception of knowledge and thus lends itself to the perpetuation of domination. There are many variants of this charge, but whatever their differences all advance what is essentially a *moral* objection to the enterprise of empirical theory: the focus is on how empirical theory distorts just or humane conduct and institutions. Such objections do not however exhaust the practical case against empirical theory, for besides the charge of moral deficiency there is the judgment that empirical theory misunderstands the character of human action, of social life, and of politics, and is therefore *theoretically* incapable of generating knowledge which is appropriate to practice. Applied to practice, empirical theory is a source not only of moral but of technical failure; the applied empirical theorist is not only a sinner but an incompetent. (I note without comment an apparent contradiction between the charges of moral and theoretical inadequacy, the former sometimes ascribing to empirical theory a practical potency denied by the latter.)

THEORY AS IDEOLOGY AND THE IDEA OF PRAXIS: MARX

Because of his influence on all later versions of practical criticism, as well as on the empirical social and political theory whose premises it examines, any discussion of these matters must touch on the ideas of Karl Marx. Practical criticism of empirical theory is in some ways best understood as variations on a theme by Marx. The theme is the theory of ideology.

It is well-known that Marx initially formulated his conception of theory and practice in a critique of the philosophy of Hegel. It is instructive to consider the reasons Marx gives for the importance of critique for both theory and practice. One of the central themes of the Hegelian philosophy concerns the importance of ideas in human history. History is indeed the history of ideas, the growth of knowledge as cumulatively achieved through the experience of successive civilizations, each a stage or epoch in the universal history of mankind. History is the process of realization, through the flourishing of successive civilizations each possessing its own characteristic culture or "spirit," of a cumulative truth only partly reflected in the culture of particular civilizations. This Hegel called "absolute spirit" and he identified it with the ideas of reason and divine providence. Marx conceived his own project as one of taking this idealist theory of history and translating it into a scientific theory of human development. The spirit of the age, said Marx, is not the moving principle of history, but only a reflection of the real moving principle, which is to be found in the activities of the human species. Epochs have characters which reflect the acts of living, working human beings—not mere conceptions. History is the record of successive forms of work and interaction, and of the various legal, political, religious, and philosophical forms that arise from the kinds of economic arrangements that are technologically possible at different times.

Despite his mystical talk of spirit, Hegel was worth being understood because the Hegelian system, properly interpreted, contained the basis for an empirical science of human nature and conduct. Part of what Hegel had to say seemed to Marx to be true: the idea of progress through dialectical confrontation and reconstruction at a higher level of awareness. The rest—the idealist metaphysics, the talk of spirit, the theology—was false. Behind the layers of myth could be found a core of truth that needed to be uncovered. But until the Hegelian philosophy is corrected in this way it is not only false, it constitutes an obstacle to truth. And this is the other source of its interest for Marx: it constitutes a set of illusions that mask the reality of existing conditions. Hegel's philosophy is not merely a set of half-truths. Rather, it reflects and rationalizes the economic, social, and political situation of Germany in the first third of the nineteenth century: politically backward, dominated by economically based elites (chiefly a landed aristocracy and a growing commercial middle class), with the mass of its inhabitants increasingly bound in servile, dehumanizing labor. By failing to reveal the actual causes of social and political change, and by confusing political ideals with the reality of existing political institutions, Hegel's philosophy of politics amounts to a justification of the existing order. It therefore constitutes, in Marx's language, an "ideology"—a set of illusions that arises in given economic circumstances and that serves to justify and in a marginal way perpetuate the social order it reflects. As such, it must be unmasked. There cannot be radical change until people, freed from the domination of their illusions, realize that things need changing. Hence the importance of the criticism of religious belief, of philosophy, of legal conceptions concerning property and the family, and of political thought.

The impulse behind the Marxist analysis is practical as well as theoretical. The criticism of ideology is required in order to establish the intellectual basis for altering society. The result is a double role for theoretical activity, which has continued to be a source of confusion within the tradition of empirical social science as well as the Marxist tradition. The confusion concerns the relationship of "theory" and "practice," and occurs because each of these terms stands at once for several different notions; and to make matters worse, the terms occasionally stand for the same notion (Lobkowicz 1977: 24). "Theory" was identified by Marx initially with the Hegelian philosophy and then with its criticism. Later this criticism, and hence the idea of theory, was generalized into a critique of all aspects of contemporary society, and finally came to include the effort to describe and explain the workings of that society. Social scientists today would recognize this effort as an attempt to develop empirical theory.

The ambiguities of "theory" are compounded by those of "practice." For the Greeks, from whose language these words derive, "practice" (*praxis*) refers to the activity of the politically active citizen, the way of life of a free member of the political community. It is distinct from the *bios theoretikos*, the life of the seeker of scientific knowledge. To theorize, for the Greeks, was to be concerned with the world of nature, with the realm, that is, of the eternal and the necessary; it did not include the effort to make sense of human action, which was understood as a realm of change and contingency (Aristotle, *Nichomachean Ethics*, VI: 3–5). Modern science, however, no longer accepts this rigid distinction between the natural and the human spheres, and so the categorical distinction between theory and practice made by the ancients is no longer plausible. We now search for the eternal and necessary in society and politics—that is, we are concerned to uncover scientific laws and not mere contingent regularities in human behavior. Theory, in other words, has invaded what was once held to be the exclusive realm of practice. But where the impulse behind the activity of theorizing is a practical one—where one seeks to understand the world in order to change it—practice in turn invades the world of theory. To engage in the criticism of existing conditions is both to theorize and to act.

These are important insights, but the traditional dichotomy between theory and practice not only makes it hard to express them, but indeed sets the stage for misunderstanding. As a result, Marxist thinking about *praxis* has tended to oscillate between identifying it with intellectual criticism and with such forms of political action as worker organization and armed struggle. The idea that *praxis* involves more than the criticism of ideas appears at a very early stage, in Marx's rejection of what he portrays in *The German Ideology* as the empty posturing of the "Young Hegelians" who, despite their attacks on "phrases" in no way threaten the existing order, and indeed merely echo it. As used by the Young Hegelians, the term *praxis* implied a philosophy aimed at political change and not merely at a theoretical understanding of politics. The call for *praxis* was a call for "relevant theory." Marx himself attempted to sketch a conception of *praxis* that was limited neither to the critique of ideology nor to the attempt to develop an empirical theory of society as the basis for an applied theory of change. *Praxis*, furthermore, was never identified with the mere call to the barricades that he ridiculed in other revolutionary activists. It is on the contrary a developmental process involving a dialectic between collective action by the working class and existing social structures, in which association with others alters the consciousness of the worker directly through the experience of collective action and indirectly by altering the social structures that influence this consciousness. *Praxis*, then, refers to those forms of activity that are capable of changing society through the growing self-awareness of the working class as a class—and this, Marx believed, is in the circumstances of capitalist society ultimately a revolutionary consciousness. Criticism and scientific inquiry are necessary elements of *praxis*, but they do not exhaust its content.

CRITICAL THEORY: HORKHEIMER AND THE FRANKFURT SCHOOL

Prominent among those who have questioned the empirical social and political theory of our own time from the perspective of specifically practical concerns are the writers of the "Frankfurt School," as they have come to be called. Through the work of thinkers like Max Horkheimer, Theodor Adorno, and Herbert Marcuse, the Marxist criticism of ideology was revived and applied to current conditions. The most significant discussion of empirical theory by any of these thinkers is that offered by Horkheimer in his 1937 essay on "traditional theory," by which he means the knowledge sought both by the natural sciences and by the attempt to understand human conduct and institutions on the model of the natural sciences. Horkheimer makes many of the points that are today the stock in trade of the radical critique of empirical social and political science. When the proponents of "a new political science" or "radical peace research" express the need for theory that reflects a commitment to peace, justice, and human welfare rather than a spurious value neutrality, a theory that is at once critical of existing society and capable of providing the basis for political change, they are expressing a wish that goes back to Marx and the Young Hegelians. The forms that the expression of this wish took in the writings of the Frankfurt School during the 1930s are important because it is through them that the Marxist criticism of ideology was explicitly applied to empirical social and political theory as we understand it, and in particular as it is presently understood within conflict research.[4]

Horkheimer argues that a better society cannot be created through the application of traditional—that is, empirical—theory, but that it requires the articulation of "critical theory." The basis of this critical theory is to be "the dialectical critique of political economy" (Horkheimer 1972: 261; first published in 1937). "Critique," in other words, is understood in specifically Marxist terms. Why? According to Horkheimer, it is the Marxist analysis that best illuminates modern society, in which most people believe themselves to be at the mercy of forces beyond their power to influence. This self-conception is true, he suggests, for individuals are in fact unable to determine the conditions of their own existence. But it is not *necessarily* true; the proposition is one that can be made false if society were to be restructured in such a way as to emancipate humanity from its repressive constraints. Criticism can help make us aware of the reasons for this powerlessness, dependence, indeed servility. But to overcome it requires more than a puncturing of the illusions through which the present system is rationalized and made acceptable. It requires a practical concern with social and political change. This is Marx's criticism of the Young Hegelians restated.

Horkheimer then turns to "traditional theory," which he characterizes in a manner that will be recognized at once as applicable to empirical social and political theory, or at least to the empiricist's conception of such theory:

> Theory for most researchers is the sum-total of propositions about a subject, the propositions being so linked with each other that a few are basic and the rest derive from these. The smaller the number of primary principles in comparison with the derivations, the more perfect the theory. The real validity of the theory depends on the derived propositions being consonant with the actual facts. If experience and theory contradict one another, one of the two must be reexamined. [Horkheimer 1972: 188]

Compare this characterization with Ted Robert Gurr's definition of a theory as an interrelated set of general propositions, some of which at least are logically derived from others and are precisely enough stated so that the empirical validity of the whole construction can be tested through controlled observation (Gurr 1970b: 16–17, 1978: 303). Neither definition as I have abstracted it is complete, but the essential similarity of the two is apparent. And in each case the definition reflects an ideal, for the features specified are more often sought than achieved.

The two definitions also share a similar conception of the relationship between theory and practice. Horkheimer emphasizes the practical character of empirical theory, which reflects a conception of knowledge appropriate to the manipulation of economic and social mechanisms as if they were a part of physical nature. The social sciences, in imitating the natural sciences, have extended instrumentalist thinking into the moral and political sphere of human life. The origins of modern social science, it is pointed out, are not in the tradition of the humanities but rather in practically oriented activities such as agricultural and market research. Its methods are thus more appropriate to a managerial approach to human life than to one moved primarily by a desire to understand. Managers need to know what they must do to produce a desired result. They seek to understand human conduct only insofar as it is necessary to influence it, in contrast to the ideal of the theorist as a disinterested observer. Because of the circumstances in which it has evolved and is pursued, and as a consequence of the methods upon which it relies to facilitate its tasks, empirical theory does not ordinarily seek a comprehensive understanding of its subject matter, but instead tends to limit itself to the search for explanations in terms of those factors that will facilitate prediction (regardless of their theoretical adequacy) or that are capable of being altered in order to produce desired outcomes. Not only does this foster an instrumentalist approach to the application of the resulting knowledge, but it also represents a limitation and hence, from the point of view of knowledge itself, a deficiency in the character of empirical theory as knowledge.

Although the search for theory is practically motivated, the practical application of theory is not itself part of the theoretical thinking. The scientist is a citizen, but the activities of scientific research and political participation are distinct. The scientist's theories are objective explanations of reality, and if they are accurate they can be put to use for any practical purpose to which they are relevant. Again, comparison with the empiricist conception of theory is illuminating. Empirical conflict theory, it is suggested, "can become a guide to action as well as comprehension," although it is in danger of being "put to unethical as well as ethical ends" (Gurr 1970b: ix–x). Empirical theory, if true, provides the basis for effective political action on behalf of a variety of ends, but it does not specify the nature of those ends. As Gurr argues, "empirical theories do not aim to praise or condemn but rather to explain. This is the only way in which they can help to resolve moral dilemmas: by showing that one way out may be more feasible or costly than another" (Gurr 1978: 307). The relationship of theory to practice is the application of technical knowledge of means to the pursuit of independently premeditated ends.

This conception of theory, according to Horkheimer, represents a misunderstanding of its character. The empirical theorists see their work as a distinct mode of activity, logically unrelated to the practical concerns of everyday life and politics. Scientific research, even though its products may be put to practical use, appears to be autonomous and self-sufficient. But this is not the case. Scientific research is an activity within the division of labor and is thus an aspect of the adaptation of a society to its environment at a particular stage in its history (Horkheimer 1972: 197). The self-determination of the empirical theorists is an illusion. They believe that their activity is determined by its subject, but in truth it is shaped by the demands of the economic, social, and political environment in which they work: in theorizing, they are responding to the workings of a complex social mechanism, most directly to those parts of it that call for and support scientific education and research. Their understanding of theory is thus an aspect of what Horkheimer refers to as "the false consciousness of the bourgeois savant" (Horkheimer 1972: 197).

It does not follow from this analysis of the social circumstances of scientific research (which remarkably anticipates more recent developments in the history and sociology of science) that empirical theory is bad in itself. The point is rather that such theoretical activity is circumscribed by its social conditions. It fails to pursue inquiry according to the dictates of the unfettered theoretical imagination because of the perpetual pressures on the theorist to respond to the practical concerns of those whose support or mere tolerance make it possible in the first place. Economics, for example, focuses on relations within the capitalist economy because that is what the economy needs and demands; meanwhile, the larger comparative, historical, and critical inquiries that depart from the premises of this culturally parochial economic science are neglected.

Horkheimer's proposed remedy for the deficiencies of the social theory of his day emerges dialectically out of the categorical distinction between theoretical and practical activity in which empirical theory is entrapped. Truth presupposes social conditions under which it can be freely pursued. Empirical theory is content to work within the cage provided by a society in which these conditions are absent. Critical theory is not content to do so because, unlike empirical theory, it is aware of the cage—aware that it *is* a cage. The critical theorist thus understands that the activity of theorizing violates its own commitment to truth unless it moves beyond thinking, including critical thinking, to *praxis:* that is, to action designed to create the conditions for its own self-fulfillment. Horkheimer thus gives a Marxist twist to the Socratic ideal when he remarks that "the characteristic mark of the thinker's activity is to determine for itself what it is to accomplish and serve" (Horkheimer 1972: 242). By failing to do this, empirical theory "betrays the very essence of thought." Thus, he concludes, the nature of theory itself "turns it towards a changing of history and the establishment of justice among men" (1972: 243).

I think that there can be little doubt that the arguments of Horkheimer and the other founders of "critical theory" are more thoughtful and interesting than those advanced by the radical critics of peace research. In particular, the writers of the Frankfurt School have attempted to clarify a conception of *praxis* that is more than merely another version of the mechanistic instrumentalism of which they accuse the empirical theorist. Part of the needed conception is already present in the Greek distinction between *praxis* and *poiesis*. *Praxis* is usually translated as "action" or "doing," *poiesis* as "fabrication" or "making." "Making and acting are different," says Aristotle (*Nichomachean Ethics*, VI: 4–5). "For while making has an end other than itself, action cannot; for good action itself is its end." Both action and fabrication are teleological ideas, but the ends associated with each are of a different character. The end of fabrication is to create a product that represents the completion of the activity and provides its rationale: a chair, a poem, a dinner. The activity of fabricating is pursued primarily for its results. The purpose of action, in contrast, is to act in a certain way: more precisely, it is to subscribe to certain conditions in acting. The end of action, in other words, is to do whatever one is doing skillfully, morally, lawfully, piously, or in some other adverbially qualified manner. For the Greeks, the pre-eminent example of *praxis* was political activity. To engage in the public life of the *polis* was understood not simply as a matter of achieving results, of producing "policy outcomes" corresponding to some extrinsic set of "values," but as acting well according to the community's ideals of citizenship and statesmanship.

Something like this distinction is made by Anatol Rapoport in distinguishing "fights" from "games" (Rapoport 1960). Like fabrication and action, fighting and playing are ideal types. The end of fighting is to win, and this (as Clausewitz insisted) is logically to employ whatever means are conducive to this end. The end of playing, however, is to stay within the rules: to conduct oneself at best skillfully and at the very least without ignoring the rules that define the game, even if this means that the result of besting the opponent must be foregone. To "win" within the context of a game thus has a very different meaning from defeating an enemy in a fight; a chess player does not win by leaping up toward the end of a tournament and throttling his opponent. Thus the end of fighting is external to the activity, something to be achieved *through* it, whereas the end of playing a game is to play well, and this is something that can be achieved only *in* the activity.

Modern society, the Frankfurt critique suggests, has, because of the logic of scientific and commercial thinking, come to approach all of its activities through the category of fabrication. Hence the Frankfurt School's distrust of instrumental reason and their perception of a strong link between it and "domination." Just as the artisan cuts and hammers the raw material into the form required by the intended result, so in politics the managerial mentality lops and chops to produce a desired state of affairs. In making this analysis, the Frankfurt writers were both aided and hindered by their Marxist premises, because if Marxism provided the concepts they required to articulate an emancipatory rather than an instrumentalist conception of *praxis*, it also has been made to support the very model of fabrication against which the critical theorist is reacting. For the idea of fabrication, in the guise of "work" or "labor," has been a recurrent element of Marxist thought. It is present in the "early" as well as the "later" Marx, a point not always appreciated by those who ascribe the origins of Stalinism to Marx the social scientist, and prefer the ideas of the young, humanist, Marx. In *The German Ideology,* for example, all human activity is interpreted through the notion of "production"—a word that as used by Marx and Engels includes more than economic production (manufacturing) and physical labor. Human beings also produce their own physical environment through deforestation, cultivation, settlement, and construction. They "re-produce" themselves by bearing children. Most important, they "produce" each other through social interaction, for individuals become what they are by learning a language, receiving an education, pursuing a career, and in various other ways participating in the practices of a particular society and class. They are, in other words, "the product" of the social circumstances of their experience. Nothing in this way of thinking necessarily commits us to an instrumentalist approach to practice, but it is easy to see how such an approach might be based on it.

In some versions of Marxism the metaphor of production does in fact lead to an instrumentalist conception of *praxis* as the production of a new state of affairs, a new society in which human beings would be freed from the physical and intellectual bondage of modern existence understood as a result to be achieved not *in* but *by means of* revolutionary action. Instead of consciousness raising we get the liquidation of the kulaks. In opposition to this conception of *praxis*, which is that of the Soviet state, the critical theory of the Frankfurt School interprets Marx's conception of *praxis* in a way not readily expressed in Aristotelian terms. The dialectic between "subject" (the working class) and "object" (society as it exists) is not instrumental action, for the actors are initially unaware of what they are doing. And even though the process set in motion is one in which the working class gradually becomes more aware of itself as an acting subject, *praxis* cannot quite be understood as fabrication because it is not action directed toward a *predetermined* end. On the other hand, it is not "action" in the

Aristotelian sense, either. In contrast to Aristotle's conception of *praxis* as individual action in an unchanging society, Marx's concept of *praxis* involves the idea of collective action, which, in changing the actor, also changes and ultimately transforms the society in which it takes place. Class consciousness is not a prelude to revolution: it is the revolution.[5]

How plausible is this attempt to develop a theory of *praxis* that is not just another version of the technological rationality of the empirical theorist? Can critical theory really avoid degenerating into the dehumanized instrumentalism of which it accuses empirical theory? It is at least arguable that even Horkheimer's moving plea for theory to show the way to a world in which it can realize its true character seems unable completely to escape the model of fabrication, because it makes the task of critical theory that of producing the conditions for its own flourishing, and this entails the destruction of capitalism. The "justice among men" to which he believes the critical theorist is committed is a substantive end to be achieved rather than a set of limits to be observed in acting; it refers to a future condition of society that corresponds more closely to human needs. The logical consequence of this conception of justice is that acts that tend toward the actualization of this future condition are "just," even if they violate existing rights. The latter, as part of the superstructure of capitalism, must give way to the necessities of revolutionary action. A more consistent Marxist would not draw back, as Horkheimer seems to do, from defending "progressive" violence.[6] Implicit in his argument is the idea of fidelity to standards of truth that are not particular to the social conditions of the present—a fidelity that recalls the Greek conception of *praxis*. But there is a tension here which, if resolved in favor of adherence to existing standards, leads to "revisionism"—that is, to an acceptance of the intellectual and moral framework of the existing order. On the other hand, if this tension is resolved in favor of results, the danger is that a complete abdication of these standards will follow, the consequence of which will be a reversion to an instrumentalism potentially as ruthless as that from which critical theory has sought to distance itself.

The most recent attempts to clarify the task of critical theory continue the effort to articulate a conception of *praxis* that is activist without being instrumentalist. Juergen Habermas (1971, 1973), for example, starts from the observation that the social sciences in their interpretive as well as their empiricist forms are liable to be corrupted; just as empirical theory can provide the basis for a manipulative approach to politics, the resources of the interpretive social sciences can be used to deceive. Under present conditions, Habermas suggests, all the sciences regardless of their character tend to become instruments of a domination masked by ideology. The task of critical theory is to free us from this domination by making possible the collective self-awareness that would dispel the illusions of ideology. Habermas's favored analogy is psychoanalysis; in the same way that the analyst helps patients to cure themselves of neurosis through self-criticism leading to a more objective awareness of themselves, so the critical theorist can help foster the collective self-criticism through which society might rid itself of its false consciousness. Habermas thus seems to avoid the dangers of *praxis* by staying at the level of criticism—a reversion, some have charged, from Marxism to the Young Hegelians. Criticism as a means to "consciousness-raising" is also central to Brian Fay's (1975, 1977) "educative model" of theory and practice. So conceived, critical theory appears to leave room for empirical theory as a valid part of the social sciences. If we avoid making exaggerated claims for it, and recognize its limitations, empirical theory surely has a role to play in facilitating the self-awareness that, for the critical theorist, is a prerequisite both of the pursuit of knowledge and of noninstrumentalist practice. This indeed is one of Habermas's main points.

SOME IMPLICATIONS OF PRACTICAL CRITICISM FOR CONFLICT RESEARCH

It is not my intention to suggest that the critical theorists are correct in their analysis of empirical theory, nor do I wish to refute the various critical arguments that I have discussed. What I have tried to suggest, however, is that practical criticism can be turned with effect on the enterprise of critical theory itself. My own view is that from the perspective of a concern with the relationship of theory and practice, the dispute between the empirical and the critical theorist is a family quarrel rather than the Armageddon it is sometimes made out to be. And because this is so the participants share much that can provide the basis for a dialogue. For the empirical theorist of conflict there are lessons both in what the practical critic has to say about empirical conflict research and in what the empirical theorist can learn from the errors of the practical critic.

CRITICISM AND THEORY

The first lesson is that criticism is an integral part of theorizing. To theorize without subjecting one's own premises to scrutiny is to invite blindness and virtually to guarantee that one's understanding will be partial and conditioned by unconscious assumptions. But just what this means is hard to specify and has indeed become a source of controversy between empirical and critical theorists. Each tradition in its own way has recognized the necessity for criticism, indeed, has enshrined its own conception of criticism in a series of procedures that are followed even when they are not understood and that tend to degenerate into methodological ritual and incantation. Each, I would argue, needs to become more aware of the limitations of its own conception of criticism. Criticism, for the critical theorist, is identified with the "critique of ideology," and this means that it is pursued on the basis of a set of Marxist assumptions themselves badly in need of criticism and revision. Empirical theory, on its part, recognizes the need for criticism in its identification of truth with testable theory, and in its consequent concern with method. The criticism to which empirical theory subjects itself is the criticism of data: the most telling point that can be made against a theory is to show that it is unable to account satisfactorily for what are taken to be "the facts." Too often, however, the empirical theorists forget what in their more alert moments they know well, that theory guides the definition and interpretation of facts.

The way out of the resulting circle is seldom found through the assembling of more and more data, hypotheses, and findings, but rather through an awareness of the need to alter one's theoretical presuppositions. What is required is that a more philosophical conception of criticism be admitted as a legitimate part of the activity of science itself, that scientists be less insistent on getting on with the job of science by excluding criticism of their own methods. Science, no less than philosophy, must be a critical enterprise; the scientist fails as a scientist if hypotheses are framed and data collected on the basis of unexamined concepts. And yet because conceptual criticism is not regarded as part of the scientific enterprise, as understood by the empirical theorist, the conceptual foundations of empirical theory are often far weaker than they need be, or then they would be if the empirical theorist would devote some serious effort to conceptual self-criticism and to learning from those who have made it their business to consider what such reflection involves.

The need for conceptual criticism as an integral part of the activity of empirical theorizing is well-illustrated by the example of how conflict theory has been led astray in its use of the concept of "violence." One of the most common theoretical approaches to the study of violence in politics has at its core the notion that violence represents a deviation from institutionalized patterns of conduct. This notion is usually not the conclusion of an argument, but rather a premise incorporated within basic theoretical concepts such as "social disorganization" or "collective behavior." Yet the notion of violence as uninstitutionalized action seems ill-adapted to the explanation of phenomena such as warfare or state terror. These phenomena seem in many significant ways to count as violence, yet appear to be highly institutionalized practices scarcely comprehensible as deviations from institutionalized conduct as such. In many societies violence is part of a settled way of life rather than an interruption of it (Huizinga 1954, G. Clark 1958, Walter 1969). One of the consequences of conceptualizing violence as uninstitutionalized behavior has been the identification of violence with the conduct of radical groups but not with that of organizations like the police that are part of what the critical theorist would call the "dominant" institutions of society. In this view, the infliction of harm by "deviant" groups counts as violence, but harm done by the authorities does not. There are contexts in which it is appropriate to make such distinctions. The error of empirical theorists, however, was to define riots, revolutions, and civil wars as if they were attacks by deviant groups against the dominant institutions, rather than as interactions among contending groups in which violence might be employed by all sides. This approach exaggerated the irrationality of revolt and the rationality of governmental responses to it (often labeled "conflict management" even as it is exacerbating the conflict), and focused the attention of researchers almost entirely on the phenomena of nongovernmental violence at the expense of inquiry into the violence of political authorities. Moreover, this approach led to a number of theoretical confusions because of a lack of correspondence between the conceptual definitions of violence embodied in theory and the measures of violence used to collect the data against which the theory was to be tested (Nardin 1973: 99–102).

Conflict research has to some extent responded to conceptual criticism of this sort. But it remains doubtful whether the larger lesson, which is that continuing criticism is a necessary part of empirical theorizing itself, has been learned. I suspect that the common attitude continues to stress getting on with the task of theorizing as it has been understood within the empiricist tradition. Definitions of theoretical terms continue to be hastily stipulated in the rush to collect data and test hypotheses, and conceptual criticism once again takes the back seat until some new blunder is exposed by critics outside the tradition. A deeper acquaintance with critical theory might help conflict research to overcome this pattern.

THE PRACTICAL CONSEQUENCES OF THEORY

Empirical theory does not deny that theory has practical consequences. On the contrary, two of its moving impulses have always been the observation of how the inadequate theories of received wisdom have led us astray and the desire to improve practice by providing it with a more adequate theoretical basis. The lesson of critical theory is that we need to be concerned not only with the practical inadequacies of the substance of our theories, but also with those of their form. The practical critic is suggesting, in other words, that it is not only the empiricist's theories but the empiricist's *conception* of theory that supports ineffective and morally objectionable policies. Theory and practice are thus related at two levels, that of substance and that of form. If in fact empirical theory in its search for causes implies a technological approach to conduct, it follows that any empirical theory regardless of its substantive content would display this feature. For example, the practical application of stimulus-response psychology is a therapy of behavior modification, regardless of the sort of behavior to which the theory is applied. Similarly, an interpretive theory of conflict that identifies conflict with misunderstanding points toward undistorted communication and the correction of impressions through dialogue as a practical approach to dealing with conflict. And critical theory, because of the weight it assigns to false consciousness as a factor in the perpetuation of domination, has among its practical implications the enlightenment of the masses concerning their true situation.

Central to the practical criticism of empirical theory is the suggestion that such theory, however accurate within its own narrow sphere, is insensitive to the most important dimensions of social and political life. If this is so, it follows that the knowledge based on empirical theory provides an inadequate basis for social and political practice. The critical theorist has been far more open than the empirical theorist to the suggestion that what is distinctive of human existence is that it takes place within a world of meanings which must be understood before they can be responded to. To illustrate the point with a simple example, a human being alone in a primitive, uninhabited wilderness exists in an environment untouched, except for his presence, by human activity. The knowledge such a person requires is a knowledge of terrain, of weather, of edible and inedible plants, of the habits of animals—all phenomena capable of being understood fully as aspects of a natural, not a social, world. But should this person come across some sign of human intelligence—a footprint, say, or some other evidence of human habitation—the character of the surrounding world is instantly transformed. Now the possibility must be entertained that other elements in the environment may be manifestations of human intelligence, rather than of natural processes: the grove of trees may be an orchard, the pit a well, the pile of stones a shrine. Understanding now requires that the data of experience be considered from the point of view of their possible place within a context of meanings: that is, as evidence of intentions or manifestations of human agricultural, technological, or religious activity.

If human conduct can be fully understood only in terms of explanatory factors that require a correct interpretation of ideas and practices, then no approach to understanding and explanation that ignores such factors can be theoretically adequate. This is perhaps least true of those activities that come closest to being mere biological functions, although even these—birth, eating, sex, death—may be endowed with symbolic significance according to which, for example, the behavior of feeding becomes the practice of dining. In complex human activities, however—and most people would include political life here—the interpretive element is of overwhelming significance. Although it does not follow that empirical theory cannot make a contribution to either the theory or practice of politics, the practical critic's suggestion that the understanding it provides is radically incomplete because of its neglect of the interpretive dimension of human conduct is certainly plausible enough to warrant sustained consideration by the empirical theorist.

There is another point about the importance of interpretation which, although it has not been stressed by the critical theorists, is of the utmost importance for understanding the relationship between theory and practice. And this is that any theory, regardless of whether it is "empirical," "causal," or "behavioral" on the one hand, or "interpretive" on the other, must itself be interpreted in being applied to the understanding of particular cases or to action in particular circumstances. It is on the basis of this insight that Aristotle was led to distinguish between "theoretical" and "practical" knowledge, the former concerned with the necessary, the latter with the particular. To engage in practice—that is, to act in the world—is to deal with contingencies. Theory may be relevant, but only if one knows which theory applies to the particular circumstances faced in acting. "This," says Aristotle, "is why some who do not know"—that is, who lack theoretical understanding—"and especially those who have experience, are more practical than others who know" (*Nichomachean Ethics*, VI: 8). Theoretical knowledge can be reduced to rules, but rules alone cannot determine actions. The rules must be applied, and in being applied, interpreted. Kant makes this point when he argues that the application of theory to practice always requires judgment. The general rules of theory

> must be supplemented by an act of judgment whereby the practitioner distinguishes instances where the rule applies from those where it does not. And since rules cannot in turn be provided on every occasion to direct the judgment . . . theoreticians will be found who can never in all their lives become practical, since they lack judgment. [Kant 1970: 61; first published 1793]

These observations apply to "practice" in the broad sense that includes fabrication (*poiesis*) as well as in the strict sense of *praxis*. Only one who is experienced in cooking can skillfully and successfully use a recipe—unless the recipe is very simple or one's standards are very low. The point would seem to apply with even greater force to the political practitioner wishing to make use of conflict theory. Experience does not guarantee successful practice any more than inexperience absolutely precludes it. But the idea (which the theoretician is prone to find attractive) that theoretical knowledge can serve as a substitute for experience is an illusion.

THEORY AND MORALITY

The mistrust of science which underlies critical theory is dramatically revealed in the myth of Faust, the savant who contracts with Satan for the means of achieving any end he might choose. Faust's sin is one of pride, which though an ancient failing is one that becomes increasingly dangerous with the growth of the evidently demonic power of modern science and technology. Capable of achieving more, man can aspire to more. Faust gives his soul in return for the infinite power that knowledge appears to confer, but in doing so forgets that power is only a means not an end. The tragedy of Faust is that lacking an appropriate end, knowledge brings not happiness but misery. The man to whom it gives the power of a god in the event becomes a beast.

The experience of the present century, most notably the destructiveness of totalitarianism and total war, has been taken as vindicating this venerable conception of the limits of mere instrumental reason, which is all that empirical theory is capable of providing. But it is not necessary to point to extreme experiences to make the point that the misuse of the scientific understanding of human conduct is not limited to totalitarian societies. This observation is fundamental to the Frankfurt critique of empirical theory. The proposed remedy, as we have seen, is to turn the theorist into a revolutionary—to argue, that is, that the theorist is necessarily committed to the restructuring of society so as to alter the circumstances in which knowledge is pursued. The argument of critical theory is that empirical theory, in accepting the view that the ends of action are extrinsic to theory, in effect excludes itself from participation in practical life except as a mere tool. Critical theory seeks to avoid this result by postulating certain ends as intrinsic to the activity of theorizing as such. Thus Horkheimer argues that because the activity of theorizing presupposes freedom of inquiry, it is committed to action directed toward the end of creating a free society, which he understands to be one based on the principles of social justice rather than on the partial and spurious freedom of capitalism. Habermas (1971: 314–315) makes essentially the same point: pure theory, or "knowledge for the sake of knowledge," is practically grounded in an interest in emancipation, because only in a free society can theory rid itself of ideological contamination. All action is determined by interests; moral conduct is action determined by an interest in social justice and is designed to promote the realization of a just society.

This conception of justice, or morality, and of moral conduct is not limited to Marxism and critical theory. Others have drawn the conclusion that because science gives us a knowledge of means but not of ends, what we need is "normative theory," to be understood as an effort to clarify and defend the values to be pursued through personal and political action. Empirical and normative thinking are to be integrated in a new set of "policy sciences" devoted to the promotion of such values as peace, economic welfare, human dignity, and ecological balance. We are urged to explore "alternative world futures" in terms of their potential for the realization of these values and to consider how the present world can be transformed into the ideal world imagined by the normative theorist. The trouble with all such solutions is that they perpetuate instrumentalist thinking rather than transcend it. The lesson of practical criticism with which I am concerned here is thus one that is to be learned as much from the failures as from the teaching of practical criticism. We are unlikely to escape the limitations of an instrumentalist conception of practice until we abandon the notion of moral conduct as the pursuit of good ends. For to think of morally justified practice in this way is to allow practical reasoning to be controlled by the logic of the concepts of means and ends, and thus to conceive practice as action employing the most effective available means for creating the conditions under which the postulated values can be realized.

The alternative is already contained in the idea of *praxis*, if only we could avoid misunderstanding it. In this respect I think the critical theorists are right, although I am not persuaded that they have succeeded in articulating a coherent and unambiguous conception of *praxis*. In seeking to adapt the idea to modern conditions, Marxist theorists have had difficulty in avoiding the very attitudes from which they attempt to free practical reason. I do not mean to imply that the Greek conception is complete or appropriate in its particulars to modern society; my suggestion is simply that in the idea of *praxis*, as expounded, for example, by Aristotle, one can find a conception of moral conduct that is categorially different from the instrumentalism that so pervades modern thought. This alternative conception is one that has been explored by many subsequent thinkers, most notably by Kant in his ethical writings and in our own period by Michael Oakeshott (1962, 1975). Practice, according to these thinkers, is not only action directed toward an end but also that which respects certain limits regardless of its end. Language is a practice, for to speak well is not to say things characterized by a certain content but to deploy the resources of language skillfully. Moral conduct is also a practice in this sense. To act morally is not to pursue good ends, but to take account of the considerations embodied in the ideas of the appropriate moral tradition concerning duty, fairness, propriety, respect, and the like that together constitute its language of moral discourse and give shape to its conception of moral conduct. Morality, in this view, does not tell us that there are particular ends we must pursue, but rather that as we go about the business of life we must adhere to the considerations and respect the limits which it is the task of moral inquiry to elucidate. To do so may restrict or even rule out altogether the pursuit of some ends we think of as good, but if so it is not because these ends will have been shown to be bad in themselves but because their pursuit is incompatible with the requirements of a common morality.

Critical theory attempts to escape technological rationality by proving that empirical theory is committed by its own nature to the pursuit of certain ends. Such a conception of theory endangers the standards of truth and justice society has so far been able to evolve, for truth and justice become ends to be achieved by means of action rather than considerations entitled to govern it. If the argument I have been making is correct, the empirical theorist appears after all to be on solid ground in stressing the autonomy of theoretical activity as an ideal even under present conditions. But the empirical theorist is likely to join the critical theorist in identifying moral conduct with the pursuit of good ends, and moral theory with the attempt to define these ends and to justify action by appealing to them. Both are thus trapped by an end-oriented conception of morality, although neither is necessarily barred from escaping it. Each in its own way has allowed the teleology of instrumentalism to drive out the quite different teleology of *praxis* understood as moral conduct. Conflict research, whether guided by empiricist or Marxist premises, acquiesces in this development by making itself the servant of social purposes. The vocation of the theorist is not to change the world but to interpret it.

NOTES

1. Studies of attitudes and beliefs can for the most part only partly bridge the gap between behavior and ideas. There are really two distinctions that are relevant here: on the one hand between what might be called "behavioral" and "attitudinal" data, and on the other between *behaviors* and what those behaviors *signify* to the agent and to those who have to respond to them. Techniques such as opinion surveys and content analysis cannot in themselves get at this dimension of significance or meaning and, if employed by observers who do not already possess a good grasp of the cultural and historical context in which behavior takes place, are likely to generate "data" that distort rather than illuminate. What is required is not only an interpretation of observable data on conflict events according to ideas supplied by the observer, but also an understanding of the ideas according to which behaviors have meaning for those whose actions and reactions the observer wishes to understand, in terms of which the observer can grasp the significance of event data.

2. Two useful discussions of the debate within peace research are those of Eide (1972) and D. J. Dunn (1978).

3. Much of the research inspired by the radical critique has been undertaken by Scandinavian and West German scholars publishing in the *Journal of Peace Research*. Some representative studies are those of Galtung (1970, 1971), Eide (1974), Senghaas (1971, 1973), Rittberger (1973), Gantzel (1973), and Krippendorff (1973, 1975). Some of these studies are evaluated, from different perspectives, by Onuf (1975) and by Reid and Yanarella (1976).

4. One of the few explicit attempts to consider peace research from the standpoint of the Marxism of the Frankfurt School is that of Reid and Yanarella (1976), who mention with approval the work of the German practitioners of "Kritische Friedenforschung" cited in note 3, above. Unlike the empirical theory of North American peace and conflict research—which is described as "parochial," "theoretically vacuous," "ahistorical," "value-obscured," and "unself-reflexive" (Reid and Yanarella 1976: 316)—the new European peace research is said to have successfully achieved a synthesis of empirical and critical approaches.

5. The interpretation of Marx's conception of *praxis* favored by the Frankfurt School was originally worked out by Lukacs (1971; first published in 1923) and is cogently argued by Avineri (1968: chapter 5). I owe my formulation of the difference between the Aristotelian and Marxian conceptions of *praxis* to Paul Diesing.

6. As an example of how the attempt might be made to justify revolutionary violence within the framework of a "humanist" interpretation of Marxism, see

Merleau-Ponty (1969: 1); justifiable violence for Merleau-Ponty is that which tends toward its own suspension by hastening the arrival of true communism. A similar argument is made within the Frankfurt tradition itself by Marcuse writing *On Liberation* (1969), for whom *praxis* has become a revolt of the enlightened against the resistance of the deceived masses. Both arguments, it should be noted, postulate a knowledge of social processes certain enough to allow one to predict the long-term consequences of present acts, and to serve as the technical foundation for revolutionary action.

CHAPTER 13

Conflict Research, Political Action, and Epistemology

J. David Singer

As ONE READS THROUGH THE ESSAYS in this volume, two rather contradictory thoughts occur. The first is that political science has come a long way in a relatively short time, with a steady increase both in the number of competent and creative researchers and in the amount of existential and correlational knowledge that they are generating.[1] The second thought is as discouraging as the first is encouraging: the likelihood that this expanding body of knowledge will be applied to the amelioration or solution of serious political problems, especially problems of political violence, remains painfully low. This pessimism is, of course, partly a response to the fact that many of these problems are so deep-seated that knowledge alone will not suffice. It also is due partly to the fact political elites are seldom competent to understand and evaluate, let alone apply, social science findings.

In addition to these two considerations, there is a third: the relative failure of the researchers themselves to comprehend fully the knowledge–action relationship. It is to that set of considerations that this brief concluding essay is addressed. In my view there is a continuous and intimate feedback loop that connects the researcher, the general public, the political elite, and the counterelite (by whom I mean those with roughly the same expertise and concerns as members of the elite, but who are not now in positions of high political influence). Until that loop is more fully examined and more clearly understood, our research findings will continue to have marginal consequences at most. There are, of course, several points at which we might break into this feedback loop, but given the fact that the acquisition and codification of knowledge must necessarily precede its application, let us begin there.

Before doing so, however, let me try to dispel one of the more recurrent and destructive myths surrounding applied social science, particularly with respect to political violence. This is the suggestion that conflict and peace researchers are either knaves or fools, inasmuch as they seek to provide the knowledge by which political elites and "the establishment" in general may placate and perhaps subjugate those who might otherwise resort to violence as a means of redressing injustice. Whereas it is indeed possible that such knowledge can be (and has been) so exploited, the problem is not inherent in the findings of these researchers. Rather it lies partly in the failure to get these findings to those who may be disadvantaged by asymmetries in knowledge; hence the importance of getting our findings to the counterelites who most often speak and act on behalf of the disadvantaged.

But a corollary of this is that the counterelites of the world had better turn away from what is often a Luddite mentality. As long as the reformers and the radicals hold to the view—as they seem to do in many parts of the world these days—that applied social science is inherently reactionary, if not pure sham, no amount of high quality research findings will be of use to the victims of exploitation and/or incompetence. Peace researchers of a scientific bent need not be, and usually are not, devoted to law and order at the expense of social justice, or to system maintenance in place of system transformation. Our aim is not to *eliminate* conflict, but to decrease the likelihood that it will be violent and reactionary and to increase the chances that it will have constructive and creative outcomes.

THE ACQUISITION AND CODIFICATION OF KNOWLEDGE

Turning to some of the more interesting problems that arise in the acquisition and codification of knowledge that might later be applied, I find it difficult to side-step the most obvious issue of all: does knowledge matter, and do ideas play any role in the modification or perpetuation of the properties of the social system and its behavioral regularities? In my view, these mental phenomena have been and always will be as important to the understanding of social systems as are more tangible phenomena such as resources, wealth, power, and institutions. The behavior of individuals and collectivities is a consequence, among other things, of the perceptions, predictions, and preferences that are brought to and accompany that behavior. Such behavior helps either to perpetuate or to modify existing social conditions. This is not to accept, of course, any simple-minded and extreme form of philosophical idealism. To the contrary, every social condition and human event is itself the result of a complex and still barely understood interaction among three sets of phenomena: voluntaristic, deterministic, and stochastic. Further, the voluntaristic component is itself a consequence of both deterministic and stochastic processes as well as of prior voluntaristic acts. Although so abstract a statement provides little in the way of knowledge, analyses that run afoul of its epistemological implications are bound to be scientifically flawed.

A second and closely related issue is not whether ideas affect the behavior of elites, counterelites, and the public, but whether that effect in turn makes a science of social phenomena impossible. That is, the Karls Mannheim and Marx are quite correct in urging that each individual's ideas are indeed influenced by the time, place, role, and status of the individual. But their overly enthusiastic disciples are quite incorrect insofar as they urge that our ideas are *fully determined* by such immediate contextual factors. Clearly, the genetic heritage, social background, and specific experiences of each of us—and all of these *precede* our ideas of the moment—cannot be neglected in any explanation of a given individual's perceptions, predictions, and preferences. The implication is important in that it makes possible—and certain epistemological schools of the past and present notwithstanding, does not render impossible—the generation of fairly objective scientific knowledge about social events and conditions. Rather, the essential purpose of scientific method is to make our biases and predispositions quite visible, and our procedures thoroughly public and reproducible.

Of course, the scientific style does not guarantee the generation of socially useful knowledge; it is necessary, but not sufficient. To produce high quality knowledge that can be applied to the resolution of political conflict, several other criteria must be satisfied, and it is to some of these that we now turn.

Perhaps the most crucial criterion for socially useful knowledge is this: we must have reproducible observations, measurements, and records of the phenomena (past or unfolding) we wish to describe or explain, as well as of the phenomena that are introduced in the search for explanation. This, in turn, requires the invention and use of explicit, operational, and public procedures such that our observations are highly reproducible from one person to the next and from one observation to the next. In the language of science, we must utilize *reliable indicators* of the presence, absence, strength, direction, and so on, of whatever phenomena we invoke in our efforts at description and explanation. A second criterion is that our indicators be valid as well as reliable. By validity we mean the extent to which our indicators provide an accurate representation of the phenomena that we hope and claim to measure. This criterion is more difficult to satisfy because, unlike reliability—which can be tested by comparing independently reproduced observations—there is no direct and absolutely convincing test of the validity of a measure. Rather, through a variety of well-known strategies we test and improve the validity of our indicators, knowing that they must always be regarded as approximations. More to the point here, neither the reliability nor the validity problem can be solved in the absence of conceptual clarity, and it thus behooves us to attend to that particular issue here.

One precondition of conceptual clarity is the obvious need for verbal precision; less obvious is the need to distinguish between the phenomenon that we seek to explain and those phenomena that we invoke in attempting that explanation. Both of these points will be, I trust, illustrated in the definitional overview that follows. Three concepts that are essential to peace research are science, knowledge, and theory, yet all are still used in a confusing and inconsistent variety of ways. By science, we mean nothing more than a body of procedures (and their underlying assumptions) that have so far proven superior to other sets of procedures in the acquisition, codification, and evaluation of knowledge. Thus the scientific enterprise is quite content-free and in principle need never foreordain the outcome of an investigation that adheres to its spirit and letter.

Whereas the basic assumption of science—that physical, biological, and social phenomena all manifest certain lawlike regularities, only some of which are now understood—is certainly a meta-theoretical one, and clearly conveys certain ontological as well as epistemological premises, it nevertheless remains essentially atheoretical. In other words, the "radical critique" of social science, while making some telling points along the way, must be rejected when it alleges that the scientific method *inherently* contains a conservative theoretical/ideological bias.[2] Although many practitioners of social science proceed from conservative theoretical premises, these premises are not inherent in the basic methodology itself but rather arise from the psychology and the social environment of the researchers and perhaps from their particular applications of scientific method. The epistemology of the scientific method, because it recognizes our ultimate reliance upon intersubjective agreement among scholarly specialists, contains more opportunity and incentive for self-correcting procedures than any of the rival epistemologies. To paraphrase Shakespeare, the fault lies, dear critic, not in our epistemology but in ourselves.

Related to this view of science is the need to drop certain invidious adjectives that continue to plague our enterprise. No one would suggest that the problems, models, and research strategies of the social sciences are identical to those of the physical and biological sciences, but it is equally misleading to exaggerate the differences. Hence reference to the "natural sciences" is to suggest that they are inherently superior in content and method and to ignore the interdependence of physical, biological, and social phenomena. Not only are the social sciences not unnatural; they are also, to take another pejorative label, not inexact. Any familiarity with the biological sciences indicates that in many realms of research, the social scientists' phenomena are indeed quite "natural" and our procedures of observation, measurement, and analysis equally or more exact, precise, and operational.

If the adjectives associated with the word "science" are misleading and confusing, those associated with "theory" are downright disastrous. Let me deal with some examples by first defining theory—at least in the scientific sense of the word—as a body of codified knowledge. To satisfy that definition, we need to have a series of logically consistent propositions, all of which are stated operationally and thus are susceptible to empirical or logical disconfirmation. Further, most of them should have been empirically tested and found largely consonant with the referent social phenomena that they allegedly describe. In addition, since the purpose of a theory is to explain or account for some regularity in an empirical phenomenon (including its direction and rate of change), that regularity and variation therein must first have been established. To devote untold time and energy to the construction of "theories," the distributions of whose outcome variable may have nothing in common with reality, might be a healthy intellectual exercise but is hardly a direct contribution to knowledge.

It follows that such distinctions as empirical versus speculative theory or positive versus normative theory are not particularly helpful. Any scientific theory is, of course, a mix of empirical evidence, disciplined speculation, and tight logic, and to speak of "speculative theory" is to speak, at best, of a model or a set of hypotheses or hunches. Speculation is that with which we begin, and we have no theory until our speculation has been systematized, operationalized, and largely confirmed vis-à-vis the empirical evidence. In sum, any scientific theory *must* be empirical. Further, a theory must be "positive" as the economists usually term it, and to speak of normative theory seems singularly unfortunate. To accept the positive-normative distinction means that we invoke high procedural standards when dealing with the world as it is or has been, but throw these standards to the winds when we come to the world as it should be or might be. To put it another way, normative theory is a contradiction in terms, and we might do better as policy-oriented scientists if we kept in mind that *theories provide the knowledge base from which we can try to move toward certain normatively preferred outcomes.* The more solid our theories, the more accurate will be our contingent forecasts, and such accuracy is essential both to the social usefulness of our research and to its credibility to those who make, shape, or challenge public policy.

By *contingent* forecast I mean only to emphasize that social scientists should insist that their forecasts are conditional upon certain preconditions and that unless those specified preconditions are satisfied, "all bets are off." As a matter of credibility, one ought to specify which behaviors by which actors, occurring in which context, will lead to which outcomes with which probabilities. And as a matter of usefulness to counterelites and elites, we must similarly be able to identify which actions they would need to propose or to take in order to achieve or avoid a given outcome, and with which probability. To continue this digression a step further, it is worth noting that the basis for such a contingent forecast may range from sheer hunches, through observed correlation patterns from the past (or from highly analogous settings), to theories. The latter are, of course, the preferred basis for contingent forecasts, inasmuch as they not only take account of changes in correlation patterns over time, but also include some explanation as to why the specified outcomes might be expected.

Turning specifically to the need for conceptual clarity in our models and theories, I want to restate that a scientific theory is composed of logically consistent propositions so formulated as to be empirically or logically disconfirmable. Yet so many of the models (not to mention putative theories) in the social sciences run afoul of this requirement. One recurrent problem is the tendency to confuse a taxonomy and a model or theory. While a good taxonomy is necessary to the extent that it identifies the variables and classes thereof that will be used on the outcome or the explanatory side of a model, it is far from sufficient. Until we explicitly postulate the direction and strength of the empirical (as distinct from definitional or logical) associations between and among our variables, we do not have a model, and until most of those postulated associations have been empirically vindicated, we do not have a theory. Thus one way to recognize that we have something less than a model is to look for—and fail to find—explicitly hypothesized empirical associations between and among the variables. Were we to invoke this simple test more often, we would be less gullible, confused, and confusing. Similarly, we cannot claim to have a theory unless we have a model, outcomes predicted by it, and an explanation for those outcomes.

Empirical propositions, whether hypothesized or demonstrated, must meet standards of conceptual clarity. They must be articulated in ways that differentiate a given outcome from its putative causes and consequences and from the motivations of the actor. It is one thing to hypothesize the causes or consequences of a given set of behaviors, but quite another to embed both the act and its associated phenomena in the same variable. One of the more glaring examples is found in the so-called pattern variables of Parsons (1951), which classify behavior not by the action actually taken, but by its "meaning" for the social system and its alleged purposes and/or consequences: pattern maintenance, integration, goal attainment, and adaptation. Whether a given act has a given consequence, not to mention whether that consequence was intended, should be a matter of empirical observation, rather than a priori assertion (Singer 1980). Nor, one might add, does it help to use categories whose mutual exclusiveness and logical exhaustiveness are dubious. Whereas the need to differentiate between an event on the one hand and its cause, purpose, or consequence on the other may seem self-evident, one detects in the social sciences today a remarkable willingness to describe events in terms of their "deep structure" and "meaning" for those involved or for the system in which they occur. Such premature "explanation" is no more likely to produce powerful theories than the mere piling up of unrelated observed correlations.

THE APPLICATION OF KNOWLEDGE

The problems diagnosed above represent but a fraction of the difficulties that stand in the way of a systematically developing body of knowledge regarding political violence. Nonetheless they provide a partial explanation for our lack of progress. Let us turn next to some of the problems associated with the *application* of conflict research findings. The first problem is that of goal selection by political actors, the second is what affects the realization of these goals. A widely shared notion among social scientists and social practitioners, many of whom differ sharply in other respects, is that the selection of goals (or preferred outcomes) is a purely normative, and hence subjective, matter. That easy and familiar assumption needs to be challenged on two counts. One is that humans are not really as divergent as is claimed when it comes to preferred outcomes. If we look far enough ahead in time, and use sufficiently general values, we find rather broad agreement among people of quite disparate nations, classes, ideologies, and personalities. For the global system and its regional, national, and other subsystems, most people would like to see high levels of physical security, material well-being, freedom from coercion, opportunity for self-actualization—and a relatively equal distribution of these four individual values (Singer 1971).

Even if we get more specific and more immediate, I suspect that the convergence would remain rather high. The more difficult problem comes only when we recognize the extent to which we differ on the *means* to these ends. And although normative considerations enter into one's choice of social instruments and procedures, these preferences are more dependent than we often appreciate on one's theoretical biases, knowledge about social dynamics, and the epistemological criteria invoked in evaluating social arguments. In other words—and this is the second count—we probably support, acquiesce in, or oppose social policies to a considerable degree according to the credibility of the contingent forecasts upon which they rest.

To the extent that this assertion is correct, it follows that our task is not just one of discovering which conditions and events are most and least conducive to nonviolent conflict resolution in which types of setting. To bring these discoveries to bear on the political process, it is essential that those whom we seek to reach are sufficiently sophisticated to distinguish between reproducible evidence and mere authoritative assertion, to take the extreme ends of the knowledge–belief continuum. Thus it behooves us to attend as much to the education of our audiences as we do to the solidity of our research; credibility depends as much on the recipient's cognitive competence as on the sender's skill and style. From this it follows that we dare not play the game of political persuasion in the traditional ways. If we do—and thus rely on the rhetorical tricks that reactionaries, radicals, and reformers have all used over the centuries—we will not only perpetuate the appalling mix of cynicism and gullibility that have marked the erratic and often disappointing road to a decent social order, we will also lose most of the political arguments, given the preference of the epistemologically naïve for simple solutions and less complex scenarios. Thus, in addition to the positive need for epistemological education in the schools, the media, and the corridors of power, there is a negative warning. No matter how urgent the specific issue may seem, we should refrain from the sort of simplistic rhetorical argument that short-sighted activists have used with fatal frequency since time immemorial. Their use will achieve little more than the recontamination of social communication channels.

Closely related to this issue is the issue of audience selection. All too often, we find incremental reformers concentrating on the political elites, and radical revolutionaries concentrating on the urban or rural masses. Assuming that most of us who do research on the causes of violence and the conditions of nonviolent conflict resolution are radical incrementalists (that is, we see the need for radical changes in the structure and culture of the social order, but find compelling the moral and empirical arguments for an incremental strategy), I would urge greater attention to the counterelites. This is because the elites seldom have the incentive, the vision, or the competence (recall Weber's felicitous allusion to "a trained incapacity") to reconsider their assumptions, their goals, or their criteria of evidence, whereas the masses seem likely to continue in their cycles of alienation and activism until serious reform in political debate as well as in political action has taken root. The counterelites, on the other hand, may well have that combination of concern and competence that could make them considerably more responsive to reproducible evidence and close reasoning in the pursuit of incremental, but radical, reform. This is not to suggest that we ignore the others, but that, as a matter of pragmatism and tactics, we address our evidence and our associated epistemological premises primarily to those who are most free to consider major system changes and most able to evaluate complex contingent forecasts.

In addition to these rather long-range considerations, let me suggest one possible payoff from our research in the short run. I refer to the construction and testing of "early warning indicators" that might serve two purposes of a pragmatic sort. First, even though we may be some distance from reasonably solid explanatory theories in our respective fields, there can be some valuable spinoff in the form of findings that show under which conditions or in the train of which events certain types of conflicts turn ugly and violent. If, for example, we discover (as we have in ongoing research of the Correlates of War project) that 75 percent of the 225 major-power confrontations occurring since 1816 ended in war under conditions of military parity and rapidly escalating expenditures, whereas the overall frequency of such escalation was only 13 percent, we can suggest two policy implications. One is that under these conditions it is particularly crucial to avoid confrontations and the other is that if history is any guide any effort to move from parity to superiority is a highly dangerous enterprise. Such knowledge in the hands of opponents and critics of contemporary security policies in the United States and the Soviet Union might enhance the credibility of their warnings.

The second purpose of such indicators is to call attention to the flimsy base of knowledge upon which such decisions often rest and to emphasize the importance of bringing more knowledge—even of a purely correlational sort—to bear on the policy process. In a recent anthology (Singer and Wallace 1979) one finds nine papers that utilize quantitative indicators to postdict the escalation of a variety of intra- and international conflicts. Some of the work in this area even demonstrates the direction and rate of change over time in the accuracy of certain indicators of warning and/or assurance. Thus there may well be some "redeeming social value" in data-based conflict research, even though in most areas we have yet to construct explanatory models which are decisively confirmed.

CONCLUSION

In this brief essay I have chosen not to lay out yet another blueprint for achieving a just and peaceful social order. Too many such plans have already been put forth, and the knowledge base on which they rest is much too thin. What we do know about effective conflict resolution and social change is much less than we need to know, and basic research must remain our highest priority. Rather I have chosen to assume that as our research goes forward and cumulative theory-building leads to a growing body of applicable knowledge, we will be in a better position—morally and intellectually—to propose and advocate specific political, economic, and social reforms.

As we move toward a more solid basis for understanding and reducing political violence, it will be essential that we help to prepare the mental climate in which our arguments, rival hypotheses, and contending predictive models can be intelligently and honestly evaluated and acted upon. This will require a degree of across-the-board educational work that few of us have yet appreciated. But if the reorientations suggested in the second section of this essay are to lay the groundwork for the systematic application of our research findings, those elaborated in the first section must first be acted upon. If our own epistemological house is in a state of disarray, there is little likelihood that the requisite knowledge will ever be acquired and codified, much less applied.

NOTES

1. By existential knowledge I mean empirical facts as expressed in data sets, and by correlational knowledge I mean the extent to which two or more data sets co-vary with one another across time or across cases. By explanatory knowledge, I mean the extent to which we can demonstrate "why" the phenomena represented in these data sets co-vary as they do. Of course, explanatory knowledge is the same as a theory, and it is to that end that our research is and must be devoted.
2. These and related issues raised by "radical" peace researchers are covered in a telling fashion by Nardin in Chapter 12.

Bibliography

ABEL, T. (1938) *The Nazi movement: Why Hitler came to power.* New York: Atherton, 1966.

ABELES, R. D. Relative deprivation, rising expectations, and black militancy. *Journal of Social Issues*, 1976, 32:119–137.

ABELL, P. Why do men rebel? A discussion of Ted Robert Gurr's "Why men rebel." *Race*, 1971, 13:84–89.

ABERBACH, J. D., and WALKER, J. L. Political trust and racial ideology. *American Political Science Review*, 1970, 64:1199–1219.

ADAMS, H. E. The origins of insurgency. Ph.D. dissertation, University of Lancaster, 1970.

ADELMAN, I., and MORRIS, C. T. *Economic growth and social equity in developing countries.* Stanford: Stanford University Press, 1973.

AGRANOFF, B. W. Memory and protein synthesis. *Scientific American*, 1967, 216: 115–122.

AHLUWALIA, M. S. Income distribution and development: Some stylized facts. *American Economic Review*, 1976, 66:128–135.

AJZEN, I., and FISHBEIN, M. The prediction of behavioral intentions in a choice situation. *Journal of Experimental and Social Psychology*, 1969, 5:400–416.

ALBERTINI, R. VON. The impact of two world wars on the decline of colonialism. *Journal of Contemporary History*, 1969, 4:17–35.

ALCOCK, N. Z., and LOWE, K. The Vietnam war as a Richardson process. *Journal of Peace Research*, 1969, 2:105–112.

ALKER, H. The long road to international relations theory: Problems of statistical non-additivity. In M. Kaplan (ed.), *New approaches to international relations.* New York: St. Martin's, 1968(a).

ALKER, H. The structure of social action in an arms race. Paper given at the Conference of the North American Peace Research Society (International), Cambridge, Massachusetts, 1968(b).

ALKER, H. R., and RUSSETT, B. M. The analysis of trends and patterns. In Russett

502   *Bibliography*

et al. (eds.), *World handbook of political and social indicators.* New Haven: Yale University Press, 1964.

ALLISON, G. *The essence of decision: Explaining the Cuban missile crisis.* Boston: Little, Brown, 1971.

ALLISON, G., and HALPERIN, M. Bureaucratic politics: A paradigm and some policy implications. In R. Tanter and R. Ullman (eds.), *Theory and policy in international relations.* Princeton: Princeton University Press, 1972.

ALMOND, G., and COLEMAN, J. (eds.). *The politics of developing areas.* Princeton: Princeton University Press, 1960.

ALMOND, G., and VERBA, S. *The civic culture.* Boston: Little, Brown, 1963.

ALPERS, B. J. Relation of the hypothalamus to disorders of personality. *Archives of Neurology and Psychiatry,* 1937, 38:291–303.

ALROY, G. C. *The involvement of peasants in internal wars.* Princeton: Center of International Studies Research Monograph No. 24, 1966.

ALTFELD, M. *The reaction of third states toward wars.* Unpublished Ph.D. dissertation, University of Rochester, 1979.

ALTFELD, M., and BUENO DE MESQUITA, B. Choosing sides in wars. *International Studies Quarterly,* 1979, 23:87–112.

AMES, E., and RAPP, R. T. The birth and death of taxes: A hypothesis. *Journal of Economic History,* 1977, 37:161–178.

AMSEL, A. Frustration nonreward in partial reinforcement and discrimination learning: Some recent history and a theoretical extension. *Psychological Review,* 1962, 69:306–328.

ANDERSON, C. W., and NESVOLD, B. A. A Skinnerian analysis of conflict behavior: Walden II goes cross-national. *American Behavioral Scientist,* 1972, 15:883–909.

ANDREANO, R. (ed.). *The economic impact of the American civil war.* Cambridge: Schenkman, 1962.

ANDRESKI, S. *Military organization and society,* 2nd ed. Berkeley: University of California Press, 1968.

ARCHER, D., and GARTNER, R. Violent acts and violent times: A comparative approach to postwar homicide rates, *American Sociological Review,* 1976, 41:937–963.

ARDANT, G. Financial policy and economic infrastructure of modern states and nations. In C. Tilly (ed.), *The formation of national states in Western Europe.* Princeton: Princeton University Press, 1975.

ARDREY, R. *African genesis.* New York: Dell, 1961.

ARDREY, R. *The territorial imperative.* New York: Atheneum, 1966.

ARENDT, H. *On revolution.* New York: Viking Press, 1963.

ARISTOTLE. The Nichomachean ethics. In R. McKeon (ed.), *Introduction to Aristotle.* New York: Modern Library, 1947, 308–543.

ARISTOTLE. (ca. 322 B.C.) *Politics.* As excerpted in J. C. Davies (ed.), *When men revolt and why.* New York: Free Press, 1971.

ARON, R. *War and industrial society.* London: Oxford University Press, 1958.

ARON, R. *Peace and war: A theory of international relations.* New York: Praeger, 1960.

ARONOFF, J. *Psychological needs and cultural systems.* New York: Van Nostrand, 1967.

ARROW, K. *Social choice and individual values.* New York: Wiley, 1951.

ASPIN, L. T. An analysis of the relational determinants of international coopera-tion: United States cooperative behavior, 1958–1968. Unpublished Ph.D. dissertation, Purdue University, 1975.

ASTIN, A. W., ASTIN, H. S., BAYER, A. E., and BISCONTI, A. S. *The power of pro-test.* San Francisco: Jossey-Bass, 1975.

ATKINSON, J. W. *An introduction to motivation.* Princeton: Van Nostrand, 1964.

AVINERI, S. *The social and political thought of Karl Marx.* Cambridge: At the Un-iversity Press, 1968.

AZRIN, N. H., HUTCHINSON, R. R., and HAKE, D. F. Extinction-induced aggres-sion. *Journal of the Experimental Analysis of Behavior,* 1966, 9:191–204.

BACHRACH, P., and BARATZ, M. Decisions and non-decisions: An analytical frame-work. *American Political Science Review,* 1962, 56:947–952.

BALOYRA, E. A. Oil policies and budgets in Venezuela, 1938–1968. *Latin Ameri-can Research Review,* Summer 1974, 9:28–72.

BANDURA, A. *Aggression: A social learning analysis.* Englewood Cliffs: Prentice-Hall, 1973.

BANKS, A. S. *Cross-polity time-series data.* Cambridge: M.I.T. Press, 1971.

BANKS, A. S. Patterns of domestic conflict: 1919–39 and 1946–66. *Journal of Con-flict Resolution,* 1972, 16:41–50.

BANKS, A. S., and GREGG, P. M. Grouping political systems: Q-factor analysis of a cross-polity survey. *American Behavioral Scientist,* 1965, 9:3–6.

BANKS, A. S., and TEXTOR, R. B. *A cross-polity survey.* Cambridge: M.I.T. Press, 1963.

BARBERA, H. *Rich nations and poor in peace and war: Continuity and change in the development hierarchy of seventy nations from 1913 through 1952.* Lex-ington: Heath, 1973.

BARNES, S. M., KAASE, M. et al. *Political action: Mass participation in five West-ern democracies.* Beverly Hills: Sage, 1979.

BARROWS, W. L. Ethnic diversity and political instability in Black Africa. *Com-parative Political Studies,* 1976, 9:139–170.

BAUMGARTNER, T., BUCKLEY, W., and BURNS, T. Relational control: The human structuring of cooperation and conflict. *Journal of Conflict Resolution,* 1975, 19:417–440.

BAUMGARTNER, T., BUCKLEY, W., BURNS, T., and SCHUSTER, P. Metapower and the structuring of social hierarchies. In T. Burns and W. Buckley (eds.), *Power and control: Social structures and their transformation.* Beverly Hills: Sage, 1976.

BAY, C. *The structure of freedom.* Stanford: Stanford University Press, 1958.

BEALS, A. R., and SIEGEL, B. J. *Divisiveness and social conflict: An anthropologi-cal approach.* Stanford: Stanford University Press, 1966.

BEAN, R. War and the birth of the nation state. *Journal of Economic History,* 1973, 33:203–221.

BEARDSLEY, P. L. Substantive significance vs. quantitative rigor in political in-quiry: Are the two compatible? *International Interactions,* 1974, 1:27–40.

BEARDSLEY, P. L. On the statistical implications of normatively charged variables

504 *Bibliography*

and the prospects for overcoming them, as illustrated by "dependency," "exploitation," and the like. *Political Methodology*, 1979, 6:173–216.

BEER, F. *Peace against war: The ecology of international violence.* San Francisco: Freeman, 1979.

BEHAR, M. Prevalence of malnutrition among preschool children of developing countries. In N. S. Scrimshaw and J. E. Gordon (eds.), *Malnutrition, learning, and behavior.* Cambridge: M.I.T. Press, 1968.

BELL, D. V. J. *Resistance and revolution.* Boston: Houghton Mifflin, 1973.

BELL, J. B. *The myth of the guerrilla: Revolutionary theory and malpractice.* New York: Knopf, 1971.

BELL, J. B. The chroniclers of violence in Northern Ireland: A tragedy in endless acts. *Review of Politics*, 1976, 38:510–533.

BELL, J. B. *A time of terror: How democratic societies respond to revolutionary violence.* New York: Basic Books, 1978.

BENDIX, R. *Nation-building and citizenship: Studies of our changing social order.* New York: Wiley, 1964.

BEN-DOR, G. Institutionalization and political development: A conceptual and theoretical analysis. *Comparative Studies in Society and History*, 1975, 17: 309–325.

BENNETT, J. P., and ALKER, H. R., Jr. When national security policies bred collective insecurity: The war of the Pacific in a world politics simulation. In K. W. Deutsch et al. (eds.), *Problems of world modeling: Political and social implications.* Cambridge: Ballinger, 1977.

BERGQUIST, G. Some relationships between foreign and domestic conflict: An examination using a cross lagged quasi-experimental design. Unpublished Ph.D. dissertation, Florida State University, 1976.

BERGSTEN, R. C. Social mobility and economic development: The vital parameters of the Bolivian revolution. *Journal of Inter-American Studies*, 1964, 11:367–376.

BERKOWITZ, L. *Aggression.* New York: McGraw-Hill, 1962.

BERKOWITZ, L. (ed.). *Roots of aggression.* New York: Atherton, 1969.

BERKOWITZ, W. R. Socioeconomic indicator changes in ghetto riot tracts. *Urban Affairs Quarterly*, 1974, 10:69–94.

BERMAN, P. *Revolutionary organization.* Lexington: Lexington Books, 1974.

BERRY, B. J. L. Basic patterns of economic development. In N. Ginsberg (ed.), *Atlas of economic development.* Chicago: University of Chicago Press, 1961.

BETTELHEIM, B. *The informed heart: Autonomy in a mass age.* New York: Free Press, 1960.

BETZ, M. Riots and welfare: Are they related? *Social Problems*, 1974, 21:345–355.

BIENEN, H. *Violence and social change.* Chicago: University of Chicago Press, 1968(a).

BIENEN, H. (ed.). *The military intervenes: Case studies in political development.* New York: Russell Sage, 1968(b).

BIENEN, H. *Kenya: The politics of participation and control.* Princeton: Princeton University Press, 1974.

BIERSTEKER, T. *Distortion or development: Contending perspectives on the multinational corporation.* Cambridge: M.I.T. Press, 1979.

BINDER, L., COLEMAN, J. S., LAPALOMBARA, J., PYE, L. W., VERBA, S., and

WEINER, M. *Crises and sequences in political development*. Princeton: Princeton University Press, 1971.

BLACKEY, R. *Modern revolutions and revolutionists: A bibliography*. Santa Barbara: Clio Press, 1976.

BLAINEY, G. *The causes of war*. New York: Free Press, 1973.

BLASIER, C. The United States and the revolution. In J. Malloy and R. Thorn (eds.), *Beyond the revolution: Bolivia since 1952*. Pittsburgh: University of Pittsburgh Press, 1971.

BLOM, H. W. Re-testing violence: A case study in theory-model interdependence. Mimeo. Rotterdam: Nederlandse Economische Hogeschool, 1973.

BLUM, A., and FISHER, G. Women who kill. In I. L. Kutash et al. (eds.), *Violence: Perspectives on murder and aggression*. San Francisco: Jossey-Bass, 1978.

BLUMENTHAL, M. D., CHADIHA, L. B., COLE, G. A., and JAYARATNE, T. E. *More about justifying violence*. Ann Arbor, Mich.: Institute for Social Research, University of Michigan, 1975.

BOBROW, D. B., and CUTLER, N. E. Time-oriented explanations of national security beliefs: Cohort, life-stage, and situation. *Peace Research Society (International), Papers*, 1967, 8:31–57.

BOBROW, D. B., HOPMANN, P. T., BENJAMIN, R. W., and SYLVAN, D. A. The impact of foreign assistance on national development and international conflict. *Journal of Peace Science*, 1973, 1:39–60.

BODIN, J. *Six books of the commonwealth*, Abridged and trans. M. S. Tooley. Oxford: Oxford University Press, 1955.

BOROCK, D. M. Universal and regional dimensions of domestic conflict behavior. Ph.D. dissertation, University of Cincinnati, 1967.

BOULDING, K. E. *Conflict and defense: A general theory*. New York: Harper & Row, 1962.

BOULDING, K. E. Reflections on protest. *Bulletin of the Atomic Scientists*, 1965, 21:18–20.

BOULDING, K. E. *Ecodynamics: A new theory of societal evolution*. Beverly Hills: Sage, 1978.

BOULDING, K. E., and GLEASON, A. H. War as an investment: The strange case of Japan. *Peace Research Society (International), Papers*, 1965, 3:1–17.

BOWEN, D. R., BOWEN, E., GAWISER, S., and MASOTTI, L. H. Deprivation, mobility, and orientation toward protest of the urban poor. In L. H. Masotti and D. R. Bowen (eds.), *Riots and Rebellion*, Beverly Hills: Sage, 1968.

BOWLBY, J. *Attachment*. New York: Basic Books, 1969.

BOWLBY, J. *Separation*. New York: Basic Books, 1973.

BOZEMAN, A. B. Civilizations under stress: Reflections on cultural borrowing and survival. *Virginia Quarterly Review*, 1975, 51:1–18.

BOZEMAN, A. B. War and the clash of ideas. *Orbis*, 1976(a), 20:61–102.

BOZEMAN, A. B. *Conflict in Africa: Concepts and realities*. Princeton: Princeton University Press, 1976(b).

BRECHER, M. Input and decisions for war and peace: The Israel experience. *International Studies Quarterly*, 1974, 18:131–178.

BREMER, S. A. The trial of nations: An improbable application of probability theory. Mimeo, 1975.

BREMER, S. A., SINGER, J. D., and LUTERBACHER, U. The population density and war proneness of European nations, 1816–1965. *Comparative Political Studies*, 1973, 6:329–348.

BREMER, S. A., and MIHALKA, M. Machiavelli in machina: Or politics among hexagons. In K. W. Deutsch et al. (eds.), *Problems of world modeling: Political and social implications.* Cambridge: Ballinger, 1977.

BRINTON, C. *The Jacobins: An essay in the new history.* New York: Macmillan, 1930.

BRINTON, C. (1938) *The anatomy of revolution.* New York: Vintage Books, 1956.

BRITO, D. A dynamic model of an armaments race. *International Economic Review*, 1972, 13:359–375.

BRITO, D., and INTRILIGATOR, M. Some applications of the maximum principle to the problem of an armaments race. *Modeling and Simulation*, 1973, 4:140–144.

BRODIE, B. *War and politics.* New York: Macmillan, 1973.

BROGAN, D. W. *The price of revolution.* New York: Harper, 1951.

BRONSON, F. H., and DESJARDINS, C. Aggression in adult mice: Modification by neonatal injection of gonadal hormones. *Science*, 16 August 1968, 161:705–706.

BROOKS, R. Domestic violence and America's wars: A historical interpretation. In H. D. Graham and T. R. Gurr (eds.), *Violence in America: Historical and comparative perspectives.* New York: Praeger, 1969.

BROZEK, J. Semi-starvation and nutritional rehabilitation. *Journal of Clinical Nutrition*, 1953, 1:107–118.

BUENO DE MESQUITA, B. Measuring systemic polarity. *Journal of Conflict Resolution*, 1975(a), 19:187–216.

BUENO DE MESQUITA, B. *Strategy, risk, and personality in coalition politics.* New York: Cambridge University Press, 1975(b).

BUENO DE MESQUITA, B. Systemic polarization and the occurrence and duration of war. *Journal of Conflict Resolution*, 1978, 22:241–268.

BUENO DE MESQUITA, B. Coalition payoffs and electoral performance in European democracies. *Comparative Political Studies*, 1979, 12:61–81.

BUENO DE MESQUITA, B. *The war trap.* New Haven: Yale University Press, 1980.

BUENO DE MESQUITA, B., and SINGER, J. D. Alliances, capabilities and war: A review and synthesis. *Political Science Annual*, 1973, 4:237–280.

BULL, H. War and international order. In A. James (ed.), *The bases of international order: Essays in honour of C.A.W. Manning.* London: Oxford University Press, 1973.

BULLOCK, P. *Watts: The aftermath.* New York: Grove Press, 1969.

BURKE, E. (1790) *Reflections on the revolution in France.* Indianapolis: Bobbs-Merrill, 1955.

BURROWES, R., and SPECTOR, B. Conflict and cooperation within and among nations: Enumerative profiles of Syria, Jordan, and the United Arab Republic, January 1965 to May 1967. Presented at the meetings of the International Studies Association, 1970.

BURROWES, R., and SPECTOR, B. The strength and direction of relationships between domestic and external conflict and cooperation: Syria 1961–67. In J. Wilkenfeld, *Conflict behavior and linkage politics,* New York: McKay, 1973.

Buss, A. *A psychology of aggression.* New York: Wiley, 1961.

Button, J. W. *Black violence: Political impact of the 1960s riots.* Princeton: Princeton University Press, 1978.

Button, J., and Scher, R. Impact of the civil rights movement: Perceptions of black municipal service changes. Department of Political Science, University of Florida. Forthcoming.

Bwy, D. P. Dimensions of political conflict in Latin America. *American Behavioral Scientist,* 1968(a), 11:39–50.

Bwy, D. P. Political instability in Latin America: The cross-cultural test of a causal model. *Latin American Research Review,* 1968(b), 3:17–66.

Calhoun, D. Review of M. Stohl, War and domestic political violence. *Journal of Interdisciplinary History,* 1978, 9:189–193.

Calvert, P. A. R. *A study of revolution.* Oxford: Clarendon Press, 1970.

Campbell, D. T. On the conflicts between biological and social evolution and between psychology and moral tradition. *American Psychologist,* 1975, 30: 1103–1126.

Cannell, C., and Robison, S. Analysis of individual questions. In J. B. Lansing, S. B. Withey, and A. C. Wolfe (eds.), *Working papers on survey research in poverty areas.* Ann Arbor: Institute for Social Research, 1971.

Cantril, H. *The politics of despair.* New York: Basic, 1958.

Cantril, H. *The pattern of human concerns.* New Brunswick: Rutgers University Press, 1965.

Caplan, N. S. The new ghetto man: A review of recent empirical studies. *Journal of Social Issues,* 1970, 26:59–73.

Caporaso, J. A. Introduction: Dependence and dependency in the global system. *International Organization,* 1978, 32:1–12.

Caporaso, J. A., and Roos, L. L., Jr. *Quasi-experimental approaches: Testing theory and evaluating policy.* Evanston: Northwestern University Press, 1973.

Caplan, N. S., and Paige, J. M. A study of ghetto rioters. *Scientific American,* 1968, 219:15–21.

Carneiro, R. L. A theory of the origin of the state. *Science,* 1970, 169:733–738.

Carneiro, R. L. Political expansion as an expression of the principle of competitive exclusion. In R. Cohen and E. R. Service (eds.), *Origins of the state: The anthropology of political evolution.* Philadelphia: Institute for the Study of Human Issues, 1978.

Carroll, B. A. Peace research: The cult of power. *Journal of Conflict Resolution,* 1972, 16:585–616.

Carter, W. E. Revolution and the agrarian sector. In J. M. Malloy, *Beyond the revolution: Bolivia since 1952.* Pittsburgh: University of Pittsburgh Press, 1971.

Cassinelli, C. W. *Total revolution.* Santa Barbara: Clio Press, 1976.

Cattell, R. B. The dimensions of culture patterns by factorization of national characters. *Journal of Abnormal and Social Psychology,* 1949, 44:443–469.

Cattell, R. B. The principal culture patterns discoverable in the syntal dimensions of existing nations. *Journal of Social Psychology,* 1950, 31:215–253.

Cattell, R. B., Bruel, H., and Hartman, H. P. An attempt at more refined definition of the cultural dimensions of syntality in modern nations. *American Sociological Review*, 1951, 17:408–421.

CHADWICK, R. W. An analysis of the relationship of domestic to foreign conflict behavior over the period 1955–1957. First year paper, Department of Political Science, Northwestern University, 1963.

CHADWICK, R. W., and FIRESTONE, J. M. Intrastate sociopolitical and empirical conflict models: A selective review and appraisal. Research Paper no. 20. Center for Comparative Political Research. Binghamton, New York: State University of New York, 1972.

CHASE, H. P., and METCALF, D. R. Undernutrition and brain development. In J. W. Prescott et al. (eds.), *Brain function and malnutrition*. New York: Wiley, 1975.

CHERKIN, A., ECKHARDT, M. J., and GERBRANDT, L. K. Memory: Proline induces retrograde amnesia in chicks. *Science*, 1976, 193:242–244.

CHOROVER, S. L. Big brother and psychotechnology. *Psychology Today*, 1973, 7: 43–54.

CHOUCRI, N. *Population dynamics and international violence*. Lexington: Lexington Books, 1974.

CHOUCRI, N., and NORTH, R. C. The determinants of international violence. *Peace Research Society (International), Papers*, 1969, 12:33–63.

CHOUCRI, N., and NORTH, R. C. *Nations in conflict: National growth and international violence*. San Francisco: Freeman, 1975.

CITRIN, J. Comment: The political relevance of trust in government. *American Political Science Review*, 1974, 68:973–988.

CITRIN, J. Political alienation as a social indicator: Attitudes and action. Paper delivered at the Cambridge Conference on Social Indicators, Cambridge, England, 1975.

CLARK, G. *War and society in the seventeenth century*. Cambridge: At the University Press, 1958.

CLARK, R., Jr. *Development and instability: Political change in the non-western world*. Hinsdale: Dryden, 1974.

CLAUDE, I. L. *Power and international relations*. New York: Random House, 1962.

CLAUDE, I. L. The problem of evaluating war. In G. L. Goodwin and A. Linklater (eds.), *New dimensions of world politics*. New York: Wiley, 1975.

CLAYTON, J. L. Vietnam: The 200-year mortgage. *The Nation*, 26 May 1969, 208:661–663.

CLUTTERBUCK, R. Northern Ireland: Is there a way? *Washington Review of Strategic and International Studies*, 1978, 1:52–64.

CNUDDE, C. F. Theories of political development and the assumptions of statistical models. *Comparative Political Studies*, 1972, 5:131–150.

COHAN, A. S. *Theories of revolution: An introduction*. New York: Wiley, 1975.

COHEN, E. A. *Human behavior in the concentration camp*. New York: Grosset and Dunlap, 1953.

COHEN, R. Introduction. In R. Cohen and E. R. Service (eds.), *Origins of the state: The anthropology of political evolution*. Philadelphia: Institute for the Study of Human Issues, 1978.

COLBY, D. The effects of riots on public policy: Exploratory note. *International Journal of Group Tensions*, 1975, 5:156–162.

COLEMAN, J. S. *Community conflict*. New York: Free Press, 1957.

COLEMAN, J. S. (ed.). *Education and political development*. Princeton: Princeton University Press, 1965.

COLEMAN, J. S. *The mathematics of collective choice*. Chicago: Aldine, 1973.

COLLINS, J. N. Foreign conflict behavior and domestic disorders in Africa. In J. Wilkenfeld (ed.), *Conflict and linkage politics*. New York: McKay, 1973.

CONELL, C. *Was holding out the key to winning strikes? Massachusetts, 1881–1894*. Working paper No. 187. Ann Arbor: Center for Research on Social Organization, 1978.

CONNOR, W. Nation-building or nation-destroying? *World Politics*, 1972, 24: 339–355.

CONVERSE, E. The war of all against all: A review of the *Journal of Conflict Resolution*, 1957–1968. *Journal of Conflict Resolution*, 1968, 12:471–550.

COOK, S. D. Coercion and social change. In J. R. Pennock and J. W. Chapman (eds.), *Coercion*. Chicago: Aldine-Atherton, 1972.

COOPER, M. N. A reinterpretation of the causes of turmoil: The effects of culture and modernity. *Comparative Political Studies*, 1974, 7:267–291.

CORNELIUS, W. A. Urbanization as an agent in Latin American political instability: The case of Mexico. *American Political Science Review*, 1969, 63:833–857.

CORNELIUS, W. A. The political sociology of cityward migration in Latin America. In F. F. Rabinovitz and F. M. Trueblood (eds.), *Latin American urban research*. Beverly Hills: Sage, 1971.

CORNELIUS, W. A. Urbanization and political demand making: Political participation among the migrant poor in Latin American cities. *American Political Science Review*, 1974, 68:1125–1146.

CORWIN, E. S. *Total war and the constitution*. New York: Knopf, 1947.

COSER, L. A. *The functions of social conflict*. New York: Free Press, 1956.

COSER, L. A. The termination of conflict. *Journal of Conflict Resolution*, 1961, 5: 347–353.

COTLER, J. Political crisis and military populism in Peru. *Studies in Comparative International Development*, 1971, 6:95–113.

CRAGG, B. G. The development of cortical synapses during starvation in the rat. *Brain*, 1972, 95:143–150.

CRAIN, R. L. *The politics of school desegregation*. Garden City: Anchor Books, 1969.

CRAMER, M. R., and BETZ, M. Letters. *Social Problems*, 1974, 22:304–310.

CRAWFORD, T. J., and NADITCH, M. Relative deprivation, powerlessness, and militancy: The psychology of social protest. *Psychiatry*, 1970, 33:208–223.

CREWS, D. The hormonal control of behavior in a lizard. *Scientific American*, 1979, 241:180–187.

CROSBY, F. A model of egoistical relative deprivation. *Psychological Review*, 1976, 83:85–113.

CROSBY, F. Relative deprivation revisited: A response to Miller, Bolce, and Halligan. *American Political Science Review*, 1979, 73:103–112.

CROWLEY, R. W. Long swings in the role of government: An analysis of wars and government expenditures in Western Europe since the eleventh century. *Public Finance*, 1971, 26:27–43.

CUTRIGHT, P. National political development: Measurement and analysis. *American Sociological Review*, 1963, 28:253–264.

DAHL, R. *Pluralist democracy in the United States: Conflict and consent.* Chicago: Rand-McNally, 1967.

DAHL, R. *After the revolution?: Authority in a good society.* New Haven: Yale University Press, 1970.

DAHRENDORF, R. *Class and class conflict in industrial society.* Stanford: Stanford University Press, 1959.

DALY, W. T. *The revolutionary: A review and synthesis.* Sage Professional Papers in Comparative Politics. Beverly Hills: Sage, 1972.

DARWIN, C. (1859). *The origin of species.* New York: Modern Library, n.d.

DAVIES, J. C. Toward a theory of revolution. *American Sociological Review*, 1962, 27:5–19.

DAVIES, J. C. The J-curve of rising and declining satisfactions as a cause of some great revolutions and a contained rebellion. In. H. D. Graham and T. R. Gurr (eds.), *Violence in America: Historical and comparative perspectives*, New York: Praeger, 1969.

DAVIES, J. C. Violence and aggression: Innate or not? *Western Political Quarterly*, 1970, 23:611–623.

DAVIES, J. C. Aggression, violence, revolution, and war. In J. N. Knutson (ed.), *Handbook of political psychology.* San Francisco: Jossey-Bass, 1973.

DAVIES, J. C. Ions of emotion and political behavior: A prototheory. In A. Somit (ed.), *Biology and politics: Recent explorations.* The Hague and Paris: Mouton, 1976.

DAVIES, J. C. Political socialization: From womb to childhood. In S. A. Renshon (ed.), *Handbook of political socialization.* New York: Free Press, 1977(a).

DAVIES, J. C. The priority of human needs and the stages of political development. In. J. R. Pennock and J. W. Chapman (eds.), *Human nature in politics.* New York: New York University Press, 1977(b).

DAVIES, J. C. The development of individuals and the development of polities. In R. Fitzgerald (ed.), *Human needs and politics.* Rushcutters Bay, Australia: Pergamon Press, 1977(c).

DAVIES, J. C. Communications: The J-curve theory. *American Political Science Review*, 1978, 72:1357–1358.

DAVIS, H. T. *Political statistics.* Evanston, Ill.: Principia, 1948.

DAVIS, W. J. *The seventh year: Industrial civilization in transition.* New York: Norton, 1978.

DAVIS, W. W., DUNCAN, G. T., and SIVERSON, R. M. The dynamics of warfare: 1816–1965. *American Journal of Political Science*, 1978, 22:772–792.

DEANE, P. War and industrialization. In J. M. Winter (ed.), *War and economic development: Essays in memory of David Joslin.* Cambridge: At the University Press, 1975.

DEBRAY, R. *Revolution in the revolution? Armed struggle and political struggle in Latin America.* New York: Grove, 1967.

DEHIO, L. *The precarious balance: Four centuries of the European power struggle.* Trans. C. Fullman. New York: Knopf, 1962.

DELGADO, J. M. R. *Physical control of the mind.* New York: Harper & Row, 1969.

DENCIK, L. Peace research: Pacification or revolution? *Proceedings of the International Peace Research Association Third General Conference, 1: The Philosophy of Peace Research.* Assen: Van Gorcum, 1970.

DENTLER, R. A., and CUTRIGHT, P. *Hostage America: Human aspects of a nuclear attack and a program of prevention.* Boston: Beacon, 1963.

DENTON, F. H. Some regularities in international conflict, 1820–1949. *Background*, 1966, 9:283–296.

DENTON, F. H. Factors in international system violence—1750 to 1960. RAND Corporation Paper, P–4216. Santa Monica: RAND, 1969.

DENTON, F. H., and PHILLIPS, W. Some patterns in the history of violence. *Journal of Conflict Resolution*, 1968, 12:182–195.

DeSCHWEINITZ, K., Jr. *Industrialization and democracy.* New York: Free Press, 1964.

DEUTSCH, K. W. Toward an inventory of basic trends and patterns in comparative and international politics. *American Political Science Review*, 1960, 54: 34–57.

DEUTSCH, K. W. Social mobilization and political development. *American Political Science Review*, 1961, 55:493–514.

DEUTSCH, K. W. *Nationalism and social communication: An inquiry into the foundations of nationality*, 2nd. ed. Cambridge: M.I.T. Press, 1966.

DEUTSCH, K. W. *The analysis of international relations.* Englewood Cliffs: Prentice-Hall, 1968.

DEUTSCH, K. W. *Politics and government: How people decide their fate*, 2nd. ed. Boston: Houghton Mifflin, 1974.

DEUTSCH, K. W., and SINGER, J. D. Multipolar power systems and international stability. *World Politics*, 1964, 16:390–406.

DEUTSCH, M. *The resolution of conflict: Constructive and destructive processes.* New Haven: Yale University Press, 1973.

DEWEY, E. R. The patterns of war. In E. R. Dewey and O. Mandino, *Cycles: The mysterious forces that trigger events.* New York: Hawthorn, 1976.

DIESING, P. *Patterns of discovery in the social sciences.* Chicago: Aldine-Atherton, 1971.

DIVALE, W. T., CHAMBERIS, F., and GANGLOFF, D. War, peace and martial residence in pre-industrial societies. *Journal of Conflict Resolution*, 1976, 20: 57–78.

DOLBEARE, K. M. (ed.) *Public policy evaluation.* Beverly Hills: Sage, 1975.

DOLIAN, J. P. Military coups and the allocation of national resources: An examination of thirty-four sub-Sahara African nations. Ph.D. dissertation, Department of Political Science, Northwestern University, 1973.

DOLLARD, J., DOOB, L. W., MILLER, N. E., MOWRER, O. H., and SEARS, R. R. *Frustration and aggression.* New Haven: Yale University Press, 1939.

DOMINGUEZ, J. I. *Cuba: Order and revolution.* Cambridge: Harvard University Press, 1978.

DORAN, C. F. *Domestic conflict in state relations: The American sphere of influence.* Sage Professional Papers in International Studies, No. 02–037. Beverly Hills: Sage, 1975.

DORAN, C. F. Regional integration and domestic unrest: A comparative study in Europe and Central America. *International Interactions* 1976, 2:67–82.

DORAN, C. F. Political instability, U.S. foreign aid and dependence: A push-pull hypothesis. Unpublished paper, 1978.

DORAN, C. F., PENDLEY, R. E., and ANTUNES, G. E. A test of cross-national event reliability: Global versus regional data sources. *International Studies Quarterly*, 1973, 17:175–203.

DORAN, C. R. *The politics of assimilation: Hegemony and its aftermath.* Baltimore: Johns Hopkins University Press, 1971.

DOWNS, A. *An economic theory of democracy.* New York: Harper & Row, 1957.

DOWNTON, J. V., Jr. *Rebel leadership: Commitment and charisma in the revolutionary process.* New York: Free Press, 1973.

DOWTY, A. Conflict in war potential politics: An approach to historical macro-analysis. *Peace Science Society (International), Papers,* 1970, 13:85–103.

DUFF, E. A., and McCAMANT, J. F., with MORALES, W. Q. *Violence and repression in Latin America: A quantitative and historical analysis.* New York: Free Press, 1976.

DUNCAN, G. T., and SIVERSON, R. M. Markov chain models for conflict analysis: Results from Sino-Indian relations, 1959–1964. *International Studies Quarterly*, 1975, 19:344–374.

DUNCAN, O. D., CUZZORT, R. P., and DUNCAN, B. *Statistical geography: Problems in analyzing areal data.* New York: Free Press, 1961.

DUNN, D. War and social change. In F. S. Northedge (ed.), *The use of force in international relations.* New York: Free Press, 1974.

DUNN, D. J. Peace research. In T. Taylor (ed.), *Approaches and theory in international relations.* London: Longman Group, 1978.

DUNN, J. M. The success and failure of modern revolutions. In S. Bialer and S. Sluzar (eds.), *Radicalism in the contemporary age, Vol. 3: Strategies and impact of contemporary radicalism.* Boulder: Westview Press, 1977.

DURKHEIM, E. (1897) *Suicide: A study in sociology.* New York: Free Press, 1951.

DUVALL, R., and WELFLING, M. Determinants of political institutionalization in Black Africa: A quasi-experimental analysis. *Comparative Political Studies,* 1973(a), 5:387–417.

DUVALL, R., and WELFLING, M. Social mobilization, political institutionalization, and conflict in Black Africa. *Journal of Conflict Resolution,* 1973(b), 17:673–702.

DYE, T. *Policy analysis: What governments do, why they do it and what difference it makes.* University, Alabama: University of Alabama Press, 1976.

EAST, M. A. Status discrepancy and violence in the international system: An empirical analysis. In J. Rosenau, V. Davis, and M. A. East (eds.), *The analysis of international politics.* New York: Free Press, 1972.

EAST, M. A., and GREGG, P. M. Factors influencing cooperation and conflict in the international system. *International Studies Quarterly*, 1967, 11:244–269.

EASTON, D. *A framework for political analysis.* Englewood Cliffs: Prentice-Hall, 1965(a).

EASTON, D. *A systems analysis of political life.* New York: Wiley, 1965(b).

EBERWEIN, W. D., HUBNER-DICK, G., JAGODZINSKI, W., RATTINGER, H., and WEEDE, E. Internes und externes Konfliktverhalten von Nationen, 1966–67. *Zeitschrift für Soziologie,* 1978, 7:21–38.

ECHOLS, J. M. Politics, budgets, and regional equality in communist and capitalist systems. *Comparative Political Studies*, 1975, 8:259–292.

ECHOLS, J. M. The comparative impact of socialism on racial and ethnic inequality. *Comparative Political Studies*, 1980, 13 (forthcoming).

ECKHARDT, W., and YOUNG, C. *Governments under fire: Civil conflict and imperialism.* New Haven: Human Relations Area File Press, 1977.

ECKSTEIN, H. (ed.). *Internal War: Problems and approaches.* New York: Free Press, 1964.

ECKSTEIN, H. On the etiology of internal wars. *History and Theory*, 1965, 4:133–162.

ECKSTEIN, H. *Division and cohesion in democracy: A study of Norway.* Princeton: Princeton University Press, 1966.

ECKSTEIN, H. Political science and public policy. In I. de Sola Pool (ed.), *Contemporary political science: Toward empirical theory.* New York: McGraw-Hill, 1967.

ECKSTEIN, H. Authority relations and governmental performance: A theoretical framework. *Comparative Political Studies*, 1969, 2:269–325.

ECKSTEIN, H. *The evaluation of political performance: Problems and dimensions.* Sage Professional Papers in Comparative Politics No. 01–017. Beverly Hills: Sage, 1971.

ECKSTEIN, H. Patterns of authority: A structural basis for political inquiry. *American Political Science Review*, 1973, 67:1142–1161.

ECKSTEIN, H. Case study and theory in political science. In F. I. Greenstein and N. W. Polsby (eds.), *Handbook of political science, Vol. 7, Strategies of inquiry.* Reading: Addison-Wesley, 1975.

ECKSTEIN, H. *Support for Regimes.* Princeton: Center of International Studies, Research Monograph No. 44, 1979.

ECKSTEIN, H., and GURR, T. R. *Patterns of authority: A structural basis for political inquiry.* New York: Wiley, 1975.

ECKSTEIN, S. How economically consequential are revolutions? A comparative study of Mexico and Bolivia. *Studies in Comparative International Development*, 1975, 10:48–63.

ECKSTEIN, S. *The impact of revolution: A comparative analysis of Mexico and Bolivia.* Sage Professional Papers in Comparative Sociology, No. 06–106. Beverly Hills: Sage, 1976.

EDELMAN, M. *The symbolic use of politics.* Urbana: University of Illinois Press, 1964.

EIDE, A. Dialogue and confrontation in Europe. *Journal of Conflict Resolution*, 1972, 16:511–522.

EIDE, A. International law, domination, and the use of force. *Journal of Peace Research*, 1974, 11:1–20.

EIDSON, B. White public opinion in an age of disorder. In D. Bossel and P. Rossi (eds.), *Cities under siege.* New York: Basic Books, 1971.

EINAUDI, L. The military and government in Peru. In C. Thurber and L. Graham (eds.), *Development administration in Latin America.* Durham: Duke University Press, 1973.

EINSTEIN, A., and FREUD, S. *Why war?* Paris: International Institute of Intellectual Cooperation, 1932.

EISENSTADT, S. N. *Revolution and the transformation of societies: A comparative study of civilizations.* New York: Free Press, 1978.

ELLIOT, R. S. P., and HICKIE, J. *Ulster: A case study in conflict theory.* London: Longman, 1971.

ELLSBERG, D. The crude analysis of strategic choice. In J. Mueller (ed.), *Approaches to measurement in international relations: A non-evangelical survey.* New York: Appleton-Century-Crofts, 1969.

ENLOE, C. *Ethnic conflict and political development.* Boston: Little, Brown, 1972.

ERIKSON, E. H. *Young man Luther: A study in psychoanalysis and history.* New York: Norton, 1962.

ERIKSON, E. H. (1950) *Childhood and society,* 2nd. ed. New York: Norton, 1963.

ERIKSON, E. H. *Gandhi's truth: On the origins of militant nonviolence.* New York: Norton, 1969.

ETZIONI, A. *A comparative analysis of complex organizations.* New York: Free Press, 1961.

FABBRO, D. Peaceful societies: An introduction. *Journal of Peace Research,* 1978, 15:67–83.

FABRICANT, S. *The rising trend of government employment.* New York: National Bureau of Economic Research, 1949.

FAINSTEIN, N. I., and FAINSTEIN, S. I. *Urban political movements: The search for power by minority groups in American cities.* Englewood Cliffs: Prentice-Hall, 1974.

FANON, F. *The wretched of the earth.* New York: Grove, 1966.

FARLEY, R. Trends in racial inequalities: Have the gains of the 1960s disappeared in the 1970s? *American Sociological Review,* 1977, 42:189–208.

FARLEY, R., and HERMALIN, A. I. The 1960s: A decade of progress for blacks? *Demography,* 1972, 9:353–370.

FAY, B. *Social theory and political practice.* London: Allen and Unwin, 1975.

FAY, B. How people change themselves: The relationship between critical theory and its audience. In T. Ball (ed.), *Political theory and praxis: New perspectives.* Minneapolis: University of Minnesota Press, 1977.

FEAGIN, J. R., and HAHN, H. *Ghetto revolts: The politics of violence in American cities.* New York: Macmillan, 1973.

FEIERABEND, I. K., and FEIERABEND, R. L. Aggressive behaviors within polities, 1948–1962: A cross-national study. *Journal of Conflict Resolution,* 1966, 10:249–271.

FEIERABEND, I. K., and FEIERABEND, R. L. The relationship of systemic frustration, political coercion, and political stability. In J. V. Gillespie and B. A. Nesvold (eds.), *Macro-quantitative analysis: Conflict, development, and democratization.* Beverly Hills: Sage, 1971.

FEIERABEND, I. K., AND FEIERABEND, R. L. Systemic conditions of political aggression: An application of frustration-aggression theory. In I. K. Feierabend, R. L. Feierabend, and T. R. Gurr (eds.), *Anger, violence, and politics: Theories and research.* Englewood Cliffs: Prentice-Hall, 1972.

FEIERABEND, I. K., and FEIERABEND, R. L. Violent consequences of violence. In H. Hirsch and D. C. Perry (eds.), *Violence as politics: A series of original essays.* New York: Harper & Row, 1973.

FEIERABEND, I. K., FEIERABEND, R. L., and LITELL, N. G. Dimensions of political unrest: A factor analysis of cross-national data. Presented to the Annual Meeting of the Western Political Science Association, Reno, 1966.

FEIERABEND, I. K., FEIERABEND, R. L., and NESVOLD, B. A. Social change and political violence: Cross-national patterns. In H. D. Graham and T. R. Gurr (eds.), *Violence in America: Historical and comparative perspectives.* New York: Praeger, 1969.

FEIERABEND, I. K., NESVOLD, B. A., with FEIERABEND, R. L. Political coerciveness and turmoil: A cross-national inquiry. *Law and Society Review,* 1970, 5:93–118.

FEIERABEND, R. L., and FEIERABEND, I. K. Appendix: Invitation to further research—designs, data, and methods. In I. K. Feierabend, R. L. Feierabend, and T. R. Gurr (eds.), *Anger, violence, and politics: Theories and research.* Englewood Cliffs: Prentice-Hall, 1972.

FESTINGER, L. A theory of social comparison processes. *Human Relations,* 1954, 7:117–140.

FESTINGER, L. *A theory of cognitive dissonance.* Stanford: Stanford University Press, 1957.

FINER, S. E. State and nation-building in Europe: The role of the military. In C. Tilly (ed.), *The formation of national states in Western Europe.* Princeton: Princeton University Press, 1975.

FINIFTER, A. W. Dimensions of political alienation. *American Political Science Review,* 1970, 64:389–410.

FINK, C. F. Some conceptual difficulties in the theory of social conflict. *Journal of Conflict Resolution,* 1968, 12:412–460.

FINK, C. F., and BOULDING, K. (eds.). Peace research in transition: A symposium. *Journal of Conflict Resolution,* 1972, 16:463–619.

FISHBEIN, M. Attitude and the prediction of behavior. In M. Fishbein (ed.), *Readings in attitude theory and measurement.* New York: Wiley, 1967.

FISHER, R. Fractionating conflict. In C. Smith (ed.), *Conflict resolution: Contributions of the behavioral sciences.* Notre Dame: University of Notre Dame Press, 1971.

FISHER, R. Third party consultation: A method for the study and resolution of conflict. *Journal of Conflict Resolution,* 1972, 16:67–94.

FLANIGAN, W. H., and FOGELMAN, E. Patterns of political violence in comparative historical perspective. *Comparative Politics,* 1970, 3:1–20.

FLANIGAN, W. H., and FOGELMAN, E. Patterns of democratic development: An historical quantitative analysis. In J. V. Gillespie and B. A. Nesvold (eds.), *Macro-quantitative analysis: Conflict, development, and democratization.* Beverly Hills: Sage, 1971.

FLORES, E. Land reform in Bolivia. *Land Economics,* 1954, 30:112–124.

FOGELSON, R. M. *Violence as protest.* Garden City: Doubleday, 1971.

FORWARD, J. R., and WILLIAMS, J. R. Internal-external control and black militancy. *Journal of Social Issues,* 1970, 26:75–92.

FOSSUM, E. Factors influencing the occurrence of military coups d'état in Latin America. *Journal of Peace Research,* 1967, 4:228–251.

FRASER, P. The impact of the war of 1914–1918 on the British political system. In M. R. D. Foot (ed.), *War and society: Historical essays in honour and memory of J. R. Western, 1928–1971.* New York: Barnes & Noble, 1973.

FREEMAN, M. Review article: Theories of revolution. *British Journal of Political Science*, 1972, 2:339–359.

FREEMAN, M. Edmund Burke and the theory of revolution. *Political Theory*, 1978, 6:277–297.

FREUD, S. (1921) *Group psychology and the analysis of the ego.* New York: Bantam Books, 1960.

FREY, F. W. Communication and development. In I. de Sola Pool and W. Schramm (eds.), *Handbook of communication.* Chicago: Rand-McNally, 1973.

FRIED, M. H. Warfare, military organization, and the evolution of society. *Anthropologica*, 1961, 3:134–147.

FRIED, M. H. The state, the chicken, and the egg: Or, what came first? In R. Cohen and E. R. Service (eds.), *Origins of the state: The anthropology of political evolution.* Philadelphia: Institute for the Study of Human Issues, 1978.

FRIED, M. H., HARRIS, M., and MURPHY, R. (eds.). *War: The anthropology of armed conflict and aggression.* Garden City: Natural History Press, 1968.

FRIEDMAN, M. Price, income, and monetary changes in three wartime periods. *American Economic Review*, 1952, 42:612–625.

FROMM, E. *The anatomy of human destructiveness.* New York: Holt, 1973.

FRUCHTER, B. *Introduction to factor analysis.* New York: Nostrand, 1954.

GALTUNG, J. A structural theory of aggression. *Journal of Peace Research*, 1964, 1:95–119.

GALTUNG, J. Violence, peace, and peace research. *Journal of Peace Research*, 1969, 6:167–191.

GALTUNG, J. Feudal systems, structural violence, and the structural theory of revolutions. *Proceedings of the International Peace Research Association Third General Conference, 1: The Philosophy of Peace Research.* Assen: Van Gorcum, 1970.

GALTUNG, J. A structural theory of imperialism. *Journal of Peace Research*, 1971, 8:81–117.

GALULA, D. *Counterinsurgency warfare: Theory and practice.* New York: Praeger, 1964.

GAMSON, W. A. *Power and discontent.* Homewood: Dorsey, 1968.

GAMSON, W. A. Violence and political power: The meek don't make it. *Psychology Today*, 1974, 7:35–41.

GAMSON, W. A. *The strategy of social protest.* Homewood: Dorsey, 1975.

GAMSON, W. A. Understanding the careers of challenging groups: A commentary on Goldstone. *American Journal of Sociology*, 1980, 85:1043–1060.

GANONG, W. F. *Review of medical physiology.* Los Altos: Lange Medical Publications, 1969.

GANTZEL, K. J. Dependency structures as the dominant pattern in world society. *Journal of Peace Research*, 1973, 10:203–214.

GARCIA, A. Agrarian reform and social development in Bolivia. In R. Stavenhagen (ed.), *Agrarian problems and peasant movements in Latin America.* Garden City: Doubleday, 1970.

GARNHAM, D. Dyadic international war, 1816–1965: The role of power parity and geographical proximity. *Western Political Quarterly*, 1976(a), 29:231–242.

GARNHAM, D. Power parity and lethal international violence, 1969–1973. *Journal of Conflict Resolution*, 1976(b), 20:379–394.

GARROW, D. J. *Protest at Selma: Martin Luther King, Jr. and the Voting Rights Act of 1965*. New Haven: Yale University Press, 1978.

GARVER, N. What violence is. *The Nation*, 1968, 206:819–822.

GEBER, M. L'environement et le développement des enfants africains. *Enfance* (Paris), 1973, 3–4:145–174.

GEERTZ, C. The integrative revolution: Primordial sentiments and civil politics in the new states. In C. Geertz (ed.), *Old societies and new states: The quest for modernity in Asia and Africa*. New York: Free Press, 1963.

GEORGE, A., and SMOKE, R. *Deterrence in American foreign policy: Theory and practice*. New York: Columbia University Press, 1974.

GERSCHENKRON, A. *Economic backwardness in historical perspective*. Cambridge: Harvard University Press, 1964.

GERTH, H. H., and MILLS, C. W. (trans.). *From Max Weber, essays in sociology*. Fair Lawn: Oxford University Press, 1946.

GIAP, V-N. *People's war, people's army*. New York: Praeger, 1962.

GIARINI, O., and LOUBERGÉ, H. *The diminishing returns of technology*. Oxford: Pergamon, 1978.

GILLESPIE, J. V., and NESVOLD, B. A. (eds.). *Macro-quantitative analysis: Conflict, development, and democratization*. Beverly Hills: Sage, 1971.

GILLESPIE, J. V., ZINNES, D. A., and RUBISON, R. M. Accumulation in arms race models: A geometric lag perspective. *Comparative Political Studies*, 1978, 10:475–496.

GILLESPIE, J. V., ZINNES, D. A., TAHIM, G. S., SCHRODT, P. A., and RUBISON, R. M. An optimal control model of arms races. *American Political Science Review*, 1977, 71:226–244.

GOCHMAN, C. S. States, power and interstate conflict: The major powers, 1820–1970. Paper delivered at the meetings of the International Studies Association, Washington, D.C., 1975(a).

GOCHMAN, C. S. *Status, conflict, and war: The major powers, 1820–1970*. Unpublished Ph.D. dissertation, University of Michigan, 1975(b).

GOLDSTONE, J. C. The weakness of organization: A new look at Gamson's *The strategy of social protest*. *American Journal of Sociology*, 1980, 85:1017–1042.

GOMEZ, W. Bolivia: Problems of a pre- and post-revolutionary export economy. *Journal of Developing Areas*, 1976, 10:461–484.

GOUREVITCH, P. The second image reversed: The international sources of domestic politics. *International Organization*, 1978, 32:881–912.

GOY, R. W. Early hormonal experiences on the development of sexual and sex-related behavior. In F. O. Schmitt et al. (eds.), *The Neurosciences: Second study program*. New York: Rockefeller University Press, 1970.

GRAHAM, H. D., and GURR, T. R. (eds.). *Violence in America: Historical and comparative perspectives*. New York: Praeger, 1969.

GRAHAM, H. D., and GURR, T. R. (eds.). *Violence in America: Historical and comparative perspectives*, rev. ed. Beverly Hills: Sage, 1979.

GRANIT, R. *The purposive brain.* Cambridge: M.I.T. Press, 1977.

GRANOVETTER, M. Threshold models of collective behavior. *American Journal of Sociology,* 1978, 83:1420–1443.

GREENSTEIN, F., and POLSBY, N. (eds.). *Handbook of political science: International politics,* Vol. 8. Reading: Addison-Wesley, 1975.

GREGORY, P. R., and STUART, R. C. *Soviet economic structure and performance.* New York: Harper & Row, 1974.

GROFMAN, B. N., and MULLER, E. N. The strange case of relative gratification and potential for political violence: The V-curve hypothesis. *American Political Science Review,* 1973, 67:514–539.

GUEVARA, E. *Che Guevara on guerrilla warfare.* New York: Praeger, 1961.

GULICK, E. *Europe's classical balance of power.* Ithaca: Cornell University Press, 1955.

GUMPLOWICZ, L. (1885, revised 1905) *Outlines of sociology.* New York: Paine-Whitman, 1963.

GURR, T. R. *New error-compensated measures for comparing nations.* Princeton: Center of International Studies, Research Monograph No. 25, 1966.

GURR, T. R. A causal model of civil strife: A comparative analysis using new indices. *American Political Science Review,* 1968(a), 62:1104–1124.

GURR, T. R. Urban disorder: Perspectives from the comparative study of civil strife. *American Behavioral Scientist,* 1968(b), 11:50–55.

GURR, T. R. A comparative study of civil strife. In H. D. Graham and T. R. Gurr (eds.), *Violence in America: Historical and comparative perspectives.* New York: Praeger, 1969.

GURR, T. R. Sources of rebellion in Western societies: Some quantitative evidence. *Annals of the American Academy of Political and Social Science,* 1970(a), 391:128–144.

GURR, T. R. *Why men rebel.* Princeton: Princeton University Press, 1970(b).

GURR, T. R. The calculus of civil conflict. *Journal of Social Issues,* 1972(a), 28:27–47.

GURR, T. R. *Politimetrics: An introduction to quantitative macropolitics.* Englewood Cliffs: Prentice-Hall, 1972(b).

GURR, T. R. The revolution–social change nexus: Some old theories and new hypotheses. *Comparative Politics,* 1973(a), 5:359–392.

GURR, T. R. Social change and the interplay of internal and international political conflicts. Mimeo. Presented to the 9th World Congress of the International Political Science Association, Montreal, 1973(b).

GURR, T. R. The neo-Alexandrians: A review essay on data handbooks in political science. *American Political Science Review,* 1947(a), 68:243–252.

GURR, T. R. Persistence and change in political systems, 1800–1971. *American Political Science Review,* 1974(b), 68:1482–1504.

GURR, T. R. *Rogues, rebels and reformers: A political history of urban crime and conflict.* Beverly Hills: Sage, 1976.

GURR, T. R. Burke and the modern theory of revolution: A reply to Freeman. *Political Theory,* 1978, 6:299–312.

GURR, T. R. Political protest and rebellion in the 1960s: The United States in world perspective. In H. D. Graham and T. R. Gurr (eds.), *Violence in*

America: Historical and comparative perspectives, rev. ed. Beverly Hills: Sage, 1979.

GURR, T. R., et al. *Comparative studies of political conflict and change: Cross national datasets.* Ann Arbor, Mich.: Inter-University Consortium for Political and Social Research, 1978.

GURR, T. R., et al. *World patterns and correlates of conflict,* forthcoming.

GURR, T. R., and BISHOP, V. Violent nations and others. *Journal of Conflict Resolution,* 1976, 20:79–110.

GURR, T. R., and DUVALL, R. Civil conflict in the 1960s: A reciprocal theoretical system with parameter estimates. *Comparative Political Studies,* 1973, 6: 135–170.

GURR, T. R., and DUVALL, R. Introduction to a formal theory of conflict within social systems. In L. A. Coser and O. N. Larsen (eds.), *The uses of controversy in sociology.* New York: Free Press, 1976.

GURR, T. R., and LICHBACH, M. I. A forecasting model for political conflict within nations. In J. D. Singer and M. D. Wallace (eds.), *To augur well: Early warning indicators in world politics.* Beverly Hills: Sage, 1979.

GURR, T. R., and MCCLELLAND, M. *Political performance: A twelve nation study.* Sage Professional Papers in Comparative Politics, No. 01–018. Beverly Hills: Sage, 1971.

GURR, T. R., with RUTTENBERG, C. *The conditions of civil violence: First tests of a causal model.* Princeton: Center of International Studies, Research Monograph No. 28, 1967.

GUSFIELD, J. R. Mass society and extremist politics. *American Sociological Review,* 1962, 27:19–30.

HAAS, E. The balance of power: Prescription, concept or propaganda? *World Politics,* 1953, 5:442–477.

HAAS, E., and WHITING, A. *Dynamics of international relations.* New York: McGraw-Hill, 1956.

HAAS, M. Societal approaches to the study of war. *Journal of Peace Research,* 1965, 4:307–323.

HAAS, M. Social change and national aggressiveness 1900–1960. In J. D. Singer (ed.), *Quantitative international politics: Insights and evidence.* New York: Free Press, 1968.

HAAS, M. Societal development and international conflict. In J. Wilkenfeld (ed.), *Conflict behavior and linkage politics.* New York: McKay, 1973.

HAAS, M. *International conflict.* Indianapolis: Bobbs-Merrill, 1974.

HABERMAS, J. *Knowledge and human interests.* Boston: Beacon Press, 1971.

HABERMAS, J. *Theory and practice.* Boston: Beacon Press, 1973.

HAGOPIAN, M. N. *The phenomenon of revolution.* New York: Dodd, Mead, 1974.

HAHN, H. Civic responses to riots: A reappraisal of Kerner Commission data. *Public Opinion Quarterly,* 1970, 34:101–107.

HALABY, C. N. Hardship and collective violence in France: A comment. *American Sociological Review,* 1973, 38:495–500.

HALLPIKE, C. R. Functionalist interpretations of primitive warfare. *Man,* 1973, 8:451–470.

HALPERIN, M. *Bureaucratic politics and foreign policy.* Washington: Brookings Institution, 1974.

HAMILTON, E. J. The role of war in modern inflation. *Journal of Economic History,* 1977, 37:13–19.

HAMMOND, T. T. (ed.). *The anatomy of communist takeovers.* New Haven: Yale University Press, 1975.

HARLOW, H. F. The nature of love. *American Psychologist,* 1958, 13:673–685.

HARLOW, H. F. Love in infant monkeys. *Scientific American,* 1959, 200:68–74.

HARMON, W. *An incomplete guide to the future.* San Francisco: San Francisco Book Co., 1976.

HART, H. The logistic growth of political areas. *Social Forces,* 1948, 26:396–408.

HARTMANN, F. (1957) *The relations of nations.* New York: Macmillan, 1978.

HAUPT, H. G. Zur historischen Analyse von Gewalt: Review of Tilly et al. (1975). In R. Tilly (ed.), Sozialer Protest. *Geschichte und Gesellschaft,* 1977, 3:236–256.

HAYES, M. D. Policy consequences of military participation in politics: An analysis of tradeoffs in Brazilian federal expenditures. In C. Liske, W. Loehr, and J. McCamant (eds.), *Comparative public policy: Issues, theories, and methods.* Beverly Hills: Sage, 1975.

HAZLEWOOD, L. A. Concept and measurement stability in the study of conflict behavior within nations. *Comparative Political Studies,* 1973(a), 6:171–195.

HAZLEWOOD, L. A. Externalizing systemic stress: International conflict as adaptive behavior. In J. Wilkenfeld (ed.), *Conflict behavior and linkage politics.* New York: McKay, 1973(b).

HAZLEWOOD, L. A. Diversion mechanisms and encapsulation processes: The domestic conflict–foreign conflict hypothesis reconsidered. In P. J. McGowan (ed.), *Sage International Yearbook of Foreign Policy Studies.* Vol. 3. Beverly Hills: Sage, 1975.

HAZLEWOOD, L. A., and WEST, G. T. Bivariate associations, factor structures, and substantive impact: The source coverage problem revisited. *International Studies Quarterly,* 1974, 18:317–337.

HEISLER, M. O. Managing ethnic conflict in Belgium. *Annals of the American Academy of Political and Social Science,* 1977, 433:32–46.

HELMER, J. *Bringing the war home: The American soldier in Vietnam and after.* New York: Free Press, 1974.

HEMPEL, C. G. *Aspects of scientific explanation.* New York: Free Press, 1965.

HENLEY, E. D. et al. Catecholamine uptake in cerebral cortex: Adaptive change induced by fighting. *Science,* 8 June 1973, 180:1050–1052.

HESS, E. H. *Imprinting: Early experience and the developmental psychobiology of attachment.* New York: Van Nostrand, 1973.

HIBBS, D. A. *Mass political violence: A cross-national causal analysis.* New York: Wiley, 1973.

HIBBS, D. A. Problems of statistical estimation and causal inference in time-series regression models. In H. L. Costner (ed.), *Sociological methodology 1973–1974.* San Francisco: Jossey-Bass, 1974.

HIBBS, D. A. Industrial conflict in advanced industrial societies. *American Political Science Review,* 1976, 70:1033–1058.

HIBBS, D. A. On the political economy of long-run trends in strike activity. *British Journal of Political Science*, 1978, 8:153–175.

HIRSCH, F. *Social limits to growth*. Cambridge: Harvard University Press, 1978.

HIRSCH, L. P., and WIEGELE, T. C. Voice stress analysis as a tool for political research. Paper presented at the annual meeting of the International Society of Political Psychology, Washington, D.C., May 1979.

HIRSCHMAN, A. O. *Exit, voice, and loyalty*. Cambridge: Harvard University Press, 1970.

HIRSCHMAN, A. O. The changing tolerance for income inequality in the course of economic development. *Quarterly Journal of Economics*, 1973, 87:544–566.

HOADLEY, S. J. *Soldiers and politics in Southeast Asia: Civil-military relations in comparative perspective*. Cambridge: Schenkman, 1975.

HOBSBAWM, E. J. *Primitive rebels*. Manchester: Manchester University Press, 1959.

HOBSBAWM, E. J. *Bandits*. Harmondsworth: Penguin, 1969.

HODGES, D. C. *Philosophy of the urban guerrilla: The revolutionary writings of Abraham Guillén*. New York: Morrow, 1973.

HOERDER, D. *Crowd action in revolutionary Massachusetts 1765–1780*. New York: Academic Press, 1977.

HOFFER, E. *The true believer*. New York: New American Library, 1958.

HOFFMANN, S. *Gulliver's troubles, or the setting of American foreign policy*. New York: McGraw-Hill, 1968.

HOLDEN, C. Russians and Americans gather to talk psychobiology. *Science*, 12 May 1978, 200:631–634.

HOLLIST, W. Alternative explanations of competitive arms processes: Tests on four pairs of nations. *American Journal of Political Science*, 1977(a), 21:313–340.

HOLLIST, W. An analysis of arms processes in the United States and the Soviet Union. *International Studies Quarterly*, 1977(b), 21:503–528.

HOLST, E. VON, and ST. PAUL, U. Electrically controlled behavior. *Scientific American*, 1962, 206:50–59.

HOLSTI, K. J. Resolving international conflicts: A taxonomy of behavior and some figures on procedures. *Journal of Conflict Resolution*, 1966, 10:272–296.

HOLSTI, K. J. *International politics: A framework for analysis*, 3rd ed. Englewood Cliffs: Prentice-Hall, 1977.

HOLSTI, O. R. External conflict and internal consensus: The Sino-Soviet case. In P. Stone et al. (ed.), *The general inquirer*. Cambridge: M.I.T. Press, 1966.

HOLSTI, O. R., and ROSENAU, J. N. Vietnam, consensus, and the belief systems of American leaders. *World Politics*, 1979, 32:1–56.

HOLSTI, O. R., and ROSENAU, J. N. Cold war axioms in the post-Vietnam era. In O. R. Holsti, R. M. Siverson, and A. George (eds.), *Change in the international system*. Boulder, Colorado: Westview, 1980.

HOLSTI, O. R., HOPMANN, P. T., and SULLIVAN, J. D. *Unity and disintegration in international alliances*, New York: Wiley, 1973.

HOLSTI, O. R., NORTH, R., and BRODY, R. Perception and action in the 1914 crisis. In J. D. Singer (ed.), *Quantitative international politics: Insight and evidence*. New York: Free Press, 1968.

HOLSTI, R. *The relations of war to the origin of the state.* Helsingfors, Finland: Helsingin Uusi Kirjapaino-Osakeyhtio, 1913.

HOLT, R. T., JOB, B. L., and MARKUS, L. Catastrophe theory and the study of war. *Journal of Conflict Resolution,* 1978, 22:171–208.

HOPMANN, P. T. International conflict and cohesion in the communist system. *International Studies Quarterly,* 1967, 2:212–235.

HORKHEIMER, M. Traditional and critical theory. In M. Horkheimer, *Critical theory: Selected essays.* New York: Herder, 1972.

HOROWITZ, I. L. (ed.). *The rise and fall of project Camelot: Studies in the relationship between social science and practical politics.* Cambridge: M.I.T. Press, 1967.

HORTON, P. B., and LESLIE, G. R. *The sociology of social problems.* Englewood Cliffs: Prentice-Hall, 1974.

HORVATH, W. J. A statistical model for the duration of wars and strikes. *Behavioral Science,* 1968, 13:18–28.

HORVATH, W. J., and FOSTER, C. C. Stochastic models of war alliances. *Journal of Conflict Resolution,* 1963, 7:110–116.

HOWARD, M. *War in European history.* London: Oxford University Press, 1976.

HUBEL, D. H. The brain. *Scientific American,* 1979, 241:44–53.

HUIZINGA, J. *The waning of the Middle Ages.* New York: Doubleday, 1954.

HULA, R. C. Calcutta: The politics of crime and conflict, 1800 to the 1970s. In T. R. Gurr, P. N. Grabosky, and R. C. Hula, *The politics of crime and conflict: A comparative history of four cities,* Part V. Beverly Hills: Sage, 1977.

HULSE, F. S. Warfare, demography, and genetics. *Eugenics Quarterly,* 1961, 8: 185–197.

HUNTINGTON, S. P. Patterns of violence in world politics. In S. P. Huntington (ed.), *Changing patterns of military politics.* New York: Free Press, 1962.

HUNTINGTON, S. P. Political development and political decay. *World Politics,* 1965, 17:386–430.

HUNTINGTON, S. P. *Political order in changing societies.* New Haven: Yale University Press, 1968.

HUNTINGTON, S. P., and NELSON, J. M. *No easy choice: Political participation in developing countries.* Cambridge: Harvard University Press, 1976.

HUREWITZ, J. C. *Middle East politics: The military dimension.* New York: Praeger, 1969.

HURWITZ, L. An index of political stability: A methodological note. *Comparative Political Studies,* 1971, 4:41–68.

HURWITZ, L. Contemporary approaches to political stability. *Comparative Politics,* 1973, 5:449–463.

HURWITZ, S. J. *State intervention in Great Britain: A study of economic control and social response, 1914–1919.* New York: Columbia University Press, 1949.

IGLITZIN, L. B. Violence and American democracy. *Journal of Social Issues,* 1970, 26:165–186.

INGLEHART, R. *The silent revolution.* Princeton: Princeton University Press, 1977.

INTRILIGATOR, M. Some simple models of arms races. In J. Mueller (ed.), *Ap-*

proaches to measurement in international relations: A non-evangelical survey. New York: Appleton-Century-Crofts, 1969.

IRIS, M. Systems in crisis: American and Israeli response to urban ethnic protest. Ph.D. dissertation, Department of Political Science, Northwestern University, 1978.

JACKMAN, R. W. Politicians in uniform. *American Political Science Review*, 1976, 70:1078–1097.

JACKMAN, R. W., and BOYD, W. A. Multiple sources in the collection of data on political conflict. *American Journal of Political Science*, 1979, 23:434–458.

JACKSON, S., RUSSETT, B., SNIDAL, D., and SYLVAN, D. Conflict and coercion in dependent states. *Journal of Conflict Resolution*, 1978, 22:627–657.

JACKSON, W. D. *The seventh year*. New York: Norton, 1979.

JACOBSON, A. L. Intrasocietal conflict: A preliminary test of a structural-level theory. *Comparative Political Studies*, 1973(a), 6:62–83.

JACOBSON, A. L. Some theoretical and methodological considerations for measuring intrasocietal conflict. *Sociological Methods and Research*, 1973(b), 1: 439–461.

JAMES, C. L. R. (1938). *The black Jacobins*. New York: Vintage, 1963.

JAMES, W. (1890). *The principles of psychology*. New York: Dover, 1950.

JANIS, I. L., and KATZ, D. The reduction of intergroup hostility: Research problems and hypotheses. *Journal of Conflict Resolution*, 1959, 3:85–100.

JANOWITZ, M. *The military in the political development of new nations*. Chicago: University of Chicago Press, 1964.

JENNINGS, E. T., Jr. Urban riots and welfare policy change: A test of the Piven-Cloward theory. In H. Ingram and D. Mann (eds.), *Why policies succeed or fail*. Beverly Hills: Sage, 1979.

JERVIS, R. *Perception and misperception in international politics*. Princeton: Princeton University Press, 1976.

JOHNSON, C. *Revolutionary change*. Boston: Little, Brown, 1966.

JOHNSON, C. *Autopsy on people's war*. Berkeley: University of California Press, 1973.

JOHNSON, J. J. (ed.). *The role of the military in underdeveloped countries*. Princeton: Princeton University Press, 1962.

JOHNSON, J. J. *The military and society in Latin America*. Stanford: Stanford University Press, 1964.

JONES, S. D., and SINGER, J. D. *Beyond conjecture in international politics*. Itasca: Peacock, 1973.

JÖRESKOG, K. C. A general approach to confirmatory maximum likelihood factor analysis. *Psychometrica*, 1969, 34:183–202.

JUKAM, T. O., and MULLER, E. N. Political support in the United States. Paper delivered at the Latin American Studies Association Meeting, Pittsburgh, April, 1979.

KAASE, M. Bedingungen unkonventionellen politischen Verhaltens in der Bundesrepublik Deutschland. *Politische Vierteljahresschrift*, 1976, 17:179–216.

KAHN, H. *On thermonuclear war*. Princeton: Princeton University Press, 1960.

KANT, I. (1781) *Critique of pure reason*. New York: St. Martin's, 1929.

KANT, I. *Kant's political writings*. Cambridge: At the University Press, 1970.

KAPLAN, M. *System and process in international politics*. New York: Wiley, 1957.

KAUFMAN, R. *Transitions to stable authoritarian regimes: The Chilean case?* Beverly Hills: Sage, 1976.

KAUTSKY, J. H. Revolutionary and managerial elites in modernizing regimes. *Comparative Politics*, 1969, 1:441–67.

KAUTSKY, J. H. *Patterns of modernizing revolutions: Mexico and the Soviet Union*. Sage Professional Papers in Comparative Politics, No. 01–056. Beverly Hills: Sage, 1975.

KEEGAN, J. *The face of battle*. New York: Viking, 1976.

KEGLEY, C. W., RICHARDSON, N. R., and RICHTER, G. Conflict at home and abroad: An empirical extension. *Journal of Politics*, 1978, 40:742–752.

KEIM, W. D. Nations and conflict individuality. *Journal of Peace Research*, 1971, 3–4:287–292.

KELLY, W. R., and SNYDER, D. Racial violence and socioeconomic changes among blacks in the United States. Unpublished paper, Department of Sociology, Indiana University, 1978.

KELMAN, H. Processes of opinion change. *Public Opinion Quarterly*, 1961, 25: 57–78.

KENDE, I. Twenty-five years of local wars. *Journal of Peace Research*, 1971, 1:5–22.

KENDE, I. 116 wars in 30 years. In *Arms Control and Technological Innovation*, International School of Disarmament and Research on Conflict, 1977.

KENDRICK, M. S. *A century and a half of federal expenditures*. New York: National Bureau of Economic Research, 1955.

KENT, E. (ed.). *Revolution and the rule of law*. Englewood Cliffs: Prentice-Hall, 1971.

KENT, G. The application of peace studies. *Journal of Conflict Resolution*, 1971, 15:47–53.

KERBO, H. R. Foreign involvement in the preconditions for political violence, *Journal of Conflict Resolution*, 1978, 22:363–387.

KEYS, A., BROZEK, J., HENSCHEL, A., MICKELSON, O., and TAYLOR, H. L. *The biology of human starvation*, Vol. 2. Minneapolis: University of Minnesota Press, 1950.

KIESLER, C., and KIESLER, S. *Conformity*. Reading: Addison-Wesley, 1969.

KIKER, B. F., and COCHRANE, J. L. War and human capital in western economic analysis. *History of Political Economy*, 1973, 5:375–398.

KIMBLE, D. P. *Psychology as a biological science*. Pacific Palisades: Goodyear, 1973.

KLEIN, L. R. The role of war in the maintenance of American economic prosperity. *Proceedings of the American Philosophical Society*, 1971, 115:507–516.

KLINGBERG, F. L. The historical alternation of moods in American foreign policy. *World Politics*, 1952, 4:239–273.

KLINGBERG, F. L. Predicting the termination of war: Battle casualties and population losses. *Journal of Conflict Resolution*, 1966, 10:129–171.

KLINGBERG, F. L. Cyclical trends in American foreign policy moods and their policy implications. In C. W. Kegley, Jr., and P. J. McGowan (eds.),

Challenge to America: United States foreign policy in the 1980s. Beverly Hills: Sage, 1979.

KLITGAARD, R. Gandhi's non-violence as a tactic. *Journal of Peace Research,* 1971, 8:143–153.

KNUTSON, J. N. *The human basis of the polity.* Chicago: Aldine-Atherton, 1972.

KOESTLER, A. *The ghost in the machine.* New York: Macmillan, 1967.

KOGON, E. *The theory and practice of hell.* New York: Berkley, 1950.

KOHLER, G. Imperialism as a level of analysis in correlates-of-war research. *Journal of Conflict Resolution,* 1975, 19:48–62.

KORNHAUSER, W. *The politics of mass society.* New York: Free Press, 1959.

KORPI, W. Conflict, power and relative deprivation. *American Political Science Review,* 1974, 68:1569–1578.

KOWALEWSKI, D. A., and SCHUMAKER, P. D. Protest outcomes in the Soviet Union. Unpublished manuscript, University of Kansas, n.d.

KRIESBERG, L., and KLEIN, R. Changes in public support for U.S. military spending. *Journal of Conflict Resolution,* 1980, 24: in press.

KRIPPENDORFF, E. Peace research and the industrial revolution. *Journal of Peace Research,* 1973, 10:184–201.

KRIPPENDORFF, E. Chile, violence, and peace research. *Journal of Peace Research,* 1975, 12:179–194.

KUGLER, J. The consequences of war: Fluctuations in national capacity following major wars 1880–1970. Unpublished Ph.D. dissertation, University of Michigan, 1973.

KUZNETS, S. *Postwar economic growth.* Cambridge: Belknap, 1964.

LADURIE, E. *Times of feast, times of famine.* Garden City: Doubleday, 1971.

LAMPTON, D. M. Performance and the Chinese political system: A preliminary assessment of education and health policies. *China Quarterly,* 1978, 75:509–539.

LAMPTON, D. M. The roots of interprovincial inequality in education and health services in China since 1949. *American Political Science Review,* 1979, 73:459–477.

LANE, F. C. The economic meaning of war and protection. *Journal of Social Philosophy and Jurisprudence,* 1942, 7:254–270.

LANE, F. C. Economic consequences of organized violence. *Journal of Economic History,* 1958, 18:401–417.

LANG, K. *Military institutions and the sociology of war: A review of the literature with annotated bibliography.* Beverly Hills: Sage, 1972.

LAPP, R. *The weapons culture.* New York: Norton, 1968.

LAQUEUR, W. Revolution. In *International encyclopedia of the social sciences,* Vol. 13. New York: Macmillan and Free Press, 1968.

LASSWELL, H. D. (1930) *Psychopathology and politics.* New York: Viking, 1960.

LASSWELL, H. D. (1948) *Power and personality.* New York: Viking, 1962.

LATOUR, S. Some determinants of preference for modes of conflict resolution. *Journal of Conflict Resolution,* 1976, 20:319–356.

LAZARSFELD, P., BERELSON, B., and GAUDET, H. *The people's choice.* New York: Columbia University Press, 1944.

LE BON, G. *The crowd: A study of popular mind.* London: Unwin, 1908.

LE BON, G. *The psychology of revolution.* New York: Putnam, 1913.

LEE, J. S. The periodic recurrence of internecine wars in China. *The China Journal of Science and Art,* 1931, 14:111–115.

LEE, M. T. The founders of the Chinese communist party: A study in revolutionaries. *Civilisations,* 1968, 13:113–27.

LEEDS, A. The functions of war. In J. H. Masserman (ed.), *Science and psychoanalysis,* Vol. 6, *Violence and war.* New York: Grune & Stratton, 1963.

LEHTINEN, D. W. Modernization, political development, and stability. *Stanford Journal of International Studies,* 1974, 9:219–245.

LEITES, N., and WOLF, C., Jr. *Rebellion and authority: An analytic essay on insurgent conflicts.* Chicago: Markham, 1970.

LERNER, M. The state in war time. In W. Waller (ed.), *War in the twentieth century.* New York: Random House, 1940.

LEVITAN, S. A., JOHNSTON, W. B., and TAGGART, R. *Still a dream: The changing status of blacks since 1960.* Cambridge: Harvard University Press, 1975.

LEWIS-BECK, M. S. Some economic effects of revolution: Models, measurement, and the Cuban evidence. *American Journal of Sociology,* 1979, 84:1127–1149.

LI, R. P. Y., and THOMPSON, W. R. The "coup contagion" hypothesis. *Journal of Conflict Resolution,* 1975, 19:63–88.

LICHBACH, M. I., and GURR, T. R. The conflict process: A self-generative model. *Journal of Conflict Resolution,* forthcoming.

LIFTON, R. J. *Death in life: Survivors of Hiroshima.* New York: Random House, 1968.

LIFTON, R. J. *Home from the war: Vietnam veterans: Neither victims nor executioners.* New York: Simon and Schuster, 1973.

LIFTON, R. J. *The life of the self: Towards a new psychology.* New York: Simon and Schuster, 1976.

LIJPHART, A. Review article: The Northern Ireland problem: Cases, theories and solutions. *British Journal of Political Science,* 1975, 5:83–106.

LINEBERRY, R. L. *American public policy: What government does and what difference it makes.* New York: Harper and Row, 1977.

LINZ, J. J., and STEPAN, A. (eds.). *The breakdown of democratic regimes.* Baltimore: Johns Hopkins University Press, 1978.

LIPSET, S. M. Some social requisites of democracy: Economic development and political legitimacy. *American Political Science Review,* 1959, 53:69–105.

LIPSET, S. M. *Political man: The social bases of politics.* Garden City: Doubleday, 1960.

LIPSKY, M. Protest as a political resource. *American Political Science Review,* 1968, 62:1144–1158.

LIPSKY, M., and OLSON, D. J. *Commission politics: The processing of racial crisis in America.* New Brunswick: Transaction Books, 1977.

LOBKOWICZ, N. On the history and theory of practice. In T. Ball (ed.), *Political theory and praxis: New perspectives.* Minneapolis: University of Minnesota Press, 1977.

LOCKE, H. G. *The Detroit riot of 1967.* Detroit: Wayne State University Press, 1969.

LODHI, A. Q., and TILLY, C. Urbanization, crime, and collective violence in 19th-century France. *American Journal of Sociology,* 1973, 79:296–318.

LORENZ, K. (1963) *On aggression.* New York: Harcourt, 1966.

LOWIE, R. H. *The origin of the state.* New York: Harcourt, 1927.

LUCIER, C. Changes in the value of arms race parameters. *Journal of Conflict Resolution,* 1978, 22:17–40.

LUKACS, G. *History and class consciousness.* Cambridge: M.I.T. Press, 1971.

LUTERBACHER, U. Bipolarity and generational factors in major power military activity 1900–1965. *Journal of Peace Research,* 1975, 12:129–138.

LYON, P. New states and international order. In A. James (ed.), *The bases of international order: Essays in honour of C. A. W. Manning.* London: Oxford University Press, 1973.

McCARTHY, J. D., and ZALD, M. N. Resource mobilization and social movements: A partial theory. *American Journal of Sociology,* 1977, 82:1212–1241.

McCLELLAND, C., and HOGGARD, G. D. Conflict patterns in the interactions among nations. In J. N. Rosenau (ed.), *International politics and foreign policy,* rev. ed. New York: Free Press, 1969.

McCORD, W., and HOWARD, J. Negro opinions in three riot cities. *American Behavioral Scientist,* 1968, 11:24–27.

McCRONE, D. J., and CNUDDE, C. F. Toward a communications theory of democratic political development. *American Political Science Review,* 1967, 61:1002–1009.

McDOUGALL, W. *An introduction to social psychology.* Boston: Luce, 1908.

McGOWAN, P., and ROOD, R. Alliance behavior in balance of power systems: Applying a poisson model to nineteenth-century Europe. *American Political Science Review,* 1975, 69:859–870.

McGUIRE, M. C. *Secrecy and the arms race.* Cambridge: Harvard University Press, 1965.

MacINTYRE, A. Ideology, social science, and revolution. *Comparative Politics,* 1973, 5:321–342.

MACK, A. Numbers are not enough: A critique of internal/external behavior research. *Comparative Politics,* 1975, 7:597–618.

MACK, R. W., and SNYDER, R. C. The analysis of social conflict: Toward an overview and synthesis. *Journal of Conflict Resolution,* 1957, 1:212–248.

MACKENZIE, W. J. M. *Biological ideas in politics.* Harmondsworth: Penguin Books, 1978.

McKINLAY, R. D., and A. S. COHAN. A comparative analysis of the political and economic performance of military and civilian regimes. *Comparative Politics,* 1975, 8:1–30.

McKINLAY, R. D., and A. S. COHAN. Performance and instability in military and nonmilitary regime systems. *American Political Science Review,* 1976, 70:850–864.

MacLEAN, P. D. The brain in relation to empathy and medical education. *Journal of Nervous and Mental Disease,* 1967, 144:374–382.

MacLEAN, P. D. Cerebral evolution and emotional processes: New findings on the striatal complex. *Annals of the New York Academy of Sciences*, 1972, 193:137–149.

MacLeod, R., and MacLeod, K. War and economic development: Government and the optical industry in Britain, 1914–18. In J. M. Winter (ed.), *War and economic development: Essays in memory of David Joslin*. Cambridge: At the University Press, 1975.

MacLeod, W. C. The origin of the state reconsidered in the light of the data of aboriginal North America. Ph.D. dissertation, University of Pennsylvania, 1924.

MacLeod, W. C. *The origin and history of politics*. New York: Wiley, 1931.

MacNeil, W. *Plagues and peoples*. Garden City: Anchor, 1976.

McPhail, C. Civil disorder participation: A critical examination of recent research, *American Sociological Review*, 1971, 36:1058–1073.

Malloy, J. M. *Bolivia: The uncompleted revolution*. Pittsburgh: University of Pittsburgh Press, 1970.

Malloy, J. M. (ed.). *Beyond the revolution: Bolivia since 1952*. Pittsburgh: University of Pittsburgh Press, 1971.

Mannheim, K. The problem of generations. In K. Mannheim, *Essays on the sociology of knowledge*. London: Routledge & Kegan Paul, 1952.

Mao Tse-Tung. *On the protracted war*. Peking: Foreign Language Press, 1954.

Marano, L. A. A macrohistoric trend toward world government. *Behavior Science Notes*, 1973, 8:35–39.

Marcuse, H. *An essay on liberation*. Boston: Beacon, 1969.

Marighella, C. Minimanual of the urban guerrilla. *Tricontinental Bimonthly* (Havana), January-February 1970, 16–56. Reprinted in P. B. Springer and M. Truzzi (eds.), *Revolutionaries on revolution*. Pacific Palisades, Cal.: Goodyear, 1973.

Mark, V. H., and Ervin, F. R. *Violence and the brain*. New York: Harper & Row, 1970.

Markus, G. B. Coercion and political instability: Cross-national patterns. Senior Thesis, San Diego State College, 1970.

Markus, G. B., and Nesvold, B. A. Governmental coerciveness and political instability. An exploratory study of cross-national patterns. *Comparative Political Studies*, 1972, 5:231–244.

Marr, W. L. The expanding role of government and wars: Further elaboration. *Public Finance*, 1974, 29:416–421.

Marsh, A. Explorations in unorthodox political behavior: A scale to measure protest potential. *European Journal of Political Research*, 1974, 2:107–129.

Marsh, A. *Protest and political consciousness*. Beverly Hills: Sage, 1977.

Martic, M. *Insurrection: Five schools of revolutionary thought*. New York: Dunellen and Kennikat, 1975.

Martin, H. P. Nutrition: Its relationship to children's physical, mental, and emotional development. *American Journal of Clinical Nutrition*, 1973, 26:766–775.

Marwick, A. The impact of the First World War on British society. *Journal of Contemporary History*, 1968, 3:51–63.

Marwick, A. *War and social change in the twentieth century: A comparative study of Britain, France, Germany, Russia and the United States.* New York: St. Martin's, 1974.

MARX, G. T. Riots. In *Encyclopaedia britannica*, vol. 19, 1970.

MARX, G. T. Perspectives on violence. *Contemporary Psychology*, 1972, 17:128–131.

MARX, K. (1867). *Capital.* New York: Modern Library, n.d.

MARX, K., and ENGELS, F. *The German ideology.* New York: International Publishers, 1970.

MASARYK, T. G. (1913). *The spirit of Russia.* London: G. Allen and Unwin, 1919.

MASLOW, A. H. A theory of human motivation. *Psychological Review*, 1943, 50: 370–396.

MASSELL, G. J. *The surrogate proletariat: Moslem women and revolutionary strategies in Soviet Central Asia, 1919–1929.* Princeton: Princeton University Press, 1974.

MAY, E. R. *"Lessons" of the past: The use and misuse of history in American foreign policy.* New York: Oxford University Press, 1973.

MAYER, A. J. *Dynamics of counter-revolution in Europe 1870–1956: An analytic framework.* New York: Harper & Row, 1971.

MAZLISH, B. *The revolutionary ascetic: Evolution of a political type.* New York: Basic Books, 1976.

MERKL, P. H. *Political violence under the Swastika: 581 early Nazis.* Princeton: Princeton University Press, 1975.

MERLEAU-PONTY, M. *Humanism and terror.* Boston: Beacon, 1969.

MESA-LAGO, C. (ed.). *Revolutionary change in Cuba.* Pittsburgh: University of Pittsburgh Press, 1976.

MEYER, A. Function of the mediator in collective bargaining. *Industrial and Labor Relations Review*, 1960, 13:159–165.

MIDLARSKY, M. I. *On war: Political violence in the international system.* New York: Free Press, 1975.

MIDLARSKY, M. I. Analyzing diffusion and contagion effects: The urban disorders of the 1960s. *American Political Science Review*, 1978, 72:996–1008.

MIDLARKSY, M., and TANTER, R. Toward a theory of political instability in Latin America. *Journal of Peace Research*, 1967, 3:209–227.

MILLER, A. H., BOLCE, L. H., and HALLIGAN, M. R. The new urban blacks. *Ethnicity*, 1976, 3:338–367.

MILLER, A. H., BOLCE, L. H., and HALLIGAN, M. R. The J-curve theory and the black urban riots: An empirical test of progressive relative deprivation theory. *American Political Science Review*, 1977, 71:964–982.

MILLER, J. G. Living systems: Basic concepts. *Behavioral Science*, 1965, 10:193–237.

MILLER, N. E. The frustration-aggression hypothesis. *Psychological Review*, 1941, 48:337–342.

MILSTEIN, J. S. American and Soviet influence, balance of power and Arab-Israeli violence. In Bruce M. Russett (ed.), *Peace, war and numbers.* Beverly Hills: Sage, 1972.

MILSTEIN, J. S., and MITCHELL, W. Dynamics of the Vietnam conflict: A quantitative analysis and predictive computer simulation. *Peace Research Society (International), Papers,* 1968, 10:163–213.

MILWARD, A. S. *War, economy and society, 1939–1945.* Berkeley: University of California Press, 1977.

MITCHELL, C. *The legacy of populism in Bolivia: From the MNR to military rule.* New York: Praeger, 1978.

MITCHELL, E. J. Inequality and insurgency: A statistical study of South Vietnam. *World Politics,* 1963, 20:421–438.

MODELSKI, G. War and the great powers. *Peace Research Society (International), Papers,* 1972(a), 18:45–59.

MODELSKI, G. *Principles of world politics.* New York: Free Press, 1972(b).

MODELSKI, G. Wars and the great power system. In L. L. Farrar (ed.), *War: A historical, political, and social study.* Santa Barbara: ABC-Clio, 1978(a).

MODELSKI, G. The long cycle of global politics and the nation-state. *Comparative Studies in Society and History,* 1978(b), 20:214–235.

MONTAGU, A. *Man and aggression.* London: Oxford University Press, 1973.

MOORE, B., Jr. *Social origins of dictatorship and democracy: Lord and peasant in the making of the modern world.* Boston: Beacon, 1966.

MOORE, C. H. The politics of urban violence: Policy outcomes in Winston-Salem, *Social Science Quarterly,* 1970, 51:374–388.

MOOS, R. H., et al. Fluctuations in symptoms and moods during the menstrual cycle. *Journal of Psychosomatic Research,* 1969, 13:37–41.

MORGENSTERN, O. *The question of national defense.* New York: Random, 1959.

MORGENTHAU, H. *Politics among nations,* 5th ed. New York: Knopf, 1973.

MORRISON, D. G., MITCHELL, R. C., PADEN, J. N., and STEVENSON, H. M. *Black Africa: A comparative handbook.* New York: Free Press, 1972.

MORRISON, D. G., and STEVENSON, H. M. Political instability in independent Black Africa: More dimensions of conflict behavior within nations. *Journal of Conflict Resolution,* 1971, 15:347–368.

MORRISON, D. G., and STEVENSON, H. M. Integration and instability: Patterns of African political development. *American Political Science Review,* 1972(a), 66:902–927.

MORRISON, D. G., and STEVENSON, H. M. Cultural pluralism, modernization, and conflict: An empirical analysis of sources of political instability in African nations. *Canadian Journal of Political Science,* 1972(b), 5:82–103.

MORRISON, D. G., and STEVENSON, H. M. Measuring social and political requirements for system stability: Empirical validation of an index using Latin American and African data. *Comparative Political Studies,* 1974, 7:252–263.

MORTON, L. War, science, and social change. In K. H. Silvert (ed.), *The social reality of scientific myth: Science and social problems.* New York: American Universities Field Staff, 1969.

MOWRY, G. E. The First World War and American democracy. In J. D. Clarkson and T. C. Cochran (eds.), *War as a social institution: The historian's perspective.* New York: Columbia University Press, 1941.

MOY, R. F. *A computer simulation of democratic political development: Tests of the Lipset and Moore models.* Sage Professional Papers in Comparative Politics, No. 01–018. Beverly Hills: Sage, 1971.

MOYAL, J. E. The distribution of wars in time. *Journal of the Royal Statistical Society*, 1949, 112:446–449.

MOYER, K. E. Internal impulses to aggression. *Transactions of the New York Academy of Sciences*, 1969, 31:104–114.

MOYER, K. E. *The physiology of hostility*. Chicago: Markham, 1971.

MUELLER, C. The potential of riot violence as a political resource. *Journal of Political and Military Sociology*, 1978, 6:49–63.

MUELLER, J. E. Presidential popularity from Truman to Johnson. *American Political Science Review*, 1970, 64:18–34.

MUELLER, J. E. Trends in popular support for the wars in Korea and Vietnam. *American Political Science Review*, 1971, 65:358–375.

MUELLER, J. E. *War, presidents and public opinion*. New York: Wiley, 1973.

MULLER, E. N. Correlates and consequences of beliefs in the legitimacy of regime structures. *Midwest Journal of Political Science*, 1970(a), 14:392–412.

MULLER, E. N. The representation of citizens by political authorities: Consequences for regime support. *American Political Science Review*, 1970(b), 64: 1149–1166.

MULLER, E. N. A test of a partial theory of potential for political violence. *American Political Science Review*, 1972, 66:928–959.

MULLER, E. N. Relative deprivation and aggressive political behavior. Paper presented at the Annual Meeting of the American Political Science Association, 1975.

MULLER, E. N. Ein modell zur vorhersage aggressiver politischer partizipation. *Politische Vierteljahresschrift*, 1978, 19:514–558.

MULLER, E. N. *Aggressive political participation*. Princeton: Princeton University Press, 1979.

MULLER, E. N., and JUKAM, T. O. On the meaning of political support. *American Political Science Review*, 1977, 71:1561–1595.

MURRAY, H. A. *Explorations in personality*. New York: Oxford University Press, 1938.

MURRAY, P. T. War and riots: International conflict as a cause of American racial violence. Unpublished paper, 1977.

MUSGRAVE, R. A., and CULBERTSON, J. M. The growth of public expenditures in the United States, 1890–1948. *National Tax Journal*, 1953, 6:97–115.

NAESS, A. A systematization of Gandhian ethics of conflict resolution. *Journal of Conflict Resolution*, 1958, 2:140–155.

NAFZIGER, E. W. The economics of political violence: The Nigerian-Biafran war in comparative perspective. Unpublished manuscript, Department of Economics, Kansas State University, 1979.

NAGEL, J. Inequality and discontent: A nonlinear hypothesis. *World Politics*, 1974, 26:453–472.

NARDIN, T. *Violence and the state: A critique of empirical political theory*. Sage Professional Papers in Comparative Politics, No. 01–020. Beverly Hills: Sage, 1971.

NARDIN, T. Conflicting conceptions of political violence. In C. P. Cotter (ed.), *Political Science Annual, 4*. Indianapolis: Bobbs-Merrill, 1973.

NAROLL, R. Imperial cycles and world order. *Peace Research Society (International), Papers,* 1967, 7:83–101.

NAROLL, R. Deterrence in history. In D. G. Pruitt and R. C. Snyder (eds.), *Theory and research on the causes of war.* Englewood Cliffs: Prentice-Hall, 1969.

NAROLL, R., and DIVALE, W. T. Natural selection in cultural evolution: Warfare versus peaceful diffusion. *American Ethnologist,* 1976, 3:97–129.

National Academy of Sciences. *Long-term worldwide effects of multiple nuclear weapons detonations.* Washington: National Academy of Sciences, 1975.

National Advisory Commission on Civil Disorders. *Report.* New York: Bantam Books, 1968.

NEF, J. U. *War and human progress: An essay on the rise of industrial civilization.* Cambridge: Harvard University Press, 1950.

NEILANDS, J. B., ORIANS, G. H., PFEIFFER, E. W., VENNEMA, A., and WESTING, A. H. *Harvest of death: Chemical warfare in Vietnam and Cambodia.* New York: Free Press, 1972.

NELSON, J. M. The urban poor: Disruption or political integration in third world cities? *World Politics,* 1970, 22:393–414.

NELSON, J. M. Sojourners versus new urbanites: Causes and consequences of temporary versus permanent cityward migration in developing countries. *Economic Development and Cultural Change,* 1976, 24:721–757.

NELSON, K. L. (ed.). *The impact of war on American life: The twentieth-century experience.* New York: Holt, 1971.

NELSON, L. *Cuba: The measure of a revolution.* Minneapolis: University of Minnesota Press, 1972.

NESVOLD, B. A., and MARTIN, A. E. Analysis of time-lag relationships between coerciveness and conflict. Paper presented at the Annual Meeting of the American Political Science Association. Chicago, 1974.

NEUBAUER, D. Some conditions of democracy. *American Political Science Review,* 1967, 61:1002–1009.

NEWCOMBE, A. G. Towards the development of an inter-nation tensiometer. *Peace Science Society (International), Papers,* 1970, 13:11–27.

NEWCOMBE, A. G., and WERT, J. The use of an inter-nation tensiometer for the prediction of war. *Peace Science Society (International), Papers,* 1973, 21:73–83.

NICHOLSON, M. *Conflict analysis.* London: English Universities Press, 1971.

NIEBURG, H. L. The threat of violence and social change. *American Political Science Review,* 1962, 56:865–873.

NIEBURG, H. L. *Political violence: The behavioral process.* New York: St. Martin's, 1969.

NISH, I. *The Anglo-Japanese alliance.* London: Athlone, 1966.

NORDLINGER, E. A. Soldiers in mufti: The impact of military rule upon economic and social change in the non-Western states. *American Political Science Review,* 1970, 64:1131–1148.

NORDLINGER, E. A. *Soldiers in politics: Military coups and governments.* Englewood Cliffs: Prentice-Hall, 1977.

NORTH, R. C., and DE SOLA POOL, I. Kuomintang and Chinese communist elites.

In H. D. Lasswell and D. Lerner (eds.), *World revolutionary elites.* Cambridge: M.I.T. Press, 1965.

OAKESHOTT, M. The tower of babel. In M. Oakeshott, *Rationalism in Politics and Other Essays.* New York: Basic Books, 1962.

OAKESHOTT, M. *On human conduct.* Oxford: Clarendon Press, 1975.

OBERSCHALL, A. Rising expectations and political turmoil. *Journal of Development Studies,* 1969, 6:5–22.

OBERSCHALL, A. *Social conflict and social movements.* Englewood Cliffs: Prentice-Hall, 1973.

OBERSCHALL, A. Theories of social conflict. *Annual Review of Sociology,* 1978(a), 4:291–315.

OBERSCHALL, A. Locker strukturierter kollektiver konflikt: Eine Theorie und eine Illustration. *Politische Vierteljahresschrift,* 1978(b), 19:497–513.

ODELL, J. S. Correlates of U.S. military assistance and military intervention. In S. J. Rosen and J. R. Kurth (eds.), *Testing theories of economic imperialism.* Lexington: Heath, 1974.

O'DONNELL, G. *Modernization and bureaucratic-authoritarianism,* Studies in South American Politics. Berkeley: Institute of International Politics, 1973.

OGBURN, W. F. On inventions and the state. In O. D. Duncan (ed.), *On culture and social change.* Chicago: University of Chicago Press, 1964.

O'KEEFE, M. F., and SCHUMAKER, P. D. Violence and protest effectiveness in Southeast Asia. Paper read to the Southwestern Political Science Association, 1979.

OLDS, J. Self-stimulation of the brain. *Science,* 14 February 1958, 127:315–324.

OLSEN, O. J., and JARVAD, J. M. The Vietnam conference papers: A case study of a failure of peace research. *Peace Research Society (International), Papers,* 1970, 14:155–170.

OLSON, M. Rapid growth as a destabilizing force. *Journal of Economic History,* 1963, 23:529–552.

ONATE, A. D. The conflict interactions of the People's Republic of China, 1950–1970. *Journal of Conflict Resolution,* 1974, 18:578–594.

ONUF, N. Peace research parochialism. *Journal of Peace Research,* 1975, 12:71–78.

OPHULS, W. *Ecology and the politics of scarcity.* San Francisco: Freeman, 1977.

ORGANSKI, A. F. K. *World Politics,* 2nd ed. New York: Knopf, 1968.

ORGANSKI, A. F. K., and KUGLER, J. The costs of major wars: The phoenix factor. *American Political Science Review,* 1977, 71:1347–1366.

ORGANSKI, A. F. K., and KUGLER, J. Davids and goliaths: Predicting the outcomes of international wars. *Comparative Political Studies,* 1978, 11:141–180.

ORGANSKI, A. F. K., and KUGLER, J. *War ledger.* Chicago: University of Chicago Press, 1980.

OSTROM, C. Evaluating alternative foreign policy decision-making models. *Journal of Conflict Resolution,* 1977, 21:235–265.

OTT, M. C. Mediation as a method of conflict resolution: Two cases. *International Organization,* 1972, 26:595–618.

OTTERBEIN, K. F. Internal war: A cross-cultural study. *American Anthropologist*, 1968, 70:277–289.

OTTERBEIN, K. F. *The evolution of war: A cross-cultural study*. New Haven: Human Relations Area Files Press, 1970.

OTTERBEIN, K. F. The anthropology of war. In J. J. Honigmann (ed.), *Handbook of social and cultural anthropology*. Chicago: Rand-McNally, 1973.

OTTERBEIN, K. F. Warfare: A hitherto unrecognized critical variable. *American Behavioral Scientist*, 1977, 20:693–710.

OTTERBEIN, K. F., and OTTERBEIN, C. S. An eye for an eye, a tooth for a tooth: A cross-cultural study of feuding. *American Anthropologist*, 1965, 67:1470–1482.

PACKENHAM, R. Approaches to the study of political development. *World Politics*, 1964, 17:108–120.

PAIGE, J. M. Inequality and insurgency in Vietnam: A reanalysis. *World Politics*, 1970, 23:24–37.

PAIGE, J. M. Political orientation and riot participation. *American Sociological Review*, 1971, 36:810–820.

PAIGE, J. M. *Agrarian revolution: Social movements and export agriculture in the underdeveloped world*. New York: Free Press, 1975.

PALMER, M., and THOMPSON, W. R. *The comparative analysis of politics*. Itasca: Peacock, 1978.

PAPEZ, J. W. A proposed mechanism of emotion. *Archives of Neurology and Psychiatry*, 1937, 38:725–743.

PARANZINO, D. Inequality and insurgency in Vietnam: A further reanalysis. *World Politics*, 1972, 24:565–578.

PARET, P. *French revolutionary warfare from Indochina to Algeria: The analysis of a political and military doctrine*. New York: Praeger, 1964.

PARSONS, T. *The social system*. New York: Free Press, 1951.

PARVIN, M. Economic determinants of political unrest: An econometric approach. *Journal of Conflict Resolution*, 1973, 17:271–296.

PATCH, R. Bolivia: The restrained revolution. *Annals of the American Academy of Political and Social Science*, 1961, 334:123–131.

PAUKERT, F. Income distribution at different levels of development: A survey of evidence. *International Labor Review*, 1973, 108, 2–3:97–125.

PAVLOV, D. V. *Leningrad 1941: The blockade*. Chicago: University of Chicago Press, 1965.

PEACOCK, A. T., and WISEMAN, J. *The growth of public expenditure in the United Kingdom*. Princeton: Princeton University Press, 1961.

PEARSON, F. S. Foreign military interventions and domestic disputes. *International Studies Quarterly*, 1974(a), 18:259–290.

PEARSON, F. S. Geographic proximity and foreign military intervention. *Journal of Conflict Resolution*, 1974(b), 18:432–460.

PEARSON, F. S., and BAUMANN, R. Research note: Foreign military intervention by large and small powers. *International Interactions*, 1974, 1:273–278.

PELOWSKI, A. L. A quasi-experimental design in the study of international organization and war. *Journal of Peace Research*, 1971, 3:279–286.

PERKINS, D. *The American approach to foreign policy,* rev. ed. New York: Atheneum, 1968.

PERKINS, D. Dissent in time of war. *Virginia Quarterly Review,* 1971, 47:161–174.

PERSKY, H., et al. Relation of psychologic measures of aggression and hostility to testosterone production in man. *Psychosomatic Medicine,* 1971, 33:265–277.

PHILLIPS, W. The conflict environment of nations: A study of conflict inputs to nations in 1963. In J. Wilkenfeld (ed.), *Conflict behavior and linkage politics.* New York: McKay, 1973.

PINARD, M. A reformulation of the mass society model. *American Journal of Sociology,* 1968, 73:682–690.

PIRAGES, D. *Modernization and political tension-management: A socialist society in perspective.* New York: Praeger, 1972.

PIRAGES, D. *The new context for international relations: Global ecopolitics.* North Scituate: Duxbury, 1978(a).

PIRAGES, D. (ed.). *The sustainable society.* New York: Praeger, 1978(b).

PIVEN, F. F. The social structuring of political protest. *Politics and Society,* 1976, 6:297–326.

PIVEN, F. F., and CLOWARD, R. A. *Regulating the poor: The functions of public welfare.* New York: Random, 1971.

POLENBERG, R. *War and society: The United States, 1941–1945.* Philadelphia: Lippincott, 1972.

POPPER, F. J. Internal war as a stimulant of political development. *Comparative Political Studies,* 1971, 3:413–423.

PORTER, R. C., and NAGEL, J. H. Declining inequality and rising expectations: Relative deprivation and the black urban riots. Fels Discussion Paper no. 96. School of Public and Urban Policy, University of Pennsylvania, 1976.

POWELL, E. H. War, social cohesion, and anomie: Reflection on the power of danger. In *The design of discord: Studies of anomie.* New York: Oxford University Press, 1970.

POWELL, J. D. Adequacy of social science models for the study of peasant movements. *Comparative Politics,* 1976, 8:327–338.

PRICE, D. J. DE S. *Science since Babylon.* New Haven: Yale University Press, 1961.

PRIDE, R. A. *Origins of democracy: A cross-national study of mobilization, party systems, and democratic stability.* Sage Professional Paper in Comparative Politics, No. 01–012. Beverly Hills: Sage, 1970.

PRYOR, F. L. *Public expenditures in communist and capitalist nations.* Homewood: Irwin, 1968.

PRYOR, F. L. *Economic system and the size distribution of income and wealth.* Bloomington: International Development Research Center, Indiana University, 1971.

PUSTAY, J. S. *Counterinsurgency warfare.* New York: Free Press, 1965.

PUTNAM, R. D. *The comparative study of political elites.* Englewood Cliffs: Prentice-Hall, 1976.

PYE, L. W. *Guerrilla communism in Malaya: Its social and political meaning.* Princeton: Princeton University Press, 1956.

PYE, L. W. *Aspects of political development.* Boston: Little, Brown, 1966.

QUANDT, W. B. *Revolution and political leadership: Algeria, 1954–1968.* Cambridge: M.I.T. Press, 1969.

RANSFORD, H. E. Isolation, powerlessness, and violence: A study of attitudes and participation in the Watts riot. *American Journal of Sociology*, 1968, 73: 581–591.

RAPOPORT, A. Lewis F. Richardson's mathematical theory of war. *Journal of Conflict Resolution*, 1957, 1:249–299.

RAPOPORT, A. *Fights, games, and debates.* Ann Arbor: University of Michigan Press, 1960.

RAPOPORT, A. Games which simulate deterrence and disarmament. *Peace Research Reviews*, 1967, 1:1–76.

RAPOPORT, A. Can peace research be applied? *Journal of Conflict Resolution*, 1970, 14:277–286.

RAPOPORT, A. Mathematical methods in theories of international relations: Expectations, caveats and opportunities. In D. A. Zinnes and J. V. Gillespie (eds.), *Mathematical models in international relations.* New York: Praeger, 1976.

RATNAM, K. J. Charisma and political leadership. *Political Studies*, 1964, 12: 341–354.

RATTINGER, H. Armaments, detente and bureaucracy: The case of the arms race in Europe. *Journal of Conflict Resolution*, 1975, 19:571–595.

RATTINGER, H. From war to war to war: Arms races in the Middle East. *International Studies Quarterly*, 1976, 20:501–531.

RAY, J. L. Status inconsistency and war involvement in Europe, 1816–1970. *Peace Science Society (International), Papers*, 1974, 23:69–80.

RAY, J. L. Status inconsistency and "aggressive" war involvement in Europe, 1816–1970. Paper presented to the International Science Association, February 1978.

RAY, J. L. *Global politics.* Boston: Houghton Mifflin, 1979.

REDMOND, D. E., et al. Behavior of free-ranging macaques after intraventricular 6-hydroxydopamine. *Science*, 1973, 181:1256–1258.

REID, H. G., and YANARELLA, E. J. Toward a critical theory of peace research in the United States: The search for an "intelligible core." *Journal of Peace Research*, 1976, 13:315–341.

REIS, D. J., et al. Predatory attack, grooming, and consummatory behaviors evoked by electrical stimulation of cat cerebellar nuclei. *Science*, 1973, 182: 845–847.

REJAI, M. *The comparative study of revolutionary strategy.* New York: McKay, 1977.

REJAI, M., with PHILLIPS, K. *Leaders of revolution.* Beverly Hills: Sage, 1979.

REMMER, K. L. Evaluating the policy impact of military regimes in Latin America. *Latin American Research Review*, 1978, 13:39–53.

RENSHAW, E. *The end of progress.* North Scituate: Duxbury, 1976.

RENSHON, S., ed. *Handbook of political socialization.* New York: Free Press, 1977.

RICHARDSON, L. F. *Arms and insecurity: A mathematical study of the causes and origins of war*. Pittsburgh: Boxwood Press, 1960(a).

RICHARDSON, L. F. *Statistics of deadly quarrels*. Pittsburgh: Boxwood Press, 1960(b).

RIEZLER, K. On the psychology of modern revolution. *Social Research*, 1943, 10: 320–366.

RIKER, W. *The theory of political coalitions*. New Haven: Yale University Press, 1962.

RIKER, W., and ORDESHOOK, P. *An introduction to positive political theory*. Englewood Cliffs: Prentice-Hall, 1973.

RITTBERGER, V. International organization and violence. *Journal of Peace Research*, 1973, 10:163–184.

RITTER, A. R. M. *The economic development of revolutionary Cuba: Strategy and performance*. New York: Praeger, 1974.

ROAZEN, P. *Erik H. Erikson: The power and limits of a vision*. New York: Free Press, 1976.

ROBINSON, J. P., RUSK, J. G., and HEAD, K. B. *Measures of political attitudes*. Ann Arbor: Institute for Social Research, University of Michigan, 1972.

ROBINSON, M. A. Federal debt management: Civil War, World War I, and World War II. *American Economic Review*, 1955, 45:388–401.

ROGOWSKI, R. *Rational legitimacy*. Princeton: Princeton University Press, 1974.

ROSECRANCE, R. N. *Action and reaction in world politics*. Boston: Little, Brown, 1963.

ROSECRANCE, R. N. Bipolarity, multipolarity, and the future. *Journal of Conflict Resolution*, 1966, 10:314–327.

ROSEN, S. J. A model of war and alliance. In J. R. Friedman, C. Bladen, and S. Rosen (eds.), *Alliance in international politics*. Boston: Allyn & Bacon, 1970.

ROSEN, S. J. War power and willingness to suffer. In B. M. Russett (ed.), *Peace, war, and numbers*. Beverly Hills: Sage, 1972.

ROSENAU, J. N. Foreign intervention as adaptive behavior. In J. N. Moore (ed.), *Law and civil war in the modern world*. Baltimore: Johns Hopkins University Press, 1974.

ROSENBERG, K. M., et al. Effects of neonatal castration and testosterone on rat's pup-killing behavior and activity. *Physiology and Behavior*, 1971, 7:363–368.

ROSENBERG, N. The direction of technological change: Inducement mechanisms and focusing devices. *Economic Development and Cultural Change*, 1969, 18:1–24.

ROSKIN, M. From Pearl Harbor to Vietnam: Shifting generational paradigms. *Political Science Quarterly*, 1974, 89:563–588.

ROSS, A. M., and HARTMAN, P. T. *Changing patterns of industrial conflict*. New York: Wiley, 1960.

ROTBERG, R. I. *Haiti: The politics of squalor*. Boston: Houghton Mifflin, 1971.

ROTTER, J. B. Generalized expectancies for internal versus external control of reinforcement. *Psychological Monographs*, 1966, 80:No. 609.

ROUSSEAU, J.-J. *The social contract*, 1762(a).

ROUSSEAU, J.-J. *Emile*, 1762(b).

ROWE, E. T. Aid and coups d'etat. *International Studies Quarterly,* 1974, 18: 239–255.

RUBENSTEIN, R. E. *Rebels in Eden: Mass political violence in the United States.* Boston: Little, Brown, 1970.

RUDÉ, G. *The crowd in the French revolution.* Oxford: Oxford University Press, 1959.

RUDÉ, G. *The crowd in history: A study of popular disturbances in France and England 1730–1848.* New York: Wiley, 1964.

RUHL, J. M. Social mobilization and political instability in Latin America: A test of Huntington's theory. *Inter-American Economic Affairs,* 1975, 29:3–21.

RULE, J., and TILLY, C. 1830 and the unnatural history of revolution. *Journal of Social Issues,* 1972, 28:49–76.

RUMMEL, R. J. The dimensions of conflict behavior within and between nations. *General Systems Yearbook,* 1963, 8:1–50.

RUMMEL, R. J. Testing some possible predictors of conflict behavior within and between nations. *Peace Research Society (International), Papers,* 1964, 1:79–111.

RUMMEL, R. J. Dimensions of conflict behavior within nations, 1946–50. *Journal of Conflict Resolution,* 1966(a), 10:65–73.

RUMMEL, R. J. Some dimensions in the foreign behavior of nations. *Journal of Peace Research,* 1966(b), 3:201–204.

RUMMEL, R. J. Dimensions of dyadic war, 1820–1952. *Journal of Conflict Resolution,* 1967, 11:167–184.

RUMMEL, R. J. National attributes and foreign conflict behavior. In J. D. Singer (ed.), *Quantitative international politics: Insights and evidence.* New York: Free Press, 1968.

RUMMEL, R. J. Dimensions of foreign and domestic conflict behavior: A review of empirical findings. In D. G. Pruitt and R. C. Snyder (eds.), *Theory and research on the causes of war.* Englewood Cliffs, N. J.: Prentice-Hall, 1969.

RUMMEL, R. J. The roots of faith. In J. N. Rosenau (ed.), *In search of global patterns.* New York: Free Press, 1976.

RUSSELL, C. A., and MILLER, B. H. Profile of a terrorist. *Terrorism: An International Journal,* 1977, 1:17–34.

RUSSELL, D. E. H. *Rebellion, revolution, and armed force.* New York: Academic Press, 1974.

RUSSELL, F. M. (1936) *Theories of international relations.* New York: Arno Press, 1972.

RUSSETT, B. M. The calculus of deterrence. *Journal of Conflict Resolution,* 1963, 7:97–109.

RUSSETT, B. M. Inequality and instability: The relation of land tenure to politics. *World Politics,* 1964, 16:442–454.

RUSSETT, B. M. *What price vigilance? The burdens of national defense.* New Haven: Yale University Press, 1970.

RUSSETT, B. M. The Americans' retreat from world power. *Political Science Quarterly,* 1975, 90:1–21.

RUSSETT, B. M., and HANSON, E. C. *Interest and ideology: The foreign policy beliefs of American businessmen.* San Francisco: Freeman, 1975.

Russett, B. M., et al. *World handbook of political and social indicators*. New Haven: Yale University Press, 1964.

Russett, B. M., and Monsen, R. J. Democracy and polyarchy as predictors of performance: A cross-national examination. *Comparative Political Studies*, 1975, 8:5–31.

Russett, B. M., and Nincic, M. American opinion on the use of military force abroad. *Political Science Quarterly*, 1976, 91:411–431.

Russo, A. J., Jr. Economic and social correlates of government control in South Vietnam. In I. K. Feierabend, R. L. Feierabend, and T. R. Gurr (eds.), *Anger, violence, and politics*. Englewood Cliffs: Prentice-Hall, 1972.

Salert, B. *Revolutions and revolutionaries: Four theories*. New York: Elsevier, 1976.

Salert, B., and Sprague, J. The dynamics of riots. Paper presented to the Midwest Political Science Association, Chicago, April 1978.

Salisbury, H. E. *The 900 days*. New York: Avon, 1969.

Sanders, D. An empirical investigation of Huntington's gap hypothesis. M. A. dissertation, University of Essex, 1973.

Sanders, D. Away from a general model of mass political violence: Evaluating Hibbs. *Quality and Quantity*, 1978, 12:103–129.

Sanders, D. Changes and challenges: Patterns of interrelationship among four types of political instability. Paper presented to the European Consortium Workshops, Brussels, 1979.

Satow, R. Political repression during wartime: An empirical study of Simmel's theory of conflict. Ph.D. dissertation, New York University, 1972.

Scalapino, R. A. (ed.), *The communist revolution in Asia*. Englewood Cliffs: Prentice-Hall, 1965.

Schaich, W. A relationship between collective racial violence and war. *Journal of Black Studies*, 1975, 5:374–394.

Schattschneider, E. *The semi-sovereign people: A realist's view of democracy*. New York: Holt, 1960.

Schelling, T. C. *The strategy of conflict*. Cambridge: Harvard University Press, 1960.

Schelling, T. C. *Arms and influence*. New Haven: Yale University Press, 1966.

Scheuch, E. K. Cross-national comparisons using aggregate data: Some substantive and methodological problems. In R. L. Merritt and S. Rokkan (eds.), *Comparing nations: The use of quantitative data in cross-national research*. New Haven: Yale University Press, 1966.

Schmid, H. Peace research and politics. *Journal of Peace Research*, 1968, 5:217–232.

Schmid, H. Peace research as a technology for pacification. *Proceedings of the International Peace Research Association Third General Conference, 1: The Philosophy of Peace Research*. Assen: Van Gorcum, 1970.

Schmitt, D. E. *Violence in Northern Ireland: Ethnic conflict and radicalization in an international setting*. Morristown: General Learning Press, 1974.

Schmitter, P. C. Military intervention, political competitiveness and public policy in Latin America: 1950–1967. In M. Janowitz and J. van Doorn (eds.), *On military intervention*. Rotterdam: Rotterdam University Press, 1971.

SCHMITTER, P. C. Paths to political development in Latin America. In D. A. Chalmars (ed.), *Changing Latin America*. New York: Academy of Political Science, 1972.

SCHMITTER, P. C. Foreign military assistance, national military spending and military rule in Latin America. In P. C. Schmitter (ed.), *Military rule in Latin America: Function, consequences and perspectives*. Sage Research Progress Series on War, Revolution and Peacekeeping (Vol. 3), Beverly Hills: Sage, 1973.

SCHMITTER, P. C. *Corporatism and public policy in authoritarian Portugal*. Sage Professional Papers in Contemporary Sociology, 1, 06–011. Beverly Hills: Sage, 1975.

SCHNEIDER, P. R., and SCHNEIDER, A. L. Social mobilization, political institutions, and political violence: A cross-national analysis. *Comparative Political Studies*, 1971, 4:69–90.

SCHRODT, P. A. Statistical problems associated with the Richardson arms race model. *Journal of Peace Science*, 1978, 3:159–172.

SCHUELLER, G. K. The politburo. In H. D. Lasswell and D. Lerner (eds.), *World revolutionary elites*. Cambridge: M.I.T. Press, 1965.

SCHUMAKER, P. D. Policy responsiveness to protest-group demands. *Journal of Politics*, 1975, 37:488–521.

SCHUMAKER, P. D. The scope of political conflict and the effectiveness of constraints in contemporary urban protest. *Sociological Quarterly*, 1978, 19: 168–184.

SCHWARTZ, D. C. Political alienation: The psychology of revolution's first stage. In I. K. Feierabend, R. L. Feierabend, and T. R. Gurr (eds.), *Anger, violence, and politics: Theories and research*. Englewood Cliffs: Prentice-Hall, 1972.

SCHWARTZ, D. C. Health processes and body images as predictors of political attitudes and behavior. Paper presented at the Congress of the International Political Science Association, Montreal, 1973(a).

SCHWARTZ, D. C. *Political alienation and political behavior*. Chicago: Aldine, 1973(b).

SCHWARTZ, N. Conflict resolution and impropriety in a Guatemalan town. *Social Forces*, 1969–1970, 48:98–106.

SCHWEITZER, A. Theory of political charisma. *Comparative Studies in Society and History*, 1974, 16:150–181.

SCOLNICK, J. M. An appraisal of studies of the linkage between domestic and international conflict. *Comparative Political Studies*, 1974, 6:485–509.

SCOTT, J. P. Biology and human aggression. *American Journal of Orthopsychiatry*, 1970, 40:568–576.

SCOTT, J. P. Theoretical issues concerning the origin and causes of fighting. In B. E. Eleftheriou and J. P. Scott (eds.), *The physiology of aggression and defeat*. New York: Plenum, 1971.

SCOTT, J. P. Violence and the disaggregated society. *Aggressive Behavior*, 1975(a), 1:235–260.

SCOTT, J. P. *Aggression*, 2d ed. Chicago: University of Chicago Press, 1975(b).

SCOTT, J. P. Agonistic behavior: Function and dysfunction in social conflict. *Journal of Social Issues*, 1977, 33:9–21.

SEARS, D. O. Black attitudes toward the political system in the aftermath of the Watts insurrection. In D. Bossel and P. Rossi (eds.), *Cities under siege*. New York: Basic Books, 1971.

SEARS, D. O., and McCONAHAY, J. B. *The politics of violence: The new urban blacks and the Watts riot*. Boston: Houghton Mifflin, 1973.

SEEMAN, M. The signals of '68: Alienation in pre-crisis France. *American Sociological Review*, 1972, 37:385–402.

SEGAL, J., HUNTER, E. J., and SEGAL, Z. Universal consequences of captivity: Stress reactions among divergent populations of prisoners of war and their families. *International Social Science Journal*, 1976, 28:593–609.

SEMMEL, B. *Imperialism and social reform*. Cambridge: Harvard University Press, 1960.

SEN, A. *Collective choice and social welfare*. San Francisco: Holden-Day, 1970.

SENGHAAS, D. *Kritische Friedenforschung*. Frankfurt: Suhrkamp Verlag, 1971.

SENGHAAS, D. Conflict formations in contemporary international society. *Journal of Peace Research*, 1973, 10:163–184.

SERVICE, E. R. *Origins of the state and civilization: The process of cultural evolution*. New York: Norton, 1975.

SERVICE, E. R. Classical and modern theories of the origins of government. In R. Cohen and E. R. Service (eds.), *Origins of the state: The anthropology of political evolution*. Philadelphia: Institute for the Study of Human Issues, 1978.

SETON-WATSON, H. Twentieth century revolutions. *Political Quarterly*, 1951, 22:251–265.

SHANKS, M. Survey based political indicators: The case of political alienation. Paper delivered to the American Political Science Association, San Francisco, 1975.

SHAPIRO, G., and DAWSON, P. Social mobility and political radicalism. In W. D. Aydelotte, A. G. Bogue, and R. W. Fogel (eds.), *The dimensions of quantitative research in history*. Princeton: Princeton University Press, 1972.

SHAWCROSS, W. The third Indochina war. *New York Review of Books*, April 6, 1978, 15–22.

SHORTER, E., and TILLY, C. *Strikes in France, 1830–1968*. Cambridge: At the University Press, 1974.

SIGELMAN, L., and SIMPSON, M. A cross-national test of the linkage between economic inequality and political violence. *Journal of Conflict Resolution*, 1977, 21:105–128.

SIGELMAN, L., and YOUGH, S. N. Some "trivial" matters that sometimes matter: Index construction techniques and research findings. *Political Methodology*, 1978, 5:369–384.

SILBERNER, E. *The problem of war in nineteenth century thought*. Princeton: Princeton University Press, 1946.

SIMAAN, M., and CRUZ, J. A multistage game formulation of arms race and control and its relationship to Richardson's model. In W. Vogt and M. Mickle (eds.), *Modeling and simulation*. Pittsburgh: Instrument Society of America, 1973.

SIMMEL, G. *Conflict and the web of group affiliations.* New York: Free Press, 1956.

SIMONTON, D. K. Interdisciplinary and military determinants of scientific productivity: A cross-lagged correlational analysis. *Journal of Vocational Behavior,* 1976, 9:53–62.

SINGER, J. D. The level-of-analysis problem in international relations. In K. Knorr and S. Verba (eds.), *The international system: Theoretical essays.* Princeton: Princeton University Press, 1961.

SINGER, J. D. *Deterrence, arms control, and disarmament.* Columbus: Ohio State University Press, 1962.

SINGER, J. D. *Individual values, national interests, and political development in the international system.* Beverly Hills: Sage, 1971.

SINGER, J. D. Variables, indicators, and data in macro-political research. In Karl Deutsch (ed.), *Methods of political behavior research.* New York: Free Press, 1980.

SINGER, J. D. (ed.). *Quantitative international politics.* New York: Free Press, 1968.

SINGER, J. D., and BOUXSEIN, S. Structural clarity and international war: Some tentative findings. In T. H. Murray (ed.), *Interdisciplinary aspects of general systems theory.* Washington: Society for General Systems Research, 1975.

SINGER, J. D., BREMER, S., and STUCKEY, J. Capability distribution, uncertainty and major power war, 1820–1965. In B. M. Russett (ed.), *Peace, war and numbers.* Beverly Hills: Sage, 1972.

SINGER, J. D., and CUSACK, T. Periodicity, inexorability, and steersmanship in international war. In R. L. Merritt and B. M. Russett (eds.), *From national development to global community.* London: Allen & Unwin, 1980.

SINGER, J. D., and SMALL, M. The composition and status ordering of the international system, 1815–1940. *World Politics,* 1966(a), 18:236–282.

SINGER, J. D., and SMALL, M. National alliance commitments and war involvement, 1815–1945. *Peace Research Society (International), Papers,* 1966(b), 5:109–140.

SINGER, J. D., and SMALL, M. Alliance aggregation and the onset of war, 1815–1945. In J. D. Singer (ed.), *Quantitative international politics: Insights and evidence.* New York: Free Press, 1968.

SINGER, J. D., and SMALL, M. *The wages of war, 1816–1965: A statistical handbook.* New York: Wiley, 1972.

SINGER, J. D., and WALLACE, M. D. Inter-governmental organization and the preservation of peace, 1816–1965: Some bivariate relationships. *International Organization,* 1970, 24:520–547.

SINGER, J. D., and WALLACE, M. D. (eds.). *To augur well: Early warning indicators in world politics.* Beverly Hills: Sage, 1979.

SKJELSBAEK, K. Shared membership in inter-governmental organizations and dyadic war, 1865–1964. In E. Fedder (ed.), *The United Nations: Problems and prospects.* St. Louis: University of Missouri, Center for International Studies, 1971.

SKOCPOL, T. A critical review of Barrington Moore's *Social origins of dictatorship and democracy. Politics and Society,* 1973, 3:1–34.

SKOCPOL, T. France, Russia, China: A structural analysis of social revolutions. *Comparative Studies in Society and History*, 1976, 18:175–210.

SKOCPOL, T. *States and social revolutions: A comparative analysis of France, Russia, and China.* Cambridge: At the University Press, 1979.

SKOLNICK, J. H. *The politics of protest: Report to the National Commission on the Causes and Prevention of Violence.* New York: Ballantine, 1969.

SLOAN, S. The functionality of violence in the new states of Asia and Africa: A reassessment of developmental theory. Unpublished paper given to the American Political Science Association, 1971.

SLOAN, T. J. The association between domestic and international conflict hypothesis revisited. *International Interactions*, 1978, 4:3–32.

SMALDONE, J. P. Review article: Rebellion, revolution, and war: Perspectives on mass political violence. *Armed Forces and Society*, 1976, 3:147–160.

SMALL, M., and SINGER, J. D. The war proneness of democratic regimes. *Jerusalem Journal of International Relations*, 1976, 1:49–69.

SMALL, M., and SINGER, J. D. Conflict in the international system, 1816–1977: Historical trends and policy futures. In C. W. Kegley, Jr., and P. J. McGowan (eds.), *Challenge to America: United States foreign policy in the 1980s.* Beverly Hills: Sage, 1979.

SMELSER, N. J. *Theory of collective behavior.* New York: Free Press, 1963.

SMITH, B. L. R. The politics of protest: How effective is violence? In R. H. Connery (ed.), *Urban riots: Violence and social change, Proceedings of the Academy of Political Science,* 1968, 29:113–130.

SMITH, P. H. *Labyrinths of power: Political recruitment in twentieth-century Mexico.* Princeton: Princeton University Press, 1979.

SMOKER, P. Fear in the arms race: A mathematical study. *Journal of Peace Research*, 1964, 1:55–63.

SNOW, P. G. Commentary on: D. P. Bwy: Political instability in Latin America: The cross-cultural test of a causal model. *Latin American Research Review*, 1968, 3:74–76.

SNYDER, D., and TILLY, C. Hardship and collective violence in France, 1830 to 1960. *American Sociological Review*, 1972, 37:520–532.

SNYDER, D., and TILLY, C. How to get from here to there. *American Sociological Review*, 1973, 38:501–503.

SNYDER, D. Theoretical and methodological problems in the analysis of governmental coercion and collective violence. *Journal of Political and Military Sociology*, 1976, 4:277–293.

SNYDER, D. Collective violence: A research agenda and some strategic considerations. *Journal of Conflict Resolution*, 1978, 22:499–534.

SNYDER, D., and KELLY, W. R. Industrial violence in Italy, 1878–1903. *American Journal of Sociology*, 1976, 82:131–162.

SNYDER, G. *Deterrence and defense.* Princeton: Princeton University Press, 1961.

SOBEL, E. The aggressive female. In I. L. Kutash et al. (eds.), *Violence: Perspectives on murder and aggression.* San Francisco: Jossey-Bass, 1978.

SOFRANKO, A. J., and BEALER, R. C. *Unbalanced modernization and domestic instability: A comparative analysis.* Sage Professional Papers in Comparative Politics, No. 01–036. Beverly Hills: Sage, 1972.

SOREL, G. (1915) *Reflections on violence*, trans. T. E. Hulme. New York: Peter Smith, 1941.

SOROKIN, P. A. *The sociology of revolution*. Philadelphia: Lippincott, 1925.

SOROKIN, P. A. (1937) *Social and cultural dynamics: Fluctuations of social relationships, war, and revolution*, Vol. 3. New York: Bedminster, 1962.

SPEER, A. *Inside the Third Reich*. New York: Avon, 1971.

SPILERMAN, S. The causes of racial disturbances: A comparison of alternative explanations. *American Sociological Review*, 1970, 35:627–649.

SPIRO, H. Comparative politics: A comprehensive approach. *American Political Science Review*, 1962, 56:557–595.

SPITZ, R. The role of ecological factors in emotional development in infancy. *Child Development*, 1949, 20:145–155.

SPITZ, R. *The first year of life: A psychoanalytic study of normal and deviant development of object relations*. New York: International Universities Press, 1965.

SPITZER, A. B. The historical problem of generations. *American Historical Review*, 1973, 78:1353–1385.

STARR, H. *War coalitions*. Lexington: Heath, 1972.

STARR, H. "Opportunity" and "willingness" as ordering concepts in the study of war. Mimeo, 1974.

STARR, H., and MOST, B. A. The substance and study of borders in international relations. *International Studies Quarterly*, 1976, 20:581–620.

STARR, H., and MOST, B. A. A return journey: Richardson, "frontiers" and wars in the 1964–1965 year. Mimeo, 1977.

STAVRIANOS, L. S. *The promise of the coming dark age*. San Francisco: Freeman, 1976.

STEEDLY, H., and FOLEY, J. The success of protest groups: Multivariate analysis. *Social Science Research*, 1979, 8:1–15.

STEIN, A. A. Conflict and cohesion: A review of the literature. *Journal of Conflict Resolution*, 1976, 20:143–172.

STEIN, A. A. Conflict, mobilization, and change: Domestic effects of war on nation–states. Ph.D. dissertation, Yale University, 1978.

STEIN, A. A. *The nation at war*. Baltimore: Johns Hopkins University Press, 1980.

STEIN, Z., et al. Nutrition and mental performance. *Science*, 1972, 178:708–713.

STEINER, J. Nonviolent conflict resolution in democratic systems: Switzerland. *Journal of Conflict Resolution*, 1969, 13:295–304.

STEINER, J.-F. *Treblinka*. London: Weidenfeld & Nicolson, 1967.

STEPAN, A. C. *The military in politics: Changing patterns in Brazil*. Princeton: Princeton University Press, 1971.

STEPAN, A. C. (ed.). *Authoritarian Brazil*. New Haven: Yale University Press, 1973.

Stockholm International Peace Research Institute. *Ecological consequences of the second Indochina war*. Stockholm: Almqvist & Wiksell, 1976.

STOESSINGER, J. *The might of nations*. New York: St. Martin's, 1973.

STOGDILL, R. M. *Handbook of leadership: A survey of theory and research*. New York: Free Press, 1974.

STOHL, M. Conflict and community: Some observations. First year paper. Department of Political Science, Northwestern University, 1970.

STOHL, M. Linkages between war and domestic political violence in the United States, 1890–1923. In J. A. Caporaso and L. L. Roos, Jr. (eds.), *Quasi-experimental approaches: Testing theory and evaluating policy.* Evanston: Northwestern University Press, 1973.

STOHL, M. Theory and method in studies of the relationship between foreign and domestic conflict and violence. Paper presented to the Fifth International Peace Research Association Conference, Varanasi, India, 1974.

STOHL, M. War and domestic political violence: The case of the United States 1890–1970. *Journal of Conflict Resolution,* 1975, 19:379–416.

STOHL, M. *War and domestic political violence: The American capacity for repression and reaction.* Beverly Hills: Sage, 1976.

STOHL, M., and CHAMBERLAIN, M. Alternative futures for peace research. *Journal of Conflict Resolution,* 1972, 16:523–530.

STRAUSS, H. J. Revolutionary types: Russia in 1905. *Journal of Conflict Resolution,* 1973, 17:297–316.

STUCKEY, J., and SINGER, J. D. The powerful and the war-prone: Ranking the nations by relative capability and war experience, 1820–1964. Paper presented at the conference on Poder Social: America Latina en El Mundo, Mexico City, 1973.

SUEDFELD, P., TETLOCK, P. E., and RAMIREZ, C. War, peace and integrative complexity: UN speeches on the Middle East problem, 1947–1976. *Journal of Conflict Resolution,* 1977, 21:169–184, 427–442.

SULLIVAN, J. D. International consequences of domestic violence: Cross-national assessment. Paper presented to the American Political Science Association, New York, September 1969.

SULLIVAN, M. *International relations: Theories and evidence.* Englewood Cliffs: Prentice-Hall, 1976.

SUMNER, W. G. *Folkways.* Boston: Ginn, 1906.

SUMNER, W. G. *The science of society.* New Haven: Yale University Press, 1927.

SWISHER, C. Civil liberties in war time. *Political Science Quarterly,* 1940, 55: 321–347.

SYLVAN, D. A. Consequences of sharp military assistance increases for international conflict and cooperation. *Journal of Conflict Resolution,* 1976, 20: 609–636.

TAAGEPARA, R. Growth curves of empires. *General Systems Yearbook,* 1968, 13: 171–175.

TAFT, P., and Ross, P. American labor violence: Its causes, character, and outcome. In H. D. Graham and T. R. Gurr (eds.), *Violence in America: Historical and comparative perspectives.* New York: Praeger, 1969.

TAI, C.-S. The effects of revolution: A quasi-experimental analysis of six revolutions. Ph.D. dissertation, Department of Political Science, Northwestern University, 1974.

TAI, C.-S. Linkages between revolution and change in Korea. *Asian Profile,* 1979, 7:25–36.

TANTER, R. Dimensions of conflict behavior within nations, 1955–1960: Turmoil and internal war. *Peace Research Society Papers,* 1965, 3:159–183.

TANTER, R. Dimensions of conflict behavior within and between nations, 1958–1960. *Journal of Conflict Resolution*, 1966, 10:41–64.

TANTER, R. Towards a theory of conflict behavior in Latin America. Paper presented to the International Political Science Association, Brussels, September, 1967.

TANTER, R. International war and domestic turmoil: Some contemporary evidence. In H. D. Graham and T. R. Gurr (eds.), *Violence in America: Historical and comparative perspectives*. New York: Praeger, 1969.

TANTER, R., and MIDLARSKY, M. A theory of revolution. *Journal of Conflict Resolution*, 1967, 11:264–280.

TAYLOR, A. J. P. *The struggle for mastery in Europe, 1848–1918*. Oxford: Clarendon Press, 1954.

TAYLOR, C. L. Communications development and political instability. *Comparative Political Studies*, 1969, 1:557–563.

TAYLOR, C. L., and HUDSON, M. C. (eds.). *World handbook of political and social indicators*, 2nd ed. New Haven: Yale University Press, 1972.

TAYLOR, M., and HERMAN, V. M. Party systems and government instability. *American Political Science Review*, 1971, 65:28–37.

TAYLOR, M., and RAE, D. An analysis of crosscutting between political cleavages. *Comparative Politics*, 1969, 1:534–547.

TEFFT, S. K., and REINHARDT, D. Warfare regulation: A cross-cultural test of hypothesis among tribal peoples. *Behavior Science Research*, 1974, 9:151–172.

TEITELBAUM, P. The biology of drive. In G. C. Quarton et al. (eds.), *The neurosciences: A study program*. New York: Rockefeller University Press, 1967(a).

TEITELBAUM, P. *Physiological psychology: Fundamental principles*. Englewood Cliffs: Prentice-Hall, 1967(b).

TERHUNE, K. The effects of personality in cooperation and conflict. In P. Swingle (ed.), *The structure of conflict*. New York: Academic Press, 1970.

TERRELL, L. M. Societal stress, political instability, and levels of military effort. *Journal of Conflict Resolution*, 1971, 15:329–346.

TERRELL, L. M. Patterns of international involvement and international violence. *International Studies Quarterly*, 1972, 16:167–186.

THELEN, M. H., and RENNIE, D. L. The effect of vicarious reinforcement on imitation: A review of the literature. In B. A. Maher (ed.), *Progress in experimental personality research*, Vol. 6. New York: Academic Press, 1972.

THOMAS, K. W. Conflict and conflict management. In M. D. Dunnette (ed.), *Handbook of industrial and organizational psychology*. Chicago: Rand-McNally, 1976.

THOMAS, W. I. (1927) *On social organization and social personality*. Chicago: University of Chicago Press, 1966.

THOMPSON, E. P. *The making of the English working class*. New York: Random House, 1963.

THOMPSON, R. *Defeating communist insurgency: The lessons of Malaya and Vietnam*. New York: Praeger, 1966.

THOMPSON, W. R. *The grievances of military coup-makers*. Sage Professional Papers in Comparative Politics, 01–047. Beverly Hills: Sage, 1973.

THOMPSON, W. R. Regime vulnerability and the military coup. *Comparative Politics*, 1975, 9:255–276.

THORN, R. S. The economic transformation of Bolivia. In J. M. Malloy (ed.), *Beyond the revolution: Bolivia since 1952*. Pittsburgh: University of Pittsburgh Press, 1971.

TILLY, C. *The Vendée*. Cambridge: Harvard University Press, 1965.

TILLY, C. Collective violence in European perspective. In H. D. Graham and T. R. Gurr (eds.), *Violence in America: Historical and comparative perspectives*. New York: Praeger, 1969.

TILLY, C. Review of "Why men rebel" by Ted Robert Gurr. *Journal of Social History*, 1971, 4:416–420.

TILLY, C. The chaos of the living city. In H. Hirsch and D. C. Perry (eds.), *Violence as politics: A series of original essays*. New York: Harper & Row, 1973(a).

TILLY, C. Does modernization breed revolution? *Comparative Politics*, 1973(b), 5:425–447.

TILLY, C. (ed.). *The formation of national states in Western Europe*. Princeton: Princeton University Press, 1975(a).

TILLY, C. Revolutions and collective violence. In F. I. Greenstein and N. Polsby (eds.), *Handbook of political science*, Vol. 3. Reading: Addison-Wesley, 1975(b).

TILLY, C. *From mobilization to revolution*. Reading: Addison-Wesley, 1978.

TILLY, C., and LEES, L. Le peuple de juin 1848. *Annales*, 1974, 29:1061–1091.

TILLY, C., TILLY, L., and TILLY, R. *The rebellious century 1830–1930*. Cambridge: Harvard University Press, 1975.

TITMUSS, R. M. (1958) War and social policy. In *Essays on "the welfare state."* Boston: Beacon Press, 1969.

TOYNBEE, A. J. *A study of history*, Vol. 9. London: Oxford University Press, 1954.

TRIMBERGER, E. K. *Revolution from above*. New Brunswick: Transaction, 1978.

TRISKA, J. F., and FINLEY, D. D. Soviet-American relations: A multiple symmetry model. *Journal of Conflict Resolution*, 1965, 9:37–53.

TRUMAN, D. *The governmental process*. New York: Knopf, 1951.

TUCKER, R. C. The theory of charismatic leadership. *Daedalus*, 1968, 97:731–756.

TURNBULL, C. M. *The mountain people*. New York: Simon & Schuster, 1972.

TURSKY, B., LODGE, M., and CROSS, D. A bio-behavioral framework for the analysis of political behavior. In A. Somit (ed.), *Biology and politics: recent explorations*. The Hague: Mouton, 1976(a), 59–96.

TURSKY, B., LODGE, M., et al. Evaluation of the cognitive component of political issues by the use of classical conditioning. *Journal of Personality and Social Psychology*, 1976(b), 34:865–873.

U.N. Demographic Yearbook, 1966. New York: United Nations, 1967.

U. S. Congress, Joint Economic Committee, Subcommittee on Economy in Government. Hearings: *The military budget and national economic priori-*

ties. Part 1. 91st Cong., 1st sess. Washington: U.S. Government Printing Office, 1969.

VALENSTEIN, E. S. Stability and plasticity of motivation systems. In F. O. Schmitt et al. (eds.), *The neurosciences: Second study program.* New York: Rockefeller University Press, 1970.

VATIKIOTIS, P. J. (ed.). *Egypt since the revolution.* New York: Praeger, 1968.

VAYDA, A. P. Research on the functions of primitive war. *Peace Research Society (International), Papers,* 1967, 7:133–138.

VINCENT, J. E. *Project theory: Interpretations and policy relevance.* Washington, D.C.: University Press, 1979.

VOEVODSKY, J. Quantitative behavior of warring nations. *Journal of Psychology,* 1969, 72:269–292.

VOEVODSKY, J. Crisis waves: The growth and decline of war-related behavioral events. *Journal of Psychology,* 1972, 80:289–308.

VON DER MEHDEN, F. R. *Comparative political violence.* Englewood Cliffs: Prentice-Hall, 1973.

VON HOLST, E., and VON ST. PAUL, U. Vom Wirkungsgefüge der Triebe. *Die Naturwissenschaften,* 1960, 18:409–422.

WAHLKE, J. C. Prebehavioralism in political science. *American Political Science Review,* 1979, 73:9–31.

WALLACE, M. D. Power, status and international war. *Journal of Peace Research,* 1971, 1:23–36.

WALLACE, M. D. The radical critique of peace research: An exposition and interpretation. *Peace Research Reviews,* 1972(a), 4:24–51.

WALLACE, M. D. Status, formal organization, and arms levels as factors leading to the onset of war, 1820–1964. In B. M. Russett (ed.), *Peace, war and numbers.* Beverly Hills: Sage, 1972(b).

WALLACE, M. D. Alliance polarization, cross-cutting and international war, 1815–1964: A measurement procedure and some preliminary evidence. *Journal of Conflict Resolution,* 1973(a), 27:575–604.

WALLACE, M. D. *War and rank among nations.* Lexington: Lexington Books, 1973(b).

WALLACE, M. D. Clusters of nations in the global system, 1865–1964: Some preliminary evidence. *International Studies Quarterly,* 1975, 19:67–109.

WALLACE, M. D. Arms races and escalation: Some new evidence. Revised version of paper presented at Social Science History Association, Ann Arbor, Michigan, 1977.

WALLERSTEIN, I. *The modern world system: Capitalist agriculture and the origins of the European world economy in the sixteenth century.* New York: Academic Press, 1974.

WALSH, M. N. (ed.). *War and the human race.* Amsterdam: Elsevier, 1971.

WALTER, E. V. *Terror and resistance: A study of political violence.* New York: Oxford University Press, 1969.

WALTON, R. *Interpersonal peacemaking: Confrontations and third party consultation.* Reading: Addison-Wesley, 1969.

WALTZ, K. N. *Man, the state, and war.* New York: Columbia University Press, 1959.

WALTZ, K. N. The stability of a bipolar world. *Daedalus,* 1964, 93:881–909.

WALTZ, K. N. Theory of international relations. In F. Greenstein and N. Polsby (eds.), *Handbook of political science: International politics.* Vol. 8. Reading: Addison-Wesley, 1975.

War and society newsletter: A bibliographical survey. Freiburg, Germany: Militärgeschichtliches Forschungsamt, 1973.

WARD, M. D. *The political economy of distribution: Equality versus inequality.* New York: Elsevier, 1978.

WATT, K. *Principles of environmental science.* New York: McGraw-Hill, 1973.

WATTS, M. W., and SUMI, D. Studies in the physiological component of aggression-related social attitudes. *American Journal of Political Science,* 1979, 23: 528–558.

WAYMAN, F. W. *Military involvement in politics: A causal model.* Sage Professional Papers in International Studies, No. 02–035. Beverly Hills: Sage, 1975.

WEAVER, J. L. Assessing the impact of military rule: Alternative approaches. In P. C. Schmitter (ed.), *Military rule in Latin America: Function, consequences, and perspectives.* Beverly Hills: Sage, 1973.

WEBER, M. *From Max Weber: Essays in sociology.* Edited with an introduction by H. H. Gerth and C. W. Mills. New York: Oxford University Press, 1958.

WEBER, M. *The theory of social and economic organization.* Edited with an introduction by Talcott Parsons. New York: Free Press, 1964(a).

WEBER, M. *Wirtschaft und Gesellschaft.* Studienausgabe. Cologne: Kiepenheuer & Witsch, 1964(b).

WEEDE, E. Conflict behavior of nation-states. *Journal of Peace Research,* 1970, 7: 229–235.

WEEDE, E. Nation-environment relations as determinants of hostilities among nations. *Peace Science Society (International), Papers,* 1973, 20:67–90.

WEEDE, E. Unzufriedenheit, Protest und Gewalt: Kritik an einem makropolitischen Forschungsprogramm. *Politische Vierteljahresschrift,* 1975, 16:409–428.

WEEDE, E. Overwhelming preponderance as a pacifying condition among contiguous Asian dyads, 1950–1969. *Journal of Conflict Resolution,* 1976, 20: 395–412.

WEEDE, E. *Hypothesen, Gleichungen und Daten: Spezifikations- und Meßprobleme bei Kausalmodellen für Daten aus einer und mehreren Beobachtungsperioden.* Kronberg: Athenäum, 1977.

WEEDE, E. U.S. support for foreign governments, or domestic disorder and imperial intervention, 1958–1965. *Comparative Political Studies,* 1978, 10: 497–527.

WEINER, M. Urbanization and political protest. *Civilisations,* 1967, 17:44–50.

WEISS, H. K. Stochastic models for the duration and magnitude of a "deadly quarrel." *Operations Research,* 1963, 11:101–121.

WELCH, S. The impact of urban riots on urban expenditures. *American Journal of Political Science,* 1975, 19:741–760.

WELCH, S., and BOOTH, A. Crowding as a factor in political aggression: Theoretical aspects and an analysis of some cross-national data. *Social Science Information*, 1974, 13:151–162.

WELFLING, M. B. Models, measurement and sources of error: Civil conflict in Black Africa. *American Political Science Review*, 1975, 69:665–685.

WESLEY, P. Frequency of wars and geographical opportunity. In D. Pruitt and R. C. Snyder (eds.), *Theory and research on the causes of war*. Englewood Cliffs: Prentice-Hall, 1969.

WESSON, R. G. *The imperial order*. Berkeley: University of California Press, 1967.

WESSON, R. G. *State systems: International pluralism, politics, and culture*. New York: Free Press, 1978.

WEST, G. T. The dimensions of political violence in Latin America, 1949–1964: An empirical study. Ph.D. dissertation, University of Pennsylvania, 1973.

WESTING, A. H., and PFEIFFER, E. W. The cratering of Indochina. *Scientific American*, 1972, 226:20–29.

WHEELER, H. G. The effects of war on industrial growth 1816–1975. Ph.D. dissertation, University of Michigan, 1975(a).

WHEELER, H. G. The effects of war on industrial growth. Paper presented at the International Studies Association Meeting, Washington, 1975(b).

WHEELER, H. G. The effects of war on industrial growth: Further findings. Paper presented at the Peace Science Society (International) Meeting, Midwest Section, Chicago, May 1975(c).

WHEELER, H. G. Effects of war on industrial growth. *Society*, 1975(d), 12:48–52.

WHITE, H. Notes on the constituents of social structure. Mimeo. Harvard University, n.d.

WHITE, J. W. *Political implications of cityward migration: Japan as an exploratory test case*. Sage Professional Papers in Comparative Politics, No. 01–038. Beverly Hills: Sage, 1973.

WIEGELE, T. C. Decision-making in an international crisis: Some biological factors. *International Studies Quarterly*, 1973, 17:295–335.

WIEGELE, T. C. The psychophysiology of elite stress in five international crises: A preliminary test of a voice measurement technique. *International Studies Quarterly*, 1978, 22:467–511.

WILES, P. *Distribution of income: East and west*. Amsterdam: North-Holland, 1974.

WILES, P., and MARKOWSKI, S. Income distribution under communism and capitalism: Some facts about Poland, the UK, the USA, the USSR. *Soviet Studies*, 1971, 22:344–370, 487–511.

WILKENFELD, J. Domestic and foreign conflict behavior of nations. *Journal of Peace Research*, 1968, 1:56–69.

WILKENFELD, J. Some further findings regarding the domestic and foreign conflict of nations. *Journal of Peace Research*, 1969, 7:147–156.

WILKENFELD, J. Models for the analysis of foreign conflict behavior of states. In B. M. Russett (ed.), *Peace, war and numbers*. Beverly Hills: Sage, 1972.

WILKENFELD, J. (ed.). *Conflict behavior and linkage politics*. New York: McKay, 1973(a).

WILKENFELD, J. Domestic conflict in the Middle East: An analysis of international inputs. Paper presented at the 9th World Congress of the International Political Science Association. Montreal, 1973(b).

WILKENFELD, J. Conflict linkages in the domestic and foreign spheres. In S. Kirkpatrick (ed.), *Quantitive analysis of political data*. Columbus: Merrill, 1974.

WILKENFELD, J. A time series perspective on conflict behavior in the Middle East. In P. J. McGowan (ed.), *Sage International Yearbook of Foreign Policy Studies*, Vol. 3. Beverly Hills: Sage, 1975.

WILKENFELD, J., LUSSIER, V., and TAHTINEN, D. Conflict interactions in the Middle East 1949–1967. *Journal of Conflict Resolution*, 1972, 16:135–154.

WILKENFELD, J., and ZINNES, D. A. A linkage model of domestic conflict behavior. In J. Wilkenfeld (ed.), *Conflict behavior and linkage politics*. New York: McKay, 1973.

WILKIE, J. W. *The Bolivian revolution and U.S. aid since 1952*. Los Angeles: University of California Press, 1969.

WILKIE, J. W. *The Mexican revolution: Federal expenditure and social change since 1910*, 2d ed. Berkeley: University of California Press, 1970.

WILKIE, J. W. Public expenditures since 1952. In J. M. Malloy (ed.), *Beyond the revolution: Bolivia since 1952*. Pittsburgh: University of Pittsburgh Press, 1971.

WILLHOITE, F. Jr., Primates and political authority: A biobehavioral perspective. *American Political Science Review*, 1976, 70:1110–1126.

WILLIAMS, A., and TARR, D. W. (eds.). *Modules in security studies*. Lawrence: University Press of Kansas, 1974.

WILLNER, A. R. *Charismatic political leadership: A theory*. Princeton: Center of International Studies, Research Monograph no. 32, 1968.

WILSON, E. O. *Sociobiology*. Cambridge: Belknap-Harvard University Press, 1975.

WINICK, M. Malnutrition and the developing brain. In F. Plum (ed.), *Brain dysfunction in metabolic disorders*. New York: Raven, 1974.

WINICK, M., and Rosso, P. Malnutrition and central nervous system development. In J. W. Prescott et al. (eds.), *Brain function and malnutrition*. New York: Wiley, 1975.

WINTER, J. M. (ed.). *War and economic development: Essays in memory of David Joslin*. Cambridge: At the University Press, 1975.

WOHLSTETTER, A. The delicate balance of terror. *Foreign Affairs*, 1959, 37:211–234.

WOHLSTETTER, A. Is there a strategic arms race? *Foreign Policy*, 1974, Summer: 2–21.

WOLF, E. *Peasant wars of the twentieth century*. New York: Harper & Row, 1969.

WOLFENSTEIN, E. V. *Revolutionary personality: Lenin, Trotsky, Gandhi*. Princeton: Princeton University Press, 1967.

WOLFF, R. P. On violence. *Journal of Philosophy*, 1969, 66:601–616.

WOLFSON, M. A dynamic model of present world conflict. *Peace Science Society (International), Papers*, 1973, 20:43–66.

WOLIN, S. The politics of the study of revolution. *Comparative Politics*, 1973, 5: 343–358.

WRIGHT, C. W. The more enduring economic consequences of America's wars. *Journal of Economic History*, 1943, 3(supplement):9–26.

WRIGHT, H. T. Toward an explanation of the origin of the state. In R. Cohen and E. R. Service (eds.), *Origins of the state: The anthropology of political evolution*. Philadelphia: Institute for the Study of Human Issues, 1978.

WRIGHT, J. D. *The dissent of the governed*. New York: Academic Press, 1976.

WRIGHT, Q. (1942) *A study of war*. Chicago: University of Chicago Press, 1965.

YOUGH, S. N., and SIGELMAN, L. Mobilization, institutionalization, development and instability. *Comparative Political Studies*, 1976, 9:223–232.

YOUNG, O. *The intermediaries: Third parties in international crises*. Princeton: Princeton University Press, 1967.

ZALD, M. N., and ASH, R. Social movement organizations: Growth, decay and change. *Social Forces*, 1966, 44:327–341.

ZANCHETTI, A. Subcortical and cortical mechanisms in arousal and emotional behavior. In G. C. Quarton et al. (eds.), *The neurosciences: A study program*. New York: Rockefeller University Press, 1967.

ZELDITCH, M. Review essay: Outsiders' politics. *American Journal of Sociology*, 1978, 83:1514–1520.

ZIMMERMANN, E. Dimensionen von Konflikten innerhalb und zwischen Nationen: Eine kritische Bestandsaufnahme des faktoranalytischen Ansatzes in der Makro-Konfliktforschung. *Politische Vierteljahresschrift*, 1975, 16:343–408.

ZIMMERMANN, E. Factor analyses of conflicts within and between nations: A critical evaluation. *Quality and Quantity*, 1976, 10:267–296.

ZIMMERMANN, E. Crises and crises outcomes: Towards a new synthetic approach. *European Journal of Political Research*, 1979, 7:67–115.

ZIMMERMANN, E. *Political violence, crises, and revolutions: Theories and research*. Cambridge: Schenkman, 1980.

ZINNES, D. A. An analytical study of the balance of power theories. *Journal of Peace Research*, 1967, 4:270–288.

ZINNES, D. A. The expression and perception of hostility in prewar crisis: 1914. In J. D. Singer (ed.), *Quantitative international politics: Insight and evidence*. New York: Free Press, 1968.

ZINNES, D. A. Some evidence relevant to the man-milieu hypothesis. In J. N. Rosenau, V. Davis, and M. A. East (eds.), *The analysis of international politics*. New York: Free Press, 1972.

ZINNES, D. A. Research frontiers in the study of international politics. In F. I. Greenstein and N. W. Polsby (eds.), *Handbook of Political Science*, Vol. 8. Reading: Addison-Wesley, 1975.

ZINNES, D. A. *Contemporary research in international politics: A perspective and critical appraisal*. New York: Free Press, 1976.

ZINNES, D. A., and GILLESPIE, J. V. Analysis of arms race models: USA vs. USSR and NATO vs. WTO. In W. G. Vogt and M. H. Mickle (eds.), *Modeling and simulation*. Pittsburgh: Instrument Society of America, 1973.

ZINNES, D. A., GILLESPIE, J. V., and TAHIM, G. S. Transforming a nation-dominant international system. *Journal of Conflict Resolution*, 1978, 22: 547–564.

ZINNES, D. A., NORTH, R., and KOCH, H., Jr. Capability, threat, and the outbreak of war. In J. Rosenau (ed.), *International politics and foreign policy: A reader in research and theory*. New York: Free Press, 1961.

ZINNES, D. A., and WILKENFELD, J. An analysis of foreign conflict behavior of nations. In W. F. Hanrieder (ed.), *Comparative foreign policy: Theoretical essays*. New York: McKay, 1971.

ZONDAG, C. H. *The Bolivian economy, 1952–65: The revolution and its aftermath*. New York: Praeger, 1966.

ZWICK, P. Intrasystem inequality and the symmetry of socioeconomic development in the USSR. *Comparative Politics*, 1976, 8:501–523.

Index of Names

Index of Subjects

M